Mike Nichols
and the Cinema
of Transformation

Mike Nichols and the Cinema of Transformation

J. W. WHITEHEAD

McFarland & Company, Inc., Publishers

Jefferson, North Carolina

All photographs provided by Photofest unless otherwise indicated.

LIBRARY OF CONGRESS CATALOGUING-IN-PUBLICATION DATA

Whitehead, J. W., 1962–
Mike Nichols and the cinema of transformation / J. W. Whitehead.
p.   cm.
Includes bibliographical references and index.

ISBN 978-0-7864-7145-4 (softcover : acid free paper) ∞
ISBN 978-1-4766-1642-1 (ebook)

1. Nichols, Mike—Criticism and interpretation.   I. Title.
PN1998.3.N54W48 2014   791.4302'33092—dc23   2014013773

BRITISH LIBRARY CATALOGUING DATA ARE AVAILABLE

Printed in the United States of America

On the cover: director Mike Nichols on the set
of *Regarding Henry*, 1991 (Paramount Pictures/Photofest)

McFarland & Company, Inc., Publishers
Box 611, Jefferson, North Carolina 28640
www.mcfarlandpub.com

For Kathryn and Jessica,
for my parents,
and for J. F.

Table of Contents

Acknowledgments   ix
Preface   1

PART I. TAKING THE STAGE

1. The Little Exile, the Cabaret Comic, the Broadway Midas   13

PART II. THE AUTEUR

2. "Peel the label": *Who's Afraid of Virginia Woolf?* (1966)   25
3. "This afternoon's feature attraction": *The Graduate* (1967)   36
4. "*Like* us": *Catch-22* (1970)   52
5. "Just act natural": *Carnal Knowledge* (1971)   73
6. "Man is bad": *The Day of the Dolphin* (1973)   89
7. "I must be dreaming": *The Fortune* (1975)   103

PART III. THE PRO

8. "A moral imperative": *Silkwood* (1983)   115
9. "Willing to play the game": *Heartburn* (1986)   129
10. "You have to take sides": *Biloxi Blues* (1988)   137
11. "She's your man": *Working Girl* (1988)   144
12. "Not like in the movies": *Postcards from the Edge* (1990)   155
13. "Say when": *Regarding Henry* (1991)   170
14. "What God meant": *Wolf* (1994)   183
15. "Family values": *The Birdcage* (1996)   192
16. "True believerism": *Primary Colors* (1998)   201
17. "Like a human being": *What Planet Are You From?* (2000)   216

PART IV. THE LATE NICHOLS

18. "A little allegory of the soul": *Wit* (2001)   225

19. "Threshold of revelation": *Angels in America* (2003)   236

20. "RU4 real?": *Closer* (2004)   273

21. "We'll see": *Charlie Wilson's War* (2007)   286

PART V. AMONG THE STARS

22. Tempered Optimism: The Cinematic Legacy of Mike Nichols   297

Filmography   309

Chapter Notes   313

Bibliography   323

Index   327

Acknowledgments

While I was working on my previous book, *Appraising* The Graduate: *The Mike Nichols Classic and Its Impact in Hollywood*, some of my readers suggested that I ought to write the first book to survey Nichols' entire cinematic career. The idea was daunting but irresistible, and three years later, in having completed it, I'm grateful for their encouragement.

As a full-time academic, I have scant extra time to take on a book-length, five-decade retrospective project like this, so I must thank Wheeling Jesuit University for granting me a position as Scholar in Residence during the fall 2013 semester in order to complete this manuscript. Special thanks are due to Rob Phillips, who as faculty chair of the Research and Grants committee approved my application and who, having subsequently assumed the position of Chief Academic Officer, supported the configuring of my schedule for maximum leave time to research and write. Thanks also to Steve Stahl, Rob's predecessor as CAO, who began the machinations that ultimately resulted in the leave time. There is no resource quite so valuable to the scholar as time. If time is the *inestimable* commodity, the faculty development grant I received to defray the expense of the illustrations in the text is fully calculable, and I wish to thank Wheeling Jesuit University as well for its support of faculty academic research. Thanks also to my departmental colleagues Kate, Paula, Amy, and Georgia for their cooperation and encouragement.

In the early stages of formulating this book, I was assisted by one of my most talented students, Shelby Sleevi (WJU '10), who did my preliminary literature review of the secondary critical response to Nichols' films. My previous work on the book about *The Graduate* had prepared me for a lack of sustained scholarly dialogue about Nichols' films, and Shelby's careful work confirmed my suspicions that I would have to blaze some trails in Nichols scholarship.

My research was both local and far-flung. Thanks as always to Kelly, Paula, Betty, and Barb at Wheeling Jesuit University's Bishop Hodges Library for helping me gather resources. I also wish to express my deep appreciation to the staff at the Edwin Fox Foundation Reading Room of the British Film Institute's Reuben Library. The British Film Institute is a mecca for film scholarship and connoisseurship; given a free day in London, I am hard-pressed to choose between the National Gallery and the BFI Southbank, which usually means that I split my day between the two sides of the Thames. Special thanks to the librarian who, on my last afternoon of my last day at BFI researching for this book, understanding my nonnegotiable next-day airline ticket and the immovable forces of other researchers stationed at each of the reading room's microfiche viewers, took pity on me, disappeared into the library's back rooms, and returned half an hour later with copies of the pages I sought, gratis. Thanks also to Ron Mandelbaum at Photofest for helping me locate images that illustrate my argument.

I wish to express my gratitude to the West Virginia Humanities Council, a state affiliate of the National Endowment for the Humanities, which provided me financial support to defray the costs of research travel and the purchase of the twenty feature films Mike Nichols has released during his half-century in Hollywood. Having the films close at hand for reference over the two years of writing time has proven invaluable to close comparative analysis. Any views, findings, conclusions, or recommendations herein do not necessarily represent those of the West Virginia Humanities Council or the National Endowment for the Humanities.

Finally, thanks as always to my family and friends for their support. Now that I'll have some free time again, let's watch some movies.

Preface

"All my pictures turn out to be all about transformation,"[1] Mike Nichols once said, from a retrospective vantage point in 1999, more than three decades into the half-century during which he has remained at or near the top of the American entertainment industry. That Nichols would see *transformation* as a central tenet of his work is hardly coincidental, given that Nichols has been as protean as any of his characters. Since his early days in the naked spotlight of stand-up comedy, Nichols has been conscious of the public gaze. Forsaking a stage presence and verbal agility in improvisation that earned Nichols and his late–1950s comic partner, Elaine May, a long-running 1960 Broadway show and a Grammy for 1962's Best Comedy Album, Nichols moved behind the curtain and promptly directed six consecutive Broadway hits, including three Tony Awards for Best Director. For more than half a year, from late 1966 to mid-summer 1967, Nichols had an astonishing four hit plays running simultaneously on Broadway, during which time his first Hollywood feature, the adaptation of Edward Albee's 1962 play *Who's Afraid of Virginia Woolf?*, also became a popular and critical success. For such a Midas touch, Hollywood was inevitable, and despite no experience in film, Nichols was an A-list director the moment he arrived in Los Angeles; his first two films (*Virginia Woolf* in 1966 and *The Graduate* in 1967) earned a total of 20 Oscar nominations, including two nominations (and the 1968 Oscar) for Best Director. He wasn't done shape-shifting, however: he would enter the world of television production in the next decade with the ABC network drama *Family*, which ran, to considerable acclaim, from 1976 to 1980, and he would eventually conquer the small-screen medium as a director as well, winning consecutive Emmys for his vivid direction of the cable adaptations of two other Broadway plays, *Wit* (2001) and the mini-series *Angels in America* (2003), both for HBO. He has returned regularly to the theater throughout his career, eventually piling up seven Tony Awards for Best Director, the first in 1964, his most recent in 2012. Indeed, even as a Hollywood filmmaker, he has remained a man of the theater, having adapted for the screen plays by Albee, Neil Simon (with whose work he'd had his first Broadway success, in 1963's *Barefoot in the Park*), Margaret Edson, Tony Kushner, and Patrick Marber. Douglas Kennedy writes that, "unlike so many other Americans who have attempted simultaneously to work in theatre and film (Elia Kazan, for example, or Arthur Penn), Nichols has consistently managed to remain on the A-Team in both arenas."[2]

Not long after the box-office failure and critical static that attended his much-anticipated 1970 adaptation of Joseph Heller's novel *Catch-22*, Nichols would lose his way so completely in Hollywood that, for an extraordinary eight years, 1975–1983, he made no narrative feature films.[3] He returned to the stage. His first play directed during his Hollywood hiatus was in 1976: David Rabe's *Streamers*, an aggressive ensemble drama on Vietnam; by the following year, Nichols as producer had delivered the iconic musical *Annie* into the hearts of the populace, thus securing for himself a new fortune but further muddying what might be called an auteurist sense of Nichols the narrative artist.

Nichols would return triumphantly to Hollywood after his strange interlude of nearly a decade, his first film of a resurrected career the noble, genre-bending *Silkwood* (1983), which earned him his third Oscar nomination as Best Director, but as the new films piled up through the 1980s and 1990s, he was all but unrecognizable as the auteur filmmaker of the late 1960s; he'd become an industry professional, cranking out entertainments within a largely anonymous stylistic sensibility that referred back for its inspiration to the work of Jean Renoir as well as to the Hollywood Golden Age of "Invisible Style" and assembly-line manufacture: "[B]y the time that you're in the middle to late years, your technique should have burned away," Nichols says. "It should be invisible. [...] What is a great Renoir shot? I have no idea. I don't think there is one. He just shoots it. It's just people who happen to be alive as you're watching them doing recognizable, slightly mysterious, very enjoyable things."[4] In 1991, Nichols identified "the fun of making movies" as using "these technical things to make people completely unaware of technical things."[5]

Nichols' long-time friend Buck Henry, who collaborated with Nichols on three of his early films, the adored *The Graduate*, the vilified *Catch-22*, and the dismissed *The Day of the Dolphin*, regrets Nichols' weakness for seemingly safe and unchallenging material: "'He knows I don't like a lot of the stuff he does. I think it's beneath him.'"[6] Joan Juliet Buck writes, "[Nichols'] career has been confusing to those looking either for auteurist rigor or for confirmations of the status quo."[7] David Thomson, writing in his obsessive and impassioned *Biographical Dictionary of Film*, now in its fifth edition, has been on record for many years as a critic of Nichols—not just Nichols the Bland Professional of the 1980s, but also Nichols the Hyper-Expressive Auteur of the 1960s. Even Nichols' late critical and popular revival with the HBO films has failed fully to mollify Thomson's frustration: "Mike Nichols is an unquestioned figure in our culture, a smart man, a funny man, a proven success in cabaret, on records, as a stage director, and as a deliverer of talking-point movies [...] Yet I find it hard to grasp a him in there, a movie director: [...] is there anything more substantial than a high reputation and a producer's instinct for what people might want to see? Is there soul, intelligence, theme, or character holding these films together in series?"[8]

What Thomson implies in his culminating question is an expectation of auteur consistency in a film artist's work, the stylistic and thematic autograph that announces we are watching a distinctive "brand": the Orson Welles film, the Alfred Hitchcock film, the Robert Altman film, the Woody Allen film. These last two eminences in particular are roughly chronological contemporaries of Mike Nichols, though Altman got his start in industrial filmmaking and television, while Allen's beginning were, similar to Nichols, in comic cabaret performance. Both Altman and Allen have been well scrutinized by the academic presses, while Nichols' career has gone largely unexamined. Until now, the only monograph on his Hollywood career was published by H. Wayne Schuth in 1978, when Nichols was a mere decade into filmmaking. Lee Hill laments "the puzzling lack of sustained critical study" of Nichols' career: "Outside of the usual film junket type publicity, there has been little serious commentary about Nichols' work."[9] Gavin Smith muses, "it's rare to see any recognition of [Nichols'] visual gifts, and the extent to which he is one of America's most accomplished filmmakers."[10] The only other book published about Nichols has been my 2011 study of his most iconic film, called *Appraising* The Graduate: *The Mike Nichols Classic and Its Impact in Hollywood*. Is it possible, Thomson's question demands, for cinephiles and scholars to identify the Mike Nichols "brand"—or is there only the anonymous professional, making sure that all the cogs turn smoothly in the Hollywood machinery?

The purpose of this book is to propose several, sometimes conflicting answers, in the form of distinct phases of Nichols' career—to satisfy Thomson's question, "Is there soul, intelligence, theme, or character holding these films together in series?" Despite a prevailing silence in the scholarly community, an ongoing cultural dialogue persists in the popular press concerning Nichols' legacy, though even here, there seems to be a tendency to take him for granted, as if the apparent ease of Nichols' talent makes critical valuation superfluous. Where Nichols has increasingly been acknowledged and feted is within his industry. Few individuals in American entertainment have been as recognized by their peers for their achievement. In 1999 he was accorded a Gala tribute by the Film Society of Lincoln Center, was in 2003 a recipient of the Kennedy Center Honors, and in 2010 received the American Film Institute Lifetime Achievement Award. His multiple talents have led to a much rarer distinction (reflective of his career transformations): with his Emmy for *Wit* in 2001, Nichols became one of a dozen rarefied show-business personalities who have earned the unofficial "Entertainer's Grand Slam" of competitive awards: the Emmy, Grammy, Oscar, and Tony (or, EGOT). He is only the second person to do so mainly as a director (three were musical composers, the rest actors and actresses); yet to acknowledge that Mel Brooks was the stage and screen director who preceded Nichols to the EGOT Slam is itself an implied commentary on industry standards, one way (of several) to demonstrate a context for Nichols' career. Brooks has been a wellspring of comic mayhem for two generations, but no one's idea of an auteur heavyweight; the Tony-winning successes of Brooks and Nichols during the first decade of the new millennium were, respectively, in *The Producers* (2001) and *Spamalot* (2005): smart, funny, crowd-pleasing, ultimately forgettable evenings out.

Thomson's lament for a consistency of artistic vision in Nichols is, in fact, everywhere apparent in Brooks, who has been the self-appointed Fool in the court of Western cultural tradition since doing his Grammy-winning impersonation of the "2000 Year Old Man" in 1961, when Nichols and May ruled Broadway with their comic sketch show. It may not be unreasonable to claim that there is a distinct "brand" known as the Mel Brooks film, but constancy may not automatically equate to what film criticism would call auteur achievement; Thomson dismisses Brooks precisely because of a consistent, too-easy reliance on the meta-gags of parody.[11] The greater variety and weight of Nichols' work presents a more complex cinematic vision. Nichols' filmmaking method may be part of the cause for critical consternation about his legacy: "The frequency and facility with which he adapts other people's material make Mr. Nichols' own sensibility hard to pin down, and he has never been one to make grand claims for himself as an artist."[12] Regardless of the origins of his cinematic stories, however, Nichols remains the selector, and he has self-identified a unifying thread in his films as "transformation,"[13] an idea this book will explore at length, not only within his cinematic protagonists but also within the broader context of Nichols' *own* transformations as an artist: those professional transformations already noted as well as the artistic transformations undertaken during the length of his film career, which I ultimately divide into three distinct phases covered in three separate sections: his early auteur films; his mid-career work as a less-distinctive Hollywood professional; and the ambitious late films, beginning with his work for HBO.

Despite these three distinct phases I have identified in Nichols' film career, my larger contention in this book is that it is possible to find a through-line in all of Nichols' work, regardless of style, tone, and relative ambition of each individual film: an intelligent critic

of social manners is always engaged and readily apparent. "The first question," Nichols has
said many times in characterizing the dialogue between artist and audience, "is the one the
audience asks: 'Why are you telling me this?' And you have to know why. And then you ask
the audience a question, the only question I know to ask. You say, 'Is this like your life?'"[14]
The narrative energy of Nichols' work, even when it devolves into manic, caricatured farce,
resides in a critique of the way we live now, what may be called the destructive objectification
at work on individuals in contemporary culture. Nichols is a man of his time, rarely exploring
eras beyond his current milieu; when he does, these narratives are typically either thinly disguised analogs of his own time (as in *Catch-22*'s Vietnam-era appropriation of the chaos of
the European theater in World War II) or else nostalgic recreations of the proving grounds
of his own generational sensibilities (as in the post-war, college-boy cultural awakenings of
Carnal Knowledge or *Biloxi Blues*, two films that otherwise are profoundly different in psychological tone). Tellingly, the retreat to the Depression in *The Fortune* and the leap to the
futurist, science-fiction premise of *What Planet Are You From?* reflect Nichols at his least
convincing. Rather, Caryn James calls Nichols "the ultimate mainstream director, who senses
the movement of American culture half a beat before the rest of us and, like a reconnaissance
man, presents us with a map of the territory where we will all arrive shortly."[15] Buck observes,
"The great appeal of Mike Nichols is that he seems to know the bitter truth about life but
to be able to rise above it with a wit and a charm unequaled in America."[16] Nichols' ironic
posture towards contemporary social values and codes of conduct suggests what Timothy
Bewes refers to as "The Anxiety of Late Capitalism," the sub-title to his book *Reification*
(2000), an attempt to argue for the "redemptive" transformation imminent in conscious
awareness of reified experience, which for Nichols begins in objectification. "If your life is
ruled by things,'" he has said since his earliest pronouncements as a filmmaker, "'you become
a thing,'"[17] which can promote the objectifying "danger of treating yourself or other people
as things."[18]

Borrowing the term "Anxiety" from Kierkegaard's *The Concept of Anxiety* (1844), Bewes
posits that "anxiety" is a manifestation of consciousness, specifically the intellectual awareness
of reification. Reviewing Marxist and Neo-Marxist interpretations of culture at length, Bewes
argues that, in a culture whose values pre-fabricate us either as agents of or aliens to the culture, reification contains within it a Kierkegaardian "education in possibility."[19] (Education
metaphors and motifs are rife in Nichols' films.) Bewes observes, "[T]he *concept* of reification,
as Lukács discovered very quickly, is itself reifying. The education in possibility is an education in the simultaneity of the anxiety towards reification with its opposite, liberation
from it."[20] Bewes eventually identifies the qualities of "inversion" and even "redemption"[21]
as latent within reification, dependent for their actualization upon the conscious awareness,
or "anxiety," of the reified—for Bewes "the spirit of possibility."[22] The radical hope or possibility inherent in the otherwise demoralizing processes of reification is, paradoxically, that
reification can itself be objectified, "imbu[ing] existing reality with an otherness which, at
the level of consciousness and beyond, ensures its imminent and radical transformation."[23]

Nichols himself chooses the word "transformation"[24] to describe his artistic vision of
humanity; in addressing David Thomson's question, about whether it is possible to understand Nichols' oeuvre as "holding [...] together in series," I will argue that it is a thematic
rather than a stylistic constancy that emerges from a careful and considered examination of
his film career. John Lindsay Brown observed early in Nichols' career that "the sheer range
of Nichols' eclecticism is not contained by it. Instead, it would seem that stylistically Nichols
is very much at the mercy of his collaborators."[25] Nichols' immersion in the "Invisible Style"

of Hollywood studio filmmaking during what I am calling his second career phase only strengthened this general impression of Nichols the filmmaker. Of Nichols' "place in the cinematic order," Peter Applebome concludes that every Nichols "film comes pre-certified for intelligence, wit and style, and few directors have such a gift for getting performances out of actors."[26] For Thomson, who grants these qualities, this is not enough. Mike Nichols' cinematic narratives hold together in series because they offer an interpretation of *transformation* as the success or failure of individuals to accept the responsibilities inherent in their reified anxiety. "I love the idea of a second chance," Nichols has said. "I'm very interested by the possibility of redemption."[27] Having been the object (often literally) of reification and its "education in possibility," a Nichols protagonist either achieves a transforming measure of liberation from reification via the wisdom available in its attendant anxiety or else remains bound in an ironic stasis, aware of the necessity to move yet powerless to act. Reification's potential wisdom may best be captured in a recurring phrase from the grand, summative work of Nichols' last phase as a film director, his 2003 adaptation of Tony Kushner's *Angels in America*. In this majestic six-hour film made for HBO as a mini-series, two main characters, Harper Pitt (Mary-Louise Parker) and Prior Walter (Justin Kirk) use the phrase "threshold of revelation" as their shared way of verbalizing the uncanny experiences of prophetic vision they undergo during their processes of transformation, as they begin to see beyond the veil of objectifying cultural abstractions each in very different ways has long accepted. Prior and Harper are prime agents of reified anxiety, and their prophetic visions evolve steadily from self-pitying stasis towards redemptive transformation.

The first four films in Nichols' oeuvre—each in its own way a masterpiece—are emblematic of a spectrum of protagonist response to the encounter with reified anxiety. The first two narratives, *Who's Afraid of Virginia Woolf?* (1966) and *The Graduate* (1967), create an allusive foregrounding in the notion of "education in possibility" since both make vigorous, ironic use of university life—the assumed promise of higher education and its actual disappointments. In *Virginia Woolf*, George and Martha reside on a college campus where he is chair of the History department and she is the sharp-witted (and sharp-tongued) daughter of the college president. In *The Graduate*, Benjamin Braddock is the precocious valedictorian of a prestigious eastern university and recipient of a graduate fellowship to prepare for a teaching career,[28] and Elaine Robinson is a diligent Berkeley co-ed, attending classes and studying for tests. Despite the manifest signifiers of culturally accepted "success" attendant upon academic performance, all four protagonists of Nichols' first two films are awash in failure. The "education in possibility" must derive from some other source than traditional educational systems, which are as susceptible to reified entrapment as any other forces of hegemonic culture. Nichols' third film, *Catch-22*, revolves around servicemen with little or no time for the niceties of academic philosophy, immersed as they are in the foxhole-pragmatism of men facing encroaching death. Ironically, only Yossarian, the non-intellectual protagonist of *Catch-22*, unambiguously embodies throughout his narrative the redemptive anxiety Bewes would argue is inherent in his concept of reification, and it is no coincidence that, as we last see him in the film, Yossarian is in motion and in transition. In its long-shot vantage of Alan Arkin's spring toward and escape into open water, the film's ending is faithful to the last sentences of Joseph Heller's novel: "'When Yossarian runs away in the end,' says Heller, 'I never said that he would get all the way. I wrote: "The knife came down, missing him by inches, and he took off." But he tries, he changes. That's the best that can be said for any of us.'"[29] The ironies of his small paddle's effectiveness against the incessant beating of the ocean's current notwithstanding, this is heroic action Yossarian's world would dismiss as craven. Finally, in his fourth film, *Carnal Knowledge*, Nichols captures a glimpse of what reified blindness looks like, in the blank stare of Bobbie (Ann-Margret), knowing the commitment she intends to express to Jonathan (Jack Nicholson) is doomed, but finally and most emphatically in the command performance of phallocratic ascendancy by Jonathan, coaching his hooker Louise (Rita Moreno) to say the lines as he has written them for her.

If Yossarian embodies the spirit of "imminent and radical transformation" as articulated by Bewes in dissecting reification, Benjamin Braddock is just as persuasive as the victim of a failed transformative awakening, the reified "award-winning scholar" and "track star" (as he is repeatedly packaged by others in the film) who finally believes he has a goal to run towards, but who ultimately runs himself (and Elaine) back into conformity's grip, all his incessant motion of the film's last ten minutes (and his intoned command to "Move!" at the church) subsumed by his failure to imagine some worthier goal than the apparent dead ends offered by the preceding generation (marriage, materialism, and social status). The final shot of Benjamin is as long in duration as the shot of Yossarian at the end of *Catch-22*, but *The Graduate*'s ending offers a tableau of paralysis, Benjamin and Elaine passively carried into a future where Nichols himself publicly condemned their failed transformation; Nichols notoriously enraged the film's initial audiences during a college publicity tour in 1968 with his prophecy that, in five years, Benjamin and Elaine will have become their parents.[30] Jonathan in *Carnal Knowledge*, from the generation of Benjamin's parents, keeps abreast of the material comforts of his Manhattan life as the Braddocks and Robinsons do in Beverly Hills, and with as little satisfaction. Their "success" is all performance, empty of any meaning other than the commodified one assigned by majority culture.

In George and Martha, the mated protagonists of *Virginia Woolf*, Nichols offers the most ambiguous resolution of a relationship to reification presented in any of these first four films. George and Martha have been simmered in their reified anxiety for many years, stuck without advancement at a small college, childless and conjuring a marriage-full of illusions. They are not callow, non-verbal, inexperienced youths like Benjamin and Elaine (the best the young protagonists of *The Graduate* can manage in articulating their reified predicament is to admit they are "confused," while George and Martha fume at great verbal length, inventing stories as "games" to vent their outrage—even more eloquently than the plain-spoken Yossarian). While there is undeniable cruelty in George and Martha's seismic "game-playing," there is also something heroic. The very essence of their games identifies their reification through their conscious anxiety, ultimately revealing the possibility of their liberation from illusion. The film ends with George and Martha confronting a dawn that is either their destruction or a reinvented freedom. Or perhaps it is both: Bewes writes, "[R]edemption, I would claim, and not 'construction' or 'reconstruction,' is the true alternative to deconstruction, and its logical consequence."[31] The dawn finds George and Martha clinging to each other because no reified illusions remain to which they may cling, as had always been their default. *Carnal Knowledge* ends with an emphatically, unambiguously negative resolution; each of Nichols' first three films ultimately leaves dramatic resolution suspended, in essence transferring reified anxiety (and the responsibility to understand and act upon one's reified awareness) into the hearts and minds of an audience that has been largely unwilling or unable to accept this challenge. I discuss this failure of popular response at length in *Appraising The Graduate*, and return to the argument in this book.

Three decades later in his career, in adapting *Angels in America* for HBO, Nichols offered an immensely complex network of narrative intersections with an even wider range of responses to reified anxiety than in his first four films combined. Roy Cohn (Al Pacino) and Joe Pitt (Patrick Wilson), the reified mentor and his craven acolyte, are in their homophobic homosexuality even less able to act than Benjamin, less willing to act than Jonathan, while Louis Ironson (Ben Shenkman) spends much of the narrative in petrified guilt for his treatment of Prior, and is finally liberated less by his love for Prior than by his brief, intimate contact with Joe's fearsome entrenchment in denial. The women in particular—Joe's long-suffering, drug-addled wife, Harper, and his fundamentalist Mormon mother, Hannah (Meryl Streep)—are capable of transformative leaps of "possibility" that, it's implied, only Belize (Jeffrey Wright), the gay nurse and long-time friend of Prior, has heretofore negotiated with something like complete success. In a climactic act of genuine, multi-layered compassion, Belize is able to arrange for the Kaddish over the antagonist Roy Cohn's still-warm corpse while simultaneously scheming to ensure the delivery of thousands of dollars of hotly sought, experimental AIDS drugs into the hands of his loved ones in need. The epic's truest (if not the most literal) depiction of an angel, Belize is, in his reified wisdom, among the most liberated characters in Mike Nichols' long cinematic career. A. O. Scott, in an excellent retrospective essay on Nichols, argues that *Angels in America*, "his most ambitious recent work, is about the decision to live as though the world were comic—which is to say, secular, forgiving, forward-looking—in the face of growing evidence that it is, more often and more fundamentally, the opposite."[32]

In the best biographical overview to date of Nichols' career, John Lahr writes that, because of the injustices and sorrows he was made to bear from a young age, Nichols "saw, and still sees, [the world] as predatory and cruel."[33] Scott notes that, "at some point [in any Nichols film], you will catch a glimpse of the selfishness and cruelty that lie beneath a surface that seems so polished and civilized."[34] Films from all phases of his career explore the "darkness" ("My old friend," as the choral soundtrack from 1967's *The Graduate* puts it) of this worldview—and yet the "kindness" that Belize embodies (tempered, of course, by his razor-sharp insights into the hypocrisy and cant of friends and enemies alike) has become an increasing preoccupation of Nichols' films. Glimmers of that kindness may be glimpsed in the darkness of even Nichols' earliest films, in the fierce, loyal tenderness with which George and Martha face the dawn together in *Virginia Woolf* or in Maggie's longsuffering support of Jake in a remarkably similar ending to *The Day of the Dolphin*. By contrast, the utter absence of anything like kindness in the scrum for control in *Carnal Knowledge* and its reboot of chamber-ensemble misery more than three decades later in *Closer*, as well as in Roy Cohn's demonic appetite for manipulative control in *Angels in America*, makes clear that Nichols knows atavistic cruelty remains a human default. In *Silkwood*, "kindness" becomes a subject, as Karen must learn to appreciate the consolation of Drew's uncommon common-man tenderness, as she comes to understand her own tolerance of Dolly has often been less than kind. Sergeant Toomey in *Biloxi Blues* dismisses "kindness" as the problematic source of humanity he intends to drill out of his recruits in order "to save these boys' lives," given the commodified identities they've been assigned by the military. *Regarding Henry*, distressingly pilloried by popular criticism for its unabashed sentimentality, was Nichols' first feature-length exploration of "kindness" as a philosophical option: Henry (Harrison Ford) journeys from a life of empty, grasping manipulation to a simpler life of shared kindnesses, modeled for him by his wife and therapists, as well as by his own child, who teaches him the positive counterpoints to all those negative lessons he's passed down from his own father. Henry forsakes his old life in an act of kindness to people he has wronged in court, distinguishing between the patronizing shows of kindness done for him by his law firm post-trauma and the genuine kindness he feels obliged to embody in his redemption. In *Primary*

Colors, Nichols found his way into the labyrinth of Jack Stanton and his campaign for the White House via the "kindness"[35] he locates at the core of the donut shop scene, which revealed the aching empathy of Stanton's motivations, saving grace to the corruptive overtures of global power.

In the extraordinary HBO films, with their invitation to "television's intimacy,"[36] Nichols foregrounded kindness again as the climactic act, as in *Regarding Henry*. *Wit*'s Vivian Bearing (Emma Thompson) avers, "Now is a time for simplicity. Now is a time for, dare I say it, kindness." In her newfound wisdom, she may be forgiven her temporal specificity; the brief retrospective glance she casts back over her own professional life as a university scholar and teacher makes cringingly manifest her own failures of kindness in her classroom at times when cruelty only built walls and sabotaged pedagogy. Uncomfortable in her vulnerability as she hungrily absorbs the kindnesses offered by Susie (Audra McDonald), Vivian remains a work in progress at her death, still as terrified of the vulnerability of needing the kindness of strangers as she is of death itself. Nichols' admiration for the text of his next project, *Angels in America*, came in his sense of the "rare" quality the play possesses, "in which acts of kindness were such a major event."[37] While Belize is at the climactic peak of these moments late in *Perestroika* (the second half of Kushner's epic), Hannah Pitt (Meryl Streep) may be the most dramatically transformed of all the characters who enter Kushner's drama as kindness-starved as they are kindness-challenged. Prior, newly awakened from his darkest night of wrestling with the Angel of "cessation, of Death," is happy to see Belize but is just as much in need of seeing Hannah. As she leaves to get some rest, he campily trots out Tennessee Williams' oft-quoted "I have always depended upon the kindness of strangers," to which Hannah snaps as instinctively reactive a response as might Vivian Bearing: "Well that's a stupid thing to do." Indeed, in a predatory world, vulnerable interdependence can be quite dangerous, and yet reified wisdom, having rejected the reductive atavism of competition and control, must seek some alternative structure for living one's life. Tony Kushner calls this the "double vision" of "empathic imagination" and "skepticism," through which we may develop "critical consciousness": "I believe in the power of theater to teach and to heal through compassion."[38] James Fisher writes, "Kushner's view of the interconnectedness of all humanity, regardless of race, sexual preference, religion, or politics and of the primacy of loyalty and commitment to others and to society"[39] reflects reified wisdom and what comes after: transformed action. This is what Nichols means by "citizenship,"[40] the final prophetic aspiration Prior Walter asserts in *Angels in America*'s coda ("We will be citizens"): "kindness had become like gold in the '80s—rare and invaluable," Nichols recalls; while acknowledging subsequent social progress, he adds, "I think the impact of these characters finding their lives and finding someone when they can is going to mean something to people any time," concluding "being a citizen" is the main subject of *Angels*.[41] "Kindness" is a typically rich word, after all, with its denotative and connotative associations with consideration and helpfulness, and its literal, etymological implications of likeness or fellow feeling: citizenship is a mutual recognition of one's kind, and the wisdom reified awareness affords is able to blast through manipulative artificial categories and classifications of a person's "kind" to the essential reality of human kinship. That even Belize, after his not-so-random but rather carefully considered acts of kindness at the climax of *Angels* must excuse himself to go "home to nurse my grudges" is a cautionary reminder that all transformation is process. True citizenship and its attendant kindness are endless tasks of becoming.

This book will cast its retrospective gaze over Mike Nichols' artistic life beginning, in "Part I: Taking the Stage," with a time before he ever thought about Hollywood, when he was a master of improvised cabaret comedy after two desultory years at the University of Chicago, with the Compass Players, precursor of the Second City comedy troupe, and then in New York, first as a comic performer with Elaine May, and then as one of the most successful directors in the history of Broadway theater. In some of its essential thematic and even stylistic elements, Nichols' comedy career serves as entrée into his thematic preoccupation with reified conformity as well as characteristic rhetorical strategies of his films. His work as a comedian was rarely solo; as a filmmaker, Nichols' creative process is fundamentally as an improvisatory collaborative artist rather than as a solo genius, a man whom actors and technicians revere for his ability routinely to conjure their best work. There has never been a question, from his earliest productions, about Nichols' authority, but his willingness to experiment with script and storyboard, trusting not only his own instincts but also those of his assembled talent during production, may suggest why he does not have a more distinctive "brand." He is cherished for providing a winning combination of collaborative autonomy and auteur autocracy: Billy Wilder called the secret ingredient of Nichols' working method "'inner content,'"[42] an instinctive dramatic compass which Nichols employs to guide a company to its best work. Richard Burton said that Nichols "conspires with you, rather than directs you, to get your best.'"[43] After this initial chapter, which traces the personal and professional journey that led to the initiation of Nichols' film career in 1966, this book's shape conforms to the three phases that distinguish his filmmaking, examining each of his 20 narrative feature films in discrete chapters (and excluding the Gilda Radner concert film he released in 1980, during his eight-year hiatus).

The first phase—from his debut in 1966 until he lapsed into eight years of cinematic silence after the miscalculations of *The Fortune* in 1975—was the most distinctly auteurist in character, and I have thus called this part of the book "The Auteur." The patron cinematic saints presiding over his early career were the towering eminences of film: Hollywood auteurs and European grand masters. Andrew Sarris characterized Nichols' "neatly eclectic style" as having been "borrowed from directors as disparate as Federico Fellini and George Stevens, Ingmar Bergman and Richard Lester, Michaelangelo Antonioni and Orson Welles."[44] The films during his first phase were stylistically and thematically aggressive, confrontational. There were stars on screen (a constant Nichols trademark across the three phases), but they were typically rivaled during this first phase by an equally formidable impression made by the *star behind the camera*. Joseph Gelmis, for example, gave Nichols a prominent place in his 1970 collection of interviews called *The Film Director as Superstar*, and Mel Gussow published a fawning article in *Newsweek* in 1968 entitled, "Director as Star." Crowing about *Carnal Knowledge*, the third film his company produced, Joseph E. Levine claimed, "'We don't even care who's in the film. We don't need stars in a Nichols film.'"[45] Nichols' most popular film in this era (still the most cherished of his career, a fixture in the upper reaches of the American Film Institute lists for Best Film and Best Comedy) was *The Graduate* (1967), a semi-independent sleeper that broke box-office records. Nichols commented that *The Graduate* "took off almost on a career of its own, even places where criticism has no impact."[46] He expressed his alarm at the unreflective mass embrace of his film as countercultural document, as in this deconstruction of his "revolutionary" audience in 1970: "[I]t depresses me to see dissent turned so instantly into a market, which is the way this country always disarms it. 'You want dissent? Wonderful, darling. Sweatshirts that say Revolution are $2.50 apiece.'"[47] My earlier book on that film details the problematic reception of *The Graduate* by audiences and mainstream film criticism[48]; though Nichols was adamant that the film was not so much an affirmation of the counter-culture as a negative satire of reified capitalist conformity, Nichols and Dustin Hoffman, the off–Broadway character actor Nichols plucked from obscurity, ironically became objects of cultural idolization. It is impossible to examine Nichols' career without frequent allusions to the most permanent of his works in the public imagination; Nichols himself even makes sly allusions to *The Graduate* twenty-three years later in *Postcards from the Edge*. There is, duly, a chapter on *The Graduate* in this present book and additional, frequent references back to the film in relation to Nichols' other films, but for the detailed exploration the film deserves (and rewards), please see my monograph. During the first half of this first phase, Nichols' reputation was so inviolable in the industry that a backlash was inevitable, to which he was and remains, in his essential desire to please audiences, acutely sensitive. "'I never said all that stuff about me,'" he told Nora Ephron as *Catch-22* was in production in Mexico. "'I'm not happy about this thing that's building up about me, because it has nothing to do with me. I mean, the things I've done are neither as good as the people who carry on say they are, nor are they as bad as the reaction says they are.'"[49]

When he returned to filmmaking in the 1980s, particularly after 1983's *Silkwood*, which was almost like a second debut given the length of the cinematic silence that had preceded it, Nichols was a different filmmaker. Nichols says of his return to filmmaking with *Silkwood*, "[T]he movie was about an awakening, and I felt as though it were an awakening for me."[50] I have called this part of the book "The Pro"; it features the films typically understood as his most commercially calculated in both style and substance. One could argue that Nichols' transformation ("a sea change," Hill calls it[51]) mirrored transformations underway in the culture at large: the various revolutions of the 1960s yielding to Reagan-era accumulation and assimilation. Richard T. Jameson writes that Nichols' return to Hollywood was "a major turning point" in his career: "Abandoning his well-nigh absolute adherence to the long take and a European (or arthouse) tolerance for duration, he became less an *homme due cinema*, more a guy who made movies."[52] Jameson argues that *Postcards from the Edge* (1990), *Wolf* (1994), and *Primary Colors* (1998), all ambitious films from this second phase that performed poorly at the box office, are "grievously underrated."[53] One of Nichols' most popular films of this second phase of his career, 1988's *Working Girl* (his fourth Oscar nomination as Best Director), reflects the uncertainty of how to understand both the filmmaker's vision in mid-career and the larger machinations of the culture. Some critics, including Thomson, recognize the film as a light-hearted, feminist "Cinderella" set in corporate America,[54] while Roger Bowen, a fellow comic among the improvisational Compass Players in Chicago during Nichols' earliest professional life, represents another camp, calling *Working Girl* "'a Republican fairy tale.'"[55] Despite the polemical division, what most reviewers and critics seem willing to agree upon is that the film is lightweight. While Nichols' work in this second phase is deceptively pro-social in appearance, my book will examine these second-phase films as carefully as the films of the other two phases; what emerges is a sense of Nichols' subversive point of view latent in even the most seemingly celebratory films of status quo conformity. As in my argument in my 2011 monograph about the heavily ironized point of view of *The Graduate*, which the mass audience failed fully to grasp in championing Benjamin Braddock (Dustin Hoffman) as a hero of the counter-culture, I argue in this book that a woman like Tess McGill (Melanie Griffith) gets exactly what she has wished for in *Working Girl*, and she literally disappears at film's end, consumed by the concrete canyons of Lower Manhattan's Financial District. As this long second phase continued, Nichols actually offered some unambiguously positive portraits of protagonists—positive not because they have succeeded in majority culture on its own terms, but because they have opted out of the prevailing culture's presumptions and prejudices. To dismiss Nichols as a fabulist of conformity is to skim the surface of his work. As Hill notes in his excellent, concise overview, "Nichols' ironic sensibility remains remarkably consistent in the second half of his filmmaking career. It is a form of irony that may be out of fashion with those for whom irony means never having to think too deeply about any one idea for too long, but for those trying to reconcile the gap between dream and nightmare in their waking life, Nichols' work continues to resonate."[56]

Yet a third phase has arguably emerged late in Nichols' career, and as with *The Fortune* in 1975, the critical and box-office failure that prompted his self-exile and transformation into the second phase of his career, this third phase seems to have been signaled by another low point in high-concept farce: *What Planet Are You From?* (2000). I have called this part "The Late Nichols," a phrase that alludes to the phenomenon of artistic autumn's colorful burst of renewed creativity, as in "The Late Rubens" or, in Nichols' own medium, "The Late Kurosawa." While no temporal demarcation like the eight-year hiatus until *Silkwood* exists for this second transition into a new phase, the return to subjects and style of memorably ambitious and consistent gravity is undeniable beginning with *Wit* in 2001. His most recent film, *Charlie Wilson's War*, was the ill-timed last of a long, dutiful Hollywood season of anti–Afghanistan War films to be released in Fall 2007; Nichols' film was easily the most effective because of an artistic willingness to modulate tone, incorporating both comedy and drama, as Nichols' films often will. While Nichols' silence as a filmmaker has now stretched to seven years as this book is published, his name continues to be attached to intriguing adaptations—of Patricia Highsmith's *Deep Water*, a collaboration with Chris Rock on a remake of Kurosawa's *High and Low*, and of the aptly named *One Last Thing Before I Go*, a novel by Jonathan Tropper.

When relevant, I include references to the production process of a film, though the primary objective of this book is critical interpretation and response rather than historical documentation. As previously mentioned, Nichols' work has received scant scholarly scrutiny, but I incorporate a representative sampling of what has been published on Nichols within my discussions. In three instances, I have included within my discussion of a film a synopsis of the film's plot. In two cases, *Catch-22* (1970) and *Angels in America* (2003), the inclusion of a plot summary is because the action of the film is not merely complex but potentially disorienting. Both *Catch-22* and *Angels* jumble chronology and routinely present events that are surreal—imagined, dreamed, hallucinated. Understanding plot in these two narratives is part of the work of interpretation. In the third case, I have included a plot summary of *The Fortune* because it is the one film in Nichols' oeuvre not readily available in a digital format, and thus may prove inaccessible to curious viewers. The perfunctory summary represents the main action of this hard-to-find film.

Finally, in "Among the Stars," I offer a brief evaluation of Mike Nichols' legacy as a Hollywood filmmaker. The chapter's title has a double meaning: Nichols as an actor's director, and Nichols' place in the firmament of filmmakers. Nichols has been a star's director since his famous debut with the most celebrated screen couple of the era, Elizabeth Taylor and Richard Burton. Most of the greatest names in his era of Hollywood history have lined up to work with him—Dustin Hoffman, George C. Scott, Warren Beatty, Jack Nicholson (four times), Meryl Streep (four times), Harrison Ford (twice), Gene Hackman (twice), Annette Bening (thrice), Emma Thompson (thrice), Julia Roberts (twice), Tom Hanks, and Philip Seymour Hoffman have all done memorable work with Nichols, garnering a shining array of Oscar, Golden Globe, and Emmy nominations and hardware. But my final chapter's title also refers to Nichols as a star in his own right, a director who has managed to maintain

A-list status decade after decade. While discussing Nichols in relation to contemporaries like Altman and Allen, I will also assert a sort of continuum of Hollywood practice via a line of inheritance from Orson Welles to Nichols to Sam Mendes. Each was a precocious talent whose initial success came elsewhere in the performing arts than in filmmaking. All three were lured to immediate cinematic achievement by an initially mutual infatuation with Hollywood—its multi-track, hyper-expressive montage medium and its incomparable command of the broad audience and thus of enormous reserves of capital. None has had an unambiguously productive and happy Hollywood career. Welles, Nichols, and Mendes all have been transformed by their experience of Hollywood and have, in turn, had a transforming influence in Hollywood. Most notably for my book's thesis, all have taken as a central (in Nichols' case, essential) theme of their work what Nichols himself identifies as the core of his narrative sensibility: the possibility (and difficulty) of human transformation.

1

The Little Exile, the Cabaret Comic, the Broadway Midas

"'The older I get,'" Mike Nichols told Sam Kashner in 2012, "'the more I think that the life I started with—I was insanely, unfairly, ridiculously lucky. All Jews went to the camps, but we not only didn't go to camps, we were allowed to leave the country. We got to America, and everything that happened was luckier and luckier. I didn't finish college. I just stopped going to class, and I got a job on the radio. I didn't know anything. I couldn't get a diploma in anything! Over and over I was luckier than I had any right to be.'"[1] Elaine May, who for a brief, shining moment in the second half of the 1950s teamed with Nichols to make the comic duo of Nichols and May, listens to Nichols' protestations of luck alongside Kashner, having consented to one of her exceedingly rare interviews, and corrects her former partner: without Nichols' talent and intelligence, his luck wouldn't have meant a thing in the entertainment world. In fact, for many years after he arrived in the U.S., not until he'd entered college, Nichols would have called himself nothing more than a survivor. He was a terribly unhappy child in an unhappy home, and while undeniably gifted, he clearly fits the model of those who have *made* their luck.

He was born Michael Igor Peschkowsky in Berlin on November 6, 1931, his family already in exile from Russia after the Revolution. His mother Brigitte's parents were culturally distinguished: his mother's mother had written the libretto to Richard Strauss' opera *Salome*, and her husband, Gustav Landauer, was martyred by German soldiers in 1918. Nichols' father, Paul Peschkowsky, was a successful physician; his Russian patronymic, Nicholaiyevitch, was the source for the Anglicized "Nichols" when the family moved from Europe to America, thanks to the two years that the Stalin-Hitler Pact was in force. Young Michael's early schooling in Berlin was in segregated schools. Beyond the systemic anti–Semitism oppressing the family, Nichols himself had a terribly unlucky physiological trauma as a four-year-old. Administered a whooping-cough vaccine, he was left permanently hairless. The stigma of this physical oddity, of his ethnicity, and of the genteel poverty into which his family in time sank in New York all formed a core identity for him as an outsider.

By 1938, it was clear that something irreversible had become entrenched in Germany. Paul left his wife, too sick to travel, and his young sons behind and sailed to America to establish a medical practice on the Upper West Side. He sent for his family a year later, but only the boys were healthy enough for the trip; they sailed together, unchaperoned (Michael was seven, Robert three). Their mother didn't join them for another year and a half. Nichols recalls being so struck by seeing Hebrew in a delicatessen window their first night in America that he anxiously asked his father if this were allowed. His father was a talented but essentially cold man who, ill at ease with two young boys suddenly in his charge, made a deal with an English family he was treating: they would take in Michael and Robert.[2] Again Nichols felt stigmatized, as the parents would kiss their own children good night, then shake hands with their young, parentless boarders. Not until Brigitte finally arrived did the boys resume living with their own family.

School resumed all the objectifying lessons begun in Germany. Michael was bald; he wore a cap everywhere. Though quick to learn English, he carried an alienating accent. And he was Jewish. Nichols told Henry Louis Gates in the PBS documentary *Faces of America*, "I never really heard anything anti–Semitic till I was in P.S. 87 and, for the first time, somebody said something about a Jewish kid—me—and it was one of the teachers. It wasn't in a particularly friendly tone, and so I came home a little concerned about it. My mother was great. I remember she sort of put an arm around me [...], and she told me about Jews and what it meant to be a Jew and what the problems were, and none of this had ever been spoken of before or she wouldn't have had to have this little talk."[3] His lifelong friend Buck Henry, whom he first met at the exclusive Dalton School on the Upper East Side where his father's practice could afford to send him, says, "'The kid was as far outside as an outsider can get.'"[4] Nichols now understands the gift inside that early struggle: "'I think there is an immigrant's ear that is particularly acute for "How are they doing it here? What must I do to be unnoticeable, to be like them?" [...] At its highest and most extreme form, it leads to great artists like Joseph Conrad and Stoppard and Nabokov. They've somehow both digested a new language and culture and made it more expressive in some way. You're forever looking at something as someone who just got here.'"[5] A. O. Scott acknowledges that this is a generational phenomenon in Hollywood between the wars: "The fact of his German birth and Russian-Jewish parentage links him to the great generation of Central European émigrés whose style and sophistication imported both classicism and modernity to Hollywood's studio era. Mr. Nichols may be the last of a venerable line that stretches from Ernst Lubitsch through Billy Wilder. He is, if you'll forgive the pun, a tamer Wilder in a wilder time."[6]

During the course of *Faces of America*, Gates' researchers turned up records indicating that two of Nichols' uncles who had remained behind in Russia perished in 1938 for "counter-revolutionary activities" condemned by the Stalin regime. Nichols said to Gates, "I'm so used to knowing that I'm *beyond* lucky—it's like a joke, this luck—and what a putz to ever have complained about anything for even a moment. And of course the only way to deal with guilt other than bury it is to try to do a little something. And so you do what you can find, and you do what you do."[7] For Nichols, doing what you can do is cinematic storytelling, and the various kinds of social objectifications he endured early in life gave him a point of view he could carry into all the different kinds of films he has made over the course of his long career. More than a formal "style," this thematic sensibility—the ways in which identity is constructed *and thus constricted* by hegemony, and the transforming wisdom available in awakening to one's reification—constitutes the consistent auteur quality of Nichols' work. In an early interview, having just completed *Who's Afraid of Virginia Woolf?* (1966) and long before *The Graduate*'s reception in 1968 and 1969 would catapult him to an undreamed level of superstardom, Nichols expressed his admiration for the great directors (he named Fellini and Truffaut in the interview) who possess the ability to take "the specifics of one life"[8] and find a universal point of contact. "If you're ruthless enough about your own life, and accurate enough, you can reach others. [...] The only way you reach a person is to reach into yourself."[9]

Some would call Nichols' filmography eclectic; others have carped that he has sought too often to please when he could have challenged. "'I can only feel my own excitement,' Nichols says. 'Sometimes I wish it were more high-minded, and sometimes I'm glad that it's not. I have no choice either way. I don't think *The Graduate* and *Carnal Knowledge* were any different from what I'm doing now.'"[10] This study argues that, at least in thematic intention, Nichols' seemingly facile claim is in fact deeply considered and accurate. In that 1966 interview on the cusp of international celebrity, enthusing about Fellini (an enormous influence on Nichols' first three films, through 1970's *Catch-22*), Nichols says, "I think that's the most enviable thing in a director, [...] a powerful view of life."[11] Nichols received his vision of life early. Whether making tragedy or melodrama or farce, Nichols *does what he can do* as a way of conveying the outrage and redemptive possibility his various stories can offer us in our own reified circumstances. When Nichols claims to "have no choice either way," he is referring to the autocracy of his inner response to a prospective film. "'You can't make your decision about a film on the basis of "Is it important enough? Is it serious enough?" It's either alive or it's not for me. If it's alive, I want to do it.'"[12]

Having his mother rejoin the family was, at best, a mixed blessing: Paul and Brigitte were not happily married; they fought bitterly and each took many lovers. Nichols' father died of leukemia, at 44, when Mike was 12, before he could show his father his particular aptitudes and promise. With his father's death came a swift reduction in the family's means, which led to a succession of uncomfortably small, grubby apartments for the three of them on the Upper West Side. Mike's enormous intellect allowed him to continue on scholarship at exclusive New York schools; he read prodigiously in literature and haunted theaters and cinemas as he was able. He and a date were transfixed by the legendary Elia Kazan production of *A Streetcar Named Desire* with Brando as Stanley Kowalski; it gave Nichols a clear sense of his future, in the theater. Yet the experiences of living in such close proximity to a hypochondriac mother, wearing a wig to school to avoid appearing totally hairless, never having an extra penny when his classmates and associates were among the wealthiest circle of New York—all fostered his sense, as a teenager, of the unfairness of life. "'I thought about revenge a lot in those days,'" he says,[13] but in the next phase of his life, he would discover a creative outlet for his vengeance: comedy. For Nichols, comedy is "'the ability to get revenge instantly'"[14]—at least as it is plied by comedians like Mike Nichols in the form of devastating social satire, the predominant formal means he has used since college to express his artistic point of view.

Nichols told *The New Yorker* in 1961 that both he and May went to the University of Chicago because they were "'on the lam from their childhoods.'"[15] It was an opportunity for reinvention among "'other weirdos like me.'"[16] Long before he met May on campus, he met Susan Sontag in line to register for classes. No slouch as a prodigy (she was 15 at matriculation), Sontag would say later that she was curiously attracted to Nichols despite the physical strangeness of his hairlessness.[17] He entered college as a pre-med student and managed to complete two years at Chicago despite less than diligent attention to his studies and a succession of increasingly ridiculous part-time jobs (most notoriously, he was fired as a Howard Johnson's food server for suggesting a patron try the chicken-flavored ice cream). He was most happy when engaged in theatrical productions. The first time he saw May was while he was literally performing a servant's role in a production of August Strindberg's *Miss Julie*. He was aware that May was aware that the production was no good (in small part because Nichols had no theatrical credibility playing a valet), yet he was helpless to communicate his awareness to her. Independently, through mutual friends, each learned the other was the only rival on campus in hostility and barbed wit. When they finally met in a Chicago train station, it was as if their meet-cute had been scripted—but then, brilliant improvisational comedians make their scripts instantly. When Nichols walked over, sat down, and broke the ice, May launched without warning into a thick Russian accent and an implied, imaginary scenario in which they were spies communicating in code. They wound up having dinner at his place (and perhaps a brief romantic fling) before settling into inseparable platonic friendship. Nichols left for New York in 1954, before discovering his destiny with May, so he could enroll in Method acting classes taught by Lee Strasberg. To make ends meet, he took a job as a classical radio station announcer in Philadelphia and commuted twice a week for his lessons. "What I learned from Strasberg was much more about directing than acting," Nichols would eventually conclude.[18] Even then, without any inkling, Nichols was preparing for what would make him a theatrical and Hollywood legend. But the path to directing for Nichols led through performing, and there was really only one other performer with whom he ever established a stage presence as an actor: Elaine May.

May was among the founding members of an improvisational theater troupe that had taken up residency in an old Chicago hall called the Compass and thus called themselves the Compass Players. When a slot opened, in 1955, Nichols moved back to the Midwest and became a Compass Player, his first regular paycheck in show business. At the University of Chicago, Nichols had already come across Ed Asner (who was for a time a roommate of Nichols, much as, a decade later in New York, Nichols would discover Dustin Hoffman as his Benjamin in *The Graduate* while Hoffman was sharing rent with Robert Duvall and Gene Hackman). With Compass, Nichols rubbed shoulders with more future stars. Besides Nichols and May, Barbara Harris and Shelley Berman were among the cast; Berman was briefly part of a comic *threesome* with Nichols and May in Chicago. Nichols and May were indisputably the brightest lights of the Compass lineup. Jay Landesman, who ran a venue in St. Louis called the Crystal Palace where Compass hoped to expand, claims "Nichols and May were 'so good, they eventually threw the company off balance, leaving the other members out on a limb.'"[19] Opinion remains divided about whether Nichols was truly a gifted improvisational actor or whether he could keep up with an endlessly inventive talent like May's purely because of the agility and swiftness of his intellect. In any case, he felt a unique simpatico in performing with May that he felt with no one else in the group, and they swiftly became a regular pairing. Through never at ease in the quintessential uncertainties and formlessness of improvisation, Nichols nevertheless found an almost religious intensity in the experience: "The great joy of Compass and then, after, working with Elaine was that once every six weeks you would be possessed. [...] I don't mean to sound mystical, but such things did happen. Like doing twenty minutes of iambic pentameter that we had not thought of but just came pouring out. That was thrilling, and you'd be drained and amazed afterwards, and you'd have a sense of your possibilities."[20] While Nichols had of course been asked to do improvisation under Strasberg, the crucible manifest in performing with Compass was "the pressure from the audience. I think that over the months, and finally over the years, that pressure from the audience taught everyone to answer the unspoken question the audience asked—'Why are you telling us this?'"[21]

Becoming peculiarly sensitized to the demands of the audience was one of the central discoveries of the future director. But he also learned what improvisation could uncover in an actor: "You got so that under the stress of performing and improvising for an audience, instead of being crushed by it and made smaller, as one is to begin with, you could actually become more than yourself and say things you couldn't have thought of and become people you didn't know."[22] A critical juncture for Nichols and for Compass came in 1958. Nichols had married for the first of what would eventually be four times, to Chicago singer and television personality Pat Scot; during the week, May would platonically share Nichols' St. Louis hotel room, then yield the bed to Scot for conjugal weekend visits. Other Compass players began expressing disgruntlement that Nichols and May were given preferential treatment; Nichols claims Berman's jealousy signaled to him that the end was near: "'One day he came offstage and said, "Hey, guys, Mike had three scenes in that set, and I only had two." It was a whole new idea in Eden to count. The group was finished in six months.'"[23] A further complication was a Compass edict that any material the actors had developed on the Compass stage belonged to Compass, which rankled Nichols, knowing he and May had written and honed some classic material.

The first significant piece Nichols and May developed eventually came to be called "Teenagers." Two young people make out in a car, and the piece requires both physical and verbal dexterity. At one point they're so entangled that passing a shared cigarette becomes a comic ordeal; this is also the origin of the moment in *The Graduate* when Benjamin first kisses Mrs. Robinson in the Taft Hotel bedroom, and she exhales a cloud of held cigarette smoke as soon as he's done. At one of the comic peaks of the piece, May as the girl protests that she can't go on or the boy will cease to respect her, and Nichols as the boy ardently assures her that if she acquiesces, he will respect her "like crazy." The pettiness of some of the other Compass performers, the proprietary nature of the Compass administration, and the sense of limitless possibility that Nichols and May had begun to feel about their own future as performers led to Nichols reaching out to the New York agent Jack Rollins in 1958. Over lunch in the Russian Tea Room, Nichols and May ad-libbed a dazzling set of improvisations for Rollins, who booked them into the Blue Angel with the Smothers Brothers and to open for Mort Sahl at the Village Vanguard. Rollins bought Nichols a new shirt and his wife bought May a new dress, and "Nichols and May" was born as an act.[24] They were now post–Compass, improvising a new professional direction together.

Within a month, they were nationally known, and soon after a juggernaut. Rollins began booking them on television spots as a way of increasing their exposure. Their first TV spot was an enviable appearance on the *Tonight* show with Jack Paar, but they tanked—the audience didn't understand the dynamic of a sketch-comic scene suddenly erupting on the stage, and Paar actually chided Nichols and May to *hurry up and finish*. A subsequent appearance on Steve Allen's show was much more successful, and the true ice-breaker was an uninterrupted fifteen minutes on Alistair Cooke's Sunday afternoon *Omnibus* (Nichols and Nora Ephron would later lovingly send up Cooke's calmly omniscient mien in the hallucinatory vignettes experienced by Meryl Streep's character Rachel Samstat while watching television in 1986's *Heartburn*). After their performance on Cooke's show, Nichols and May were headliners. The next logical moves were from cabaret slots to ticketed "concerts" in larger halls as well as recording some of their routines on vinyl. And it was here, in the enormous success they enjoyed in commanding a following that clamored to hear their "routines," that the seeds of Nichols and May's undoing as an act were sown. May, enthralled by the derring-do of improvisation's high wire, came to hate the *routine* of performing "routines" and would happily have continued to act without a net, while Nichols, in awe of the "dybbuk" they could occasionally conjure while improvising,[25] was ultimately far more interested in polishing: "'I became more and more afraid,'" he told Lahr; "'I wasn't happy with getting paid a fortune for something and not having tried it out in advance.'"[26] Though he was still years away from his first directing gig (a 1962 collaboration in New Jersey with Stephen Sondheim on a comic-musical revue of Jules Feiffer cartoon sketches[27]), Nichols effectively became the

Mike Nichols would later be even more famous as a Broadway director and as a Hollywood film-maker, but his first celebrity came as one half of the comic-sketch duo Nichols and May. Nichols met Elaine May while they were students at the University of Chicago, and they later became members of the improvisatory comedy troupe the Compass Players. May was and remains Nichols' first choice as an artistic collaborator and, beyond their two official collaborations (on 1996's *The Birdcage* and 1998's *Primary Colors*), she has polished many other Nichols film scripts prior to production.

director of Nichols and May. Jack Rollins says, "Elaine would go one forever if you let her. She is insanely creative, but she had no sense when to quit. Really, the editor was Mike, because he lives in this world—I call him Mr. Practical—and she lives in her own world, completely disconnected from the practical world.'"[28] Rollins' producing partner, Charles H. Joffe, is even more frank: "Everyone who saw them thought that she was the backbone of the act, and we knew it was him.'"[29] Elaine May was thus the first major actress in a long line that Nichols would make even better with his skills as a director. Meryl Streep, Emma Thompson, Annette Bening, and Julia Roberts don't line up over and over again to work with just anyone.

The act that Nichols honed for them (and that May eventually took to wearing as her very stylish straitjacket) was a social satirist's tour of gendered social proscriptions and liberal pretension. Very few pieces in Nichols and May's repertoire directly target the enemies of liberal ideology. "What their comedy traced," Adam Gopnik writes, "was the true phenomenon of the time: not 'rebellion' but the spread of college education and in-group conformity, and the growth of the university as a central symbolic switching station of American life."[30] In this sense, Nichols and May as an act is the warm-up to *The Graduate*'s distrust of collegiate credentialing as anything more than initiation into a reified club. Nichols deconstructed the success of Nichols and May as more evidence of the lockstep conformity of the popular landscape: "'[W]e became a fashion in the usual way. [W]e were written about in *The New Yorker*. The first week or two at the Blue Angel, nobody much laughed at us. But when *The New Yorker* came out, *how* they laughed. We were horrified. We didn't know such things were possible. We'd just been in Chicago, where people laughed if it was funny; if it wasn't they didn't. We had to be approved, accredited. Once they said we were like the Lunts, they laughed when we came onstage.'"[31] *The New York Times* declared that Nichols and May had "'both snob and mob appeal' like Chaplin and the Marx Brothers."[32] The phrase, delivered so early in Nichols' career, would become very much the dilemma with which Nichols has wrestled throughout his filmmaking career, veering between prickly work with lofty artistic ambitions and reassuringly mainstream work calculated to please audiences. Ironically, some of the films that would seem to have been initiated as much for their box-office appeal as for artistic ambition—Harrison Ford as a recovering accident victim and workaholic in the sentimental *Regarding Henry* (1991); Michelle Pfeiffer and Jack Nicholson as werewolves in *Wolf* (1994); John Travolta and Emma Thompson as Clinton Avatars in the much-anticipated 1998 adaptation of Joe Klein's bestselling political satire, *Primary Colors*; and Garry Shandling as a sex-obsessed alien in *What Planet Are You From?* (2000)—were financial disappointments, though Nichols' artistic reunion with Elaine May in *The Birdcage* in 1996, more than three decades after their professional breakup, was another industry sure-thing that more than delivered on its producers' crowd-pleasing expectations.

Three recordings preserve the energy, invention, and satiric attack of Nichols and May. Oddly, two of their most frequently referenced routines, the aforementioned "Teenagers," and "Pirandello," a nearly 20-minute tour de force of physical and verbal humor, were not among the tracks on any of the three albums (likely because these two pieces depend more than many of Nichols and May's routines on visual as well as verbal effects). The premise of "Pirandello," whose title alludes to the post-modern Italian playwright of metaphysical alienation, chronicled nothing less than the entire life cycle of a couple, from early childhood games of house through old age and death. As the children play, they mimic the backbiting they have learned from their parents; eventually, they have *become* their parents (echoed in Nichols' vision of Benjamin and Elaine becoming their parents after the end of *The Grad-*

uate[33]), squabbling for domestic control. Reduced in later age to metaphoric assertions of power via games (the last of which is chess), their final scene in the earliest versions of the sketch has the woman fall over and lie prone in death, just as the man has finally won their match. In the impoverished spirituality of their relationship, her death is of far less consequence than his having finally won a game against her.[34] It's a vision of human interaction as essentially atavistic. "[O]ur mutual aim became pinning down behavior, making fun of human behavior," Nichols says.[35] If anything, the completed, mature "Pirandello," while less far-reaching in its recording of the stages of life, is also darker, and it produced their most cataclysmic moment on stage. Anticipating Nichols' career-long fascination with examining "transformation,"[36] the routine still traced two metamorphoses beyond the "children" that begin the piece: the first metamorphosis remained the same, as the mimicking children become their parents, then morph again, this time into versions of themselves, actors on stage in a turf war with each other over control of the scene they are playing. By this point, "Pirandello" was the attention-grabbing centerpiece of the show they intended to take to Broadway with Arthur Penn directing. Yet the theatrical show threatened to destroy May, who could not bear the rote repetition of what had begun in adventurous experimentation. The show's routines had been polished to a high gloss by Nichols the director-in-formation, and now were subject to further honing by Penn during its trial run in Westport, Connecticut. While it's unclear whether May's frustration with her entrapment within lines that comically dramatize the entrapment of their characters was the source of the on-stage meltdown between them, Nichols and May morphed one extra time on a certain night in Westport, from actors playing actors to actors no longer *playing* at all. The rote climax of the piece called for the two actors literally to grapple, until the penultimate line, "What do you think you're doing?" produced the final punchline of the act: "I'm doing 'Pirandello.'" On this night, however, Nichols actually began to slap May, while May clawed at his chest until she drew blood. "They brought down the curtain and we cried a lot," Nichols said. "It never happened again. But that one time, it suddenly actually did take us over."[37] The show eventually ran for nearly a year—308 Broadway performances. "'What happened is what happens to all long runs,'" says Nichols. "'It got so dehumanized and so unreal by the time we'd played it a year.'"[38] Nichols was first objectified as a Jew in Europe and then in exile; the commodification of Nichols and May was a very different demonstration of the individual subject to mysteriously potent social forces of constriction.

The first of their three recordings, released in 1959, is entitled *Improvisations to Music*, and indeed, a wide variety of piano accompaniments (by Marty Rubinstein) essay styles from cocktail tinklings to classical impressions of Bach and Chopin; there is even a tinny dance-hall number. This anomaly, whose title, "Everybody's Doing It," forcefully broadcasts its theme, is the most overt statement of the commodification of human experience (and artistic culture) by the commercial impulses of late capitalism to be found in the work of Nichols and May. Each performer takes turns in oracular, stylized cadences that sound like knockoffs on the poetry of Modernists like Pound or Eliot and, later in the piece, of the contemporaneous Beat Poets: "Today there is no more but the echo of the wild throng of wild crowds ..." The repetition of "wild," however, signals not a poeticized stratagem but a literary bankruptcy that continues to devolve; May concludes the sentence, "... with their 'Poop-poop-pee-doo' and 'Rooty-too.'" Two sentences later, she has ceded all originality to the Madison Avenue doggerel of "'Do you see the USA in your Chevrolet?'" before veering again into "poetry": "... and see those voices alive in images no longer echoes but begging, crying for something more than the slogan of an artless age ..." As Nichols reenters, he refers directly to the 1950s iconography of Institutional Man: "You did it, you son of a gun in your gray flannel suit! You drowned the poets, the flannel in the mouth choking the voice of the silver bird that cries no more. 'Winston tastes good like a cigarette should.' 'You get a lot to like in a Marlboro.'" The routine is far less "funny" than, for instance, the parody of David Lean's *Brief Encounter* (1946), with a dentist and patient in a guilt-wracked affair ("Do you know, when you looked in my mouth and said, 'It's rotten,' I thought, 'Nothing can happen now'"). Yet "Everybody's Doing It" is an early glimpse of what Nichols would explore in dramatic form in his film career.

A year later, after their Broadway show had opened on October 8, 1960 as an instant smash, Nichols and May committed four of the show's beloved routines to vinyl in an album entitled, like the show itself, *An Evening with Nichols and May*. With a live audience responding to the scenes, the contemporary listener may make the nearest approach to experiencing the exuberant energy and comic acting of Nichols and May's performances (a few of their early television appearances are also available on the internet). Each of the four tracks on the 1960 album is a permanent classic of the 1950s new comedy. In "Telephone," Nichols plays a man who desperately needs to place a call, has lost his dime in the payphone, and must submit to the impenetrable bureaucratic logic of the telephone company as personified in May's implacably unsympathetic and officious operator. At one point, he imploringly inquires whether there is "someone else I can speak to, a *human*." In the light of Nichols' later film career, it is obvious from "Telephone" why adapting *Catch-22* and its impenetrable bureaucratic illogic was so appealing to Nichols. "Adultery" takes up where "The Dentist" from *Improvisations to Music* left off, examining the national character of Americans, the British, and the French, using the scenario of an affair. "Disc Jockey" bites every hand extended by the entertainment monolith. The album closes with "Mother and Son," in which Nichols and May send up their overbearing Jewish mothers, and reverses, in as dark a tone, the metamorphoses of "Pirandello," as the astronaut-son and his mother regress to cooing baby talk.

Their final album of new material (before the inevitable "greatest-hits" repackaging of previous recordings) was 1962's *Mike Nichols and Elaine May Examine Doctors*, and while still inspired, its one-dimensionality of subject matter can't help but diminish its power in comparison with the diversity of satiric targets represented on the first two albums. One addition offered at the end of this album is a cut called "Nichols and May at Work," a rehearsal session in which May again plays the archetypal overbearing Jewish mother, intent on manipulating her son via the reflex of social expectation. What is striking about the performance is the delight they clearly take in their creative process—they are their own first audience, and Nichols bubbles with laughter at May's metamorphosis into character. Perhaps the charm of these albums is that, like the Beatles, there is no enormous tailing off: the work is uniformly solid because confined to a brief epoch and uncompromised by reunion recordings and cash-in concerts. Nichols and May did perform a few more times: at fund-raisers for George McGovern and Jimmy Carter, for instance, but these were not the sort of events that could properly be called formal reunions, subject to the manipulative spin-cycle of hype and a colorization of their black-and-white legacy. What we have are the second-person accounts of their on-stage chemistry, a few video excerpts, and the three albums of recorded material, a brief comedy comet gone before they could burn out their creative energy.

When May said she could no longer do the show, Nichols was less certain of what came next than May. She'd written a play, *A Matter of Position*, for Nichols to star in as the lead, in the role of a man so stymied by uncertainties about his life that he spends the majority of the play in bed. The strain between them began in the fact that Nichols himself had inspired her characterization, but what broke their trust was that she was no longer performing beside him; now she was the playwright sitting coolly beside Fred Coe, the director, out beyond the stage lights, critiquing his performance and conveying her displeasures indirectly. The play never made it to New York, closing after 17 performances in Philadelphia. Their parting was strained, and while they made those political appearances and also starred as George and Martha in a well-regarded 1980 New Haven revival of *Who's Afraid of Virginia Woolf?*,[39] they would not officially collaborate together again in making comic stories for another 35 years (when she wrote and he directed her back-to-back adaptations of *The Birdcage* and *Primary Colors*).[40] When May's play written for and about Nichols flopped, in part because of his own failings, Nichols suddenly was that guy without impetus: "I really felt for a long time that what I was able to do came from my special connection with Elaine. Without her, there was not much I could do."[41] Nichols was coaxed into taking a job directing Oscar Wilde's *The Importance of Being Earnest*, and Broadway producer Arnold Saint-Subber contacted Nichols to work with a young Neil Simon on a new play, *Nobody Loves You*, and do a trial run at the Bucks County Playhouse outside Philadelphia. There were no guarantees that Nichols would be the director who would take the play to Broadway, but Nichols, given a cast that included Robert Redford and Elizabeth Ashley, turned the play into *Barefoot in the Park*, and Nichols suddenly had a new sometimes-partner (he and Simon would collaborate on four Simon comedies on Broadway over the next decade, and on 1988's *Biloxi Blues* on the big screen); Lahr calls their collaboration "probably the most successful commercial partnership in twentieth-century American theatre."[42] More important, Nichols had his new career: "In the first fifteen minutes of the first day's rehearsal I understood that this was my job, this was what I had been preparing to do without knowing it. [...] Everything I learned from Strasberg, from improvising, from performing with Elaine, was preparing me. I felt what I had never felt performing: I felt happy and confident and I knew exactly what I wanted to do."[43] Lahr writes that Nichols' amazing string of Broadway hits throughout the 1960s "made him the most successful Broadway director since George Abbott."[44]

Such a claim, unambiguously intended as praise, begins to suggest the ephemerality and insularity of the Broadway bubble. George Abbott was indisputably a volcanic force in the American theater during the first half of the twentieth century, but he is hardly now a household name. While Nichols found his true calling in the theater beginning with *Barefoot in the Park*, it is more difficult to find first-hand evidence of the genius of his theatrical career than in the permanent documents of his comic career or his life as a filmmaker. One becomes dependent upon the accumulation of hardware (nine Tony awards) and the testimonials of his peers. In all the various permutations of his professional life in entertainment, he has made the people with whom he works better. Simon is a case in point. Inevitably, Nichols' working method, drawing on his years of improvisation in Compass and with Elaine May, draws out new discoveries in a play's scenario and characters. As "the first [theatrical] director to demand, and get, a share of the author's royalties,"[45] Nichols takes on a kind of secondary authorship of every script and screenplay he accepts and nurtures towards performance. Simon confesses his conflicted feelings about this legal maneuvering by Nichols: "I wasn't pleased with [sharing royalties with] him, but I can't argue with it. [...] I would rather have him do it and have the play be great. I never worked with anyone in my life—nor will I ever work with anyone—as good as Mike Nichols."[46]

When Elizabeth Taylor was searching with Ernest Lehman for someone to direct her as Martha in the screen adaptation of Edward Albee's *Who's Afraid of Virginia Woolf?*, Nichols was a natural choice. They'd fallen into an easy friendship when Nichols and May were performing each night next door to where Richard Burton was holding court in *Camelot*. Nichols' extraordinary run of success on Broadway had given him the credentials to link to the instinctual trust Taylor felt for Nichols. Beginning his Hollywood career with back-to-back Oscar nominations (and winning for his sophomore effort, *The Graduate*, when many artists "slump") justified Taylor's sense of his capabilities. Perhaps putting such a complex play and two such stratospheric stars as Burton and Taylor in the hands of a neophyte cinematic director may be construed as risky, but Nichols wasn't a neophyte of anything but cinema itself. He was also a man whose quick wits enabled him to counter each new challenge with an improvised methodology for success, not merely survival.

After initial and phenomenal success as an avant-garde auteur in the European tradition in his early films, Nichols stumbled repeatedly at the box office, eventually retrenching during an eight-year Hollywood silence in which he returned to the two earlier phases of his professional life, mounting Broadway plays and directing a feature-length film, *Gilda Live* (1980), that celebrated the comic-cabaret acting of Gilda Radner. When he returned to filmmaking, it was as a Hollywood pro in the A-movie tradition: big stars, high production values, genre storytelling formulas. Steven Spielberg says, "'Every development executive, every studio president, has a list of directors [...] and Mike has never been off the A-list.'"[47] At an advanced, late-phase age when many people in other professions would have long since retired, Nichols has mounted some of his most successful box-office (2005's *Spamalot*) and critical (2012's *Death of a Salesman*) Broadway productions while once again returning to riskier, more challenging work in his films. Each of the films he has made since turning 70 in 2001—*Wit* (2001) and *Angels in America* (2003) for HBO, *Closer* (2004) and *Charlie Wilson's War* (2007) for wide theatrical release—has been well received by the critical establishment. He has been both lucky and good. "'He can go on and on until he chooses not to go on anymore,'" Spielberg says admiringly of Nichols as Hollywood director.[48] Spielberg's claim about Nichols' status as a self-determining force at this stage of his professional life can be applied equally to his position as the most important stage director of his generation, able to command the starring husband-wife team of Daniel Craig and Rachel Weisz on Broadway in late 2013 as the leads in a revival of Harold Pinter's *Betrayal*. Spielberg says, "'You want him because you know that he's going to tell the story better than it was told in the screenplay you bought. You're going to be getting basically two scripts for the price of one.'"[49] Nichols' life prior to Hollywood gave him background in writing, acting, and directing, and it gave him his consistent thematic preoccupations. By the time Taylor and Hollywood came calling, Nichols was ready for his next creative life, whether he fully realized it at the time or not.

2

"Peel the label"

Who's Afraid of Virginia Woolf? (1966)

The film career of Mike Nichols was set to begin, appropriately enough, in the adaptation of a bildungsroman, Charles Webb's *The Graduate*, but its producer, Lawrence Turman, struggled to find studio backing for a project with a little-known source text and no star attached to the titular role. In the meantime, Ernest Lehman, who'd burst into Hollywood in the 1950s as the writer of prestige projects like *Sweet Smell of Success* (Alexander Mackendrick, 1957) and *North by Northwest* (Alfred Hitchcock, 1959), had optioned Edward Albee's spectacular 1962 Broadway play *Who's Afraid of Virginia Woolf?*, adapted the script for the screen, and sought out Nichols, the hottest director of 1960s Broadway, to direct his film version. Nichols sought and received Turman's blessing to make this film first. As fitting as the bildungsroman would have been for Nichols' debut in Hollywood, the organic transition from stage to screen of a laceratingly funny tragicomedy was an equally appropriate way for Nichols to begin his long and varied career in Hollywood filmmaking.

The proposed film of *Virginia Woolf* had the sort of thoroughbred pedigree that makes for enormous expectations. The play ran for over a year and a half on Broadway and won the 1963 Tony and Pulitzer (although the latter award was revoked prior to presentation because of the play's profane language and frank sexual content). Not only was Nichols, the toast of Broadway, attached to direct, but Lehman as screenwriter and producer brought prestige to the project, and when Richard Burton and Elizabeth Taylor agreed to play the lead roles of George and Martha, the battling married couple whose college-campus home is the setting for Albee's play, an even loftier level of celebrity and anticipation resulted. From the first day of rehearsals, the production would be plagued by paparazzi, as well as by the astonishing A-list of friends "the Burtons" attracted to the set (including, but not limited to, Marlene Dietrich and the Duke and Duchess of Windsor). The appetite of the public for the production was so enormous that Nichols, Burton, and Taylor appeared on the cover of *The Saturday Evening Post* before a single roll of film had left the camera.

Such expectations could have produced paralyzing pressure on the small company that traveled to Smith College in Northampton, Massachusetts to begin filming, but Nichols was so confident that he understood Albee's play that he did not doubt what he'd been hired to do. This in turn translated to the cast. Burton, first a man of the stage (like Nichols), depended on his director to give him readings from George's part in order to interpret his lines, and was awed by Nichols' preternatural talent in empowering actors: "'He appears to defer to you,'" Burton told *Newsweek*, "'then in the end he gets exactly what he wants.'"[1] Lehman assembled a harmonious partnership of director and stars: Burton and Taylor were already close friends with Nichols as a result of the proximity of their theaters during 1960, when *An Evening with Mike Nichols and Elaine May* (directed by Arthur Penn) played next door to Burton, appearing in *Camelot*. The resulting level of trust in and commitment to Nichols for two actors who would be asked to submit to enormous and sometimes humiliating exposure in Albee's story was essential. Quite apart from his manifest talent in interpreting story and character and motivating cast and crew, Nichols understood the care and feeding of two mercurial, self-doubting, gifted stars.

Nichols the stage director insisted on several phenomena that marked him as a screen novice. The location shooting in New England, across the continent from his new employers at Warner Bros. in Hollywood, was the first and most obvious example. The authentic collegiate atmosphere was more help to the psychology of the actors than to Richard Sylbert's art direction and Haskell Wexler's cinematography—only a few night shots of the campus are part of the final cut, and even these are so non-descript that they do not project the image of an eastern campus (Nichols would return to Smith a half-decade later to shoot some more-distinctive campus scenes in *Carnal Knowledge*). Nichols freely admits in hindsight that taking the production on the road for an entire month was an unnecessary extravagance; when Turman finally secured funding to make *The Graduate*, Nichols was willing to let the University of Southern California campus "stand in" for Berkeley in some shots, to suit the limited production budget. For its part, Smith took the studio's money but asked not to be singled out for acknowledgment in the credits, given the scabrous depiction of academia rendered by Albee's play.[2] Nichols also set aside three weeks of rehearsal for his four-person main ensemble, Burton and Taylor plus George Segal as Nick and Sandy Dennis as Honey, as he would do again on *The Graduate* and subsequent films. Nichols also showed a reverence for Albee's original text that protected it from meddling; when the film was in rough-cut form, he invited Albee to Hollywood to view it, unbeknownst to Lehman, and Albee expressed "'relief'" that Nichols "had a pretty good idea of what the play was about. There was at least one considerable intelligence at work."[3] Later that year he was asked in an interview if this would be the first of many such cinematic adaptations of his work, and Albee replied, "'I'd rather stop while I'm ahead. I may not get Mike Nichols as director next time.'"[4]

Warner Bros. anticipated a Technicolor release that would do justice to the extraordinary eyes (and numerous anticipated close-ups) of their two leads, but Nichols remained adamant that the film would be shot in black and white, or it would have a different director. Federico Fellini's *8½* had only just been released in the U.S. within the previous year as preproduction on *Virginia Woolf* began, and Nichols had been much taken by the lustrous black and white textures of Fellini's surrealist masterpiece (*8½* would remain a lingering influence, in various ways, on each of Nichols' first three film projects). In asserting his absolute conviction concerning photography of the production, Nichols was beginning to voice his cinematic interpretation of Albee's play, an artifice aware of its artificiality, not a work of kitchen-sink realism. "The whole idea of movie as metaphor changed with color," he has said; in *Virginia Woolf*, "the whole thing is an *idea* of reality."[5] Presenting the narrative in black and white in an era (given Burton and Taylor's infamous Technicolor emoting in 1963's *Cleopatra*) in which color was an increasingly standard default of the industry foregrounds, as clearly as does the celebrity of the lead actors, Nichols' intent that the audience be aware of the medium and thus of the aesthetic behind choices made in presentation—not only at the level of Wexler's cinematography but also of narrative itself. (Nichols was still exploring self-conscious performance in late work like the 2003 HBO mini-series of Tony Kushner's *Angels in America*.)

Nichols' aesthetic of filmmaking asserts, "A good movie is about something and also about something else."[6] While this statement is one he attaches to all of his films, he has made the statement specifically in the context of *Virginia Woolf*, a film in which particular damage may be done by misinterpreting its action as realistic, in the same way that the characters do damage to each other when their linguistic games, fraught with ever increasing brinksmanship, become literally as serious as death. In his very first film, this aesthetic led the fledgling director into pitched confrontation with his writer-producer, Lehman, whose initial adaptation lovingly preserved much of Albee's language and situations—only to betray them in the narrative's final act. Lehman's adaptation changed the metaphoric center of the play's action, the imaginary child created in secret conspiracy by George and Martha, into an *actual child* who killed himself on his birthday. Lehman has the screenplay's action occur on the anniversary of the child's death, by hanging; George and Martha have subsequently covered over the scene of the suicide, in a closet of their current house, walling up and papering over the closet doorway.[7] While there is provocative metaphoric value in the "empty space" vacated by the son within an upstairs room superficially cosmeticized beyond daily view, this is not Albee's vision; Lehman's reinterpretation managed to fumble away the secret nature of "Sunny Jim" and his very "existence," which was, pointedly, a *fabrication*. Nichols says he understood himself to be making a "movie in which there is an imaginary child and somebody gets this upset about saying he's dead,"[8] intending "a movie that forces you—*forces* you—to consider metaphor and what it could possibly mean."[9]

All the faculty of New Carthage would have known about the son who hanged himself; newcomers like Nick and Honey would have been warned in whispered gossip of the sad story papered over inside the house they were scheduled to visit after leaving Martha's father's party. The play (and subsequent film) would have been a thinner thing if this had been its story: a play about tragic loss, not reified disappointment. It would certainly have been a story worth telling (indeed, it's a variation of the story George tells Nick about the tragedies in the life of a certain 15-year-old), but it would not have been *Who's Afraid of Virginia Woolf?* As directed by Mike Nichols, *Virginia Woolf* remains Albee's story, not Lehman's— the story of a grand conspiracy and an epic "performance." Discussing the film as "camp," Harry M. Benshoff argues that Nichols "foregrounds the performative nature of identity" in Albee's play, "continually theatricalizing the quotidian."[10] To give George and Martha's son "real" life (and death), as Lehman had proposed, is to ignore the artistic consequences of both the artifice of his construction and, most important of all for the redemptive qualities inherent in reification, the performance of his exorcism late in the narrative. "Sunny Jim" must die, of course, but for the purposes of Albee's and Nichols' redemptive vision, all must agree that he was never alive at all.

* * *

Who's Afraid of Virginia Woolf? is classically dramatic, adhering to the unities of time and place; Nichols and Lehman take advantage of the plasticity of cinema to expand the mise-en-scène to include the opening walk across the late-night campus and the later car trip to the roadhouse for dancing. Albee's play makes reference to *Walpurgisnacht*, a pagan and later Christian rite of spring in which the Dionysian is complicated by the supernatural or the surreal. Nichols did not choose to foreground Albee's allusion, and yet the nighttime, nightmare vibrations of the narrative, with the spring softness of moths swarming the porch lights (a meticulous detail of Sylbert's production design) and George and Nick idling by the tree swing are redolent of a late-semester evening. Martha wears a coat home from her father's party, but it is not a heavy coat; George and Martha stroll without urgency along the campus' lamplit walks, taking the air. This opening sequence is, of course, an addition to Albee's play, in which their arrival in their own house is the play's opening action; Nichols and Lehman's slow and stately title sequence establishes that, whatever the audience associations with the venom in George and Martha's marriage, there is an undeniable companion-ability between them as well. It is crucial that, through all that follows, much of it vile, vindictive, and injurious, we retain an understanding of this essential companionship. Nichols has been utterly unambiguous about it: "'They are suffering for one another, and they love each other beyond measure, which is how and why we're able to stand the whole thing.'"[11]

Only one of the four competitors in the games that comprise the after-party activities at George and Martha's house in *Virginia Woolf* is actually an athlete: Nick, representing Biology, the blonde, blue-eyed, firm-bodied specimen who does everything well. He's a former champion boxer, but he also completed a Master's degree in the same time that some of his slower peers were finishing high school. At 28, he's caught the eye of the New Carthage College President, who has bestowed upon him the greatest of honors: the directive that his daughter Martha and her husband George, an Associate Professor in the History department, pay special attention to Nick and his wife Honey. Nick is the physical embodiment of George and Martha's dream child, their Sunny Jim; Nick's vitals and demographics are the "historical inevitability" of a culture's yearning for an ideal of perfection. And the irony is that Nick is everything he's supposed to be, a striver, with a naked ambition that seeks implacably to ascend and, if necessary, assail. He's the punch line to the old witticism, *Be careful what you wish for.*

The arena of his ambition seems small, even hermetic (the academic world of tenure and promotion), which only intensifies the irony of the desperate competition enacted in the narrative. The battles in academia are so pitched because the stakes are so low. It's a world at one move from reality, the abstraction of peering at life through the distancing agent of the microscope or monograph. It's another reminder of the metaphoric intention of Albee's narrative. These people have devoted their lives to scratching and clawing for dominance of a neat half-acre of next to nothing, and they will sacrifice anything—especially themselves— to have it.

George arrived at New Carthage as a promising scholar and, as we learn from Martha, proceeded to impress her father and, what's more, charm Martha herself. "I actually fell for him," she tells Nick, who listens in a solemn, embarrassed silence, "and the match seemed practical, too. For a while, Daddy really thought that George had the *stuff* to take over when he was ready to retire." The classical references (Carthage, the Punic Wars) overlay a dynastic, imperial context on George's career, and the puniness not only of George's accomplishments but, more ironically, of Martha's and her father's ambitions emerges. "I had it all planned out: first he'd take over the History department, then when Daddy retired, he'd take over the whole college ... and Daddy thought it was a good idea, too—for a while, until he started watching for a couple years ... and started thinking that maybe it wasn't such a good idea after all, that maybe Georgie-boy didn't have the stuff, that maybe he didn't have it in him." Her speech, inflected by Nichols and Sam O'Steen, his editor, with cutaways to handheld close-ups of Nick and Honey spectating in paralyzed silence, is a performance, intended to goad George toward his next move in their marriage match.

George warns her not to continue her aggressive escalation, citing her earlier transgression in having "mentioned" their son. The imaginary child, their "Sunny Jim," has been their secret for a decade and a half of barrenness. Now he becomes an item of living-room theater.

Performing the drama that leads to the "death" of Sunny Jim begins in having the right audience, and Nick and Honey, the ambitious, conniving analogues to George and Martha's younger selves, are the perfect spectators, like performing before a distorted mirror. A sense of the past but also of the present locks into place during Martha's speech. Their present disappointment and anger find roots in the high hopes and desire of their origins as a couple, anointed by Martha's father with the responsibility not only of success but of succession. George and Martha were attracted to each other for "practical" reasons: she is the highest and best prize to be won in the fun and games of campus politics, and George is the emperor-in-training. Yet Martha's speech is further colored by an impractical consideration: that she "fell for" George. The carefully selected diction is rich in connotative suggestions: there is, on its surface, the pop slang for romance; but there are also metaphoric and sinister associations: of having been duped or conned; of having diminished or lowered herself. Her connection to George has reduced her status. It's why her first identity on campus remains as the "President's daughter" rather than as "George's wife" (to say nothing of simply being known as *herself*: Martha). In the cultural competition for power on campus, George is a "bog" she has sunk into rather than a throne to which she has ascended. George is "swampy." He is a "flop." And all of this imagery of falling and flopping is sexually suggestive of impotence, yet another area of dynastic disappointment.

If this narrative were purely a negative satire (like Nichols' next film, *The Graduate*, which concerns itself with a critique of majority culture rather than positing alternatives to it), perhaps George's brandishing a gun at Martha would not be an act-one false climax but a third-act tragic crescendo, and the grasped potency of a real gun, loaded, cocked, and disgorged would have served to indict a culture obsessed with power and objectified control. *Virginia Woolf* does in fact eviscerate social-materialist brinksmanship (as does *The Graduate*), but there is another dimension to George and Martha that has nothing to do with the practicalities of ambition. They love each other. Unlike Benjamin and Elaine, children playing at love who hardly know each other, George and Martha know everything about one another. "Martha's a romantic at heart," George says snidely, and Martha can only agree. By the end of the night, they've long since demonstrated it's true, and they have recognized that their illusions of what constitutes romance will have to be discarded along with all other illusions. What holds them together through disappointment and the total war declared in the roadhouse parking lot is not a false hope that, after their long "fall" into each other's arms, they will somehow find the wherewithal to rise and make good on the promise of their social capital (long since squandered). Rather, they see in together the dawning of a new day because they love and admire each other and reject the received illusions of "success" that have so long guided them. After Martha has had her failed clinch with Nick and the two of them have retired to the kitchen, Nick makes the mistake of disparaging George, and in Martha's most profound speech of the entire film, when she stupefies Nick by declaring George a prince among men, she confesses, "I will not forgive [George] for having come to rest, for having seen me and having said, 'This—this will do.'" The disillusionment she describes here is redemptive if only she can stop seeing it as a source of self-hatred. Having so little respect for herself and what she has become, she can't help but lose respect for George when he falls for *her*.

This is why the gun must be a "false" gun, a toy, for play-acting, for performing potency. In a narrative filled with misfiring guns (George and Martha's barrenness; Honey's "hysterical" pregnancy; Nick's late-night, liquor-induced impotence), the tragicomedy ends with the death of an *illusion*, not a character. Sunny Jim must die not because it will hurt Martha (though of course it does, and George's motives in creating the "telegram" are far from pure), but because their "son" represents their imprisonment in a world of performance and expectation. Their potency—their worthiness as dynastic successors—is predicated upon a *demonstration* of potency. For both of them, this presupposes performance, production. George must churn out intellectual content (books, papers, lectures); Martha must churn out progeny. Correcting their usage errors, Martha reminds the others that she went to college, but we have no sense of why, other than that it is the family business. What did she study? Was it, perhaps, "Art," like Mrs. Robinson, who capitulated to the values assigned to her? Did Martha harbor any intellectual aspirations? Would it matter if she did, if her only thought of what intellectual capital might yield is academic power and prestige?

In this sense, Sunny Jim is an illusion because George and Martha construct him as compensation for their disillusionment, rather than seeing the process of *dis-illusion* as a liberating, alternative power in its own right. They have in their reach a true marriage, but see only a "bog"; family, but see only a harbored fantasy; a home, but see only a "dump." George and Martha have something Nick and Honey do not (though they could learn something from the ordeal they witness): George and Martha truly, genuinely, have each other. Yet their conformity to the pre-packaged values of their culture obscures this recognition, or rather, horrifies them when they do in fact recognize it. This is the substance of Martha's bristling confession to Nick: George falling into Martha's arms is evidence of his unworthiness. He should have known better. He should have wanted *more*. The games they have played for years are the "games people play" for power and status, for control in all social situations including one's love match. The games they play on this Walpurgisnacht are, by contrast, culminating, and ironically denounce—exorcise—the playing of games.

The very first line of the narrative initiates all the levels of game-playing in the film: "What a dump!" Martha exclaims, when they enter their small, book-glutted and untidy house. She has just turned on the lights (which George will turn off at daybreak, at show's end). We at first assume no irony in the statement; we take it to be the unvarnished sentiment of a dissatisfied, inebriated woman, but Martha is also playing a part, delivering a line from "some goddam Warner Brothers epic." The first game of the night, then, is "Name That Epic," and George loses, because that's what George, being like most of the rest of his species, does. Nichols and Lehman are delighted to have this early exchange from Albee's play serve as the overture to the evening, not least because, even before the full moon and the leafy shots of the campus and Elizabeth Taylor's name appear, *Virginia Woolf* brandishes the familiar "WB" of the Warner Bros.' logo. We are in fact *watching* a "Warner Brothers epic." Albee's original casting choices—Bette Davis and James Mason—would have had Davis ascending to what Benshoff calls "Pirandellian excess"[12] in reprising the line from her own epic, quoting her character Rosa Moline from *Beyond the Forest* (King Vidor, 1949), Davis' final role for Warners. It's the first of Nichols' many reminders in the film that his film is a performance of people performing.

There is drama, too, simply in Taylor's having snapped on an unflattering overhead light, of Taylor deglamorized for the camera as never before. When casting was set, Nichols tasked Taylor with gaining weight for the part, which Taylor apparently accepted "with relish." She showed up heavy enough that Nichols in panic put her on a diet.[13] The ironies of the mixed agenda are enormous, given Nichols' heartfelt awareness that the film is a condemnation of surrender to social construction. Nichols fully intended Taylor's deglamorized depiction as the aging, dissolute, and coarse Martha, but the health of the film as commodity would be jeopardized if they went too far in ravaging their beautiful star, the film's most prominent asset.

In the shifting voices she uses to deliver and re-deliver Davis' line, Taylor conveys self-consciousness that could lead to self-awareness: she is her first audience, but it is only a performance she pursues because it may further be projected to George. For his part, George appears the soul of disinterest, though this too is an affectation. Upon Nick and Honey's arrival, Nichols and Wexler demonstrate George's artificial diffidence in the blocking and framing of the early scenes in the living room, particularly when Martha has Nick pinned on the sofa with her while George, detached, sits behind the battlement of his desk. At times George even represents himself as reading a book, the very epitome of rude inhospitality. The shots often render Martha and Nick in foreground, George diminished and separate behind them, and Honey fittingly off-screen altogether. Yet it is more difficult to command attention via passive disinterest, as George does, than by aggressive, libidinous pursuit, as Martha does. This is the cause of George's abrupt change in performative strategy: after the wet-blanket "sulking" nets him fewer battles won than Martha, George becomes more active and aggressive in performance, a change dramatically announced during the gun sequence.

Again, Nichols dialogues with the audience during this powerful episode. In the parameters of staged performance, George must exit the stage for several minutes while Martha's critique continues to resound in his ears. Like much of what follows, Martha's performance is for George; Nick and Honey's presence merely formalizes the dynamics of spectacle, as well as affording George and Martha additional props for staging their improvised action. George understands this; so does Nichols. Availing himself of the flexibility of cinematic presentation, Nichols' camera follows George "off-stage" with a series of tracking shots that take George deeper into the house, to a storage room where the gun rests on a top shelf. George has the authority of the camera's gaze; it's his performance, not Martha's, that commands our central attention.[14] The rendering of sound in this scene is anything but realistic: walls are no obstacle for the wrecking-ball power of Martha's voice. One of Alex North's infrequent musical intrusions upon the action shimmers and trembles beneath Martha's monologue. As Nichols insists, George's moment alone is a rendering of "his experience, period"[15]: George has heard this catalogue of his faults before, and it runs in a loop in his head whether he's in earshot or not. The return to the living room, startling the fragile Honey and concluding his elaborate joke with the flourish of the umbrella, evokes laughter, applause, and Martha's enflamed desire for him, all of which he makes an elaborate pretense of ignoring. The brinksmanship has begun.

That all of this happens before "an audience" is no accident. What Albee creates (and Nichols preserves against the one-dimensional literalism of Lehman's original adaptation) is ritualized performance, the Greek drama of catharsis, updated via the Latin mass of exorcism. The play *is* the thing, as in Hamlet's play improvised to provoke a crisis in his family's dysfunctional dynamics, but while a secondary consequence for George and Martha may be to convict and redeem their audience, the equally complicit, commodified Nick and Honey, the urgency of the improvisational games George and Martha play is primarily for themselves and their own future. In the roadhouse parking lot, the stakes are presented as absolute: "Before I'm through with you," says Martha, "you'll wish you'd died in that automobile," and George counters that Martha has "moved bag and baggage into your own fantasy world." They end up agreeing upon "Total War." In his glowing review for the *New York Times*, Bosley Crowther calls it "surprisingly significant that [...] in the middle of the night, making outrageous noises and racing about in cars, the couples are awesomely surrounded by only darkness, silence and doom" and that the roadhouse itself is "empty [... and] a hollow, friendless place."[16] Kashner and Schoenberger write "the parking lot's harsh neon light shines pitilessly on the couple, like a prison searchlight examining every hidden corner of their marriage, sparing no one"[17]—least of all the child they have constructed to compensate for what they have been taught they lack. We may connote innocence with the child they have imagined—both the innocence of Martha's description ("A beautiful boy") and the innocence of George and Martha's organic but ultimately futile desire to reproduce. Yet in "total war," the innocent are destroyed along with "legitimate targets" and indeed, the child, as illusion, is always endangered, and never quite innocent. (George and Martha accuse each other of having corrupted or defiled their "son.") The clearest sense the narrative offers of the illusion's endangerment is the strange and repeated reference to the child as "the little bugger"—this is not quite tenderness, and the phrase's connotative undertones are far from innocent. Sunny Jim is another of the games George and Martha have played, their most darkly elaborate and private. The spectacular ending to this film is their improvisational gambit, initiated brazenly by Martha and courageously accepted by George, to end all games: disillusionment of the most desirable sort.

George must sense in Martha's channeling of Bette Davis and her "hard day at the grocery store" as a "housewife" who "buys things" a restlessness, predisposed to changing rules that have needed changing since the moment, many years ago, when George and Martha first capitulated to them. This is why he warns her not to tell Nick and Honey about their son. Perhaps he's also been warned by his own behavior at the party, when, according to Martha, he'd roared at her "Virginia Woolf" pun in feigned amusement. Their self-consciousness about what is expected of them provides the source of so much of their self-disgust. Nick and Honey do not hide their hunger to conform and conquer, and George and Martha are thus constantly confronted throughout the night by the reflection of their own weaknesses. Nick and Honey praise Martha's father; they praise the house; they laugh politely as long as they can and become mutely accepting after laughter can no longer be appropriate as a response to what they witness. All of them are prisoners: George and Martha serve at her father's pleasure as much as Nick does, and Nick and Honey aspire to nothing more or less than to some day assume George and Martha's place. As such it is unthinkable for them to leave when the opportunity to ingratiate themselves arises, or when the potential of destroying a crucial alliance could be as close as an inopportune departure. "How do you like it here?" George vaguely asks, and Nick stumbles all over himself to indicate what a nice time he's having, though he's in the middle of someone else's nightmare with no inkling that it is his nightmare, too. Half as accusation, George asks, "What made you decide to be a teacher?" Nick's execrably politic answer is, "Oh, the same things that motivated you, I imagine." George calls him immediately on the lazy, non-committal vapidity of such an answer, but part of what alarms George about the answer is that its emptiness may be an accurate representation—for both Nick and himself.

The devastating irony of Albee's narrative, commanded to the full by Nichols in Taylor's performance, is the appearance that Martha is in control and that George is everything she calls him—a bog, a swamp, a coward. Nichols knows that George is actually in control,[18] and while it may seem that his motivation to kill the imaginary child upon hearing Honey comment upon the door chime is inspired by cruelty and a desire for revenge upon his cuckolding, he has also imagined the checkmate at the end of their long game. Yet neither George nor Martha is ultimately powerful enough without the other to destroy what they have in complicity created, and this is the grace of what they encounter in their marriage as they attend to the death of their illusions. Their alliterative games—Get the Guests, Hump the Hostess, Humiliate the Host—culminate in their cruelest, riskiest, and most redemptive games of all: Truth and Illusion, and Peel the Label. "Labels" are Albee's most overt reference to the constructed-ness of social identity. "Nick and Honey *are* constructs," says Nichols. "They don't love each other, they don't know who they are, they're pure façade."[19] George and Martha have peeled their labels to find "nothing": in the roadhouse parking lot, Martha says, "You can't come together with nothing, and you're nothing. Snap!" She snaps her fingers as if performing magic. But their recognition of the "nothing" beneath their respective labels is what distinguishes them from Nick and Honey, who never get to this insight. Honey flatly refuses reified wisdom: "I don't want to know anything," she says, when Nick is upstairs with Martha. Later, Martha gives Nick advice: "Relax. Sink into it. You're no better than anybody else." Nick's reply, "I think I am," speaks volumes for his lack of self-awareness. He still believes there is intrinsic value in his assigned labels: championship athlete, agile scholar, upwardly mobile professional. He hasn't seen the "nothing" from which a human, free of labels, may actually begin to take some distinctive shape.

In the end of the narrative, the baroque gusts of language are stripped away to ever-simpler phrases and even infantile baby-talk ("Honey funny bunny"); what also gets stripped away is the artifice, at least for George and Martha, though not until after the most elaborately performed ritual, the intoned Latin of the Mass. Nichols the improvisational performer would have recognized in George and Martha's game-playing brinksmanship the rarest kind of improvisational theater, that rejects the easy set-up for the chance at a richer dramatic reward. One of the highest compliments Martha pays George (naturally, not in his hearing—though he knows, because they know everything about one another) is that he "can keep learning the games we play as quickly as I change them." In fact, George has seen through the games to the possibility of a post-games landscape; he is in control, but he guides them both towards a place where control or power will be irrelevant. He *goads* her to "total war" in the roadhouse parking lot, and the casualty is their default mode, the endgame to end all their games. "I don't know when you people are lying or what," Nick says, to which George responds, from the depths of his reified paranoia, "You're not supposed to."

Timothy Bewes argues that reification implies self-consciousness, an awareness of one's cultural condition.[20] The surgical method by which George and Martha dissect one another and their guests indicates how profoundly, consciously reified they are, and thus their latent redemption becomes a part of their awareness. In this sense, George is truly the one in control. He steers them to their disillusionment by "killing" their "son," because it comes to him that this can be their new beginning, an acceptance without judgment of the lives they have made, rather than illusions that can only stand in tormenting judgment upon their failures. The exorcism rids them of the spirit of captive performance, of the myth of potency. George and Martha do indeed "come together" at the end of this film in order to *destroy*, not create, and in so doing paradoxically create the possibility, for the first time, of a genuine future, not one circumscribed by hegemonic and dispiriting values.

In the film's final moments, which remain reverently faithful to Albee's play, language is further reduced to the humility of short sentences and repeated simple phrases, to a Beckett-worthy sense of exhaustion that nonetheless, in its tenderness, underscores a tenuous, literally dawning hope. The exemplary last shot of the film, lasting more than three minutes, begins in close-up on George as he turns out the lamp: the performances are at an end. The camera tracks and zooms into a two-shot as George crosses to the window where Martha sits, the morning light startling and strange behind her after so much night. The "fun and games" begin to recede in much the same way that nightmares will. "It will be better," George posits, and Martha's doubt humbles him without emasculating him. Even here, ritually cleansed of their illusions, Martha deferentially and out of long habit posits a rule change, perhaps some new, small, innocent game: "I don't suppose, maybe, we could …" George's reply is tender and yet pointed, authoritative but loving: "No." In context, he could utter no more *affirmative* word.

Taylor won the Academy Award for many moments in the film. Her third-act speech to Nick in the kitchen, exposing the pain of her self-loathing and its transfer onto her beloved husband's weary shoulders, is among her greatest: George, she ruminates, "can make me happy—and I do not wish to *be* happy. Yes, I *do* wish to be happy." Here is the film, condensed nearly to a haiku: the paradoxical mass of contradiction the reified individual feels just before redemptive possibility opens one's perspective. In the film's final lines, Taylor is twice asked to interpret the same complicated impulses, using the most minimal language: "Yes. No." Each time she is equal to the challenge. In Martha, Taylor must have found the embodiment of many of the commodifying issues—studio domineering, typecasting, failed love and marriage, weight gain, aging—that threatened to devour her. As George begins softly to sing the song she was once, for no good reason, so proud of, we might reasonably expect that what

The "total war" between George (Richard Burton, left) and Martha (Elizabeth Taylor, center) in *Who's Afraid of Virginia Woolf?* reaches its climax in the "exorcism" of the malignant spirit they have conjured together—a child, their "Sunny Jim"—as an illusory refuge against the barren disappointments of their lives. Their "Walpurgisnacht" is performed for a captive audience: the social-striving couple Nick (George Segal) and Honey (Sandy Dennis), a fun-house mirror of George and Martha's younger selves. As the film ends in dawn's pale light, some equally pale yet palpable hope for post-war kindness emerges.

we're hearing is mockery; it certainly was earlier, when George echoed it in the dance that sent Honey diving for "the euphemism." Now, in the softness and stillness of the new day, there is affection in it, and sorrow. Performance anxiety prompted her punning song at the party, the restless quest for attention and the power that accrues to it. When she answers the song's by-now rhetorical question ("I am, George. I am"), the meaning of her answer speaks to a fear of defaulting to ingratiating complicity again, but also to a more generalized fear of the unknown, of what a *dis-illusioned* life might be like. Taylor's posture assumes a modified bow, and the camera zooms to a close-up of their joined hands, as in a wedding photo. Their marriage, so long a *boxing* match that supplants love with power, is transformed by the sacrifice of their illusions into a genuine *love* match, in which games and winning are no longer the point. They finally trust each other with the reverence that marriage avows.

It is an intensely theatrical tableau, a hushed waiting for the curtain. The performance of George and Martha may be coming to an end in the dawn of their disillusionment; the performance of Burton and Taylor and Nichols has come to an end; the human inclination to socially proscribed performance may never end.

3

"This afternoon's feature attraction"

The Graduate (1967)

Few films have benefitted from a more felicitous conjunction of talent, truth-telling, and timing than *The Graduate*, the cinematic adaptation of a tepidly reviewed and largely ignored 1963 first novel by Charles Webb. The story of a precocious recent college graduate with a bright future he doesn't want resonated with an emerging audience of Baby-Boom college students to create a cultural phenomenon. In its time, the film was a box-office blockbuster of nearly unprecedented proportions, running in theaters from late 1967 (in order to qualify for the 1968 Academy Awards) through the entire calendar year of 1968 and well into 1969, "eventually [becoming in its time] the third-most successful movie in history, surpassed only by *The Sound of Music* and *Gone with the Wind*."[1] The estimable Stanley Kauffmann called it "'a milestone in American film history.'"[2] Its mega-success surprised everyone including its producers (functioning in semi-independent status in rented space at Paramount, where the film was largely shot on custom-built sets); Lawrence Turman, the man who bought the rights to Webb's novel because he responded to the story's cultural alienation but also because the little-known source text was just within his tiny price range, knew that even modest success would recoup the investment and get his foot in the door of Hollywood (he had rejected the steady work his father's garment business offered). Turman's luckiest stroke was that Mike Nichols, hottest stage director in New York, also responded to Webb's book in a deeply personal way. With Nichols on board, Turman was eventually able to secure financing, albeit beyond the big studios, through Joseph E. Levine's independent production house that imported racy European art films and made B-movie exploitation films.

What no one could anticipate was the cultural wave cresting just as post-production was wrapping in the fall of 1967. The concerns of a generation increasingly estranged from the post–World War II sense of earned entitlement to material accumulation and the mounting tensions of the Cold War and America's entanglement in Asian conflicts first in Korea and then in Vietnam reinforced fears that, as Benjamin Braddock, protagonist of *The Graduate*, puts it, "It's like I've been playing some kind of game, but the rules don't make any sense to me. They're being made up by all the wrong people. No, I mean no one makes them up; they seem to've made themselves up." Despite minimal publicity and largely respectful but far from unanimously rapturous reviews,[3] the popular embrace of *The Graduate* was immediate, decisive, and clamorous. Originally released in only two movie theaters in the country, both of them in midtown Manhattan, lines began forming daily around the block;

the film received seven Oscar nominations (winning for its sophomore director), and eventually it seemed the entire country was humming Simon and Garfunkel's "Mrs. Robinson." Hoffman went from unknown character actor to cultural symbol overnight: "'I was an object,'" he recalled, ironically describing himself exactly as his character Benjamin has been treated by his parents. "'No one knew my name. I wasn't a human being to them. I was the Graduate.'"[4]

Nichols, no stranger to the love of an audience, was utterly unprepared for this extremity of mass devotion. The Broadway world is comparatively hermetic and a mere fraction of the audience that Hollywood commands. To have a run of hit plays, as Nichols had during the first half of the 1960s, made him the toast of the town, but in the rest of the country, a vague shadow of the east-coast entertainment scene. His earlier run of success with Elaine May as a comic was similarly spectacular in a relatively limited way: the triumph of the Arthur Penn-directed two-person Broadway show and companion, Grammy-winning recording. Nichols was a New York cultural celebrity, not a national celebrity. In directing Burton and Taylor in what became his first film, the extraordinary 1966 adaptation of Edward Albee's *Who's Afraid of Virginia Woolf?*, Nichols stepped into a broader, more intense spotlight, but the luminosity of his two stars and chamber-cinema methodology of the production reinforced Nichols' reputation, where it was known at all beyond the greater New York cultural zone, as a man of the theater. *Virginia Woolf* has far too much cinematic vivacity and ingenuity to be dismissed as a filmed play, yet its Albee pedigree and unities of time, place, and action permit a lazy assumption of Nichols as having brought Broadway to Hollywood rather than having succeeded in Hollywood's distinct medium. With *The Graduate*, Nichols' expressive, formalist embrace of the deliberate and idiosyncratic language of European art cinema of the 1950s and 1960s announces the star *behind* the camera. While Dustin Hoffman, a struggling character actor already a trifle old (at 30) to start a career, was transformed by his performance as Benjamin Braddock, the true star of *The Graduate* was its auteur. Nichols discovered the expressive possibilities of the medium during the long production and post-production phases of *The Graduate*: "A movie, although it's very technical in the shooting stage, really puts you much more in touch with your own unconscious and the unconscious of the audience," he has commented, adding, "Which is, I think, the great hold that it gets on us all."[5] As Richard T. Jameson writes, Nichols' education in cinematic language was also an education for his mass audience: "[N]o other film in going-on-seven-decades had so decisively or deliciously made so many people notice the kinds of selection and design that go into making the movie experience."[6] In the delirious aftermath of the film's reception by a young audience hungrily poised to embrace a cinematic analog of its own social alienation, Nichols also became aware of the irrational power of cinema, as he watched in profound helplessness as the audience saw what it wanted to see, remaking the film in its own self-congratulatory image. The roots of Nichols' eventual withdrawal from avant-garde style to a more conventional, traditional style of cinematic communication (demonstrated particularly after the box-office debacle of 1970's *Catch-22* and its heavily accented formalism) may be traced in part, ironically, to box-office success: the alarm and dismay he encountered in having his carefully orchestrated film appropriated and misinterpreted by an audience hundreds, even thousands of times larger than he had ever encountered in his greatest earlier successes.

The Graduate is relatively faithful to Charles Webb's 1963 novel. Richard Corliss denounced Buck Henry's adaptation as "retyping,"[7] though Henry was rightfully acknowledging the cinematic qualities already latent in Webb's story. The film opens with Benjamin

Braddock (Dustin Hoffman) having graduated from a phenomenal collegiate career. In the novel and in earlier drafts of the screenplay, we also learn that Benjamin has served as vale-dictorian of his class, despite the fact that he has yet to turn 21 years old. He is the recipient of the Frank Halpingham Award, which we learn in Webb's novel is specifically given to a student who displays promise as a future teacher. While we do not glimpse that promise for ourselves—Benjamin seems extraordinarily non-verbal for much of the film—the larger implications of the award are clear: Benjamin has been identified by the system of education as a promising agent to perpetuate the goals of the educational system that produced him. He can serve as a molder of young men and women precisely because he has so cooperatively yielded to his own molding. Similarly, at home in Los Angeles, where his parents meet him at the airport (oddly eschewing attending their only child's graduation—was their social calendar too full? Too much planning to do for his graduation party?), Mr. and Mrs. Braddock (William Daniels and Elizabeth Wilson) anticipate a life of conformist inheritance for Ben: their big Beverly Hills house and pool become the battleground for several scenes depicting the 1960s "generation gap" between the parents who collectively won World War II, reaping its spoils, and their children, who came to question a nation of gender and racial inequality, nationalist incursion, and "soulless wealth" (as Lyndon B. Johnson characterized it in his 1964 Great Society speech).[8]

Andrew Sarris writes that, "whereas Nichols merely transferred *Virginia Woolf*, he tran-scended *The Graduate*."[9] Nichols' second film was, in many ways, an absolute departure from his first. The most obvious visual differences are that the solemnity of Haskell Wexler's neo-noir black-and-white photography, capturing largely nighttime interiors, gives way to the polychromatic vibrancy of sun-splashed Beverly Hills and the San Francisco Bay area. Steven Spielberg calls *The Graduate* "'a visual watershed'" in Hollywood.[10] *Virginia Woolf* cast two of the most famous celebrities of Hollywood and put one or the other (and usually both) in virtually every frame of the film; *The Graduate* casts an unknown (about whose undeniably ethnic features and maladroit early screen tests everyone had grave doubts) as its center of gravity, its only potential "star" (Anne Bancroft, who'd won the Tony and subsequent Oscar as the saintly Annie Sullivan in *The Miracle Worker*) dimmed by her role as the film's great antagonist, Mrs. Robinson. The milieu of *Virginia Woolf* is distinctly east-coast, cerebral, verbal, set outside the "real world" in the halls of academe (and a decidedly small-time, low-power academe at that); in *The Graduate*, we are on the west coast, among largely non-verbal or inarticulate members of the commercial world, in which physicality assumes prominence. Most significantly (for the audience reception of the two films), the protagonists of *Virginia Woolf* are firmly entrenched in middle age, with its attendant crises and regret over lost opportunities, while *The Graduate*, despite giving us long glimpses of middle-aged ennui, offers protagonists who could be enrolled in George's classes, and whose crises are formational rather than foundational. George and Martha know who they are and spend the majority of their narrative in trying to decide whether to confront or continue to ignore this knowl-edge; Benjamin and Elaine have no idea who they are but suspect that they need to become something other than what their parents' generation—George and Martha's generation—has bequeathed to them.

And yet the constancy of Mike Nichols' vision as a filmmaker emerges, in these first two films of his long career, in the fact that, despite all these differences, *Virginia Woolf* and *The Graduate* share a horror of the distortions and desecrations of human personality wrought by status and the pursuit of power. George and Martha's all-night, all-*marriage* sparring match for manipulative control of each other and illusionary spin on the sorry, unfulfilled realities of their shared life ultimately ends in the only way that points to a positive dawn: with their shared defeat. No one wins their final game, and as losers, they are free to lose their illusions and get on with the business of being fully, interdependently human. Ben and Elaine are far younger and far less wise than George and Martha. They don't understand as clearly how deep the ruts of reification run. Each of Nichols' first two films shows two generations held fast in the grip of cultural conformity regardless of profession, age, or privilege. Higher learning in both narratives reveals itself to be one of the most insidious agents of reified stasis: neither George, tenured but tenuous in his "authority," nor Benjamin, the "award-winning scholar" nauseated by whatever he has "learned back there in the east," is able to think his way out of his cultural box. George, however, has Martha, who provides him a "worthy adversary" and who, by accident, initiates the game (telling somebody about their "son") that leads them eventually to the light of the day. All Benjamin has is Elaine (Katharine Ross), and vice versa. Elaine can share in Benjamin's confusion about the future (her understanding of his situation is not a negligible thing; in fact, it's a source of his obsessive attraction to her), and she can commission him to imagine a "definite plan" for his future. Yet however bright they are purported to be by their culture (whose interests lie in securing their conformity), they are largely inert and malleable; "clean-cut and stupid."[11] Having rejected the problematic lives they've been told to lead, Benjamin and Elaine are nonetheless of little aid to each other in imagining an alternative to the future offered with such anxious insistence by their parents. "'We very consciously thought of the movie as a dream,'" Nichols says, "'and just beginning to wake up from it at the very end.'"[12]

What shocked and alienated Nichols about the unreflective enthusiasm with which the mass audience promoted Benjamin and Elaine as iconic counter-culture couple was Nichols' own understanding of his protagonist as having "drown[ed] among objects and things, committing moral suicide by allowing himself to be used finally like an object or a thing by Mrs. Robinson, because he doesn't have the moral or intellectual resources to do what a large percentage of other kids like him do—to rebel, to march, to demonstrate, to turn on. Just drowning."[13] Nichols told Peter Bart while making the film, "'Benjamin has been surfeited with objects. Even his girls are regarded as objects. Benjamin himself has become an object to his family.'"[14] Lee Hill concludes that *The Graduate* remains a powerful fable about the difficulties in rebellion in a consumer culture where choice is rampant and yet illusory."[15] *The Graduate* is "a focus on individual freedom versus collective repression,"[16] an ironic warning to a more insidious level of conformity than the mass audience was aware of—Benjamin runs, but as a track star, he runs on a circular track. Without any alternative finish line in his head, he is bound to return to what he knows, as Nichols predicts, to "become his parents."[17]

* * *

In the years since its initial blockbuster run in theaters, the reputation of *The Graduate* has grown in inverse proportion to the fulfillment of its prophetic pronouncement upon the counter-cultural revolutions of the 1960s. Many of those individuals who announced their intentions to "drop out" of conformist culture eventually became their parents, returning to the culture and its values either in resignation of an experiment they could not sustain or happily reacquainting themselves with the material comforts they had missed. The argument of *The Graduate*'s narrative is that counter-motion is, in itself, unsustainable: movement purely away from the undesirable will result in inertia unless the movement can be reignited by a positive goal worth moving towards. In *The Graduate*, Ben may be a superbly performing

student, but his professors must not have required him to do much genuinely original thinking—he is alarmingly inarticulate about his objections to the prevailing culture and purely
mute on viable alternatives.

Why, for instance, has he even boarded the plane that returns him to Los Angeles from
the east? The film's opening shot, a close-up of Hoffman, reveals an unhappy young man,
grim-faced; the zoom-out reveals that his isolation is in a cabin-full of people, being
instructed by a disembodied voice from the cockpit. Simon and Garfunkel's "Sounds of
Silence" makes its first of three commentaries on the film's action as the next shot is introduced, a long take of Benjamin passively conveyed along a moving walkway at LAX. A cut
to a shot of his suitcase conveyed along a similar belt suggests an analogy between man and
luggage: each is an object carried towards its pick-up point. Within the first fifteen minutes
of the film, the Braddocks throw two parties for their son, both of which are naked grasps
at status enhancement for the Braddocks at Ben's expense. As bad as the graduation party
is, it pales before the hyper-anxious performances of father and son in front of the assembled
guests at the birthday party. Mr. Braddock, with his statuesque trophy wife, trophy house,
and trophy pool, has pinpointed Benjamin as his status difference-maker: anyone with money
can buy a big house and attract a suitably glamorous partner who projects his conspicuous
values, but a son who tore up the racing tracks and the classrooms at a prestigious east-coast
school is an item that money alone can't buy.

To his credit, Benjamin objects to this bankruptcy of values, not least because it commodifies him. In the film's very first dialogue, before his parents misbehave at the first of the
parties in his honor, he hides in his childhood room from his parents' friends, and his father
demands to know what's the matter so that they can get him downstairs and start showing
him off. Nichols blocks and frames the stationary camera's shot so Benjamin can remain
static, establishing Benjamin's pervasive psychological point of view: "It's a highly subjective
film with everything filtered through the eyes of its protagonist."[18] His father (and later his
mother) moves in and out of the shot, obstructing the sight line from Ben to camera. "What's
wrong," his father says, impatiently. Benjamin haltingly admits only that he wants his future
to be "different." We assume that this is the habitual reticence of the emotionally bullied
child, who fears the consequences of uttering a discouraging word. Yet distance from his
dictators later in the narrative does not promote greater eloquence. His longest speech, about
who makes the rules in society, is to Elaine on their first (and only) formal date, when he
concludes that the rules "seem to've made themselves up." This is a long way from an articulate, reasoned social critique, though it does suggest inklings of reified reality. We begin to
understand why he boarded the plane and returned to a place that clearly makes him miserable: he can't think of any better place to go.

The mise-en-scène of his childhood room, to which he retreats from his parents and
their parties (as well as after his estrangement from the Robinson women), encapsulates his
malaise: it is, visibly, still a child's room, with its tiny bed, arrayed toys and decorations, and
comfortingly burbling aquarium. The tank, lit a soft underwater green, features a tiny *plastic*
diver, a foreshadowing of his own transformation into a diver, posed by his parents in the
backyard aquarium, an exotic prized fish on display. Shooting Benjamin in close-up framed
by the tank in this early dialogue with his father, Nichols invites us to see the aquarium and
larger room as a metaphorical womb-space of a young man his father keeps calling a "boy"
(in his barker's patter at the birthday demonstration of the diving suit). Ben has retreated
to this safe womb-space from the graduation party after a few breathless, claustrophobic
moments lost in a crowd of adults demanding to know his plans for the future or, in the case

of Mr. McGuire of the "Plastics" speech, *predicting* his future, like a balmy, avuncular oracle.

Mrs. Robinson's invasion of the womb-space, which Murray Pomerance refers to as Benjamin's "horrifying, self-contained cyst,"[19] is thus an especially queasy transgression, given what we know to be her ulterior motive. Benjamin is made anxious and aroused by this quasi-maternal figure (the camera's gaze—Ben's psychological point of view, which eventually is literalized by subjective camera—has already rested briefly upon her, sitting alone at the party). She barges in with an unlikely excuse, since she has probably visited this house enough times to know where its bathrooms are, then maliciously tosses his car keys into the aquarium, upsetting the diver, when Ben has offered to loan her his new car. At her house, the parent-child dynamic continues with Mrs. Robinson alternating flirtation and scolding until locking herself naked in her daughter's room with her prey. Both this night and the night they meet for the first time at the Taft Hotel, Ben's objections to what she proposes center on appearances: what his parents and Mr. Robinson would say. His sense of impropriety is inherited from his parents, and it is based not in a moral code but in social performance (literally, imagining a disappointed audience).

This received value is tenuous because not his own, and because there is so much in his parents' world to which he objects. At the birthday party, what residual or habitual allegiance Benjamin feels to their will is irreparable. Mr. Robinson has advised Ben to "have a good time while you can"—it's a vague and ominous reference, later fleshed out during Ben's "conversation" with Mrs. Robinson, to the unhappy circumstances in which the Robinsons happened to marry, victimized by incautious physical desire and consequential social proscription. In a matched set of voice overlaps between successive scenes, Nichols and his editor, Sam O'Steen, stitch together a causal connection between three events: Mrs. Robinson's offer, the Braddocks' humiliating birthday performance, and Benjamin's acceptance of the offer. As Benjamin walks away from the Robinsons to his car, Mrs. Robinson calls, "I'll see you soon I hope." The next voice we hear, as Benjamin is still clambering into the Alfa Romeo, is his father's: "Ladies and gentlemen, your attention please, for this afternoon's feature attraction." The entire birthday scene is played as an analogy to the reticent performer whose stage fright only increases the anxiety of his exposed partner. It is the scene that most clearly announces the thematic intentions of the film.

Daniels and Hoffman, who respectively play Braddock father and son, are small men; Wilson, who plays Mrs. Braddock, is statuesque by comparison. Centered on the lawn and surrounded by his smaller family is a brawny man in a bathing suit. Nichols uses the diminutive size of his two main performers in the scene to underscore psychological imbalances or inadequacies they feel. Mrs. Braddock as played by Wilson is big and brassy (recall her near-hysterical bray of joy when Ben announces his intention, later in the film, to marry Elaine); Mrs. Braddock is given to grand, attention-grabbing gestures, like the thrown-back head (as in the engagement "announcement") signaling, in a publicly demonstrative way, her delight or pleasure. To Mr. Braddock's weak jokes to warm up the crowd before the "feature attraction," she laughs to the sky, performing her role as the model audience. Not a moment feels natural until Benjamin, behind the patio door, breaks from script and improvises his dismay about what's expected of him. Nichols and Robert Surtees, the veteran cinematographer, shoot up from a low angle on Daniels; as in the earlier scene in which Mr. Braddock breaks in on his son's privacy and breaks down Ben's resistance in the aquarium-lit bedroom, father upstages son, mugging to the crowd, which begins to heckle the host when the "show" threatens to fall flat.

In fact, the more carefully examined psychology of this scene suggests that, when Benjamin balks, the show becomes more, not less, interesting to the invited guests: if they thought they were socially bound to witness the Braddocks' brinksmanship in flaunting the status of an award-winning scholar in the family, the unannounced developments that lead to the humiliation of two generations of Braddocks offer them an unexpected windfall of status-capital. One may in fact assume that the new party, thrown so soon after the old one, may itself have been a status reassertion by the Braddocks, after the embarrassment of Benjamin's disappearance from his own graduation festivities. Again a lucrative gift is at the center of the party's attention, a scuba suit whose cost is with pointed casualness identified: "And it better work," jokes Mr. Braddock, still warming the crowd, "or I'm out over two hundred bucks." Unspoken is the reality that, if it doesn't work, he could also be out a *son* ... but in the world of status maintenance, his son's personhood is of small concern. "Dad, can you listen?" comes from a voice with no corporeal reality for the master of ceremonies—which is why Mr. Braddock *can't* listen.

And so Benjamin is finally brought on stage, infantilized to the extreme of taking a toddler's steps in the ridiculously inappropriate flippers. All the psychological assertions of Benjamin's point of view—his parents' domineering upstaging of his interests, Mrs. Robinson grotesquely commingling the maternal and seductive, Mr. Robinson's noir scariness in giving Ben advice about sowing some wild oats—is finally summarized in the shift to Ben's literal, subjective-camera perspective inside the mask. The Braddocks' stagy gestures of encouragement mimic the condescending cheers of young parents coaxing their baby to walk, but, a few moments later, their firm hands pressing the subjective-camera mask back under the pool's surface have a more sinister tone. Nichols has characterized Benjamin as "drowning in things, and [confronting] the danger of becoming a thing, the danger of treating yourself or other people as things"[20]; this chilling shot suggests that the "drowning" was not accidental: Benjamin is too weak to resist the material burdens thrust upon him, which laden him down to the bottom. As his father's desperate pleas for Ben to perform have suggested, Mr. Braddock has himself sunk long ago under the weight of accumulation, and his misguided sense of love for his son endangers the next generation.

The voice overlap that extends this sequence, in which Ben calls Mrs. Robinson from the Taft Hotel to begin their affair, creates a causal link in which the birthday party is the final status-inflicted humiliation Ben allows his parents to perpetrate upon him. (Ironically, once he has arrived at the Taft Hotel, he will be commissioning all the humiliations under his own power.) If the film were truly a counter-cultural film with alternatives to propose, these first 25 minutes would have been well spent in a comic, hyperbolic (Benjamin's distorting point of view) skewering of a world of consumerist conformity, status anxiety, and disingenuous performance. Having argued decisively against that world, it could then use its last 80 minutes to dramatize the difficult rewards of taking a road less traveled, arguing for a genuine alternative to the social proscription to which so many fall victim.[21] But this is not the narrative route chosen in *The Graduate*, which remains throughout its entire length a negative satire of reified conformity. In his rave review, Roger Ebert praised *The Graduate* "because it has a point of view. That is to say, it is against something."[22] However, Benjamin's point of view, steeped in critical insights about his culture that might have portended the beginning of wisdom, ultimately ignores the redemptive qualities of self-knowledge and inherent self-correction because of a failure of imagination. Unlike the reified heroes who transform themselves and their circumstances by whatever limited means are available to them (as for instance, George and Martha do at the end of *Virginia Woolf*, or Meryl Streep's title character does in *Silkwood*, or as several characters do in *Angels in America*), Benjamin understands his reified dilemma but literally can't imagine an alternative. From the bottom of the pool, Ben could decide to think about somebody else for a change: join the Peace Corps, teach in a disadvantaged urban or rural school district, coach a juvenile-offender track squad. He could explore philosophical alternatives, or join a religion or a political party. Instead, the only alternative that occurs to him is to try "to be suave" with Mrs. Robinson, a choice that redoubles his humiliation. It's the only choice that matters, because it curses all future choices he attempts. In the logic of *The Graduate's* narrative, his choice to become a deceptive adult just like all the adults he knows, with their secrets and betrayals and power struggling, transfers the blame for the ruin of his life from his parents, who want to imagine his future for him, to his own shoulders. Nichols describes Hoffman's "expressionless" portrayal of Benjamin during the famous "Sounds of Silence"/"April Come She Will" montage as his self-conscious desperation "trying not to become an object," but which devolves into the increased "despair of an affair that is just below the waist and he has no real connection to it, so the montage is how it goes on once conversation fails."[23] Having been so uniformly objectified, Benjamin's instinctive response to the two Robinson women is to objectify them both. Søren Birkvad argues, "sex is a battlefield of power play and projections" in which Mrs. Robinson is the "whore" objectified as isolated body parts (most often legs, but also breasts and belly) and Elaine the "Madonna" objectified as her enormous, mega-lashed eyes[24] and flustered, chaste embarrassment when "not dressed" in her own room or contemplating her mother's sexuality in Benjamin's Berkeley room. Benjamin is ultimately no better (or even different) at imagining his future than his parents were. They want him to call up Elaine Robinson the next time she's down from Berkeley and begin the dynastic succession; when he rejects the world of his parents and their values, Benjamin winds up in Berkeley, bird-dogging Elaine.

The central insight of *The Graduate* is that Benjamin doesn't come any closer to establishing a viable alternative to performing the reified roles ascribed to him when he is with Elaine than when he is with her mother. (This was the failure of audience response when the film was initially embraced as an iconic utterance of the counter-culture: during what Nichols calls the "fantasy prettiness"[25] of the film's second half, many have missed the ironized treatment of Benjamin's desire for marriage and happily ever after as a Machiavellian means to get the upper hand on the Robinsons; at this moment, Benjamin behaves as cynically as the Robinsons in Santa Barbara.) When Benjamin calls Mrs. Robinson from the hotel, we watch in resigned horror the comic nightmare of his performance anxiety, from the frying pan of his parents' home to the fire of Mrs. Robinson's bed. He bumbles against the cocktail table, failing to get a waiter's attention, failing to get a room, failing even in the simple task of conveying the room number. "Shall I just stand here?" he asks Mrs. Robinson as she begins to undress. "I mean, I don't know what you want me to do." He isn't even good at *watching*. Ultimately, she must cruelly goad him at the root of masculine vanity and insecurity: "inadequate" performance. The affair's consummation comes, predictably, in anger, where love is never even an afterthought. But is the relationship with Elaine any less bound up in pretense and received expectation? Certainly a second potential turning point looms during Ben's date with Elaine, calculated to end all the calculating of the Braddocks and Mr. Robinson. He dons the adult's mask of sunglasses, even in the nighttime environments of the Strip and the strip club, and performs the misanthrope's role learned from Mrs. Robinson until, sunglasses removed, he recognizes this is who he has become, but not the person he understands he should be. It's a moment that returns him to desiring something "different" for his future, and yet the "drowned" choice he has made in the pool continues to doom subsequent choices. When he has the opportunity to confess fully the particulars of his affair, he withholds the most salient detail, knowing Elaine will be lost to him forever if he reveals the truth. He assumes another *role*: the individual in command of the agency of his personhood, wiser for his mistakes. Ironically, his sober mien only seems to inspire admiration in Elaine; she has no idea it's a fantasy he's performing for her. Later, when Elaine's own alienation from her parents' expectations (as embodied in Carl Smith, demographic dream-boy of the older generation) pushes her back into Benjamin's arms, his monomania for marriage as a solution to problems of social status is a cynical default to what the Robinsons attempt to do to their daughter in Santa Barbara with Carl. The audience too facilely absorbed (as Benjamin is) in the genre conventions of romantic narrative may thus fail (as Benjamin does) to see this irony for what it is: a skewering of the culture's master narrative of conformity, of course, but also a critique of the individual who, equipped with reified awareness and thus knowing better, allows himself nonetheless to be consumed. Benjamin and Elaine will become their parents precisely because they don't have a single other choice in their heads.

If the "birthday party" is when Benjamin "drowns," forced by his parents into a choice he flubs, the other key moment of the film comes not in the incomplete anagnorisis at the strip club but earlier, in the failed anagnorisis during the "conversation." This crucial scene, one of the most important of Nichols' film career, marks the most obvious appearance of the hand of Nichols the stage director: for much of the scene's nearly 10-minute length, the camera is stationary, set at eyeline on the Taft Hotel bed where Mrs. Robinson and Benjamin have met for their latest assignation. More audaciously, whole minutes go by with the screen dark. The object of the scene is Benjamin's determination to prove to himself that the affair is something other than the soul-killing dead end he knows it to be. The previous scene, between Benjamin and his mother and assembled with yet another voice overlap implying further causation, is the closest anyone comes to staging a meaningful intervention in Benjamin's life. Yet even in this confrontation with her son, Mrs. Braddock is revealed as invasive and performative. Sexy in her peignoir, she invades the steamy bathroom where her half-naked son shaves for his night out. Contextually, each is in the final stages of preparing for a bedroom performance. The atmosphere is murky, unwholesome. Mrs. Braddock, by her own description, proceeds to "pry" into Benjamin's "affairs," causing her son's visible recoil (he slices into his thumb with the safety razor) but verbal resistance. She exits with a mother's cliché: "I'd rather you didn't say anything at all than be dishonest." Benjamin's empty imploring for her to "Wait a minute" provides the overlap to the "conversation," in which the unmistakable rustling of bed linens in a dark room as he asks again, "Will you wait a minute, please?" implies a conjunction between his mother and Mrs. Robinson. (Actually, the Braddocks have completed a psychological foursome in the affair throughout the summer, if only in Benjamin's paranoid imagination: in the voice overlap that ends the famous "drifting" montage of Benjamin in the pool, in his parents' house, and at the Taft Hotel room with Mrs. Robinson, the shot of Ben thrusting onto a raft that becomes Mrs. Robinson ends with his father asking, "Ben? What are you doing?" as if having burst in on them in their illicit love nest. His parents' voices ring constantly in Benjamin's guilty ears.)

His mother's preference of silence to dishonesty meets her son's default to the sounds of silence by the end of the "conversation" with Mrs. Robinson. There is no other scene in the film (which arrives at nearly the narrative's midpoint and spiritually serves as its fulcrum) that so sustains a dialogue between two people; Elaine and Ben certainly never have such a conversation: on their "date," dishonest performance by Benjamin negates the value of their sharing; in his Berkeley boarding house, her scream cuts short his opportunity to tell the whole truth; in subsequent conversations, he has set marriage as the single and perpetual topic. With Mrs. Robinson, however, this one time only, they begin to peel away the layers of performative artifice (the middle-aged siren in command of younger flesh; the more-than-"adequate" young stud) toward the truth. The voice overlap from the inconclusive conversation with his mother suggests that Ben begins the "conversation" scene as a performance for his mother in absentia; he wants to prove to her (via convincing himself) that she is wrong about his empty nights.

The provocative confusion of the voice overlap ("Wait a minute") receives a clarifying illumination when Benjamin coldly reaches across Mrs. Robinson, switches on the night table lamp, and addresses her as usual, with her formal name: "Mrs. Robinson, do you think we could say a few *words* to each other first this time?" The light will remain an ongoing motif in this iconic scene. It is most obviously a rhetorical assault, intended first by Benjamin (when he snaps on the light here at the beginning of the scene, as if to spotlight his desire to make their affair something that can be scrutinized and found worthy of meaning) and then by Mrs. Robinson (who summarily dismisses his suggestion that they talk when she says, "I don't think we have much to say to each other," and snaps the light off again). In a searching but ultimately failed critique of the film, Farber and Changas argue that her claim "proves to be quite accurate, but it doesn't expose her shallowness, as Nichols seems to have intended, it exposes *Ben's*."[26] Actually, it's pretty clear that Nichols intends her dismissal to expose them both—one for his naivety, the other for her cynicism. The entire scene, with its stage properties of the lamp switch, bed sheets, and underwear, is a relentless staging and re-staging of *exposure*.

In particular, Nichols uses the lamp's light to comment critically on his characters—both of them, not just Mrs. Robinson (whom Benjamin's prevailing point of view will increasingly demonize in the traditional iconography of melodramatic villainy: an ogress, a witch). When Mrs. Robinson snaps the room back into darkness, she commands this directorial control of the scene Benjamin has attempted to improvise. He will not turn the light on or off after this point; she is master of illumination or concealment. She needs to light a cigarette. Rather than fumbling in the dark, she turns on the light to locate lighter and package; she happens to do so just as she has suggested, with deadpan irony, that he might begin this conversation he has proposed by talking about his "college experiences," thus illuminating the temporal and cultural gulf between them. The light displays him in abject position, on his knees, head buried. She extinguishes the light, but he continues to insist, and a false start results: an abortive dialogue about art. What they have in common, it turns out, is merely whom they know: they talk about Mr. Robinson and then, as the light comes on again when Mrs. Robinson has admitted to her pregnancy and hasty marriage, about her daughter Elaine. Clearly Mrs. Robinson has switched on the light, but why? Given the clear establishment of the light as an expression of control, we would expect to see Mrs. Robinson swiftly move to master this situation, but she doesn't. She has, in a moment of unaccustomed vulnerability, revealed a truth kept even from Elaine: that the Robinsons' marriage was a proscribed duty to appease the gods of appearance. The subsequent two decades of loveless marriage (which throws a retrospective spotlight on Mr. Robinson's advice to Ben to have "a good time while you can") have been one terribly long and trying performance.

But now, with the light on, she pleads for Benjamin not to "tell Elaine," although he seems barely to know the Robinsons' daughter. Propped on an elbow, Benjamin looms above her, provided an unexpected jackpot of ascendant power. This is a dynamic moment for them both: in their sudden intimacy (after months of carnal embrace without emotional depth), she has confessed her most carefully guarded secret of social propriety. For Ben, the revelation leads to further curiosity about her personhood, contemplating her as a bright young college student: "What was your major?" he asks. Her evasion, turning away from him, suggests a crossroads where two people meet—one a master manipulator whose entire adult life has been an endless role-play of maintained appearance, the other an apt pupil who unfortunately is incapable of imagining any life for himself other than what his culture has already projected for him. The pupil appears accidentally to have unlocked the master's weakness. To his genuinely innocent question, the kind he might have been expected to ask a campus acquaintance, she answers, in resignation, "Art." Reified convention required that, two decades ago, Mrs. Robinson's just-beginning life as a student ended and another, her life as a wife and expectant mother, began. But her major subject has a deeper resonance in the etymological associations with "artifice" that subsequently have become her command performance.

Remembering her earlier avowal that she doesn't "know anything about it," he pauses, hovering above her in the room's illuminated space, the award-winning scholar solving a puzzle. In the silence, her enormous wedding ring diamond catching the light, the history of Mrs. Robinson's commodification (and, by analogy, his own) unfolds behind his furrowed brow. What he says next will be as momentous as the choice he made at the bottom of his parents' swimming pool. Available to him is the opportunity to open up in a similar way to Mrs. Robinson, to communicate his exasperations with a life seemingly as predetermined as her own, in which parents and their values decide their children's lives. It is hard to imagine what Mrs. Robinson might do with such confessional vulnerability (maternal solicitude would be awkward, for instance). He offers a carefully modulated sympathy in his polite response, "I guess you kind of lost interest in it over the years," and again she offers vulnerability: "Kind of." For Nichols, this is "the very heart of Mrs. Robinson, and therefore of the movie: namely, her self-hatred and the extent of her sadness about where the exigencies of her life had taken her, as opposed to where she had originally wanted to go."[27] *The Graduate* is poised to be a different kind of film altogether if Benjamin sympathetically and meaningfully connects to Mrs. Robinson's reification before he ever even meets and connects with her daughter's reification. But Benjamin backs away from the intimacy into a calculated, childish prurience, cajoling her to offer copulative particulars including the make and model of their make-out car (a "Ford"). Her scolding "That's enough" rights their relationship in the familiar power dynamic of her superiority, and she confirms that reassertion of control via the switch that plunges them back into darkness. When she switches on the light one last time a moment later, she has a fistful of his scalp and is back to giving autocratic commands: "Don't you *ever* take that girl out."

What are we to make of the one aberrant exception to the rhetorical rule of light in this scene? When Mrs. Robinson switches on the lamp, having been found out for her complicity in the Robinsons' two-decade social performance, she is behaving out of character. This would have been a predictable moment to take another diversionary poke at his codified sense of masculine potency, to issue a command, to threaten to cut off his supply of no-attachments eroticism. Instead she sheds a light on her own vulnerability, as if in delayed capitulation to his having turned the light on when he initiated the call for a conversation. While it might be within reason to say that, in the moment, she has been caught off-guard by the unanticipated turn the conversation has taken, recognizing in Benjamin a deeper simpatico than the lost and alienated victim-in-waiting she sensed at his graduation party, there is another explanation for the light coming on during this crucial part of the conversation: beyond Mrs. Robinson's direction of the relationship stands Mike Nichols' direction of the scene and the film. We must be made to see what Benjamin sees in *The Graduate*—his sometimes literal, always psychological point of view—and in this moment, particularly as he pauses upon learning her major subject in college, what Benjamin sees is how both of them have been processed and packaged as objects. *Beyond* what Benjamin sees and understands, however, is the ironic subtext Nichols invites the audience to grasp: that Benjamin, out of socially conditioned politeness and a failure of nerve, rejects responsibility for what he has glimpsed, ultimately refusing (by the end of the scene) to pursue any of the instincts he knows to be right. He continues the affair and foregoes any further pursuit of meaningful conversation. He's had enough of the truth. As if to remind us of the motif of illumination and failed action, Nichols ends the scene with the two fighters nearly naked, static in their opposite corners of the frame, and this time it is clearly the *director's* prerogative to return the scene, via fade-out, to darkness, the "old friend."

All action after this midpoint of the film is mere sound and fury, the illusion of direction, as Benjamin's sprinting across campus and neighborhood, up and down the California coast, and even to the church on time is doomed by his incapability or unwillingness ever to take that full, potentially redemptive glimpse into the reified void that he beholds, briefly, propped on an elbow over Mrs. Robinson, and then to act appropriately on what he has seen. The fantasy of happy ever after with Elaine that caused the proto-feminists of 1968 to argue that the films' misogynistic point of view demonizes the mother and denatures the daughter is Benjamin's (not Nichols') fantasy. In the conversation scene, the film allows sympathy for Mrs. Robinson; it is Benjamin who refuses to be informed in future action by the reified wisdom available during the conversation. Benjamin's point of view plays with genre at the end (he has a lot of time on his hands, driving the roughly 1,100 miles between Berkeley and Beverly Hills, round-trip, then back down as far as Santa Barbara again): perhaps with the echo in his head of Mr. Robinson's jocular "Standing guard over the ol' castle?" quip the night Mrs. Robinson first tried to seduce him, as well as with the feudal pressures to solidify partnership alliance by arranging a relationship between Braddock boy and Robinson girl, the climactic confrontation at the church vibrates with the timbre of the chivalric romance. As he storms the (nearly) fortified castle and penetrates towards its improvised keep, he becomes, in the psychology of the film's complicated, multi-layered point of view, both the knight determined to rescue the virginal damsel and the silly young man with a chivalric fantasy in his head, chasing after a woman he can't possibly expect will be able to transcend the baggage of his having slept for an entire summer with her mother.

An examination of the location site Nichols and his filmmaking team selected for filming this climactic confrontation underscores Nichols' intentionality in projecting Benjamin's romanticized self-image as chivalric interventionist. The church structure, the United Methodist Church of La Verne, half an hour's drive east of Los Angeles, is a high-modernist, post–Saarinen fortress with only a single public conduit of ingress and egress. When Benjamin's final sprint up the sidewalks of "Santa Barbara" reaches the church, Nichols and O'Steen add in a strummed, Latinate guitar chord by Paul Simon, an evocation of the soundtrack trope of the climactic Hollywood Western showdown. In this inflected moment, Nichols conflates medieval knighthood with its modern Hollywood avatar, the old–West cowboy-hero. Yet the design of the existing church structure in La Verne offered only one way in, through the double glass doors (which we see Benjamin barring with the cross at the end of the confrontation with the Robinsons and the wedding party). Audaciously, Nichols and company negotiated with the church to build a second door—the one the Robinsons neglect to lock—on the second-story street-side of the building, complete with a set of stairs to this auxiliary portal. After Benjamin runs to the main doors and finds them locked—a sure sign of an appropriation of a house of God for some unholy rite—he runs to these stairs built by Nichols' crew, throws open the door cut by Nichols' crew, and disappears inside to find himself in the cry room high above the sanctuary, still the boy in the bubble, held at bay by his elders, but no longer willing simply to acquiesce in his social consignment. Despite his lack of a "definite plan" (which Elaine has asked him to formulate in Berkeley before she submits to her parents' definitive plan), Benjamin raises holy hell against the Robinsons' unholy manipulation of marriage. After the shoot in La Verne wrapped, all the work done to create this auxiliary access to the building was immediately undone, the door removed and the wall seamlessly restored, the stairs disassembled. To visit the church now is to find no evidence of this side entrance Benjamin used to enact his rescue, as if he (and we) imagined it, as in a sense we do in the fantasy momentum of his chivalric action.

The United Methodist Church of La Verne, half an hour's drive east of Los Angeles, became the more convenient stand-in location for the climactic, romanticized rescue of Elaine by Benjamin from her coerced marriage to Carl Smith in Santa Barbara. Prior to filming *The Graduate*, Nichols and his crew actually built a stairway and cut a door in the second-story side of the building (the first bay on the left) to underscore the sense that Benjamin has breached the castle-like defenses of the Robinsons. However, the conclusion of the film ironically deflates the sense of principled valor, in hollow, directionless victory (photograph by the author).

That there is a wedding at all is more evidence of willful ignorance of the insight available in reification. The Robinsons, having endured two decades of enforced matrimony, might be expected to want something more for their own daughter than her similarly objectified sacrifice upon the altar of social manipulation and appearance. No one—not the Robinsons, not Carl Smith, not Benjamin—pursues marriage for its sacramental intention: the union of two souls. Marriage for all concerned has a far less exalted end: the manipulation of status. Marriage in both generations is merely a power move. Elaine, easily Benjamin's equal in passivity, allows herself to be shuffled along the squares of the marriage chessboard over the film's final half-hour. Nichols masterfully inflects the minute in which Benjamin, trapped behind glass above the wedding, taps and bellows for Elaine's attention. Nichols has Hoffman call Elaine's name no less than 20 times, a suspense-building projection of romantic longing as old as Romeo and Juliet, Paolo and Francesca, Jacob and Rachel. During this din,

The Graduate **became an icon of the New Hollywood in the brief period between the old Studio System era and the rise of the new corporate business model in the 1980s. The ambiguous final moment on the Santa Barbara bus, an improvised surprise Nichols sprung on Katharine Ross as Elaine Robinson and Dustin Hoffman as Benjamin Braddock by keeping the camera rolling after the script ran out, yields the brief, non-synchronized smiles on the two escapees from the conformity factory—smiles that settle into the resigned expressions of two people still trapped in "sounds of silence" without a "definite plan."**

Nichols cuts between close-ups of the Robinsons, Elaine, and Benjamin; we hear Carl Smith only as an off-screen voice, asking, "Who *is* that guy? What's he doing?" At the end of the sequence is when we get our first and only close-up of Carl in the film. Significantly, it announces that the camera has adopted a second subjective point of view: Elaine's. She looks at her mother, lips twisted in obscene invective directed up at Benjamin. After a cut back to Elaine, shifting perspective to find her father, the camera offers her vantage of Mr. Robinson, similarly engaged in mute obscenity towards the glassed cry room. Again the film returns to Elaine, and she turns to look in the opposite direction; the cut to Carl staring directly into the camera, face contorted as he directs his abuse directly at *her*, ends the sequence. When Nichols cuts back to Elaine, she is ready to call for his help. The self-fashioned knight descends into the fray as Errol Flynn might have, leaping a balustrade and subduing the feudal lord and company, cross held high. Birkvad writes, "Although, in the end, he apparently acts like a crusader for free love [...] Ben is still a child of the instant-gratification mentality of southern California."[28] What an audience may extrapolate is the happy ending to the fantasy conjured in Ben and Elaine's ingenuous heads: "a heteronormative love triumphing over every obstacle to achieve blissful harmony and nothing more."[29] The "rescue" scene rarely fails to provoke in its audiences a laugh of delight, mingled, Nichols must have hoped, with a sense of incredulity for the ridiculous pomposity of the symbolism.

But he has largely hoped in vain. As a culture, we love our genre formulas uncompromised by reminders of our more meager reality. The avant-garde techniques Nichols and his team integrated from the variety of their cinematic influences "gave *The Graduate* an exceptionally 'contemporary' look, even though, in the end, the movie's story could be regarded as an updated example of one of the most worn of Hollywood clichés—'love conquers all.'"[30] Jacob Brackman reported in a long, mostly negative 1968 essay in *The New Yorker* about *The Graduate* phenomenon that, when he saw the film in a packed theater, the audience instinctively knew the film was over when the boy won back the girl, and they noisily began to debrief, putting on their coats, as the Santa Barbara bus pulled back into the flow of traffic.[31] The extraordinary 40-second shot of Hoffman and Ross, playing young people numbed by the enormity of their directionless future, was a product of the improvisatory instinct of its director: "Mike told the camera operator to run the reel out and just let them sit," recalls Henry. "Being good actors and nice people they just sat there, waiting for an instruction. Their look of discomfort was partly out of lines with nothing more to do and the camera was still on. All that fit perfectly into a film about lives in stress with an uncertain future."[32] The profound ambiguity of the ending was largely lost in the initial-run audience's enthusiasm for its own counter-cultural fantasy. The reality of the film's formal design introduces a circular structure that Nichols returns to as a formal means to imply transformative opportunities squandered: after all the peripatetic movement in the second half of the film, Benjamin surrenders to passivity, carried by mechanized forces at film's end (the bus) just as he was at the beginning (the plane, the moving walkway), with the return of Simon and Garfunkel's "Sounds of Silence" magnifying our sense of his stasis. Nichols disenchanted college audiences by concluding, "'At the end he is just as lost as he was in the beginning,'" a prelude to his notorious pronouncement that Benjamin and Elaine will revert to the default inheritance of their parents' commodified world.[33] "The enchanted fairytale conclusion to *The Graduate* is moving precisely because of the ambiguity within Benjamin," writes John Lindsay Brown.[34] The brief, dolorous coda on the bus is what comes after the happy ever after. Murray Pomerance poses the rhetorical question, "Was it really this and only this, we must wonder, that Ben's important education was preparing him for?"[35] Henry recalls, "I think [Hoffman and Ross] thought the camera was going to run out a few seconds after they smiled: a happy ending. [...] No dialog, however classic and witty that I could have written, could have conveyed that feeling in quite the same dramatic way."[36] Hoffman and Ross had run out of script; so have Benjamin and Elaine, passively conveyed thus far in their lives and, despite their prominent educational experience, at a loss for next steps. Education remains one of the most prominent motifs of Nichols' subsequent films; formal education typically only seems to prepare characters to take their objectified places in the world, while the reified education in possibility is available to all, regardless of limiting distinctions of, for instance, class or gender. By the time the box-office (gold) dust had settled on *The Graduate*, the film had become a sacred object of its generation,[37] in which its own avatars, Benjamin and Elaine, were largely immune from the merciless satiric glare directed at all members of the older generation in the film; even critics who objected (like Pauline Kael, most comically vehement of the backlash reactionaries to Nichols; Farber and Changas; and Brackman) failed to see the film's ironic scrutiny of Benjamin and Elaine's failure. But in ignoring the imaginative failures of the film's protagonists, the audience fails not only to see Benjamin's surrender, but perhaps its own.

4

"Like us"

Catch-22 (1970)

In 1968, Mike Nichols was as close as dramatic entertainment came to a sure thing. He'd won the Grammy as a comedian, multiple Tonys as a stage director on Broadway, and the Oscar as a film director for *The Graduate*. Amidst all the hoopla of his new and white-hot Hollywood career, he'd even managed to open a new play in February 1968, Neil Simon's *Plaza Suite*, two months after *The Graduate* had opened, and once again won the Tony for Best Director. After touring college campuses as part of the Joseph E. Levine publicity band-wagon for *The Graduate*, Nichols, nearly ubiquitous in popular culture for more than a decade, disappeared for a year. He didn't stop working; he'd embarked on the quixotic task of adapting Joseph Heller's legendary 1961 novel *Catch-22*.

Hollywood was in transition from its old working method—an assembly line of inter-changeable "talent" (technicians, writers, and actors) under contract to a particular studio—to a new model of production predicated upon the deal, in which the talent was free to assemble wherever the money flowed. The Studio System was all but dead, and the big studios would soon be gone or altered beyond recognition. Nichols was emblematic of these devel-opments. He'd made his first film for Warner Bros., dealing with Jack Warner himself, as well as with the studio's practice of being "thrown off" the lot after delivering his final cut (so that an in-house editor could put Warner's stamp on the finished product; fortunately for Nichols, Sam O'Steen, the Warners' editor, had become a Nichols man during the pro-duction). *The Graduate*, however, was quasi-independent; Levine's Embassy Pictures rented studio space for Nichols at Paramount to make the film. Now, for *Catch-22*, Nichols was working for a third production company, Filmways (run by two independent producers, John Calley and Martin Ransohoff), in association with Paramount. Nichols' subsequent two films would complete an obligation to Embassy, and the last film of his first phase, before nearly a decade of feature-film silence, was at Columbia. Nichols was an early model of the New Hollywood era that stretched from semi-feral location shoots in the wilderness during the late 1960s (Dennis Hopper's *Easy Rider* and *The Last Movie*) through legendary boon-doggle shoots of the late 1970s like Michael Cimino's *Heaven's Gate* in remote Montana.

These were the final days of the old technology as well. In 1968, Stanley Kubrick was finalizing his space epic, *2001: A Space Odyssey*, which upon its release would vie with *The Graduate* for the cultural imagination and its box-office receipts; *2001* introduced stunning innovations in special-effects technologies that pointed the way toward the next Hollywood boom. By the end of the 1970s, George Lucas and Industrial Light and Magic had embarked upon the cinematic odyssey to Computer-Generated Imagery (CGI). But in the late 1960s and early 1970s, the old equipment serviced a new generation of film brats who used the inexperience of their new corporate producers to make their idiosyncratic, often indulgent films. This was the era when William Friedkin rode back-seat camera through New York's streets at high speeds in *The French Connection* (1971), and Francis Ford Coppola squandered enormous reserves of emotional and fiscal capital in the Philippines trying to make *Apocalypse Now* (1979).

Nichols had already demonstrated the self-indulgent mindset of the free-agent auteur in taking his *Virginia Woolf* company across the country to Smith College rather than making do on a soundstage at Warner's.[1] Authentic location shooting on Joseph Heller's massively popular novel of World War II would require far more exotic travel than western Massachusetts, however, since the story takes place on a military base in the Mediterranean theater, as well as in Rome. Yet Nichols and his by-now regular collaborators—production designer Richard Sylbert and editor Sam O'Steen, both returning for their third film with him, as well as Buck Henry, returning for his second as adapting screenwriter—took the money and ran. One destination was Italy; Rome's Piazza Navona figures prominently in scenes of the soldiers on leave. But the majority of principal photography, set on the fictional Army base of Heller's novel, took place in a remote location along the northwestern coast of Mexico, in the state of Sonora. There Nichols' company built genuine stone buildings, including the base headquarters, in which they would film for months and then, in creating the air raid the base flies against itself, blow to bits. Henry recalls, "We were in Mexico at the time of the student unrest of 1968. Units of the Mexican army were posted on the perimeter of our base to keep Mexicans from the planes, weapons, and dynamite that we were using."[2] The landing strip and ruins of the set built by the film company for the Army Air Force planes of the bomb squadron still remains, one of Guaymas' tourist attractions.

Nichols, who would become a consummate pro in his second phase by reining in the financial and stylistic excesses of the New Hollywood auteurs, insists his indulgences were not deliberate but instead the result of naivety and ignorance of the industry's standard operating procedures. Living in Mexico with a troop of famous actors and technicians was a liberty of the time; staying for months while working out shots and re-rehearsing scenes that left everyone, Nichols included, enervated with boredom was the license such liberty failed to revoke. The film far exceeded shooting schedule and budget. Millions of feet of film fell to the cutting-room floor, making a major character like Major Major (Bob Newhart) minor and making a relatively minor character like Hungry Joe (Seth Allen) merely a faraway pair of legs, falling from a deck into the sea.

People had been daydreaming about making a film of *Catch-22* since its publication in 1961. For years Orson Welles had lobbied to direct the adaptation, and Heller had given his blessing; predictably, given the combative nature of his ongoing relationship with the studios, Welles had been unable to secure financing. The book had gained cultural momentum year by year not solely as an anti-war document during the ideological battles of the 1960s but also as an anti-establishment broadside against the narcotic ease of conformity, the surrender to a collective, corporate will so pervasive its source could scarcely be traced. By the time Buck Henry was hired by Nichols to adapt the script, Heller's *Catch-22* had become an oracular presence in the counter-culture, one of the handful of artistic manifestos (Nichols' own *The Graduate* was another) that the younger generation coming of age pointed to as its collective voice. This is another way of saying that the person or persons who embarked upon this project of making the literary saga of Yossarian's revolt a cinematic saga would do so at high risk of getting a talismanic object "wrong." It's also a way of saying that Nichols, in love with the book and supremely confident in his abilities to make compelling dramatic narrative on stage and screen, strode with purpose into his first, almost-guaranteed failure.

Catch-22 as adapted by Buck Henry and made into a film by Mike Nichols is not a failure. In fact, it remains a remarkable document, filled with wondrous cinematic effects, memorable actors, and a story that does not diminish Heller's epic satirical scope and vision even as it vastly reduces its mass. In an excellent analysis of the film just after its release, Chuck Thegze writes that Nichols and Henry achieved this by focusing much more than Heller did on Yossarian as the constant central character of the narrative, excising powerful material from the novel when it did not directly dovetail with Yossarian's experience of the war.[3] *Catch-22* didn't stand a chance with critics and the general public due to the overwhelming and unreasonable weight of expectation, given the combination of accumulated adoration for Heller (silent as a novelist in the decade after *Catch-22*'s publication) and Nichols (dramatic Midas of all he touched) as well as the year-plus of hyped hysteria for Nichols' enormous, multi-million-dollar undertaking on two continents and three countries. Nichols' *Catch-22* couldn't help but be something other than what its audience thought it wanted. The film received only one glowing major review, from Vincent Canby in the *New York Times*; other reviewers mixed admiration with frustration, as in Stephen Farber's assessment in *Sight and Sound* that it "is unquestionably a failure, [...] but its intermittent dramatic intensities, its arresting experiments with time in relation to point of view, and the power of Alan Arkin's performance make it worth seeing."[4] Nichols knows he might have worked harder to please the crowd with his adaptation, but years later, looking back, he remains firm: "What I like very much about it are its ambitions."[5]

The film also suffered from poor timing within the industry itself. Yossarian's prickly personality as the film's central character, the confusing complexity of the hallucinatory structure, and the cool alienation explicit in the narrative point of view were no match commercially for the juggernaut of Robert Altman's very free adaptation of *M*A*S*H**, released several months earlier the same year. Hawkeye Pierce (Donald Sutherland) and Trapper John (Elliott Gould) were cruel, manipulative, exploitative, and self-serving, but they were also charmingly charismatic rogues, good at saving lives in the operating room, good at athletics, good with women. Though more of a mensch, Yossarian was also more of a schlemiel, a Nichols specialty since Benjamin Braddock in *The Graduate*. Yossarian may provoke some admiration in the audience for the persistence of his resistance, but he does not inspire a following, even on screen. Audience members would be hard-pressed to find themselves yearning for a place opposite him in his tiny open boat on the ocean as the film ends. However, in *M*A*S*H**, the audience watches Hawkeye and Trapper win over nearly everyone, and as the community parts to go separate ways home at the end of their tours of duty, the audience is invited to feel the loss as keenly as any of the members of the "Swamp." In *Catch-22*, Yossarian can't run away fast enough from the complicit conformity of his base. Given the inevitable consumer's choice between near-simultaneous releases of two allegorical, satiric treatments of America's current foreign military intervention in Vietnam, via stories set during earlier military engagements (Korea in *M*A*S*H**, World War II in *Catch-22*), the consumers opted overwhelmingly for the one that ends with victory, both literal (the football game/betting war) and symbolic (Hawkeye and Trapper John's co-opting of the camp to their own alternately libertine and humanist sensibilities).

"But," as a long feature in *Time* pointed out as the film debuted, "Nichols was not making *Super-M*A*S*H**. From the beginning, he was aware that laughter in *Catch-22* was, in the Freudian sense, a cry for help. It is the book's cold rage that he has nurtured."[6] *Catch-22* has a complicated cast of characters, even in its cinematic adaptation (which reduces the host of dramatic personalities by more than half). Its protagonist is an angry complainer, sympathetic in situation more than personality. And Nichols and Henry accentuated the surrealism of Heller's narrative, making the filmed version a quite literal fever-dream of associative transitions, within which many in the audience became hopelessly lost. There was also the inherent problem that the tone of the story Heller's *Catch-22* tells promotes polarization. The so-called Silent Majority, many of whom had fought in Europe in World War II, or in the Pacific in World War II and Korea, were always going to struggle with a narrative that questions the moral prerogative (and staying power) of the United States as a world power. Even for those open to the satiric accusations the book and film level at American triumphalism and the military-industrial complex, Heller's narrative as well as the necessarily reduced screenplay by Henry have little warmth. Heller, who was greatly impressed and relieved by the faithfulness of Nichols and Henry's intentions, acknowledges this choice: "If a certain objective had to be striven for, I was pleased that it was a grim one, a melancholy one. The easy way would have been to emphasize the sex and the comedy."[7] For all its lampoonish, surreal humor, *Catch-22* as novel and as film is an angry story about emotional isolates. It isn't a film an audience can cozy up to. It can be admired, but it cannot easily be loved. Nichols knew this as soon as he previewed the film, he told Steven Soderbergh: "It's not a film anyway that leads to a huge audience reaction. The first two films I made *did* lead to a huge audience reaction and cheering and carrying on."[8]

At the end of *Catch-22* (which in the narrative's logic is chronologically the beginning, just before Nately's whore stabs him and sets in motion the fever-dream of associations that make up the bulk of the film), there is one final catch for Yossarian (indelibly played by Alan Arkin, in his first starring film role; he and Nichols had worked together on Broadway in 1964's *Luv*, which ran for over two years) to negotiate. The two-headed Colonel-monster of Cathcart (Martin Balsam) and Korn (Buck Henry) appeals to Yossarian to join with their efforts to win the hearts and minds of "the folks at home." Most basically, in an eerie echo of the contemporary social-network euphemism, they implore Yossarian to "like" them. Yossarian's instinct for self-preservation is put to its greatest test in this munitions-free moment of the narrative. It is obvious to all where the threat to identity comes from when in the turret of a bomber absorbing flak above a strategic target. But on friendly turf, in the presence of smiling commanding officers who have promised to put him on "easy street," the risk is less apparent (and therefore much more insidious). Indeed, Yossarian initially takes their offer, and Nichols and David Watkin, the film's director of photography, zoom in to a depersonalized shot of their clasped hands sealing the deal. In the surreal logic of *Catch-22*, this is when Yossarian is at his most vulnerable, and Nately's whore thus may do her worst. We protest his innocence in vain—the man who has acquiesced to Cathcart and Korn's deal may be many things, but he is not innocent.

"The passage of time reveals that there is very little wrong with Nichols' film," writes Lee Hill, assessing it as "one of the finest achievements of the era. If only all 'failed films' were this well crafted, thoughtful, full of comic energy, and beautiful to look at."[9] Nichols himself, reflecting on the film, recognizes the enormous accomplishment of "something that is not trying to be a mass movie," even as he second-guesses choices he made (all of which he made to accentuate the atmosphere of surreal alienation).[10] Any of these choices might have invited a wider audience appeal if he'd opted for accessibility over the seeming chaos that the film's world required: the vast acreage of the film with no musical accompaniment to provide emotional cues; the sudden, unexplained knife-attack on Yossarian that might have more clearly identified Nately's whore as assailant; and using "a warmer actor, more connected to the audience, for Yossarian—like Dustin [Hoffman, title character of *The Graduate*]."[11] None of these would have made the film a more successful aesthetic experience, however. All are phenomena that, in Nichols' mind, would have better served to endear the film to its audience, a goal Nichols has always prized as an entertainer, and which he admirably sacrifices in *Catch-22* (and his next film, *Carnal Knowledge*) for the greater good of cool, dark satire. "Most comedies are brightly lit, very visible," Henry observes. "In *Catch-22*, the darkness gives an eerie, dreamlike quality, which is part of the tone and content of the story, like a fever, which is how I thought about it."[12]

In Nichols' artistic laments for a work doomed by its own prickliness to the margins, one senses the mass-audience entertainer's appetite to please, to be "liked," in combat with his conviction of the organic truth of a narrative. Coming on the heels of *The Graduate*, a film adored (at times for the wrong reasons) by the most massive audience Nichols would ever command, *Catch-22* feels like a corrective aesthetic measure both for himself and his audience. Nichols' conflicted emotions about the film remain. The film failed to earn back its investment upon initial release, and whatever his aesthetic convictions, this failure would have shaken the auteur's sense of utter confidence in his instincts. In the metaphoric terms of his own film, Nichols was at a decisive point, balanced between the often mutually exclusive imperatives of artistic ingenuity and commercial viability. He made the right choices artistically in *Catch-22*, but as a likable man who wants to be liked, Nichols has carried the dilemma of *Catch-22* into every subsequent production. In every sense, *Catch-22* was a life-changing experience.

* * *

The plot of *Catch-22* could not help but be truncated; over nearly 500 pages of densely episodic prose, Joseph Heller layers on a thick impasto of absurdity that argues against the assumption that the paradox of the novel's title is to be located exclusively in military life and thinking. (The biography of Major Major Major Major is but one isolated example of the scores of textured incident, background, and character study that could not transfer from book to feature film.) While the book focuses on the military mindset, the madness of existence extends beyond the military into civilian life. Buck Henry's adaptation of the novel for the cinema has no such luxury, settling instead for a vision of total war in which the madness inherent in World War II seeps into the surrounding culture until, as the old woman at the Roman whorehouse explains it, all seemingly random acts of violence and injustice can be attributed to "Catcha–22." Hill writes, "in spite of the film's picaresque quality, Nichols' film, thanks to Buck Henry's script, with its repeating dream sequence set in a damaged bomber cockpit, is as immaculately structured as one of Harold Pinter's celebrated screen adaptations."[13] Of the adaptation, Heller was surprised by what it had managed to achieve: "'I expected to be disappointed—after all, I had no part of it. But I saw what Mike had done. He didn't try to make it just an antiwar movie or an insane comedy. He caught its essence. He understood.'"[14]

While Captain Yossarian is the central presence of both book and film, the film rarely makes the pretense of a larger, all-encompassing point of view. We encounter *Catch-22* largely via the alienation of Yossarian. Thegze argues that, within the insular, hallucinatory circularity of Yossarian's point of view, the film renders nothing less than the psychological transformation of Yossarian from enraged but helpless victim of the pervading military-industrial mind-think (the madness of "Catch-22" logic) to conscientious objector, opting out of a madness he can recognize for what it is. The film opens with his stabbing because, in the Catch-22 logic of the world in which Yossarian finds himself, only an attempt on his life can save his soul. His sick-leave meditations, which comprise the majority of the film's running time in a dense web of flashback and fantasy, are his time to summon himself for what he knows he must do: reject the enticements of Cathcart and Korn and assume the hard responsibilities of life in opposition to hegemony. "The Yossarian one meets at the beginning of *Catch-22* is, one can be assured, a permanently changed Yossarian,"[15] argues Thegze, indicating in particular what Yossarian has encountered in the death of Snowden and in the military detachment from that death at Snowden's funeral, when Milo is more concerned about candy-coating his capitalist missteps with Egyptian cotton than in grieving a fallen friend. Thegze's characterization of Yossarian's change as "permanent" is, however, premature: Yossarian quite willingly shakes hands with men whose mien and morals he detests, motivated by nakedly cynical self-interest. Nately's whore saves his soul by giving him more time—recuperative, therapeutic, healing time—to contemplate and reject the deal he has made. Yossarian knows the right thing to do in confronting the reality of the military's indifference to human life and death, but he needs to be stabbed by the woman who carries Nately's memory more acutely than Yossarian himself in order to bring him into full possession of what he knows.

After a stunning time-lapse photograph of sunrise over the Mediterranean, we watch as the squadron of an Army Air Force base prepares for takeoff[16]; in a bombed-out headquarters building (later we learn it has been destroyed by its own munitions), Yossarian (Alan Arkin) shakes hands with Colonels Cathcart (Martin Balsam) and Korn (Buck Henry), though we have no idea what has transpired between them (later we learn he has made a corrupt deal in order to be sent home). Yossarian departs the building, descending to field level, where he pauses briefly to watch the planes in formation; there he's stabbed by an enlisted man (whom we later learn is neither) and falls to the ground, his face a rictus alluding to iconic depictions of war-time atrocity from Rubens to Goya to Picasso. The associative logic of the film's narrative, which Henry carried over from his work with Nichols on *The Graduate*,[17] emerges in the overlapped dissolve from Yossarian's suffering to the first of five sequences in the turret of the bomber where Yossarian, the plane's bombardier, must attempt to aid Snowden (Jon Korkes), a young, wounded soldier in the turret with him. "'The picture will be cut as if Yossarian's delirium were cutting it,'" Henry told Nora Ephron.[18] After another brief dissolve, which establishes Yossarian as the one who is being attended to (he's on a stretcher in the back of an Army ambulance), Nichols and his editor, Sam O'Steen, cut immediately to Yossarian among his friends at dinner in the mess hall—Dobbs (Martin Sheen), Orr (Bob Balaban), McWatt (Peter Bonerz), Aardvark (Charles Grodin), and Nately (Art Garfunkel, in his first film role). Introduced (so that it may be echoed at the ending, when the film's narrative will have argued persuasively for it) is Yossarian's philosophical argument: asked, "Just suppose everyone felt the same way you do [about opting out of the mortal risks of warfare]," he responds, "Then I'd be a damn fool to think any different." Continuing the associative leaps of this opening section, or overture, of the film, Nichols and O'Steen cut to Yossarian in one of his many wheedling conversations with Doc Daneeka (Jack Gilford), another friend, who can't ground Yossarian for craziness as long as Yossarian desires, sanely, to be grounded—our first encounter with "Catch-22" logic.

The next sequence of the film would seem to be from the omniscient perspective of Heller's narrator, since it does not depict Yossarian, and yet it is the first external illustration in the narrative of Yossarian's internal preoccupation with human madness (as he lies in his hospital bed, free-associating in fevered infection, recovering from his knife wound). Milo Minderbinder (Jon Voight, just after *Midnight Cowboy*), acting mess officer, presents an ambitious proposition to base commander Cathcart: Milo hopes to begin trading with various military and civilian partners "to give the men in this squadron the finest cuisine in the entire world." His subtextual goal is to create a corporation—M&M Enterprises—to operate his commodities exchange, and his first brainstorm is to trade vast cartons of silk for Egyptian cotton. The "catch" is that the silk comprises all of the material of the squadron's parachutes, and Yossarian is wounded in the leg during the flight mission in which he discovers this. Another overlapped dissolve to Snowden (and to Yossarian drowning) takes us to Yossarian in the hospital, presumably recovering from the leg wound he suffered in the bomber rather than the knife wound that begins the narrative—though the point is already emerging that we should understand a certain fluidity to events and thus to sensibility in all we're encountering: the narrative is a summative argument by Yossarian, recovering from his stabbing, just before he goes AWOL.

In the hospital, Yossarian latches on to Captain Tappman (Anthony Perkins), the base chaplain, as a potential spokesman for his grounding, asking Tappman to talk to Cathcart. Yossarian, captive in the infirmary, watches two nurses attending to the "soldier in white," a man swathed like a chrysalis in plaster casts from head to toe. As the nurses blithely exchange full catheter for empty saline drip, effectively recirculating the man's own toxins through his system, Yossarian meta-theatrically breaks the "fourth wall" of the film for the one and only time, regarding us, the camera, as he screams his disbelief. Everything we witness in this film is an emblem of the madness Yossarian fears will consume him along with everyone and everything else in its path.

A long, Yossarian-free sequence follows (now haunted by his Catch-22 understanding of the world), in which Cathcart promotes Captain Major (Bob Newhart) to squadron commander (upon the death of Major Duluth, killed off-screen in action while flying a raid). Major also receives a concomitant promotion in rank, inevitably to Major. (In the austerities of delivering a two-hour running time, the film does not allow itself to revel in the Hellerian absurdities that Major's first and second given names are also Major, thus rendering him, upon promotion, "Major Major Major Major.") When Chaplain Tappman comes to Major Major's office, he is only permitted to see the major when the major is out, more "Catch-22" thinking at its finest, but personalized to suit the needs of a particularly alienated officer. The Chaplain is whisked to Cathcart's office, where he finds Orr waiting, sopping wet, freshly pulled from the sea after his fourth air crash; Cathcart's purpose for seeing the chaplain is to command him to think up "some snappy prayers" for pre-raid services, which Cathcart hopes will get him featured in the *Saturday Evening Post*, as a British colonel and his squadron were. The chaplain attempts to use this opportunity to question Cathcart's serially raising the minimum number of missions soldiers must fly before completing the requirements of their tour of duty, but he gains no traction. Tappman is dismissed with the assurance that it is "None of your business" to worry about the well being of the men of the squadron. Cathcart and Korn indulge in cruel daydreams about how General Dreedle, whose arrival for base inspection is imminent, would handle a troublemaker like Yossarian.

The fate they ultimately imagine is administered, in jump cut, not by military protocol but by a more private skirmish for tender territory, waged on a beach dune between Yossarian and Nurse Duckett (Paula Prentiss). In Yossarian's associative logic, this short, painful scene overlaps the ceremonious arrival of Dreedle (Orson Welles), accompanied by his son-in-law, Lt. Col. Moodus (Austin Pendleton), and a WAC (Suzanne Benton), selected by Dreedle for obvious objectifying anatomical reasons. Dreedle interrupts a briefing in progress by Major Danby (Richard Benjamin) for the imminent bombing of Ferrara, and Cathcart, to curry favor, raises the mission ceiling again, this time to 75. Yossarian and his friends discuss Cathcart's mania for polishing the brass over spaghetti in the Piazza Navona in old Rome, our first chance to get to know Nately, an angelic innocent intent upon marrying a certain whore (Gina Rovere) always seen in company of her kid sister (Fernanda Vitobello). It's also our first extended glimpse of Aardvark, a pipe-smoking and puritanical patrician intent on chastening into chastity the whores he meets. To the familiar strains of Richard Strauss in "Thus Spake Zarathustra" (ubiquitous in late 1960s culture because of Stanley Kubrick's use of the piece in *2001: A Space Odyssey*), Yossarian first sees Luciana (Olimpia Carlisi) and trails after her until thwarted by a supply caravan directed by Milo Minderbinder.

The mission to Ferrara is a spectacular failure, in which the squadron drops its tonnage in "marvelous bomb pattern" into the ocean beyond the port (that Ferrara is in fact significantly inland off the Adriatic coast is, in this sense, simply more of the film's absurdity, and indeed, the port town is never expressly identified as Ferrara—it could still be that the 5–10 minute flight inland was the strategic intention). Yossarian was the instigator of the bomb dump, we learn; he is unable to understand why they are to bomb a non-military target, and attracted by the notion that they are obliged to return to base the instant they have dropped their load in order to avoid exposure to retaliatory fire, he has initiated the premature drop. Cathcart arranges for medals to be awarded, thus countering any potential publicity about the absurd cost of the wasted mission, and Yossarian shows up for the ceremony naked, much to Dreedle's disgust. He gives the medal he receives to Luciana. In a third overlap to the Snowden death scene, Yossarian learns that Milo has not only traded away their parachutes but also their morphine.

What comes next is undoubtedly the most shockingly surreal moment in Yossarian's long fever-dream: the death of Hungry Joe. "Gruesome and pointless—a bit like war itself, then," it is "perhaps the bleakest moment in any anti-war satire."[19] In the novel, Hungry Joe dies "off stage"; in Nichols' film, Hungry Joe is an innocent bystander (if, as the film queries, there can be such a thing), killed as collateral damage of yet another "Catch-22." McWatt dive-bombs Yossarian, back on the beach making time with Nurse Duckett; McWatt is driven to this jealous demonstration because she ought to be with McWatt, since she likes McWatt better—even though she "can't stand" him. On one of McWatt's low passes over the beach, he swoops too low too soon and slices Hungry Joe in half at the waist. Hungry Joe's stricken lower half remains upright for a memorable instant before crumpling into the sea. McWatt's plane wobbles furiously out of control over distant mountains, where it crashes into a cliff. In one of the great absurdist motifs in Heller's novel, Doc Daneeka has been a phantom signature on the manifests of his friend McWatt's missions so he can avoid flying yet still receive credit for having done so. As they watch McWatt crash in the film, Doc is among the small company that helplessly witnesses the deaths of Hungry Joe and McWatt. Sgt. Towser (Norman Fell) laments, with Doc standing next to him, that Doc's name was on the manifest, and they are all crestfallen when they don't see Doc jump from the plane before impact. For the remainder of the narrative, the official record as entered in the manifest trumps Doc's actual, corporeal presence, which even Doc ultimately comes to accept. The scene of the deaths of Hungry Joe, McWatt, and Doc Daneeka is followed by a funeral—for someone else, naturally. It's Snowden's funeral, which Yossarian commemorates by once again eschewing uniform of any kind for nakedness— and attendance via nearby tree limb. Milo asks him to try some chocolate-covered cotton, because the market flooded with Egyptian cotton just after he traded all their parachutes.

In Rome on leave, Yossarian proposes to Luciana but is met by more "Catch-22" thinking: she won't marry a crazy man, and Yossarian must be crazy because he wants to marry her. Nately engages the 107-year-old proprietor (Marcel Dalio) of the whorehouse he frequents in the most overtly philosophical dialogue of the film, in which the old man explains his secret of endurance, delivered in the parlance of "Catch-22": "We will certainly come out on top if we succeed in being defeated," referencing the doomed overreaching of imperial ambition in ancient Rome, Greece, and Persia, as well as in modern Germany and the United States. Nately accuses the old man of opportunism, and Yossarian enters on cue with perspective: Cathcart has just raised the number of missions to 80 in his rage that Orr has just crashed for a fifth time.

The next sequence of scenes reveals two very different sorts of secret schemes in motion: Milo cryptically warns Yossarian and friends that the base is on alert, while Yossarian begins to reflect upon the equally cryptic suggestions the "accident"-prone Orr gave him before his most recent crash: "If you were smart, you'd fly with me." Back on base, Yossarian finds Milo's caution has been heeded: the base is all but deserted; he encounters only isolates like Major Danby and Doc Daneeka; contemplating Orr's latest disappearance, he flashes back to Doc Daneeka's awkward request to pretend he is a soldier named Harvey who has just died, in order to provide comfort for Harvey's family, which has traveled 5,000 miles to spare him the indecency of dying alone. Yossarian agrees on the condition that Doc files a form to ground him, and Doc immediately warns him "there's a catch": military brass has to approve the request, and brass' policy is not to approve requests. Harvey's family mournfully enters, and black comedy ensues, with Yossarian assenting to be called Harvey and Harvey's brother John (Richard Libertini) correcting his parents (Liam Dunn and Elizabeth Wilson, who was Mrs. Braddock in *The Graduate*) when they call Yossarian Harvey. "What difference does it make?" asks Harvey's mother in exasperation. "He's dying." Her pronouncement unnerves Yossarian, serving as the associative trigger to return a fourth time to the Snowden death scene. By now the scene takes us deep enough into the moment to see Yossarian has gingerly established a tourniquet on Snowden's leg wound. Snowden responds to Yossarian's question about pain in his leg with a vague gesture toward his torso, and Yossarian uncovers Snowden enough to reveal that Snowden's entire right side is awash in blood.

On base, Nately seeks Yossarian's help to stop Dobbs, who has vowed to kill Cathcart. Yossarian promises to help in the assassination if Cathcart dares to raise their mission number again. Dobbs and Nately scuffle and Nately is knocked cold. Then, suddenly, Yossarian and Dobbs are caught in floodlights and, soon after, the hellish choreographed conflagration of a raid on the base. The nighttime explosions are worthy of a Bosch landscape. Yossarian opens fire, but Milo warns him to take cover and stop shooting his own men: "This is an M&M Enterprises operation," he announces. Cathcart confirms what Milo has claimed, explaining that, to unload the cotton Milo bought with their parachutes, M&M has crawled into bed with the Germans, whose demand was that the Americans save them the risk and expense of a raid by bombing their own base. Yossarian tries to kill Cathcart on the spot, but his gun is empty from shooting at the planes. He discovers Nately was killed in the bombing of headquarters.

The narrative jumps to Yossarian's subjective camera point of view, on the operating table with his stab wound. In the midst of the bloodied surgeons, an oily figure in black (Felice Orlandi) arises, impossibly, from what can only be Yossarian's own viscera. "We've got your pal," the man says. So begins the last Roman sequence, in which, after the base bombing, Yossarian seeks out Nately's whore to tell her the terrible news. The film began with a sunrise; in this last Roman sequence, it is now the dead of night. Yossarian runs into Aardvark, with another young Italian girl (Wendy D'Olive) we assume he means to protect from the exploitative life of wartime. At the whorehouse, Yossarian learns from an old woman (Evi Maltagliati) that the whores have been herded away by the "white heads," the white helmeted MPs, citing "Catcha–22" as their right of action. On the street he sees other whores being herded by the MPs, and a motorcade led by Milo roars through the streets; Yossarian attempts to attack Milo in vengeance for Nately's death, and Milo's MPs subdue him. Milo implacably offers to direct Yossarian to Nately's whore, which he can do authoritatively because prostitution is now a wholly owned subsidiary of M&M Enterprises. Yossarian walks past a blocks-long line of silent G.I.s awaiting their turn in the M&M whorehouse and finds Luciana working the desk of the whore factory; "Everybody works for Milo" she intones ominously, and she hands Yossarian the key to the room of Nately's whore, charging him $10.

Nately's whore pulls a small knife and attempts to kill him when Yossarian tells her Nately is dead; she and her kid sister pummel him until he escapes out a window, and he wanders the back streets of old Rome, witnessing sad vignettes of degradation everywhere he turns. Distantly, *Una furtiva lagrima* ("A Furtive Tear") from Donizetti's opera *L'elisir d'amore* plays, one of the few instances of musical inflection in the film, fading only when Yossarian discovers that Aardvark has raped and killed the young woman he was squiring. Yossarian hears the MPs ascending the stairs and assumes confidently that they can successfully negotiate the morality of *this* moment, but they ignore Aardvark and instead place Yossarian in custody, for being AWOL.

Cathcart and Korn, anxious to be rid of Yossarian's constant agitation of his fellow soldiers, offer him a deal: he may go home, but "Of course, there's one catch": Yossarian must "like" them. They offer him "easy street," and explain, "all you have to do is [...] tell the folks at home what a good job we're doing." Surprisingly, Yossarian assents. With his handshake, we realize we've reentered the scene from the beginning of the film, when he is stabbed while watching his squadron forming on the runway. This time we hear the impassioned female voice of Nately's whore as she drives the knife home and escapes, and just as when we witnessed the scene the first time, it dissolves into the Snowden death scene. This is our fifth and last revisiting of the occasion of Snowden's death. After Yossarian has treated Snowden's leg wound he attempts to deal with the newly revealed damage to Snowden's torso, only to be horrified by the sloughing of Snowden's vital organs from his chest and abdomen to the floor of the turret. Yossarian is tormented by the ineffectuality of his comforting, "There, there."

Near the end of his three-week hospital stay after the stabbing, Yossarian receives two visitors: Major Danby and Captain Tappman. The substance of their conversation is that Cathcart and Korn intend to uphold their end of the bargain and have spun the knife attack as Yossarian's selfless act of sacrifice to save the colonels from assassination. Yossarian decides he "can't play Cathcart's game" and vows to break the deal: "I've flown 55 missions. I've been fighting for my country for three years. Now I'm going to start fighting for myself." Danby echoes Dobbs' question from early in the film, "Suppose everyone felt that way?" and Yossarian's answer remains firm: "Then I'd be a damn fool to feel any different." He recites a list of all his friends lost as casualties of the war, but Danby corrects him when he names Orr; Orr has reputedly washed ashore in Sweden. The chaplain proclaims it "a miracle," but Danby corrects him: "It's no miracle—he has to have planned it!" Inspired by finally understanding Orr's method amidst the madness, Yossarian leaps from the window of the infirmary and

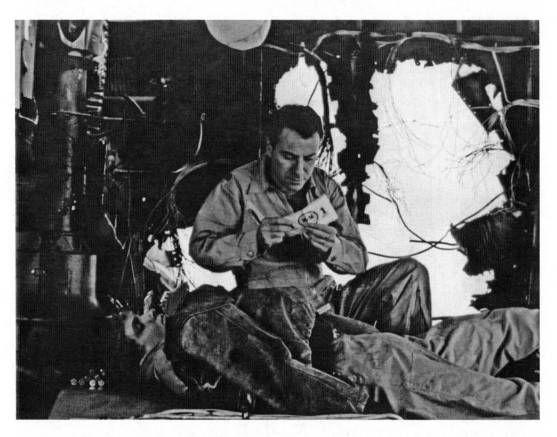

One moment repeatedly returns in *Catch-22*: Yossarian (Alan Arkin) tends to the wounded Snowden (Jon Korkes) in the bombardier's nest of a compromised B-25. Much of the film is Yossarian's associative fever-dream, experienced while recuperating in the infirmary from a near-fatal stabbing; the Snowden sequence recurs in his mind because it epitomizes Yossarian's own tenuous existence, his powerlessness to provide anything more than cold comfort ("There, there"), and his objectification by a military-industrial complex that makes all decisions based on corporate profit (the scrip in Yossarian's hand, where morphine should be).

runs for the ocean. When last we see him, he is emulating Orr, a tiny figure in a raft stroking determinedly against the immense, implacable blue of the ocean.

* * *

Catch-22, the 1961 novel by Joseph Heller, is and will remain a phenomenon, one of the rare literary works whose influence is so vital and contagious that popular usage has outstripped literary allusion. Most people know what a "Catch-22" is without having any idea that its source as a phrase derives from a work of black humor. In taking on a book that, in the decade after its initial publication, had ascended to status as a counter-cultural touchstone, Nichols may well have meditated upon the absolute adoration his audience had felt for Benjamin Braddock in *The Graduate*. In Yossarian, genuine anti-hero of *Catch-22*, Nichols may have felt he could in all confidence present to his audience a bona fide icon of resistance (sometimes passive, other times, as when he shoots at Milo in the tower and aims a gun he still believes is loaded at Cathcart, very aggressively active). There is a world of difference in Nichols' treatment of what appear on the surface to be two very similar endings:

The Graduate's Benjamin Braddock running away after rescuing Elaine Robinson and *Catch-22*'s Yossarian running away after leaping from the infirmary window. Both Benjamin and Yossarian have attempted to "play by the rules," only to find, as Benjamin puts it to Elaine once the date from hell settles into boy meets girl, "It's like I'm playing some kind of game, but the rules don't make any sense to me. They're being made up by all the wrong people. No—I mean no one makes them up; they seem to have made themselves up." Both Benjamin and Yossarian have, in fact, rejected hegemonic structures they understand to have little interest in their welfare, only their submission. Each is, in our last glimpse of him, finished physically running, and each is in a state of surrender to larger currents of motion (in Benjamin's case, the random Santa Barbara bus he and Elaine have flagged down and boarded; in Yossarian's case, the tiny raft). Yet there remains a distinction between Benjamin's case and Yossarian's case: Benjamin has no inspirational role model in his head, while Yossarian has the example, however quixotic, of Orr's persistence in non-compliance—Orr's very surname is a summation of the contrarian principle, his many test-crashed missions the sanest madness in an ocean of wartime absurdity. Orr has made a separate peace in Sweden, and it is what Yossarian will be thinking about during the sun-blistered days and cold, wet nights that await on his way north. All Benjamin can think about is what his parents have wanted: for him to settle—into marriage, career, mortgage, the compliant life of the majority.

The pervasiveness of socially proscribed games and rules is among the most consistent preoccupations of Nichols' career. George and Martha create an evening of performance art from the "games" they've felt compelled to play during the course of their adult lives, and Benjamin, the track star, is no stranger to performance; it's what attunes him to the insight about games that he makes to Elaine on their date. In *Carnal Knowledge*, Nichols' film that followed *Catch-22*, the intellectually nimble main characters are fully reified in that they understand and can articulate the violence done to them by commodification (and acknowledge their own tacit—even at times eager—complicity in these objectifying systems); Sandy (Art Garfunkel) even has a culminating speech in the film's coda about the "games" social systems expect us to play with one another. By *Heartburn* in 1986, the metaphor of the "game" has found its way into the choric commentary of Carly Simon's song "Comin' Around Again," which opens and closes the film with its references to complicit willingness "to play the game" of performing the rote, doomed roles of courtship. *Catch-22* is the least overt of Nichols' first four films in referencing this culture of artificiality via the "game" metaphor, but this may only be a result of its sublimation within the coined title metaphor, which characters either adapt to and use to their advantage (like Cathcart and Korn, Major Major, Milo, and even Orr) or else oppose with overwhelmingly adverse consequences (like Yossarian, who never quite finds a way to make the "logic" of "Catch-22" work for him). Benjamin in *The Graduate* can't let go of the mainstream system's values, even as he seeks to break the hold the mainstream system has on him. His perspective—which perceives monsters of conformity and misanthropic surrender all around him—fails to identify his own commitment to the master narratives whispered in his ear by his culture, to be the *hero* and ride off into the sunset with the beautiful maiden (her maidenhood still, in the nick of time, intact). Yossarian has long since been cured of the propaganda-spread disease of heroism, of self-negation in the pursuit of some pretty illusion. In the Snowden scenes in the bombardier's turret (where Yossarian himself could easily have been the one to absorb the deadly fire Snowden has sustained), and in the chaos of Yossarian's own wounding and in the aborted bombing run on Ferrara and its decorated aftermath, Nichols extracts any potential glamour or nobility from the pressurized moment, deconstructing the Hollywood war-film trope (a popular oversimplification of Hemingway's ethos of grace under pressure) of the serene right-ness of young men flying repeatedly into the teeth of death. Alan Arkin's prickly, antic inhab-itation of these scenes offers us anti-heroism of the most literal sort. This is not *alternative* heroism—what cultural connotation, in our hunger for models of action in dramatic art, seeks to discover in counter-culture storytelling—but a position *opposed* to heroism, that is anti-*heroes*, because heroes of any kind beget conformity. In the absence of legitimate cultural values, then, heroism is a chimera, and only a "damn fool," in Yossarian's parlance, would conform to such a patently false construction.

Like *The Graduate*, *Catch-22* appears before our eyes as something other than realism. Nichols says, "*Catch-22* is a dream; [...] it has the lack of boundaries that dreams have, and the repetitiveness and the lack of reality."[20] Nichols would eventually make some films grounded in realism, but this was not the mode in which he began his Hollywood career. We are asked to see the world not as it "is," but as it appears within the subjective distortions of a particular character. Poisoning the outsider's perspective of Benjamin in *The Graduate* are his intense naivety, his residual desire for assimilation, and his ferocious self-justification; as a narrative eye, he is unreliable. Despite the fact that much of *Catch-22*'s narration is the jumbled, associatively obsessive fever-consciousness of Yossarian as he recuperates from his stabbing by Nately's whore, we are more inclined to accept his reliability than Benjamin's. Farber writes, "This non-rational structuring (flashbacks, flash-forwards, fantasies within flashbacks) approximates the movements of consciousness better than most subjective films, and creates a powerful sense of inner disorientation"[21]—but the disorientation is physical; psychologically, Yossarian is pulling things into coherency. The direction in which Yossarian's "consciousness" is moving, argues Nichols, is therapeutic, the redemptive embrace of reified wisdom: "'That's what the movie is. [Yossarian] does not remember the end of Snowden, and he's trying to and it gets cut off and when he does fully remember Snowden he breaks down and is reconstituted and makes his decision. It is exactly parallel to psychoanalysis.'"[22] Yossarian shows no particular desire to protect his own ego-territory, only his skin. He ques-tions the morality of the Ferrara mission (when Nately takes the patriot's cop-out that "it's not our business" to question a military objective, Yossarian raves, "Whose business *is* it?"), but recognizes his limitations in confrontation with the monolith of the military-industrial complex. Nor does he want to profit from the war, the biggest "business" of all, only survive it. When Cathcart and Korn make their appeal to him to "Tell the folks at home what a good job we're doing," they do not differentiate, as Yossarian does, between themselves and the abstraction of country. "Haven't you got any patriotism?" asks Cathcart. "Wouldn't you give your life for your country? Wouldn't you give your life for Colonel Korn and me?" Yos-sarian has long since seen through the mirage of an officer's uniform or a military stratagem; these men will cheerfully bomb their own base if it's in the service of their capitalist reward. *Catch-22* "tell[s] the folks at home what [...] we're doing," rather than spinning propaganda about "a good job," with its attendant confections of decorated, heroic action.

Only in a satire could political philosophy be expounded from within the parlor of a whorehouse, but the logic is sound: the whorehouse removes a man's accumulated emblems of acculturated authority and conformity, reducing him to a single, primal urge that tran-scends all ideologies and socially constructed desires. The 107-year-old man who runs the whorehouse has seen men stripped of all pretense for generations and thus understands how temporal are even the grandest of pretensions: "In a few years," he tells Nately, "you'll be gone and we will *still* be here. You see, Italy is a very poor, weak country, and that is what makes us so strong, strong enough to survive this war and still be in existence long after your country has been destroyed. [...] Rome was destroyed. Greece was destroyed. Persia was destroyed. Spain was destroyed. All great countries are destroyed. Why not yours?" Both he and Nately (whose surname suggests his infantile ingenuousness) will be dead before the narrative's end; the mojo of "Catch-22" is more powerful than the old man's pragmatism or the young man's idealism. Given that those who not only endure but thrive are Cathcart and Korn and, most of all, Milo, the film underscores the triumph of capitalism as ironic philosophy: Milo is among the lowest of enlisted men as the narrative begins, pitching his entrepreneurial schemes for improving base rations, but by the end of the film, he has established nothing less than a cult of personality that commands a fascist motorcade through Rome and bowing and scraping of officers like Cathcart and Korn. Milo is the minister of expediency, commodifying both sex and death and paraphrasing the old General Motors bromide of Big Business: "I feel what will be good for M&M Enterprises will be good for the country." Thegze observes that, while Yossarian was the first principle of intensified focus in reducing Heller's novel to a two-hour film, Milo was a secondary choice of focus, and in so choosing, Henry underscored not only the anti-war message of the film (ultimately far clearer than in *M*A*S*H**) but also the critique of the commodifying forces of capitalism. "[I]n a war under capitalism the decisions, especially the moral decisions, begin to be made by the money— not the people who have the money, but the money itself. And that's what happens in this picture. Rules like Catch-22 are generated by the morality of the money, and everything serves that."[23]

In Nichols' original conception of the film, the shoot on the set in Sonora was to be populated by hundreds of extras, all of whom were needed to establish the realism of a thriving base community in the European theater during World War II. But this was a misstep Nichols recognized when he began to see the dailies: "I said, 'It's just an air-force movie.' And as soon as we got rid of the extras, you begin to get a little more sense of a dream, that these guys are here alone, which is of course impossible [in a purely realist, documentary sense], and it seemed more correct."[24] The decision to send away the extras also had its practical side: there was the care and feeding of them day after day, and to wrangle so many individuals into intricately choreographed scenes with long takes and vast depth of field was enormously time-consuming and expensive. Nor was sending them away without risk: once they were gone, the remoteness of the location all but cemented the style of the film as surrealist rather than realist, with the attendant challenge to audience sensibility of consuming something that operated under assumptions inherently other than the default (that what we hear and see is objectively "real"). It was the effect he'd aimed for in *The Graduate*, in the "pretty fantasy" of Benjamin's perspective in the film's second-half "love story," and it had failed to register as such for a majority of his audience—ironically generating box-office gold. In *Catch-22*, the decision to depopulate the base revokes any safe, marketable footing in cinematic realism, a courageous but, in retrospect, financially devastating step away from the audience. The deceptively cozy setting and fiery performances of the quartet in *Virginia Woolf* created a filmic intimacy with the audience; the intended ironies of *The Graduate* melted in the audience's passionate, proprietary need for a counter-cultural rallying point; but in *Catch-22*, Nichols finally conveyed exactly the cool, cinematic distance he intended to wed to Heller's absurdist military world. *Catch-22*, Nichols asserts, "is not trying to be a mass movie."[25]

Catch-22 juxtaposes loud, action-packed visions of hell with solemn, meditative visions of purgatory, and Nichols himself found the film's identity not in the action but in its reflective moments of inactivity. The core of the film, despite the indisputably memorable quality of these set pieces, is not Milo blowing up the base, nor McWatt killing Hungry Joe and then himself, nor Aardvark killing the young whore. Rather, it's a dense nucleus of alienated despair. Before Yossarian goes into Rome for the final time, only to find the rot so deep and so thorough that he, and not Aardvark, is the one the MPs have come to arrest, he wanders the base. Many of his friends are dead. Orr, his bunkmate (consistently depicted laboring alone in their barracks over some small item of aeronautic machinery beneath a single bare bulb—a cartoon vision of the idea-man), has disappeared. And so Yossarian on his ramble encounters only fellow isolates, exposed to the realities of reified wisdom but paralyzed into inaction: Doc Daneeka on the beach, mournfully meditating on his official status as persona non grata (after being reported a casualty of McWatt's crash); and Danby alone in the mess hall, plaintively but without expectation looking up when Yossarian appears. Nichols identifies this shot of Danby as the moment his *Catch-22* "begins to be about something. It begins to be about all their loneliness and separation from each other."[26] These are the other victims, the ones Nichols' *Catch-22* is really about, the ones who don't appear on any list of the "casualties."

If Yossarian is *not* an alternative, counter-cultural hero but a stridently dedicated *non*-hero, opposed to the objectifying notion of heroism of any ideological stripe, *Catch-22* is a film as stridently dedicated to opposing generic appetites for war narratives and heroes. "Because *Catch-22* stays away from any scenes of combat, it never inadvertently glamorizes war or makes it seem exciting: the most effective anti-war movies are almost invariably the most indirect."[27] The film offers many characters who endure but are not assimilated: Danby, Doc, Chaplain Tappman, even Major Major (who is too isolated and despised, not to mention self-exiled and self-despising, to capitalize as the other officers do on Milo's epiphany that war is big business). All but Major Major are well-wishers of Yossarian, if not quite friends. None of these characters can possibly be mistaken for heroes—much less so the demonstratively pro-social characters like Dreedle, Cathcart, Korn, or Milo. Of all the film's characters, only Yossarian is consistently courted by hegemony for assimilation; the others have readily acceded to their labels and been ignored. Yet Yossarian's labels don't stick. When he drops his tonnage into the bay to abort the mission over Ferrara, the base command, anxious to appease General Dreedle, determines to decorate Yossarian and the rest of his crew; when Yossarian reports for the pinning ceremony naked, he reveals his understanding of the 107-year-old man's wisdom: that the commodifying social labels of military (and other) institutions are an illusion that hegemony uses to distract socially constructed beings from their essential equality. (More than three decades later, it's the same wisdom Harper Pitt has come to accept near the end of *Angels in America*, when she stands naked before her husband Joe and demands to know the truth of what he sees, and thanks him when he admits that he sees "nothing." Such reified insight rarely provokes joy; instead, it offers the consolation of naked clarity.) As Dreedle discovers, it is difficult to decorate a naked man, whose reified insight assures him of the emptiness of a culturally constructed signifier like a uniform (or its even more abstract attendant rank and privileges). Nichols uses a startlingly "naked" artifice in the lead-in to the medal ceremony to underscore the point.

There are indelibly convincing cinematic illusions in *Catch-22*, a work with far fewer post-production special effects than one might imagine. Ironically, for all the surrealism of *Catch-22*'s mood, the film was shot in long takes of carefully choreographed "realism" captured by the camera as they unfolded. McWatt's plane crash, for instance, involves no crashed plane but an intricately timed detonation of explosives high on a rock-face just as the stunt plane disappears from view beyond the mountain. Yet when Cathcart and Korn accompany

Dreedle as the officers make their way across base to the medal ceremony, "honoring" the participants of the Ferrara raid, Dreedle's manipulation of power compels the colonels to run behind his jeep. Welles, playing as always not only whatever part he'd been assigned but also the one he'd assigned himself decades earlier, as "Orson Welles," made the autocratic suggestion to Nichols in front of the company that a platform be attached to the back of the prop jeep in which his character rides, and that Balsam and Henry as the colonels be made to jog in place on the platform to simulate running and thereby remain consistently in sound- and shot-range. The result is disastrously fake, and in fact Balsam and Henry continue to jog in place at least a step after the jeep has jerked to a full stop, which should have sent them sprawling into the jeep's back bumper. To reshoot was doubly impossible: Welles would have been adamant about his idea, and once Welles flew away, there was no bringing him back to the remote location shoot (and small desire to do so under the best of circumstances). Rather than cut the shot in regret at its failure to approach even minimal standards for cinematic illusion, however, Nichols holds onto it in the film's final cut to underscore the pervasive *unreality* of the mise-en-scène and thus, of all we see in the game-playing of hegemonic identity politics. It's a moment of supreme visual irony.[28]

The culminating insight of Joseph Heller's novel comes in its penultimate chapter, entitled "Snowden," in which Yossarian's recurring flashback to watching a young soldier die an inglorious, meaningless death ends in the "grim secret Snowden had spilled all over the messy floor. It was easy to read the message in his entrails. Man was matter, that was Snowden's secret. [...] The spirit gone, man is garbage."[29] It is a scene delivered in typically cool Hellerian deadpan, and yet the outrage, particularly in the selection of the word "garbage," is palpable. Heller's picaresque narrative piles up the documentary evidence for how "spirit" may be extracted from a person long before the bullet shatters bone and brain. The institutional men of the officer class have made their various deals with the devil of hegemony and perpetuate a mechanized process of dehumanization that consumes both the enlisted and the promoted. Heller and Nichols each propose various outbreaks of resistance to the resigned conformity of the military-industrial complex; in Nichols and Henry's film, Major Major, Doc Daneeka, Orr, and Yossarian represent various kinds of counter-responses to the madness. Major Major, promoted to squadron commander when Major Duluth is killed in action, resists soothing by the bromide, "We all have to do our part, sir." Major Major's solution is to abet his already long-standing status as persona non grata by becoming invisible, and indeed, Nichols resists the obvious, crowd-pleasing impulse to give Bob Newhart additional comic set-pieces later in the film (despite Newhart being stranded in the desert with the rest of them). After Major Major establishes his official "presence" in the office (he can only be seen when he is out, and under no circumstances may he ever be seen when he is in), Newhart's character disappears from the film. This disappearance has nothing to admire in it; it is expediency alone, with no attempts on Major Major's part to intersect with or counter the powers that be. In its way, it is an equally cynical abuse of power to that of any of the other officers in the narrative.

Doc Daneeka's "disappearance" is even more absurd; he becomes a bureaucratic exception, the accidental persona non grata who ceases to exist because the official record says so. Doc's retiring personality has made him one of those awful paradoxes of the military machine: a healer who fits men to reenter the killing maw of battle. A medic understands "Catch-22" logic as well as anyone. Early in the film, Yossarian recalls the conversation with Doc where he is first able fully to articulate the essential madness of "Catch-22," in grasping that the insanity defense can never be used in this man's Army because only a sane man would try to use it to escape the insanity. Yossarian whistles: "That's some catch, that Catch-22." Doc rejoins brightly, with a kind of demented pride, "It's the best there is!" Doc has had his essential life-affirming nature (and vocation) co-opted by war, and it has made him a little crazy. It has not destroyed his essence, however. In one of the film's most powerful chamber scenes, Doc enlists Yossarian to play a dying man, Harvey, for the victim's family, to provide them in the spirit of tender compassion a comforting illusion of a last word with their loved one. The problem is, of course, that Yossarian is not Harvey. Yossarian objects that they will know this, that the illusion will convince no one, and anyway, he isn't dying. Doc interjects soberly, "Of course you're dying; we're all dying." Doc has been gazing into Heller's "grim secret" of our entrails much longer than Yossarian has. "One dying boy is just as good as another," he muses. "Or just as bad." Yossarian wrangles a deal from Doc that he will finally give Yossarian his long-sought recommendation for a Section 8, though Doc cautions that there is a "catch": the administration has a policy not to approve Section 8s. That Yossarian assents suggests he is capable of generosity when there is no self-preserving percentage in it. The evening visit with Harvey's family is how the skits of Abbott and Costello might have played if they'd been nihilists. The family accepts the "Catch-22" logic of the dying as if having caught a camp infection, assenting to call Yossarian by his actual name while believing him to be Harvey in near-death delirium. The recurring phrase of the scene suggests the absurd futility: "What difference does it make?" And indeed, Harvey's family departs with no sense of particular comfort or of having brought comfort to their lost loved one. For Yossarian, the episode has been a palpable reminder of his mortality, and it is no surprise (in Yossarian's fevered, associative logic as he recuperates from the stabbing by Nately's whore) that he revisits the Snowden scene again immediately after his encounter with Harvey's family, or that he recalls Dobbs' plot to kill Cathcart (and his own role in stopping Dobbs) immediately after discovering Snowden's blood-sodden torso: Yossarian clings tenaciously in the surreal associative logic of Catch-22's narrative to the conviction that causation—even if it promotes personal guilt and shame—still offers the hope of meaning in an absurd world. Unlike Major Major, who simply disappears, or Doc Daneeka, whose life-sustaining impulses are trumped by the Army's death-dealing impulses, Yossarian never stops believing in his responsibility to individual agency, though the form his action will take evolves over the course of the narrative, moving from a conviction that he can reason with systems rigid with circular illogic to a reified heterodoxy that, by film's end, has only one true believer: Yossarian himself.

Yossarian is the man who would become Orr, though he resists this transformation through much of the narrative, a product not of Yossarian's failures of recognition so much as Orr's powers of concealment. Yossarian has never found a way to counter "Catch-22" with an alternative logic of his own—but Orr has. Accepting the premise that he will fly missions in ever-increasing minimum numbers until the odds of his survival become impossibly small, Orr comes to the epiphany that he will work within "Catch-22" and its systemic illogic rather than attempt to extricate himself entirely from what is ordained by forces larger than himself. Yossarian spends much of the narrative in futile attempts to reason with impenetrable forces of unreason, to his great exasperation. Orr serenely accepts those impenetrable forces and finds his own Catch-22 methodology *within* "Catch-22": *the only way to survive is to crash*. Nichols does not offer us images of Orr as a man among men. He is a man apart, depicted beneath the naked bulb of his midnight inspiration, poring over the tiniest of mechanisms in the enormous momentum of the war's machinery for the life-giving gasket that will deliver his separate peace. He becomes an expert of mayhem, a genius of accident. As played by Bob Balaban, he's a cipher, and Yossarian never gets close enough to him before

Orr's "final" crash to understand the method in Orr's madness. In a brief moment of near-disclosure in his otherwise clandestine effort to fight "Catch-22" with his own Catch-22, Orr makes a discreet invitation to Yossarian: "If you were smart," he says during one of these late-night mechanic's tinkerings, "you'd fly with me." Yossarian, thinking only of the apparently "unlucky" number of Orr's crashes (and not that Orr has "luckily" managed to survive every one of them), says, "There isn't anyone in the squadron who wants to fly with you." Orr, perversely inspired by "Catch-22," answers, "They're crazy." In fact, Orr's loner persona and obsessive flight record yield the unavoidable conclusion that he's the crazy one, and while hindsight tells us he's been crazy like a fox, there is a maddened intensity and death-defiance in Orr that can only come from a pendulum swing away from the institutionalized master brand of madness.

Yossarian, until the film's conclusion, experiences this mad extremity only in brief, fleeting moments. The first to appear in the film's jumbled chronology is when Yossarian has been hospitalized with a wounded leg and observes the preoccupied bombshell nurses attending to the soldier in white cocooned in full body cast; the nurses' sole ministration as they distractedly gossip is to exchange the soldier in white's urine collection for his empty saline bag. Nichols has Arkin as Yossarian regard us before screaming in horror. It's an arresting black-humor moment, a metaphor to do justice to the madness of a system in which even life-giving medicine merely recirculates death, as Doc Daneeka knows. It's no accident that Yossarian is in this same infirmary dormitory—locus of "healing"—when he has his final epiphany and goes AWOL at film's end. The sole direct address to the camera is inarticulate but highly expressive—perhaps the only appropriate utterance worth projecting beyond the frame. It is the message Nichols intends for us to carry away with us: the very sound of madness, performed not for dramatic context but as metanarrative commentary. Orr's personality is a counter-methodological madness kept under wraps; Yossarian's personality, recognized early on by the brass as holding the potential to influence and lead men, is a long and sustained wail of outrage. Much more than Orr, Yossarian has attempted to articulate a verbal counterweight to "Catch-22." The repeated catechism (in which, in an effort to compel his compliance with commonly held assumptions about institutional behavior, he is asked to imagine what would happen to the status quo's order and discipline if "everyone felt the same way you do") elicits his unvarying response, "Then I'd be a damn fool to think any different." Buck Henry as screenwriter does a good job of extracting the essence of a baggy monster of a novel by taking his cues from Heller's own repeated refrains and climactic flourishes. In *The Graduate*, Henry needed to make few excisions, and those he did (as for instance the largely superfluous trip to northern California Benjamin takes ostensibly to find meaning in American experience) only sharpen the film narrative's causal logic of commodified despair. In the adaptation of *Catch-22*, Henry retains the novel's essence and takes the transitional devices (mainly visual dissolves and visual and sound overlaps) he learned while working with Nichols on *The Graduate* as his means of creating Yossarian's fever-dream logic while in recovery from the stab wound. The anti-conformist catechism in which Yossarian asserts his independence ironically by a defiant appeal to logical solidarity is as close as Nichols and Henry come to positing Yossarian as counter-cultural icon. "Don't follow leaders," Bob Dylan had warned in 1965 in "Subterranean Homesick Blues," and Yossarian, a man whom Cathcart and Korn fear has stirred the enlisted men to reflect upon the absurdity of their status, has leadership potential. It is the essential irony of counter-cultural non-conformity: how can such an impulse ever "organize?" Ultimately, Yossarian will have to learn the Tao of Orr.

If his inarticulate scream beyond the fourth wall initiates Yossarian's reified counter-response, his single most maddened act of antagonism to the status quo in the film comes during the raid on the base, revisited later in his nighttime confrontation with Milo's cortege in old Rome. Dobbs has come to Yossarian seeking a partner in assassinating Cathcart, who has once again raised the minimum number of missions, this time to 80 (provoked, we learn, by his anger that Orr has ditched yet another plane, and this time has gone MIA). Although Dobbs insists that he is not only *not* crazy for plotting to kill Cathcart but that, in fact, "It's the first sane thing I've ever done," Yossarian talks him into delaying. He promises to help Dobbs should Cathcart raise the number beyond 80. Yet when Yossarian witnesses what Milo and the brass have agreed to do to their own base, Yossarian's madness erupts with potentially killing force. That he is inept as a killer is secondary to his will to destroy. He ineffectually fires a handgun on Milo in the control tower, then has no bullets left when he takes point-blank aim at Dobbs' originally proposed target, Cathcart. "A contract's a contract," Cathcart reminds him. "That's what we're fighting for."

Yossarian reels away into the maelstrom of the base under attack, and Nichols and Henry punctuate the scene with Yossarian's discovery of Nately's blown-up corpse. We are not given a look at what he sees; presumably, it is a vision similar to the soft sloughing of internal organs onto the bomber-turret's floor in the final Snowden scene. Nichols and O'Steen instead cut to the scene when Yossarian is on the operating table after the stabbing, fighting for his life, and the oily man in black appears out of his own viscera with ominous, cryptic assurance, "We've got your pal." (Heller is able to give this moment its due gravity by its placement near the book's conclusion, in the chapter entitled portentously, "Catch-22.") The surgeons assume Yossarian to be hallucinating and ignore him; while we also understand him to be hallucinating, we have no such luxury of ignorance. Yossarian's accrued outrage has led us to this moment, and from thence we follow the associative thread of his logic through the Roman nighttown, in which Yossarian encounters the old woman at the deserted whorehouse (Heller's own choice for the "most effective scene" in the film[30]) and learns that all the world is awash in "Catcha–22." Yossarian reenacts his ineffectual assault on the base commander during the self-imposed air raid by undertaking an equally ineffectual assault on Milo, the progenitor of the precious contracts they're "fighting for." Yossarian howls his outrage at Milo for the death of innocence as embodied in Nately, the angelic patriot martyred by friendly fire. What follows is an exchange written by Henry that Nichols claims Heller paid the ultimate compliment of having wished he'd written himself.[31] Milo implacably reassures Yossarian that Nately died with 60 shares in M&M that his parents will receive. Yossarian protests the cold comfort of money to people who are already rich, and Milo's cool response summarizes the (big) business of war's commodification of human life: "*Then they'll understand.*" The montage of Roman darkness Nichols assembles—of cruelty and degradation to human and animal alike, climaxes in Aardvark's rape and murder of the pretty Italian girl we'd seen him with earlier. Yossarian posits, "You can't take the life of another human being and get away with it—don't you understand that?" The white heads of the MPs promptly ignore Aarfy and arrest Yossarian. The MPs carry out in microcosm what Milo's M&M Enterprises and the Army have institutionalized. Milo shares with Nately's parents an "understanding" of the world based in commodity; it's Yossarian who doesn't—won't—understand.

Unlike Orr, Yossarian has repeatedly attempted formalized rebellion via dialogue. Now, at film's end, he is finally able to grasp Orr's vision of an alternate Catch-22 to "Catch-22" that acknowledges the ineffectuality of imposing responsibility on philosophically irresponsible systems. In *The Graduate*, Henry wrote a brief speech for Benjamin to share with Elaine at the drive-in during their date, in which he articulates a vision of a rule-making *other* composed of "all the wrong people. No—I mean no one makes [the rules] up; they seem to have made themselves up." It is an articulated comprehension of reification. Heller points to an early introduction in his novel of the disembodied and ultimately identity-less "they" whom, for example, Clevinger accuses of wanting to kill him. "It is the anonymous 'they,' the enigmatic 'they,' who are in charge," Heller later wrote about his novel. "Who is 'they?' I don't know. Nobody knows. Not even 'they' themselves."[32] This, too, envisions a paranoid reality of enculturated malevolence, a socially proscribed death force. At film's end, Nichols and Henry conflate the conversations Heller has written for Yossarian in separate chapters, incorporating them into a single scene of dialogue in the infirmary. Heller has Yossarian recount his vision of the oily man who'd attested to having gotten Yossarian's "pal," and the chaplain confirms Yossarian in his interpretations of the vision. Beyond all the dead and missing of Yossarian's pals, there are those like the chaplain gripped by the death-force of institutional "Catch-22": "I like to think that I'm your pal, Yossarian, [...] and they certainly have got me. They've got my number and they've got me under surveillance, and they've got me right where they want me."[33] In the film, the chaplain and Danby, two of the base misfits, join together to spur Yossarian to his climactic insight, the Orr insight: a civilization in the grip of reified force must save itself one person at a time, because no system will seek anything but to consume the individual. The very idea of a mass revolution against reified conformity is a Catch-22. "What would you do if you were me?" Yossarian asks them. "Imagine you're me." Chaplain Tappman's poignant response echoes his contention (in the novel) that "they certainly have" him: "That's hard. Sometimes I even have trouble imagining that I'm *me*, if you know what I mean."[34] This scene, one of the longest takes in any Mike Nichols film (at four and a half minutes of uninterrupted rolling camera) begins a slow zoom on Yossarian shortly after the chaplain's despairing remark. This has been and will remain Yossarian's story, and we watch as, in his final climb to Orr's insight, the film narrows its range of focus to him, and to his responsibility to his own life.

Nichols and O'Steen luxuriate in slow motion and three angles of Yossarian's existential leap from reification's grip, as he is now in the grip of Orr's alternative vision: a separate peace in Sweden, sitting out the war. Danby and the chaplain hurl potential problems at him, and Yossarian runs through or around their worst scenarios. As the distance from them grows, we understand their voices to be in his head (as has been much of what we've seen during the course of the narrative, Yossarian's long counter-logical reverie building towards this incipient choice of action): "'It's an unreal situation,'" Nichols says. "'It's a conversation that could not be held and it seems right and feels right when you're watching it because it says, We're not talking about something literal here; we're talking about a moral decision.'"[35] Yossarian running away is Heller's last word on the subject[36]; Nichols and Henry, however, extend the narrative to incorporate the helicopter shot of Yossarian leaving the land to strike out in his tiny open boat. The Sousa parade on the base serves up the ideological dream of "Stars and Stripes Forever," the final word of whose title may be interpreted as a cultural assumption of dynastic inevitability. The only "permanent change"[37] Yossarian can reasonably effect is the change within. Cathcart and Korn coerce Yossarian's cooperation with a deal; now Danby's voice warns Yossarian of the life of dissent, with its attendant alienation and exile—the life of Orr: "You'll be on the run with no friends! You'll live in constant danger of betrayal!" Yossarian can only respond, without breaking stride, "I live that way now!"

In his first three films, Mike Nichols presents three conclusions that set protagonists adrift: George and Martha clinging to each other against the approach of a post-games dawn;

Benjamin and Elaine in the belly of a packed city bus, passively conveyed wherever the city fathers have ordained its route should go; and now Yossarian, beating on against the ocean's vast current. Of the three, Nichols treats George and Martha's resolution with the most dignity and the least irony. Despite their brokenness, George and Martha are ennobled by their shared commitment to each other and a post-illusion future. Benjamin and Elaine's resolution is *awash* in irony, as the generic signifiers of "happily ever after" (damsel rescued, captors thwarted, boy and girl reunited to ride off into the sunset) dissolve in the 40-second shot of their blankness on the bus and the reprise of Simon and Garfunkel's "Sounds of Silence." Benjamin is passively conveyed *into* the film (via jet and conveyor-belt walkway), and he is passively conveyed *out* of the film (via Santa Barbara bus). Neither George and Martha nor Benjamin and Elaine project certainty of a next step, and yet George and Martha are far more united in their hands-clasped resolve to make that next step in solidarity. Benjamin and Elaine ride together, alone. Yossarian has no companion at all, and as we last see him, he is actively stroking towards his future, presumably embracing Orr's course for Sweden. Nichols says, "'It's a picture about choosing at what point you take control over your life and say, "No, I won't. *I* decide. *I* draw the line."'"[38] We are told Orr has made it, presumably by the same route (from his ruined plane), but the film does not grant us an independent certitude that "Sweden" and its separate peace is anything but a fantastical mirage, for Yossarian or, for that matter, the legendary Orr. Instead, Nichols offers the zoom-out, ironic perspective of a God's eye view shot from a helicopter, reminiscent of the deterministic American Naturalism of Crane, Dreiser, and Norris: Yossarian on the ocean, a tiny man in a tiny raft with an even tinier oar. The Sousa triumphalism is cognitive dissonance against what our eyes see: this is positive movement in only the most abstracted sense. Nichols as a cinematic storyteller is a critic of culture, not a counter-cultural visionary. He dissects present ills of reification rather than providing articulated alternatives. If he has defined himself as a storyteller of "transformation,"[39] his focus has typically been upon the moment of decision and the necessity to decide, rather than upon the long-term consequences. He is indeed a filmmaker of "*transformation*" rather than of the *transformed*. In his next three films, *Carnal Knowledge*, *The Day of the Dolphin*, and *The Fortune*, which complete the first phase of his Hollywood career, he would adopt three very different genres to pursue the same question: whether transformation is, in fact, even possible. Not until he returned to filmmaking after artistic transformations of his own would he return to the depiction of protagonists busy in the project of re-making themselves, rather than reshaped within the iron grip of commodifying desires.

5

"Just act natural"

Carnal Knowledge (1971)

The experience of making *Catch-22* and having it fail to resonate with the mass audience to which he'd long since grown accustomed in three separate entertainment careers shook Mike Nichols, who took on, as his fourth feature-film project, a narrative that feels worlds away from his pacifist war movie. The enormous, vaudevillian cast of *Catch-22* is replaced in *Carnal Knowledge* by a chamber ensemble of seven (one of whom, Carol Kane as Jennifer, has only one scene and no lines, and another, Rita Moreno as Louise, appears only in the film's final scene). *Carnal Knowledge* is a simpler film with more complex characters. It is more like the films Nichols himself says are his instinctive subject.[1] While *Carnal Knowledge* has an epic sweep of time from the late 1940s to the early 1970s, it unfolds as an intimate drama, a character study of the sexual evolution of two men against the broad context of the sexual revolution within the culture. Unlike *Catch-22*, for which the large-cast, big-production assumptions of a mass-audience appeal (as in *The Graduate*) had to be re-scaled for the niche, art-film audience it actually served, *Carnal Knowledge* never presumes to be a film for everyone. Like *Who's Afraid of Virginia Woolf?*, *Carnal Knowledge* continues pressing at the edges of what is depictable in the realities of human relationship (both films notoriously also helped to shatter the assumed limits entrenched by the old production code in Hollywood).[2] The frankness of adult language and situation make these early films Nichols' most "European," by the standard assumptions of the late 1960s and early 1970s. John Calley, the Hollywood film executive and long-time friend and collaborator of Nichols, says, "'It changed my life and the lives of many friends. It wasn't this runaway hit that seemed to catch a generation in the palm of its hand like *The Graduate*, but as a [...] work of art, it was very, very important."[3] Perhaps the time-capsule quality of its depiction of the growing pains inherent in the sexual revolution of the 1960s will leave some to conclude that the film has not aged gracefully, but thinking about the film in relation to a remarkably similar narrative from relatively late in Nichols' career—the 2004 adaptation of Patrick Marber's 1997 stage play *Closer*—reveals that Nichols' 1971 film still offers insights not bound by its time and place. In Marber's play, Larry (the Clive Owen character in Nichols' adaptation) says, "Everyone learns, nobody changes,"[4] the very essence of reified despair. In returning to variations on *Carnal Knowledge*'s objectified sexuality in *Closer*, Nichols models his tempered optimism as a film artist, acknowledging our reticence to change but also the perpetual redemption available in reified awareness. Ernest Callenbach writes that *Carnal Knowledge* is "about the sexual chauvinism which is America's *machismo*, and which is very far from dead now even though the fifties may have been its heyday"; Callenbach concludes, "It is a cold and merciless film, but then artists are not required to stand in for the Red Cross. They document disasters, and it is we the viewers who must clean them up, in our own lives."[5]

Of *Catch-22*, Nichols has said, "[T]hat's not my kind of movie, because it's not about interpersonal things at all. [...] There is no subtext, [...] there is no underneath, when the underneath is what draws me; it's why I make movies. The things people don't say."[6] In this sense, *Carnal Knowledge* is a therapeutic return for Nichols from a self-imposed exile in the chilly surrealism of Heller's world. He had chafed while in the isolation of the Mexican desert, and he had similarly found himself restricted by the broad picaresque nature of Heller's vision, in which character development is oxymoronic. For all the notorious frankness of *Carnal Knowledge*'s screenplay by Jules Feiffer, much of the interest of the two main characters is located in Sandy's, Susan's, and Bobbie's utter subjugation to Jonathan, disparities of power that ultimately make it impossible for any of them to be fully frank and honest with one another. Sandy's is the only potentially dynamic character in the film, but all the characters are given abundant opportunities for insight, change, and growth that they squander. Their failure is indicative of the tone intended by Feiffer, the satirical New York cartoonist who originally created the narrative as a stage play for Nichols to direct. Of Nichols' first three films, all of which unfold in tonal darkness, *The Graduate*'s tone is deceptive, because the film is agleam with sparkly Southern California light and situational comedy (as well as with the color-saturated dreaminess of the romantic genre fantasies of the film's second half). *Carnal Knowledge*'s tonal darkness is as chilly as its settings (filmed on location mostly back on Smith College's campus in the late autumn leaves and snow, and in wintry British Columbia): cold overcast days at college; at the Wollman Ice Skating Rink on Fifth Avenue in New York; on a gray, chilly day for tennis.[7] Referring to it as "perhaps Nichols' greatest film," Peter Biskind writes, "*Carnal Knowledge* was easily as original and savage as *Virginia Woolf*, but it lacked even the whisper of affirmation that saved *Virginia Woolf* from total bleakness."[8] Nichols calls it "the darkest movie I ever made."[9]

Art Garfunkel, who made his Hollywood debut in *Catch-22* in a supporting role as the angelic and well-meaning naïf Nately, assumes an entirely different level of acting responsibility in *Carnal Knowledge*. He begins in the same sort of wide-eyed innocence as in portraying Nately, and the lightness and gendered ambiguity of his character's name, Sandy, suggest a similar relationship to the wider world. While not as close to the center of the narrative as his best friend, Jonathan (Jack Nicholson, in the first of four roles for Nichols), Sandy is ultimately the most interesting character in the film. Like George and Martha in *Virginia Woolf*, Benjamin (and to a lesser degree Elaine) in *The Graduate*, and Yossarian in *Catch-22*, Sandy has a reified recognition about himself and his relationship to larger forces in the world and must either act or fail to act on what he has learned. Sandy's journey is from Nately-like innocence; in the film's first half, his ingenuousness is rarely shaken, and Jonathan and even Susan (Candice Bergen) can startle him with what appears to be the forthrightness of their spoken desire. Jonathan in particular uses his misogynistic distrust and air of phallic entitlement to provoke titillated giggles or opened-mouth awe from Sandy. The only phenomenon that can jar Sandy's default optimism about romantic experience is his marriage to Susan, and this is when he deliberately allows Jonathan to become for a brief time his teacher, with disastrous effects on both his marriage *and* the affair with Cindy (Cynthia O'Neal) that Jonathan abets for him. The final scenes of the film suggest that, despite his steadfast efforts at maintaining companionship with Jonathan, Sandy may have left his old mentor behind. Yet he hasn't quite become his own man; instead, he has subjugated himself to a girl young enough to be his daughter and adopted her vocabulary and vision: Jennifer is his "love teacher." It's an indication of the darkness of the film that, at the moment Sandy makes this pronouncement, we are less apt to celebrate his enlightenment than to sneer at him along with Jonathan (Sandy's "hate" teacher), a character from whom we've been profoundly distanced during the course of the narrative because of his cruelty and duplicity.

What is less ambiguous in the film's conclusions is that the roots of unhappiness in *Carnal Knowledge* are militantly patriarchal, seated in the minds of men who, as Nichols characterizes them, "think of [women] as mere sex objects."[10] Jonathan, the film's center, is unapologetic in his refusal to adapt to the changing cultural landscape, in which the assertion of feminist identity and sexuality is the pervasive subtextual catalyst. The film's point of view, largely via Jonathan's aggressive misogyny, reflects this: while the two lead women in the film, Susan and Bobbie (Ann-Margret), are substantial roles (earning Ann-Margret an Oscar nomination for Supporting Actress), each woman unceremoniously disappears from the film well before the end, precisely because Jonathan's disgust has willed her expunging. Even Sandy, clearly Jonathan's longest-standing and perhaps only friend, vanishes before the end, with the implication that, were the film to continue further into the future (with Jonathan as a corporate take-over specialist of the 1980s, perhaps), it would do so without Sandy either. Increasingly, Jonathan must retreat into a world of fantasy performance, given his painful inadequacies in asserting traditional dominance. The indelible vignette Cynthia O'Neal creates in her brief appearance as Cindy suggests that there's no exit from patriarchy if women's liberation simply entails their becoming duplicitous men. But the near invisibility of Jennifer, who watches Jonathan's misogynist slide show in stunned silence, leaves us to try and glimpse her exclusively in what transformations she may have wrought in Sandy, who gushes about her masterful personality. *Carnal Knowledge* isn't ultimately about feminism; it's about the endangerment of patriarchal hegemony, in which women and men alike are "struggling in the strait jacket of a morality that divides women into madonnas and whores and men into make-out artists and losers."[11] Responding to the myopic charge that Nichols and Feiffer have created a misogynist film, Vincent Canby observes, "If anything, "Carnal Knowledge" is exploitative of men, not, heaven knows, as sex objects, but as exploiters."[12] The film, especially in the ironic depiction of flaccid phallocracy in the final scene, would seem to be announcing the endangered species of the phallocrat, but it is far from unambiguously optimistic about patriarchy's extinction.

The film was the second of Nichols' three productions with Joseph E. Levine and AVCO-Embassy, for which the prurience of subject and the prospect of Candice Bergen and Ann-Margret in bedroom scenes were reason enough for crusty Levine's eye-winking patronage. For the fourth consecutive film, Nichols worked with a different Director of Photography (the legendary Guiseppe Rotunno, who shot *The Leopard* for Visconti and who had just begun a long working partnership with Fellini), many other contributors were familiar faces to Nichols' productions, editor Sam O'Steen and production designer Richard Sylbert chief among them. Nichols typically asked cast and crew to capture long takes, with the logistical demands on blocking, lighting, acting, and camera movement. For all the phenomenal instances of montage transition in *The Graduate* and *Catch-22*, many of the essential thematic ideas are encapsulated via long take. The final moment on the bus in *The Graduate* is a profoundly revealing image wrought by leaving the camera running, as were the "conversation" between Mrs. Robinson and Benjamin and the closing debate Yossarian has with Danby and Tappman in the base hospital. This affinity for the long take may quite naturally be attributed to Nichols' instinct for the power of live theater—people exploring conflict by talking to each other as they maneuver around each other. And while Nichols became more comfortable with cutting for desired effect, his work has continued to demonstrate an affection for the cinematic potential of judiciously used long takes: "I still love a long [take], if enough is happening, because it has a certain mesmerizing quality."[13]

In *Carnal Knowledge*, the long take has particular emphasis as a part of Jonathan's religion of surface appearance and "glamour." Susan, Bobbie, and finally Louise all have their long-take close-ups in *Carnal Knowledge*, and in each case, there is an irony in the world seen at length through Jonathan's eyes. Gavin Smith observes that the famous long take of Benjamin and Elaine on the bus, consigned to scrutiny by the rest of the bus patrons but also by the audience, suggests "the point of departure for the style of *Carnal Knowledge*."[14] Having already assigned himself an objectified role as a traditional male, Jonathan can only see these women in their status as objects of his fickle desire (which trumps what he perceives as their own inevitably fickle nature). He's a mess, and so he makes sure to leave greater messes wherever he goes. As in *The Graduate*, *Carnal Knowledge* ends in role-playing and pretense rather than in any wholesome solidification of identity, but Nichols, burned by the mass-audience's tone-deafness to the ironies of generic fantasy in *The Graduate*, makes the performative commodification as overt as possible in *Carnal Knowledge*. "The keynote of these relationships," writes John Lindsay Brown, "is exploitation."[15] The "games" of social performance (clawing at power in marriage and career in *Virginia Woolf*, conspicuous consumption as social brinksmanship in *The Graduate*, and the bartering of human lives in *Catch-22*) continue unabated in *Carnal Knowledge*.

* * *

The white-hot spotlight of *The Graduate* radiates not only within the first phase of Mike Nichols' film career but within the larger context of *all* the films he's released, none of which has approached the cultural resonance and ubiquity of his second film. One way of re-contextualizing *Carnal Knowledge* is that, in the progress of the generation, Sandy and Jonathan are east-coast contemporaries not of *The Graduate*'s Benjamin Braddock, but of Benjamin's *parents*, and the Robinsons. Jennifer, the young woman Sandy brings with him in the scene in which Jonathan presents his misogynistic slide show, is only a few years younger than Elaine Robinson. The film is not in any sense within the point of view of Elaine or Jennifer's generation, though Jennifer certainly serves as mute, horrified witness to the ruins of the preceding generation. *The Graduate* is a kid's self-serving fantasy as a way of negotiating the problems posed for him by his parents' generation, in which the satirical eye of the film turns increasingly ironic, particularly in the film's second half, revealing the failures of counter-culture kids unable to imagine alternatives to the cultural defaults they're set to inherit. We get only brief glimpses of the older generation's sensibility, most acutely during the "conversation" Benjamin insists upon with Mrs. Robinson before one of their frequent assignations at the Taft Hotel, when Mrs. Robinson lets slip some revealing vignettes of her brief youth in college. *Carnal Knowledge* backtracks to those salad days, to reveal that Mrs. Robinson's unplanned pregnancy was only one variant of social determinism for those who came of age immediately after the war.

Jonathan is the dark mind of *Carnal Knowledge*, demonstrated as his voice rises out of the dark screen (the title's sex euphemism printed in red lettering), amidst the nostalgic strains of Glenn Miller, to ask a question of seemingly naked vulnerability: "Would you rather love a girl or have her love you?" The film thus introduces a potential distinction between its title (sex) and the apparent, stated preoccupation of its characters (love), but as Jacob Brackman observes, "Continually looking for fulfillment from mere fornication, never understanding the erotic as a metaphor for one's deeply felt connectedness, [the characters are] doomed to fall short of satisfaction forever."[16] Sandy immediately, instinctively puts Jonathan's hypothetical question about love into dispute, balking at the artificiality of Jonathan's either-or absolutism, but his challenge is in the spirit of sophomoric dorm-room debate rather than genuine seeking for mature wisdom. Their snickering, prurient conjecturing reveals them to be as blank as the screen in terms of experience. The intimacy of the darkness seems at first to include us, their voices as close as the person in the next theater seat, but we soon learn that each is disingenuous in his own way, undercutting the illusion of intimacy. They veer inconsistently between valuing interior qualities of romantic love (wanting someone to talk to and who will understand one's inner life) and superficial qualities of lampooned sexual attraction (a girl who's "built"). Their debate conveys a friendship based in mutual exploration of social formation: they try ideas out on each other in the seemingly safe social vacuum of their nighttime dorm room, prior to venturing out into the social gambit of dating. Even in this brief three-minute exchange, the two young men betray their sensibilities: Sandy, an essentially timid, nice person, is looking for someone "nice." Jonathan, an essentially manipulative, cold person, confesses, "Every time I start being in love, the girl does something that turns me cold." Each feels dread and anticipation in embarking upon his sexual and sentimental education, and Sandy, the more forthright if less frank of the two, gets the last word on this anxiety they're articulating in the dark: "I feel the same way about getting laid as I feel about going to college. I'm being pressured into it."

Nichols has rendered cinematic conversation against a dark screen before, of course, in the epic conversation Benjamin Braddock tries to have with Mrs. Robinson as a desperate way of re-humanizing their dehumanized affair. In *Catch-22*, Nichols again presents key conversations in a metaphorically revealing darkness. Orr tries slyly to hint to Yossarian in their barracks that there may be a genuine method in the apparent madness of his continuing to fly despite his serial crashes, and later, Yossarian receives a tutorial in "Catch-22" logic from the old woman left behind at the whorehouse after it has been cleaned out by Milo's MPs in M&M's hostile takeover of the business. These conversations in the dark confound cinematic expectation; not only do they emphasize the revelation of spoken word but also ironize those revelations that emerge in the darkness and fail to illuminate. In the case of Benjamin and Mrs. Robinson, the conversation serves both to confirm Benjamin's instinct that dialogue humanizes, promoting understanding, and to undercut the potential for meaningful connection in a relationship when neither partner is willing to sustain honesty and understanding. Orr, lit by the single bulb shining on a gasket from his plane engine, half-trusts Yossarian with his secret, but in the paranoia of the military environment, he cannot risk a full declaration; it's every man for himself. The old woman's implacable explanation of all injustice and suffering as the self-evident product of the mysteriously pervasive "Catcha–22" has Yossarian yearning for insight from a stranger with little English, so accustomed is he to the difficulties and obfuscations of human discourse. Coming as the first scene in *Carnal Knowledge*, and more boldly obliterating *any* pictorial representation from the screen than in the least-lit "darkness" scenes of *The Graduate* or *Catch-22*, Nichols presents an overture on alienation: the presumed intimacy and underlying deception that encapsulate the uneasy contradictions whenever two people talk. The admixture of fear and need is as likely to compel people into playing roles as to be themselves.

As the titles end, our first image is of Susan, her fair beauty emerging from a darkness as if Sandy and Jonathan's dialogue during the titles has conjured her, and in a sense, it has—the dialogue is an anticipation of the social "mixing" that awaits them as part of the pro-

scribed ritual of courting and mating. Susan is in this sense a construction of their imaginations, and their imaginations are a construction of their reifiying culture. Sandy and Susan's
conversation is rich in meta-analysis of the social "act." Nichols has her enter the room where
the mixer is being held as if from the darkened wing of a brightly lit stage, and Sandy and
Jonathan become her obvious audience. They are all on display for one another at the mixer,
including the two men in relation to one another. Before either of them talks to Susan, they
play with the prerogatives of male proprietorship; Jonathan magnanimously announces to
Sandy, "I give her to you." Yet his gift masks a more malicious intention, using Sandy as his
advance man, a way to manipulate both Sandy *and* Susan. Jonathan, as usual, says what everyone is thinking—except for his hidden subtext. Having given Sandy suggested ice-breakers,
including the "unhappy childhood" routine he later trots out himself, Jonathan warns Sandy,
"But don't make it like an act." This is not quite the same thing as admonishing Sandy to
"Just act natural." It's an acknowledgement of the rules of social commerce and an observation
that triumph comes in the most artful "act."

Sandy has already failed to perform his first time in Susan's presence, and it takes Susan
breaking the ice for them to begin a conversation. They instantly gravitate to their shared
self-conscious antipathy for the ritual of performed socialization, and an intrinsically romantic quality the two young men have already conjured as their ideal in the darkened dorm
room ("She should be very understanding," Jonathan has specified. "We'd start the same sentences together") here comes to sudden life, as Susan's observation, "Everybody puts on an
act," becomes the opening of a sentence Sandy is dying to conclude: "So, even if you meet
somebody, you don't know who you're meeting." Susan even provides a coda to the thought:
"Because you're meeting the act." The inherent wisdom of this opening exchange fails to
protect Sandy and Susan from what will become a heavily reified courtship and decades-
long marriage of disillusionment and reduced expectation, in which every move is codified
within a preexistent set of assumptions for what constitutes "success" and "satisfaction."

Susan argues a line of logic that consigns all relationships to reified performance ("If
they think it's an act they feel better because they think they can always change it"). Instead
of accepting her warning, he patronizingly refers to her as "a lady lawyer," and when she asks
if he likes Amherst, he muses, "My parents worked very hard to send me. I'd better like it."
Sandy thus renders a version of himself as dutiful—sensitive to the proscribed behavior of
son and, soon enough, lover. His proscribed role as a man becomes the subject of several
campus dialogues with Jonathan, intercut with scenes of Sandy attempting to perform this
assumed role with Susan. Almost all of these early moments of turf conflict are waged on
the playing field of Susan's body, as Sandy makes his halting way around the sexual bases.
Jonathan embodies Sandy's perceived sense of expected performance, with his talk of having
"won" the "big fight" over kissing. With Susan on their dates, Sandy talks not in terms of
desire but performed expectation: "If I could kiss you once last week, I should be able to
kiss you at least twice tonight," and "Because the way we're going, by this time I should be
feeling you up." Genuine desire is nowhere in evidence; indeed, when Susan challenges him
to explain what "fun" is available to him in her coerced performance, he immediately retorts,
"I didn't say it was fun." The entire experience of intimacy becomes a rote negotiation of
reciprocal responses, of quid pro quo. Later in the same date Susan learns that Sandy is *not*
an experienced young wolf on the prowl, and she modulates her performance based on this
new information: a sexual advance commences, initiated by her. This new development,
dutifully carried back to campus where Sandy can at last take pleasure not in the experience
itself but in the status it confers, is the event for which Jonathan has been waiting. Knowing

from Sandy that Susan is both sensitive and sexually yielding, he gives her a call. Nichols underscores the performed quality of the entire sequence by having Sandy and Jonathan celebrate—at high volume—Sandy's breakthrough, then cutting abruptly to a one-shot of Jonathan's call, from a phone booth in the highly presumptive location of the Smith campus. His story that, "taking a drive," he was "practically on" her campus, is not overly far-fetched, since the two colleges are only about eight miles apart. Jonathan is not above poaching on his best friend's girl, and Susan, we're even more surprised to learn, is not above being poached.

As they begin to warm to the task in a campus bar, their talk returns the script to meta-analysis, the same reified self-consciousness that characterized Sandy and Susan's initial conversation at the mixer. Jonathan holds forth on the hidden agendas that serve as the default parlance of most relationships: "Most girls I talk to, it's like we're both spies from foreign countries and we're speaking in code. Everything means something else." As with Sandy, Susan intuitively understands and can contribute further insights, to which Jonathan's "You're very sharp. I like that," elicits her "And that means something else." The irony of the entire exchange is that their self-conscious awareness of their complicity in the games people play is a kind of license for the awkward transgression of betraying Sandy, throwing subsequent debriefings between Jonathan and Sandy into ironized complexity, as when Sandy says to Jonathan, "I can say things to her I wouldn't dare say to you." While this enthusiastically reported intimacy becomes the bone of contention between Jonathan and Susan, it is an entirely accurate representation of Jonathan's own position. Jonathan has introduced their preferred mantra of "Bullshit artist" as a response to all significant romantic and sexual conquests, and the phrase is in fact an apt descriptive of each member of the triangle. Jonathan may be the impresario, but he eggs on Susan to commence and continue their affair, and he eggs on Sandy with victorious tales of his conquest of "Myrtle." Sandy never gets suspicious that his best friend won't produce this generous girl, only redoubles the inherited pressure for competitive performance, appealing to Susan to relieve him of his virginity as if of a disreputable social stain. For her part, observes Brackman, Susan is complicit in her commodification, willing "to put out strategically" in order "[t]o parlay the competition for her favors into a home in the suburbs."[17]

Feiffer originally thought of *Carnal Knowledge* as a stage play, but Nichols knew a play could not deliver the alienated intimacies of *Carnal Knowledge*'s close-ups and two-shots. After the wide-open spaces of *Catch-22*, *Carnal Knowledge*'s landscapes are dorm rooms and living rooms, car interiors and hushed clinches. *Catch-22* was not Nichols' "kind of movie," he says, "because it's not about interpersonal things at all."[18] In this sense, *Carnal Knowledge* is a watershed in Nichols' career. *The Graduate* was about intimate failures of communication, but his audience misinterpreted it. *Catch-22* was about politics and grand systems of human deception, and the audience tuned out. *Carnal Knowledge* re-centered Nichols in character study as a means to the ideas he desired to explore.

The conspiracy Susan and Jonathan strike up continues unrevealed for years, though the affair itself is doomed from its inception, like all relationships predicated in falsified performance. Feiffer and Nichols assert this falseness by returning again to another motif introduced in Sandy and Susan's initial conversation, when Jonathan recommends Sandy talk about his "unhappy childhood" without making it "like an act." In fact it's *Jonathan* who trots out the "very messed-up childhood" story for Susan: "I'm another person with her," he tells Sandy, though in fact he's always what Susan initially described to Sandy at the Smith mixer ("I think people only like to think they're putting on an act, but [...] they're the act.

The act is them"). He's a "bullshit artist" who wants to crow about his conquests and doesn't want to hear about Susan's sexual relenting with Sandy. Nichols and O'Steen use a dancing scene to access the toxins that have permeated the triangle: Jonathan and Susan dance together with animated pleasure; Sandy and Susan dance together in an awkward choreography of obligation. The cuts are hidden by other dancers crossing in front of the camera, producing the vertiginous sensation for the viewer that we are uncertain who will be with whom next. But it's the long next shot, the three friends seated together at a bar table, that illustrates how manic their performance has become. In a long-take close-up, Susan screams with laughter at some unheard punchline about a chronically mispronounced word. The unease we saw on the dance floor is masked by an inflated performance of "fun," completely out of scale to the modest payoffs of other mispronounced words. Jonathan's and Sandy's voices derive from off-screen during the entire take. They aren't the focus, nor can they see her as we see her. They can only see her from where they sit. She's the piece of meat between two hungry carnivores. Sandy can grasp the concept of socially proscribed performance without ever grasping its applicability; Jonathan cynically grasps at the concept as an arch justification of his manipulative actions. Susan, who has articulated a clear-headed vision of how reified performance works, here dances as fast as she can to keep both her lovers happy. It won't work, and the rest of *Carnal Knowledge*'s first section, featuring Susan, devolves into a protracted breakup.

Feiffer's script keeps pouring on the ironies: Susan is the only one who "gets" the escape hatch in reification, but isn't the one who escapes. Instead it's Jonathan who exits the affair, having found the basis of his objection to a girl who gives him regular sexual access: she can tell Sandy his thoughts, but she can't reciprocate with Jonathan. There's real anguish as Susan acknowledges this, and convincing despair in Jonathan's demand. What goes unsaid between them is *why* Jonathan's mind remains opaque to her: he's too much within the fortified walls of his invulnerability to ever allow a genuine thought to project. Nor can she do the other task Jonathan requires of her: to tell Sandy that they have fallen in love with each other. "He looks at me with such trust," she says. Jonathan, recoiling, asks, "How do *I* look at you?" Told he conveys "bitterness," he replies, bitterly, "At least you know my thoughts." But bitterness and mistrust have always been Jonathan's response to the other sex, from the opening dialogue in the dark where Gloria's sexual provocation and Gwen's sexual fastidiousness—the two sides of intimate performance—both prove to be turn-offs for Jonathan. His anxiety about performing becomes more acute with accrued performances.

Although Susan's name continues to pop up in the story (as Sandy's off-screen wife), Susan disappears from the plot after Jonathan breaks up with her. The breakup conversation comes via telephone call, accentuating the distance they've always had to negotiate as a couple. The ultimatums Jonathan has given her—to read his thoughts, to tell Sandy the truth about their relationship—all end in Susan's failures to deliver (at least from Jonathan's point of view), and in the next scene, the film's point of view is refined to identify Jonathan as its source. Susan's last on-screen line is the breakup cliché, "I'll always be your friend," to which Jonathan responds, "I hope not," reducing her first to tears, and then, in her last scene, to a purely off-screen presence. The point of view is ironic, however—Jonathan's is an increasingly unsympathetic perspective. In essence, Nichols invites us into the mind of a monster; too encyclopedic in his distastes to be called merely misogynistic, Jonathan is misanthropic, his contempt for his best friend Sandy palpable from the earliest moments in the film, having "given" Susan to Sandy only as a means to keep his thumb on them both. Jonathan's obsession with power and control are organic byproducts of his learned masculinity, invulnerable defenses against vulnerability. Because she is "sharp," Susan is dangerous—she has angles that can cut. She is capable of holding up her end of their conspiracy, perhaps more capable in her own way even than Jonathan, given her comparatively greater intimacy with Sandy. Candice Bergen's slender angularity makes her an ideal physical type for the "sharp" role, a pronounced contrast to the zaftig curves and softly rounded passivity of Ann-Margret as Bobbie, Susan's replacement as the occupied center of Jonathan's point of view.

In Susan's last scene in the film, we can still hear her but can't see her, because Jonathan's autocratic point of view forbids it. Sandy and Susan are packing for a camping trip that pointedly does not include Jonathan. The take, a single close-up of Jonathan, is initially reminiscent of the close-up of Susan in the bar after dancing, screaming in exaggerated laughter. But in that scene, performance is the preoccupation: everyone is watching Susan—the audience, Sandy (in adoration), Jonathan (with suspicion). In fact, the long-take close-up of Jonathan in this scene, while it demonstrates in Susan's bright tones her having launched herself entirely into the role of Sandy's lover, is less a reminder of Susan performing than a harbinger of Jonathan's shrinking worldview; it's a shot that shares a greater affinity with the final shot of the film, another close-up of Jonathan, who, by narrative's end, is not quite post-woman but is adamantly post-relationship. In the dorm-room close-up, Jonathan's gloom seems to goose Susan's off-screen demeanor. She's a parodic performance of chipper affability, although her direct addresses to Jonathan have zero effect: "Isn't he being silly, Jonathan?" and "Isn't he a nut, Jonathan?" do not stir Jonathan from his brown study. It's the last trace of Susan in the film's diegesis. He obliterates her from his consciousness (though not from his slide show, which retains all, harboring every grudge and slight of his lifelong turf war with the female sex). Nichols and O'Steen fade this final scene of the collegiate triangle.

There are comparisons to be made here to the narrative transitions in *The Graduate*, although in *The Graduate* the transitions typically are punctuated by black, the "darkness" of Simon and Garfunkel's "Sounds of Silence." The essential similarity is that these transitions—Benjamin's slamming the bathroom door at the Taft Hotel to plunge himself into the empty affair with Mrs. Robinson; the fade to black after Elaine discovers the truth of the affair and Benjamin is banished by two generations of Robinson women—demarcate an intensifying alienation in the protagonist, as they do, in white blankness, in *Carnal Knowledge*. The darkness of Jonathan's character is in little doubt; the whiteness on screen is thus an analogue not to his sensibility but rather to his willed indifference, a deliberate wiping of his emotional slate. After this first occurrence, 38 minutes into the film (within a minute or so of the first blackout transition of *The Graduate*), there will be two recurrences: at the end of the film's second section, Jonathan's life with Bobbie up through her suicide attempt; and at the conclusion of the film's much briefer third section, the last image of the film. While the blackout transitions of *The Graduate* are accompanied by silence (interrupted only by Simon and Garfunkel's non-diegetic song), an ice-skating rink organ burbles maddeningly to each of the three whiteout transitions in *Carnal Knowledge*. It is music that compels gaiety and that has no cultural meaning outside performance. The ice dancer, her long exposed limbs a public provocation in the wintry scene, performs.

There is no certainty of identification of the skater, and thus she is emblematic of all the narrative's various performers aware of their desirability and consumable status. The initial sensation of the skater's appearance is, for the audience, disorientation: how did we get from the Amherst dorm room to this bright, open, sun-splashed place? Who is this woman? Through whose eyes do we see her? Having wiped clean his emotional slate of nagging vulnerabilities, Jonathan has emerged fifteen years after college[19] as a successful New Yorker (his firm did the taxes of a minor celebrity with whom, he boasts to Sandy, he has slept). Yet in another sense, little has changed: he is still ogling women from afar in the company of his old college roommate Sandy. While we (and they) watch the skater, Feiffer's largely off-screen dialogue fills us in on what we've missed: Jonathan has yet to settle down into marriage and family, while Sandy and Susan have married and Sandy has a successful medical practice. Jonathan needs little encouragement to launch into a paranoid, misogynist screed about emasculation, terrified and enraged by feminine power—in the *early* sixties, before the full cultural assertion of feminist autonomy.

As Sandy takes cues from Jonathan's miserable attitude to suggest monogamy as a potential solution, Jonathan directs his most frontal assault on Sandy's reified life. "You're so well off?" he challenges, and Nichols and Feiffer cut to a new scene in which, we imagine, the dialogue has continued from visit to visit. This is Garfunkel's momentous close-up (Bergen and Nicholson have already, as noted, been scrutinized in close-up, and Ann-Margret will have her memorable, post-coital moment of creeping devastation propped against the wall behind her bed). Sandy is talking to Jonathan, who is the camera. He is selling himself one or another of the oft-sold Manhattan bridges, an apologia for a marriage that, if Susan were in the room with them, would be humiliating. Gone is the bravado of his earlier claim, "Susan's plenty enough woman for one man"; in its place is resignation to a proscribed life of passionless material partnership. A reverse shot of Jonathan listening reminds us that Sandy's speech reinforces in Jonathan's mind a sense of how easily he can triumph in his life's competition with Sandy. Sandy confesses his life is "not glamorous or anything," and tries desperately to believe "There are other things besides glamour." Of course there are, but whether Sandy finally comes to embrace rather than resignedly accept this truth is left in doubt.

The immediate cut by Nichols and O'Steen after Sandy's claim, to a screenful of Ann-Margret at her most bountifully glamorous, makes Jonathan's position on the claim abundantly clear: his restless pursuit of accumulation and display never ends. Julian Jebb writes, "She is the *Playmate* personified: huge-breasted, submissive, smiling, co-operative"[20]; Paul D. Zimmerman adds, "she is everyone's adolescent dream but her own."[21] For Jonathan, there is *only* "glamour," and when he can't help but see through that illusion, it intensifies the inauthentic, culminating in the film's haunting final scene with Louise the prostitute, rehearsing potency. *Carnal Knowledge*'s small ensemble is perfectly cast, but there is no greater coup for Nichols in the casting of his fourth film than his having risked an important part on Ann-Margret, Scandinavian bombshell of notoriously superficial cinematic glamour, as Bobbie, majestically carnal, spiritually in need. Nichols believed in Ann-Margret's rightness as Bobbie as he'd once believed in Elizabeth Taylor as Martha or Dustin Hoffman as Benjamin Braddock or Alan Arkin as Yossarian, in spite of the registered doubts of producers and industry experts. The easy part for Nichols in casting Ann-Margret was in seeing the physical type. The cut to Ann-Margret hunkered with Jonathan at a tablecloth restaurant, bursting from her black cocktail dress, is cinema in full command of comic irony: her hair and features and mannerisms and voice are all much, much larger than life, Jonathan's answer to Sandy's attempted devaluation of glamour. If Jonathan is going to embrace the consolations of material "success," he's going to be as performative as possible, a Manhattan power broken out on the town with his trophy, and then to bed. Casting Ann-Margret as Jonathan's object of desire was surely no stretch; finding within the bimboid persona of the screen's female Elvis a genuinely soulful existential presence is the astonishment at the heart of *Carnal Knowledge*: the human soul requires other things besides being—or having—Ann-Margret.

In Manhattan's Rainbow Room, Bobbie and Jonathan are on their flirtatious first date, seated over dinner. This and the next three scenes—in the cab, entering the apartment, and at climax—constitute an encyclopedia of knowing, reified clichés of the proscribed courtship ritual. In the restaurant, they wrangle over her age before arriving at an agreement on "twenty-nine," one of the perpetual markers of female vanity, after which Jonathan, who is also in his thirties, zings her with his crack about preferring "older women." Nuzzling in the cab, their conversation becomes increasingly intimate; strikingly, it mirrors the subject of Susan and Sandy's first conversation: an awareness of the familiar roles they are assuming. While Susan and Sandy's dialogue was a series of meta-analytical insights whose wit was cool and distant, Bobbie and Jonathan pursue a franker, farther-reaching improvisation on the course not only of courtship but its deterministic endgame: marriage, domesticity, and divorce ("I'll take you for every cent you've got"). Bobbie is joking, and yet we know enough about Jonathan's misogyny to recognize Bobbie's lampoon of the gold digger as part of Jonathan's paranoid vision of gendered performance—this is no joke. The scene is playfully sexy and as full of doom as Yossarian's surrealist vision of drowning just beyond carnal salvation with the beauty on the floating dock in *Catch-22*. Yet while Yossarian dedicates himself to attempting to reverse his reified life, Jonathan is powerless in the grip of glamour to extract himself from a misery he understands awaits him. His fault in this misery will be a failure to recognize he has always played his role too well: in possessing his trophy, he all but obliterates her.

Nichols accesses the movie cliché of passion with his slow track across the discarded clothing strewn in the moment's heat in a trail to the bedroom, where the inarticulate ejaculations of the lovers move toward a temporary, annihilating satisfaction. The scene is not quite believable, precisely because it is so self-referentially cinematic: it's what the conventions of film genre compel us to want. In this film whose courting lovers are so hyper-aware of their performed roles, a long take like the one that trails across a room, down a corridor, through a door, and up to the bed of unwitting characters is a reminder of film's manipulative medium. We're being asked to play our proscribed role as moviegoers, yet we're also asked to stand at a meta-critical remove to examine this proscription. In other words, we as a movie-going audience are in precisely the same predicament as Susan and Sandy and, later, Bobbie and Jonathan are as courting lovers: aware of and in thrall to our manipulation. This is the nature of reification, which carries within it meta-cognitive recognition. Nichols, who learned his lesson in projecting narrative irony in the wake of *The Graduate*'s juggernaut of non-reflective adoration, leaves no room for misapprehension here. If that slow track to veritable intercourse of the gods does not alert us to a sense of our complicity in fetishizing the performance of glamour, we are as much to blame as Jonathan.

The seeming idyll of ecstatic sensuality and satisfaction depicted in the first four scenes of the relationship between Bobbie and Jonathan receives a coda in a brief morning-after scene, reading the Sunday paper with breakfast in bed, an easy, Edenic nudity suggestive of all masks discarded, roles renounced in favor of genuine contact. They play a game in which they take on acknowledged, cliché roles of nurse and patient, secure for the moment in who they are when they are together. Yet in the following scene, which in time reveals to us that several equally idyllic weeks must have passed since their first night together, Bobbie challenges Jonathan's primacy (and autonomy) by suggesting they "shack up." His ease evaporates instantly, and his evasive response devolves into a halting, cautionary legalism that she eventually euthanizes with a sharp insult. The moment just before her suggestion is their last moment of happiness in the film; he leaps up for one of the many showers we see him take during this section of the narrative (a physical manifestation of that psychological fastidiousness to wipe clean the emotional slate), and Bobbie is caught by the camera in a long and pensive close-up against a wall dominated by blankness, "the finest shot in the film."[22] (Eventually, we see more of the apartment's interior, whose central decorative element is a stunningly glamorous headshot of Bobbie caught in mid-spin in the model's studio; in contrast, Nichols and Rotunno's gorgeous close-up of the woman herself, in the grip of equal and opposed forces of desire and anxious caution, is more beautiful for being *alive*, not *posed*, *captured*.) Ann-Margret convinces us of the difficulty of this moment, listening to her lover's cheerfully tin-eared voice in the shower and afraid that the feelings she's about to reveal will bring them both only heartache. She knows she ought to hastily dress and walk away. Zimmerman praises Ann-Margret's "quiet, soft, moving performance that catches the pathos of so many women who never develop their inner resources because men seem so satisfied with their exteriors."[23] Yet she is complicit as well in the prophecy she and Jonathan have teasingly enacted in the cab their first night, since she has entrapped someone she instinctively knows better than to love, because she knows (or knows soon enough) that he has no love to return, only possessive worship. When she makes her proposition, she's as emotionally naked as she is physically naked; Jonathan adroitly wraps himself in a towel and in convenient clauses of caution, ultimately analogizes her proposition to "business deals I've seen come to grief." Feiffer's word choice here reveals the default assumption Jonathan carries into all human transactions, whether personal or professional: everything is always about negotiation and acquisition. If Bobbie persists (as she does), it will be with the understanding that

In the apartment Jonathan (Jack Nicholson) comes to share with Bobbie (Ann-Margret) at the heart of *Carnal Knowledge*, the most prominent decoration is a glamorous, larger-than-life photograph of Bobbie from her days as a fashion model. It is a harrowing evocation of the objectifying perspective from which Jonathan regards her, and the brooding prospect captured in this image indicates how little satisfaction he actually derives from the conquest and possession of a socially constructed "trophy." As Nichols had first argued in *The Graduate*, a life predicated upon restless acquisition can never be at peace.

she is a commodity she has bartered at the price of her own self-worth. She becomes Jonathan's prisoner, but she has slipped on her own chains.

The careful structure Nichols and Feiffer impose on *Carnal Knowledge* demonstrates that, despite varieties of type and temperament, cultural conformity homogenizes experience. Susan and Sandy's first conversation pessimistically summarizes their decades-long relationship; Bobbie and Jonathan's does the same. Competition (and thus, power) motivates action. Sandy makes his first sexual power moves based on the "success" Jonathan has reported with "Myrtle," not because of an inner urge to express sexual passion (which isn't the predicating motivation for Jonathan, either). Later, the editing sequence implies that Jonathan bedding Bobbie is predicated upon Sandy's defensive assertion that glamour is not the zenith of human achievement; indeed, Jonathan's sense of aggressive, superficial possessiveness and desire to win points are what cause him to possess whomever and whatever he possesses. (When in the brief last section of the film, as Sandy and his new, young girlfriend Jennifer visit Jonathan and endure his slide show, Jonathan explains the circumstances under which a venereal 16-year-old to whom he paid $20 in the Village has found her way into the show, Jonathan suggests that Jennifer might know her and thus sets up the implication that, in different circumstances, he'd have been as likely to proposition her.) Sandy's speech "de-glamorizing" glamour is delivered in close-up to the camera; after Bobbie's proposition, Jonathan addresses the camera, sitting across from Sandy at dinner. It is remarkable as one of the few, albeit brief, moments of Jonathan's vulnerability left exposed. He confesses to occasional impotency, no doubt confident that Sandy in his role as physician is more accustomed than the average man to such disclosures and much more inclined to confidential respect for the information (as opposed to the opportunistic exploitation Jonathan would likely pursue). Yet the closest he can come to vulnerability with Bobbie is to mask it with excessively obvious displays of traditional masculinity, demanding food, demanding that Bobbie desist from pursuing her independent life and career. Terrified of dependence, he moves to instead make her entirely dependent on him, and his utter success consumes him with loathing for them both, displayed in brow-beating her for not having beer in the refrigerator. Yet when she offers to go to the store, then asks if he'll accompany her, he concludes in disgust, a forecast of Jonathan's alienated life as the film ends, "I may as well go myself." It's a painful acknowledgement to them both of the illusion of intimacy—the illusion is by this point all they share.

The last of the close-up monologues in this second section of the film belongs again to Sandy, who, perhaps inspired by Jonathan's own admission of vulnerability, confesses to the physical deadness of his marriage to Susan. The ironic weight of these close-ups has begun to accrue by this point: close-ups are a cinematic trope of self-revelation, but as these characters get further and further from genuine intimacy with one another, the close-ups mock true revelation. Jonathan uses this opportunity—patiently awaited for decades—to suggest Sandy have an affair, which will afford Jonathan new turf to invade and conquer. He's nursed his grudge against Susan and Sandy since college; now he'll destroy their marriage bond and, having found Sandy a lover, once again claim her as his own. The contextualization of all Jonathan's action within competition and winning can hardly be in doubt in the site of Sandy's first date with Cindy, on a late-autumn Manhattan tennis court. Initially, the men strut and preen for the women; Cindy watches with appetite, while Bobbie quickly loses interest. Cindy is invited to "take on" Jonathan, despite Bobbie feebly protesting it's her "turn." She has been usurped by a deglamorized, masculinized woman. If she is aware that Jonathan has procured Cindy for Sandy, she doesn't let on her position about this premed-

itated infidelity. Rather, she appears to be meditating on how low Jonathan can go, as if she
has glimpsed all the future chess moves required to bring them all to "mate"—on Jonathan's
terms.

The next sequence is the last to feature Bobbie (who, like Susan, becomes a spectral
presence after marriage, a foregone possession). It is the scene that confirms Jonathan's bad
intentions in having brought Cindy into the picture—he means to betray both Bobbie and
Sandy, ironically by pushing them into each other's arms. The sequence unfolds in three
scenes, the first of which is a culminating argument between Bobbie and Jonathan before
Cindy and Sandy drop in on their way to a party, followed by Jonathan's bait and switch
proposal to Sandy to trade partners for the evening, and capped by the very different behaviors of the two women to Jonathan's condescending manipulations: Bobbie begs for marriage,
only to have Jonathan frankly compare it to a death sentence; Cindy chides him for plotting
without her consent and promises a future assignation only if negotiated on her terms. In
Cindy, Jonathan has met his match: her cold detachment in deflecting his play for her is cruelly contemptuous of everyone but herself: "You want to come around sometime by yourself,
that's one thing. I've been expecting that. But you tell Sandy if he lays one hand on that tub
of lard in there not to come home." She leaves without bothering to tell Sandy herself.

Cindy's man-eating frankness of desire is a distortion worthy of inclusion in Jonathan's
slide show; Bobbie and Cindy are bookends in the sequence that represent Jonathan's spectrum of disgust, from the women like Bobbie who emasculate by smothering a man, to the
women like Cindy who forget that they are "the weaker sex" and, in emergent liberation,
assert the prerogatives of primacy that transcend gender. The entire sequence plays as an
elaborate variation on "Catch-22" logic. Bobbie understands her dissolution as a perpetuating
cycle: "The reason I sleep all day is I can't stand my life," she says, but it is clear she could
just as easily invert the two clauses. She doesn't want anything except for Jonathan to love
her, but he replies, in a narcissistic caricature of self-disclosure, "I'm taken—by me!" He
commands her to "get out of the house" and "do something useful," though of course he's
previously commanded her to quit her job and stay at home. In a line that could have fit in
Catch-22, Jonathan asserts in exasperation, "I'd almost marry you if you'd leave me." Her suicide attempt makes his statement prophetic. Though defiantly screaming his resolve not to
be manipulated over her prone body, his resistance is futile. He is, by his own confession,
impotent.

The skater's waltz and whiteout screen return; we understand that, in the internal logic
of the film, more time will have passed, and with it, another illusory attempt by Jonathan at
redeeming the time via wiping the emotional slate. Predictably, his carapace continues to
harden around him with the passing years. Feiffer's screenplay identifies Jonathan, when we
finally see him at the conclusion of his slide show, as "in his forties."[24] The urban minimalism
of his furniture, Sandy's groovy facial hair: the diegesis has finally found the present, the
film's 1971 release date.[25] The slide show itself is baroque in its misogyny. Sandy seems too
shell-shocked by what he has witnessed to confront Jonathan when Susan's image appears,
though he must be exploring the possibility that this could be the mysterious "Myrtle" he'd
heard so much about.

Sandy has shown his old friend contempt while rescuing Bobbie from her overdose;
now his disapproval seems to have moved beyond words. But as their final conversation
reveals, it's Jonathan who can barely contain his contempt for his perennially naïve friend,
while Sandy can afford to be magnanimous about Jonathan's many malevolencies because
of Jennifer's nubile body and mature wisdom. It seems reasonable for Sandy to conclude that

he, not Jonathan, has won. "I found out who I am," Sandy claims, and he laments "[a]ll those games" they have allowed themselves to play. The sermonette on overcoming the culture of "games" can't help but echo the socio-terrorism of the game playing in *Virginia Woolf.* The ferocity with which George and Martha perform their "exorcism" from the reified cycle of "success" games they've been waging for years on domestic and academic playing fields is more convincing as a transformation than Sandy's cliché-strewn testament to his own evolving sense of identity. Jonathan, for his part, does not believe a word he's hearing, and heaps scorn on Sandy for the clichés and the naivety. He will never permit someone he's so easily fooled to be his advisor. After hearing one too many of Sandy's hippie appropriations, he says, "'Bad vibrations.' Sandy, I love you, but you're a schmuck. Well, you were always young, Sandy. Open. You were schmucky a lot of the time but maybe schmuckiness is what you need to stay young and open." In this line of logic, Jonathan has never been "schmucky," because he could never be "young and open." That way lies vulnerability and weakness. In another throwaway line that could easily have been one of the linguistic knots in the *Catch-22* script, he says, "Listen, don't listen to me."

He concludes, "You're doing great and I'm making money." It's as nice as Jonathan gets: there's enough success to go around, as long as Jonathan gets a bigger share. Sandy will not relent: "You can find what I've found, Jonathan." Sandy, it turns out, will not agree to let Jonathan win, and it prompts the last words Jonathan says to Sandy in the film, words that could easily spell the end of the illusion of their "friendship": "Don't make me insult you." What has kept these two together all these years is Sandy's "schmuckiness" and Jonathan's easy avenue to feel superior. There may be only one true friendship among all the relationships represented in Mike Nichols' first four films, and it's the notorious donnybrook of a marriage between George and Martha in *Virginia Woolf.* (In his next film, Nichols would work with Buck Henry to explore another genuine marriage-based friendship, the life's work of Jake and Maggie Terrell in *The Day of the Dolphin*.) There is never an opportunity for such a friendship between Benjamin and Elaine, because they never allow themselves to think beyond a codified future in which marriage is a means of social manipulation. There is never an opportunity for such a friendship between Yossarian and any of the various isolates and misfits on his base in *Catch-22*, or with Luciana, who couldn't marry anybody crazy enough to want to marry her. Certainly there has never been enough genuine honesty between Sandy and Jonathan to sustain such a friendship—Jonathan simply is not capable of it. He's too good at winning. In the logic of "Catch-22," Jonathan's compulsive winning dooms him to a lifetime as a loser.

Sandy has referred to Jennifer as his "love teacher," but we get no opportunity to verify the claim, only the faintly ridiculous sound of these hippie phrases in his mouth. But the film has never been about Sandy anyway. The film's perspective begins, literally, in darkness; it ends in a different kind of darkness, in the warmly lit apartment of a prostitute, with money exchanged, lines of potency rehearsed, and a final wipe of the slate via the return of the skater and the maddening organ music. Jennifer clearly has principles and a vocabulary she's imparting to her avid disciple Sandy, who seems always ready for the next revision of his philosophy; in Jonathan's world, on the other hand, there can be only one teacher, one philosophy. He's "taken." His phallocentric commitment is made nauseatingly overt in the script he has written for Louise. The performance he teaches her is corrupt at so many levels: predicated in money, not love; instigated from the autoerotic rather than the erotic impulse; and ultimately a controlled pretense in which the smallest, off-script improvisation can literally deflate the project. The film ends with one final monologue in close-up, the only one given to someone other than one of the main quartet: Louise pep-talks Jonathan through a meditation on phallic power, the oldest lesson in patriarchy, and the only one Jonathan has managed to retain. But this is *not* Louise talking: this is Jonathan pep-talking himself in the script he has created for her to perform, to "summon an inner power so strong that every act, no matter what, is more proof of that power." Following his rave for *Catch-22* with two separately published raves for *Carnal Knowledge*, Vincent Canby in the *New York Times* lamented that the film had to end as soon as it did,[26] but the film *has* to end where it ends— Jonathan can devolve no further without opting out of life's project altogether. He is the purely misanthropic man. Of all the darkness of Mike Nichols' first four extraordinary films, there is no darker moment than this.

6

"Man is bad"

The Day of the Dolphin (1973)

In sheer genre terms, only the werewolf-horror film entry *Wolf* (1994) in Mike Nichols' filmography is as strange an excursion as Nichols' fifth feature, a paranoid-conspiracy thriller starring George C. Scott and "talking" dolphins. Nichols' long exile from urbanity in Mexico during production of *Catch-22* had now sufficiently faded from memory to allow Nichols to book himself another lengthy, remote location shoot, this time on a remote coast in the Bahamas. Instead of working with vintage airplanes, he would now work for the first (and last) time with animals among the dramatic leads. Significant passages in the film elapse without dialogue; indeed, *The Day of the Dolphin* is intensely cinematic; the ecstatic marine cinematography is reminiscent of the "pretty" ironies of the Berkeley idyll in *The Graduate*; the simple beauties of the world (and of the cinema) are not as they appear.

This was the golden age of the paranoid-conspiracy thriller in Hollywood, borne of the era that offered the Pentagon Papers and the secret bombings of Cambodia, the Watergate break-in and the subsequent White-House cover-up. It would have been impossible for a 1973 audience not to have cultural associations with a plot that features a battery of recording devices and tapes that disappear in order to facilitate a whitewash. Alan J. Pakula became the auteur of the genre in the loose trilogy of films *Klute* (1971), *The Parallax View* (1974), and *All the President's Men* (1976), but many other directors in the Hollywood firmament explored the genre as well, including Francis Ford Coppola in *The Conversation* (1974; he was nominated against himself and *The Godfather, Part II* for Best Picture and Best Director at the Academy Awards) and Roman Polanski in *Chinatown* (1974). Polanski had originally been attached to write and direct *The Day of the Dolphin*, in 1968 (he had been laboring unenthusiastically over the script in London when his pregnant wife, Sharon Tate, died of multiple stab wounds inflicted by the Charles Manson gang, and he was understandably unable to refocus on the project afterwards).[1] For Nichols and Henry, the genre offered a logical and novel excursion into insights they'd already been making about the causes and effects of self-delusion in reified systems.

Every one of his first five films shares a thematic preoccupation with the problem of communication. *Dolphin* foregrounds this meditation, since it presents as its protagonist Dr. Jake Terrell (Scott's character), biologist, zoologist, and *linguist*. Vincent Canby, who for the first time was unable to give Nichols an unqualified review, dwells on the source material that inspired Robert Merle to write the novel Buck Henry greatly simplified for the screen: the work of Dr. John C. Lilly. "Unlike Dr. Lilly," writes Canby, "who finally gave up his work on the grounds that it was cruel to take away the dolphins' freedom in the interests of research, the hero of "The Day of the Dolphin" pursues his [linguistic and behavioral] experiments to their successful conclusion." He concludes that not even Scott is immune from the undignified tone inevitably introduced by talking fish: "No matter what he does," Canby argues, "the dolphin is bound to uptank him."[2] Polanski had bailed out of the project, unsure of how to create a dignified thriller from a Dr. Doolittle premise; the reviewers had a field day savaging the film with witty puns and hyperbolic exclamations about the creaking plot; Pauline Kael was at her most venomous, calling it "the most expensive Rin Tin Tin picture ever made" and wondering, "if Mike Nichols and Buck Henry don't have anything better to make movies about than involving English-speaking dolphins in assassination attempts, why don't they stop making movies?"[3] As a matter of fact, they did: it was their last collaboration.

But while *Dolphin* suffers the inevitable slings and arrows of the backlash that had been waiting for just such an invitation to their ridicule, the film is anything but literal in its intentions. Nichols' next foray into the paranoid conspiracy thriller would be in *Silkwood*, where among the intimate relationships of another strong ensemble cast, the shadowy conspiracy is secondary to the trespasses of friends and lovers. The many critics who carped at the silliness of *Dolphin*'s conspiracy plot (and this was nearly everyone) missed the point: Nichols isn't a thriller director, and he didn't suddenly become one for his "talking-fish film." While previous Nichols films dramatized the limits of language or the unwillingness of characters to reveal themselves through language, *Dolphin* offers an inquiry into the evolutionary morality of language. Like those earlier films, its conclusions about our dysfunctional species are dark—so dark that, in the language of the scientific hypothesis that serves as the prologue to the film ("Why, after millions of years as a land animal, [... the dolphin was] compelled—or decided—to return to the sea"), Terrell implies humans may constitute an evolutionary cul de sac rather than progress.

* * *

After the very brief title sequence offers the inscrutable image of a dolphin's eye, regarding us under a baleful scratch of strings in Georges Delerue's Oscar-nominated score, *Dolphin* begins in performance, a highly self-conscious presentation by Scott, noted actor of Broadway stage and Hollywood screen, who squints and growls directly at the camera in close-up with a pure-black backdrop. Scott was a star. Nichols clears the set of all distractions and lets the performer perform. But what the performer is performing is his character's performance: as we eventually learn, he is Dr. Jake Terrell, beneficiary of a Franklin Foundation grant to conduct research into animal behavior, specifically of dolphins, and what we are witnessing (when Nichols finally allows us an establishing shot of Terrell before his audience) is one of the indentured performances the Foundation periodically extracts from its beneficiaries as in-kind payment for its largesse. Terrell's first word, "Imagine ..." suggests yet another level of referenced performance, however: Nichols the filmmaker addressing his audience with a paraphrased invocation of Coleridge's suspended disbelief. What Terrell and Nichols are asking us will require our cooperation in art's shared act of hypnotic suggestion. We're being asked to believe that dolphins can speak toddler–English.

But whether we do or not is not the point of the film. Nichols is not making a statement about marine behavioral conditioning circa 1973; the film is about objectification, commodification, and exploitation, and the conceit in which dolphins can talk provides a metaphor for the manipulative hegemonic exploitation of the purest and least corruptible. Scott's performance as the trained and performing researcher is a fascinating study in self-delusion:

Terrell believes he is protecting the dolphins from the exploitation of a cynical outside world, but he has failed to protect them from himself. In the opening monologue, there is a richly provocative balance between hubris and reserve in Terrell's manner, and it simultaneously makes his claim as a scientist more credible while also allowing us the inference that he knows more than he's telling and enjoys the control. Nichols helps to create this impression of covert reticence via ironic insertions of vignettes in Terrell's research laboratory, where the dolphins perform for a man we will later know as "Mahoney." The dolphin show is a variation on two early-childhood activities: shape differentiation and object retrieval. Mahoney watches, impassive, as first one shape than another is retrieved; then he asserts his will and introduces a "trick," substituting an already retrieved shape. The dolphin, consternated, awaits Mahoney's recognition of his "error." The vignette plays without diegetic sound, only Delerue's anxious score inflecting tone. Terrell has just been declaiming the ingenuous rationality of the dolphin point of view as a "perfectly accurate receptor of information about the world for miles around"—which presumes that the world for miles around will be a perfectly accurate *transmitter* of information. As the ensuing narrative implies, in the conduction of information, the human is a far less reliable and thus far more dangerous species than even the shark, the dolphins' most natural enemy.

Terrell's presentation sets down certain basic premises of dolphin reality: its existence is "ecstatic," reliable, enviable in its efficiency of communication; it's a life of "two worlds"— the water and the air. Nichols again interjects a brief vignette, of an obviously distressed dolphin bound by canvas harness and human hands and wired to various laboratory technologies recording vital signs, and Terrell assures us the dolphin has "few natural enemies." We sense simultaneously Terrell's belief that he is not an enemy of the dolphins and an ironic detachment, via these insertions, of the cinematic narrator from Terrell's implied self-assessment, in which he has distinguished himself from "certain clumsy scientists" who investigate via vivisection rather than non-invasive observation. Nichols' inserted vignettes puncture the absolute authority Scott's presence otherwise commands as Terrell, and we understand Terrell's performance to be about more than adding to the sum of scientific knowledge: he's doing his dance for a private foundation's continued patronage and protesting too much— attempting to subdue the malignant doubts he has about his own motives as a researcher.

He ends his presentation with what may at first seem pure immersion in the realities of his science: a short documentary film of the birth of his star subject, "Alpha," so named because he was the first dolphin to be born at the Terrell Center, to a mother who died soon after Alpha's birth. His pride in Alpha is as palpable ("We raised him ourselves") as it is patriarchal: Terrell is "Pa" to Alpha, and Terrell's wife, Maggie, is "Ma." Asked about the military's interest in dolphin intelligence, Terrell sounds either naïve or willfully ignorant when he claims, "The government and I pay very little attention to each other. [...] I'm not a *political* scientist. My degrees are in biology and zoology." The film he has shown his audience is ideological, a projection of his belief that his method is hands-off and non-invasive, but most important, organic, the equivalent of the proud father showing snapshots of his child. Also reminiscent in this staged performance is another performing patriarch, Mr. Braddock (William Daniels) in *The Graduate*, intent on maintaining status via the show he alone can command: his progeny's performance, and its redounding glory. We must understand Dr. Jake Terrell as in the grip of objectifying forces as he presents Alpha to audiences: his objectifying scientific will, in which the dolphins are inevitably a means to the end of knowledge; and his financial necessity, in which both he and the dolphins are commodities the Foundation must market to maintain, in turn, its own solvency and credibility.

Nichols further erodes the dramatic authority of Dr. Terrell/Scott by permitting audience insolence: a woman presses the intelligence issue, wondering if the dolphin she'd heard about that can count to eight in recognizable English is the product of "some kind of trick or something." Terrell's response is a condescending smile and a parroting of her own vocabulary: "Yes, I'd say—yes, just a trick." The matter-of-fact acceptance of this default currency of human interaction, the "trick" or deceptive illusion, would have a powerful enough irony simply by our having sensed Terrell's withholding—he, too, has been engaged in a "trick," in collusion with his assistants and the Foundation. But as the woman turns to talk to her neighbor, the camera reveals Mahoney among the audience members (prominent, even if we don't recognize Paul Sorvino, because he is one of the few men in the room), and we sense the conspiracy is deeper and, because in the first inserted vignette we've already seen Mahoney attempt to trick the dolphin and thus expose the Terrell Center as a sham of rote conditioning rather than logical decision-making, we presume that Terrell's "trick" is merely a wheel within wheels, of tricks far deeper than the ones he himself has performed at the Center and on this stage.

The immediate aftermath of the public event, which to all appearances has been a strategic success for the Foundation, suggests the commodified, transactional relationship the Terrell Center has with the Franklin Foundation, as manifested in the Terrell's interaction with Harold DeMilo, his Foundation liaison. Questions persist about Terrell's enormous bills for recording equipment; Terrell wheedles a ride to his boat from DeMilo (despite its being significantly out of DeMilo's way). DeMilo attempts to modify Terrell's thinking about his command performances ("It's all in the name of good public relations," he says—a tombstone aphorism for a man like DeMilo, who has staked his reputation upon appearances), and Terrell, one foot already on the pier, reminds DeMilo he needs more money. There is professional courtesy between them, but what underlies all is manipulative negotiation of power.

And then Jake Terrell has left behind the land for his own private island, a bubble of supposed autonomy. In his brief exchange with Mike (Edward Herrmann, looking something less than nautical in a job where his spectacles would be perpetually sprayed to opacity with salt), we learn that Maggie has suffered some injury from Alpha and that Jake is more concerned with Alpha than with his wife; Jake repairs below deck and commands, "Wake me before we get there." He wants to have resumed full control of his faculties before resuming full control of the compound as he steps off the boat; yet the emphasis upon entering a dream world as he moves from the land to his liminal compound and its shimmering, watery laboratory poses a way of understanding Terrell's relationship to the wider world. In the longest philosophical dialogue in the film, between Jake and Maggie after it is inevitable that they must surrender Alpha's secrets to general consumption, Maggie refers to Jake's anger: "because the world is coming in here and interfering with your little kingdom, all those people who carry whatever disease you think the outside world has." Jake will come to recognize that this "disease"—commodification—is one he has brought with him into their dream world he has constructed for the meeting of the species.

Certainly his arrival at the compound suggests that, if this is paradise, there is nonetheless trouble here. Jake is palpably drawn toward the lab, a striking piece of poured-concrete architectural sculpture that sits at the heart of the compound, but his assistants all assume he will want to see his wife first. As portrayed by Scott's real-life spouse, Trish Van Devere, Maggie is resigned to Jake's ill-temper and distraction, releasing him to Alpha as a worldly continental wife might permit him to see his mistress. In a moment of roughhousing, Alpha has bitten Maggie's leg, which is depicted in the foreground of the composition, shapely and bandaged, as Jake enters. Maggie is displayed on the bed less like an invalid than a Titian *Venus*, and yet Jake barely notices her. "Was he—excited?" Jake asks, with an avidity that suggests a sexualized subtext. "That's what—the third time this week." Maggie playfully asks, "Getting jealous?" but as he leaves, she's the object of desire ignored. At the tank, David (Jon Korkes) refers to Alpha's maturation as well: "I think his Ma and Pa aren't enough for him anymore." In ironic hindsight, we can read this as David steering Jake towards adding another dolphin to the secret training sessions, to improve his conspiracy's odds of success. And we wince at Jake's order to install an intercom system between the lab and the house, an impulse to improve communication that has such keen cultural associations with deception. It's another of Jake's attempts to control his reality, and like the listening devices that were bringing down a Presidency as this film was released (the Senate Watergate Hearings opened three days before *Dolphin*), it's a technology ripe for misuse.

Jake clears the lab to be alone with Alpha; after Nichols cuts back to Maggie, alone and preoccupied by Jake's preoccupation, a long shot pans from Maggie at their bungalow across the compound to the lab's locked doors, inside of which (via dissolve to the lab's interior tank window with its movie-screen-sized dimensions) the film finally locates a version—Jake's version, from which everyone, even Maggie, is excluded—of paradise, in the gorgeous underwater photography capturing Jake swimming with Alpha, who has just recognized him, tenderly, by name: "Pa." The camera lingers in close-up on Jake's hand, stroking, patting; his wedding band glints in the light, and we wonder at the odd exchange Jake has had with Maggie, so detached from genuine intimacy through habitual familiarity and professional distraction. It's yet more evidence that Terrell, smartest man on the island, is oblivious to certain essential realities that will leave all of them vulnerable, especially the dolphins who have guilelessly entrusted themselves to his care.

We already know—or assume we know—some things about Mahoney, to whom we are finally introduced by name in the next scene, when he calls on DeMilo at the Foundation. Mahoney is oily; our reservations about him are only deepened by his brazen lack of a convincing story for why he wants an introduction to Dr. Terrell and his research center. Told "Terrell doesn't want visitors—strangers—at the Center," Mahoney shoots back, "Why, is he hiding something? [...] Is he scared somebody's going to run off with that good-looking little girl he's married to?" While DeMilo has inspired little warmth in us, his contempt for Mahoney's apparent tastelessness seems well-founded, leading him to a direct question: "Are you a blackmailer, Mr. Mahoney?" Mahoney demurs, yet also says, "I have access to a lot of files, public and private, all kinds of sources—when we get to know each other better, I'll tell you some things about your*self* that will simply astound you." We know from Mahoney's later admission to the Terrells that this is an oblique reference to DeMilo's closeted sexual orientation, which DeMilo demonstrates he is willing to protect at the cost of more than merely Jake Terrell's project; caving in to Mahoney compromises the Foundation's conspiracy as well. He's such a slave to projecting a conformist image that he's willing to risk everything: "All in the name of good public relations." Among Mike Nichols' many characters over the course of his film career, only Joe Pitt (Patrick Wilson) and Roy Cohn (Al Pacino) of *Angels in America* seem more deeply terrified by who they actually are and by what it might mean if this identity should become public knowledge—but there is genuine anxiety in many of Nichols' narratives about full disclosure of oneself, given the risks of lost potency or control involved in the surrender of one's secrets. While not as extreme as the gendered taboos Joe, Roy, and DeMilo face, characters as different as George (Richard Burton) and Martha (Elizabeth Taylor) in *Virginia Woolf*, Jonathan (Jack Nicholson) in *Carnal Knowledge*, Stewart (James Spader) in *Wolf*, Val (Dan Futterman, who plays the image-conscious son of Armand and Albert Goldman) in *The Birdcage*, all politicians in *Primary Colors*, and "Alice" (Natalie Portman) in *Closer* all keep the truth of themselves to themselves as protection against cultural vulnerability.

DeMilo's exclamation about the Terrells' island, "It's like being in another world!" must have its attractions for DeMilo, and he seems hurt when the Terrells suggest he may have come to visit with a hidden agenda, though of course that's exactly what he's done: he threatens the Terrells with loss of funding, and Jake deals Maggie out of the conversation. Nichols and his director of photography, William A. Fraker, leave her centered, alone, and dwarfed by an enormous vacant picnic table, a reminder of other times Jake has left her alone to pursue research business. Far from emphasizing her passivity or victimhood, however, *Dolphin* attaches to Maggie a fierce loyalty to those she loves that can't be distracted or dissuaded (as can her husband's). In their long philosophical conversation at the center of the film, it's clear she's been advising Jake all along, to little effect. Jake may be the more advanced intellect, but Maggie has the advanced heart; she's the most centered and admirable character in the film, despite Jake's serial marginalization of her. She's a prototype of the kind of character Nichols would turn to in the rest of his career, beginning with Meryl Streep as Karen Silkwood and culminating with Belize in *Angels in America*—strong iconoclasts who glimpse the redemptive truths inherent in reification and who understand or come to understand an alternative way of being in the world.

What follows is the first of Jake and Alpha's command performances, and it opens with Jake doing his best impression of a director, editing together his narrative of interspecies communication. The "screen" of Alpha swimming in the tank glows blue in the background, where DeMilo is asked to take a seat. "What do you know about linguistics, semantics?" Jake asks, then follows, condescendingly, with, "Okay, lesson number one," a reference he could be making either to the first tape he plays of his lessons for Alpha in English morphemes or to teaching DeMilo the rudiments of his work. Either way, there is an imperial air to his performance, an assumed mastery quite at odds with what we know to be the conspiratorial chaos gathering around him. His hubris is on full display here, though it takes the board's later visit to turn it into self-righteous arrogance. The narrative of Alpha's metamorphosis moves from initial problem (the dolphin's unintelligible, though intelligent, battery of clicks, whistles, and other noises) through progressive complications towards a climactic counting of numbers from one to ten, not the mere *eight* that the woman had asked about during Terrell's last public appearance on behalf of the Foundation. Jake's performance has its desired effect, as Delerue's melodious score implies. Jake even permits DeMilo to see Alpha's introduction to Beta, the female dolphin Jake hopes will stimulate Alpha to even faster learning. As DeMilo leaves, the men default to their quid pro quo interaction with each other: while DeMilo promises confidentiality and full support, he asks a "favor" as well: "There's a man I know," which he quickly amends to "an old friend of mine, Curtis Mahoney." Nichols cuts to Maggie on the bungalow verandah, watching the men talk in the distance, out of earshot. We know what Maggie knows: that Jake's ambition is blinding him to sense. The sequence ends with Jake's uneasy gaze at the departing plane and the last purely harmonious "dolphin dance," Fa and Be (as they are known in the simplicity of single-morpheme nicknames to facilitate their learning) in a synchronized movement to Delerue's romantic "Nocturne," the main theme of the soundtrack score. As we are its only witnesses, there is a sense in which the diegetic narrative does not classify it as "performance" in the same way as it has treated

Jake's public displays; it is a time-out from the narrative, a moment of "purity" amidst the projected image-making. Jake may delude himself he has found a separate peace, a return to Edenic simplicity of motive; the swim to "Nocturne" reminds us that not even Jake's motives are pure, and that for true transparency of motive, we must turn to the "lower" mammals.

Two weeks have passed when we encounter Jake and Maggie, spatially (and spiritually) separated by a research tank, wringing their hands about Fa's "regression" to his own language, learned from Be. Jake's uncompromising behaviorist methodology forbids him to award a morsel to Fa so long as his prized pupil remains uncooperative, but Maggie clearly has a less conditional sensibility. Jake looks on in disapproval as Fa and Be reap unearned reward from his wife, purely out of affection. For all his disgust with the meretricious strategies of the "land" world (the Foundation as "tax write-off" for the super-rich, the general public one insatiable appetite for "freak-show" consumption), Jake can only understand relationships as transactions. DeMilo has wheedled information about the research project from Jake by threatening to revoke his funding; while this infuriates Jake, he has established no less commodified a relationship with Fa, and the imminent relationship with Mahoney gains no traction because each has typed the other as unwilling to negotiate any connection beyond the purely transactional.

Nichols' and Henry's structural design in this suspense melodrama takes the familiar editing technique of the cross-cut, typically employed at the climax of the action, and applies it throughout, less often to juxtapose simultaneous actions than to present apparent contrasts or oppositions. In this section of the film, two newcomers have entered the liminal space of the Terrell Center, one (Be) from the sea, the other (Mahoney) from the land. Be is instantly and profoundly welcomed by Fa; Mahoney is given the "scenic route" through turbulent waters by Mike's water-taxi and washes up at the Center looking half-drowned, wrung out by nausea. Given the glimpses we've had of Mahoney, the narrative tempts us to a point-of-view sympathy not with Mahoney but with all those he has come to "invade." Jake and his staff (acting on Jake's orders) engage in a campaign of half-truths and subterfuge, fobbing off an unnamed dolphin as Fa and claiming ignorance of any communicative rapport with dolphins. Again Nichols frames Jake and Maggie with the research facility between them; seated on their verandah, they parry their anxieties about Mahoney, DeMilo, and "the good ol' Establishment" until Jake autocratically concludes, "Let Mr. Mahoney do his job, whatever that is, and get out, and we'll go on about our business." Jake's confidence that he can control and manipulate the world he's built is matched only by his naivety that such control is in his power. The next scene demonstrates this, when Mahoney catches David and Lana (Victoria Racimo) in a cover-up; that night, Maryanne (Leslie Charleson), working alone in the lab, hears someone trying to enter. Mahoney departs the next morning with the prophecy that Jake will need to reach him "when the time comes" and the assurance, "We're all on the same side."

Nichols and O'Steen wittily cut to a sliding metal lock between the main and holding talks, Jake's latest strategy in the war of wills with Fa, his lately recalcitrant prodigy: Jake intends to *impose sides*. The fascinating, nearly 10-minute sequence that follows dramatizes the tedium of behavior modification, as Jake commodifies both relationships and communication by withholding Be (and his own affections) from Fa until the dolphin relents to the superior, controlling will of man. The sequence ends with Delerue's triumphal, neo–Baroque brass voluntary, joyfully leaping dolphins, and, in a comic lampoon of the narrative's critique of all the objectifying impulses of even the most well-meaning humans in the narrative, a nighttime beach party at which the celebratory centerpiece is a culinary confection in the shape of a dolphin, soon to be sliced and served for the revelers' consumption.

A brief exchange Jake has with Larry (John David Carson) reminds us again of the "dream"-like quality of their liminal, island-based position between two worlds, even as Jake has Larry checking the Center's underwater barriers for evidence of other infiltrators, like sharks. Jake admits that, "since Alpha started speaking, I've had a feeling I haven't had since I was your age [...] that there are infinite possibilities." Again the narrative undercuts Jake's vaulting ambitions via ironic parallel cutting: a call from DeMilo, whose agenda Jake reveals in a night-shot meeting with the staff. Mahoney has learned about the breakthroughs with Alpha and Beta and intends to publish what he's found out; the Foundation's public-relations damage control requires Jake to get out ahead of the story and reveal the Center's work. In another husband-wife composition, Jake is foregrounded, Maggie silently backgrounded, and the Center focally between them; their philosophical argument at the core of the narrative is mere minutes away. The scene ends with Jake's paranoid lament, "They're sneaking up on us," and Henry's screenplay once again relies on cross-cut to make concrete Jake's lurid fear, as Mahoney and his partner Stone reach the island's shoal by small, unlighted trawler. Nichols' cinematic language continues to characterize Mahoney as the invader, though in retrospect we can revise our understanding of Mahoney's motives—he's gathering his facts to "expose" Terrell's work so it cannot be co-opted for service to some covert, antagonist ideology. We don't believe Mahoney and Jake are "on the same side" until Jake does (and with as little satisfaction, given Mahoney's distasteful methods).

By Nichols' standards, the Terrells' philosophical argument in their bungalow's bedroom is a model of terse economy. At just under two minutes, it is a mere fifth as long as the most notorious "conversation" in Nichols' filmography—the one in the Taft Hotel bedroom between Benjamin and Mrs. Robinson in *The Graduate*. Jonathan and Sandy have several longer conversations in *Carnal Knowledge*, and even Sandy and Susan speak for as long when they first meet, at the Smith College mixer. Of course, George and Martha's theatrical conversations dwarf any subsequent conversations in Nichols' films for sheer volume (temporal or sonic). Yet there is a frank maturity to Jake and Maggie's exchange (ironic, given Maggie's accusing Jake of being a "baby") that is never possible in any of these previously presented conversations. One reason why none of those other conversations stand a chance of accomplishing true exchange is because the participants are not proceeding from a desire for equal footing. Mrs. Robinson and Jonathan lord their Machiavellian stratagems over Benjamin and Sandy, respectively. George and Martha have been engaged in a decades-old linguistic wrestling match. Sandy and Susan project ironic social avatars at one another to hedge against the vulnerabilities of exposure. These aren't conversations so much as no-holds-barred competitions for an upper hand. Another, related reason these conversations don't promote full and free exchange is that one or both parties in each remain unable or unwilling to look squarely at reified reality and to acknowledge it for what it is. In Jake and Maggie Terrell's conversation about Alpha and the future of their research, Maggie has the courage of her convictions: she knows she is right, and will not stand down from that truth. As important, the two genuinely love each other (if Jake remains too easily distracted), and his respect for her wisdom is palpable as she lays out for him a vision of reified awareness.

Maggie's word-choices signal her less-than-wholly supportive position on Jake's conduct as a researcher; besides his being a "baby," Jake has set up his own "little kingdom," and he dreads "whatever disease" the "outside world" carries. All of this diction is encoded with angry critique that Jake could respond to with righteous indignation. That he doesn't storm away is one measure of how much he values her perspective. Jake not only fails to deny any of their judgments upon him, but he confirms how profoundly he's convicted of the threat of this "disease": "it can kill Alpha and Beta [...] by turning them into 'valuable properties.'" His paranoia is the vision of the reified: the dolphins' commodification by the socio-economic establishment. He can see the "disease" of the reified "outside world," but isn't quite able to see that he is himself a carrier. Maggie does, however. "Jake," she says, creeping across the bed and into close-up, something the dynamics of the Jake-centric mise-en-scène have not often afforded her (or, as in the first shot of her, lounged across the bed, have served only to objectify her), "if they're going to be exploited, who's responsible? You taught them our language. Why? To become like you?" Nichols and O'Steen cut back to Jake, reassuming his centrality, though his faith in himself and his mission as a researcher has been shaken. Admitting he may have been "wrong," Jake sits on the bed near Maggie's lounging form. The resulting composition is as comfortably intimate as any shot of the couple thus far, though Scott's noble profile still juts imperiously above Van Devere's penetrating gaze. "We should have become like them," Jake says wistfully. "Like what they are: instinct, and energy." Maggie's solution foreshadows the film's conclusion: "Then let them go. Send them back to the sea." In despair, or with residual calculation, or most likely in a combination of these two states, Jake replies, "I'm afraid it's too late. They wouldn't know what to do or where to go. We've changed them." And he leaves, rejecting Maggie's reified wisdom to prepare Alpha for his biggest performance yet, before the Foundation's board of directors.

Jake and Maggie Terrell (the real-life husband and wife team of George C. Scott and Trish Van Devere) attempt to cross the liminal space between land and water and between species in *The Day of the Dolphin*, Nichols' conspiracy thriller released during the summer of the Watergate hearings in 1973. Everywhere among the "land mammals" is duplicity and mistrust; the dolphins bring a literal, "face-value" understanding of reality into their meetings with humans, but even the most well-intentioned of men (like Jake) prove to be confusingly two-faced in their objectifying motives for making interspecies contact.

The performance, which takes place not in the research tank but at the pier, at the most obviously liminal of meeting points between land and sea, is a complicated, multi-level admixture of presentations. On its face, the event is a scientific demonstration for the project's sponsors. Yet for Alpha, the moment is merely the progeny's willing performance for his master. For Terrell, the performance is a celebration of all he has accomplished; Maggie has acknowledged this at the beginning of their philosophical conversation, when she says realistically, "The world has to find out about this sooner or later; that's all part of it. What's all this work been for?" The question hangs in the air between them much in the same way that Mr. Braddock hectors his son floating in the pool in *The Graduate*: "Would you mind telling me what those four years of college were for? What was the point of all that hard work?" Benjamin, adrift, replies pointedly, "You got me." Similarly Jake, less confrontational but no less adamant than Benjamin, admits, "I don't know any longer." In his first phase as a filmmaker, Nichols crafted narratives that built not so much toward the expected crescendo of epiphany as toward revelatory exhaustion. Stymied by a grasp of the pointlessness of socially proscribed action, key characters in all of Nichols' early films find themselves at a loss for motivational momentum. They are stronger on the question of what *not* to want than on an ambition worthy of their future effort. Nichols' satiric vision is the realist's perspective, exploring the way we live now less than how we once lived, or ought to live. When Jake comes up against the bankruptcy of motives for why he has built the Terrell Center, he concludes what a veteran showman must conclude: *on with the show*. Terrell's show with Alpha stands as an ironic conflation of father and son in the birthday-party scene in *The Graduate*, where Mr. Braddock all but drowns in his own flop-sweat trying to show off his award-winning son and another expensive present he's bestowed, the diving gear. Jake, like Benjamin, hates the commodifying aspect of his life, but like Mr. Braddock, is compelled to conformity to satisfy the version of himself in which he has so heavily invested over time.

But the strata of performance in this scene are visually underscored by the strata of the mise-en-scène: the sea on the lowest plane, inhabited by Alpha; Jake still perched in his liminal space on the landing dock; and the board members arrayed along the upper promenade of the dock. As we eventually learn, the Foundation's board also projects an identity and interest other than its true, conspiratorial agenda. Accompanied by DeMilo, they sit in a line like judges, peering down upon Terrell and the dolphins, and during the performance, the camera alternates between high-angle shots down on Terrell, Fa, and Be below and low-angle shots from Terrell's vantage point up on the board members. Terrell is the one whose potency is in jeopardy—he must perform for their continued sponsorship—and the conversation with Maggie has shaken his previously unquestioned sense of professional achievement. However, the board's boorishness, particularly exemplified in the tone-deafness of Wallingford (John Dehner), permits Terrell to regain his illusion of superiority. He has trained Alpha to perform for food; the board (and the scientific Establishment to which its largesse gives Terrell entrée) has trained Terrell to perform as well. And there is yet another audience to this performance: hidden by ground cover across the cove, Mahoney and Stone view the show via field glasses. Mirroring Terrell's perspective, the camera treats Mahoney as the threat and the board as locus of legitimate power, the body that can command performance.

The performance in essence constitutes a second round of philosophical conversation, commencing with Alpha's assertion, "Man is good." However, unlike the Terrells' conversation, conceived in frank and forthright exchange between equals in an atmosphere of love and respect, this conversation is fraught with complications from power, deception, and objectification. Only the animals are guileless and without false motive in this exchange. The subject of sharks—predatory violence—becomes the board's preoccupation in testing Alpha's conceptual apparatus. Wallingford stands, exaggerating his assumed hierarchical position in the meeting, and pompously begins a hypothetical scenario about a shark that Terrell gently corrects. Wallingford bulls forward, stating, "There is a shark in the tank," spooking Be out of the holding area. An impromptu performance of damage control ensues: Jake sends Fa to retrieve Be, a demonstration of the enormous trust the dolphins have invested in their master (thus unwittingly manifesting their vulnerability to manipulation, precisely what the board has come to see). When Alpha returns with Be, he shares an insight with Terrell: "Man say things not." It is Alpha's first conscious experience of mendacity. Wallingford asks for clarification, and Terrell, secure in his illusion of ethical superiority, happily translates: "He's calling you a liar." Terrell goes on to explain that, while the dolphins' sonar communicated no warning of imminent predators (unlike Jake himself, who has no such heightened sensory awareness of the danger in his midst), "they trust us more than they do their own instinct." Because she has not been privileged with depiction in the scene, we're startled to hear, off-screen, Maggie add, "They've never been lied to before." Her voice, relegated once again to marginality, indicates how swiftly her quiet moral authority has been subjugated to her husband's compulsive desire to perform. The board members, having learned the most important single item they've come to confirm, politely suggest moving to "less emotional questions," such as swimming speed and future language acquisition, ancillary items in their plot. Suspecting nothing, in his willful desire for innocence like that of the dolphins, Terrell seizes the opportunity to demonstrate Alpha's emotional devotion to and dependence upon him. The scene ends with Alpha nuzzling Terrell's leg like a subservient house pet, prompting Terrell's smugly defiant (and terminally naïve) gaze of triumph.

His command performance immediately begets another: the Foundation compels him to return immediately to the mainland with them, and Maggie, hoping to protect her husband, offers to leave the island as well—an unexpected coup for the conspirators. The next time Terrell will see Alpha, the dolphin will have completed a crash-course in human mendacity. DeMilo confesses his own dishonesty about Mahoney, blaming Mahoney's "pull with the people in the government." Terrell confides in Maggie that he intends to "out" Mahoney at the press conference, still naively believing he can control events, and ironically intending the same tactic Mahoney has used to manipulate DeMilo (exposing hidden secrets as a means of assuming power). At this point, the film settles into the machinery of the thriller formula—Stone's breeching of the lab's secure perimeter (and subsequent assassination); the theft of the dolphins (based in faked telephone communication by David and false promises made by the staff to the dolphins); the stonewalling of the Terrells by the Foundation, who have never had the slightest intention of communicating with the public about Terrell's advances and thus exposing a key component of their conspiracy; and the programming of the dolphins to commit murder. Alpha and Beta are kept captive just beyond reach of their natural habitat, hovering above the ocean in ergonomic slings and having their inherited philosophical premise, "Man is good," irrevocably altered.

And so, when Mahoney returns to the compound and demonstrates—another dramatic performance, this one in utter silence—how David compromised the confidentiality even of the Terrells' private quarters, Mahoney is transformed in Jake's assessment from oily enemy ... to oily ally. He is, indeed, on their "side," yet his tactics are deplorable, as they learn in his admission of manipulating DeMilo. During a slow zoom across the dark compound to a close-up of Jake, Mahoney reveals David's true identity and allegiance to "the guys you work for." Jake blusters his demurrals, but Mahoney implacably rejoins, "Oh really? I always thought you work for the people that pay you." The unpleasant truth of the observation stuns Terrell to silence, and the camera begins a slow pan of the huddled, half-lit faces of the loyal remaining staff, beginning with Maggie, who manages a meager, "That's not fair." She knows its truth, has known or suspected it longest of anyone other than Mahoney at the table. In the tradition of Hollywood paranoid-conspiracy thrillers, vague but potent questions about the conspiratorial vulnerabilities of the nation's governance become part of the conversational mix, but Nichols and Henry remain committed to metaphysical rather than political inquiry. The question of whether government is good is far less pressing than establishing or disproving the essential veracity of Alpha's claim that "man is good." Attendant upon this central preoccupation is the danger of surrender to commodified delusion. Late in their counter-conspiratorial dialogue, Mahoney abrasively asks Terrell, "[H]ave you been living on this planet?" In his own estimation, Terrell has not; it's what has been revealed in the philosophical conversation with Maggie. He has naively believed he could insulate himself from the "disease" of the land by repairing to his liminal retreat between land and sea, there to have a meeting of the minds with the ingenuous, instinctual other. Yet he has taken the Foundation's money and fed his voracious ego in the training of a dolphin in his likeness, carrying the "disease" of commodified value into this tropical paradise. The next day, as Jake, Maggie, and Mahoney attempt to anticipate what nefarious use to which the Foundation may direct the dolphins, Nichols and Fraker compose a gorgeous shot of Maggie and Mahoney seated at the table, the iconic research facility a vivid gray-green reflection in a window behind them. Terrell has just recognized the end of all this: he has trained the dolphins to be used for the grand illusions of man and with no regard for their intrinsic value. The only wrinkle in his plan is that the conspirators have stepped into *his* place.

Nichols and O'Steen return to cross-cutting, now in its more conventional rhetoric as parallel, simultaneous actions. The Terrells undertake the heavy-hearted process of dismantling what little remains of their dream, beginning with the release of the other dolphins that have been under their control. On the conspiratorial yacht, David's lies about "Pa" being on the boat and extorting his cooperation by withholding Be exacerbate Fa's precocious adaptation to the manipulative dishonor of men. With Be in hand to deliver the "ball" (the bomb to be affixed by the dolphins to the hull of the President's yacht), Wallingford assembles a firing squad to eliminate Alpha, who escapes, returns to the Terrell Center, and, having been instructed by Terrell that the men are bad and that the "ball" is also bad, Fa is discharged to solve the problem. He intercepts and coaches Be to save herself by off-loading the bad "ball," and since the dolphins' only understanding of off-loading is the affixing of "ball" to "boat," they return the "ball" to its rightful owners. The conspirators are silenced; all that remains is to silence the conspiracy, and the resolution of *Dolphin* dramatizes this process as it is concluded on the mainland, the island, and in the sea. Much of this film has been preoccupied with communication, beginning with Terrell's opening presentation, directly to the camera, and foregrounded in the drama of interspecies linguistics. But nearly all that communication has been bound up in pretense and objectified performance. In this sense, the coda of *Dolphin* depicts a capitulation to those various social forces that have undermined genuine, free exchange. The last seven minutes are a series of variations on subsidence into silence, and *Dolphin*'s narrative arc thus traces, across its tidy 100-minute length, a similar trajectory to the ten-minute "conversation" Benjamin attempts with Mrs. Robinson in *The Graduate*, which begins in Benjamin's desperate effort to establish some meaningful connection with Mrs. Robinson beyond the purely carnal and ends in resigned defeat: "Let's not talk at all."

With the debris of the conspirator's yacht still smoking in the sea, O'Steen jump cuts to Elizabeth Wilson as Mrs. Rome, emerging from behind a closed door with a leather portfolio clamped to her breast. In a fluid, single take that suggests the efficiency with which the Foundation manages all its secrets, Fraker's camera tracks her through the Foundation's corridors, her grim face alternately lit by the false smiles she must offer to staff she passes. She enters DeMilo's corner office with its spectacular sea views and hands him a single-page memo he reads and promptly shreds—end of shot, end of the narrative's business with DeMilo and the Foundation: silence on the mainland. The form cut from the shredded memo to a shot of papers being incinerated in an old drum on the beach at the Terrell Center acknowledges that Terrell and company are just as anxious to leave no trace of the past and its illusions: silence on the island. The human animal can will silence and thus revise history, but dolphins cannot. Their understanding of the world is too literal; it wouldn't even occur to them that reality could be reconstituted by language and possessive control.

When they return, the dolphins offer their story without embroidery or abridgment, and without apology: the "ball" and David are "not." Terrell reels under the recognition that his prized pupils have become remorseless killers. As a plane begins to buzz the island, perhaps bringing retributive silence, Terrell embarks upon the capstone performance of his compromised relationship with the dolphins. He has taught Alpha "man is good," but he has awakened to the reality that, at best, his species has an ambiguous relationship to moral authority. To save the dolphins' lives, he must deny all—his love for them and his life's work. He begins sentimentally, with assurances of love that are ardently returned by Fa, prompting an exasperated Mahoney, agitated by the appearance of the plane, to exclaim, "Everybody loves everybody! Now let's get out of here!" Mahoney was unceremonious about his partner's death and unsentimental at the prospect of ruining the lives of DeMilo and his family; he's a man denatured by life in the shadows—not a "bad" man, but a man who understands life as permanently characterized by ideological "sides" and the objectifying struggle for power that such divisions imply. Terrell announces to Alpha his intention to abandon the great liminal experiment of the island: "Listen, Fa: Pa and Ma go to land. Fa and Be go to water. Fa not see man, not talk to man." In a moment of verbal irony, Fa summarizes: "Not talk." Terrell confirms: "Not talk. Swim, eat, play—not talk." His unsentimental rationality at the approach of the "bad" men appears to convince Alpha: "Fa go now," and they turn away. Yet Maggie cannot resist the moment's last opportunity for affection, prompting Terrell, back turned to the water, to snap: "Pa is *not*"—a profound, metaphoric admission of his failures. Terrell's utterance is the ultimate ironic use of language, negating himself via performance.

The staff disperses, literally running for cover. Jake and Maggie also move towards cover, obviously to give whoever is in the plane more difficulty in finding them, but the instinct seems more organically to derive from shame and a desire to hide themselves from Alpha, who has not yet retreated into resigned silence. He intrepidly calls to them from the sea. The two-shot close-up of the Terrells walking up the beach towards the tree line shows the sea and the Center behind them, a final reminder of the liminal dream they'd briefly, falsely conjured out of Jake's willingness to chase his own version of commodified success. "Don't turn around. Keep moving" are Jake's final words of existential wisdom in a narrative that began with his exhortation to "Imagine" and, at its midpoint, still found him marveling at "infinite possibilities." Eventually the strategy is a success, and Alpha stops calling and swims away: silence, finally, from the sea. The film's final, melancholy shot returns to the familiar compositional strategy of bisecting the Terrells via the physical bulk of their research center in the background. The shot, a half-minute take in which the only movement is of

Maggie's hair and the vegetation in the soft, tropical breeze, fades in the same fashion as the Terrell's dream. Their dream is "not."

An era of Nichols' life as a filmmaker ended with the completion of *The Day of the Dolphin*. It satisfied his contract with Joseph E. Levine and AVCO-Embassy, always for Nichols a profoundly uncomfortable fit.[4] *Dolphin* was also the last of his three collaborations with adapting screenwriter and close friend Buck Henry (who makes indelible small-part appearances in the other two films—as the intimidating Taft Hotel desk clerk in *The Graduate* and as Colonel Korn in *Catch-22*, but who only appears, uncredited, in an early audience scene in *Dolphin*, though he has a large, off-screen presence in the film because it is his voice, electronically treated, that serves for the dolphins[5]). Henry and Nichols both felt themselves to be under attack due to what they believed to be knee-jerk Hollywood mistrust of New York talent; Henry describes his thinking about the dissolution of the partnership with Nichols as both organic and an acquiescence ("Let them have other targets"[6]), though he's since gone on record as disapproving some of Nichols' subsequent, middlebrow filmmaking ambitions.[7] While Nichols would make one more film, *The Fortune*, before vanishing from feature-film production for nearly a decade, by the time he returned he was a transformed filmmaker, chastened by his early auteur celebrity (and its critical backlash).

Unlike the grotesqueries of perspective in *The Graduate* or the outsized, Vaudevillian madness of *Catch-22*, the narrative of *Dolphin* is an unabashed presentation of an imagined rather than reflected world, in which the dim possibility of rational, interspecies communication in human language is asserted as the accepted reality. What nonetheless makes this a Nichols film is how the science-fictive overlay reflects the usual dysfunction between people—friends, lovers, business associates—as a result of capitulation to the default power dynamics of majority culture. In his opening lecture, Jake Terrell the evolutionary scientist has posed his curiosity about "Why, after millions of years as a land animal, [the dolphin's] species was compelled—or decided—to return to the sea." Nichols the psychological realist has proposed an answer: the land may be too inhospitable a place, dominated as it is by that most predatory of all species, the ultra-territorial, hegemonic homo sapiens. We are everyone's worst enemy, including our own. Men like Wallingford are the monsters of objectification; men like DeMilo are their willing or helpless enablers and accomplices; men like Mahoney are reified cynics, aware of but numbly philosophical about their own denaturing. The Terrells are reified dreamers; awakened to the "disease" of the outside world they've never quite managed to escape. Jake's ambitions have ended at the sea, but in Maggie Terrell rather than in her brilliant, blustering, hubristic husband, Nichols made an early discovery of what would become his central narrative focus when he returned to filmmaking after his eight-year hiatus: the woman—or powerfully feminized man—resistant to the marginalizing assumptions of patriarchy. Nichols would explore this archetype in fascinating variations through, for example, Meryl Streep's tour de force portrayal in *Silkwood*, Harrison Ford as the rehabilitated title character in *Regarding Henry*, Streep again as Suzanne Vale in *Postcards from the Edge*, and the Pitt women (Streep and Mary-Louise Parker) and Jeffrey Wright as Belize in *Angels in America*, but Maggie Terrell is Nichols' first tentative step towards this new kind of hero.

7

"I must be dreaming"

The Fortune (1975)

Casting about for a next project after the critical drubbing of *The Day of the Dolphin*'s sober melodrama, his partnership with screenwriter Buck Henry at a cordial end, his three-film deal with Joseph Levine and AVCO-Embassy satisfied, Mike Nichols found himself reading a 325-page screenplay[1] by Carole Eastman, writing as Adrien Joyce, writer of *Five Easy Pieces* (Bob Rafelson, 1970), which earned her an Oscar nomination. Jack Nicholson, star of Rafelson's film and a familiar face to Nichols from *Carnal Knowledge*, handed him the script. Whether Nichols' films to that point were best categorized as comedy or drama may have been a point of contention; what few questioned was the essential gravity of purpose. Nichols was a serious filmmaker—seriously funny, as bespoke his roots in stand-up and Broadway comedy—but with art-house intentions. And on his lap landed a strangely massive yet slight, slapstick farce "without an ending, which I had to carve like a block of ice."[2] "According to Nichols," writes Peter Biskind, "he read half the script, given to him by Nicholson, on the first leg of a flight to Poland, and the second half sitting on his suitcase in the Warsaw airport waiting to get through customs. In those circumstances, the phone book would have been entertaining."[3] Not only was Nicholson interested, but so was another Hollywood A-list actor, Warren Beatty. While Nicholson was still a film away from his stratospheric performance as Randall P. McMurphy in *One Flew Over the Cuckoo's Nest* (Milos Forman, 1975), he certainly had box-office bona fides; Beatty was well into his second decade as one of Hollywood's biggest stars, and Nichols, although none of his post-*Graduate* films had approached that film's phenomenal success, remained a Hollywood prestige director. (Hollywood was about to change, however—*was* changing, given the dawn of the block-buster era, with two *Godfather* films already in the bank and *Jaws* set to launch a month after *The Fortune* would be released.) Hollywood wisdom suggested that the star power and Nichols' first film purely in his element (of comedy) gave *The Fortune* can't-miss credentials. And yet it did miss—and it served as Nichols' last word in Hollywood until he returned eight years later with Meryl Streep in *Silkwood*.

As if to make up for the slightness of the story, Nichols allows the three principals—Nicholson, Beatty, and a fresh-faced Stockard Channing in her film debut—to camp and vamp for the camera: shrill voices, disheveled hair and costumes, lots of fighting and throwing things. Nicholson actually licks his lips to show his libidinous desire. Set in the 1920s with the sexual revolution's nostalgic smirk at the Mann Act era, the film seems a naked overture to audiences that had swooned over costumed between-the-wars nostalgia in *Paper Moon* (Peter Bogdanovich, 1973) and *The Sting* (George Roy Hill, 1973), both of which were comic offspring of Beatty's own New Hollywood harbinger, *Bonnie and Clyde* (Arthur Penn, 1967), released in the same year as *The Graduate* and similarly a favorite of the counter-culture. As an allusion to Beatty's fame as the notorious hick-bankrobber-folk-hero, *The Fortune* is playful, and there are breathtaking moments, as when Channing's character Freddie emerges in flesh-colored satin lounging pajamas from a shipping trunk at the edge of the ocean: the image suggests a farcical reinvention of the Birth of Venus as imagined by a silent comedienne. Indeed, the film's nostalgia is less about the era itself than about the films produced in Hollywood during that era when silents were giving way to sound. When Beatty and Nicholson perform the near-impossible unloading and reloading of the aforementioned trunk atop a vertiginously steep bus in the middle of the night, the stunt is filmed in its entirety as trunk descends into Beatty's waiting arms; if Buster Keaton had accepted the trunk, he'd have wound up under or in it, to comic effect, but Beatty, gamely doing his own stunt, manages to look fragile and determined as the trunk descends. He just isn't terribly funny (his frenetic anxiety plays to much better comic effect in a contemporary film like *Shampoo* (Hal Ashby, 1975), released three months earlier. The inanities of the Adrien Joyce script are largely without clever subtext; the actors' broad gestures and frantic motion, the infectiously expressive ragtime soundtrack adapted by David Shire, and the sight gags and lyric tableaus would have rewarded a modified silent film (music but no dialogue) more than this film, where people talk a lot. The next year, Mel Brooks would release his *Silent Movie* parody, also keyed to the nostalgia wave. The next year would also be the first of Nichols' eight years of literal silence.

The Fortune is very much of its own times, referencing the Hollywood nostalgia boomlet of the 1970s. Beatty again plays a handsome, down-on-his-heels grifter with a movie-star jaw and a willingness to kill to get ahead in a world without even breaks. *Bonnie and Clyde* had briefly and powerfully meditated on the emptiness of the gang's pursuit of cash. Just after Bonnie has her brief, ominous meeting with her mother, treated by Penn with a surreal finality that suggests they're already in the afterlife, Bonnie (Faye Dunaway) asks Clyde, "What would you do if some miracle happened and we could get out of here tomorrow morning and start all over again, clean? No record, and nobody after us." Clyde meditates upon that a moment, then concludes, "Well, I guess I'd do it all different. First off, I wouldn't live in the same state where we pull our jobs ..." Clyde can imagine no other way to live his life; the Depression-era setting suggests none of them has the economic freedom to live as they choose. The film was contextualized by the counter-culture in the 1960s as a dramatization of American class struggle, and some of its more extreme fringe element saw in the Barrow gang's armed assertion of autonomy a manifesto for violent revolution. In casting Beatty in a return to a role as a dim sharpie of yesteryear, *The Fortune* is self-conscious in its projection of the dead end of scheming to circumvent entrenched systems of materialist greed. Nick is an even less likely candidate for nefarious success than Clyde Barrow.

The Fortune is the only one of Mike Nichols' 20 feature films not available on DVD. Is it fair that *The Fortune* should languish inaccessibly while, for instance, *What Planet Are You From?* remains available? Each signals the end of a phase of Nichols' career, which he would follow with a galvanizing reinvention of himself. Nichols told Mel Gussow that *The Fortune* was "'less black, less socially oriented' than his other comedies."[4] *The Fortune* nevertheless has themes consistent with Nichols' earlier, more serious films. The rogues played by Nicholson and Beatty commodify Channing's Freddie as part sex-toy, part golden-goose, with a trust fund worth marrying and later killing for. There is also a gender studies subtext of performed heterosexuality and repressed homoeroticism that is most overt when Channing dons some of Beatty's clothes and inflames Nicholson to seduction. The film's narrative logic, with its screwball lampooning of the noir inheritance caper, dooms the three of them to a life as an entrapped trio, though the film's light tone suggests that neither they nor we should get too worked up about their fate. Vincent Canby in the *New York Times* returned to his default position of admiration for Nichols' work, but the *Times* also published John Simon's savage dismissal. The film would mark Nichols' third box-office failure in the four films after the blockbuster success of *The Graduate*. Neither as bad as its initial failure would suggest nor as good as any of Nichols' previous films or its strong cast would promise, *The Fortune* is a meringue that draws to a close the decade-long banquet of Nichols' first phase as a filmmaker.

* * *

The plot of *The Fortune* is one of the simplest of Nichols' career; only *Wit*, a stage play adapted for HBO in 2001, may be simpler (though it is prodigiously more complex in its themes, language, and characterization). Frederica Quintessa Biggard, or Freddie (Stockard Channing), a Hudson Valley heiress, elopes with her boyfriend Nick (Warren Beatty), though because he has not yet extricated himself from his marriage to a woman we never meet, named Beatrice (who is apparently better-looking than Freddie), Nick has enlisted a friend in mutual need, Oscar (Jack Nicholson), to marry Freddie. Oscar is running from an incident as an embezzling bank teller. The necessity of marriage seems at first the exigency of love, then of criminal evasion (the Mann Act, as well as Oscar's thievery), and finally of a confidence game: to bilk Freddie of her fortune.

The three flee across the country by car, train, and plane to California, thence to settle as husband, wife, and curiously affectionate brother in a rented bungalow. Oscar becomes increasingly vocal about feeling unattended, a "fifth wheel." A prurient busybody, Mrs. Gould (Florence Stanley), serves as landlord and audience to their various role-plays. Nick quickly gets a job as a car salesman; Oscar and Freddie are each happy to laze about the bungalow all day, Oscar because he's a grifter conning the conman, and Freddie because she's never known a day in her life when she wasn't attended to, her whims swiftly, satisfyingly addressed. Oscar uses the gift of a baby chick and some sweet talk to seduce Freddie one lonely day, and when Nick threatens to throw him out, counters by reminding them he's the husband and, via the recent consummation of the marriage, has left "no loopholes." Freddie accuses them both of desiring only her money and vows to "give it all away," banishing them both from her bedroom.

The two men, sitting at a closed filling station in the middle of the night, idly daydream, and Oscar self-dramatically begins to speak of suicide: "I'd like to get a gun and just—bang!— solve all my problems." He has pointed the imaginary gun unambiguously at his own head, but Nick, in a moment of inspiration, twists the idea, pretending he has misunderstood: "You could do that to her?" And thus is hatched the idea of the film's second half: a series of elaborate attempts at an "accidental" death for Freddie, with one stipulation: "Nothing 'accidental' could happen before the birthday," when Freddie is old enough to inherit.

Nick poses as a fakir so they can buy a venomous rattlesnake up in the hills; they take it home and put it to the test with Freddie's chicken, now full-grown. In the morning, inevitably, the takers find they have been taken: the chicken paces over the dead snake's corpse. To the ever-interested Mrs. Gould, Nick confides a story of marital dissatisfaction between his "sister" and "brother-in-law"; they get Freddie drunk (an easy task, since a few sips always incapacitate her), and she passes out—but when they try to drown her in the court fountain

The Fortune, an antic farce set in the Mann Act era, was Mike Nichols' last film before an unplanned hiatus that stretched to nearly eight years (1975 to 1983). Nick (Warren Beatty, center) and Oscar (Jack Nicholson) plot for the inheritance of an airy heiress, Freddie (Stockard Channing). While at first their dim-witted plan is to get rich through marriage, they later turn to attempted murder—a strange conflation of tones that proved too much for audiences. Despite learning the truth about each other, the three default joylessly to their triangular arrangement, as if consigned by punitive sentence.

(really no more than an elaborate birdbath), she merely turns face-up out of harm's way and continues sleeping. Mrs. Gould finds her there, and the boys are back at square one.

This initiates their climactic, most elaborate caper: not wanting to waste Freddie's drunken stupor, they bundle her into a shipping trunk and escape to dump the trunk in deeper water and drown her. They blow a tire before they're able to get out of the neighborhood, and so they lug the trunk across town to Nick's car lot, where the only vehicle that will start is an enormous old bus. More slapstick ensues on a deserted old bridge; as they attempt to unload the trunk, first one car then another headed the opposite direction appear in the dead of night. Eventually a full-blown traffic jam has erupted. They reload the trunk, unsnarl the jam, and drive to the ocean. Startled by a car with lovers (Catlin Adams and a very young Christopher Guest) hoping for a quiet snuggle by the sea, Oscar gives the trunk a panicked shove, and the deed is done. They head home, but panic anew that Freddie's drowning inside a trunk may not match the facts of the distraught wife's suicide note they've typed out for her. They turn the bus around and head back to the coast.

Meanwhile, Freddie's trunk washes up at Long Beach, and she emerges, dazed and understandably confused by where she has awakened. A passing car driven by an eager-looking John the Barber (Tom Newman) happily shelters the drenched Venus. Nick and Oscar find the empty trunk and return home, madly inventing their story for the police. Oscar appears to be the potential weak link, worried he can not keep their story straight. Freddie and John, in an amorous clinch at his place, negotiate the collection of her things from the bungalow; she, too, is trying to think up a story she can tell, though hers is for John, not the law.

The police, led by Chief Detective Sergeant Jack Power (Richard Shull) show up at the bungalow. Before they can state their business (an inquiry about the missing bus Nick could easily explain away), Oscar has blurted enough sinister (if incoherent) details to get them carted off to the station where, finally with a rapt audience, he confesses all. The police return with Nick and Oscar in handcuffs to the bungalow to collect evidence; Freddie and John, retrieving her belongings, narrowly escape out the back door, but she remembers her chicken and returns. Oscar and a policeman spot her and the entire assembly pursues. Having apprehended her, Detective Power relates Oscar's confession to Freddie, and Freddie refuses to press charges: "I would never believe that in a million years." John and the police are dismissed; Freddie returns with the two boys to the bungalow, and as the film ends, Mrs. Gould edges toward the house, hoping for another scandalous glimpse inside.

* * *

Nichols' love of the long take immediately reappears in the opening shot of *The Fortune*, in which a Hudson Valley mansion in the pre-dawn gloaming sits stolidly as a tiny figure capers down the manicured path to the gate. This is Freddie, the Quintessa feminine napkins heiress, who has fallen under the sway of an older man, Nick, who waits in his running car just beyond the gate to sweep her off to the justice of the peace. A title card has set the scene for this first shot: "During the 1920's in the United States the law known as the Mann Act was much feared. It prohibited transporting a woman across state lines for immoral purposes. Because of the Mann Act, a man who wanted to run off with a woman and was unwilling—or unable—to marry her, would sometimes go to unusual lengths." The title card plays under a jaunty period orchestration of a 1927 pop song written by Al Dubin, Pat Flaherty, and Al Sherman, "I Must Be Dreaming." The song continues as the lovers embrace and Nick offers a flask, from which she accepts a generous measure of courage before smothering him in kisses. The song, with its female vocalist, instantly adheres to Freddie: she is the dreamer, breaking with the staid, patrician future that awaits her behind those gates to elope with a handsome older man.

The suggestion from the opening shot of the film that humans are dreamers is reminiscent of earlier Nichols conceits: the dawning day after the Walpurgisnacht nightmare of exorcised illusions in *Who's Afraid of Virginia Woolf?*, the dulled awakening of Benjamin and Elaine to the enormity of the consequences of that post-wedding bus ride into the future, Yossarian's fever-dream that comprises much of the associative narrative of *Catch-22*, the nubile ice-dancer gliding and twirling in and out of focus to the organ swirls of Jonathan's alienated lust in *Carnal Knowledge*, and the illusory paradise of the Terrell Center and its Edenic harmony of the species in *The Day of the Dolphin*. "What is strongest, by far, in Mike Nichols' movies," Jacob Brackman concludes, "is his reconstruction of waking nightmares people sometimes find themselves lost in."[5] In every case, except perhaps for *Catch-22*, when the absurdity of dreams and illusions is more than matched by the absurdity of systemic madness (what passes for "reality"), dreams in these narratives are typically blinding illusions that *captivate*, in the most literal and malignant sense of the term. Read this way, the typical Nichols narrative during his first phase offers a drama of dreamers called to awakening. In *The Graduate*, Benjamin is literally awakened by Elaine in his room in Berkeley. His response, "What's happening?" is far more existential than the more predictable "Who's there?" It's as if he's been waiting for something to happen, which in fact he has. Yet this is the moment when Benjamin and Elaine, faced with an opportunity to reject the lives they've been handed and to choose lives of their own making, default instead to children's games of playing "house," where all talk begins and ends with the conventional narrative of adult conformity: marriage—the unhappy trap of their parents' generation, and the one that, ironically, their fathers had conspired all summer to set into motion by conjuring a first date.

Endings are thus crucial for what they reveal about human responses to disillusionment. In *Virginia Woolf*, *Catch-22*, and *Dolphin*, awakening has hardly been a cause for celebration, and yet there are degrees of fragile hope (Brackman alludes to them as "reassurances"[6]) implied in their respective closing scenes: George and Martha tenderly bearing each other up into the light of day, Yossarian beating his small oar against the inexorable tides, Jake Terrell chastened and hunkering with Maggie in the shadows beyond the walls of his research center, his paradise lost. In all these films there is a rekindled awareness of what is real and how this differs from the dreams they've conjured against reality's harsh light, though the palpable distance settling between Jake and Maggie looks less like the solace of George and Martha than like the alienation of Benjamin and Elaine on the back bench of the Santa Barbara bus headed who knows where. None of these awakenings is unambiguously positive: the typical Nichols character in his first phase as a filmmaker "is trapped by his past culture. He cannot break out; he can only achieve understanding."[7] The ending of *Carnal Knowledge* is the most unequivocally dark of all these narratives: Jonathan is now paying to sustain the always-threatened illusion of his potency, paying even for the illusion of companionship. He is at his most diminished in this deliberate pretense. *The Fortune*, while a farce and thus without the responsibility to realism's gravitas, nonetheless presents a willed blindness that persists past many invitations to awaken. In a film where even attempted murder is played for slapstick laughs, the audience must do the work of tonal translation through much of the film, though the last shot, a mirror-reverse of the long opening take, with Freddie headed away from camera toward her new, much more modest residence, begins to suggest some of the melancholy of the choice she has made in remaining with Nick and Oscar. In the cartoon-like tone of *The Fortune*, we emerge from the film world saying these three deserve each other; we might have said something similar about George and Martha or Jake and Maggie in their subdued but unmistakable communion at the end of their respective films, but the statement would have had an entirely different meaning. Those couples have earned the privilege of communion's solace; Freddie, Nick, and Oscar, so constant in their inconstancy, are consigned to it in perpetuity. *The Fortune* thus offers deliberate self-delusion as a tool of farce rather than its more familiar use as harbinger of tragic alienation.

All three principal characters are subject to self-delusion that is socially constructed. Freddie has convinced herself Nick is genuinely in love with her (and that Oscar's protestations of love are also genuine), because she is as desirous of a "different" future than the one arranged by her parents as Benjamin Braddock is during his early talk with his father, while his graduation party thrums below them. However, in the very first shot of *The Fortune*, as she runs the length of the estate's ceremonial promenade to where Nick is waiting with the car running, we are the only ones watching. As the camera pans down to find her emerging from the estate's broad-gated entry to greet Nick, we see that he has been preoccupied with preening in the rearview mirror: this life-changing event of elopement means less to him than whether he has a strand or two of hair out of place. Before the credit sequence and its attendant song are ended, she also submits willingly to a more generalized pretense: Nick and Freddie pick up their "fifth wheel," Oscar, and the three of them proceed to the Justice of the Peace, where the camera pans and then zooms in a window to the perfunctory marriage ceremony of Freddie ... to Oscar. Comic tone is cemented by her bypassing the "groom" to give Nick, ostensibly a mere witness, a long soul-kiss. Avoiding Oscar's opportunist attempts to steal a kiss as part of the show they are performing, she accepts a glass of cheap champagne, takes a sip, and, having mixed this alcohol with whatever was in Nick's flask, collapses in a stupor as "I Must Be Dreaming" comes to its equally abrupt end. Freddie is a victim of her own imagination, quicker to invent fairy tales than even the grifters she's fallen in with. Nick can't marry her *yet*, because he's still married; the marriage to Oscar is a legal fiction designed to outwit the Mann Act authorities, but in fact, like many a duped and deluded lover before her, Freddie has outwitted herself, accepting Nick's promises that a divorce is coming and entangling herself in the ridiculous legalities of a marriage of convenience. The deeper delusion is not that Nick will keep his none-too-dependable word about leaving his wife; rather, it's her assumption that, as a person, she commands the essential attraction that holds Nick, when in fact her needy, narcissistic, mercurial personality and, to Nick's mind, her questionable pulchritude are no match for her trust fund.

On the train, Oscar gets his first good, daylight look at Freddie and observes in an aside to Nick that she's "not as good-looking as your wife," more indication that Nick's motives may be less than pure. Oscar goes on and on about liking Freddie more from the front than from the side; given Freddie's taste in clothes, which pursue the Flapper-era's gender-bending unisex designs until they reach their logical extreme with her donning knickers and vest, the references to views of Freddie have a homoerotic subtext. Her young girl's body is less obviously female viewed from the front than the side, where breasts less easily resolve against the chest's plain. Oscar and Nick have a never-spoken attraction to each other, which even Freddie once, in exasperation, notes, as a provocative stab at regaining their primary attention, before filing it away to ignore again: "You're several times more interested in each other than you are in me." It's only one of the culminating insights to which she gives voice during the cathartic melee in the bungalow at the film's midpoint, and she ignores all insight for the rest of the film, up to and including when the police review her self-delusions with her before she opts to return with the boys to the bungalow in the film's final shot.

Oscar's coveting of Nick's and Freddie's attention is given overt expression on the plane ride to Los Angeles, when his attempts at polite conversation are trumped by engine noise and the essential disinterest of his targets. His subsequent "wing-walk" garners plenty of attention from all concerned (the rest of the passengers collect autographs upon landing) but merits only a scolding from Nick—and not for concern about Oscar's safety: Nick reminds Oscar that they ought not to be calling undue attention to themselves. "All this whole trip you've been ignoring me," whines Oscar, like a neglected wife. "You should pay some attention to the fact that I'm here, too." Later, Oscar cultivates a pencil moustache like Nick's, which Nick instantly pegs as a "monkey-do" effort to emulate and subsume, even consume, Nick. Freddie is collateral damage in a sub-conscious impulse to sustain their life together. When they talk about what will happen to the inheritance, they discuss it in mutual terms, without talking of parting ways. She becomes their surrogate for each other. Confessing to Nick her having consummated the marriage to Oscar, Freddie dismissively refers to their coupling as "some stupid thing, I don't even know what—I was faced to the stupid wall"—a description of a non-traditional position that may have allowed Oscar the fantasy that he was actually with Nick, an interpretation further emphasized by her immediate observation that she feels herself to be depersonalized by their threesome in the men's greater interest in each other. Having met but failed to cross this forbidden social frontier, Nick and Oscar have negotiated an unspoken, even unconscious sublimation of desire within the object of Freddie, who at first misunderstands their preoccupation with each other on the car ride to the picnic ("Love has turned to hate!"), but by the time of the bungalow melee at the film's midpoint has recognized she, not Oscar, is the non-essential partner in their triangle.

The melee in the bungalow is valuable for articulating the reified insights they all happily ignore thereafter. The melee opens with Nick gone to work, again expectant (against all good reason) that a ne'er-do-well like Oscar will seek a job to contribute to household maintenance. Oscar is as happy to be Nick's kept man as Freddie is to be Nick's kept woman. Alone with Oscar, Freddie cedes to him the ascendant traditional-female role Nick has abetted and dresses in Nick's clothes as a knowing provocation to the latent homoerotic tastes of the boys, and as she reminisces about previous experiences in cross-dressing ("I did feel like a real individual"), inflames Oscar to their assignation with her facing the wall. Nichols further complicates the scenario by having the camera retreat outside during the consummation, there to huddle with Mrs. Gould on the side lawn between houses to listen vicariously. Mrs. Gould's canned proscription against Hollywood-style debauchery when this suspiciously arranged threesome first inquires about the bungalow has thus been revealed as a disingenuous pretense, while her apparent naivety in permitting two older men to move in with a young female is actually a voyeur's fond anticipation of vicarious trespass. When Nick comes home unexpectedly for lunch (while Mrs. Gould watches), Oscar pours himself out the bedroom window onto the turf at her feet, and she comments in satisfaction, "Are we practicing 'The Bandito' today?"—a comically prurient acknowledgment of performed sexplay. Soon she's listening to Nick and Freddie, never batting an eye at what otherwise would have been a breaking of one of the most powerful of social taboos. Mrs. Gould assumes that nothing anyone tells her as a covering backstory is true, which only inflames her appetite for what carnality may be hidden beneath the social pretense.

Nick finds an unfamiliar condom carton in the bed, which sends him accusingly out to the kitchen in search of Oscar. As their argument escalates, they are joined by Freddie, whose attempts to intervene in the central mano-a-mano dance of desire are thwarted. Her forlorn "You're several times more interested in each other than you are in me" is a calculated effort to refocus them on their ostensible heterosexual objective, but their preoccupation only intensifies. Oscar proudly confesses his sexual interest in Freddie that morning has been purely to preserve his claim to her fortune, and Nick's deepening rage has less to do with sympathetic insult to Freddie than with having been outwitted. A second time, Freddie attempts a forlorn observation in hopes of eliciting protested assurances: "I'm getting the funny feeling that money is all anybody cares about in this room." A second time she is correct, though as with her earlier gambit, her impure motive to manipulate with what she thinks are emotional incendiaries fails to have an effect on her intended targets or, indeed, on her own perspective. Freddie knows and speaks the truth, and it fails to set any of them free, because her intended audience is uninterested, and because she has only spoken the truth by accident, hoping to be coercive. She will never come closer to reified redemption than she does in these two utterances, and the boys never come close at all. Instead, they sublimate their desires in a kitchen-destroying series of violent clinches, their only socially sanctioned form of close contact.

Later, standing outside the locked bedroom where, within, Freddie lavishes fetishistic strokes upon the downy innocence of her cheeping chick, Nick and Oscar appear to be a pair of jilted lovers. They are exiled in the next shot to the darkness beyond the house, hanging out at the closed filling station, the composition a variation upon Edward Hopper paintings like *Gas*, in which a small outpost of civilized "order" appears to offer little security when seen against the massed volume of velvety darkness in the encroaching woods. Our social constructions are a tenuous hedge against the wildernesses beyond and within us, and the subsequent dialogue bears this out: the boys put Freddie in a conceptual strong box, grimly objectifying her as a means to the end of her fortune. Nick swiftly transforms Oscar's moment of grandstanding self-negation into a solution to their unspoken problem: sharing Freddie's money without Freddie, a happily ever after they could never articulate. "You wanna sleep on it?" ends the wee-hours daydream that has become, improbably, a plan, and with this verbal allusion to sleep, *The Fortune* cuts to a glittering curtain of beads encircling a ballroom dance floor where, in an intricate series of cuts reminiscent of the dancing triangle of Jonathan, Sandy, and Susan in *Carnal Knowledge*, Nick and Oscar take turns with Freddie dancing to a tango, an instrumental variation on the same song from the opening sequence, "I Must Be Dreaming." It's the birthday of Freddie's majority, a cause for celebration for all their various dreams—Nick and Oscar's dream of female-free riches; Freddie's dream of the competing affections of not one but two ardent men with whom to play house (as in the scene soon after when she attempts to cook them a disastrously unappetizing breakfast). All three are more comfortable with dreaming than with the reality of identity, desire, and consequence.

If *The Fortune* is ultimately a far simpler story than any of the five films preceding it in Nichols' first phase of his Hollywood career, this is because the hysterical key of the slapstick genre never allows the characters to explore nuance and dilemma that promote complexity. The plots and schemes that absorb the rest of the story reveal a variety of coping strategies for dissatisfaction with real experience. Nick is most tirelessly committed to pretense; though not especially bright or inventive (Beatty has invested half a career in playing characters whose furrowed brows hope, but fail, to conceal a lack of wits within), he struggles manfully toward the next improvised role he feels expected to play. Oscar is the exact opposite: wearied to enervation by keeping Nick's increasingly inane stories straight, he gratefully confesses whatever he can to anyone who will listen, though this too is a pretense, motivated not by genuine contrition but by the pleasure of being on a stage, playing a part he, not Nick, controls. Freddie's experiences in the film's second half are the most passive of the three; indeed, she is insensate for a large portion of the time, her objectified status not as sexual commodity but purely financial property comically symbolized by her literal containment within a box, the storage trunk. In her emergence, Venus-like, from the box, she is afforded the cinematic possibility of rebirth—who else could have put her in this box and set her adrift but Nick and Oscar? Yet she quickly squanders this insight on the first leering passerby, an otherwise anonymous "John" with whom she uses her sexuality as a commodities exchange for John's warm car and promise of genuine desire (he only commodifies her sexually, knowing nothing of her identity as the Quintessa heiress).

Planting the seeds of his latest ruse with Mrs. Gould, Nick is treated to this bit of homespun platitudinizing from his landlady and neighbor: "I don't know why, in such a glorious world as we've been provided with—birds, sunshine, of beautiful trees and flowers—and the radio—why people don't get on any better than they do." *The Fortune*, like earlier Nichols films, posits an essential answer to this question: because no one takes such a question seri-

ously, because no one *asks* such a question seriously. Mrs. Gould, with her elaborate orna-
mental birdbath and constant garden watering, is only interested in the glories of nature as
a pretext for the voyeuristic glimpses into forbidden windows that her gardening affords.
Whatever small insights her comment may contain, they are of no interest to her, and certainly of no interest to anyone in the adjacent bungalow. Like Freddie, who allows potential
insights to be obscured by trivializing desire for self-gratification, Mrs. Gould wouldn't know
nature if she stumbled over it. In her paean to the natural world, her culminating example
of the glories of nature is ... "the radio."

When Oscar and Nick return home empty-handed, having found the trunk but no
Freddie, Nick determines that they will wait a while, to "see what happens." After all the
contrivances to premeditate an "accident," they will finally allow nature to take its course.
Rehearsing their story, the "natural" quality of the story becomes of the highest priority:
"We show a natural concern as to her whereabouts?" "How does that sound, more natural?"
"To me, it's more natural." Yet nature has long since been preempted by the contrived "accident" of Freddie's disappearance, an assertion of control that itself has been lost in a pack
of misbegotten accidents and bungling. One of the insights that emerges from the first phase
of Nichols' career is that prevarication and particularly denial are what constitute the "natural" in the human condition. Freddie is drawn back to the bungalow not by a desire to
collect her things and start a new life but by an organic, instinctual awareness that any such
rebirth is not what she really wants, and that no new life actually awaits her. In this sense,
it's no accident that in the clockwork mousetrap of *The Fortune*'s plot, she has returned yet
again (after seemingly having evaded detection by the police or the boys in fetching her
belongings), this time to retrieve her chicken, that once-fragile symbol of her innocence,
now grown into a mature hen and stronger than a snake. John would merely have been
another variation on Nick and Oscar. She may as well stay as go.

The police bring along a photographer (John Fiedler) in tow, to "document" the "reality"
of their enforcement of laws that, as the plot's end reveals, have yet to be broken, thus demon-
strating their own complicity in performed "order." The natural state of the world is slapstick,
The Fortune argues. "Dear Nicky," we hear Chief Detective Sergeant Jack Power read out from
Freddie's letter to the assembled cops and crooks in the bungalow's living room, waiting for
yet another photo to be snapped, "this is to inform you that things have changed." This is the
lifeblood of drama, the recognition and reversal documented by Aristotle in the *Poetics*. But
among the dreamers in *The Fortune*, change is a mirage. Power offers Freddie a final chance
to heed her own statement, to reject her objecthood and strike off in some new direction,
in quest of the authentic. Nichols and his director of photography, John A. Alonzo, create
a subjective tracking shot through the archway of the bungalow development from Nick
and Oscar's perspective: they move toward Freddie, who holds in her hands her chicken—
and their fates. "We are not about to cause you harm," the police promise her. They manage
to seat her on the running board of their car; the chicken roams the street. "I must inform
you of a series of somewhat bizarre events," Power says, "attested to by a man who is apparently
your husband." By the time he's completed this sentence and launched upon the "facts" of
the case, the camera has tracked through the archway of the development where they've been
living and has begun its inexorable centering on Freddie; the opening version of "I Must Be
Dreaming" fades up into the soundtrack mix. As the camera's gaze is close enough now to
depict the nuances of Freddie's expression, we believe we understand her body language to
be rigid, dignified shock at all she's being asked to absorb—a reconfirmation of all she's
known since, at least, the inflammatory insights she'd voiced during the kitchen melee.

"Oh no," she finally says to the detective, her face in close-up tear-streaked and mascara-stained, "I would never believe that in a million years." There is barely contained outrage in Channing's delivery, a wonderfully ambiguous rendering of the line that can as easily imply her outrage is directed at the detective for pricking her bubble, at the boys for having disappointed her so profoundly, at herself for being so endlessly predisposed to "dreaming," or at a cosmos that only offers her a cavalcade of boy-men like Oscar, Nick, and John. Nichols has used this device of the recurrent non-diegetic song to propose, in formal terms, a confirmation of dramatic stasis: things have *not* changed. In *The Graduate*, Benjamin begins and ends the film in unmoving, passive conveyance toward an unknown future, while Simon and Garfunkel's "Sounds of Silence" serves as a kind of folk-rock Greek chorus commenting upon his alienation. Despite all his potential opportunities for insight and transformation, Benjamin remains rudderless, "drifting" from beginning to end. In *The Fortune*, Freddie runs toward the camera in a long take that seems to portend her active pursuit of destiny, while the song that plays ironically undercuts her dreamy romanticism (or at least does so in retrospect, as we come to understand the bill of goods Nick has sold her, and she has sold herself). Now, at film's end, she sits exhausted by her experience, allowing the camera (and Nick and Oscar) to advance upon her. The camera in close-up on Channing's face, as she turns to look up at Nick and Oscar standing over her, awaiting her judgment, is at the same angle Nichols and Robert Surtees used in *The Graduate* to shoot Elaine just before she yells "Ben!" at the church. Yet Freddie's outrage is more complete, and more debilitating, than Elaine's: Elaine still thinks she has a way out when she yells for Ben—at least until reality intrudes as they settle in on the back seat of the Santa Barbara bus. Freddie is merely going back to the bungalow with the boys.

The reverse shot from Freddie's subjective-camera perspective shows us Nick and Oscar, their awareness dawning that they are about to be uncuffed and set free, remanded to the custody of one another and of Freddie, and this is the point of the film's long, complicated final shot, which returns us to Freddie's upturned, stained, and bitterly resolved face, which we will not have an opportunity to see or read again. The camera pans 180 degrees, slowly enough to allow Nick and Oscar to collect her things from John's car and for Freddie to collect her chicken, to watch John drive away and to take in the mute stares of the neighbors raptly consuming the spectacle, and finally—as the lyrics to the song begin by asking, "Who am I to think that you would care for me the way you do?"—to see Nick, Oscar, and Freddie returning resignedly to the bungalow, their refuge and their condemnation, and several steps down in class from the estate from which she escaped in the opening shot. *They deserve each other*, a comic inversion of the romantic formula that lovers are *meant for each other*, is the subtext of the decidedly non-triumphant resolving shot. The camera lingers long after the three have quietly disappeared together inside the bungalow and the cops have vacated the scene, until we see that Mrs. Gould has edged, hose at the ready as covering pretense, back into position to see whatever lurid developments may next ensue.

The anti-climax of the film's ending matches the anti-climax of the film's reception. Paul D. Zimmerman writes that the film is doomed by its attempt to hybridize a bleak vision of human nature with a hyperbolic comic form like farce, proclaiming *The Fortune* "a comic 'Chinatown,' a moral wasteland of mean motives and faithless acts in which comedy cannot flourish."[8] It is Nichols' least known film, though enthusiasm for it emerges from powerful sources; the Coen Brothers, for instance, are long-time admirers.[9] While arguably a trifle in comparison to the films Nichols made before it, *The Fortune* is a playful deconstruction of the cultural appetite for nostalgia at the expense of examining our real lives. Taking a retrospective view of Nichols' career, Caryn James in the *New York Times* calls it Nichols' "last risky comedy," which "seems to cut close to our cultural dreams and failures."[10] Like Mrs. Gould, our culture in the late 1960s and early 1970s happily peered in at these sepia-toned vignettes from bygone eras (*The Godfather* saga, *The Sting*, *American Graffiti*, etc.) as ways of re-packaging a past that distracted us from the dizzying, revolutionary changes swirling in the present. Nichols retrenched after *The Fortune*, and, given the enormous achievement of *Silkwood*, the film with which he eventually returned eight years later, this seems to have been the right instinct at the right time. In *Silkwood*, Nichols juxtaposes the romanticized image of bygone America (the heartland imagery of the film's opening shots) with the economic realities of contemporary life, when the agrarian past has collapsed into the dreaming of an exploitative technological future.

8

"A moral imperative"

Silkwood (1983)

It is rare that a Hollywood director of Mike Nichols' stature should remain silent for more than eight years, as Nichols did between 1975, the year in which he released *The Fortune*, and 1983, when *Silkwood* appeared. It is rarer still that the silence is not the concentration of an artist upon some grand project that requires a longer gestation. Nichols had proven himself to be a quite dependable and efficient filmmaker, delivering six films in nine years—a steady rate of production that would cheer any executive producer. While Nichols was away, he was hardly inactive—just not making films. "Of course, I've had slumps in my work," he says, "but at the time, I just couldn't find a movie I wanted to do."[1] Nichols worked with Neil Simon on a script called *Bogart Slept Here* and actually commenced a first week of shooting with Robert De Niro in the lead, but he and Warner Bros. mutually agreed to pull the plug, and Simon later revised the script into *The Goodbye Girl*. Nichols re-grounded himself in Broadway, directing George C. Scott in Chekhov's *Uncle Vanya*, debuting David Rabe's Vietnam drama *Streamers* (later adapted for the screen by Robert Altman), and making a mint as a producer of the blockbuster musical, *Annie*. He also dabbled in television production (ABC's drama *Family*) and made a feature-length film recording of Gilda Radner's live stage show, released in 1980. While he was away, however, Hollywood changed irrevocably. *The Fortune* was released the same year that Steven Spielberg made his first fortune, with *Jaws*; Spielberg's friend George Lucas inadvertently introduced a new corporate franchise model two years later with *Star Wars* (1977), and Hollywood has been unrepentantly chasing the big blockbusters ever since. His accidental mega-success with *The Graduate* notwithstanding, Nichols is not a blockbuster director. His themes are too relentlessly "adult," his characters talk a great deal (except when, thematically, they don't), and "action" in the Hollywood-generic sense is something that often takes place off-screen, when it takes place at all. During Nichols' eight-year hiatus from Hollywood, the concept of the A-list director shifted in meaningful ways. He was an A-list director before his hiatus, and he was again after, but by then there was an A-plus list for the likes of Spielberg and Lucas (and later filmmakers like Robert Zemeckis and James Cameron). Nichols took his post-*Graduate* cache and moved temporarily to Mexico to film a literary phenomenon. More than his eight years away in the late 1970s and early 1980s, his year away on location south of the border, making a film no one could warm to, shifted Nichols' place in Hollywood.

Silkwood serves as an apt transition from Nichols' first phase to the much longer, entrenched second phase. *Silkwood* is as much a chamber drama as *Carnal Knowledge* or *Who's Afraid of Virginia Woolf?* Most of *Silkwood*'s drama unfolds in a shotgun house in

Oklahoma and a couple of rooms of a nuclear production facility. *Silkwood* is about the evolution of its title character. Leonard Quart and Albert Auster argue "the film spends more time, using long takes and medium two-shots, to capture atmospheric detail—the clutter of her collapsing house—and realistically limn her difficult relationships [...] than in conveying the machinations of the nuclear power industry."[2]

Silkwood is a major film by a different filmmaker than the celebrity auteur of 1960s Hollywood. While the great films of Nichols' first phase as a director, from *Virginia Woolf* through *Carnal Knowledge*, are "idea" films, making grand statements about the culture, *Silkwood* introduces a filmmaker intent upon character, in which the particular ills or flaws in the culture recede from subject to setting. *Silkwood*'s story happens to take place within the world of nuclear power administration and accountability. Yet it is not an "idea" film, about the ethics of nuclear power, as *The Graduate*, for instance, was an "idea" film about what Lyndon Johnson called, in his "Great Society" speech, "soulless wealth," and as *Catch-22* was an "idea" film about the commodification of the enlisted man within the military-industrial complex. Nichols returned to filmmaking after losing his way by reinventing himself based on the insights he'd had about himself as an artist while making *Catch-22*. All the grand, sweeping statements about the Generation Gap (*The Graduate*) and The War (*Catch-22*) and the Sexual Revolution (*Carnal Knowledge*) and Governmental Abuses of Power (*The Day of the Dolphin*) that precede *Silkwood* in Nichols' oeuvre would suggest that a film chronicling the life and times of a nuclear-power industry whistle blower would be a referendum on the dangers of nuclear energy. Lee Hill writes, "Although *Silkwood* was an ostensibly '60s film dealing with corporate corruption, political activism, class and gender, the film was, at its core, a character study about a woman and her friendships."[3] Nora Ephron and Alice Arlen's screenplay conveys a cautionary sobriety about this enormous issue, yet (as is typical of Ephron's work in the first of two consecutive collaborations with Nichols as she moved towards directing her own films) the narrative focus is centered upon the personal, with whatever political resonances emerging as a consequence of this focus. *Silkwood*'s focus is on the title character, Karen Silkwood (Meryl Streep, in the first of her four collaborations with Nichols) awakening slowly to her reified status as a human resource of the nuclear-power industry, a resource capable of absorbing "permissible" amounts of radioactive contagion per industry regulations. "'As I began to talk to Nora and Alice about it,'" says Nichols, "'I got interested in it being about an awakening and discovered that it was my own awakening [as an artist]'"[4]

The film's subject is not about firmer nuclear regulation but feminist empowerment. Although a significantly better and more substantial film than Nichols' next release, *Heartburn* (1986), which was also a collaboration with Ephron and Streep, *Silkwood* is nonetheless in important ways the same film: the narrative of a callow woman's dawning recognition that the world rewards callowness and disavows the assertion of personal and political responsibility. What makes the difference between the two films is ultimately tonal: *Silkwood* takes the extra time to know all its main characters as more than mere types, embracing the languorous Okie pace in the long takes and slow burbling of the banjo over Georges Delerue's orchestral score. Nichols was so committed to the storytelling formula he embarked upon in his second career phase with *Silkwood* that he moved from *Heartburn* to other films—*Biloxi Blues* (1988), *Working Girl* (1988), *Regarding Henry* (1991), *The Birdcage* (1996), and *Primary Colors* (1998)—that feature characters wrestling with reified awareness and the difficult choices that result either in characters' numbed conformity or reactive transformation.

Karen Silkwood's story takes a different form than any of Nichols' previous films, because it has a definitive biographical arc, up to and including her suspicious death.[5] Benjamin and Elaine are objects of ironic incredulity at the end of *The Graduate*, in a different key than Freddie and the boys as *The Fortune* closes; George and Martha in *Virginia Woolf* carry themselves with chastened, tragic dignity as they confront their disillusionment, while Jake Terrell sits with Maggie in exiled shame at the end of *Dolphin*, knowing he should have listened to her. Jonathan in *Carnal Knowledge* festers in a hell of reflexive self-defense; Yossarian is a holy fool, beating a retreat from the absurdity of convention. In the context of the growing spectrum of Nichols' characters and their responses to reified reality, Karen Silkwood is Nichols' first martyred saint of enlightenment. Maggie Terrell is a harbinger of this new kind of Nichols character, the humble vessel of moral authority whom the other characters ignore at everyone's peril, including their own. What vests Karen with authority for an anti-authoritarian visionary like Nichols is how relatively little of the time Karen spends in certitude about the authority the film confers upon her (beginning with its title). "It is that complexity," writes Tom Doherty, "the refusal to hew to a party line, that makes *Silkwood* stand apart from so many ideologically correct, emotionally dry films."[6] Karen remains the prey of reifying impulses throughout the film, fishing for commodifying sexual reassurances of her value from nearly every man with whom she has meaningful contact, even as she frequently discounts or ignores the frustrated sexual longing of her friend and housemate Dolly (Cher, in an Oscar-nominated performance). In narrative terms, Karen's politicized disappearance affords her an eloquence and nobility she could never have consistently sustained in additional decades of life (had she lived that long with her "internal contagion").

Silkwood thus shares an essential narrative shape with *Catch-22*: the common person at war—direct, logical odds—with the prevailing culture. But while *Catch-22* delivers its narrative via surrealistic, slapstick farce, *Silkwood* presents a strange and affecting hybrid of gentle, even lyrical realism (in its domestic sub-plots) juxtaposed to a thriller formula (in its evocation of Karen's growing understanding of the Kerr McGee operation and her fact-finding about the nuclear-power industry). Nichols as a filmmaker in his first phase did not present his films in a realist's style. Taking expressionist cues from the suburban-campus "exorcism" at the climax of Edward Albee's great play, Nichols launched a vernacular with roots in the comic lampooning used by traditional Hollywood comedy and the art-house formalism of European masters like Bergman, Fellini, and Antonioni: each tradition was in its own way a stylized response to and fun-house reflection of reality. In his first phase, Nichols could accurately be called a Hollywood Expressionist, in the tradition of such eminences as Preston Sturges and especially Billy Wilder, two social satirists working in the heart of Hollywood in consecutive eras. Neither Sturges nor Wilder made films like *Silkwood*—earnest, even pious character study. Nor did Nichols himself turn exclusively to such films—but the shift away from formal expressionism and the assertion of a clearer, less ambiguous moral resolution in some of his films would provide a contrast to the murky dystopian sensibility of the early films, in which heroes are hard to find and even harder to hold on to.

* * *

The pastoral opening image of *Silkwood* belongs to a different film than the one that ensues, which is the point: in its long, slow duration before we eventually meet the film's main characters, the opening (with Georges Delerue's soundtrack score) conveys a melancholic elegy for America's agrarian past. This is Oklahoma, but it could be Kansas, or Missouri, or Iowa, or Indiana, or Ohio. In its unassuming way, it's an image that might recall other solitary houses in American iconography: the isolated Victorian farmhouses in Hopper or Wyeth canvases, the Clutter house on the Kansas prairie in Richard Brooks' *In Cold Blood* (1967) or the solitary mansions in George Stevens' *Giant* (1956) or Terrence Malick's *Days of Heaven* (1978). Yet this house is less gothic in its isolation than merely modest, a house that once overlooked a farm but no longer does. Three industrial migrant workers live here, their roots as tenuous as their profession—they assist in the production of nuclear energy. The view is from down a road very much like the one we see Karen Silkwood travel in the film's final shot, the view in her rear-view mirror, as it were: a suitable coda on a narrative and a way of life. This bucolic vista is a romantic illusion, a nostalgic evocation of a time when individuals might negotiate a life on their own terms in relationship to the natural world, small prairie communities of such individuals knitting themselves together with crops and livestock and family Bibles. The people who live in this house now and in other such houses along these rural routes come across the miles to the same destination, the true civic center of their economic well being, and in the sequence of shots from which that first pastoral image proceeds, we travel that route in company with a humble economy car that ultimately reaches its destination when it turns in at the drive marked by the "Kerr McGee Corporation's CIMARRON FACILITY Nuclear Division" sign. The first three words are relatively small on the sign, the final two relatively *microscopic*. What the sign celebrates is its greater locality, and thus the neighbors it welcomes to work every day. It is window-dressing against the reality of what its neighbors—the workforce of the Kerr McGee plant—encounter. They have been encouraged by Kerr McGee to take their lives in their hands for the good of their own household solvency and the economic future of their hometown.

When we first meet her, Karen Silkwood is hardly an admirable subject. Hoping to find someone to take an approaching weekend shift to free her for a trip to see her children in the neighboring state of Texas, she whines at and cajoles her co-workers to take her shift. There is an easy camaraderie she hopes to exploit—salt-of-the-earth types she buzzes among in the workroom and lunchroom without settling anywhere for long. We overhear flirtations, gossip, and, as a kind of sub-conscious reflection of their unspoken professional uneasiness, their shared discussions of bodily distresses, ailments, and oddities. We learn that, in Karen's workroom, they mix uranium and plutonium by hand in the "proper ratios," sifting for "impurities." We watch in horror as Karen, blowing bubble gum, has to call on Wesley (David Straithairn) to peel the gum off her face with a hand he's just removed from a secured glove; he pops part of the gum into her mouth, the rest (to general merriment) into his own, casual and unconcerned with shared contagions; the risks of what they are doing are purely abstract to most of them. We meet Thelma, a middle-aged woman wearing a very obvious wig, who worries that her daughter will have a cancer relapse. Her daughter is likely Karen's age. At lunch, we see that Karen is "with" Drew (as much as she's with anyone), and overhear his conversation about a "contaminated truck." While the others lament that the truck's operators "didn't monitor" for radiation exposure, Karen can only bemoan her own inconvenience about not finding a substitute for the weekend shift.

Karen in the film's opening scenes is as self-interested and myopic as the industry that employs her. When a safety drill ensues, reminding them to review protocols for emergencies, the company overrides the standard precaution, and Morgan (Fred Ward) muses, "Can't do the drill—might stop production for ten minutes." No one seems terribly perturbed at this cavalier approach the facility takes to its human resources, but Karen's solipsism is grotesquely distended: she's in tears with the frustration that the alarm has not signaled a genuine contamination. "If it had been the real thing," she moans, "they woulda shut down the plant. I coulda had the whole weekend." Karen's bind is economic, but in her defense, she has learned to sell herself wholesale because of Kerr McGee's methods. If Karen simply asks for a weekend off, she will be interpreted as having lost interest in her employment and will therefore be replaced by another prospective worker lined up for the next available job. In the limited options of a grateful local economy, Kerr McGee has assumed an enormous and spiritually devastating measure of control over the formation of individual identity. Needing jobs to live, the workers at Kerr McGee refuse to look at the prospects they face in juggling uranium and plutonium full-time. *Silkwood* presents a rural America in which people are dying for work.

Karen manages to extract from her friend Gilda a promise to take her shift; later that night, she comes out of the plant to her car but, distracted by noise and light at the other end of the parking lot, peers through chain-link fencing at a tractor-trailer being chopped down into parts. She appears to make no connection to what she'd overheard her own boyfriend discussing with friends that day. Making innocuous inquiry, she's shooed by a man on the other side of the fence, and she moves docilely away. There is no anxiety in Karen, no sense that she has been manipulated by socio-economic circumstance into her current bind. She seems unable to think causally about anything further removed in future time than "the weekend"—she can sense no irony, for instance, in lighting a long succession of cigarettes throughout her days, and certainly senses no irony in her vain "hope" to see the facility's work stopped by radiation poisoning. Her self-interest is nearly total, but her self-value all but non-existent.

The trip to see her children intensifies this portrait of Karen, but it also clarifies the quality of comradeship she shares with Drew and Dolly, both of whom are, in their own ways, more admirable than Karen as the narrative begins and thus, as we warm to the narrative through them, reflect well on Karen herself. They care for her more than she seems to care for herself—there must be something more to Karen than we have yet seen. Even among the powerless, Karen is particularly disenfranchised: arriving at her common-law ex-husband's house in Texas, she finds that he has made alternate plans for the children and she can only take them to lunch. The rainy drive back to Oklahoma introduces the easy camaraderie of their threesome: Drew pensively plucking at the banjo Delerue has woven into the soundtrack, Dolly quietly faithful in the back seat, and Karen singing "Amazing Grace" as a group lullaby. Nichols revisits Karen's plaintive rendition at film's end. The encore would have resonance enough simply by virtue of its placement (and Streep's performance), yet we're further cued to its significance as testimonial by a variation in its end lines: "was blind, but now I see," the more familiar John Newton lyric, appears as usual, but then is replaced by "was bound, but now I'm free." In the context of the ruined trip to Texas, the variation is an unintentional critique of her haplessness as a mother. In self-pitying effusion, she says of her children: "I had 'em in the car. I could just've headed straight for Oklahoma." Drew's response is not so much cruel as clear-headed: "What would you have done with 'em?" In fact, the children probably *are* better off in the hands of Linda (Tess Harper), who seems to have more compassion for the kids *and* Karen than Karen herself. Karen has no innate instinct for responsibility (it is the basis of her transformation in the film). The best she can muster is a suspicion that she ought, as an adult, to possess such an instinct.

The way Karen adopts an air of caring for Thelma suggests her first halting attempts at trying on responsibility. Of all the people with whom Karen works, Thelma with her aggressively unfashionable eyeglasses and ungainly wigs and plaintive, rasping voice of woe is a kind of signifier for the life they're all leading—or, more aptly, where life is leading them. Karen's concern remains an abstraction until the day Thelma is "cooked" and given a thorough scouring to eliminate her external contamination by radiation, yet Karen's only wisdom is to tell Thelma, "Honey, try not to cry—salt's gonna make it worse." Karen comes home after Thelma's ordeal and takes her latent fear and frustration out on Dolly and Drew: suddenly the careless, frat-house squalor of ripening leftovers in the refrigerator and scattered marijuana seeds on the table feels to her like a creeping contagion, and the c-word escapes into open air: "If anybody around here's going to get cancer, we're all gonna get cancer." For the first time, Karen has broached the unspoken subject of the danger they all confront each day, but Drew, albeit gently, provides her his typical reality check: You just waking up to this? What do you think we're working with over there, puffed wheat?" Like a scolded child, she mutters, "I was just asking a question," and Drew rejoins, "If you're really worried about it, stop smoking."

At this point in the narrative, Drew is awake to the reality of their lives in ways Karen will apprehend only in stages, yet Drew's vision will prove far more limited than Karen's. He can't think beyond the union of Karen and Drew. (His Confederate flag flown large above the bed is an indirect comment on his position regarding larger Unions, of which he wants no part.) Meanwhile, Karen comes to believe in a Union that encompasses the welfare of all. This includes the unfortunate likes of Thelma, but Karen's "Union" unconsciously took in its very first member when Karen adopted Dolly, whose sexual orientation would make her a pariah in small-town America (and even a figure of patronizing fun to Drew and Karen, who genuinely love Dolly, when Dolly brings Angela back to the house for the first time and Drew and Karen can hear faintly through the walls the sounds of their lovemaking). In the scene where Karen and Drew sit on the porch step and Drew chides Karen's uncritical perspective on the health risks of her job and smoking habit, Nichols makes sure we see Dolly as odd woman out when Drew and Karen retire to their sexual consolations. Dolly remains in moody isolation, and when Karen apologizes for the previous night's churlishness about Dolly's refrigerated mystery leftovers, the two women engage in an emotional tug-of-war (made tangible by the belt of Karen's bathrobe) over the gulf in their affections. If we'd had any doubts, the scene dispels them: Dolly has long carried an unrequited torch for Karen, and while Karen could be accused of leading Dolly on (and her immature craving for attention is probably one small subconscious reason to keep Dolly around), the scene ultimately plays out as Karen's unwillingness to discard Dolly simply because they are fundamentally unlike. What Karen can return are Dolly's loyal feelings; in their own way, they exchange avowals of love that not even Drew full comprehends. Dolly's and Drew's love for Karen does her credit, but Karen's love for them does her good. Her kindness to Dolly offers seeds for future redemptive transformation.

The discussion with Drew—his reference to her "waking up," in particular—cues a new Karen at work. She chides herself for not remembering the importance of a nasal smear for Thelma, and loudly reminds Thelma in the Kerr McGee parking lot to insist upon this examination. Hurley approaches when Karen, with unintentionally comic timing, intones her paranoid's warning, "there's a lot of liars around here." Yet Karen remains childishly careless at work. Nichols and O'Steen cut to a shot of a birthday cake for Gilda, displayed on a rolling waste barrel labeled, "Contaminated Material." Hurley chides them less for breaching the workroom with food (that's on them to protect themselves) than for stealing company time on a project three months and a million dollars behind schedule, and in their haste to get back to work, cake spills on the floor. Hurley orders them to clean up after shift, but Karen impetuously picks up a hunk and stuffs it into Gilda's mouth. It's during the post-shift cleanup that Karen gets to experience the intensity of contamination and its scouring aftermath, initiating both her and us into the gravity of the plant. Casually, almost flippantly waving her limbs before the monitors, she sets off the alarms, and then curls herself tightly against the wall to await the cleanup crew and its total violation.

An ironic contrast emerges in the film between the treatment of nudity on Karen's own terms and on company terms. With Drew in her own bedroom, Karen is comfortable in her own skin (abetted by Drew's adoration). Yet Karen is aware of her objecthood beyond the intimate poses she strikes for Drew. Enraged by the facility-wide assumption that she deliberately contaminated the plant to get out of work (an unjustified charge on its face since she'd wheedled Gilda into substituting for her), Karen storms through the plant to find Drew and complain. She finds him in a room crawling with men, including Quincy Bissell (Henderson Forsythe), head of the fledgling Union initiative at the plant; Curtis (J. C. Quinn), Gilda's overbearing husband; and Zachary (Norm Colvin). Karen stands out in this workroom not only because of her righteous agitation but also by gender. Zachary's undisguised ogling adds to Karen's agitation as she vents her frustration at Drew, with Quincy on a raised platform a story over her head. Drew and Quincy good-naturedly peer down at Karen, ribbing her, and Quincy takes the opportunity to interject traditional Union rhetoric: "The company's gotta blame somebody—otherwise it's *their* fault." The camera angles—up on Drew and Quincy and down on Karen—reinforce her undeserving victimhood and imply the gendered assumptions of their social environment. With an eyeline shot reestablished on her, Karen targets Zachary: "What're you lookin' at, Zachary?" She minces around him, posing, then flashes him by tearing open her coverall to expose a breast. "Get lost, okay?" she says, and Zachary flees. "Hey, Karen," Quincy deadpans, "you ever thought about going into politics?"

The gesture reveals Karen's awareness of a socially derived power she may access at will (and at peril for her self-worth). Her objectification as a vessel of desire is something she uses at various times in the film—to cast a spell on Winston (Craig T. Nelson), to be noticed by Paul Stone (Ron Silver)—but it is, of course, a fleeting power that will erode as swiftly as her physical youth and beauty. In this particular case, it is power wielded expressly in a moment of powerlessness—a cynical reduction of her person to manipulative weapon for punishing someone even more vulnerable at that moment than herself: dim-witted, idly lusting Zachary. The introduction of nudity as another strategy in the filmmaker's rhetorical toolkit of options also indicates the substantial ways Hollywood had changed since Nichols began making films. Perhaps, during their bitter "conversation" at the Taft Hotel, Benjamin and Mrs. Robinson's brief exposure of one another's vulnerabilities might have been most accurately represented by physically exposing the actors; 1967 standards of practice instead mandated that their emotional exposure be depicted using measured camera placement and framing, judicious cutting, and a thin bed sheet. Certainly when Mrs. Robinson forbids Benjamin to see Elaine and he rips the sheet out of her hands and down to the foot of the bed, this moment of exposure would have found an apt analogy in the shock of Anne Bancroft's nudity. Karen's willful self-exposure in a workroom full of men signals both her complicit objecthood and her awareness of (and submerged rage at) her objectification—two vital conditions of reification—she has yet fully to grasp. By the end of the film, she has awakened to reification's insight, and this moment of self-exposed exploitation with Zachary is echoed in the film's closing scene, when Karen, defiantly headed (against Drew's stated will) to her interview with the *New York Times* reporter, "flashes" Drew not skin but a reminder of that earlier exposure. She is simultaneously playful with her lover and purposeful in referencing a former self; she references who she was and who she is from a self-aware position of redeemed identity and faith in individual agency. The first gesture, an act of aggression aimed at Zachary but intended for hegemony, reveals nothing but an awareness that manipulation is our common currency, and she will trade on her own sexual desirability as the only capital she has. The second gesture reveals much more: the tenderness she feels about the secret history she and Drew share, her awareness of who she once was (someone who could prey upon a sorry little man like Zachary as payback for her own victimhood), an acknowledgement of the more meaningful exposures she's since come to embrace as a part of her responsibility.

Ephron and Arlen cleverly use Quincy's wisecrack about politics to foreshadow this last and most meaningful dimension of the recapitulated gesture—her acknowledgement of her politicized consciousness about and obligation to the truth of her experience. Karen has, of course, never considered politics for a moment (and if she had, would have assumed it was a right of patriarchy not open to her), but she is on her way to being politicized by her experience. Until now, that experience has been abstract: an uncomprehending glimpse of a "hot" truck being buried, a distant, pitying glimpse through glass of Thelma's old body being scraped clean of its contamination. It is significant that, while Thelma's body is exposed to the camera's eye, Karen's body in the showers is not. The violation is expressed instead via the shriek of the alarm and the close-up of her face pressed against the streaming tiled wall. We are not afforded a clinical medium shot of Karen, as Karen (and thus we) saw Thelma. The violation is immediate, total, *personal*. Delerue's score, necessarily rendered beneath the insistent rhythm of the alarm, is merely a handful of chords, played by low strings, and they resolve at the end of the shower scene in the eerily reminiscent manner of Bernard Herrmann's bass strings at the end of the most famous (and harrowing) of all shower scenes in film history, when Marion Crane (Janet Leigh) is hacked to death by "Mother" in Alfred Hitchcock's *Psycho* (1960). The tight close-up of Karen's face against the tile, enduring the assault, is another near-quote from the Hitchcock classic. While in *Psycho* the symbolism of "cleansing" fails to provide any solace against the random eruption of madness, the madness in *Silkwood* is anything but random: needy communities clamor for the privilege of endangering themselves in plants like Kerr McGee. Marion's "cleansing" produces the opposite effect: she's nothing but waste when the shower is done, her lifeblood swirling down the drain, her remains fit only to be slid into the swamp. But Karen's "cleansing" is more ambiguous. She is pronounced "clean" at its end, but she becomes increasingly skeptical about whether such regimens have any effect when countering devastating nuclear potency. The industry has scoured her into experience. If there is indisputable cleansing in this scene (and the two other, equally painful assaults she endures in the Kerr McGee showers), it is the scouring of illusion from her mind about whether the work they are performing is dangerous and whether those who administer the industry are to be trusted—or even whether they are competent. "I'm supposed to pee in it at home," she says, summarizing the company physician's instructions about the weekly urinalysis kits she's being handed. The kits will monitor whether she has internal contamination, but if a test yields a positive result, having conducted the test at home will confirm that she has spread the contagion beyond the "secure" boundaries of the facility.

Yet Ephron and Arlen's screenplay takes pains to remind us of the socio-economic bind of these rural Oklahomans dependent upon the "largesse" of the company to sustain these

Karen Silkwood (Meryl Streep, in the first of her four Nichols films) passes through radiation sensors at the front door of the Kerr McGee nuclear production plant. Karen has set off the detectors before, upon exit, and been subjected to a corrosive "cleaning" regimen; now she is stopped on her way in, carrying toxins that endanger the industry. The detection and cleaning scenes in *Silkwood* use visual and sonic tropes from horror, particularly *Psycho* (Hitchcock, 1960) to underscore Karen's victimhood—which she manages to transcend via reified "awakening" (as Nichols calls it) about herself and her world.

compromised homes they've made on the poor prairie. At home after her first ordeal in the Kerr McGee showers, we glimpse Karen after a very different kind of shower, daubing herself with lotions to heal the abrasions to her skin. She's talking with Drew, and the subject is reduced opportunity, the only kind they've ever known. "I wish I could take better care of you," he says. The comment reflects his reified assumptions of his role as the patriarchal master, compromised by economic vicissitudes. Karen reminisces about her mother's having urged home-economics classes upon her to "meet some nice boy," to package herself for social consumption as a marriageable commodity. But Karen says she defied her mother to take "science," although her motive was far from intellectual advancement (with its consequent hope of social advancement). She simply had a more practical understanding of where the boys are, a more practical approach to marketing herself. The feminist vision of Karen Silkwood's story as rendered by Nichols comes in the immediately succeeding sequence of scenes, in which Karen becomes politicized: reviewing Union handouts, asking questions at her new facility posting in the metallography workroom (using her flirtations with Winston not to build status or esteem but to gather information), and volunteering at the next Union meeting. Drew wishes he could take better care of her, but this is, first and foremost, Karen's own responsibility, and she has begun to assume it.

Ephron and Arlen introduce a sub-plot nearly an hour into the film involving Angela, the mortuary beautician Dolly brings into their shared home and into her bed. The sub-plot offers the filmmakers an opportunity to explore Karen's (and Drew's) tolerance while at the same time giving Angela an outspoken outsider's perspective on the predicament of Kerr McGee employees. "Karen, you ever been downtown?" she says, while practicing her trade on Dolly's face, covering Cher's olive complexion in a deathly pallor. "There are two big streets. One's called Kerr, and one's called McGee, and that's how I see it. They own the state, they own everybody in this state, and they own practically everybody I work on." It's as bald a statement of the reified system of socio-economic determinism as the film will allow any of its characters, who typically are less verbal, and terrified to utter the truth. An awkward comic moment ensues when Drew, having had a mini-tantrum about Karen's increasing activism, describes Angela's make-up job on Dolly as making her look like a "corpse," then learns that Angela works for Thayer's Funeral Home. "You know, Drew," she says, "I can always tell when a dead person I beautify worked for Kerr McGee, because they all look like they died before they died." The comment seems to have little effect on its intended target, but it weighs on Karen, and she says so. It's Drew's worst moment in the film; even when he leaves Karen later, his motive is at least partially to leave behind their dangerous work environment. But his other motive, and the only force driving his actions in the current moment, is his profound sense of threat at Karen's awakening to political responsibility. He reduces himself to what he almost never is elsewhere in the film: a thick-headed redneck lout. Bare-chested and covered in car grease, standing at the refrigerator drinking the last beer, he hears Karen shifting gears into her newly familiar activist's mode and pours the remainder of the can over his head. As twin rhetorical flourishes, he tosses the can casually into a corner of the room and exits with a resonant belch. It is a self-consciously artificial performance that degrades both performer and audience. *Silkwood* follows this scene with another that taps their objectified gender stereotypes. This time, Drew is out in the yard chopping wood, while Karen tries to make him see how "important" it is that she chooses the proper clothes for her first Union trip to Washington. He remains steadfastly dismissive, and Karen is reduced to accepting Angela's fashion advice.

The meeting Karen, Morgan, and Quincy have with Stone and Richter (Josef Sommer) in Washington is strictly pro forma until Karen takes the two Union organizers aside and tells them about Winston's doctored negatives in metallography. Nichols and his Director of Photography, Miroslav Ondricek, shoot the scene with Karen off-screen, tucked into an office while Stone and Richter stand together in the doorway. Her voice is timid, her manner hesitant, but as Richter asks the question, "Can you get documentation?" Nichols cuts to a close-up of Karen, followed by reverse shots of the two men: she's come into focus in the scene, suddenly worthy of the men's attention. Richter's talk of an interview with the *New York Times* and increased Union leverage in contract talks with the plant makes Karen even squirmier, and Richter increases the rhetoric: "The point is that if you're right, they could kill off two million people" as a result of knowingly producing defective fuel rods for breeder reactors and tampering with the evidence in metallography. Nichols and O'Steen cut back to Karen in appropriately startled close-up as Richter concludes, "It's a moral imperative involved here." Karen and Stone return to his office, where Morgan and Quincy are delighted to be watching the superficial pageantry of Washington as it parades by the window. Stone's matter-of-fact summation that he will "go over your statements for the AEC meeting and then, later, you and I will go over yours" registers as a concealment of motives: Karen has become Stone's political and sexual object. The final cut of the sequence is over Stone's shoulder, as

Karen meets his gaze, shifts her eyes anxiously to the two Union brethren she's just upstaged via feminine wiles, then smiles in demure satisfaction. She has just packaged herself to a better class of man. *Silkwood's* ironic point of view leaves us in no doubt about the continued transactional commodification of her encounters with men. The film is exactly at its mid-point, and its titular character, although she has learned a great deal, still has much left to learn about her complicity in her objecthood.

For Quincy, "head of the Union" at Kerr McGee, the journey to Washington is the stuff of after-dinner slide shows, in which store-bought slides of landmarks (including a blindingly snowbound Capitol Hill) are interchangeable with slides of their own visit, posing before monuments and on their hotel's steps. (Earlier, we'd even seen him snap a photo of their flight attendant as she served their lunch on the plane.) And so the "harmless" photo of Karen and Paul Stone, in a night shot arm in arm outside the hotel looking elegant, relaxed, and comfortably intimate, is merely another in the long log of their days, though Drew, seated with Karen in the dark, reads the photo's subtext instantly and withdraws his arm from around her. Actually, we learn soon enough that Drew has withdrawn even further: he's resigned from Kerr McGee. In the car, traveling home from Quincy's, Karen parrots Richter's line in countering Drew's concern about people losing jobs: "There's a moral imper-ative here." She used to belong to the company (and to Drew); now she's a "stand-up girl" (Richter's celebratory but condescending phrase) who belongs to the Union (and to Paul Stone). Her using Richter's phrase is a studied performance of rhetoric, not yet a hard-won demonstration of conviction. Drew isn't fooled by it. He gives her the option to "quit and come away with me." While Karen's contention that she "can't quit now" is complicated by her mixed motivations, there is nonetheless little of the callow Karen left, whining her wish for a convenient plant contamination to ease her life. They part with the understanding that Drew wants no part of "a problem I can't solve," a polar opposition to Karen's naïve faith that she can be a part of a solution (and have an important Washington boyfriend, too). The next morning, his things moved out, Karen attempts one last tug at his heartstrings, and he says, "Sweetheart, it's like you're two people. I'm in love with one of them, but the other one's ... " It's fitting that he can't quite bring himself to finish the sentence, since Karen is in transi-tion—he only knows one of her identities, as the simple, needy mess of a woman to whom he's become attached. The new Karen finishes the sentence he's too loving and confused to complete himself: "... a big old pain in the ass." Paul Stone's desirability may be an under-current of her attraction to her new life; she'd choose Drew and activism if they hadn't been made mutually exclusive philosophical positions. Karen is the woman Drew loves, but now she's something more. She has come to understand herself as "not simply aimed at changing company policy, but also motivated by an unstated desire to realize a greater sense of self."[7] The challenge of the short remainder of her life is for her (and Drew, as it turns out) to determine what, exactly, she has added to her identity.

So begins Karen's short, unhappy career as a Union operative. The cut to a disorienting close-up of a woman rooting through a drawer clarifies the consequences of her choice. This is the "other" Karen, the one who steals damning evidence and then, when caught, self-righteously retorts, "Well, I think you should take a person's word for something." (She takes Paul Stone at *his* word and winds up jilted, except of course as an operative providing useful intelligence.) The "other" Karen helps arrange scarifying information sessions to rally Union support. The Union's scientific expert (Graham Jarvis) terrorizes familiar and unfamiliar faces in the crowd, including Thelma and Gilda, each of whom has willingly avoided to this point confronting these stark realities: "What we don't know is how little plutonium causes cancer. The government says that the maximum permissible body burden for your lifetime is 40 nanocures. Let me tell you how much that is: that is the size of a tiny dot on a piece of paper. We say that that's too much. We say that it takes less than that to kill you. We don't say it's twice too much, three times too much; we think that that is 115,000 times too much. [...] When you inhale it, and it lodges in your lungs, you're married to cancer." The homespun romantic metaphor is juxtaposed against a two-shot of Karen and Paul, unofficial Union "couple," though Paul will throw her over because of the primacy of his own marriage to the Union. The film posits the organic necessity of interdependence, and as such the agreement to disagree that eventually facilitates Drew's return—their loving contention about her activism that they're still debating in their very last exchange—marks a definable evolution in them both.

Ephron and Arlen litter this section of the film with broken relationships—not only Drew's departure from their shared home, but also Karen's inability to get past Stone's answering machine, and Angela's dumping Dolly to return to her husband. Initially Karen and Dolly lash out at each other in their abandonment and self-pity, blaming each other (rather than themselves) for their breakups. Dolly trumps all insults when she asserts, "You took about as good care of Drew as you did of your kids." Yet this argument resolves itself on the porch, with Karen cuddling Dolly to her breast like a distraught child and soothing her with a lullaby; what is of ultimate value is not the social labels that restrict them but the alternative family they have created together. Delerue's lamenting strings segue from generic soaring to modify themselves as an accompaniment to Karen's song, a moving formal assertion of Karen's personhood in the narrative, in a way the soundtrack has previously privileged Drew's banjo and the shriek of the contamination alarms. Nichols cuts to a wide shot of the surrounding darkness and the spare light in which the two women huddle together on the porch, affording them the privacy of their disappointment and their solace.

This idyll of connection seems to be continued in the camaraderie of the Kerr McGee lunchroom, but Karen's desire to record stray remarks as potential evidence of the company's dereliction of its moral responsibility to its workers and the world quickly provokes strain. Karen learns from Gilda that her husband Curtis has been called to extra shifts four nights running, "flushing the pipes." In a paraphrase of a conversation between Nately and Yossarian in *Catch-22*, Gilda hisses, "Why don't you just concentrate on uppin' our wages, and skip what is none of our business?" Karen deadpans the double meaning back at her: "This *is* our business, honey." Increasingly, Karen's isolation at the plant derives not only from a hostile management but also from her peers, and her second contamination, while "very slight" and of an "acceptable level," results in the paranoia of the daily urinalysis. An accident at night—when she hits a deer—leaves her woozy in a ditch and thus in a weakened moment of willingness to call Drew, who recognizes the first Karen, the one he loves and who needs him: he stays the night, their last peaceful night. Her return to work in the morning brings the most serious evidence of contamination so far: she sets off the alarms as she enters the facility. Karen Silkwood is now a contagious danger to Kerr McGee. The shower that ensues is the most violent in the film, the camera literally in her face as she begs for the multiple "cleaners" to stop. It is palpably a rape. Drew, Dolly, and Karen's domestic life is over, their house stripped and quarantined by HAZMAT workers in space suits, Dolly torn away by her secret deal with the company. "Where am I gonna go now?" says Karen. "I don't have any place to go now." Hurley looms over her in her tiny car in the dirt drive before her ruined house, an ambiguous bear of a man. "We're getting a room for Dolly," he says. "We can help you. We want to help you. We can help you with a place to stay. We can help you with money." He waits expectantly for her to default to dependence, to surrender herself to the company for keeps, and her resistance and, ultimately, her refusal to capitulate to their systemic will is as soul-searching an act in its own way as was refusing Drew's call for her to quit. When Drew does a walk-through afterwards, it's given the cinematic treatment of the grieving lover, the banjo returned to a soundtrack whose lamentations have always featured a hint of resigned finality. Their makeshift family's troika of intimacy is revisited in a tight shot of the three of them together on the plane to Los Alamos for contamination testing by more sophisticated censors and screens, yet their intimacy has been contaminated by compromise and paranoia. Karen asks point-blank if Dolly, in any of her HAZMAT debriefings, told "the company about the *New York Times*" or "about the X-rays" she's been angling to steal. Dolly's reply, "Karen, they know everything about us," is well calculated to deflect blame by enflaming anxiety. Karen never does get a straight answer as to whether or not Dolly has betrayed her; we're left to ponder the significance of Hurley's citing Dolly in trying to capture Karen's signed name on the clipboard. Dolly, it would seem, told Hurley what he wanted to hear in order to secure company patronage. Dolly fades from the film soon after. During the final montage as Karen's ruined car is towed back through town, hers is one of the faces of loss, likely complicated by her compromised actions of self-interest.

The brief New Mexico pilgrimage brings only confirmation of worst suspicions: the more sophisticated the infrastructure of the nuclear industry, the more sophisticated the packaging of conveniently arbitrary "truths." Dolly and Drew are "well below permissible levels of contamination," according to the examining doctor (James Rebhorn, at his most ominously bureaucratic). Americium, produced during the disintegration of plutonium, is present in Karen's lungs and chest. "We estimate you have an internal contamination of six nanocures of plutonium. Now, the maximum permissible body burden for occupational exposure is 40 nanocures, so as you can see, you are *well* under that level." This is, of course, a very different interpretation of the data than Karen's own expert, invited to inform the Union rank and file of their accepted risk in the plant. The white-coated arbiters of what is "permissible" allow that, despite their methodological and technological sophistication, they could be missing her exact statistical contamination "by plus or minus 300 percent at this level." Karen seizes at the hopefulness of having less contamination, but is tempered by the reminder it could be more. "But even that," he adds, "would be underneath the maximum permissible body burden." Nichols allows a suite of four silent shots to render the devastation of these lives: the close-up of Karen's startled face as it dawns on her there are merely smoother confidence men than Hurley and the other Kerr McGee bosses, working their shell game of "permissible" plutonium poisoning; a return to the smug reporting physician; a close-up of Drew, who also now understands it's been a wasted trip, no comfort to *any* of them; and finally back to Karen, a condemned woman beginning her premature calculus of the end of days. What follows is coda, "a postscript without any inflated theatrics about the triumph of individual courage and virtue over the evil corporation."[8] Ephron and Arlen take us to the end of the trail of Karen Silkwood's historical record, all ambiguities firmly intact: the commitment to the *Times* interview; the uncertainty about whether she held company documents constituting a smoking gun; the inconclusiveness about the circumstances surrounding her death in the "single car accident." The film provides only the barest hint of possibility of another car on the dark road where Karen Silkwood died, and this could merely have been her paranoia. It gives no evidence of condemning documents in her possession, nor does it suggest when the alcohol and Quaaludes would have entered her bloodstream.

From the Albuquerque airport, Karen calls Stone to set up the *Times* interview; having just left the coolly calculated statisticians of Los Alamos, she's on the phone with a man who can only think of the metallography X-rays and expresses no concern about where she's just been or what she's learned about her health. Her objecthood is rarely more pronounced with the company than it is here, with the Union. On the plane ride back to Oklahoma, Drew can still enthuse, looking out over the marvelous expanses of the desert Southwest, "Man, I love it here. I love this country. I'd like to stay here forever." Back at his place, he continues on this theme of a new life in the West, the one Karen had idly mused upon while comforting Dolly on the porch after their fight, when she'd wondered if Drew was "right" and they should "quit and move someplace clean." But Karen knows there is no such thing as a "clean" place: men protecting nuclear interests have just cynically condescended to them in the deserts of southern New Mexico, site of some of the most infamous atomic tests ever conducted by her nation. At the most literal as well as the most metaphoric levels, contamination is everywhere, both internal and external, within the company and the Union and even within one's closest, neediest friends like Dolly, who sold Karen out to be kept by the company. On this subject of her contamination, Drew gets one more chance to say, "I don't care," but unlike before, when he was rejecting not only the company but also Karen's willingness to begin perceiving the truth in all its consequences, he is fighting past her defenses now that they both have the truth. It's his best moment, still quintessentially Drew, but the better class of boyfriend Karen has always secretly hoped for: Drew-plus. "I know," she says.

Karen's last day is, in *Silkwood*'s estimation, a triumph, no matter what the ambiguities of its outcome. "The filmmakers," writes David Denby, "refuse us any kind of catharsis—a big, angry speech, an emotional confrontation with corrupt officials."[9] That last lovers' quarrel on Drew's steps offers us Drew and Karen in perpetuity, ever themselves, but new and improved. Drew unrepentantly refuses to cooperate with her activist agenda; to his familiar, patriarchal "I don't want you doin' that," Karen joyously replies, "Well, I'm doin' it," Streep's beauty given its rare full radiance through the typically hardscrabble de-glamorization to which the drama has accustomed us. They agree to disagree, adults at last, and he quips, "We can always have a fight later." She gets his attention a last time before climbing into the car and driving away via "flashing" him his own borrowed shirt, self-referencing that earlier Karen, now forever the former Karen, whose sexuality was her only frame of reference to the world, and who could think only in terms of commodified relationships. Her reification offers her insights at which, however astringent, she refuses to blink. The closing montage—which sees the likes of Thelma now among the Union faithful as Streep's plaintive, homespun voice reprises "Amazing Grace"— offers no consolation other than that of the transformation of the life that preceded it from blindness to sight, from one who was bound by socially constricted identity to the empowerment of liberation. And yet the final contextual note at the end of the film reports that the Kerr McGee plant closed; as Winston had argued, this is a hard victory for a town in need of economic relief. The larger commodifying burdens of socio-economic reality remain.

With *Silkwood*, Nichols returned to Hollywood feature filmmaking at the height of the medium's powers, recommitted to his themes and characteristically capable of coaxing indelible performances from his cast and crew. He would remake his Hollywood reputation on the strength of the characters he portrayed and the actors he cast to portray them. As Lee Hill puts it, "Nichols the expressionist had become Nichols the seemless craftsman."[10] Streep, Cher, Ephron and Arlen, O'Steen, and Nichols himself (his third time as Best Director) were all nominated for Academy Awards, and Russell's and Delerue's were only the most neglected of the other sterling performances. Though indulgences and missteps would occasionally follow in the next decade and a half before he refocused through collaboration with HBO, Mike Nichols returned to filmmaking with *Silkwood* as good as ever.

9

"Willing to play the game"

Heartburn (1986)

For his eighth feature film, Mike Nichols returned to some familiar faces and places. *Heartburn* was his second consecutive film with Nora Ephron as writer; in both cases, Ephron was writing from life—in their first collaboration, using as her material the short life and mysterious death of Karen Silkwood, nuclear-energy whistle-blower, and in the second collaboration, the unhappy roman à clef Ephron had published in 1983 about her marriage to and divorce from Carl Bernstein, the journalist made famous for his *Washington Post* investigations of Watergate. *Heartburn* also marked the second Nichols film for two of its key actresses: Meryl Streep in the lead role as Ephron's alter ego, Rachel Samstat (after starring in *Silkwood*'s title role), and Stockard Channing, a lead in *The Fortune*, supporting as Julie Siegel. Perhaps most significant of all was Jack Nicholson's *third* lead role for Nichols, as Mark Forman, the man who hoodwinks Rachel into giving marriage another chance. The role Nicholson plays can be understood as a variation on the first role he played for Nichols, in *Carnal Knowledge*, as the predatory and preternaturally angry Jonathan. Any sense that Nicholson's character is a softened version of Jules Feiffer's misanthrope is less because Mark Forman is a nicer guy—he isn't, especially—but rather that the consistency of *Heartburn*'s point of view from Rachel's/Ephron's perspective allows us to see, as we couldn't quite see in *Carnal Knowledge*, how a woman might be lulled into surrendering herself into the hands of someone so patently disinterested in any endeavor that does not address his own appetites.

Heartburn's limitations make it the least accomplished of all Nichols' films to that point in his career. Its mind is made up about its characters from the title sequence on—when Rachel is moved to tears by the wedding ceremony at which she meets Mark, and the camera catches Mark so disengaged by what he's witnessing that his only concern is not to be caught drooling as he dozes in the pew. It's an introduction to how the film will do business; from the opening, as with wedding guests, it "takes sides." In retrospect, we can understand this secret glimpse of Mark—a glimpse *not* available to Rachel in the moment that it is happening—as Rachel's retrospective point of view emphasizing not only Mark's thuggish emotions but also her own culpability, having ignored so many warning signs in her headlong "dream" (as she characterizes it late in the film, just before delivering her key-lime coup de grâce) of the marriage of true minds. "I believe in love," Carly Simon declares in the most forcefully delivered line of "Coming Around Again," the song Nichols and editor Sam O'Steen, in their seventh film together, use as they did "The Sounds of Silence" in *The Graduate*, to open and close the film and provide a choric commentary on the protagonist's inner life. Simon's determined alto immediately shifts in the next line, "But what else can I do?" from conviction to an ambiguous exasperation—the inevitability of true love recast, potentially, as the helpless paralysis of the accident about to happen before one's own eyes. As Vera (Maureen Stapleton), Rachel's therapist, puts it when she takes her turn giving Rachel a wedding-day pep talk while the guests wait outside, "Divorce is only a temporary solution." Love and marriage are problems we are doomed by biological and cultural determinism to "solve" again and again.

If Nichols has previously made films about characters determined by the hard-wiring of their hearts and their reified roles, the point is that they were multi-character dramas, in which point-of-view shifts, sometimes kaleidoscopically, to give us glimpses into a variety of philosophical responses. *Heartburn* limits its point of view to Rachel and the world as she sees it, recovering from her "heartburn": as a woman reviewing a past in which she deliberately ignored the signs. The film repeatedly returns to a motif introduced with their marriage: the fixer-upper house with even more problems than promise. (The roof never does stop leaking.) Rachel launches them into the house project with fond anticipation; only in retrospect can she see the project was beyond reclamation. In the novel that forms Ephron's basis for the adaptation, Rachel acknowledges, "I'm writing this later, much much later"[1] and "if I tell the story, I control the version."[2] In roman à clef, it's a strategic decision, and in this particular scenario, which unfolds the story of the very public failure of the marriage

The most consistent motif of *Heartburn* is the gutted Washington townhouse Rachel Samstat (Meryl Streep) and Mark Forman (Jack Nicholson, right) buy and attempt to renovate from the ground up throughout their doomed marriage. They delegate much of the responsibility for the construction to a contractor, Laszlo (Yakov Smirnoff), who is often difficult to reach and, even when meeting with them, is at best a poor communicator who may in fact be cheating them. Their perpetually porous house is an apt foreshadowing of the collapse of their marriage, the result of failed communication and duplicity.

of two writers who mine their own life experience as a profession, it colors the "fictional" narrative that results. The story will end badly, we know, except that, in its telling and the retrospective wisdom of that long perspective, a silver lining presents itself: Rachel/Ephron has learned something, and the story is their cautionary tale for themselves and for us. In this sense, Rachel has moved along the road of reification to a recognition of her complicity in her victimization, the road traveled by Karen Silkwood. Until its ambiguous ending, Nichols' film doesn't turn the tables on Rachel as it does on protagonists of earlier films (Benjamin in *The Graduate*, most prominently), offering an ironic perspective on what the characters themselves can't see. There's little irony in *Heartburn* except in the use of Simon's song, which "comes around again" at film's end. The return of the song, and the song's meditation on eternal recurrence, undercuts the sense of wisdom gained in the telling of the tale. In the novel, Rachel asserts as narrator that, "if I tell the story, I can get on with [my life],"[3] which implies hard-won progress. Rachel's ambiguous relationship to the truth of her experience is on full display in the novel's final lines, however. Rachel has been recalling some of the happiest times with Mark, including "the Petunia song" he would sing to her when she was pregnant, and which made her feel "secure and loved in a way I had never dreamed possible."[4] She'd always meant to write down the words, but she'd never quite gotten around to it. "And now I couldn't remember them. I could remember the feeling, but I couldn't really remember the words. Which was not the worst way to begin to forget."[5] These, the novel's last words, invoke a more complicated idea of what might constitute "progress" for Rachel. Her heart burns, and she would like to "forget" this feeling. Her heart will burn again—both with love and its seemingly inevitable failed aftermath. In Nichols' film, Simon's song is the sly formal move to pose a shadow on all the enlightenment and awakening from dreams at narrative's end. Unlike in *The Graduate*, where the return of "Sounds of Silence" introduces an unambiguous commentary on the film's ambiguous "happy ending," the imposition of "Comin' Around Again" (which is itself ambiguous about love, believing in "next time" and, simultaneously, in the serial disillusionment of all next times) cannot similarly function as a clarification of point of view in *Heartburn*; the film ends in the confusion of its protagonist, and as such, it is the best and truest moment of a film that typically has its mind made up about what it reveals.

　　Heartburn's narrative felt familiar when first released because the real-life rift of Ephron and Bernstein was still so fresh in cultural memory; the reason the narrative feels so familiar after decades is that it constitutes a model for Hollywood fable-telling in the "woman's film" industry Ephron helped to revitalize in films like *When Harry Met Sally* (Rob Reiner, 1989) and *Sleepless in Seattle* (Ephron, 1993), which examine the compulsion to believe in the mythos of the one, inevitable, *An-Affair-to-Remember* true love. In the climactic key-lime scene, Betty (Catherine O'Hara), the blonde Washington newswoman who specializes in gathering unhappy gossip, demands of the assembled guests at her latest dinner party an answer to the question, "[H]ow is it possible to live with someone so long and not know something so fundamental" as the spouse's long-term affair? The answer is that the deceived must be complicit. Ephron's work simultaneously deals in open-eyed awakening and in blind faith. As such, it dovetails with characters Nichols has examined in earlier, better films. In *Heartburn*, Ephron offers a version of a writer for whom writing, that iconic act by which we discover ourselves and the world, offers no solace or wisdom, and our last image of Rachel (on the plane driving the other passengers crazy with a really loud series of renditions of the "Itsy Bitsy Spider") is of an older, wiser, resigned woman—an incomplete woman, because she's without a man and will be busily healing for the next round.

* * *

The narrative logic of *Heartburn* is established by the editing of the opening sequence of scenes, which take us from the wedding at which Rachel Samstat and Mark Forman first meet to the one at which they themselves are wed. Between the two weddings come four relatively short scenes, a breathless précis of courtship: the reception, at which Rachel allows herself to be picked up by Mark; the bar they go to for a drink when they leave the reception; a very brief scene on the street during which they first kiss; a wee-hours bowl of shared pasta after tumbling together into bed. The sequencing projects their marriage as a fait accompli. The narrative point of view emerges as an act of retrospection by Rachel, and in this sense, we understand her feeling of exasperated helplessness—("What else can I do?" sings Simon in "Comin' Around Again")—to be the resignation infusing all we have seen in the narrative: her foolish behavior, and Mark's relentlessly unfeeling behavior.

The film's assertion of Rachel's right of gaze comes in the opening shots, when she and Mark enter at the same time beneath the neo-gothic arch of the church where the wedding is to take place. Mark notes her, and Nicholson's distinctive eyebrows arch. She hesitates long enough for him to enter first and be seated; as she follows, we get to watch her watching him. Her use of a compact mirror to gain a rear-view peek at Mark is a visual pun on the entire experience of the film: her look backwards at a failed marriage, a hollow "dream," as she labels it during that concluding dinner-party confession. Simon's song provides the soundtrack commentary, strengthening the sense of being enveloped within Rachel's experience. Of Simon and Garfunkel in *The Graduate*, Nichols had once observed that they were "what was happening in Benjamin's head"[6]; "Comin' Around Again" establishes a similarly complex, ironic relationship to Rachel in *Heartburn*, because Rachel is able to articulate in her closing speech what Simon has introduced in the title sequence. The verses of Simon's song depict quotidian details of an inequitable relationship, in which the woman is over-burdened by domestic responsibilities while the man "breezes in." But the payoff in a pop song is its repeated refrain, and the repetitions in Simon's song are especially apt when the subject of the lyrics is itself repetition, a "game" that's coming around again." Ironically, almost two decades after Nichols attempted to persuade Paul Simon to write lyrics specifically commenting upon Benjamin Braddock's malaise in *The Graduate*, which Simon did not quite manage to do to Nichols' satisfaction,[7] Carly Simon created a single original song for *Heartburn* that beautifully incorporates and comments upon Rachel's inner life and predica-ment. And as in *The Graduate*, Nichols reprises the song at film's end, as an editorial final word that further emphasizes the circularity the song and the narrative both explore. "I believe in love," Simon sings, an avatar for Rachel, who is avatar to Ephron's autobiographical travails and—another cyclical dimension—to Simon's own failed celebrity marriage to the singer-songwriter James Taylor. The assertion—positive, courageous, even defiant—is imme-diately complicated by an inserted rhetorical aside, "But what else can I do?" and a declara-tion, among the oldest in pop balladry: "I'm so in love with you." There is both pleasure and pain in the lines, an abandonment of head to heart and, in the full context of the song (and the movie it summarizes), of the crushing abandonment that will come as a result of the heart's risk. Ephron's roman à clef is, like most of her work, a paean to the resilience (for better and worse) of the human heart.

For Nichols, the key interest of Ephron's two stories he filmed is the main character's transformation, the central idea he claims for his filmmaking.[8] The point of that self-mocking last in-joke Karen Silkwood shares with Drew, the "flash" she offers him just before driving away, is to confirm her full awareness of the forces of reification that once informed her every movement. It is similar to, but far more triumphant than, Rachel's pie to Mark's face; the pie signifies the domestic limitations to which Rachel has long acquiesced, and which she literally shoves back in Mark's face, before witnesses, when she's finally had enough. Yet *Heartburn* finds in Ephron's adaptation of her own novel a set of social rules that pervade all human interaction, and which are equally apparent in Rachel's behavior as well as in the life and choices of her father Harry (Steven Hill); Julie Siegel, who becomes Rachel's closest friend; and Betty (Catherine O'Hara), the Beltway socialite and gossipmonger.

Harry Samstat is perhaps a clue to Rachel's attraction to Mark, a gruff charmer with little knack (or interest) in empathy, because there's no percentage in it. Mark has never hidden his womanizing, nor does Harry. One of Rachel's first outrages when she discovers Mark's secret cache of hotel and florist receipts is that he's too indifferent to the clandestine nuances of infidelity to use cash, "like a normal philanderer." Harry and Mark are frankly unapologetic—Harry cheerily so, Mark with more edge—about their straying. "This is hard for me, too," Mark says to Rachel, as if that could possibly help. "You can't take its temperature every five minutes, to see if the fever has gone down." Indeed, the "fever" never breaks between Mark and Thelma Rice. Harry, with less (read: nothing) at stake in Rachel's unhappiness, is blithely unrepentant: "Men: I hate 'em. I've always hated 'em. No wonder I hang around with women. Because it's men who do things like this." He "breezes" back out of the apartment as he breezed in moments before, on his way to meet a lady and help spend her money, and with the parting wisdom, "You want monogamy, marry a swan." Although one assumes Rachel's first destination upon her return to New York at film's end will be her father's apartment, one must also assume she will be under no illusions that she'll be greeted with the paternal warmth, tact, and care she so clearly craves.

Julie Siegel offers Rachel the closest thing to female comradeship she finds in the narrative, but there are complications. Rachel first meets Julie in New York, at her father's apartment, on her wedding day. The Siegels meekly enter the deliberation room where Rachel has sequestered herself, introducing themselves as Mark's oldest friends. Their reassurances are comically counter-productive: Rachel should rest in the knowledge that she's "the only person [Mark's] ever treated decently." Upon the move to Washington, Julie and Arthur become Mark and Rachel's closest friends, there for a lunch party when Rachel's water breaks, stretched out on a West Virginia river bank with them as Rachel and Mark bicker, and close by for an endless number of other dinner parties and social engagements. When Rachel discovers Mark's infidelity, leaves briefly, and allows herself to be coaxed back, Julie becomes her confidante, but what is revealed in their exchanges is an unsettling resignation to devalued identity. Julie's default salutation to Rachel comes in the form of a question: "Are you behaving yourself?" The post-affair onus falls to the injured party: implicit in Julie's innocuous questions is a sense that Rachel must improve her performance if she is to expect alterations in the performance of Mark's role. Rachel understands the question, fielding it without rancor or indignation. She launches into a monologue of her performance as forgiving and rededicated wife. The sequence of images that accompanies this is simultaneously a recollection of her futile attempts to reinstate herself as the object of Mark's esteem and a deconstruction not only of that specific effort but of the socially bound parameters of that role. "Behaving" may be outside her power if she can no longer accept the premises that construct the behavior. Her stories of making perfect meals for Mark put words of praise literally in Mark's mouth (Nicholson merely moves his mouth to Streep's intonations); further undercutting the already artificial quality of her loving culinary acts is her continued snooping into Mark's private papers. But there is another level of undercutting as well: while she is on the phone with Julie, Annie wails in the background; without budging, Rachel bellows to

Juanita to hush Annie's crying. Rachel's monomania about herself, either as object of Mark's affection or his mistreatment, has incapacitated her other identities. She is a loving but often absent mother, despite not working; she has neglected her own talents as a writer and devolved into channel surfing across a series of networks that all focus on Mark's ill-treatment of her.

The commiserating phone exchange with Julie is most disturbing, however, in what Julie reveals about herself at its end. Rachel sums up her report on "behaving" by assuring Julie, "I'm being very good." Julie says, "I'm proud of you." "I hate this," Rachel responds. "I wish he were dead." Julie, still trying to be kind and encouraging, simultaneously validates and invalidates Rachel's experience with Mark when she casually alludes to Arthur's "little affair." There has been no previous inkling of any marital discord between Julie and Arthur (which Rachel clearly knows about but which has come as a revelation to us), nor will the narrative represent them hereafter as anything but loving and close. As Julie delivers her comic litany of daydreams about a life post–Arthur, we are left to wonder if she has saved her marriage to Arthur, or if she merely has saved their shared act as "the Siegels." Certainly the intelligence Betty later shares with Rachel in the supermarket, that Arthur has been seen meeting with Thelma Rice at the Washington Hilton, takes on an unsettling ambiguity— is Arthur keeping his professional counsel—if that's what it is, and all that it is—a secret from Julie, or is Julie keeping it a secret from Rachel along with the rest of the politely inbred society in which they both move, extolling the virtues of death fantasies as a means to perpetuate a convincing performance as the loving, capitulating wife? Arthur and Julie Siegel are what Mark and Rachel can hope for as a married couple, which may be why neither Mark nor Rachel ultimately has the stomach for "behaving."

The sequence that follows Julie's revelation suggests their impatience with their assigned roles. At yet another dinner party, Rachel does her best to bask in the glow of Mark as he holds forth from the head of the table. "That was really fun, wasn't it?" she asks Mark on the ride home, as street lights alternately illuminate her mask of contentment and his grinning rictus of satisfaction. Nichols holds the shot long enough to see Rachel's pose dissolve. The composition is reminiscent of that final bus ride we see Benjamin and Elaine take in *The Graduate*, when each of them has a smile (but not simultaneously) that fades to resignation. At home, Rachel confronts Mark, diminished by perspective (in every sense) at the other end of the hallway, with the cues he's missed, the lines he's blown in their ongoing effort at "behaving": "Yeah, it really was fun, Rachel," she says, as him. "It was just like old times, reminded me of how much fun we used to have, how much fun we could still have, honey I love you so much I don't know what got into me, I know, I know how hard this must be for you, I know how awful and cold and distant and preoccupied and self-involved I must seem, but please forgive me ..." Mark eventually rushes to her, but he can't bring himself to say any of these lines. Arthur's collaboration with Julie may have saved their marriage; it may perhaps even have strengthened their bond (though this point is left permanently ambiguous by Nichols and Ephron). But Mark's refusal to recite on cue until it's too late (during the second delivery, when he acquiesces and recounts Annie's troubled birth as Rachel undergoes another C-section) saves Rachel from additional time in the purgatory of marital pretense.

With Betty, Rachel finds an avatar of the audience for whom such pretense is performed. Betty is a consumer of misery, a newshound of the rampant social dysfunction in Washington's small circle. She is everywhere Rachel goes—not just the dinner parties, but also the stores and the salons, the everyday world Rachel inhabits and can't escape. Betty delivers in real life what Rachel's imagination conjures on her television set: a non-stop commentary on a marriage at its breaking point. In this sense, the pie scene is almost as much an attack on Betty as it is on Mark. Betty prides herself on knowing all the latest social intelligence; given bad information about Thelma's social disease, she embarrasses them all by running directly to Thelma with what she's learned. It may even be the case that Betty has enlisted in Thelma's camp in throwing the enormous party to which Thelma has expressly invited Mark and Rachel. Though not stated, implicit in such an invitation (given Thelma's rage at Rachel) should be an unspoken threat, and whether Betty is naïve to the theater she's helping to facilitate or merely *playing* at naivety, Rachel destroys the party planning (and the current dinner party) with the pie, calling an end to the production of her marriage and underscoring Betty's obtuseness. While the attack has its own artificially performed dimensions (resonating as it does in the time-honored tradition of vaudeville), it is a performance meant to convey truth rather than a superficial misrepresentation, as the time spent in "behaving" herself and "being very good" has done. It's a pie in the face of reified pretension, and it's no accident that, if Mark is its primary target, it nonetheless leaves a mess in Betty's house.

Rachel's closing monologue acknowledges what she's learned in order to answer Betty's parlor-talk question, "How is it possible to live with someone and not know something so fundamental [as whether the spouse is faithful]?" Nichols has the camera panning and zooming, virtually uncut, for the four minutes of this scene, and here, as the camera pans away from Betty as she finishes the question, it moves past Arthur, his eyes resting ambiguously on Julie seated across from him, before the camera centers on Rachel. "It *is* possible," Rachel assures them all, "to love someone so much, or to think that you want to love them so much that you just don't even see anything." Nichols cuts to Mark briefly, an ironic illustration of Rachel's statement: she sees Mark *now*. "[...W]hen things do turn out to have been wrong, it's not that you knew all along, it's that you were somewhere else." Betty interjects in disbelief, "You'd have to be living in a dream." It's the one thing in the film on which Rachel and Betty can agree.

In her conclusion, Rachel articulates what may constitute the difference between someone like Julie and someone like herself: "And then the dream dies. The dream breaks into a million tiny little pieces, which leaves you with a choice: you can either stick with it, which is unbearable, or you can just go off and dream another dream." Julie apparently has made her peace with the "unbearable" post-dream reality of love's betrayal. Rachel can't bear it. Earlier in the conversation, Betty has declared categorically that people "are *not*" capable of change. Rachel's concluding statement and the pie's punctuation create an ambiguous tension between a depiction of feminist empowerment and this other, more melancholy image of eternal recurrence, to "go off and dream another dream." Walter Goodman, writing in the *New York Times*, argues "Today's audiences remain in love with love." As such, he continues, the film's ending

> is much less daring than Nora's door slam that ends [Ibsen's] "A Doll's House." [Rachel's] walk-out affirms the high value the heroine places on home and family. [The characters in *Heart-burn*] want to be with it sexually—practically everybody sleeps around. They all have accepted feminist aspirations—every female character [...] does work of some consequence. But what the principals want most of all is nothing more novel or exciting than a steady relationship with someone of the other sex, and that seems no easier to achieve today than it ever has been.[9]

Had the film ended with Rachel demanding the keys (reliable signifier of self-agency) and closing the door on this dead-end of a life, there would exist a kind of positive energy that, while dramatic, would have nothing to do with the next day (or even later the same evening) in the life of a newly single mother of two very young children in a city from which she remains estranged. Nor would Nichols the entertainer have allowed the film to end this abruptly; the gasps and laughter of the audience must be shepherded by lingering on Nicholson as he mugs for the camera, licking whipped cream off his chin and smiling bemusedly. In fact, Rachel striding purposefully out of Betty's house and all it represents is not quite indicated in the either-or Rachel has articulated. The filmmaking rhythms at the end of *Heartburn* are almost identical to those of Nichols' most famous film, *The Graduate*. The pie in a boorish husband's face has the same broad comic effect as Benjamin swinging the cross at the denizens of reifying ritual after Elaine's empty marriage to Carl Smith. It makes audiences laugh and cheer. And the long denouement on the bus, as the soundtrack reprises Simon and Garfunkel's opening lament, meets its structural analog in Rachel's long, halting walk across the tarmac, any momentum that has swept with her out of Betty's house long since stymied by Annie's toddling steps, as Carly Simon's song about recurrence returns. In *The Graduate*, the cyclical structure suggests stasis. Benjamin is and remains a passive participant in the drama of his own life, awaiting his next role, incapable of improvising some viable alternative. In *Heartburn*, Rachel's face is as somber as Benjamin's or Elaine's, but she has been more articulate than either of these much younger people about what awaits: another round, as Simon sings, of "the game." Waiting for their plane to take them back to New York and a resumption of her life as a writer, she plays the "Itsy Bitsy Spider" game with Annie, and the resilience of the fabled spider (and of those around them in the packed space of the flight cabin) is tested by Rachel's final spoken line in the film: "Again?" This time Simon joins in, along with an entire chorus of children, all extolling the hopeful doggedness of the spider-hero of song. Simon segues back to the original song that opens the film, starting midway, with the declaration, "I believe in love." She varies what comes next, however: "But who knows where or when, but it's coming around again." The double conjunction and the sheer breadth of the unknown create suspense that is, at best, mingled hope and dread.

Karen Silkwood, far from a finished product when she met her end on a dark rural road, was nonetheless clearly the sort of character Nichols had in mind when he identified the core identity of his films as "transformation." Callow, youthful characters like Benjamin and Elaine in *The Graduate* and Freddie in *The Fortune* have been given far more privileged economic opportunity than Karen but have less evolutionary movement to show for it. Freddie and Julie, the two characters Stockard Channing has played for Nichols, are women who choose to return to lives they have seen as illusory. There is a prophetic glimpse that something similar will happen to Rachel beyond the end of *Heartburn*. Rachel will return to the unrequited adoration of her editor, Richard (Jeff Daniels), who clearly admires more than just her talent. She is, indeed, an object of desire, professional and carnal. Yet Nichols gives us no assurance that she can see beyond her objecthood as her outrage settles into the compulsions of her biology and her social roles. While she has refused to be Julie, this is not the same as being *Rachel*, whoever that is. Karen Silkwood was moving toward a new life. As with Benjamin and Elaine in *The Graduate*, the most that can be said of Rachel is that she's rejected one variation on a once and future life.

10

"You have to take sides"

Biloxi Blues (1988)

As a Broadway director, particularly during his extraordinary initial splash in the early 1960s, Mike Nichols was accustomed to having shows in production and performance simultaneously. But only once in his Hollywood film career did Nichols release two films in the same calendar year: 1988, when *Biloxi Blues* was released in the spring and *Working Girl* premiered in December, just in time to qualify for the 1989 awards season. The first is a comic drama, a period piece set in the final days of World War II almost exclusively among men in a Mississippi boot camp. The second is a comic melodrama, a conjoined variation on the capitalist fantasies of Horatio Alger and fairy tales like "Cinderella," set in the corporate battleground of contemporary Manhattan, largely among women. What the two films share in common is a naif's introduction to the reifying complications of the world, which Nichols had earlier dramatized in films like *The Graduate*, *Carnal Knowledge*, and *The Fortune*.

Biloxi Blues marks what many must have felt was Nichols' long-delayed first (and only) cinematic collaboration with long-time friend and Broadway partner, Neil Simon.[1] The screenplay is Simon's adaptation of his own stage play that premiered in 1984, the middle play of the so-called "Eugene trilogy" of Simon's semi-autobiographical works featuring the protagonist Eugene Morris Jerome, which begins with *Brighton Beach Memoirs* (premiered on stage in 1983 and as a Gene Saks film in 1986) and concludes with *Broadway Bound* (premiered in 1986 and as an ABC television movie in 1992). *Biloxi Blues* wrestles with a variety of issues related to the formation of individual and cultural identity, especially related to sexuality and ethnicity.

Eugene's relationship to the story he tells us is, in its essentials, Neil Simon's: in the final voiceover, he describes his adult life, which reflects Simon's own: marriage, two daughters, and Broadway success, most recently with a play called *Biloxi Blues*. He assures us, "Everything in it is true," though the narrative clearly blurs memoir and sentimental fantasy. The narrative is hermetic—a single point of view, a six-week boot camp bracketed by a train ride into and back out of the deep south, only two women with sizable speaking parts in the story, neither of them portrayed with a particular dedication to realism, and African-Americans fleetingly glimpsed in their Mississippi slums. Through the many references to Eugene's composition book, in which he faithfully records "everything that happens" each day, we're given to understand that the narrative has both the obvious trajectory of young men preparing to enter battle (which they never do, other than with each other and with reifying cultural systems) and the more personal arc of one young man heeding the urge to find his voice.

These young men are roughly the same age, both chronologically and historically, as Jonathan and Sandy in *Carnal Knowledge*; Eugene (played by Matthew Broderick in Nichols' film) could have been the New York Jewish kid down the hall in Jonathan and Sandy's dormitory, going to school on the G. I. Bill. He might have seemed older and wiser to Jonathan and Sandy, who begin their narrative in wide-eyed, objectifying daydreams about women's anatomy. Yet Eugene's "play" is as dreamy about women and "Justice" as anything Jonathan and Sandy might concoct in their lights-out schoolboy fantasies. *Biloxi Blues* has slick, shining surfaces to which reified anxiety, particularly about male sexuality, can adhere only briefly before sliding into pro-social resolution. Eugene ultimately has at least as much in common with the "animals," Selridge (Markus Flanagan) and Wykowski (Matt Mulhern), as he does with Epstein (Corey Parker), the man with whom he shares an ethnic "background." His fantasy, when the boys in the barracks play their game of erotic imagination, is less flamboyantly heterosexual than either of the "animals," but it nonetheless expresses the anxiety to project heterosexual potency; by contrast, the fantasy expressed by Hennessey (Michael Dolan), to spend time with his family, receives nothing but scorn from the men most invested in projecting straight virility. Hennessey, the closeted gay kid in the platoon, haunts his scenes, but not the narrative as a whole, which includes him as part of the company in the film's final voiceover without differentiating his plight—a facile sense of inclusion masking Eugene's essential conventionality. When Eugene fantasizes about the world in *Biloxi Blues*, it's to lose his virginity, meet the perfect girl, and dispense a decidedly sentimental brand of justice upon Sgt. Toomey (Christopher Walken), the certifiable company leader; yet his play offers the persecuted Hennessey only his matter-of-fact punishment, and then allows him to disappear. Without irony, the film presents a picaresque narrative, the relationship among whose various parts is that its narrator loves "every damn one" of the men with whom he's served. While it's undeniably a warm-hearted love—Simon is nothing if not a warm-hearted storyteller—the easy solution to problems is troublingly unreal. Hennessey and Sgt. Toomey are simply swooped offstage by "the Army" that processes them. During the height of the gay-scare in the barracks, Eugene gives Carney (Casey Siemaszko), the guy "you can't quite count on," the line, "It's none of our business. Just let the Army take care of this." (Carney's claim echoes similar claims made by Nately in *Catch-22* and Gilda in *Silkwood*.) Simon does exactly that in his narrative, then blankets all their fates in Eugene's nostalgic affection. *Biloxi Blues*, a shared mid-career project of two old friends of the theater, is a relatively major play of a relatively minor American playwright, and a relatively minor film of a relatively major American filmmaker.

* * *

Biloxi Blues is, like *The Graduate*, a fantasy projection of a young man's sense of himself on the cusp of adulthood. What makes the two narratives so different is not the disparity in time (Eugene is old enough to be Benjamin's father) but in ironic distance between the fantasy and the awareness of fantasy. In *The Graduate*, Benjamin Braddock believes himself to be commodified and comes to see Elaine Robinson as similarly subject to commodification (as when her parents kidnap her from school, sequester her, and hand her over to marriage with Carl Smith). Benjamin's fantasy of chivalric rescue of the distressed damsel is treated with ironic skepticism by Nichols' narrative. Benjamin is afforded no retrospective insight on his callowness; Eugene in *Biloxi Blues* sees everything through the refocusing of time and qualifies his reflections with myriad references to his writerly aspirations and to the "fantasies" in which he indulges and encourages in his peers. The ironic tension in *The Graduate* is between Benjamin's sense of identity and purpose and the narrative's revealing that his identity and purpose are shallow and self-serving. Eugene vacillates between acknowledging the writer's "responsibility" to truth and confessing his own weakness for self-serving fantasy. The elegiac tone of Eugene's retrospection, awash in the atmospheric music of the era, is perhaps more congratulatory of its narrator than it ought to be. Eugene may be more likably verbal than Benjamin, but he suffers similar problems of failure to fully process his reified circumstances.

A relatively early scene dramatizes the iconography of reified reality, when Eugene and the rest of the company watch a classic Abbott and Costello service comedy, *Buck Privates* (1941), which emblematizes the endearing camaraderie of the military, then sit soberly through a war newsreel reminding them of their noble cause; Vincent Canby writes that the scene, with its references to earlier cinematic scenes, places *Biloxi Blues* "in a very different movie-reality, in an Army that's racially segregated and in which ignorance and bigotry are the order, though, in hindsight, World War II remains the last 'good war.'"[2] Yet Eugene's nostalgia for the iconography engraved upon his imagination by the culture wages war with his innate sense of the real problems of a system in which he himself is marked for persecution and must work hard to assimilate. David Denby and Jack Kroll remind us in their reviews of the film that Epstein is Eugene's intellectual and moral consciousness,[3] more interested in social critique and justice than in ingratiating compromise. As a result, the film delivers a split perception of all it surveys, "a blend of harsh reality and blurring fantasy."[4]

Eugene is writing from the first scene of the film; the voiceover in our ears is paired with the old-fashioned, marbled composition book in his lap as he endures the troop train. Simon's theatrical punchlines begin to establish a comfortably formulaic sensibility: "It was my fifth day in the Army, and so far I hated everyone" is a comic opening statement balanced by his gushing conclusion, "I didn't really like most of the guys then, but today I love every one of them." We're given abundant invitations to see Eugene's narration as problematically unreliable (not the least in the casting of Broderick, still prominent in the American imagination as the impossibly capable and snarky Ferris Bueller from John Hughes' 1986 film). Most prominent in the narrative's unreliability is the fantasy game the enlisted men play, which culminates in the translation of the two New York Jewish boys' fantasies into reality. Eugene's two-day pass manages to net him a "perfect" day, in which he learns the secrets of sex from a maternal prostitute and manages, among a veritable tide of enlisted men washing up on Biloxi's streets with weekend passes, to invoke from the prettiest girl at the USO dance the highest of praise for an aspiring man of words—not just her time and attention (and her address in Gulfport) but also her observation, "Eugene, you didn't say one wrong thing in that whole conversation." We're still watching his fantasy. As he did in *Who's Afraid of Virginia Woolf?*, *Carnal Knowledge*, and *The Fortune*, Nichols uses dancing as a symbolic means both of intensifying and deflecting reality. Nichols has opened the film with a beautiful helicopter shot of the troop train crossing the Mississippi, while Pat Suzuki sings "How High the Moon"; Lee Hill calls this shot and its mirrored pendant at the film's conclusion "one of the most ravishing opening and closing shots in a service comedy ever made."[5] The languorously dreamy quality of the performance, accentuating the romantic longing of the lyrics, is reprised in the USO dance scene; Eugene has chosen a song for the hall's record player: "Solitude." Daisy appears, spectrally reflected in the window behind him, the summoned image of romantic fantasy for a lonely soldier. As their perfect conversation, about literary Daisies, moves them onto the floor, Eugene reveals his aspirations as a writer, and Daisy feeds him catnip: "If you ever become a famous writer, I'll be immortalized." Nichols inserts a jarring transition here, using a new lens to intensify still further the fantasy space they've entered together and replacing "Solitude" with the song most on the retrospective Eugene's mind, a reprise of "How High the Moon." What we see and hear is a deeply inflected version of Eugene's wish fulfillment. Earlier at the dance, his braggadocio about Rowena offering him a second time "on the house" is met by condescending dismissals from Wykowski and Selridge. They see through his fantasy claims immediately, and Eugene acknowledges in his summation at the end of the film, "Rowena never gave me a second one for free." Simon the one-liner joke artist can't resist a meta-allusion: "Maybe I'll leave that out if they ever make it into a movie."

"Everything," Eugene promises about his story, "is true," a statement he immediately compromises by exempting the lie about Rowena's generosity. This means, for instance, that the real-life analog to Epstein really wished for Toomey to do 200 pushups (believable enough), and that the real-life analog to Toomey really cooperated (not so much). Actually, these climactic moments of the film with Toomey strain credulity even more than Eugene's "perfect" adventures with Rowena and Daisy on his two-day leave. Money buys time with a prostitute, and the USO dances brought soldiers into chaperoned proximity to sweet young women. The rest of what Eugene relates about the two encounters may be understood as over-fond reminiscence, an organic consequence of his having commodified Rowena and objectified Daisy. The fantasy of Toomey's surrender, however, is the stuff of neatly poeticized dramatic resolution. It is, in fact, nearly a deus ex machine. It fulfills Epstein's wish, it's true; more important within the context of Mike Nichols' vision of commodified personhood, it fulfills (for a second time) Don Carney's prophecy: "It's none of our business. Just let the Army take care of this."

Carney actually offers this advice in light of the gay witch-hunt that consumes the base in the wake of the "Lindstrom" discovery (one of the two young men discovered in a homosexual clinch). This episode is the most powerful and most under-examined in the film; while the disposition of Toomey receives the pride of placement as the climactic episode of this picaresque narrative, the stigma of theft and then of homosexuality is the story's center, and Hennessey as much as Epstein is the hero who takes sides and acts on his convictions rather than merely conforming to the easy will of the crowd (as Carney does, provoking Eugene's judgment as undependable). Toomey's reduced authority at the film's climax is in direct correlation to a deepened sense of Eugene's understanding that Carney is wrong in claiming that the Army can "take care" of the intensely personal problems individuals encounter. Eugene has flaunted authority reflexively; at the end of the narrative, the challenges the enlisted men make to authority are considered, justified. Toomey is a product of his profession, a soldier intent upon the manufacture of soldiers. In his philosophical debate with Epstein after the $62 showdown, and then again during his long climactic deposition to Eugene, Toomey expresses a single guiding aesthetic: the warrior. In the dialogue with Epstein, in which Toomey meets a physically unprepossessing but intellectually formidable opponent, Epstein argues, as he ultimately does in any argument, for logic as superior to emotional or physical manipulation: "I just don't think it's necessary to dehumanize a man in order to get him to perform. You get better results raising our spirits than lowering our dignity." What Epstein's logic has failed to compute is the illogical nature of combat, Toomey's sole focus: "Men do not face enemy machine guns because they've been treated with kindness. I don't want them human. I want them obedient." The terrible irony is that, while Epstein has the moral upper hand, within the reifying context of the institution of war, Toomey has the more durable logic. Walken's ability to move convincingly among emotional extremes serves Toomey's character well in this moment, as the sergeant verges on tears as he asserts, in all the sincerity of war's Catch-22, "I'm trying to save these boys' lives."

This debate with Epstein is likely what predisposes Toomey to return to Epstein after receiving the devastatingly depersonalized letter reassigning him to retired veteran status. He can reason with Epstein, even if they agree on nothing. Eugene's intervention functions differently than would anyone else's in the company, because Toomey knows Eugene is also capable of understanding what has happened to Toomey. The two New York Jews are, in Toomey's own lexicon, the "misfits" who can see through the dehumanizing necessities of combat training to the dehumanizing nature of institutions that declare war in the first place. Having glimpsed these truths, either Epstein or Eugene is in a position to be able to understand the cruel irony of Toomey, breaker of men, himself broken by the very institution he has so passionately served. Referring to his status as "terminated," he creates a surreal vision of having the steel plate in his skull changed out for sterling silver. "That means I'll be able to hock my head in any pawn shop in this country," he says. He's understood himself to be a good soldier; he understands himself now to be defective machinery, easily and unfeelingly replaced.[6]

But if Carney's prophecy, that the Army can "take care" of aberrations to its methodology, ultimately anticipates Toomey's dismissal, its most chilling fulfillment is in the abrupt and permanent disappearance of James Hennessey from the film. The film's opening moments constitute a ritual assignment of stereotypes that quickly become ingrained, presented to us by Eugene himself, who does little to discourage them, settling only for complicating them, as when Wykowski discovers, reading about himself in Eugene's notebook, not only his "animal" characteristics but also his potential as a soldier, for all the ambiguities we understand to be inherent in such "praise." Wykowski is the dumb Polack, and Epstein is the vaguely effete Jewish bookworm. Eugene reveals something of his own failure as a student of psychology when his notebook labels Epstein the "homosexual," failing to notice the closeted gay man in their midst. Epstein questions Eugene's instincts, particularly since Eugene can offer no more evidence about, for instance, Epstein's orientation than that he never talks about girls.

In retrospect, Hennessey's courageous defenses of Epstein when facing Wykowski's anti–Semitic onslaught are the perspective of a man systematically instructed in self-loathing by an institution that once, quite literally, criminalized "deviancy." While deviancy may be connoted to mean degenerate behavior, particularly of an aberrant sexual nature, its antonym is no less pejorative: conformity. If Carney's arguing for the Army's authority may be interpreted as conformity to majority, we begin to reinterpret his failure of performance at Rowena's in a different light. Rather than "cold feet," Carney may have no relevant sex instinct to call upon in this moment of social truth, whereas Eugene, however clumsy, is driven by nature and by majority rite of passage as much as Selridge and Wykowski, the "animals" to whom he has consistently condescended. Carney's reticence, as revealed in his gratefully accepting the offer of ice cream before a trip to the whorehouse, is not simply evidence of a boy afraid to grow up but may also suggest a boy afraid that he is something other than what a culture declares to be a man, and postponing a while longer putting that fear to a concrete test. To apply logic to deconstruct the military mindset is only one way to be a misfit; lingering anxiously in the dust outside Rowena's place, surrounded by playing African-American children, Carney looks every bit the misfit. At the dance afterwards, this stigma remains.

Hennessey, however, is the film's ultimate misfit. Toomey's utter surrender to the alternative institutional logic of the Army has exiled him, but he isn't a misfit. Neither Epstein

In one of the most chilling scenes of the typically warm-hearted *Biloxi Blues* (Nichols' collaboration with Neil Simon), Sgt. Toomey (Christopher Walken) commands his men to halt their boot-camp march along a Mississippi road. Under interrogation, a recruit has just yielded the name of the man with whom he'd been spied in a homosexual tryst. The wanted man is Hennessey, the only man in the barracks who defended the Jew, Epstein, from anti–Semitic persecution. Hennessey is singled out of the ranks of the march and driven away, never to be seen again, an emblem of the codified intolerance of systemic order.

nor Eugene is the *lone* Jew, and even if he were, this "deviancy" is "merely" sociological, not legal. Epstein seems logically if not emotionally horrified by Eugene's categorization of him as gay, because there are legal repercussions to homosexuality, and as we learn in the coda, Epstein pursues a life immersed in the law and justice. Hennessey and Epstein are the odd men out of the quest for sexual experience with Rowena. Epstein's exception is his flamboyant intellectualism, while Hennessey, particularly in his little improvised theater performance about his black ancestry to teach Wykowski a lesson, displays a cunning native intelligence that has probably aided him thus far in eluding sexual detection. On the bus with the others as they descend upon the streets of Biloxi, Hennessey alights, makes contact with another enlisted man, and the two of them melt together into the crowd, against the general flow. Hennessey understands exclusion. When Wykowski asserts with conviction that Epstein the Jew has found and kept Wykowski's $62, Hennessey is the one who demurs, labeling Epstein "not the kind that steals money." Hennessey soon inserts himself into a performed role, claiming the "colored" mother. The camera lingers on his face, offering us (like Wykowski), time to mull his features, sifting for some revealing ethnic detail: the film invites our reflexive racism. Selridge uses institutional logic on the problem: "You can't be colored—they wouldn't let you in here with us." (It's the very same logic he could have used to argue that Hennessey has to be straight.) Wykowski finally rises to Hennessey's bait: "Yeah, but I guessed it. See, it was something I couldn't put my finger on, but I knew there was something wrong with you." Wykowski seems relieved, affirmed—a satisfied product of his culture. Hennessey finally steps out of the assumed role to prove Wykowski wrong: "Now we know how you think, don't we, Wykowski?" Yet while Wykowski has been easily misled about the particulars of Hennessey's misfit status, he may be right in sensing something "wrong" with the Irishman.

It's another scene Eugene witnesses in silence, like the persecutions of Epstein. In voiceover, he tells us, "I really hated myself because I didn't stand up for Epstein, a fellow Jew. Maybe it was because I was afraid of Wykowski, or maybe it was because Arnold sometimes asked for it, but since the guys didn't pick on me that much, I just figured I'd stay neutral, like Switzerland." Epstein reads this motivation in Eugene as he reads all of Eugene's behavior, as the mostly well-meaning but passive posture of a dilettante in love with the idea of being a writer rather than with the genuine discoveries about the world engendered within writing. After Epstein takes his stand against Toomey on the $62 artifice, Eugene confronts his friend to ask, "Why is it we come from the same background but I can't understand you?" Epstein replies, "You're a witness. You're always standing around watching what's happening, scribbling in your book what other people do. You have to get in the middle of it. You have to take sides. [...] Until you do, you'll never be a writer, Eugene."

Accepting Epstein's premises, which Nichols and Simon present as often annoying but ultimately deriving from the genuine wisdom that one day will make Epstein a "feared" man of legal justice and moral authority in Brooklyn, what is the verdict of *Biloxi Blues* on Eugene as a writer? The answer is complicated by Eugene's apparent moment of action when he takes Epstein's side in the most dangerous single moment in the narrative, a scenario in which Toomey implores them to take *his* side and behave as soldiers in his final glimpse of them in the pouring rain—"as long as Justice is served." Yet this moment has the look and feel of more fantasy from a man who has always aspired to a life of the imagination. Before this come many moments for Eugene of inaction and sideline-sitting, and a troubling silence about Hennessey, who had become one of them and then, on a midday march on a dusty Southern road, was "disappeared" by the Army. *Biloxi Blues* offers the portrait of a young man whose most meaningful actions come in honing his reified anxiety, when mute "witness" begins to find its voice: recording the fantasies and performances of a group of terrified young men (Eugene includes Toomey in his final tally of their number), all of whom have been indiscriminately assigned to be the men their culture has demanded. We can read Eugene's mostly modest fantasies within the context of the reified anxiety that comes into focus for him during his service, and his play is where he is best able to take a side, arguing for the reality of the terrorizing weight that cultural definition and expectation place even on a culture's most assimilated members.

11

"She's your man"

Working Girl (1988)

With *Working Girl*, Mike Nichols went Old Hollywood to tell a new fable of working-class female empowerment. With its social critique sweetened by old-fashioned star power in the service of romantic comedy, it's the kind of film Billy Wilder might have made had he permitted himself pure fantasy. Released at the end of the year, in time for the nominating season, the film pleased audiences and received six Oscar nods, including Nichols' fourth nomination as Best Director and no less than three actress nominations, Melanie Griffith for her lead role and Sigourney Weaver and Joan Cusack in support. Carly Simon was also nominated—and subsequently was the film's only winner—for Best Original Song. Replete with the comparative iconographies of Manhattan's capitalist towers and the modest blue-collar neighborhoods of Staten Island, another co-star of the film is the Staten Island Ferry, churning the liminal waters between ethnic, low-income America and the capital of capitalism. A familiar trope of Studio System romantic comedy is the mistaken, feigned, or assumed identity, which lends itself to a trademark Nichols thematic preoccupation: the pressure to assume and perform socially constructed roles. Reified performance has been at the heart of Nichols' dramas and comedies since his earliest features—the "games" George and Martha play in *Who's Afraid of Virginia Woolf?*, the "shows" Benjamin's parents mount under the guise of their loving celebration of their son in *The Graduate*, *Catch-22*'s Colonels Cathcart and Korn asserting their deal with Yossarian to "like" them and say good things about them at home, and so on. "Performance" is at the very center of the drama in Nichols' ambitious follow-up to *Working Girl*, 1990's underrated cine à clef *Postcards from the Edge*. *Working Girl*'s mingled echoes of "Cinderella" and the Horatio Alger mythology of capitalist self-invention, two of America's most persistently beguiling fantasies of rags-to-riches reward for the nobility of grit and dedication of spirit, imagine a woman afforded the opportunity to pretend her way into the *Fortune* 500.

As Tess McGill, Melanie Griffith is a contemporary Cinderella, with her little girl's voice and grown-up curves, shown over and over by Michael Ballhaus' camera. Sigourney Weaver, as Tess' new boss, Katharine Parker, is also, like Tess, reduced to reclining cheesecake by the camera's gaze when her skiing accident enforces her feminized passivity[1]; Harrison Ford as Jack Trainer, object of both women's desire, gets significant shirt-off time, as do Alec Baldwin as Tess' Staten Island boyfriend Mick and Elizabeth Whitcraft as Doreen, the woman angling to steal Mick away. In the context of Tess' Cinderella story, no shot in the film seems quite so erotically provocative in its fairy-tale allusion as the shot of Tess, madly vacuuming Katharine's house in high heels and precious little else to eliminate any trace of her past

144

weeks of living literally in Katharine's shoes (as well as her apartment, office, and identity). *Working Girl* is a Cinderella-story for adults.

The problems with audience reception of *The Graduate*—the Baby-Boomer embrace of Benjamin Braddock as counter-cultural hero despite scant evidence in the cinematic text itself—are if anything even more pronounced in *Working Girl*, which has the tidy concluding episodes of recuperative social comedy. Tess is rewarded with authorship of the deal she'd imagined and brokered under false pretenses; Katharine is punished for her malfeasance in trying—twice—to steal Tess' idea. Jack and Tess are presumably left to happily-ever-after, as are the Staten Island couples whose dreams are more modest: Cyn (Cusack) and Tim (Jeffrey Nordling), and Mick (Baldwin) and Doreen (Whitcraft). The film is either Nichols' most conventional or else one of his most subtly subversive, provoking polarized responses. Leonard Quart and Albert Auster label it "anti-feminist" in its "put down of the type of cold, manipulative superwoman" represented by blueblood striver Katharine (Sigourney Weaver's character),[2] while Deron Overpeck writes that, "at first blush, *Working Girl* appears to be an uplifting story of a woman succeeding in the corporate world."[3] Audiences could be forgiven for misreading its iconography of upwardly mobile feminist fantasy, but the final shot, a helicopter pull-back from Tess until she is lost in the glass and steel canyons of lower Manhattan, suggests the irony beneath the fantasy. In the larger context of Nichols' career spent in dramatizing reified class, gender, and ethnicity, *Working Girl* is a reified daydream of the "contradictory expectations of women during the 1980s"[4] spun from the cotton candy of "Morning in America" Reaganism.

* * *

As the title naughtily suggests, *Working Girl* is a meditation on the sexualized commodification of the human person. Certainly the film's opening moments set up the tension between the rhetorical egalitarianism of Lady Liberty in New York's harbor and the reality of gender and class politics everywhere else, specifically within corporate culture. "'I like doing stories about women,'" Nichols says, "'because they're the underclass in America.'"[5] Carly Simon's "Let the River Run" establishes a triumphalist context in its call for the "dreamers" to "wake the nation" to the shining ideal invoked in an ambiguous (and never clarified) phrase like "the New Jerusalem." Some of America's most potent icons are on display in these opening shots of the film: the 360-degree helicopter panorama around the Statue of Liberty's crown, the swoop across the water to the Battery, Wall Street, and wincingly, the World Trade Center, still 13 years from its destruction. *Working Girl* was released during the final days of Ronald Reagan's second term in office, and the astonishing explosion of prosperity in the free-market countries of the world radiated outwards from its epicenter on Wall Street, where Tess McGill toils in low-ceilinged obscurity. Nichols says that he imagined the film's opening as a "combination of immigrant and slave ship image."[6] David Denby calls the crossing of New York Harbor during the film's titles "a momentous rite of passage" and argues that the film "celebrates the yearning to belong."[7] Nichols has long commented on the act of immigration as one of the great exercises in conformist survival: "[T]he key was [...] the immigrant's ear: [...] they have to learn what's happening very fast and sound like *that*."[8]

Tess has been working avidly to improve her inherited station among the working class of Staten Island. She rides the ferry daily with her best friend, Cyn, the only woman on their commute with bigger hair. The hair is a superficial compensation, a way for two socially insignificant people to stand out in the throng, yet as the ferry disgorges them, the wide shot often loses them in the sidewalk throng. Tess, who put herself through five years of night

In *Working Girl*'s title sequence (and several subsequent returns during the film), Tess McGill
(Melanie Griffith) rides the ferry from blue-collar Staten Island to Wall Street. These crossings
mark the liminal space she occupies as a dreamer of upwardly mobile dreams (Cinderella meets
Horatio Alger) in dog-eat-dog New York at the end of the Reagan administration. The film ends
with another grand shot of New York Harbor, but Tess' victory of assimilation has now firmly
entrenched her in the financial district, where she is no longer visible—she has been consumed
within the uniformity of the concrete canyons.

school to complete her degree "with honors," remains relentless in her commitment to self-
improvement. Trying to angle Tess into skipping her latest night class (on speech elocution),
Cyn wonders in a thick New York accent, "Whaddya need speech class for? You tawk fine."
Altering her elocution will put distance between herself and her life with people like Cyn,
who becomes increasingly disapproving as Tess assumes the airs of Manhattan. (By film's
end, though Cyn is Tess' first call-out from her new office, one wonders how many more
phone calls remain in the future of this friendship—do Tess and Jack Trainer share anything
in common with Cyn and Tim?) It isn't Cyn and the other salt-of-the-earth working men
and women on Staten Island that Tess objects to, however; rather, it's the condescension of
the Manhattan power elite that has her crazy, knowing she "could do a job" (as she tells
Olympia Dukakis in the Petty Marsh personnel office) if only given a chance.

The introductory scenes in Manhattan clarify Tess' sense of gendered entrapment. For
her bosses, Turkel and Lutz (James Lally and Oliver Platt), Tess is not quite a nonentity
because she's eye-candy, but as a colleague, she's worthy only to fetch coffee and, in time of
deepest need, toilet paper. They do not take seriously her requests to be sponsored for the
"Entrée Program"; instead, they "pimp" her out to randy colleagues like Bob from Arbitrage
(Kevin Spacey) whose swinish intentions are evident from the moment he picks Tess up in

a company limo equipped with cocaine, and porn videos where the training tapes should be. After Tess retaliates by insulting Lutz on the commodities ticker, the personnel officer cautions Tess, "You don't get ahead in this world by calling your boss a pimp." To her checkered history at Petty Marsh (she's gone through three bosses in six months), Tess can only assert, "Wasn't my fault." Even if we're inclined to believe her, we're aware of the overwhelming force of patriarchal practice she's up against in rejecting business as usual. This is the way this game is played. Offering her a last chance, Dukakis' character assigns Tess to a different kind of boss than any of her previous executive administrators: Katharine Parker (Weaver).

At first glance, Katharine is everything Tess would like to be. She's smart, assertive, stylish, able to stop a male colleague's forward pass and instead turn it into her own strategic offensive. At the meet-and-greet Katharine throws for herself, Tess watches in awe when an oily colleague's advances on Katharine stray from the professional to the personal, and Katharine deftly makes herself the hunter rather than the hunted: "You get me in on the Southeast Air divestiture plan," Katharine says, shrugging off his hand, "and I'll buy *you* a drink." Although intimidated and depressed that she is a couple weeks older than Katharine, Tess takes seriously Katharine's Pygmalion overtures to mentorship. Early on in their relationship, Tess is called into a planning meeting for the meet-and-greet party. A colleague of Katharine, Ginny (Nora Dunn), has made some forceful suggestions about the catering, and Katharine makes a show of having her repeat the ideas for Tess to transcribe. Tess interjects her suggestion to replace the usual tidbits with dim sum, citing an article she's recently read in *W* magazine. Ginny expresses skepticism about Tess reading *W*, but Tess says, "You never know where the next big idea will come from." When Katharine responds readily to Tess' suggestion, it may feel to Tess as if her boss has empowered her, but the reality of the exchange has been a subtly encoded demonstration of Ginny's diminished potency. Ginny is left to reclaim what power is left to her in the room, sniping at Tess that dim sum hardly qualifies as a "big idea." Katharine's praise of Tess as the meeting breaks up is awkwardly patronizing: "Dim sum, Tess. I like it, contribution-wise. Keep it up." With such faux-laudatory power moves, Katharine is intent on pumping Tess up while keeping her down.

Later, as Katharine prepares for her ski weekend, Tess is literally brought to her knees before Katharine, buckling her boss' feet into bright red ski boots, Katharine's preferred color as a strategy of inflamed display: she's a "working girl," too, her sexuality opening rather than closing the doors because she's willing to titillate her way to what she wants. Nichols and his longtime editing partner Sam O'Steen (working his ninth of Nichols' ten feature films) alternate up-angle shots of Katharine with down-angle shots of Tess to solidify the understanding both women have of their respective places in the scheme of American corporate culture. Katharine is a player, and the psychology of corporate gamesmanship seeps into her diction about her personal life. The ski weekend, she allows Tess to understand, is about another kind of deal, one in which she has orchestrated all the details: "We're in the same city now. I've indicated that I'm receptive to an offer. I've cleared the month of June." Thus the way has been made clear for Jack Trainer's merger proposal. Tess has no sense of the manipulative properties of relationships except when dealing with men like Bob from Arbitrage and Mick, her boyfriend, both of whom see her purely as a sexual commodity who might be capable of answering phones between bouts of sex, and so she guilelessly asks, "Well, what if he doesn't pop the question?" Katharine waves away her doubt: "I really don't think that's a variable. Tess, you don't get anywhere in this world by waiting for what you want to come to you. You make it happen." Jack is, in the contextual parlance, the very essence of a "hot commodity," much as Katharine knows herself to be, and as Tess comes to see herself. This is the function of all the hot bodies on display in *Working Girl*: their vocational and social marketability is in direct correlation to their factor of physical attraction as well as their professional acumen. When Jack and Tess meet, they're able—barely—to keep their hands off each other until the Trask pitch carries. With the deal sealed, they can no longer hide their sense of shared qualification: they've *earned* each other, equally hot commodities to one another in boardroom and bedroom. On a different scale of social commodification across the harbor, Doreen has strapped herself onto Mick as Staten Island's version of upward mobility, orchestrating her own brand of hostile takeover.

"Watch me, Tess," Katharine says. "Learn from me." The offer may sound like generous mentorship, but it is actually a fairly naked maneuver to reinforce her potency; Denby writes, "Katharine really is pure actress, a faker who has perfected the appropriate corporate-female style of 'candor.'"[9] Tess takes the command to heart, and when Katharine is conveniently indisposed due to her skiing accident, Tess seizes the opportunity much as Katharine would have, had their roles been reversed. *Working Girl* offers Cinderella the keys (or security-code combination) to the palace; on a visit by Cyn to Katharine's brownstone, the two working girls watch in reverence as Tess throws a switch that lowers the entryway chandelier for dusting. Simon's "Let the River Run" goes through as many permutations over the course of the film as Tess herself, and Nichols and Rob Mounsey, the music scorer for the production, dress up the chandelier scene with a treatment of the song on pipe organ, as if there could be no more formal signifier of arrival than to command a remote-controlled chandelier in one's vestibule. The film does not hide the materialist longing of its heroine, and the film's box-office success is due to keeping the ironic undertones of skepticism about capitalism accessible but not aggressively deconstructionist. Tess' initial visit to the brownstone is, in essence, child's play-pretend: she sits at Katharine's desk, listens to Katharine's plummily intoned messages on the Dictaphone, works out on Katharine's exercise bike, applies Katharine's perfume and makeup at Katharine's vanity, looking at herself in Katharine's mirror. Indeed, she's looking at herself applying Katharine's blusher as she mimics Katharine's pronunciations when she learns a new dimension of Katharine's skill set: duplicity. On hearing Tess pitch her idea for a major deal with Trask, Katharine's implicit allegation is that Tess has misappropriated someone else's intellectual property: "No chance you overheard it, say, on the elevator?" When Tess immediately rejoins, "No. No way," Katharine offers an insultingly literalist reassertion of the same question ("Somewhere?")—as if Tess has used the loophole of not having overheard the idea on the elevator to demur. Katharine's strategy in these accusations is twofold: to cow Tess into questioning her own agency as a potential market analyst and to learn whether any genuine authority is attached to the Trask proposal. Satisfied that the idea is *merely* Tess' makes it fair game for her to poach, though Tess, as she becomes a more accomplished student in the arts of duplicity, would certainly have been able to read unintentional praise in Katharine's twice-suggested accusation that her idea has originated in a third party. When Tess hears, "Hard copy on this from my home computer. Do not go through Tess," she learns a great deal about "the rules" of the game, and the patronizing "Watch me, Tess. Learn from me" refrain takes on an unintended irony. Griffith's face in empowered, low-angle close-up is steely, clamp-jawed: "Two-way street," she says, echoing another of Katharine's often repeated and clearly insincere exhortations. And so, equipped with a complicated, comic set of performed roles she must juggle, Tess goes to work. The irony is, however, that she cannot close the deal she makes (either with Trask or with Jack) on her own, and she will at some point have to confess her own duplicity. Katharine must play an instrumental role in sealing both deals, as she is unable to stop her petty power-playing in the film's climactic scenes.

Working Girl is at its least convincing as a glimpse inside the art of the deal. The fantastic dimensions of the narrative extend to the power-grubbing effrontery of Trask's gatekeeper, whose sneering pleasure in refusing Jack and Tess' proposal is trumped (pun intended) by a mysterious phone call from Trask himself, commanding the deal to be set in motion. The scene ends with Harrison Ford, as Jack, eyeing possible hiding places for hidden cameras and the gatekeeper's assurance that Trask "knows everything." The scene plays, in other words, as commerce made mystical. A god has spoken, and some scramble for cover, while others smile with a grace bestowed. Jack Trainer, a seasoned professional (despite his recent "slump") appears as astonished by it as a neophyte like Tess. In fact, they only have this meeting because of crashing Trask's daughter's wedding, a barbaric abuse of opportunity that ought to have made Jack and Tess lepers at Trask Industries, if not across the length and breadth of the Financial District. If there is something magical about Trask, a sort of fairy-godfather of this Cinderella retelling, there is something undeniably magical inherent within Tess, as well—for all her earnest preparation and left-field ability to see lucrative connections between *Fortune* features and *Daily News* gossip, Tess has the magic of sex appeal, and she understands this. As she tells Jack when they meet cute over tequila (and Valium) at a closing party the night before her initial pitch at Dewey Stone, "I have a head for business, and a bod for sin." Jack approves of the package: "You're the first person I've seen at one of these damn things that dresses like a woman, not like a woman thinks a man would dress if he was a woman." Jack's highest praise of Tess to Trask, on the other hand, is simply, "She's your man." But a man couldn't have charmed Trask on the dance floor at his daughter's reception (nor could most women). For that particular job, it helps to be Melanie Griffith. As one might expect, in *Working Girls*, sex sells.

With her transformation from Staten Island broad to Katharine Parker wannabe, Tess' old circle can't help but notice her pretensions. Attending a party for Cyn and her fiancé, Tim, Tess butts heads again with Mick, who tells her morosely, "You look different." Without enthusiasm, he adds that she looks "Classy." The word has all the pejorative undertones that an ambitious blue-collar entrepreneur like Mick would be threatened by; despite his own ambitious reach, she's clearly reaching even further. His futile proposal, coming so quickly after his having been caught with Doreen, is as audacious in its way as Tess crashing the Trask wedding with a proposal of her own. But *Working Girl* is Tess' Cinderella story, not Mick's, and the fantastic clings to her initiatives, while we see Mick in a grittier sort of realistic success, with the less glamorous Doreen as his partner in the new boat business. Mick's transformation via American dream retains the boundaries of water—he will remain a Staten Island boy who will never be closer to Manhattan than its harbor. Tess's dream is complete; she aspires to and, in the narrative's wish fulfillment, becomes "classy"—a word uttered only by the underclass.

Tess flees Staten Island and Mick's proposal with his command that she get her "priorities straight" ringing in her ears. The next time we see her, she's attempting, simultaneously, to be two people: "Tess McGill of Petty Marsh" and "Miss McGill's secretary." Cyn watches her performance, unimpressed: "First of all, look me in the eye, and tell me you're not thinking, even in your wildest dreams, Mr. Briefcase-Let's-Have-Lunch is going to take you away from all of this." Cyn can't even imagine what Tess has been dreaming: Cyn thinks all this effort of night school self-improvement has just been to nab a higher-class husband. Cyn assures Tess, "You're gonna get your heart stomped, just like you're stomping Mick's." She functions as Tess' voice of reified resignation: "Look, all I'm saying is, if you're so smart, why don't you act smart?" The irony is that this is literally the project upon which Tess has embarked: she's play-acting a role as a Katharine Parker-style desk warrior. Assuring Cyn she knows what she's doing, her rationale is a near-paraphrase of Benjamin Braddock's outraged summation of social proscription to Elaine Robinson at the drive-in on their date in *The Graduate*: "I'm not going to spend the rest of my life working my ass off and getting nowhere, just because I followed rules that I had nothing to do with setting up." In *The Graduate*, Benjamin concludes that "no one" sets up the rules—"they make themselves up," an even more radical understanding of reified proscription than Tess' perspective on patriarchal exploitation. When the phone rings and, sitting at Katharine's power desk, she reflexively defaults to her imagined sense of power ("Tess McGill's office"), her defiance of the rule-makers that have pre-ordained her status is instantly deflated by Katharine's startled correction. "No," says Tess apologetically, "Of course it's still your office." Cyn piles on; as Tess listens to Katharine's orders entering through her phone ear, Cyn provides a parable for her free ear: "Sometimes I sing and dance around the house in my underwear. Doesn't make me Madonna. Never will."

Cyn's reference to the Material Girl is particularly apt, given Madonna's persona as a shape-shifting paragon of empowerment through reinvention, Madonna Louise Ciccone slipping her working-class roots to become a perpetual pop icon. Madonna is a kind of patron saint of canny self-commodification, always two steps ahead of the prevailing powers of her objectification, manipulating the manipulators. She would not have been out of place as the soundtrack's choral commentator on Tess' liminal passage from Staten Island ethnicity (a McGill stuck with her "Mick") to Manhattan player, apprenticed to a Trainer. Yet Carly Simon is an evocative choric presence as well, her career path working some of the same pop-exploitation territory Madonna would work a decade later: no female singer-songwriter of the 1970s more overtly sexualized her image than Simon in a series of frankly erotic album-cover portraits that interpreted her aggressive/confessional song-narratives ("You're So Vain"; "You Belong to Me"). As Nichols used variations on Simon's song, "Comin' Around Again" as both vicarious and ironic non-diegetic counterpoint to Rachel Samstat's travails in *Heart-burn*, so Nichols uses Simon's "Let the River Run" to promote the sensation of a dreamer's self-actualization.

Tess' reference to "rules" in her apologia to Cyn receives re-definition in the second half of *Working Girl*, when Katharine returns to Manhattan. Tess is immediately relegated to Cinderella-like chores, schlepping Katharine's suitcases and running her errands. The montage that immediately precedes Katharine's arrival includes the shot of Tess vacuuming, framed in a doorway like a life-size poster-portrait depicting the eroticized fantasy of patriarchy, in which the "bod for sin" is also good for menial servitude. (Sam Mendes quoted the image in *American Beauty*, his 1999 Academy-Award winner for Best Picture and Best Director, with Annette Bening as the object of desire domesticated, feverishly sweeping the carpet of one of her realty properties in her lingerie.) When Tess arrives with Katharine at the brownstone, it is shining—but Tess has "carelessly" neglected to turn off Katharine's computer. The screen reveals Katharine's memo about Trask intended for Jack Trainer, left visible by Tess as a sub-conscious accusation of her boss (otherwise, considering that the Trask deal is happening later that same day, Tess' carelessness is an air-headed error of colossal proportions). When Katharine sees the memo, she improvises, unfolding a story of Jack Trainer and unfounded allegations of ethical misconduct that ironically parallel her own misappropriation of Tess' idea (she can't know that Tess has heard her memo to herself on her Dictaphone and thus already has the accurate back story on the Trainer memo). "See, " Katharine says, "Jack got burned once. He was accused of stealing a plan for taking a company private.

He's very sticky about the ethics of reviewing other people's formative strategies. He wouldn't have looked at [the Trask idea] if I'd said it was from a colleague, and I couldn't very well say it was a secretary's notion." These last distinctions, between "colleagues" who have "ideas" and "secretaries" who have "notions," eliminates any residual qualms Tess might have had about what she's been doing while the boss was away. Katharine's rapacious exploitation of Tess makes the treachery of louts like Turkel and Lutz look like the relative amateurs they are. Where once she'd exuded to Mick, "It's so exciting. I mean, she takes me seriously. [...] There's none of that chasing-around-the-desk crap. And it's like she wants to be my mentor, which is exactly what I needed. I mean, I feel like I'm finally getting somewhere, Mick," now Tess must come irrevocably to terms with Katharine's sense of entitled ownership of Tess and whatever might emerge from her. In Katharine's eyes, Tess has no more right to her "idea" than to calling Katharine a "colleague." Intellectual property is relativized by hegemony: the best idea in the hands of the powerless is roughly equivalent to no idea at all.

Compounding her "error" in leaving the memo open on Katharine's computer, Tess "forgets" to collect her planner when she dashes from Katharine's house after delivering a pharmacy order, leaving ample evidence for Katharine to assemble to understand Tess' scheme. The film offers no definitive interpretation of these apparent gaffes, but Tess's predicament will not end with the finalizing of the Trask deal. She must discredit Katharine if she is to restore some of the credibility she will inevitably lose after confessing, as she must, that in sleeping with Jack and making a deal with Jack and Trask, she has fundamentally deceived them. If it is accidental that she allows Katharine a way into the proceedings of the deal, it is a fortuitous stroke of luck; if it is intentional that she offers Katharine clues to what she has been up to during her boss' absence, it is a brilliant stroke of strategy. Inevitably, Katharine must roar her outrage, and Tess must let her—but she would also know that she has done her homework on the Trask deal, and Katharine has not; its intricacies and Katharine's arrogant appropriation of the deal as her own without having earned its intellectual property still remain to undo Katharine and restore Tess as capable and hungry enough in a man's world to find the unorthodox side entrances—a crashed wedding, an assumed position—to command a hearing. It's possible that Tess only *appears* careless, and has in fact set Katharine up to hang herself on her own entitlement.

Working Girl is laden with mirrors and mirror-surfaces. As Katharine has spun her story at Tess, she's reflected in a mirror behind her, visually depicting the traditional cinematic trope of split identity or, more specifically in this case, two-faced deception. Yet no one in the film is reflected in more mirrored surfaces than Tess. The night of her birthday, alone with Mick, she laments she can't wear any of his pointedly erotic gifts in public; it's the first of many times we see her modeling a man's fantasy of women's lingerie, with peekaboo panels and dangling garter straps, and her reflection in the mirror sets up her divided identity as Mick's girl and Wall Street's girl. With Cyn at Katharine's house, she's back in garters again as she holds up a series of outfits to decide what to wear to surprise Jack Trainer at the party the night before their meeting, and the cocktail dress she eventually chooses is as stunning as it is stunningly out of place among the soberly masculine female couture decorating the rest of the women—like, for instance, Katharine's colleague Ginny, from whom Tess flees as if at the approaching stroke of midnight, to escape being revealed as a fraud. After leaving Katharine's house (leaving behind the incriminating details recorded in the planner), Tess pauses to appraise herself in the lobby of Trask Industries, choosing the mirrored surface of the brass Trask plaque; Griffith's prominent jaw sets with professional resolve that comes with playing her new role, as a scheming corporate deal-maker whose "two-way street" ethics make her appropriation of Katharine's status and contacts justifiable once Katharine has opened the taboo door by appropriating her idea. All these reflective doublings serve to remind us that the women in particular are held by patriarchy in the double bind of their corporate gender bending, where the narrative's highest praise from its princely hero is "She's your man."

In *Working Girl*, the Bad Girl is punished and the Good Girl is rewarded. More important, men preside over the adjudication of their cases and are the primary beneficiaries of all profits the women create. If *Working Girl* is Tess' fantasy of class climbing and gender empowerment, it's a fantasy that reverently respects its limits. While it may question the "rules" and rule-makers, it is quite comfortably recuperative on its surface. In the climactic showdown at Petty Marsh, Tess has cleaned out her desk, sobered by the collapse of a fantasy Cyn had warned her was bound by reified determinism to fail, and in the lobby, Tess falls even farther, her box of personal items jostled to the floor in the scrum at the elevators. But Jack lowers himself swiftly to his knees to help her, and his position as he speaks to her is as the wronged partner, both professionally and personally: "Just one thing: was you and me just part of the scheme, too?" Tess resignedly poses the question they all understand, from lowly cogs like Cyn to small dreamers like Mick to the fully entitled like Katharine and Jack and, at the top of the pyramid, Trask himself: "If I told you I was just some secretary you never would have taken the meeting. [...] Can you honestly tell me it wouldn't have made a difference?"

The narrative has brought them both to their knees, but Tess reminds Jack and us that there remain gradations of gendered powerlessness. Earlier, Jack has confessed to Tess his reified anxiety about the atavistic world in which they work: "One lost deal is all it takes to get canned these days." He spins a small morality tale about the little pieces of tape stuck one on top of another corresponding to the phone lines at his command on his desk—"new guys over the names of old guys, good men who aren't at the other end of the line anymore, all because of one lost deal." The dehumanizing meanness of such an environment reduces Jack physically: in a film that routinely presents Harrison Ford as beefcake, this scene allows him to look weak, anxious, diminished, a speck of bread from his sidewalk sandwich stuck to a corner of his mouth. The unmasking of his partner at the boardroom table would have been devastating had Katharine decided to ruin both Tess and Jack, but she still fancies Jack as her boy-toy, and so she is content to command, "Jack, just trust me and sit down." Where earlier in the proceedings, the salutations around the table began with "Gentlemen, and"— nodding in Tess' direction—"ladies," when Katharine waits for Tess to leave, autocratically reconvenes the walk-through of the deal's particulars, and then wisely hands the meeting back to Jack (because she has no idea about the nature of the deal), Jack's salutation to the assembly is less nuanced: "Well, gentlemen, the players may have changed but the game remains the same, and the name of the game is 'Let's Make a Deal.'" It's not Jack's finest moment. He's content to type Katharine with the rest of the men (seeing through her calculated ruse of weakness on her crutches). More important, he has just done to Tess precisely what he earlier abhorred about corporate culture: after commodifying her "bod for sin" by seducing her upon their first meeting with a deceptive concealment of his own identity, he manages now to exploit her "head for business," reaping the fruits of her idea. He's stuck a piece of tape over Tess. There's a sense in which his joining her on her knees is about his recognition of this, regardless of his expressions of injury. The "game" and its rules have consumed him, and this has not summoned his best behavior.

While Katharine has become a "man" in these climactic scenes, she retains a woman's innate sense of power inequity that must constantly be managed. Her feminine dizzy spell in the Trask boardroom may be the most blatant advertisement of her gendered status, but her response to Tess in the elevator lobby is as cliché a moment, this time the trope of the catfight for a man (Trask as much as Jack). Weaver's statuesque six-foot frame looms over Tess and Jack on the floor, and Katharine piles on, accusing Tess of attempting to steal additional files and the ideas they contain, as well as her fiancé. The best Tess can manage from her diminished position is to call Katharine "bony," a contrast to her "bod for sin" with its unmistakably generous curves; the insult is puny and ill timed and makes no impact on the players. She hasn't the spirit left for a catfight, but she rallies by mining her "head for business" and manages to shake Trask's confidence with her reference to "the hole in your deal." Now she has Trask's attention, and he deftly slips from Katharine's elevator just before it departs. By the time Katharine next sees Trask, his confidence in the deal has been restored; now it is Katharine he doubts. Katharine attempts a coup de grâce, dismissing Tess' pretentions to qualification: "Oren, we really don't have any more time for fairy tales." But she is out of luck, because that is precisely what *Working Girl* has always, unapologetically, been: a reified fairy tale of circumvented rules. Only one of the two women is able to articulate the deal's "formative strategy." Katharine, the mannish ("bony") working girl is ruined, while Tess, the hungry operator with the "bod for sin," is rewarded with an "entry-level" position at Trask. Overpeck writes, "Katharine's comeuppance draws attention to her lack of femininity. By comparison, Tess's strength is her ability to retain her femininity in the corporate world."[10]

Like Jack, Trask appears mystified by Tess' strange and apparently self-defeating behavior: "Why didn't you tell us all this in the boardroom that day?" That these supposedly intelligent men can ask such questions may be the most unrealistic element of the whole fantasy. In yet another instance when a Mike Nichols character temporarily sounds as if he or she has just stepped from the script of *Catch-22*, Tess argues, "You can bend the rules plenty once you get upstairs, but not while you're trying to get there, and if you're someone like me, you can't get there without bending the rules." Thus the narrative returns to "the rules," the auteur preoccupation of Nichols' career. The film has made a great fuss in hanging the contours of its narrative on ethical and unethical behavior, but concludes with an acknowledgement that opportune rule breaking is one of the most important rules of the culture.

The film doesn't end on this irony, however. Rather, we're given the opportunity to see Tess' wish fulfilled. Jack packs her a box lunch in a child's parody of a Rosy-the-Riveter lunch bucket, and Nichols sees this as "a dream of equalness" in which there might be "far more future for her than Benjamin [in *The Graduate*] because she and Jack [...] have the real beginning of a life together."[11] At Trask, she must endure a last role-reversal, this time with her secretary as the usurper. Alice Baxter (Amy Aquino) is not quite as ostentatiously big-haired and cosmeticized as Cyn and the rest of the Petty Marsh pool, and while she gently and apologetically corrects Tess about their stations (Tess defaulting to having misunderstood Trask's definition of "entry-level"), she also coolly corrects her about her own status: "If it's okay, I prefer 'assistant.'" Tess begins the redress of her sustained abuses in reviewing her expectations of Alice: "I expect you to call me Tess. I don't expect you to fetch me coffee unless you're getting some for yourself. And the rest we'll just make up as we go along." On a much more modest scale, this is Alice's fantasy come to life, too; Tess' allusion to making up their roles foregrounds fantasy in women's reverse conspiracy against the cabal of patriarchy.

Tess' first call from the privacy of her office is not to Jack—it's to Cyn, and Cyn's response is to rally the floor at Petty Marsh to a frenzied celebration that one of their own has achieved what amounts to a prison break. They are cheering for a friend but also for a fantasy; earlier, up on Katharine's floor at Petty Marsh when Tess is hired on the spot by Trask (who vows in the same autocratic breath to ruin Katharine), Tess and Jack kiss in full view of the deal-makers and the Petty Marsh secretarial pool, who react with sighs and applause—a veritable movie audience consuming the latest Hollywood confection. Can such things happen beyond "the movies?" In *Working Girl*, we watch it happen—but that's the point: it's a Hollywood fairy tale that deconstructs itself while delivering dependable genre rewards to an audience that was happy to lap them up, more than doubling the studio's investment in domestic box-office receipts alone. As in *The Graduate*, the mass audience is largely ignorant of irony in its sweet-toothed consumption of genre's confections.

The film's penultimate shot is of Tess on the phone with Cyn, captured from the air outside her office window. The slow zoom out gradually encompasses a grid of identical glass-and-steel offices in which, only by the greatest concentration, can we remain focused on where Tess is.[12] This shot dissolves into the final, gorgeous helicopter shot, lingering near the crown of the Woolworth skyscraper, of Tess' building, in which Tess' office is now an indistinguishable gray block in a receding labyrinth of office blocks that eventually resolves, as the helicopter drifts out over the harbor, into the southern tip of Manhattan, its western contour dominated by the Twin Towers. Subsequent events notwithstanding, there is ambiguity in the triumphalism of this final image (with Simon's voice celebrating "the New Jerusalem," which is "now an ironic counterpoint to Tess's new anonymity,"[13] in which individual dreams are subsumed within a yielding to the corporate whole.[14] If Tess can stand to make it there, she can make it anywhere, living with the anxiety of "the rules" and the omnipresent fear of becoming a mere name on an old piece of tape with newer names unceremoniously pasted on top. *Working Girl* gives its audience exactly what it wants, then asks us to consider if that's wise.

12

"Not like in the movies"

Postcards from the Edge (1990)

Of Mike Nichols' first five features after his return to Hollywood in 1983 with *Silkwood*, all but one of them were, in one sense or another, "from life." Beyond the depiction of Karen Silkwood's whistle-blower confrontation with nuclear power were *Biloxi Blues*, Neil Simon's fictionalized memoir of boot-camp xenophobia, and adaptations of two romans à clef: *Heartburn*, Nora Ephron's narrative of her marriage to and divorce from Carl Bernstein, and *Postcards from the Edge*, Carrie Fisher's fictional account of growing up talented but troubled in the shadow of a legendary Hollywood star, Debbie Reynolds. Richard Corliss calls it "a show-biz mother-daughter film par excellence—*Terms of Endearment* out of *Gypsy*."[1] In adapting Fisher's novel, however, Nichols added yet another dimension "from life": it is the film in his oeuvre that most personally explores his own relationship to cinema as a director.

It is symbolically appropriate that *Postcards from the Edge* stands at the midpoint of Nichols' career as a filmmaker, the eleventh of 20 feature films, made 24 years into a half-century of Hollywood filmmaking. *Postcards* is sturdily emblematic of his interests and themes and an appropriate mid-career stocktaking of his life as a filmmaker. In a career spent scrutinizing the often debilitating but occasionally transformative effects of socially proscribed performance, Nichols could be expected eventually to turn his satirist's gaze upon Hollywood itself, that capital of illusion and pre-fabricated performance. Fisher, who adapted her own bestselling roman à clef, acknowledges that she sent the book to Nichols as a possible staged "performance piece" (like Jules Feiffer with *Carnal Knowledge*), and as he had done with Feiffer, Nichols instead proposed to make a film that she would write. After several abortive attempts, she turned in pages with a scene between the novel's protagonist and a grandstanding mother, and Nichols encouraged Fisher to continue developing the film with this relationship as the source of central conflict.[2] The portrait of Hollywood Nichols paints is warmer than, for instance, the scabrous fun-house mirror Robert Altman would hold in front of Hollywood two years later in *The Player* (1992), with its hilarious cameo by Buck Henry in the opening shot as he tries to pitch a sequel to *The Graduate*. Indeed, that famous three-minute continuous take at the opening of *The Player* is a stylistic relative of the truth-or-illusion opening of *Postcards*, in which a complicated 150-second tracking shot is eventually spoiled by Suzanne Vale (Meryl Streep), too coked-up to keep from blowing a line. Later, looping the corrected dialogue with the film's director, Lowell Kolchek (Gene Hackman), Suzanne is convicted and mortified by her mistake, but Lowell generously acknowledges he shouldn't have been trying to do the scene "without cutaways." It's an echo of

155

observations Nichols has made about himself as a beginning filmmaker, looking back on how much he did *not* know about filmmaking as he got started.

Like everyone else with talent who has enjoyed success in the movie industry, Nichols is aware that the pressures and fish-bowl exposure of celebrity in Hollywood are realities with which one must come to terms, without protest or expectations of sympathy from the ravenous public. Lowell says as much to Suzanne in the film's most important scene, the looping session, which Lowell identifies as a perfect "metaphor" of how Hollywood is perpetually distinct from life. The entire post-production editing process offers a sense of retrospective control simply and purely unavailable as we fumble and grope our way through our lived lives. Not having an edit button to rely upon is what causes many individuals to settle into assumed identities, preferring the artificiality of reified performance to authenticity. Ironically Lowell, a Hollywood director of performances, seems able to understand and articulate this syndrome in a way that makes sense to Suzanne, assuming a parental authority her mother, Doris Mann (Shirley MacLaine), can never quite offer because of her own performance anxieties.

There's a different kind of through-line to the narratives Nichols was choosing to make mid-career. In *Working Girl*, *Postcards*, and his next film, *Regarding Henry*, the protagonists must learn how to act. They must perform a role until it potentially transforms them into better, authentic selves. In *Working Girl*, Tess McGill (Melanie Griffith) gets her Cinderella wish, via her "bod for sin," of using her "head for business." Yet the triumphalism of the ending suggests the possibility of ironic undercutting in the film's final two shots, in which Tess disappears, engulfed in the corporate labyrinth of lower Manhattan. It may be useful, in other words, to heed the old bromide to be careful what we wish for when accepting the dictates of social climbing. The ending of *Postcards* is equally triumphant in its superficial appearance, as Suzanne belts out a dynamic performance in Lowell's next film, but the ambiguities of this closing scene accrue: Suzanne is, after all, performing. Though in her element, she is not quite *herself* when we last see her, and the irony is that the old Hollywood saw has been demonstrated yet again: some of our best performers are most themselves when someone else. Not until *Regarding Henry* does Nichols depict unambiguous transformation; here, the ironies have been inserted much earlier in the narrative, since Henry (Harrison Ford) only embarks on his transformational journey unconsciously (in the most literal sense, in a recovery from traumatic brain injury). *Regarding Henry* offers its protagonist an opportunity not only to perform his way into a new, better self, but to come to terms with his old self and opt to continue playing a new "part." We see something similar offered by Tess when given Katharine Parker–like authority over an "assistant": "the rest we'll just make up as we go along" (an ambiguous line that alludes to the Cinderella fairy-tale quality of the narrative). *Postcards* accesses the improvisatory nature of identity in the complicated layering of selves in the looping scene, where Suzanne's cocaine-addled performance plays over and over, bigger than life, on the editing screen on the studio wall behind Lowell and Suzanne, and where looping can make her performance "better." Lowell suggests that Suzanne herself, post-rehab, seems "better," and clarifies this by adding, "Better because you're sober." Suzanne makes her own addition: "And worse because I'm sober." However, Lowell has the last word: "Yes, but worse in a good way." "Better" to have a "worse" Suzanne than a false, chemically enhanced Suzanne, getting by on charm and beauty and pharmaceuticals.

For Nichols, *Postcards* is a none-too-sentimental journey into his own past as a film artist, most directly by a witty accessing of his greatest celebrity in *The Graduate*. Although the entire Beverly Hills/generation-gap milieu invites reminiscence of Benjamin Braddock's disaffection among the Los Angeles nouveau riche, Nichols overtly references *The Graduate* in the homecoming party Doris throws for her daughter after rehab, which is not really a party for her daughter at all. The sequence features the most painfully self-conscious series of performances anywhere in this entire film about performers: Suzanne's coaxed and unwilling performance recalls Benjamin being goaded into descending to his graduation party and having to provide a "practical demonstration" of his parents' expensive birthday present, the scuba suit. As if to facilitate the flashback, Nichols even has his production team provide an exterior night scene at Doris' Beverly Hills house, with a pool glimmering nearby and, in the background, similar black-and-white striped awnings to those featured in the exterior décor at both the Braddock and Robinson houses. There is a conscious continuity and consistency of vision implied in this visual and dramatic reference to a much-beloved film. Yet Nichols in mid-career has mellowed towards his protagonists. The ironies and ambiguities have softened, allowing a stronger possibility of redemption latent within reified anxiety. Karen Silkwood, Eugene Jerome, Tess McGill, Suzanne Vale, Henry Turner—these mid-career Mike Nichols protagonists represent individuals less obviously imperiled by their own failure of imagination (like, for instance, Benjamin Braddock and Elaine Robinson in *The Graduate*, Jonathan from *Carnal Knowledge*, or Freddie from *The Fortune*) and thus on the cusp of the sort of "realization" that promises, in the terms Lowell and Suzanne use to describe it during the looping scene of *Postcards*, a changed life.

* * *

False appearances and performance—these are the preoccupations of Mike Nichols in his Hollywood cine à clef. Of course, these had long been preoccupations of Nichols' cinematic career, the very center of motivation in films like *Who's Afraid of Virginia Woolf?*, *The Graduate*, and *Carnal Knowledge*. The setting is, in one sense, the most momentous change: instead of academia as the origin point of role proscription, Nichols surveys his industry's back lot, a comic drama of life on the other side of the curtain. The mordant tone established by Carrie Fisher in her novel transfers intact to the screen, where, if anything, the ironies only deepen as the film captures films in production, false stage sets struck, and actors acting. In her DVD commentary track about the film,[3] Carrie Fisher reveals that when Meryl Streep, by this point a Nichols veteran from *Silkwood* and *Heartburn*, was offered the part of Suzanne Vale, the line that sold her on the film was Suzanne's terrified admission to her director, Lowell Kolchek, "I can't feel my life." Suzanne's ability to convince as an actress in a film or in her own identity is incumbent upon feeling, and yet she has been anesthetized by substances and faking her way through performances both on and off camera for so long that she no longer feels at home in the role of Suzanne (much less any other character she's been hired to play). At its heart, performance is less about transformation (its appearance) than alienation (its reality). As he has done since *The Graduate* (and again in films like, for instance, *Heartburn* and *Working Girl*), Nichols creates a narrative trajectory that ends in the profound ambiguity of generic triumph and complicated irony. In *The Graduate*, the love story of Benjamin and Elaine appears to have a happy ending, undercut by that joyless bus ride into a reconnection with "darkness, my old friend" and a directionless drift toward the future. In *Heartburn*, the slapstick, pie-in-the-face climactic dinner party and Rachel's liberation from marital indenture to an unfaithful man are undercut by the soundtrack reprise and its Nietzschean nod to eternal recurrence; in *Working Girl*, Tess makes-believe her Cinderella story all the way to Manhattan, but our last glimpse of her is obscured in the dizzying honeycomb of downtown office towers, another drone of the hive. At the end of

Postcards, Suzanne has capitulated to her mother's command performance to become a singer, and she's a star, just as Doris had predicted. It's a moment rich in those reflexive Hollywood-story dimensions: Nichols directs Streep (a producer's dream of a *Variety* headline) as Suzanne Vale, directed by a veteran studio director, much like Nichols himself—but, above all, near the rafters, hovering like the ghosts of the moguls (Zanuck, Mayer) she tosses with studied casualness into her conversations, Doris Mann is the impresario, a stage-mom on steroids (or vodka), with the clout to make her daughter over by sheer will in her own image. It's a Hollywood ending, all right, in all the rich complexity of that phrase.

The film opens twice, on idyllic long vistas of the Pacific. The first opening is to the unnamed film within the film, the genre exercise being made by Lowell Kolchek about clandestine activity in a banana republic. A foregrounded helicopter landing disturbs the tranquility of the ocean view, and a military man in stereotypic sunglasses emerges from the craft. Suzanne's character is one of three American women who have a plane to catch, but at customs, Suzanne's character is pulled aside by the soldiers, who take her into a back room and slap her around. The logistics of the take, now over two minutes old, are immense, and in an instant, the enormous choreographic effort of the scene is undone when Suzanne blows a line during her big patriotic-bravado speech: "Let me ask you something. Don't you ever get tired of acting like a cliché of a typical, generic, South American thug—yeah, great, go ahead and hit me again. Tell you something: our side'll always win, you know why? 'Cause we have more spirit and more resources than you. All it'll cost us is money. There isn't enough MOMMY in the world to further a cause like yours." Her co-actors in the scene break up at her Freudian slip; perhaps the in-joke hilarity of this daughter-of-a-famous-Hollywood-mother isn't lost on them. The tension of the scene, which has more to do with the uninterrupted take (homage to Orson Welles' audacious two-minute tracking shot to the bomb explosion that opens his 1958 Latin American noir classic, *Touch of Evil*) than with the genuinely stereotypic setting and characters and dialogue, dissolves in Suzanne looking directly at the camera, giggling, and breaking character with an oath. From off screen, Lowell yells, "Cut." We're out of cheesy melodrama and into the "real life" of Meryl Streep's character's substance abuse threatening Gene Hackman's character's film. While we may debate whether the greatest risk to Lowell's film is Suzanne's performance (what about that cliché-strewn script?), we're nonetheless introduced to Suzanne's default solutions to problems: acting. She laughs with the cast and crew, soothes Lowell with apologies, and disappears with her body double into her trailer to snort some fresh clarity. But we're also confirmed in our opinion (first incited in her blown line, then authenticated in Lowell's impatient brush-off of her apologies) that Suzanne isn't quite the actress she appears to be: when Lowell calls her out on her unprofessionalism and fires her supplier, he's vocalized a referendum on her livelihood, a performance in which it is even more crucial that she be convincing off-camera than on-.

After this initial sequence, prelude to the film's ongoing smirking about the reality of Hollywood illusion both on-screen and throughout the industry "behind the scenes," the film's "real" melodrama begins, with a refreshed long-shot vista over the Pacific and a complicated choreography of camera movement that eventually ends in two inert, debauched figures on a bed: Suzanne at the Malibu "ranch" of Jack Faulkner (Dennis Quaid). In Jack, Suzanne has found her level, a man even more committed to the performance of an act than she is. Perhaps this is what has caused her to overdose. Jack's wild Jeep ride to the emergency room has less to do with genuine care than with the ways in which the unscripted improvisation of a woman's death in his bed will affect his ability to sell the part he has grown accustomed to playing in Hollywood: the silver-tongued trophy hunter of ingénues. In the hospital's driveway, he stuns an orderly by explaining, of the semi-comatose figure in his passenger seat, "I'm dropping someone off": like Benjamin at the opening of *The Graduate*, reduced by the comparison cut to equivalency with his luggage moved along a conveyor belt, Suzanne is mere baggage to be unloaded.

Suzanne's charm is such that her incoherent mutterings on the E.R. table amuse Dr. Frankenthal (Richard Dreyfuss), who ends up sending flowers to her in rehab—an indication that Suzanne's life may have less to do with "reality" than that of the typical E.R. patient. Suzanne's roommate, Aretha (Robin Bartlett), is quick to give her the reality check that this is not how overdose-recovery usually works; Aretha's presence or absence in the film usually corresponds to Suzanne's degree of engagement with the world as it really is. New to the idea that she is in rehab, Suzanne's most visceral reaction during her admission interview is *anti*-reality: "My mother knows?" she moans. When confronted with the knowledge that "having to have your stomach pumped usually indicates fairly suicidal behavior," Suzanne's response reflects her radically disoriented relationship to her own actions: "Yeah, well, the behavior might be [suicidal], but I was certainly not." It's a kind of inverted aesthetic of the career actress.

Aretha persists at the periphery, in essence Suzanne's one "real" friend in every sense of that term: seemingly unimpressed—unlike many at the rehab clinic and elsewhere—by Suzanne and her famous grandstanding mother; consistently available to remind Suzanne of the realities of her life, good and bad; genuine in her care for and sympathy with Suzanne, without agenda. Aretha's presence invests the scenes where she appears with an assertion of Suzanne's desire to remain connected to a world beyond the industry or its influence, a world antithetical to Jack Faulkner's "lines" or even to Dr. Frankenthal's starry eyes. The film isn't about Suzanne's friendship with Aretha (we don't ever even learn why Aretha has landed in rehab, and this is perhaps because Suzanne herself has not delved this deeply into her friend's pain), but Aretha is the only friend on set when Suzanne performs her show-stopping final song for Lowell's latest genre film, with a country-western setting. Aretha, an addict, is the film's baseline for normalcy, a veteran of substance-abuse and recovery who doesn't have an interest in co-opting the vulnerabilities of the famous woman in the next bed or in manipulating her own vulnerabilities for sympathy points. This is ultimately why it's important that the narrative doesn't dwell on Aretha's story: she doesn't deny it, but she doesn't dwell on it, either. It's not her drama.

Suzanne's enforced companion is her mother, Doris Mann (Shirley MacLaine). The mechanics of the plot require that Suzanne be in the custodial care of one of her parents post-rehab as a stipulation of the insurers of her next film. Fisher readily admits that this crucial plot point is an artifice conjured to throw mother and daughter into repeated conflict, rather than an accurate reflection of industry practice.[4] If the scenario is less than convincing, the metaphor is what matters: Doris still commands her daughter's life, whether this is a contractual order or a legacy of substance dependency. Suzanne has inherited her mother's magnetism; she has also inherited her mother's vulnerability to addiction. When Doris makes her grand entrance at the rehab clinic, stagy in her lateness to ensure a full house at full attention, Suzanne does her best to stand up to her mother, but she only comes across as, by turns, impatient and cross and childish (down to cooing over some sweets her mother has brought her). When Doris embarks on her obligatory crying scene, Suzanne refuses to be her rapt audience. "Feels like I'm not talking to you sometimes," she says. "Feels like I'm talking to your drama coach."

So begins the ritualized, public humiliation of Suzanne Vale, a kind of expressionistic magnification of the non-anesthetized narcissism of the recovering addict (who dreams vivid, surreal dreams of trying to bogart pills in a luminous corridor decorated by famous overdose victims—Marilyn, Elvis, Belushi, Billie Holiday—and of being personally chided by Nancy Reagan). Her first day on the set is a disaster of bad filmmaking and producers. The film is yet one more terrible buddy-cop production. Suzanne seems almost intentionally miscast, as if to facilitate the patronizing comments of her director and a series of producers that begins, even before her first performance her first morning, with Rob Reiner bursting into her trailer demanding urine. The consensus is that she's holding back some essential quality she's capable of offering—it's our first sense of what she will later come to understand as her inability to feel her own life. This state might once, quite reasonably, have been ascribed to her substance abuse, but she is, at great cost, clean. While it will take her most of the narrative to fully come to terms with the source of her chronic numbness, the narrative immediately begins its demonstration of the source of Suzanne's—and her mother's—malaise. They are addicted to performance. *Performance* is here distinguished from *performing*, to which Doris seems far more committed than Suzanne; indeed, Suzanne expresses to anyone who will listen (as well as to her mother, who won't) her conviction that she needs to "get out of the business. If I don't I'll never have any kind of chance at a normal life." *Performing* is what both Doris and Suzanne are naturally good at, and it has paid their bills (at least until Suzanne's agent Marty steals her money and disappears). *Performance* is what they've accustomed themselves to, a falseness about their personal lives that requires booze and narcotics to live with the lies and that requires one of the foremost lies to be about the abuse of booze and narcotics. We shouldn't be distracted by the fact that those individuals addicted to performance are in fact performing professionals. They are susceptible to performance in precisely the same way, Nichols argues, as academics (*Virginia Woolf*), lawyers and doctors (*The Graduate* and *Carnal Knowledge*), the military (*Catch-22*), and so on.

Whether or not Suzanne's overdose was a premeditated act of self-annihilation, a calculated call for attention, or a desperate cry for help, there can be no questioning that the narrative of *Postcards* identifies it as a boon for Doris' performance addiction. On her way home from her disastrous first day on the cop movie, Suzanne and her mother predictably squabble and spar; Suzanne asks her mother in exasperation at being upstaged at every turn even of a private conversation: "How did we end up talking about your death from my drug test?" Her mother is just getting started, however: awaiting them at home is a Hollywood mansion full of guests assembled, in stunningly poor taste, to welcome Suzanne home from her rehab stint. More horrific is the immediate sense that the party is merely a pretext for Doris' celebration of herself. The parallels to the Beverly Hills parties in *The Graduate* thrown by the Braddocks ostensibly in honor of their son Benjamin's milestones (his college graduation, his 21st birthday) would be pronounced even if Nichols and company had not gone to the additional trouble and expense of including night exterior shots by a glowing in-ground swimming pool and of those distinctive black-and-white striped awnings so prominent in the exterior décor of both the Braddock and the Robinson houses. The chief correspondence between the parties thrown in both films is that they are transparent advertisements for the party throwers, cruelly at the emotional expense of the erstwhile honorees, the children. In *The Graduate*, the emphasis is on performance anxiety—the scenes offer little in terms of genuine performance, while great energy is expended in pep talks and crowd-handling; in *Postcards*, however, Suzanne is a more seasoned performer than Benjamin, and even more aware of her social construction as a performer. *Postcards* posits a child at a similar power disadvantage to a parent's willed conformity, but offers a more hopeful variation on *The Graduate*'s ambiguous resolution.

Doris ushers Suzanne into her amateurishly arc-lit foyer and announces, "My little girl is home." The infantilizing reference recalls Mr. Braddock's persistent allusions to "this boy" when serving as barker to Benjamin's diving exhibition at the birthday party. Suzanne is chronically trapped in the trained-monkey role as Doris Mann's "little girl," much as Doris herself remains the chronically diminished daughter of Grandma, played with homespun ferocity by Mary Wickes, demeaning all loved ones in sight. We first meet "Grandma" out on the lawn, where Suzanne escapes with Aretha for some fresh, non-performative air. Grandma storms over and makes the first direct acknowledgment of Doris' own problems with substances: "Well your mother started drinking her wine. Unless I want to sit around all night listening to her rattle off the mouth, I thought I'd hightail it on out of here." It's a brief first cameo by an old familiar Hollywood face, and she chews scenery (and Conrad Bain's ear, as the beleaguered Grandpa in early-stage dementia) and exits quickly enough that we can't help but think of it as yet another performance, short but something other than sweet, Grandma's great passive-aggressive disappearing act. There is barely time for Suzanne and Aretha to catch their breath from catching some fresh air before Doris has sent the maid out onto the lawn after Suzanne to convey her command performance. Suzanne's reaction shot with pool behind her captures her in the same entrapped position as Benjamin after Mr. McGuire's "Plastics" speech. Nichols and O'Steen cut to the gruesome symbolism of the post-rehab cake, a slab with Suzanne's headshot likeness, diced into dozens of pieces to be consumed by the party guests. It's a conceit Nichols and O'Steen have used before to achieve a similar effect, when the marine biologists at the Terrell Center in *The Day of the Dolphin* cut a cake in the shape of a dolphin, an unconscious revelation of their exploitative relationship to their fellow mammals.

Despite all the tricky business of shots within shots in *Postcards*, of showy in-production long takes like the first shot of the film or the comically inept process shots of Suzanne dangling from a high-rise ledge or shooting inexpertly from within a bobbing speedboat, the two most obvious depictions of performed expectation in the film are the back-to-back musical numbers delivered at the party by Suzanne and her mother, and Jack Faulkner's avowals of love by the sea, on the back patio of his Malibu "ranch." At the "surprise" party, the order of performance has been decadently anticipated by Doris, who offers her daughter not merely to be consumed, but to be consumed expressly as a warm-up act for her own vamping. Coaxed by Doris' audience, who perform their own expected role of ardency, Suzanne is powerless to resist this extension of her mother's will; she chooses, nonetheless, to "speak" to her mother in the old Ray Charles showstopper "You Don't Know Me" as a kind of Freudian soliloquy. Doris, whose rapt, oblivious attention basks in the glow of Suzanne's performance, acknowledges only Suzanne's appearance, not the pointed substance, of her selection: Doris nonverbally urges Suzanne to shrug off her wrap and show a little of that creamy skin that runs in the family, and Suzanne duly complies. The cutaways to Doris' delighted, stage-mom reactions are only a secondary assertion of Doris' dominance of Suzanne's performance; watching with the audience, the camera prominently frames Suzanne with Doris' painted portrait beaming down on her from the back wall.

Suzanne's song ends wistfully, her message not received, her performance charming in its vulnerability and ambivalence. She's been humbled by her fall; she lacks the unrepentant seismic authority of her coked-up self in Lowell's film, or of her mother's booze-chutzpah. (It's the quality that the producers on her current film, the bad buddy-cop picture, are asking for without knowing what it is they're asking.) Suzanne resigns the party's spotlight and, bathed in the audience's mild, admiring applause, takes a seat in the crowd, leaving her mother "awkwardly" captured in the glare of audience attention. On cue, a guest calls for Doris to sing. Even the staging of Doris' performance is staged. Doris' protesting resistance is pro forma. With melodramatized ardor, she looks at Suzanne and proclaims a reciprocity of performance: "You sang for me, I'll sing for you." In her haste to slake her thirst for the audience's thirst for her, she can't even hold the tender maternal moment; turning to the pianist, she reveals her pro's preparedness: "'I'm Still Here' in D flat." The song, about dogged, near Darwinian show-business survival, is by Stephen Sondheim, from *Follies*; it's an impeccable choice by Nichols, with his encyclopedic knowledge of theater and incomparable entertainment world connections (he'd worked with Sondheim in 1962, staging a Jules Feiffer comic-musical revue[5]), as apt a selection for Doris as Suzanne's choice of "You Don't Know Me" for herself. Nichols even had Sondheim write some additional "improvised" lyrics especially for Doris, including "giving auditions on Zanuck's lap."[6]

Heeding her own advice to Suzanne, she flashes some skin as the show starts, giving a brief glimpse of a long leg. The layers of self-aware performance keep piling up, as MacLaine, channeling Debbie Reynolds, references "Shirley MacLaine" in another line of particularly campy improvisation: "I'm feeling transcendental—am I here?" The moment is good, clean Hollywood fun in the service of Nichols' consistent inquiry into human complicity in objectification: MacLaine acknowledges her Hollywood-packaged, free-spirit iconography as entertainer and cosmic cadet while playing a woman acknowledging her Hollywood-packaged, free-spirit iconography. Doris is in fact equally adept—and content—to package and deliver both her daughter and herself, damn the costs and consequences. As the show-stopper climbs towards her performative climax, she seems to improvise a cruel, self-serving line about Suzanne's travails—"I got through all of last year, and I'm here"—but the line is original to Sondheim's song; the improvisation here is in her non-verbal gesture of "tenderness" towards Suzanne, who blanches at the public reference to her weakness and failure. It's a ghoulish stroke of good fortune for Doris that her lovely, talented daughter has hit bottom. And the vampiric energy derived from this "fortune" fuels Doris' final vamped spectacle, atop the piano, flashing every inch of leg plus the color of her panties. (Nor, we learn in a later aside, was this Doris' only scene-stealing performance at a party ostensibly for her daughter: there was an earlier showstopper at a birthday party for Suzanne, involving a flash of leg and a far more sensational view for the guests, unobstructed by underwear.)

Suzanne cheers her mother's crowd-pleasing finale, insensible in the moment's magic to the emotional expense of her mother's addiction to the spotlight, but Nichols acknowledges its toll by creating a comic jump cut to a sight-gag process-shot on the set of the buddy-cop movie: Suzanne "hanging" by her fingertips from a window ledge. The visual metaphor is, if anything, given greater comic power by being so absurdly false; it's an acknowledgment of a film audience's suspension of disbelief in accepting Hollywood's storytelling conventions. On set but off drugs, Suzanne ought to be more present than she was on Lowell Kolchek's film, but she is precisely the opposite, at least according to the buddy-cop director and producers. The irony of *Postcards* is that, newly sober and thus un-insulated against the world, she's out of touch with a world in which layers of cosmetic and chemical barriers reduce the risks inherent in confrontation with the genuine. At her lowest, hungrily eyeing someone's neglected pharmaceutical bottle, Suzanne reels from the funhouse of the Hollywood studio directly into the arms of Jack Faulkner. We recognize him long before she does. Nichols and company have great fun in the background of this scene, disassembling a suburban Hollywood street and turning it into an asphalt back lot of parked cars—another comic metaphor of willed illusion and broken spells. We know she's at a studio, bereft about her loss of power as a performer, but it *looks* like she and Jack are rekindling a high-school crush. As Jack delivers his "lines," including an impression of Jimmy Stewart and his telltale, awkward compliments about how she smells, Suzanne sways between knowing the truth of Jack's illusion and wanting to surrender to it. Nichols and Fisher offer Suzanne a brief intermission from Jack's "show" during which Suzanne returns home to witness more of *Doris'* show. Jack arrives to take Suzanne for a "drive" to his "ranch," and Doris oozes vampy charm; all that's missing is for Jack to ask, "Are you trying to seduce me, Mrs. Mann?" When Suzanne calls her on it, Doris replies testily, "Well, why can't we *share* people?" Understanding herself purely as object of desire, she can't conceive of anyone else on other terms.

In the next cut, to Jack's "ranch," Nichols and O'Steen return for a third time to the film's default opening vista: the familiar long shot of the Pacific. These shots have, by this point, ironically oriented us to the film's strange, movie-idiom logic, moving from the dreamy, romantic remoteness of the ocean to more immediate clashes between illusion and reality—banana republic intrigue yielding to flubbed dialogue; a night of love yielding to the comatose morning after; and now, Jack Faulkner's protestations of love, which scream scripted insincerity, and to which Suzanne knowingly yields. Jack's "lines" unfold during a slow zoom that, for all its gentleness, is none-too-subtle in broadcasting the tropes of Hollywood romance. His words are so transparently Hollywood woo-talk that Suzanne makes fun of them: when he "confesses" he has "feelings" for her, she parries, "How many—more than two?" Jack "acts" hurt and protests his love: "I thought I was immune to movie stars, but I've wanted you from the first moment I saw you on screen, and that never happens to me. You're the realest person I've ever met in the abstract." It's a blunderbuss approach to seduction, and inevitably, some of the scattered shot hits the target. Until now, the soundtrack has left us alone with the ambient noise of the coast and Jack's hushed entreaties, but now Nichols layers on the programmatic strings of surrender. Suzanne yields, and Jack, who ought to know a closed deal when it's laid out on the table, can't stop himself: "You'll never be sorry," he says, and Suzanne has the scene's comic last word: "You sound like a rug salesman." Jack knows enough at least not to break the spell of her reduced sales resistance by protesting this characterization, which Suzanne in any case follows with an ardent, "*My* rug salesman." This is an important moment in the film, not because it demonstrates Suzanne's reified awakening but because it dramatizes her hitting the reified snooze button. Well aware of her reified anxiety in both the welcome-home party scene with her mother and this love scene with Jack, Suzanne remains unable or unwilling to resist her own commodification. Her passivity in permitting herself to be sliced up and consumed by the narcissistic appetites of Doris and Jack makes her complicit in her ongoing suffering, the only life she can "feel."

Drugs, booze, sex—these are mere symptoms of a larger syndrome of addictive performance, in which having an audience is the greatest drug, and being an audience delivering adoration on cue is next best. Jack, Suzanne learns, is everything he says he isn't, a prodigious sexual performer who can't even limit himself to a single Hollywood actress on a given day. Suzanne's confrontation with Jack comes after a memorably casual series of confessions by Evelyn Ames (Annette Bening), who "plays the prostitute" in the picture. Through Evelyn, Suzanne learns of Jack's galling lack of originality as a seducer—most of his lines are recycled, and Evelyn, probably to be nice, but managing to dig the knife, consoles Suzanne by saying, "You're obviously getting some new stuff, which means he must like you." The conversation comes on one of those jarringly decorated Hollywood sets, where Southern California has been transformed to a wintry east-coast street of row homes at Christmastime. Suzanne drives directly from the set to Jack's house, still wearing her cop's blues, intent on "busting"

Jack. She rails at him for his falseness, her words the epitome of the Hollywood broken heart, and when she begins a familiar rhetorical phrasing (she insists, "It's not the fact that you will leave" that bothers her so much), Jack accuses *her* of the sin of dissembling: "It *is* the fact that I will leave," he says, and he assures her that he will. He's a Hollywood trope of The Cad, except he's been stricken with a brief, rage-induced truth serum. What Jack articulates is the always-unspoken compact of performance in which the sexes are to conduct their proscribed roles. Suzanne's "busting" Jack shatters the illusion of their "Hollywood romance," a terrible threat to Jack—who as a result vanishes from the narrative, never so much as referred to again, a mirage she's drawn too close to and can no longer see. The moment of truth so disarms and disillusions (in the best sense, even if she's in no condition at that moment to understand it as such) Suzanne that she simply stalks away, storming home to her mother's medicine cabinet.

So begins the climactic confrontation with her mother, which ranges over most of Doris' Beverly Hills floor plan. Suzanne has scored two tablets of some prescription drug, a tranquillizer or painkiller, and it may surprise us when she doesn't immediately pop the pills in her mouth, instead dropping them into the breast pocket of her cop costume. Her instincts are rewarded because Doris is on the prowl, and only half-accepts Suzanne's story of looking for aspirin. (The idea that Suzanne might actually kick her habit must be terribly threatening to Doris' own sub-conscious convictions about addiction, and to see Suzanne regress would thus be a twisted comfort—perhaps the reason the prescriptions in her medicine cabinet have not been removed to some secure location to begin with.) In the kitchen, as her mother constructs a health-food smoothie, Suzanne forages, eating cold pasta from a container in the refrigerator. Doris appears to be far more in control during this scene than her daughter, though Nichols and Fisher eventually reveal this to have been yet another illusory, booze-fueled performance: Suzanne looks jarringly out of place in her police blues (pills in pocket), binging at the open fridge door, while her mother has to remind her of her looping appointment at the studio with Lowell Kolchek, another of her messes for which Suzanne must accept responsibility. Doris continues to take a kind of unholy satisfaction in Suzanne's troubles; in an earlier run-in between mother and daughter, in which Doris denies an alcohol problem, she says, "I hardly think that my drinking can be compared with your drug-taking. Even if it could be, I think that your involvement with drugs has vindicated me. I hardly think you're in a position to judge me." The irony is that Suzanne's substance-abuse predicament ideally equips Suzanne to identify, sympathize with, and, in having dried herself out, "judge" Doris. Doris is a legendary performer, but Suzanne knows the ins and outs of the role by now almost as well as her mother does. She has seen through Jack; she can also see through her mother. Doris can't kid a kidder.

Doris, in need of a drink and reasserted power over Suzanne, chooses this moment in the kitchen to break her daughter, unloading the news of new public humiliation: Suzanne's agent, "Uncle Marty," has stolen her money and disappeared, and Suzanne's father's lawyer has been put on Marty's trail. Suzanne predictably flees upstairs in fresh mortification, and Nichols and MacLaine ad-lib an improvisation to Fisher's script: Doris pulls down a bottle of booze from a cabinet and liberally fortifies her health-food concoction, which she'll drink for courage through the remainder of this showdown with her daughter. When Doris goes hunting for Suzanne, she finds her, changed into civvies (providing no evidence of what has become of the pills she's cadged) and out of steam on the hall staircase. Doris pushes again (a pitch so familiar that Suzanne can finish all her lines) her desire to recast her daughter's career by producing a record album. Suzanne articulates her most threatening desire of all:

to get out of the performing business entirely. The resonance of such a threat (Suzanne surrendering the family's most deeply held addiction) must be so chilling to Doris that it flushes out into the open their most carefully guarded secrets. When Suzanne defiantly airs the truth of her own addiction ("I took the drugs; no one made me"), Doris accepts it as an attack and responds with a seeming non sequitur: "Go ahead and say it: you think I'm an alcoholic." (She's holding the "health-food" smoothie as she says it.) Not only does Suzanne rise to the challenge and confront her with this reality, but before they are through, she has laid out the final accusation of their life together: that Doris hooked her on sleeping pills while Suzanne was a pre-adolescent. The showdown collapses, both women disoriented from having broken their default "script" so completely to air the truth. Doris storms upstairs, Suzanne out to the driveway, where she revisits the rage she's felt as she roared away from Jack. This time, however, she has drugs in hand, and we see her take the two pills she'd palmed before she roars away from her mother's house. The moment is a devastating encapsulation of failure, her sobriety and her fully awakened reification seemingly squandered in a single, self-defeating act. A moment later, when she pauses at a manicured Beverly Hills curb down the street but still in view of her mother's house, she induces herself to vomit up the bolted pasta and pills before rushing down into Hollywood to meet Lowell. This is what off-script improvisation can look like: messy but *original*. Suzanne has asserted authorship of her life, no longer content with the part into which she's been cast, and which she has so dutifully performed. Vomiting has never seemed so attractive.

Nichols and Fisher construct the sequence of three scenes at the climax of the film—Suzanne's climactic crisis in the argument with her mother and her refusal to digest the pills she has swallowed; her debriefing with Lowell Kolchek about the neatness and resolution of art and the messiness and muddling irresolution of life; and her mother's climactic crisis of this same tension between art and life—as an ambiguous resolution of Suzanne's dramatic journey. Throwing up the pills (and, in the previous scene, "bringing up" her mother's and her own well-guarded secrets) is a purgative, the quintessential rejection of the toxins of the past that we see as a typical third-act staple of Nichols' narratives. George and Martha shakily enter the dawn of a new day in *Virginia Woolf.* Benjamin and Elaine flee the castle-keep at the end of *The Graduate.* Yossarian follows Orr's lead and goes AWOL at the close of *Catch-22.* Rachel decamps from Washington with her raging case of *Heartburn.* What makes *Postcards* a different narrative than any of these early resolutions is that rejecting the past isn't the final action of the film. All these earlier films focus on negative movement, a retreat from past illusion or entrapment, without indicating what Elaine desires for Benjamin to articulate when she comes to his boarding-house room in Berkeley: she wants Benjamin to leave, but she doesn't want him going anywhere until he has a "definite plan." In their *very* different ways, both *Silkwood* and *Working Girl*, two narrative journeys of working-class women towards personal and professional empowerment, offer complicated resolutions that move beyond the turning point to what might come next: a woman's first tentative attempts at establishing autonomy. (However, neither film, as we have seen, leaves such movement to be perceived except through a thick, pervasive fog of ambiguity, particularly in Karen's death, of course, but also in Tess' being swallowed up by dog-eat-dog lower Manhattan.) Lowell Kolchek, her director and the closest thing she has to a stable adult in her life, helps Suzanne articulate the wisdom available after she has rejected—literally, *ejected*—her default dependency on drugs for performance. The structure of the film has her absorb Lowell's wisdom; then it tests her on how well she has absorbed it by immediately putting her in the position of counseling Doris on the same newfound wisdom. The three performances by Streep—in

Having ruined a bravura long take while high during her last film before rehab, Suzanne Vale (Meryl Streep) meets her director, Lowell Kolchek (Gene Hackman) at the studio to loop her missed line and reflect on the difference between fixing mistakes in art and in life. Unlike similar compositions in Nichols' *Carnal Knowledge* and *Closer*, this enlarged image from the film-within-a-film in *Postcards from the Edge* reflects a woman's enlarged awareness of her complicity in her commodification—by her agent, by Jack Faulkner, even by her mother. The next scene, in which Suzanne counsels her mother as Lowell has counseled her, beautifully illustrates her absorption of reified wisdom.

Silkwood, *Heartburn*, and *Postcards*—create a loose triptych of feminized reification: Streep plays three women of exceedingly different milieus (the heartland and both coasts) who nonetheless share in common a gradually focused, edifying anxiety that provokes the possibility of meaningful transformation. (And Streep's performance thirteen years later as the middle-aged Hannah Pitt in *Angels in America* will add a fourth such character, the most unambiguously transformed by her experience.) Of the three earlier films, made within a seven-year span in the 1980s, *Postcards* offers the most triumphant resolution for its protagonist, though Nichols can't resist lingering ironic ambiguity.

Suzanne rushes into Lowell's editing studio, where he sits idle with his staff, clearly waiting on her arrival. She's abjectly apologetic, and Lowell offers an ambiguous absolution. When he says they weren't expecting her for another half an hour, he suggests there's an automatic industry recalculation for mercurial talents like Suzanne's: she's probably half an hour or more late, but not as late as the drug-addled Suzanne would have been. Her Freudian slip du jour with Lowell comes when, asked if she'd like something, she automatically requests

"Coke," and after a hyper-conscious beat in which all wait in a stunned silence, she stammers out, "... -a-cola." She's full of nervy, hand-wringing energy, still on the jag that induced her to swallow then purge the pills, and it tells us something, since we'd seen so little of the pre-rehab Suzanne, that Lowell observes in all sincerity, "You seem better now," when she seems anything but. She makes him qualify the claim twice: "Better because you're sober," and then, finally, "worse in a good way." The moment in the long take she ruined projects on the wall behind them, Suzanne in two-shot close-up, luminous and blowing her line with the "mommy" slip-up. Looking at this past self, she falls back into apology mode, and Lowell chides her gruffly, practically, "No, don't be sorry. Just *fix* it."

The scene is, from this point, saturated with meta-commentary on the art-life metaphors of performance and editing. The looped snippet of the long take rolls over and over on the back wall as Suzanne first nails the line, then breaks down in mingled exhaustion and relief during playback. Lowell asks for the room, and his crew clears out so quickly they don't power down the projection, which continues to loop her mistake like a bad memory. "What could possibly be the matter?" Lowell asks into the dense, anxious cloud of her tears. "You've gone back and corrected the past, at least in your work. What could be a better metaphor?" The essence of Lowell's advice is not about self-editing, however, which in any case is not possible except as the illusion she and her mother have practiced through denial and anesthetization. Instead, his wisdom focuses on re-creation, and it comes out of his mouth not so much like a bumper sticker (to whose reductive oversimplification she objects at the rehab clinic) but "a little like movie dialogue," which is how Lowell describes it in explaining its appeal to Suzanne. "Yeah, that's me," says Suzanne. "I don't want life to *imitate* art; I want life to *be* art." It's an articulation of the performed life so habitually remote from authenticity that, as she confesses, "I can't feel my life." The irony is that she can *feel* the terror of not feeling—precisely what the drugs had once alleviated. Lowell counsels patience as she learns to be genuine: "Growing up is not like in the movies, where you have a realization and your life changes." In real life, it takes more time; transformation is a gradual process, not a movie cut. Lowell has the power to help speed Suzanne's transformation, because he puts her back to work, in the movie with the show-stopping scene that literally ends *Postcards*. Is a Hollywood ending still a Hollywood ending if it calls into question its essential confected quality, its Hollywood-ness?

We see this final scene through the prism of innumerable Hollywood films about the corrosive glamour of Hollywood. We know enough about these stories to know that they as often end up on the front page of the supermarket tabloids as they do the front page of *Variety*—that in fact what makes the glamour of Hollywood corrosive is the symbiosis of those two different kinds of page-one headlines. They have met in Suzanne Vale's life, and they meet in Doris Mann's life at the film's climax, in the crying scene between mother and daughter after Doris, in her cups from too much health-food smoothie, wraps her vintage car around a Beverly Hills tree. As Suzanne approaches the Emergency Room, Nichols and cinematographer Michael Ballhaus set up the camera in the same location as when Jack Faulkner ran off after dumping Suzanne at the hospital. The contrast is two-fold: Suzanne is nothing like her overdosed self; in recovery, she is also nothing like Jack. She does not run from the problems of reality but to them. She's prepared to face reality as something other than a scenario to be performed.

Dr. Frankenthal remains on duty, delighted for another opportunity to bird-dog Suzanne, and while Suzanne holds him at bay, there is something appealing to her about his relative ordinariness and warts-and-all acceptance. He's seen her at one version of her worst.

For now, however, the subject is her mother, and as she steps into Doris' room, we may have trouble recognizing the profoundly deglamorized, diminished figure in the bed: half-bald, sallow, and tiny, that's Shirley MacLaine! That's Doris Mann. Lording over her own daughter's collapse in an even more direct and ghoulishly delighted way than Doris has done to Suzanne is Grandma, who bellows at Suzanne, "Oh there she is, my other monster. I can't seem to keep you two out of the hospital lately." Clearly, nothing could please her more. Suzanne kicks her out to the waiting room, and when Doris reflexively performs her role ("I suppose she means well"), Suzanne's poignant, prickly reply is: "Yeah—she sounds like that voice in your head that tells you you can't do anything."

Hollywood loves these scenes; indeed, MacLaine won the Oscar six years earlier in *Terms of Endearment* (James L. Brooks, 1983), partially on the strength of a tearful hospital-bed scene like this one, with Debra Winger as her daughter. Nichols and Fisher know the scene, know we know the scene, and deconstruct the genre of such scenes as they watch mother and daughter literalize the cosmetics of performance. Doris confesses her Norma-Desmond anxiety about her "turn" in the spotlight being "almost over," but surrenders it to her desire to see her daughter "enjoy your turn." The transformation of Doris is so quick we know it can't be total, and she will slip back into jealousy. The point is that she has accessed the truth of her experience and Suzanne's in this moment. The two prepare Doris's "face" for her latest close-up with the press, waiting in a hungry pack down the hall. Donning her white mink, her headscarf a regal turban, she comments to Suzanne, "You know what my mother said to me yesterday? She said that I've put on airs. I use big words like 'gesture' and 'devastate.' I don't think they're so awfully big, do you? What am I supposed to do, sound like a hick the rest of my life just to make her happy?" There are layers of irony to this speech, as Doris, a bit bloodied but unbowed by her very public accident, straightens to star-posture and sashays down the corridor to meet the media. Suzanne, standing with Frankenthal, watches Doris and adopts a brief, simultaneously sardonic and admiring sway to her own hips. "We're designed more for public than for private," she concludes—but this is true of us all, albeit for most to a decidedly reduced degree of magnification. We must all contend with and negotiate the social gaze; reified anxiety grants us the opportunity to gain wisdom from the way the gaze holds us in it sights, molding us and making us "act."

The entire last act of *Postcards from the Edge* is Nichols and Fisher's self-aware assertion of the potency of Hollywood's metaphors of performativity and commodification, of "hot properties" who are "larger than life." Some, like Jack Faulkner and Evelyn Ames, are content to play their roles, to accept with cynical good cheer their mutual objectification. Others, like Suzanne and, perhaps, her mother, may see a redemptive possibility along the lines of what Lowell Kolchek has articulated, rejecting inherited dysfunction and constructed limitation to declaim, "I start with me." Nichols cautions that all his film depicts is "a *small* step forward."[7] How, then, should we read the ending of *Postcards*, which adopts a familiar Nichols' narrative strategy of echoing the beginning at the end (famously first introduced in "Sounds of Silence" reprised at the end of *The Graduate* but also either literally or poetically the structural design of films as different as *The Fortune*, *Heartburn*, and *Biloxi Blues*)? In *The Graduate*, with which *Postcards* overtly dialogues, and where Nichols first established this rhetoric of recurrence, Benjamin's passivity and blankness of purpose at the end of the film mirror his countenance at the opening: he's still being defined in relation to his parents and their values, still in ineffective retreat from their wide-reaching way of life. In *Postcards*, Suzanne begins and ends the film captured in performance under the gaze of Lowell's camera, the stakes raised by her director's love of the long take. Not only does the show-stopping performance of the country-western song evoke (and eclipse) Suzanne's botched opening performance, but it also resonates with the first song we heard her sing, the coerced and reluctant version of "You Don't Know Me," a statement a default-performer can make with confidence. Aside from Lowell and perhaps some vaguely familiar faces among the crew, there are only two people on the set that we assume are there by direct invitation of Suzanne Vale. The first is Aretha, the new, true friend, who has been through the rehab wars with Suzanne and has seen first-hand (at the surprise party) where Suzanne's neuroses have their roots. Aretha's presence signals Suzanne's commitment to the ongoing project of reality. The other invited guest, Doris, was standing with Aretha but then steps away, permitting interpretations running the gamut from jealousy to a desire not to crowd her daughter's "turn." Doris becomes the payoff at the end of a long crane shot in which the camera moves us from the set floor out over the crew and up into the rafters of the building, where Doris beams down from her high roost. Another interpretation of her lofty perch is of the god who has had her way: she has made no secret of wanting to see her daughter become a singer, and now ... here she is, performing. As with "You Don't Know Me," Suzanne's song would seem to carry a message meant specifically for her mother; Nichols tapped another old friend, the poet and children's author Shel Silverstein, for his loving country-western parody, "I'm Checkin' Out (Of This Heartbreak Hotel)." (The song was nominated for an Academy Award but lost—to Stephen Sondheim, for a song he wrote for Warren Beatty's *Dick Tracy*.) As belted by Streep after a tentative opening verse, the song has the feel of a rebel yell, and it seems aimed at her mother not in defiance but in invitation: if she's breaking out, perhaps her mother would care to join her. Suzanne's performance is acknowledged by a very different response by Lowell at the end of the long take; on his previous film, her blown line and nervous hilarity had elicited only a muttered, "Cut," but this time, as she brings down the house, we hear the director say, distinctly, "Cut. Print." The film ends as it begins, as our social lives themselves inevitably do, in scrutinized performance. Our experience designs us all "more for public than for private." In her reified awakening, Suzanne is better equipped to contend with the command performances of life post-drugs, post-denial, and in an assertion of her own terms.

13

"Say when"

Regarding Henry (1991)

Mid-career, Mike Nichols became increasingly drawn, in his own words, to narratives of "transformation."[1] His second phase began with his first (of four) films with Meryl Streep, as Karen Silkwood, the Okie narcissist cum activist, a phenomenal metamorphosis in temperament and values, but Nichols sought out variations of ever-more dramatic change: the recovering substance-abusers in his previous film, *Postcards from the Edge*, constitute a significant before-after continuum, but Nichols was only warming up for the series of films that would close his second-phase run through 2000 and the major shift in aesthetics and audience represented by his films for HBO and afterwards. In *Regarding Henry*, Nichols tells the story of Henry Turner, attack lawyer for a rapacious Manhattan firm that could comfortably serve as legal counsel for *Working Girl*'s Katharine Parker (Sigourney Weaver) in her wrongful-termination suit after the whole Trask-McGill affair. More specifically, *Regarding Henry* is, as the title suggests, a close scrutiny of the literal trauma it would take to re-wire a brain as hardwired as Henry Turner's for exploitation. Because of its literal, physiological dimension, Henry's transformation is on a different scale of magnitude from the ironized fables of feminist empowerment enacted in working-class girls like Karen Silkwood or Tess McGill,[2] and yet Nichols would expand the scale still further in his next film, the 1994 horror-satire of Manhattan power brinksmanship *Wolf*, in which trans*mut*ation trumps trans*form*ation.

Regarding Henry is an early piece of melodrama from the pen of Jeffrey Abrams, who would become better known as J. J. The film's polish and its charismatic cast project a higher tone on the essential tearjerker formula,[3] and part of its interest must undeniably derive from seeing it in the context of a larger trajectory of Nichols' vision: it's another narrative in which a protagonist has the opportunity to unlearn an old life and act his way into a new role. We see Henry Turner travel farther along this road than any previous Nichols protagonist, revisiting personal and professional wrongs with repentance and a desire for wholesale do-overs. The metaphor of brain trauma accounts for such a sweeping change of mind and heart; Henry is able to turn the page on his old life because he no longer feels the reified obligation to maintaining its won turf. He can't remember what a killer he was.

At the story's center are two actors Nichols had worked with before—Harrison Ford from *Working Girl* and Annette Bening of *Postcards*, neither of whom had been utilized to full capacity. Ford in particular is asked to carry the weight of *Regarding Henry*, and his performance is largely in the key of melodrama: the pre-trauma Henry is purely unsympathetic, bullying his maternal secretary (Elizabeth Wilson), his cowed daughter (Mikki Allen, in the only screen performance of her life), and even an elderly malpractice victim in a wheelchair; the post-trauma Henry is mostly a docile child but, if the situation requires it, can summon an adult's righteous indignation at moral and ethical failures, as when he deduces that his wife Sarah (Bening) has been having an affair with his best friend and law-firm colleague, Bruce (Bruce Altman). The title could also be the subject line of any number of memos written post-trauma, about his law firm's desire to ease him back into practice until he is once again able to resume cutting throats by cutting corners, or about his firm's damage control once they've understood the full civil and penal burden Henry's transformation has forced them to shoulder. Our final images of Henry are carefree, and yet surely his own complicity in irresponsible, potentially illegal action remains to be dealt with not only by his former firm, but also by the Turners themselves, no doubt at great emotional and financial cost. Melodrama offers Henry (and us) the free pass of dramatic resolution long before there can be any hope of legal resolution. The Matthews case, which bookends *Regarding Henry*, might drag on for years, with his old firm doing all it can to throw Henry under the bus.

This transformation is the confectionary aesthetic of melodrama as observed by Lowell Kolchek, the film director in the climactic looping scene in *Postcards*: resolution in narrative is most often neatly packaged, clearly discernible and definable and, as a consequence, far more satisfying than life's ambiguities and long, halting *process*. It doesn't do to dwell too deeply on its artificiality unless the narrative's ironies demand that we do, as in the final images of films as different as *The Graduate* and *Catch-22*, *The Fortune* and *Heartburn*. *Regarding Henry* is as earnest and tonally non-ironic as any film Nichols has ever made. The transformation of Henry Turner is exemplary, a moral object lesson, and it renders the narrative of the film as a far simpler fairy tale than, for instance, the Cinderella dimensions of *Working Girl*, whose concluding ironies threaten to deconstruct the upwardly mobile ambitions of Tess McGill. Henry Turner has renounced obsessive legal atavism to be a better husband and father. (It probably is no coincidence that the film was released just over three years after Nichols married for the fourth and final time, to the television journalist Diane Sawyer, having survived a mid–1980s bout with adverse, psychologically disorienting side effects to a prescription medication. In many ways, Nichols' own life turned in as dramatic a fashion as that of his protagonist in *Regarding Henry*, whose last name, Turner, is surely no accident. Of this film, Nichols succinctly says, "It's about redemption."[4]) Although Nichols has often layered a subtext of skepticism beneath the appearance of transformation in his films, *Regarding Henry* offers no such complications. This is one of the few Nichols films with an unequivocally happy ending.

* * *

When Henry and Sarah Turner extricate themselves from the endless social competition among the New York strivers and then, in the film's conclusion, also wrest their daughter Rachel from the same human sacrifice to which Henry had once been subjected by his "work ethic" father, Nichols offers us a thoroughly unambiguous resolution of reified redemption. The Turners have stepped off the treadmill of conformist success to travel an autumnal, golden path less traveled in the film's final shot. The opening and closing images, zoom-outs from iconic American architectural forms, reflect the transformation wrought in Henry Turner. As the film begins, Nichols and his cinematographer, Giuseppe Rotunno (Fellini's collaborator who shot *Carnal Knowledge* for Nichols and who would also shoot Nichols' next film, *Wolf*), zoom slowly on the Corinthian portico of the neo-classical New York State Supreme Court, where we will soon hear Henry Turner plying his trade as attack dog of a corporate Manhattan law firm. The scene is wintry; snow sticks to the streets and sidewalks around Foley Square. The building's massive and solemn façade projects all the grandiose pretensions of civilized order, though it is housing a corruption of legal license, since Henry's summation not only attempts character assassination of an ailing, wheelchair-bound man but literally breaks the law by asserting the innocence of his client and fault of the accuser while concealing evidence to the contrary. This is the house of Henry, and like the weather in which we view it and the man holding forth within it, it is forbiddingly cold. It is a place of power, aggressively asserted by the privileged against the disadvantaged. The mirror-image shot that ends the film, a zoom-out from the neo-colonial Flagler Memorial Chapel at the Millbrook School in the Hudson Valley, contrasts to that chilly gray opening image of the courthouse in the warmth of buttery light Rotunno's camera captures on and behind the chapel; more important, Henry and his family have safely emerged from the confines of this simpler but no less institutional edifice. No institution confines them at film's end. As we know, within this building children are being lovingly but firmly indoctrinated with the ideology of capitalist domination. If Abrams' screenplay elides some of the messier details of the consequences Henry Turner will inevitably bear for whistle-blowing on his firm's (and by extension, his own) misdeeds and complicity in withholding evidence, it's because these legal questions and ramifications are secondary to the spiritual transformation that makes them possible. Henry is a changed man, as close to reborn as narrative can make him: he gets a do-over on childhood via the miracle of brain damage. He learns to feed himself, to speak, to walk, to read. He gets a second chance at learning to think. He learns to love, to be sensitive to those around him, rather than simply asserting at all times and in all things the prerogative of his will. The second time Henry does childhood, he actually grows up.

In the key of melodrama in which *Regarding Henry* unfolds, Henry Turner is a monster of self-serving arrogance, condescension, and greed. He bullies poor Mr. Matthews, the man victimized by hospital error, and he bullies the jury that, although clearly appalled by his shameless references to Mr. Matthews' personal failings, must ultimately find for Henry's corporate client because of the audacious skill of his case. (Even Bruce, his law partner, involuntarily hangs his head at the calculated attack on Mr. Matthews, a brief but telling sign that Henry does the dirty work that not even the other carnivores on the executive floor of his firm quite have the stomach to do.) On recess, Henry threatens a furniture store that has delivered the wrong table. At the office, his secretary Jessica, a veteran of Henry's multi-tasking gruffness, follows him as faithfully as a collie and accepts his cigarette butt as the closest thing she'll get to the courtesy of a goodbye. At home, he browbeats his daughter Rachel and patronizes his wife Sarah, and at the party he and Sarah rush off to so they can leave it sooner, he tells a story of the Machiavellian lengths he has gone to, at great expense, in having chartered a boat to tour New York Harbor for the express purpose of avoiding conversations with his in-laws. When he has the social authority to do so, he ignores people altogether, as he does with Eddie, the doorman of his exclusive condominium building.

It may seem surprising that Sarah is able to coax him into apologizing to Rachel when they return home, but since he has no intention (or even understanding of how) to apologize, we may interpret it as Henry's cynical averting of Sarah's will: he's not even honest enough simply to tell her no. Waking Rachel from a sound sleep, he crows about his triumph in court and lectures her again on the same tired theme of responsibility to "respect other people's things," the poison at the root of conspicuous consumption and the social marathon of success. If Henry's second chance at life, which constitutes an hour and a half of the 107-minute film, is a slow awakening towards spiritual mindfulness, the final act of his first, failed life is an errand in mind*less*ness: ignoring Sarah in favor of his self-destructive cigarettes, allowing her the indulgence of whispered telephone flirtations (we later learn they are probably shared with Bruce) from which she's startled by the police at the door; and his oblivious, belligerent entitlement upon interrupting a robbery at the corner store and expecting to bully his way out of it: "Gimme a break, will you? I just want a pack of cigarettes."

What follows is a truly profound "break"—a physiological rupturing of present from past, of Henry Turner from the man he was to an organism of ultimate submission, dependent at first upon others for everything including his next breath. Nichols and Abrams don't spend long passages of the film meditating on the stillness of the comatose Henry, yet the implication is clear well before the difficulties of his rehabilitation emerge: the perpetual striving and tyrannizing are at an end. There may be the illusion of "family" feeling in the partners waiting at the hospital, but this will bring its own disillusionment: the avuncular "We're here" of Charlie Cameron (Donald Moffatt) will dissolve time after time in relief at not being asked to extend himself beyond symbolic limits of "caring"; Phyllis (Robin Bartlett) will betray Sarah and Henry's friendship; and Bruce and Linda (Rebecca Miller) will eventually have their professional and personal duplicities unmasked—just like Sarah and Henry themselves. The rest of the film is an invitation to new beginning for the Turners, beyond the masks of pretense they all wear—but old habits of reification die hard. In these early scenes after the shooting, Sarah becomes the assumptive surrogate of all that energetic effort, striding purposefully through hospital corridors and, above all, maintaining the Turner stiff upper lip. Told by Henry's doctors that, "in some ways, he'll be starting from scratch here," Sarah coaxes back tears and puts on her brave face. She won't allow Rachel to see her father, instead confecting stories that he's getting better every day and can't wait to see his daughter. Rachel's adolescent self-absorption veers between expressing concern for her father, lobbying opportunely at a vulnerable time for a long-desired puppy, and worrying about the family's finances. She's been a pawn in the competitive brinksmanship between elite New York families: pre-shooting, Sarah and Henry's one clear moment of bonding is their glee that Rachel has been accepted to an exclusive boarding school that rejected a friend's daughter; now, post-shooting, Rachel reports overhearing a friend's mother's gleeful observation that, given Henry's condition and the way the Turners "spend money," they'll be "out on the street" inside a year. Sarah's temper flares at this, but she's clearly also convicted by it, and in a subsequent scene, touring an opulent apartment she's found for her friend Phyllis, she attempts the latest performance of her role as the brave spouse: "Actually, this whole thing's making me a stronger person. Really." Phyllis, sensing weakness, seizes on it under the guise of concern; with little prompting, Sarah breaks down and confesses her terror that their privileged lives are at an end. Phyllis' subsequent wisdom summarizes a way of life: "Don't—DO NOT—tell anyone else what you just told me. If I were you, I would go out with a few friends and spend a whole lot of money."

Sarah remains shallow enough to giggle in naughty complicity with such advice, in the same scene in which she's also able to articulate, before a grand mantelpiece mirror, that they have nothing put away and that "things will have to change." Phyllis' advice may simply be stupid, or it may be an orchestrated hastening of the fall of the house of Turner. Sarah watches with undisguised envy as Phyllis snaps up the apartment without any haggling over price, an impulse purchase by a person whose bank accounts insulate her from the consequences of acting on acquisitive impulse. Indeed, the irony of this affluent world of instant gratification is alienation from genuine feeling. Robin Bartlett, who plays Phyllis, is a useful study in contrasts of casting. Asked by Nichols to play small but essential roles in consecutive films, Bartlett moves from being Aretha, the constant signifier of authenticity in Suzanne Vale's life in *Postcards from the Edge*, to being a superficial, betraying strategist in *Regarding Henry*. Aretha is the friend Suzanne wants on set when she makes her triumphant return to the life of acting at film's end, hopefully more prepared to confine her artifice to stage sets rather than allowing it to return as her permanent mask for living. Phyllis in *Regarding Henry* appears to be, like Aretha, a compassionate, supportive friend in this early scene, but the best that can be said about her advice is that it is catastrophically impractical. Later, Phyllis reveals her cruel condescension at the housewarming party for the apartment Sarah has helped her find.

Early in the film, however, Sarah heeds Phyllis' advice as philosophical dogma, maintaining appearances literally at all costs. When Charlie, the crusty senior executive of Henry's firm, takes her out to lunch with a few of Henry's associates to catch up on Henry's progress, he waits for a moment when he's alone with her to ask, with a delicacy bordering upon distaste, "if everything's under control ... financially." He goes on to sniff, "Some things we just don't talk about," but the Turners, he explains, are "family." This is an early and decisive test of Sarah's resolve to uphold the Turner brand during their crisis. Sarah pauses long enough for us to recall her recent cleansing confession to Phyllis, as well as Phyllis' shockingly unfeeling counsel. Sarah's eventual response is carefully calculated to land just on the proper side of rude rebuff: "We're in wonderful shape. No problem." Far from taking offense, Charlie beams in what for the first time is genuine rather than condescending affection: "I knew I could count on Henry." The moment is such a distortion of paternalism that, like Phyllis' advice, it may only be understood as a reflexive axiom. To "count on" someone is, in Charlie's world, to have no consequential relationship with him at all. And Charlie's comment is all the more daft for being unable even to acknowledge Sarah independent of the Turner brand: she doesn't receive a mention in his benediction. She is subsumed under "Henry." Sarah accepts this diminishment as the rules of the game.

Regarding Henry juxtaposes Sarah's desperate maintenance of appearances with Henry's guileless reemergence into the reality of consciousness. He becomes a special case for Bradley (Bill Nunn), a burly ex-football player who serves as Henry's physical therapist. Bradley is a relentlessly cheerful presence, the first personality to coax a smile from "Hank," as he calls Henry. (For Bradley, Henry will always be "Hank," a nickname that sets no artificial store in the airs the Turners' wealth and power might otherwise command.) With Bradley, Henry learns to stand, toddle with a walker, stride without a cane. An early, often hectoring, mantra from Bradley is some variant of "stand up straight," something Henry gave only the appearance of doing in his previous life. Despite the overtures of the speech therapists, it's Bradley who cajoles Henry to utter his first post-trauma word: "Ritz." The word becomes a complicated distillation of the Henry/Hank continuum: he utters the word in the context of having been tricked into eating Tabasco-laden eggs, and Bradley is surprised to find that, instead of caviar (his stereotypical notion of what people like the Turners eat), Henry has tastes for a quotidian cracker. The word nonetheless has connotative redolences with the ostentatious affluence of the Manhattan power-broker elite, and we will come to understand, in colleague Linda's lovelorn confession late in the film, that the word has a complex symbolic association with his secret life every Tuesday and Thursday afternoon with Linda at the Ritz-Carlton Hotel. But "Hank" has no meaningful conception of this impulsive blip of memory; Bradley's simple interpretation of the word becomes "Hank's," and he not only relishes crackers as a subsequent dietary staple (assuming the unpretentious plebeian tastes of the post-trauma Henry) but paints Warholian canvases faithfully reproducing the Ritz packaging, paintings

Nichols and his set designers mischievously use in Henry's home and office to displace or provide visual competition for familiar Abstract Expressionist stylists like Mark Rothko and Adolph Gottlieb.

Henry's nature, post-trauma, is diffident and retiring. He's a blank slate, at least for the time being, and *Regarding Henry* argues that having master-tutors who are children (Rachel, his daughter) or child-like (the man-child Bradley, with his kid-in-a-candy-store appreciation of all the attractive female staff at the rehab clinic) is just the thing for a man as indoctrinated from childhood by the manipulative values of the adult world as Henry Turner has been. With Bradley, "Hank" assumes a role as a sort of slow, grinning sidekick, and so when it is time to leave the clinic and return home with Sarah and Rachel to Manhattan, "Hank" surprisingly resists change as much as any child wishing to sustain an accustomed, ordered, and pleasant life. Bradley at first tries to work on Henry to facilitate the transition, and it's interesting that, while Sarah and Bradley clearly have established a working friendship over the course of Henry's rehab, Bradley does not now approach Sarah to undertake the next stage in Henry's development. Instead, gaining no traction with Henry himself, he goes to Rachel and consults with her as he cannot, quite, with her mother, to take on the raising of her father.

Nichols and Abrams get comic mileage out of Henry's reintroduction into his old world. Not only does he remember Eddie—perhaps unlikely, since he's just remembered an hour earlier that home is synonymous with gray carpet—but he bear-hugs this unassuming servant he'd never previously even deigned to acknowledge. When he enters their home, he admires rather than decries the "turtle" table. Hollywood loves the trope of the man-child wandering out into the world to look at what adults have wrought: Tom Hanks in *Big* (Penny Marshall, 1988) is an obvious antecedent, but the most appropriate and powerful influence on the twenty minutes after Henry comes home is Peter Sellers as Chance the Gardener in the screen adaptation of Jerzy Kosinski's novel *Being There* (Hal Ashby, 1979), in which Chance's initial foray beyond the house where he has lived his entire childhood and adult life unfolds to the funked-up strains of Strauss' "Thus Spake Zarathustra," a witty allusion to Kubrick's use of the piece in *2001: A Space Odyssey* (1968). Nichols says, "We thought of the world of rich people in New York as a world to which he returned, when he came from the hospital, absolutely fresh, pretty much as someone who'd come from another planet."[5] Ford, wide-eyed on the mean streets of adulthood, accepts every curbstand offer of junk food as well as a sidewalk huckster's hustle into a porn theater, where he absorbs "performance" pressures that will contribute to his inhibitions as Sarah attempts to become his third master-tutor (after Bradley and Rachel), when she urges his return to adult intimacy. When he gets back home from this big day out, with a beagle pup for Rachel (and himself), Sarah's relief only barely outweighs her exasperation, and she storms off in frustrated tears. Henry, mystified, turns immediately back to his master-tutor for instruction: "Why is she so mad?" Rachel instructs him as she would a little brother: "If you're gonna be late, you have to *call* her." The new Henry accepts his rebukes equably, though we understand the old workaholic Henry to have been the type who unrepentantly justifies all absences (including unfaithfulness with Linda) with the holy excuse of *the job*. Rambling around the apartment without occupation in his first day home, he asks their servant, Rosella, what he does when he's here. Her charmingly indeterminate verb-tense employment casts an unintentional but accurate perspective on the old Henry: "You are working all the time. [...] You work so hard. I can't believe it." He presses her to characterize his leisure time, but she persists, "You are *always working*." His ethic comes in handy when a task presents itself: Rachel's determination that he must learn to read. With reading come his first attempts to understand his life; the narrative juxtaposes the reading lessons on Rachel's bed with sessions of looking through old photographs. He holds up a black-and-white photograph of himself and asks, "Who's this?" Rachel identifies him, then tells the only stories of his childhood that she knows, the parabolic tales of "the work ethic." Henry earnestly inquires, "What's that?" and Rachel in relief confesses, "I don't know." She has her suspicions, however—it's why her smile is so wry, and it's why she's dreading her next high-pressure years at school.

Henry's reintroduction into the adult world is far rockier than his reconnection to his daughter. His first contact within the law firm comes via Bruce, who arrives during Henry's proud, child-like announcement in the kitchen that he can read. Bruce sets up with Henry for a chat in Henry's study, where a Turner *Ritz Cracker* painting sits behind Bruce in Henry's line of sight. Henry lustily gulps down a glass of milk and registers a welcome-home gift of a picture frame about the way a six-year-old would. "Were we really good friends?" he asks, struggling to recall Bruce's name. "Of course," says Bruce, and then it's his turn to struggle: "We were partners" is the best he can do in embellishing his original claim, which clarifies nothing, particularly for Henry. At the "big party" the firm throws for Henry and Sarah, Charlie holds forth about the cutthroat dependability of Henry and of his father before him (who presumably worked himself into an early grave, since there is no other evidence of him), and when Charlie finishes, to sycophantic applause, Sarah whispers an imperative into Henry's ear. He stands hesitantly and begins, "Sarah said I should say something." The crowd laughs in anticipation of what he will say after this unintentional meta-witticism, not understanding the workings of Henry's literal mind. So effortlessly able to perform for juries in his former life, he has no instinct for how to perform now, and his halting, heartfelt plea for their patience has an anticipatable effect: indulgent applause by his suddenly superior-feeling colleagues and a sour look from Charlie, whose grudging applause seems tainted by an unpleasant odor. At the office, Henry is taken on a tour by Bruce and extravagantly condescended to by a colleague named Rudy. Bruce introduces Henry to Jessica, his long-time secretary, whose name Bruce himself can't quite recall, and she gets Henry's usual coffee with cream. Henry has apparently been coffee-free (or at least cream-free) since his recovery, because he doesn't know to stop her pouring. She finally instructs him in this small piece of etiquette: "When you've had enough, Mr. Turner, you say when." As played by Elizabeth Wilson in her fourth and final role for Nichols, Jessica is a combination of habitual solicitude to a dynamic force of the firm and a kindly schoolteacher bringing along a sweet but slow child. With more time in the film, she might have been another unlikely master-tutor to Henry, but the implications of power relationships within the firm finally render such a role impossible. Nonetheless, as the resolution of the film makes clear, she makes her impression upon him, particularly with this universally applicable piece of wisdom. At first, Jessica indulgently brings him all his requested files, as if happy to encourage any subject that fosters a child's motivation to learn; yet when his reading becomes too closely integrated with critical evaluation of what he reads, she is compelled to follow Bruce and Linda's instructions to keep Henry separated from forbidden reading material. Henry's office is moved to a far humbler space than his old one, with a nondescript view and no frills; Jessica comes to have more delegated power in the firm than he does, precisely because she must reverence the rules he no longer even understands, let alone upholds.

Henry's confrontation with Bruce and Linda, over lunch, is a kind of alternative parental education, but Bruce and Linda fail as master-tutors because they tire so quickly of attempting to help Henry understand their world; this is understandable, given that their world is not constructed for careful scrutiny. If Rachel in particular has been instructing Henry in how to be a family man—not quite a father yet, but certainly a member of an affective unit— Bruce and Linda, sitting together in solidarity across the table from him, assume the bearing of indulgent but increasingly impatient parents who move from soothing assurances to barked instructions: "Put it back in the file." Henry persists: "What we did was wrong." Instead of praise for his solitary deduction (he has begun to assume the adult's role of responsibility for his own instruction) and moral assertion, Henry receives from Bruce a combined censure and reminder of the system of values-reinforcement his old life offered: "What we did is paying for lunch." The narrative offers no representation of Henry's attempting to confide in anyone other than Bruce and Linda about his reading-based insight into the old Henry; it's natural enough that he wouldn't want to burden Rachel with this, but he makes no attempt (that we see) to confide in Sarah, either. He manifests a child's guilt; he has not yet reestablished adult intimacy and confidence with Sarah, but there is a more essential truth in his silence. Although the confrontation scene plays as if Henry is the slow-learning child and Bruce and Linda his patronizing guardians, his ease in coming to them is a tacit acknowledgement that he is *not* talking to adult authorities but peers in wrong-doing: all three of them seated at the table are children, and Henry has just advanced beyond *them* in moral development.

He seems more at home, for the first time in his life, at home. When Rachel, with impeccable timing, broaches the subject of whether she should in fact be sent off to prep school, she does so just as he is beginning to parse more adult dilemmas both within and beyond their home. They are baking cookies together: it's a task at which the old Henry would have been equally as clueless as the new one, but far more dismissive; the new Henry reads earnestly from a recipe on the counter. Rachel's appeal to him about her schooling status is so strategic because it is directed not so much to her newfound family member (for sympathy) as to her newfound *father* (for sympathetic action), just as he's come into his moral maturity. However, her plea to be excused from attending the cutthroat prep school is tabled until Henry can talk to Sarah: "I don't want you to go anywhere, but I'm not sure it's up to me. Is it up to me?" Where once Henry, in the fog of his oblivious entitlement, blithely made choices that affected anyone with whom he might come into contact, he is too tentative in his new humility to express his agency in the world. These two problems (what to do about the Matthews case, and what to do about Rachel) become Henry's twin preoccupations to solve throughout the remainder of the narrative, and his answers to these two problems, as well as to the twinned problems of Sarah's and his own marital infidelities that he encounters later in the film's final act, create the sense of whom the new Henry will be as his accelerating transformation via reified anxiety comes to its resolution.

When Henry approaches Sarah about Rachel's school enrollment, he lacks the self-possession to make his case. Sarah, no doubt thinking ahead and seeing that Henry's diminished powers will not provide the financial windfall they'd once enjoyed, has made good on his commitment to rein in their finances by moving to a new, more modest house. Henry tamely follows her though the rooms, acquiescing. Their exchange about these decisions yields a clear sense of Henry's submissiveness: "You think we should move?" Sarah: "I do." Henry: "And you think Rachel should go away to school." Sarah: "Yeah." Henry: "Okay." Depositing Rachel, Henry must be as brave and as false as his daughter. He tells a story of trepidation on a first day of school and of eventual assimilation, and it sends Rachel glumly across the quad, toward the chapel featured again in the film's final shots. Sarah is encouraged that his memory has coughed up such a specific fragment from his childhood, and he confesses guiltily that he has made it up. The odd thing about this lie by the new Henry is that it contrasts to the duplicitous old Henry in its motivation. All his lies as the old Henry were self-serving, but this newest lie (for which he feels an immediate paralyzing shame) facilitates the very thing he himself does not want, in an effort to make others' lives a bit easier. His lie is a gift to Sarah in particular, who has had to bear the brunt of this family-rending decision in her belief that it will ultimately be best for Rachel. While this benign deceit is no more than a way station on the path to his genuine self, it represents an attempt at forward movement.

In their empty nest, with Rachel no longer available to continue as his master-tutor and no longer the appropriate source of his increasingly adult experience and wisdom, Sarah ascends to her position as master-tutor, though ironically, she must grope towards true moral adulthood along with Henry. She is able to promote a renewal of intimacy, pushing past Henry's adolescent insecurities with her simple but multi-layered command, "Touch me." Thus begins the final phase of Henry's reawakening. He's had to take his cues from Bradley, Rachel, and Sarah, Jessica, Bruce, and Linda, and anyone else who has cared to instruct him (for better or worse). When he obeys Sarah's tender command, he discovers a vast well of instinct that must be acted upon if he is truly to be himself, not what the contending host of others mean for him to be. After making love this first time as the new Henry, he presents a tender command of his own: "Sarah? Tell me how we met," and he is amazed to hear with what casual audacity he ignored his own date to proposition Sarah with the promise of "great blowfish." Emboldened by these tales of heroic-sized ego, Henry begins a renewed and improved courtship of Sarah, without social constraint. Walking up Fifth Avenue by the Park, he takes her hand, and while she is delighted, she can't help remarking on how the old Henry shied from public displays of affection, niggardly in his willingness to be himself outside of his profession. In a self-dramatizing demonstration of how he doesn't "mind so much anymore"—"mind" here serving as synonymous with calculated performance—he pulls her up onto a bench and kisses her. The camera remains at eye-level up on them, and it's no surprise that they are noticed by other passersby, including Phyllis and her husband Daniel, conspicuously overdressed compared to the Turners' casual attire. The camera set-up to capture them is above eyeline, angled down, with the pronounced effect that each is getting the opportunity for a good look at the other. Henry and Daniel are inarticulately ill at ease in the brief, ensuing exchange, while Phyllis and Sarah, also uncomfortable, are more skilled at maintaining a cooing illusion of social niceties, including an invitation for the Turners to the housewarming.

This party, unlike the "big party" for Henry's homecoming, finds Henry in a place where he can begin to understand social subtexts. He gravitates to the affable hired help for conversation, and reports the ill-natured gossip he's overheard from some of the guests to Sarah as well as to the waiter, provoking their laughter. It may appear that Henry is in on the joke, but as we learn in the next gossip he overhears, he hasn't made the moral connection to how such chatter has a devastating effect on power in relationships. With Sarah, he hears the host and hostess, Sarah's supposed good friend Phyllis and her husband, exchanging disparaging asides about the Turners, including the none-too-delicate characterization of Henry as an "imbecile." (We may be reminded here of the old Henry having once described a friend's adolescent daughter as a "virtual idiot" in feeling the social superiority of Rachel's acceptance and the other girl's rejection at the prep school, and Sarah had laughed in delighted, empowered complicity.) Now the Turners stare at Phyllis and Daniel in horror and make their hasty escape. Henry refuses to leave his bed, and the narrative invites a comparison between Henry and the beagle, Buddy, who docilely sits when so commanded. Henry appears willing to take his reified cues from the world around him and to be trained in his own diminished value, though his defeat has led not to redoubled striving for assimilation as in his first life but rather to utter resignation to the role of imbecile.

Sarah's call for Bradley to return as a master-tutor elevates Henry from comparison to a dog to comparison to a powerful athlete. Bradley's story of undesired, involuntary transformation from star football player to physical therapist resonates with Henry, who confesses, "I thought I could go back to my life, but I don't like who I was, Bradley. I don't fit in." In essence, Bradley gives Henry the permission he's needed, in his submissive, post-trauma rehabilitation not only of body but of mind and identity, to be himself: "Let me tell you something, Hank. Don't listen to nobody trying to tell you who you are." This crisis of professional identity soon abuts a crisis of marital identity, as Bruce's careless use of the same stationery for the bestowal of yet another rote social gift (a homecoming present for the Turners' imminent move) provokes a memory of a secret cache of such stationery deep in the intimate recesses of Sarah's bureau, which Henry had rifled in his boredom in the days just after his move home. A conversation he'd had during the early days of his rehab with Bradley, about a wife's infidelity, has cemented his sense that his own instincts—the devastating betrayal of

The transformation of Henry Turner (Harrison Ford, left) after brain trauma in *Regarding Henry* has reached a critical phase when his wife calls in Bradley (Bill Nunn), Henry's physical therapist. Henry no longer needs Bradley's help with physical rehab, but overheard remarks from some old "friends" among the Manhattan power elite have left him uncertain about who he is. Bradley reminds him that social conformity is a trap: "Don't listen to nobody trying to tell you who you are." Soon after, Henry embarks on a series of existential errands that establish the new (and improved) Henry Turner.

trust—are appropriate to what he has uncovered among Sarah's private things. He waits, a shadowy presence backlit against a window, for Sarah, and literally flings the letters at her. It is what the old Henry would do, and when Sarah pleads with him to stay ("We were miserable. You don't remember, but I do. I was lonely"), she can only follow him to the elevator and watch him leave. Henry is on the precipice where love and power go their necessarily separate ways, and it takes Henry's confrontation by Linda to bring him face-to-face with the old, Ritz-loving Henry, whose professional and personal duplicities intertwined so completely. In the Ritz, and then on a bench in Central Park, Henry finally and fully euthanizes his old self, an act he could only commit after final and full confrontation with the enormity of that man's failures. His ride uptown on the subway at first seems nothing more than the aimless wandering of the tabula rasa Henry newly home from rehab. But the ride is far from random drift: the film ends with a brisk, ten-minute sequence of four existential errands that embody Henry's spirit of redemptive possibility.

The first of these errands is to Mr. and Mrs. Matthews, to undo what damage he has contributed to the more essential damage committed through the hospital's negligence. He hands over the evidence he and the partners have suppressed, arousing Mrs. Matthews' understandable suspicions. His apology provokes her simple, one-word question: "Why?"—an interrogative that, in its open-endedness, can as easily be interpreted, *Why are you sorry?* or *Why are you doing this?* or *Why do this now and not then?* His answer is as simple and versatile as her question and sums Nichols' self-evaluation of his aesthetic project as a cinematic storyteller: "I've changed." The second errand affords Henry an opportunity to expand on this new definition of himself: at the law firm, he plows right into Charlie's office, provoking an unprofessional epithet from Charlie in the midst of a consultation with a row of four Asian businessmen. Charlie testily condescends to Henry's farewell, mistakenly assuming Henry remains the dogged but feeble-minded shell of the former powerhouse, interrupting to say goodnight. "No, Charlie," says Henry. "I can't be a lawyer anymore." Charlie again misinterprets Henry's communication (even while speaking fluent Japanese to his clients), this time assuming Henry is finally aware that he is a charity case incapable of practicing law, rather than comprehending what Henry actually means: that his conscience can no longer permit him to continue in his old craft. Simply put, Charlie Cameron and Henry Turner no longer speak the same language. (It apparently doesn't occur to Henry—nor *must* it, to be a genuine transformation—that he could become a plaintiff's attack dog in his new minting as a lawyer, his life dedicated to redressing injustice on the side of the weak and victimized.) As Henry departs, finally having made his intentions clear (and with Charlie by now acquiescing readily in his relief from this ongoing, embarrassing headache), the lawyer for the Matthews claim has put in a phone call to Charlie's office. The narrative's naïve resolution of the crimes committed by Henry and the firm is appropriate here because it matches Henry's own reconceived relationship to justice; out beyond the film's happy ending waits an unpleasantly long and confrontational unfolding of hostile correspondence, depositions, and testimony. After leaving Charlie but before leaving the office, Henry's only other lingering goodbye is to Jessica, to whom he explains, with a witty awareness of his humbled state upon returning to the firm and submitting to her tutelage post-trauma, "Well, I had enough, so I said when." This self-conscious commentary on his professional selves, the pre-trauma wolf and the post-trauma lamb (with neither of whom he's ultimately comfortable), invites a similar deconstruction of his private selves.

His professional errands dispatched, Henry turns his attention to the domestic crises that are now, for the first time, not merely the center of his responsibilities but the basis of his conscious, voluntary identity. He offers Linda the courtesy of a perfunctory goodbye; his return to Sarah's doorstep is far more considered in its poking holes in the blowhard who once promised her blowfish. Dramatically, Henry's opening gambit in the mutual forgiveness the Turners must offer one another serves a similar deconstructive purpose as that quick flourish Karen Silkwood (Meryl Streep) shares with Drew (Kurt Russell) as he lasts see her. In *Silkwood*, Karen's gesture attests to her utter awareness of and wry commentary upon the superficial object she'd once been, flashing her ogling male co-worker to gain the upper hand, exploiting (and thus commodifying) the only power at her disposal, her sexuality, in the reified war of gendered and socio-economic manipulation that is their shared way of life. The joke she shares with Drew is evidence of her mastery of that old reified self, a declaration of independence from the old Karen and her various imprisonments within systemic commodification. Henry's line to Sarah as she opens the door and waits mutely for his verdict parodies his grotesquely overdeveloped former sense of entitlement as the old Henry Turner: he delivers a verdict upon *himself*. The man whom Sarah characterizes in the opening of the film as never able to apologize meets her apology with his own and begs to be allowed to change, inside and out. The man who has looked to Sarah as he groped toward his second identity is liberated from both his former entitlement and from the empty submission of his post-trauma blank slate; he is suddenly, volubly, and minutely articulate about his desires. "Whatever you want is fine," she says, not in resignation to traditional, gendered surrender but in grateful and loving welcome of the prodigal. Henry's first truly domestic act of leadership in his life ends the film with his fourth existential errand: "I want us to be a family, for as long as we can, Sarah, for as long as we can."

The film's closing scene begins with a series of angles on Rachel at convocation in her school's chapel. The uniform the girls all wear and the blank visages with which they passively absorb the headmistress' exhortations suggest Nichols' vantage point on this assembly. These are the sort of experiences that produced Benjamin and Elaine in *The Graduate* or Jonathan, Susan, and Sandy in *Carnal Knowledge*. In a social system broken by commodified reduction of the human person, the process of formal education becomes not the medium of enlightenment but of conformist assimilation. The headmistress' address, no doubt as advertised to the ambitious parents who have invested in these promising futures, takes as its gospel the "work-ethic" Henry had inherited from his father and, unreflectively, had intended to pass on to his daughter: "You're all learning what that means when you ask yourself, 'Why do I push myself? Why do I strive to be a harder worker? A better listener? Well, look around you." Nichols and O'Steen have cut from close-ups of Rachel to shots that place her on the periphery of a larger, otherwise anonymous group. "There are the answers to those questions," the headmistress continues: "Competition." And so among the future elite is initiated that same reified sense of essential wariness that motivated their parents to send their children here, to "get ahead" of their peers, and which they will in turn pass along to their own progeny. As the headmistress bids them to close their eyes and silently intone the work-ethic prayer ("I will work harder. I will listen better"), Henry, having entered from the chapel's narthex, lets loose the hound of his nearly lost family life. The headmistress, aware of Henry's physical and intellectual misfortune (and his attempts in his enfeebled state to call his homesick daughter), is more indulgent than we might have expected and more tolerant than she would have been if any other parent had pulled such a stunt. (The risks to fragile student-body morale of witnessing such a scene are enormous, and though the film does not depict it, one can imagine the rhetorical damage control she may have pursued after the Turners have left, citing poor Mr. Turner's "accident" and implying that he has lost his competitive edge.) Henry, the prodigal, sounds as if he is atoning not only for his own sins but the sins of his father as he apologizes (again) and explains himself: "I missed her first 11 years, and I don't want to miss any more." The camera angle down on Henry acknowledges the physical and professional deflations of the past year, yet can't undercut the essential reality of Henry's respectful defiance of institutional authority and its values. The headmistress receives his pronouncement with a display of impeccable breeding and an ambiguous magnanimity: is she happy to see the genuine love he has for his daughter, or is she simply minimizing a potential scene? Charitably, she does both, and this only reinforces the film's sense of outrage not at well-meaning individuals and their various Darwinian rationalizations for reified behavior but of the reifying systems themselves.

As in *The Graduate*, the protagonists emerge from a church, one of the most traditional settings of comic resolution. The Turner family appears to have been united by an official, ceremonial union in which they have pronounced themselves a family. Yet, as in *The Graduate*, but without the ironic layers of point of view, the anointment of institutional blessing is demonstrated to be, at best, purely pro forma when contrasted to the individual contracts we make with each other in trust and love, un-manipulated by performance pressures of reified systems of social conduct. Rachel tosses away her uniform beret in a parody of an institutionalized ritual of credentialing: the tossing of the cap at commencement. Their awakened, transformed life together commences. The Turners, true to their name, turn their backs on the illusion of success as *Regarding Henry* ends; therein lies their only hope of achieving a more lasting and meaningful success, because it is self-actualized, not passively inherited.

14

"What God meant"

Wolf (1994)

After the utterly conventional dramatic narrative of *Regarding Henry*, Mike Nichols embarked on a series of genre exercises to close the decade and the second phase of his Hollywood career: *Wolf* (1994) may be the most surprising of all, a gothic werewolf melodrama that also seasons the story with romance and with capitalist satire; *The Birdcage* (1996) followed, a gay farce adapted from the French hit *La Cage aux Folles*; then *Primary Colors* (1998), adapting Joe Klein's political campaign satire; and *What Planet Are You From?* (2000), an unlikely hybrid of sex-farce and science-fiction. In the early films of his second phase, from *Silkwood* through *Regarding Henry*, there were occasional commitments to Nichols' generic roots in comedy, most notably in *Working Girl* and, to a lesser extent, in *Heartburn* and *Biloxi Blues*. But two of the four films that close this second career phase, *The Birdcage* and *What Planet*, feature unapologetically broad humor, and while *Wolf* and *Primary Colors* may be understood to have far more sober tonal intent, *Wolf* suffers when taken too seriously. Nichols would return to consistently serious dramatic intentions after the turn of the millennium, with his move to HBO, but his output in the second half of the 1990s saw a director very much at play, because he'd earned that right, or perhaps had lost his way. Of the four films with which he closed the decade, only *The Birdcage* was an unqualified box-office success. The other three were expensive, devastating financial failures, and *What Planet* is in the small minority of Nichols' least accomplished films.

Wolf offers a demonstration of what happens when a director works too far outside his demonstrated generic vocabulary. Because it attempts more gravity than the silliness of *What Planet*, *Wolf* is actually the more alien film. Should Nichols, an acknowledged master of comedy and drama, have been experimenting with an exercise in supernatural horror? The film is probably most comfortable inside the satiric confines of the Bradbury Building, where Jack Nicholson (in his fourth and final appearance as a Nichols lead), Christopher Plummer, James Spader, David Hyde Pierce, and Eileen Atkins all enact the comedy of bad manners that passes for corporate culture in the hostile-takeover era. As the film moves closer to the natural world (on the leafy Alden estate and in Central Park), let alone in the supernatural mysticism of Om Puri's scenes, Nichols reveals himself to be literally lost in the woods.

Nichols works from a script by Jim Harrison and Wesley Strick (with uncredited revisions by Elaine May[1]); Harrison, with his debts to men's men like Ernest Hemingway and James Dickey in exploring codes of masculinity and gender roles, is at a glance an unlikely voice for Nichols to adopt in exploring his otherwise familiar preoccupations with commodified performance and reified anxiety, yet beyond Harrison's distinctive musings on the twinned instincts of savagery and the noble savage within, the critique of late capitalism makes familiar points of contact with other Nichols' films. Anthony Lane writes that *Wolf* "may be the first movie to merge lycanthropy and capitalism into a joint venture."[2] Where Harrison and Nichols most diverged was in drawing conclusions from their horror scenario: in the "return to the wild" depicted in the film's ending, Harrison sees a sloughing of civilization's bonds,[3] while Nichols believes the idea of reversion to noble beasts is a "'sentimental lie,'" because "'This is a story about somebody who loses his humanity, and you can't say that's something to be desired.'"[4] The culture introduced in *Wolf* is of "highly civilized" commercialized atavism: our species tears out the throats of its competitors not by physical assault but via the hostile takeover (whether in the boardroom or in a colleague's bedroom). Property is territory, and anything from professional position to personal relationship is property. Not surprisingly, this is a world dominated by patriarchy, represented most aggressively by Raymond Alden, leading his way into every human scrum with the noble brow of Christopher Plummer (at his most effortlessly, smugly baronial). Alden is a billionaire takeover specialist who has no personal interest in what he takes over—he's simply possessing property as its own reward. He possesses people, too—his daughter Laura (Michelle Pfeiffer) is among his key possessions, and he keeps her with more ardor and less success than his stock acquisitions. This becomes a sub-plot of *Wolf*'s inquiry into reified anxiety: can anyone refuse to be commodified?

Nichols' previous film, *Regarding Henry*, ended with a glimpse inside the reification factory—an exclusive prep school, where students are asked to look around them at their future competitive antagonists, then ask, "Why do I push myself? Why do I strive to be a harder worker?" The question may masquerade as self-improvement, but its context applies with equal ease both to internal and external comparatives—these young people are, like Henry Turner himself, being groomed for competitive dominance. In the likes of Henry Turner (Harrison Ford) and Katharine Parker (Sigourney Weaver in *Working Girl*)—Nichols has presented the corporate American of either gender as a force of late capitalist surrender to relentless acquisition. Unlike *Working Girl*, whose narrative ends in the irony of a fairy tale in which the princess gets exactly what she wished for (a hard-driving prince and a window on the anonymous canyons of Manhattan power), *Regarding Henry* offers a sincere antidote to the commodified infection. The Turners opt out of the rat race; the film ends as they take a road less traveled. The narrative trajectory of *Wolf*, although worlds apart from *Regarding Henry* in terms of genre, ends at a similar point: with the rejection of imprisonment within the imperatives of wolf-eat-wolf late capitalism. Georgia Brown writes, "Will's puncture wound is in the hand not the head, and whereas the venal, driven Henry required slowing down, the passive, defeated Will needs to be revved up."[5] Indeed, beginning with Meryl Streep as Suzanne Vale at the end of *Postcards from the Edge*, belting her declaration, "I'm Checkin' Out," Nichols introduced a string of feature films invested in a common commitment to principled exile from the majority culture. He wouldn't return to people trying to maintain principles *within* the system until *Primary Colors*, when the ambiguities between principle and compromise spike again at the film's climax and resolution, as in earlier Nichols films from *The Graduate* to *Silkwood* to *Biloxi Blues*. Suzanne's song could as easily belong to the Turners in *Regarding Henry*, excusing themselves from the bloodthirsty social competition of New York's elite. And Suzanne's song could also belong to Will Randall (Jack Nicholson) and Laura Alden, who opt out of a life predicated solely on hegemonic possession. Each has known the ignominy of being commodified; both have also tasted the power of manipulating others and found it did not agree with them. When they "go wild," there is something very different in their natures than when Stewart Swinton (James Spader, always game to play strange and unsympathetic roles) goes wild. Their wildness calls them out of the false civility of socio-economic structures. In his next film, *The Birdcage*, the last before the grand statement of *Primary Colors* returned to the question of whether individuals can change reified systems (rather than the other way around), Nichols tacks on a deliriously comic coda to this sequence of films within his oeuvre, a very broad comic finale on the topic of being "out" of the box of social conformity.

* * *

Wolf's potpourri of generic and tonal accents renders it a risky narrative experiment. Within the same narrative are the dead-earnest sentiments of the romance genre, uncomfortably close to the boisterously funny corporate satire within the gleaming walls of the historic Bradbury Building in downtown Los Angeles (where McLeish House publishing operates) and the supernatural horror elements of the werewolf formula. The parts don't always cohere gracefully. David Foster Wallace, in his classic creative nonfiction essay about cruise-ship tourism, "A Supposedly Fun Thing I'll Never Do Again," writes of feeling so trapped between ports that he takes to watching and re-watching the closed-circuit movie channel available at all hours in every stateroom. *Wolf* is one of the films in rotation during his cruise, and his one-word dismissal ("stupid"[6]) is, of course, unfair, though it does reflect the larger cultural indifference to the film. It's a telling insight into Nichols' self-knowledge as a filmmaker that his next film, *The Birdcage*, is not only an official, credited reunion of his first successful professional collaboration, with May, but also a reversion to one of his most familiar generic formulas: social comedy.

Despite all the intermittent hair and the talk of full moons and amulets, *Wolf* retains Nichols' consistent critique of commodified social structures, this time returning to Manhattan's corporate battlefield of *Working Girl*. The milieu is the executive class. Will Randall must first come to terms with his inner wolf and then reject its unnatural application within the bloodthirsty atavism of "civilized" human society. Betraying her own discomfort with the literalized genre conventions of horror, Janet Maslin writes, "So long as it stays confined to the level of metaphor, as it does in the first hour of 'Wolf,' [Will's descent into the atavistic instincts all around him] is irresistible. And Mike Nichols' own killer instincts as an urbane social satirist are ideally suited to this milieu. Just as he did in the opening, not-yet-sentimental sections of 'Regarding Henry,' Mr. Nichols knowingly captures the smooth viciousness behind his characters' great shows of sophistication."[7]

Will's deferential gentility has anesthetized his marriage to Charlotte (Kate Nelligan) and left him an aging alpha-editor at McLeish House, unwittingly provoking the primal appetites for dominance of the young would-be usurper, Stewart Swinton. When we first see Will in Manhattan, he's in close-up on the sidewalk, moving beside a chain-link fence. The camera's zoom-out reveals that we have been watching Will from within the enclosure of a construction site, and as the camera pans to follow Will, it picks out another social species in its workday habitat: the hard hats in their tight pack, hungrily watching money (men) and sex (women) passing by just beyond the fence. Coming as it does between the wintry transgression of Will on the wolf's territory in snowy Vermont, where he's bitten, and the post-takeover whisperings and closed-door stratagems at McLeish House, the brief exterior shot reminds us that the commodified world sees all as territory to be negotiated—either to pass through unmolested or, if the call of one's blood should command it, to assume the aggressor's role and consume whatever one desires.

Certainly this is Stewart's philosophy, having stolen from Will those two most palpable symbols of his self-possession: his senior executive position and his handsome wife. When Raymond Alden seeks the appropriate cutthroat to place at the helm of the new McLeish House, he does not even speak to Will about the job; rather, he hires Stewart—whom Alden confesses has irritated him with his constant, wheedling desires—and only reneges and hands the job back to Will after Will's daemon-wolf blood demonstrates that he can be sufficiently "ruthless." Alden doesn't much care for either Stewart or Will; he makes his choice purely on the man he perceives to be the dominant hunter. When Will meets Alden's daughter, Laura, her beauty does its usual stuff of attracting the male of the species, but she's utterly unimpressed by him in a way we assume she has learned by default, combatting the waves of strutting Alden "wolves" sniffing around her iconic cheekbones and enormous eyes. At their hostile first lunch together, only undertaken to establish her autonomy from her father and Will's defiance of her father's clearly communicated desire that Will be gone, neither has an awareness of any need of companionship. Will delivers a long, alienating speech that begins with the deliberately antagonizing provocation, "You know, I think I understand what you're like now." What comes out of his mouth over the course of the next two minutes are the sort of anti-romantic bromides on which one-night stands are often negotiated. Jack Faulkner (Dennis Quaid) in *Postcards from the Edge* wouldn't have felt entirely estranged from the canned sentiments Will delivers with deconstructive irony and, subtextually, a modicum of hope an old guy instinctively might find himself carrying into a conversation with a beautiful woman he wouldn't mind possessing. Laura in bored irritation barely bothers to growl, "Sorry, wrong line. I am not taken aback by your keen insight and suddenly challenged by you." She has deconstructed the deconstructionist; she wins because he doesn't score. A few moments later, what gets through her defenses are questions Will, freed from the expectations of his male prerogative, asks about her family, especially her brother the suicide (whom we can safely presume, being the only son and heir to the Alden mantle, would have been expected to carry a particularly heavy burden of constructed behavior).

For both Aldens, father and daughter, Will is a comic lampoon of obsolete deference and gentle "civility." As he is fired on the sweeping lawn of Alden's estate, Will receives Alden's assurance, "Nothing personal. C'mon. You know that you're clearly a man of taste and individuality, which I prize. These days, not only in corporate America but all around the globe, taste and individuality are actually something of a handicap." Will's civil but pointed reply clarifies his perspective on people like Stewart Swinton and the men like Raymond Alden who encourage them: "Well, just out of curiosity, on what basis did you pick my successor—vulgarity and conformity?" Indeed, Alden's hiring practices clearly reward smaller gestures made in the same key as Alden's own hostile takeovers. Alden's kiss-off indicates the satirized object of *Wolf*: "You're a nice person, Will. Thank god I replaced you." With Laura, moments later on this same lawn, Will assures her she's "safe" with him, not in the sense of his providing protection but rather of his posing no threat. As a result, her early conversations with him mingle incredulity and faint disdain, until, at their peanut-butter-and-jelly luncheon only held to annoy Alden, he scolds her: "I don't take anything for granted, Miss Alden, except some small measure of civility from my hostess."

Charlotte and Laura take different perspectives on this old wolf. While Laura's inner goodness (obscured beneath a bad-girl mask meant to goad her domineering father) innately begins to respond to a like nature in Will, Charlotte has entered into the affair with Stewart as a kind of recompense for Will's lost fire. After the wolf bite, Will needs some time to adjust physically; the initial reaction is an even greater lethargy than he'd previously mani-

In *Wolf*, the territorial objectification and atavism of corporate culture emerge in the battle between Will Randall (Jack Nicholson, left) and Stewart Swinton (James Spader) for a new senior editor position created by a conglomerate's takeover of a publishing house. The rivalry spills over into possessiveness about Will's wife Charlotte (Kate Nelligan), who, tired of Will's lethargy, has entered into an affair with Stewart. Their uneasy triangle is captured at the dinner where Raymond Alden, the man behind the takeover, hands the job to Stewart, citing the *handicaps* of Will's "taste and individuality."

fested. During the car ride home from Alden's firing party, Charlotte needles Will, less about Alden than about the man with whom, unbeknownst to Will, she's been sleeping: "Why did you let him walk away with your blessing, guilt-free?" She still wants to talk about it when they're home in bed, but all Will wants to do is sleep—which is what he does for the next 18 hours, a kind of mini-hibernation. He awakes feeling "good" but ravenous, and his appetites for her stew and for Charlotte are exactly what she's desired, for "a *very* long time." Nonetheless, she keeps a previously arranged assignation with Stewart that requires her to lie to Will (the answering-machine message about the conference in New Haven). Will, with his newfound sensory talents, literally "sniffs" out the adulterous liaison. Kate Nelligan's innate gravity offers Charlotte a humanity that would otherwise have been lost in the sexual front running she attempts with the two men vying for the restructured senior editor position under Alden. Later, when Charlotte returns to Will at his hotel and pleads to be taken back, he growls at her to "Keep away." While this is part of the feral, aggressive new Will (and the only quality eyewitnesses remember and recount to the police), the moment retains a complicating ambiguity: this is Will's embarrassingly public recoil from the woman who betrayed him, yet it is also potentially residual evidence of his goodness, the same impulse that will cause him to handcuff himself to a radiator in his hotel room and endure the searing of the amulet against his skin, all to remain civil against the temptation to ravage. He warns Charlotte for her own good, and out of his own good. Laura, watching the tense exchange, must become the beauty to his beast, though her effect does not so much tame as ennoble him.

In the days immediately after Stewart's double double-cross, however, while he is still growing into his new powers of self-assertion, Will becomes a monster of conformity, not only vowing to "get" Stewart and making good on the vow, but even matching wits with the top-dog himself, maneuvering his way to a deal for more money and power. When Alden's accountant reflexively balks at the proposal's audacity, Alden stills him and approves the deal without negotiation. As if acknowledging a self-betrayal, Will accepts Alden's praise (he's even more bloodthirsty than Stewart at this moment): "Yes, but I still have those two big drawbacks: taste and individuality." Alden is in on this sort of self-hating mockery: "Maybe I can overlook 'em," he says. The two suddenly seem made for each other in a way that does no credit to either. These are Will's nights of liberation, a free id in Midtown. By day he figuratively tears the throats from his competitors; under the moon he tears the throats out of animals and the gun-hands off of would-be muggers.[8]

In Will's brief absorption into the mainstream of corporate conformity, he and Stewart are momentarily on equal moral footing. After announcing to his longsuffering executive assistant, Mary, that "the worm's turned and is now packing an uzi," Will confronts Stewart, who assumes the same bootlicking servility with which he has previously cloaked his treachery (as at the Alden firing party, when he asks Will what he should do after Stewart has been named as his successor). Having learned that Will has double-crossed him, Stewart says to Will, "What do you want me to do? I'll do it. Resign today? Promise never to see Charlotte again? Just tell me what to do." Will's civility has never previously permitted direct confrontation and bloodletting, so it startles Stewart into honesty when Will calls his bluff and demands his immediate resignation. "Well," Stewart says, "I can't do that," and then, to himself, but loudly enough that Will (and we) can hear it, "So why did I say it?" It's a striking meta-cognitive moment: no one could be less interested in a self-examining answer, and he knows Will would be the last man to counsel him now in self-knowledge. In asking the question, Stewart plays the role of a man questioning why he is a man who reflexively plays roles. In essence, he puts a mask on his mask, and he does so knowingly, with the knowledge that his one-man audience has always known this about Stewart. It's as pure a moment of reified anxiety as Suzanne (Meryl Streep) watching her blown lines on the looping screen with Lowell (Gene Hackman) in *Postcards from the Edge*, but empty of any redemptive spirit of possibility to reverse or replace the damaging behaviors it deconstructs. Later, when Will is in trouble with the police and Alden is wavering about the deal he's made, Stewart nags at Alden with the same persistence he'd initially displayed in double-crossing Will. He learns about the complicated clauses Will has negotiated into the contract concerning succession (Roy would be next in line for Will's position), and he goes beyond even Alden's generous boundaries between civility and incivility in asserting his will to power. Alden is visibly aghast at the mirror Stewart holds up to his own aesthetic of corporate conduct, and Stewart says, "I didn't mean that," again only tangentially to his audience, as if in theatrically reflective aside. Alden demands, "Well, what *did* you mean?" Stewart is the very image of reified ambition; it will devour him. Dr. Alezais has explained that the daemon-wolf is a kind of self-revelation, consuming the non-essential appearances of a being until all that remains is "his nature, his heart. [...] The daemon-wolf is not evil, unless the man he has bitten is evil."

The "rules" of this exercise of the horror genre have asserted themselves in these dialogues Will has with Dr. Alezais, as well as with Laura in his hotel room. We come to understand what Will the wolf will do and what he won't allow himself to do. He will ruin Stewart's suede leather shoes and his professional advancement, but he will not physically attack unless provoked. He will utterly reject but will not physically attack Charlotte (at least not knowingly). He *will*, however, attack the Central Park muggers, what the New York tabloids of the era would have called a teen "wolfpack." Laura ascribes to him, with certainty hard won by years of bad experience with wolves, the status of "good man, and that's very exotic to me," she says. "I never thought I'd meet a good man who looked at me the way you do." She recognizes in Will's gaze something more than mere appetite.

As Will ultimately becomes more apparently himself under the spell of the daemon-wolf, so too does Stewart, who begins the narrative struggling to say what he truly feels after a life spent in unctuous diversion and manipulation, but who comes to find himself increasingly compelled under the spell of the daemon-wolf to say precisely what's on his mind, often to his own bemused surprise and puzzlement. At the film's climax, arriving at the Alden estate hotly pursuing both Will and Laura, he has only one thing on his mind: a demeaning objectification of Laura's sexual attraction. The guards are stunned into hostility by his frankness, but before they can subdue him, he subdues them. Having tracked down Laura, disarming directness remains his only mode. Released from the role-playing of "polite society," Stewart is frank in his reductive estimation of Laura as mere sex toy. By contrast, the ennobling power of the love Will feels for Laura reaches its apotheosis just before the film's climactic showdown between old wolf and usurper, when Will delivers a speech that expresses the goodness Laura has seen within him: "I want you to know something: I've never loved anybody this way, never looked at a woman and thought, if civilization fails, the world ends, I'll still understand what God meant, if I'm with her."

Wolf argues that the great civilizing power of the world is not law but love. Alden uses the legal system and contracts to bind and possess, his takeovers no less savage for being bloodless. In the firing party scene at Alden's mansion early in the film, Allison Janney has a brief walk-on part as a guest who gets to ask Alden a nakedly thematic rhetorical question: "I do not think of Time-Warner as another great, multinational conglomerate but as a bunch of decent, caring people, because I just don't believe money always implies ruthless ambition, Mr. Alden. Am I insane?" Alden suavely replies, "I would say so, yes," provoking approvingly sycophantic sniggering. With Stewart after Charlotte's body has been discovered in the park and Will has gone missing, Alden discusses the future in terms of legal prophecy: Will has written Roy into the succession of McLeish House authority, and Alden yields only to this power of contract law, because it is the basis of his dominion. Yet Alden has no effective legal means of manipulating Laura, to whom he remains essentially powerless. Draw up a legal document disinheriting her? It could have little effect on someone so little desirous of the trappings of his largesse. Will has a kind of possessive power over Laura that comes, ironically, from truly loving rather than possessing her. Detectives Bridger (Richard Jenkins) and Wade (Brian Markinson)—the law—similarly have no effect in exerting influence over Laura. In the hotel room when they confront Will and Laura with the news of Charlotte's death, Laura is aggressively defensive of Will's legal well-being, despite her own exceedingly precarious standing as "Miss Smith." Bridger immediately backs down, though he hungrily eyes her, also aware, as Stewart has been, that Will's alpha-male status may legitimately be challenged. In the film's coda, after Laura coyly refers to Will as "too tame" for her, using verbal irony to throw the literalist keepers of the law off the scent, Bridger confesses his attraction to her: "Yeah, that's what I thought when I saw you together at the Mayflower." As portrayed by Jenkins, Bridger is Will Randall without either a shot of daemon-wolf virility or Will's innate civility. Bridger drinks on the job, lets suspects push him around, and hopes to use the opening created by his investigation to make a run at Laura, who ought to be considered very much a person of interest in the various crimes committed around her. His ineffectuality is most manifest in the legal muddle of the film's ending: with what crimes will Stewart be posthumously charged, and with what crimes will Bridger fruitlessly pursue Will—or will he pursue Will at all? He seems interested only in pursuing Laura as the film ends, but in the closing montage, she has eyes—turning amber with the spirit of the daemon-wolf—for Will.

"There must be something wild within, an analog of the wolf," Dr. Alezais has intoned to Will during their consultation—just before Will refuses to infect Dr. Alezais with the bite of immortality. "Certain moments in Nicholson's performance (like the gentle, confused look he gives the dying Indian sage when asked to bite his hand) felt like strange, luminous celluloid flashpoints not quite like anything seen before. [...] *Wolf* in its clumsy way exudes some of its hero's torn earnestness, the beast's desperation to find a humane way."[9] Will may be wild, but he remains civil. He can't bring himself to even the most well-meaning of unprovoked attacks. The "analog of the wolf" is indeed the basis of the werewolf formula as well as the satire of late capitalism. "It feels good to be the wolf, doesn't it?" he asks Will. "Power without guilt, love without doubt." But of course the irony of Dr. Alezais' characterization of the wolf is that he unintentionally describes two very different species of animal. The amoral (or "evil") wolf wields power without reflection let alone guilt, and never doubts love because his love is terminal narcissism. This is the daemon-wolf that consumes Stewart, whose heightened senses doom him not only to registering sound and scent at extra-human levels, but also mendacity. Stewart's untrustworthy nature accentuates his suspicion of others. He is destroyed not by Will's bared teeth and claws, which always hold back their fatal force, but by Laura's bullets, because she now feels as acutely the daemon-wolf as either of the men; despite the essential gentleness beneath the hardened exterior she projects to the world, she is able to kill because Stewart is in mid-leap and Will is thus endangered. Will's "power," as Dr. Alezais refers to it, has nothing to do with the systems of reified power within which Will has found himself so ill at ease throughout his career. His short venture into conformity with manipulative power-mongering soon disinterests him once he has come to "understand [...] what God meant," contemplating Laura in the grip of a daemon-spirit of loving commitment.

Protagonists have been riding away (*The Graduate*), paddling away (*Catch-22*), singing away (*Postcards*), and walking away (*Regarding Henry*) from the constricting forces of their objectification since Nichols' earliest films. The social renunciations implicit in *Wolf*'s conclusion are consistent with such negative movement, but *Wolf* has more in common with *Postcards* and *Regarding Henry* than with earlier Nichols films of counter-cultural resistance, because there is a clearer sense of self-definition ("This is who I am") rather than merely negative definition ("Whatever I am, I am not that"). There is something hapless about Benjamin and Elaine's blank passivity at the end of *The Graduate*, and Yossarian's tiny, quixotic strokes against oceanic currents may be noble but seem equally absurd, given the impracticality of his goal. There is in *Wolf*'s resolution, in which Will and Laura happily renounce their compromised humanity for the "wild within," a familiar insight about human "evolution" that Nichols first posited in 1973, in *The Day of the Dolphin*. It is a dark vision of humanity's atavism, a devolving (rather than evolving) into ever more bloody territorial possessiveness.

In *Dolphin*, all the intellectual brilliance of Dr. Jake Terrell (George C. Scott) has been focused upon lifting the dolphins up toward the presumed pinnacle of natural selection: homo sapiens. Yet Jake's gradual epiphany is that, in fact, his attempting to shape in his own image the dolphin Alpha, born in captivity at the Terrell Center and the only "son" he and his wife have, instructing him in human language and logic, has only exposed Alpha (and his mate, Beta) to the venality of the "superior" human race and left Fa and Be complicit in the deaths of the conspirators on the boat. In the end, Jake is ironically reduced to using the system of logic with which he'd initially established meaningful engagement with another species in order to lie to them, sever ties, and thus preserve their lives from his own murdering species. It's a noble but despairing gesture, one that underscores for Jake the futility of cross-purposes at the center of human experience, our reified codes of savagery wearing the mask of humanist civility. If Jake could grow gills, perhaps he would; indeed, his happiest moments in the film, scored to the romantic strains of Georges Delerue's main theme, are when he has strapped on oxygen tank and mask and entered the dolphins' world of water (albeit always within the artificial construction of the center's aquarium, the boundaries he has imposed). What Jake realistically cannot do within the confines of the paranoid-thriller genre, Will and Laura fantastically can achieve within the werewolf formula. Thus the rhetoric of *Dolphin* banishes the Terrells East of Eden, while the conclusion of *Wolf* foresees what David Denby calls "the liberationist undertones"[10] of Will and Laura's reunion within the forest primeval, "what God meant." The satire of commodified conformity thus meets its hybridized generic conclusion in Nichols' beloved sense of "transformation,"[11] here taken to its generic transmutative extreme. Lane writes, "From 'The Graduate' onward, [Nichols] has relished the spectacle of Americans at one another's throats."[12] In *Wolf*, there is clearly more honor (among the highest human values for Nichols) to being a lone wolf of "taste and individuality" and the imperatives of love than to disappearing into the wolfpack of predatory conformity.

15

"Family values"

The Birdcage (1996)

Thirty years after his Hollywood debut in 1966 with *Who's Afraid of Virginia Woolf?*, Mike Nichols returned, in a sense, to his past. *The Birdcage*, a baroque slapstick comedy of the collision of the gay and straight worlds, is Nichols' official reunion with his first professional partner, Elaine May, who wrote the adapting screenplay (though May had worked behind the scenes with Nichols as a script doctor on many earlier films). As during their shared stage career, Nichols and May once again delivered an enormously successful, crowd-pleasing comic confection, without question the most exuberantly funny film of Nichols' career. *The Birdcage* was also the biggest hit of the decade for either Nichols or May.

The Birdcage has its origins in the French stage play by Jean Poiret, adapted into the 1978 French-language film directed by Edouard Molinaro and written by Poiret, Molinaro, Marcello Danon, and Francis Veber. David Denby conjectures that the evergreen potency of Poiret's original concept is "because it's less about homosexuality than marriage and family."[1] May's script is faithful to the original concept of the story—gay men who have raised the biological son of one member of the couple and who, upon the eve of the son's engagement to enter a heterosexual union, attempt to cover up their lifestyle for the peace of a first meeting between future in-laws—but it transports the home of the drag club at the center of the narrative from St. Tropez on the French Riviera to South Beach in Miami. May's meta-textual translation moves the original's French-culture problems and prejudices into the context of the on-going American ideological debate over "family values" (essentially, the political appropriation of gender roles and reproduction) midway through the Clinton presidency, to which it refers on several occasions. One presumes the two families would simply go their separate and very distinct ways after the eventual wedding ceremony, rather than keep up the perpetual pretense—but it's just such a contemplation that *La Cage aux Folles* and *The Birdcage* invite: even if, in the misguided name of love for one's family, one were to attempt such a pretense, the increasing complexity of the architecture of such a house of cards eventually must collapse, and nature must reveal itself. If not in linguistic ingenuity, in dramatic form both *La Cage aux Folles* and *The Birdcage* evidence the complications of Shakespearean comedy, with its exchanged and concealed gender identities and eventual resolution of differences in humanizing common cause (and, of course, a wedding). The thematic flourish in all versions of this narrative is that love and family know no distinctions of gender, orientation, or political affiliation—the gay couples in the French original and the Nichols and May adaptation are quite as capable of the stability and nurturing love espoused by "family values" conservatives as the most conventional of married, heterosexual partnerships. Richard

Corliss calls *The Birdcage* a "gently supportive comedy about gays, a sweet parable of family values."[2] *The Birdcage* may most fruitfully be read as a light and refreshing sorbet course before the heavier, satirical political entrée Nichols and May would serve in *Primary Colors*.

Of Nichols' two kinds of narratives—the reified protagonists who, awash in the anxiety of their constructed predicament, cannot or will not imagine themselves out of their imprisoning social traps, or the protagonists who sense within their reified anxiety a means to diagnose their inherited condition and imagine for themselves a redemption—*Postcards from the Edge*, *Regarding Henry*, and *Wolf*, Nichols' three previous films, are all of this latter variety, and there are other, even earlier films in this same mode. George and Martha in *Who's Afraid of Virginia Woolf?* have tentatively embarked on their first morning in such a fruitfully disillusioned existence at film's end; Yossarian rows furiously against vast systemic currents of reification; Karen Silkwood dies amidst her crusade against objectifying industrial callousness and labor-force complicity. Suzanne Vale in *Postcards* and Henry Turner in *Regarding Henry* embark upon second-act lives of post-addiction commitment to the genuine, not to the protocols of social conformity and the success myth. *Wolf* wins its transformative victory more "easily" by virtue of its generic latitude, in which transmutation (into the wolf's monogamous purity of purpose) stands in for transformation, but Will's (not quite) lone wolf status descends spiritually from Thoreau, not wolves.

In *The Birdcage*, his follow-up to *Wolf* and another utilization of non-human species as titular metaphor, Nichols allows satire and farcical fantasy to commingle, but without the supernatural as an additional element. The fantasy is that social and political conservatives can be transformed; the satire is that they must. To his son Val (Dan Futterman), Armand Goldman (Robin Williams) says, "Yes, I wear foundation. Yes, I live with a man. Yes, I'm a middle-aged fag. But I know who I am, Val. It took me twenty years to get there, and I'm not going to let some idiot senator destroy that." Armand only *has* Val as a son because of the reified confusion he was still wrestling with when Katherine Archer (Christine Baranski) seduces him into a one-night stand while cast members in a musical together. That reproductive experience nonetheless solidified his sexual orientation, and he has lived in blissful if decidedly non-quotidian partnership with Albert (Nathan Lane) ever since. For all his costume changes, Albert is always himself. It's the next generation—Val and his intended, Barbara Keeley (Calista Flockhart)—who must negotiate their own reified anxiety, the engine of this farcical plot of disguise and subterfuge. Val and Barbara take their place in Nichols' long roll call of the reified transformed by their experience to speak truth to power, however haltingly.

* * *

The Birdcage offers Mike Nichols another clever variation on his auteurist thematic preoccupations with performance, social conformity, and intolerance, though this time the protagonists are hysterically unsuccessful at trying to be anyone or anything but who and what they are. Much of the drama of reified anxiety and the possibility of transformation is worked out off-screen. Armand Goldman, for instance, has a biological son as evidence of his sexual ambivalence from a much earlier time in his history, when he experimented for a night with Katherine Archer, a big, brassy blonde ten years his junior. Armand's commitment is to Albert, from whom he's never since wavered in his devotion. We are also not invited to see the yielding of Senator Kevin Keeley and his wife Louise (Gene Hackman and Dianne Wiest) to a public acknowledgment of their ties, via Val and Barbara's marriage during the closing credits, to the Goldmans, one-time symbols of Keeley's cultural contempt. What *The Birdcage* offers is a platform for hyperbolic comedy and, as a kind of subplot, a bil-dungsroman of two young people's maturation. The only person who never dons a costume from beginning to end of the narrative is Val, but he has been the instigator of all the command performances that take place around him, implicating (and devastating) the two people who have loved him longest and best.

Nichols uses the soundtrack of *The Birdcage* to bookend the film with Sister Sledge's "We Are Family," thus foregrounding the ideological battlefield of "family values" as an ironic irritant to genuine family feeling and connection. Every one of the six members of the interfamily dinner party is motivated, at least in part, by affection for his or her nuclear family. Val and Barbara come immediately to ask for the respective blessings of their parents rather than simply eloping and sparing themselves the pain of attempting to work within family strictures. The motivation is respect, yet the application is severely lacking: each child ultimately treats his or her parents poorly as a result of a desire for their good will in a union. Val temporarily denies his parents' identity; Barbara generates a comforting series of pre-posterous lies for hers. The Keeleys take a page from the Robinsons in *The Graduate*, manipulating the rite of marriage for social gain—a gain not for their daughter but for themselves. While Barbara cowers meekly, Louise argues the merits of plunging ahead with a wedding the Keeleys hadn't originally supported: "It would restore your image," she assures her husband the Senator. "A wedding is hope, and a white wedding is family and morality and tradition." She concludes calculatedly, "Love and optimism instead of cynicism and sex—it would be an affirmation." In a private moment at the dinner party with the Goldmans, she accuses her husband of only being concerned with his career, not his daughter's welfare, and Keeley calls her on it: she's at least as guilty, given the idea was her brainstorm. The only family members willing to subvert themselves and sacrifice their own interests in deference to their loved one's needs are Armand and Albert. Val sells them down the river for the shot at a happy beginning to a shared life with Barbara; Barbara's lies estrange her from her xenophobic parents; and the Senator and his wife act first upon political, not familial imperatives. Armand and Albert are alone among the participants in this social disaster whose actions, the product of love, damage only themselves. They do all they do for Val.

The Sister Sledge song also foregrounds the sense of queer solidarity provided by a neighborhood like South Beach (or, for instance, San Francisco's Castro), further displayed by the drag club's costuming and performances. "I have all my sisters with me" has a rhetorical zing to it in the context of the zoomed camera angles on performers who, up close, are not at all what they appeared from a distance to be. Nichols and cinematographer Emmanuel Lubezki spend a minute after this first number in uninflected observation of the costume change of the most petite of all the male dancers in the "We Are Family" troupe as he strips away one costume and snaps himself into the next, with a stylized "horse" strapped around his pelvis. This is transformation made in gendered confidence about identity. What is most flamboyant at The Birdcage isn't the music, the décor, or even the costumes, but the self-expressive "pride" of the staff and patrons.

By contrast, Val Goldman is all apologies, creating confected stories about Armand and Albert and asking his father to play nice with Senator Keeley, a man who would never knowingly agree to be in the same room with them, much less come to champion one of them, as he does Albert (who is wearing the conventional uniform of heterosexual matron-hood at the time), as "Our kind of people." Val and Barbara are in the bind they're in for the same reason that star-crossed lovers have chafed at familial bonds for untold generations.

The Goldmans and the Keeleys have taught their children to cherish their inheritance, but both kids are so young they have never had to put what they've been taught to a test. Elaine May took *La Cage aux Folles* and made its central conflict emblematic of the political polarization of America: if red and blue actually had to share the world's worst seafood stew and a media scandal, might they not discover what is most human in one another?

In their very drabness, the Keeleys are every bit the stereotypical lampoon that the Goldmans are. When Louise dissolves in an outburst of tears at the film's climax, it feels like an inexpert attempt at the sort of histrionics Albert so effortlessly emotes on cue. Louise wears sensible, expensive fashions; her daughter wears excessively plain, preppy sweaters and dresses. Barbara has the unformed, dreamy quality of Honey in *Who's Afraid of Virginia Woolf?* Although her father describes her as sensible and able to take care of herself, we see little evidence of this. Even her brief stand against her parents' default intolerance near the end of the film collapses upon command. Barbara's and Louise's lives revolve around the Senator's, and his life, like that of any politician, is utterly in the grip of his political ambition and his ability to manipulate an image. The Keeleys are a cartoon of control, and their animation is in inverse proportion to their ability to maintain that control.

The Keeleys fret continually about appearance and performance: their entire lives are a projected image that can collapse at any moment under the weight of reification; the Goldmans fret about appearance and performance only when about to take the stage at the club. As *The Birdcage* begins, Armand notes that Albert has not yet appeared backstage in anticipation of his nightly appearance as Starina. He ascends to their residence and finds Albert histrionically locked in his boudoir. What follows is a parody of various kinds of reified social pressure: Armand worries about disappointing the "packed house" downstairs, sounding much like Mr. Braddock trying to coax his son Benjamin into public view at various parties in *The Graduate*. Albert moans, "That's all I am to you, isn't it: a meal ticket. Never mind about my feelings, never mind about my suffering—it's just your show. Not even *our* show. Your show." Sitting before the vanity mirror, Albert intones examples of what he's done "to make myself attractive to you," losing and gaining and losing weight again. Agador and Armand take these broad gestures in stride; indeed, Agador feeds Albert aspirin with the product stamp sanded off, to provide the illusion of a placebo effect, an Albert's Little Helper. All of it has the feeling of pre-performance ritual. After the show, Albert and Armand revert to the placid, middle-aged existence of a largely platonic marriage, their demonstrative gestures limited to an affectionate morning peck over coffee.

When Val poses the gambit of Armand and Albert performing for his future in-laws within their own living space, it throws into relief the life they've been living without reflection, naturally. Armand, the "man" of his partnership with Albert, becomes aware that, far from masculine, he is also a massive assemblage of "tells" who could no more "pass" as straight than the far more flamboyantly feminized Albert. This had never been a problem until Val makes it one, and it had never been a problem for Val growing up until his desire to share his life with someone else brought her family's version of values into juxtaposition with those of the Goldmans. "I don't care who he is," Armand says defiantly. "I don't want to be someone else. Do you want me to be someone else?" There is only one right answer to this question, and Val fails to offer it. Instead, he says, "You've done it before." Together they recall his first day of school and Armand's request of his young son to reply to pointedly xenophobic questions about his father's profession with the generic All-American characterization, "A businessman." When Val enlists Armand as his accomplice in perpetrating the fraud of Katherine's portraying "the wife," they know in the abstract it will hurt Albert. But Val becomes increasingly calloused as the time grows shorter. When Albert first learns of the plan, Val says, in a vain attempt at soothing, "It's just for tonight," to which Albert replies, with heightened, stagy emotion, "I understand—it's just while *people* are here. [...] The monster—the *freak*— is leaving. You're safe." But there is only one monster in the house, and it's Val. He also repeatedly brutalizes the Goldman's valet, Agador (Hank Azaria), who accepts the insults and barked commands like a poor stepchild.

Armand puts on a conservative dress suit and tie; in the mirror, he regards this second Armand and says, "I look like my grandfather in this suit. Dressed like this in every picture. Killed himself when he was 30." The age is significant: this was Armand's age when he became a father. Unlike his grandfather, he survived his crisis and learned to live with who he is, but the scene projects a kind of death-spirit, which Val only encourages when he instructs his father not to walk, not to gesture, not even to "talk—too much." This is just before Albert minces through the door, corrects his walk (to *John Wayne*, if John Wayne minced), and sits down across from them, revealing his flamingo-pink socks. In the silence, Nathan Lane rolls out a solid minute of exquisite physical comedy, entirely ill at ease in every treacherous gay limb and digit, until he's wrapped himself into a pretzel of anxiety. This is Val's doing, and they all know it, but Albert takes it upon himself: "What? No *good*? Why? I'm dressed just the way you are. I took off all my rings. I'm not wearing any makeup. I'm just—a *guy*." Indicating the socks, Armand says, " What about those?" With dignity, Albert says, "Those,

The caring openness of the Goldman family devolves in *The Birdcage* into secrets, conspiracies, and hurt feelings when Val (Dan Futterman, center) comes home to tell his father Armand (Robin Williams, right) that he wants to marry the daughter of a conservative senator obsessed with polarizing "family values." Val, who's been raised by his father and Albert, Armand's partner, suddenly desires an alternate version of his family life, which means Albert, Armand, and Agador (Hank Azaria), their personal assistant, must masquerade *within* demeaning stereotypes as a means of *deflecting* demeaning stereotypes.

well, one does want a hint of color." In the despairing silence that ensues, Albert boils until he bursts: "You're thinking that, dressed this way, I'm even *more* obvious, aren't you? [...] I just wanted so much to help you, and you *hate* me." Armand expends all efforts to console Albert, but Val never says a word. At the moment, neither Armand nor Albert is "just a guy," and only "just a guy" will do. Val lets them down by letting them know they've let *him* down. Yet they are nothing other than who they have always been, the two people who have never let him down.

A predatory paranoia has been unleashed inside the Goldmans' birdcage of tender, flamboyant, self-actualization, and its aggression comes in the forms of impatience, intolerance, and denial. Nichols and May have introduced this invasion of objectified assumptions early on in the film—via audience double-cross. After coaxing Albert down from his pre-performance jitters and onto the club's stage, Armand slips upstairs again, dismisses Agador for the evening, and prepares the residence for an assignation; when Val, an attractive young man, first lets himself in, we are guilty of assuming the worst stereotypic conclusions about a gay man: whatever else he is, he is helplessly promiscuous. It's as if we begin the film in the psychology *not* of any of the Goldmans—not even image-obsessed Val—but rather of the Keeleys, whom we will not meet for the first quarter-hour of the film. This is the psychology that, once injected into the Goldmans' consciousness by their adored but suddenly ashamed son, threatens to undo in a day the family solidarity the Goldmans have spent 20 years attempting to build. As we are enlightened about the true nature of the tryst and the two men involved—not unfaithful gay liaison but tender father and son reunion—our default cultural assumptions aren't swept away but rather are *sourced* and given narrative reality by Val's craven surrender to Barbara's parents' values.

The Keeleys are defined entirely by what others think of them. Both of Nichols and May's collaborations, *The Birdcage* and *Primary Colors*, Nichols' next film, offer central characters who are major United States politicians and whose every move is scrutinized and parsed by the media and just as obsessively dissected by the politicians themselves and their handlers. Authenticity becomes increasingly difficult inside such an objectifying cage, where an actual person is reduced to a representative cluster of symbols and signs. As a result, when the personal upheaval of their daughter's possible early marriage is trumped by the public scandal of Senator Jackson's spectacular indiscretion, the conservative Keeleys career as wildly in reactive, damage-controlling stratagems as the Goldmans. Perhaps rightly expressing initial alarm at Barbara's proposing marriage at eighteen (and expressing mingled distaste and longed-for ignorance when Barbara boldly discloses her sexual activity with Val), the Keeleys swiftly lose the thread of concern for their daughter's well being in questions of status. At first they fear she will make an undesirable social match and fret over Barbara and Val's characterization of "Mr. Coleman" (as Barbara pronounces the Goldmans' name) as "in the arts," a "Greek cultural attaché." Then, as the full force of the scandal literally envelops them, sealing them in their snowy house and the objectifying eye of the media, the Keeleys' thoughts turn to commodifying their daughter's future as a politicized signifier of their legitimacy.

Louise Keeley's king-making instincts reveal themselves when she happily recalibrates her perspective on Barbara's potential wedding; like the Robinsons' arranged marriage for Elaine to suit their desire for revenge on Benjamin in *The Graduate*, the most sacred of rites between two individuals is cynically co-opted for manipulative social control. The Keeleys acquiesce to their daughter's desire, but for all the wrong reasons, and to serve a self-image that has become necessarily distorted by campaign ideology. Kevin Keeley has climbed "into bed," as the pundit parlance has it, with Senator Jackson because he believes the Southern politician's ultra-conservatism more nearly approximates the nation's mood than, for instance, the middle-of-the-road politics of Bob Dole, the man who lost to Clinton in 1996. Dole is "too liberal" for the Keeleys, but they've become so out of touch with life as actually lived that such a critique is pure abstraction—a perceptive "truth" rather than reality. Yet as they begin to ponder Barbara as sacrificial political lamb, their thoughts about the "Colemans" suddenly disintegrate in revelatory paranoia: "They can't blame us for this! Eli Jackson was a common redneck; we had nothing to do with him socially." With the media massed on the frozen lawn, the Keeleys fly the coop, the birdcage they and their political team have constructed for them out of reactive genuflection to public whim and private fear. The irony is that their intolerance has caused their daughter to tell extravagant lies about her prospective in-laws, and the Keeleys consequently race toward "*Enquirer* heaven," a photo-op exposé of hypocrisy on a (Eli) Jacksonian scale.

"I don't want to be someone else," Armand has said to Val, but the infection of the Keeleys makes for the sort of terminal self-consciousness that can only come from externally derived self-definition. The Keeleys' disease is precisely that: a lack of ease in their own skins, and thus a fundamental lack of ease with others who are different, even when they are perceived as alike (as the Keeleys at first are led to believe of the "Colemans"). Having arrived at the "Colemans'" house, Keeley holds forth on the changing weather of the drive south from the snow to Miami, and his monologue devolves immediately into an epic of stump-speech pieties and platitudes, "an aria of dullness," according to Terrence Rafferty, who calls it "the best moment" in the film.[3] It certainly exposes the hollowness at Keeley's core. So long a politician thinking of other people in terms of metrics and ideologies, he is fundamentally lost as a person with other people, as ill at ease as Albert in his suit and pink socks, terrified of saying a wrong word and antagonizing the "Colemans," in whom he and Louise have irrationally focused their political rehabilitation. Out of the "Colemans'" earshot, the Keeleys stew about the impression they are making, even as they also begin a defensive counter-caricature of their hosts. Williams as Armand has just done a comic turn trying to find his way, in increasing agitation, out of the curtain-lined room. "The loveliest thing about this surefire scene," writes Denby, "with its furious machinery of entrances and exits, is that caricature turns to benevolent farce. At its best, farce does not judge; it unifies all of humanity in ridicule."[4] The Keeleys interpret Armand's discomfort and the absence of "the wife" as inevitable censure of their choice of political bedfellow: "It's this thing with Jackson—the wife probably doesn't want to be in the same house with us, and the father is a nervous wreck." Keeley begins to muse on "something about the father and the butler," and Louise scolds him, "Dad, you always think the worst." The hyper-traditional appellation suggests an acquiescence to patriarchal hegemony at the most basic levels of psychology in the family, guiding all their actions for so long that they are on a kind of ideological autopilot, and as they sense Armand's return—the curtains now proudly mastered and confidently, even dramatically swept aside, the Keeleys reassume their submissive masks. It's a stroke of exquisite comic timing by May that this is when Albert, in a mask worthy of Williams himself from his enormously successful box-office appearance in matronly drag as *Mrs. Doubtfire* (Chris Columbus, 1993), first appears, as "Mrs. Coleman."

Both Williams in the earlier film and Lane in *The Birdcage* target a grand-maternal image in the vein of Barbara Bush, emphatically and unapologetically reassuring traditional older women. The strategy releases them from sexualized identity, where they can hide, postmenopause, from the socialized "problem" of desire and all its political implications. The always excellent Wiest has to this point in *The Birdcage* been Keeleys' ideal wife because she is an idealized mother and, in practical terms, a political rather than conjugal partner; now Albert co-opts the image and, with his performative flair, threatens to replace her in the affections of a man who for so long has been in relationship only to ideas, not the people upon which the ideas have been projected. "Maybe I'm just an old-fashioned girl," says Albert winningly, playing *precisely that*, "but I pity the woman who's too busy to stay home and take care of her own." Lane's performance of Albert's performance of "Mrs. Coleman" is "a wicked parody of the Stepford moms who are the senator's ideal woman. Show business becomes an apt metaphor for family life; all are putting on the acts they think others want to see."[5] Though anything but conventional, Albert's life has in fact been dedicated to both an arch parody of and an ardent commitment to the "old-fashioned." His speech is of course an act, but it is somehow also an entirely sincere representation of his heart. For his part, Keeley can't keep himself from gushing, "Hear, hear," like a politician, and then, more personally, "It's just so nice to meet people like you." Nichols and his editor, Arthur Schmidt, here cut to a series of close-up comic reactions by Armand and Val, as Keeley administers the ironic coup de grâce with smug politicized conviction: "Our kind of people." The journey of May's screenplay is a journey off Keeley's very limited map, towards his total disorientation and an inadvertent discovery of the truth of his claim: although sensationally dissimilar, the Goldmans share with the Keeleys a desire for a stable domestic unit, symbolized by the traditional comic resolution of the plot, a wedding. The Keeleys value the family no more than do the Goldmans.

The effect, half an hour later, of seeing the Goldmans for who they really are, not as Barbara's lies and their own presumptions have distorted them, has a profoundly disorienting effect on Keeley. The spell of ideology has held him so fast for so long that, confronted with this truth, he simply can't see it. Rafferty points out that Keeley's is "the one role that has been significantly expanded" from *La Cage*; the Senator is "a four-square champion of traditional morality, whose reactionary philosophy, it's clear, is directly attributable to a stubborn, intractable intellectual incapacity. He's literally unable to see the world as it is."[6] Hackman's glazed countenance and repeated, disconsolate, "I don't understand ..." take on a kind of ritualized quality, as all six members of the dinner party take their various turns trying to help him see. Katherine has joined them by this point, and Keeley, increasingly contemptuous of "Mr. Coleman's" condescension to "Mrs. Coleman," believes he's seen through Armand's hypocrisy: the European's casual disregard for the sanctity of the marriage bond by the arrangement of a "live-in mistress." Confronting Armand, he has just delivered a triumphal blast of accusatory rhetoric: "Exactly how many mothers does your son have?" Val, in his final act of aggression towards his parents, gently tugs Barbara's loaned barrette free from Albert's wig, exposing the man beneath the mask—though this initially shocking disclosure is transformed not only by the tenderness with which Val accomplishes it but, more to the point, by his verbal assertion of responsibility, however belated, for representing the truth of himself and his family to the Keeleys: "Just one," he says, presenting Albert. "*This* is my mother." Val confesses, more shamed than sheepish, "We lied to you. Barbara and I. And everybody lied for us. These are my parents." Armand, solemn and moved by his son's newfound courage, introduces his wife, Albert, to the Keeleys, and Val's mother, Katherine, to her son, who says approvingly to Armand of Val, "You've done a good job." Armand tenderly encompasses Albert in accepting her praise on their behalf. Barbara is next to help her parents in grasping the enormity of their misassumption, deconstructing various social images culminating in their ethnicity. Louise impatiently tries to disillusion her husband:

"He's a man. They're both men," to which Keeley responds, in comic non sequitur, "He can't be," and then directly to Albert, "You can't be Jewish." Katherine attempts to explain her role in this complicated modern family, but Albert, finding his least affected voice, the one that is most *himself* (neither "Mrs. Coleman" nor "Starina"), says, "I just want you to know, Senator Keeley, that I meant every word I said to you about a return to family values and a stricter moral code." Hackman, still portraying Keeley as hilariously oblivious, delivers the line "I feel like I'm insane" with the poignancy of a man whose unconscious mind is in the midst of transforming his consciousness. It's not quite the brain damage Henry Turner undergoes in *Regarding Henry*, but there is genuine trauma. "Nothing's changed," Albert tries to reassure him, "It's still *me*." But he's wrong: something *is* changing, something that will eventually permit what Louise naively yearned for at the beginning of the plot: a "white wedding" as "an affirmation." The Keeleys simply hadn't understood at that point what true affirmation might look like, and that it might not look solely *like them*.

Louise briefly reasserts her prerogative as kingmaker and attempts to minimize further damage by rushing them out. Barbara resists but, like the under-formed youths in *The Graduate*, capitulates. In parting, though he can't any longer figure out what he should be calling them, Keeley rallies to his long-observed defaults to pander for their votes (no doubt concerned for his often-cited Florida political ally, Jeb Bush, who clearly would never have been relying on the Goldmans' votes). Yet the fear of public perception re-confronts the Keeleys as they open the Goldmans' door, and all their summoned stiff upper lips tremble and fall. There can be no freedom from identity crisis when identity is formed by social proscription. This initiates the solution to the comic plot: the Keeleys' immersion, a veritable wallowing, in alternative culture, donning the mask that redemptively unmasks them and permits them finally to *see* the Goldmans. The reprise of the club's frenetic performance of "We Are Family" voices testament to a Family of Man, a newfound simpatico between the Keeleys and Goldmans, one undertaken not for political ends (the Goldmans actually have more to gain in red-blue battleground Florida by betraying the Keeleys—as the Senator's own chauffeur cheerfully and repeatedly does) but because of the far more meaningful (because not abstracted) personal feeling they have built over this first evening together. Against all odds and informed finally by their star-crossed kids, the Keeleys and Goldmans find common ground where the Montagues and Capulets could not ... admittedly with the help of lamé, big wigs, and lots and lots of foundation makeup. Sister Sledge's anthem calls us to work our way through the reified anxiety of the birdcages in which we are complicit in our entrapment to find the common denominator of our uncommon uniqueness, our individuality as persons of value in dispiritingly dismissive systems of default hegemony. Corliss concludes, "The film is bold enough to propose the integration of gays—and by extension of anyone 'different'—into an America that at the moment seems ready to take up arms and shoot holes in the melting pot."[7] In his Foreword to May's published screenplay, Nichols observes, "Elaine's triumph with regard to the script was to ask the question, 'How would it be if this story happened right here, right now, in today's society?' She understood that you have to include every possible kind of prejudice in the telling of this story because in the final reconciliation you represent everyone—not just gays and heterosexuals but Jew and gentiles, Democrats and Republicans ... one hopes the whole country."[8] Introducing the newest performers that will include the three staid Keeleys amidst a rainbow coalition of dancers in drag, Armand makes his final announcement to his Birdcage audience, and to us—Nichols and May's simple yet radical ideological affirmation: "As we come to the end of our show, you are family, too."

16

"True believerism"

Primary Colors (1998)

After not having headlined together for well over a quarter of a century, Mike Nichols and Elaine May had such a positive experience sharing credit on *The Birdcage* that they embarked together on Nichols' next feature film, an adaptation of Joe Klein's novel, *Primary Colors*. Originally published in 1996 by Klein under the name "Anonymous," *Primary Colors: A Novel of Politics* explores a Presidential campaign administration bearing striking resemblances to the Bill Clinton White House, elected in 1992 and returned to office four years later. The novel was a bestseller and as a result became a hotly anticipated Hollywood project. Given the high-profile political satire of the original narrative, *Primary Colors* seems unlike Nichols' typical subject matter, which had rarely assumed overt political reference. Working with May on *The Birdcage* and *Primary Colors*, Nichols politicizes the deadening weight of commodification and conformity on individuals. These familiar insights are given their broadest implications in *Primary Colors*, broader even than in *Silkwood* or *The Day of the Dolphin*, Nichols' two political-conspiracy narratives, and *Catch-22* and *Biloxi Blues*, his two distinctly different armed-forces comedies that question the commodifying methodologies of militarism. In *Primary Colors*, Nichols and May posit the suddenly quite natural and obvious assumption that, if reification has a trickle-down effect on all individuals within late-capitalist systems of social construction, those charged with governance of such systems can hardly expect to be immune.

Unfortunately for Nichols and company, *Primary Colors'* release date offered a problem similar to the release of *Catch-22*. In the case of the earlier film, released in 1970 at the height of dissent about Vietnam, the timing problem came not from the external socio-political context but from its Hollywood counter-cultural competition, Robert Altman's *M*A*S*H**. Lee Hill writes that, for 1970 audiences, "Nichols' film appeared too calculated and fussy compared to the rawness of Altman."[1] *Catch-22* became an enormously expensive and painstaking flop. *Primary Colors* had no box-office rival as a Clinton administration allegory. Rather, it had the real thing: the culture was awash in the tabloid scandal of Monicagate, the nightly news a near-endless montage of Clintonian euphemisms and denials and the salacious details evidencing his appetites: "*Primary Colors* cannot hope to distinguish itself from the image-making spectacle it attempts to represent."[2] Nichols and May strangely found themselves with the insoluble problem of art trying to compete with life in that most unenviable of battlegrounds, the public imagination, where truth will always be stranger than fiction. Their character, Jack Stanton, played so convincingly by John Travolta, was up against the original on initial release. Why would anyone have been absorbed in 1998 by the scandals and foibles of a fictional Clinton avatar when a hostile Congress was rhetorically shoving the real Clinton ever closer to impeachment proceedings for the lies he'd told about his White House sexcapades? Nichols observes, "so-called current events have largely replaced fiction as the primary metaphor. [... T]hey have crowded out the metaphors that were in fiction, they've sucked up metaphor into them so that they're the main story. They're the story that everybody's watching in the way that everybody used to read Dickens and Dostoevsky in serialized form. *Primary Colors* is confusing because it's fiction and reality at the same time."[3]

As much as any Nichols film in the course of his career, *Primary Colors* requires reassessment now that time has afforded aesthetic distance, though Hendrik Hertzberg, writing in *The New Yorker* in a 1998 retrospective of Hollywood political filmmaking, was already calling it "the smartest movie ever made about American politics" and "the first product of Hollywood [...] that presents the struggle for democratic political power in all its morally and humanly complex glory and, especially, shame."[4] Lee Hill writes, "the film looked suspiciously like instant nostalgia to many viewers and critics. Like *Catch-22*, *Primary Colors* will eventually earn the respect it deserves. Few American films of recent years have cast such a thorough, critical, yet sympathetic look at the people and processes that shape public policy."[5] David Thomson, historically stingy with praise for Nichols, asserts that *Primary Colors* is "a good sharp comedy."[6] What audiences missed in *Primary Colors* was a typically extraordinary ensemble cast assembled and directed by Nichols, as well as an opportunity to glimpse the operations of a campaign staff at a level of verbal and logistical sophistication that future Nichols collaborator Aaron Sorkin (who wrote the adapted screenplay for *Charlie Wilson's War*) would match and even exceed in 1999, a year after the release of *Primary Colors*, with his NBC television series, *The West Wing*, which would run for seven seasons. The reasons for *Primary Colors'* box-office failure are not as simple as its timing, however. Flouting the generic Hollywood rules for comedy, even when hybridized to political drama, *Primary Colors* is long; at nearly two and a half hours, it is the longest theatrical feature of Nichols' career. It is also dense, populated by nearly 100 characters, a dozen of whom have major roles, and whose strategies and challenges are filled with realistic complication. Finally, despite a tacked-on coda of political triumph, the film is the very essence of narrative ambiguity, always a problematic strategy when attempting to tell commercial stories. Under the best of conditions, with no current-events static and even with its established literary pedigree, *Primary Colors* might have struggled to find a mainstream audience. Monicagate merely made inevitable what was already a distinct possibility.

John Travolta as Jack Stanton and Emma Thompson as Susan Stanton—analogs of the Clintons (who, in *Primary Colors'* allegory, have an adolescent son, Jack, Jr., rather than an adolescent daughter named for a Joni Mitchell song)—are quintessential Nichols protagonists, profoundly conflicted between their impulses to resist the prevailing culture and to take their rightful performative places as part of the conformist elite; "this is a movie about performers performing."[7] David Denby calls *Primary Colors* "a performer's view of running a campaign; it offers personality as performance."[8] But in this big, sprawling panorama of a political campaign from grass roots in storefronts and cheap motels to power suites and eventually all the way to the White House (briefly glimpsed in that triumphal coda), the Stantons are no more important to the narrative in terms of the dilemmas they face and choices they must make than two other characters in the film. Libby Holden (Kathy Bates, the sole member of the extraordinary cast nominated for an Academy Award, which she lost to Judi Dench for her brief cameo as Queen Elizabeth in *Shakespeare in Love*) is the passionate but unstable operative with whom the Stantons began their political journey two decades earlier. Libby, exiled from the Stantons' political lives by her psychological problems, returns when summoned by Susan, who will accept no substitute as the person whom the Stanton campaign will employ to investigate Jack's (and his opponents') potentially damaging political skeletons. Susan may have selected Libby because she can be trusted *not* to play fair, to hold the Stantons to a different standard than their opponents. Ironically, Susan's expectation of Libby is accurate, yet backfires: Libby does indeed hold the Stantons to a different standard based in the ardency of her affectionate respect for them, but rather than it being relaxed, the standard to which she holds them is even loftier, one that anticipates redemptive non-conformity rather than complicit conformity to the worst practices of the political system. In the first of a series of "tests" the protagonists of *Primary Colors* take near the film's conclusion, Libby passes *her* test by bringing to the Stantons the muck she has raked as the campaign's investigator. When the Stantons subsequently fail, without a moment's hesitation, the test Libby has passed along to them, the consequences are tragic.

The true protagonist of *Primary Colors*, however, is an outsider: Henry Burton (the British actor Adrian Lester), a bright, privileged African-American young man just getting started in politics, whose grandfather was one of the Civil Rights era's most prominent moral voices. "The first major contribution Nichols and May made to the film adaptation," writes James Kaplan, "was to give body and soul to Henry Burton, to make his Candide figure at once our surrogate and a suffering character in his own right."[9] Henry's character makes *Primary Colors* a bildungsroman, the narrative strategy of Nichols' most famous film, *The Graduate*. Through Henry's journey to an awareness of his personal responsibilities as a man of color in American government, *Primary Colors* dramatizes the process of inner formation of a young person. Nichols is, in this sense, more typically a cinematic poet of adult psychology—of the post-formative reassessment of cultural identity rather than the initial formation of that identity. Nor is Henry Burton at the beginning of *Primary Colors* as blank a slate as Benjamin Braddock (Dustin Hoffman), either at the beginning *or* the end of *The Graduate*. Product of the same educational and socio-economic advantages as Benjamin, Henry has done much more with his immediate post-collegiate life, though he ultimately feels a similar sense of emptiness. Working for an African-American Congressman, he has tired of the symbolic but ultimately illusory victories of minority politics, of forcing Presidential vetoes rather than enacting system-changing legislation. When the Stanton campaign comes calling, Henry is open to a new and more promising possibility, of working among the elite staff of a man who might one day hold the power of the veto.

As is often true of the bildungsroman hero, Henry must confront, assess, and absorb from a variety of developmental models in becoming fully himself. Richard Jemmons (a colorfully profane Billy Bob Thornton, playing the Stantons' James Carville) identifies Henry as suffering from "galloping T. B.," or "True Believerism," a hindrance to the cynical detachment necessary for the political operative. Both Richard and, in a decidedly softer, more attractive form, Daisy Green (Maura Tierney) offer Henry a hard-boiled way of being a political lifer, and Henry never seems convinced that their detachment is an advantage. Henry wants to connect—to attach, not detach. Henry's journey in *Primary Colors* is from icon to icon, a willing believer in each in turn. As the narrative begins, he is in the process of exiting Adam Larkin's congressional administration, and Governor Jack Stanton literally moves him to tears in scooping him up onto his political team. A sneaky reference from the Hollywood Golden Age gives us a sense of Henry's taste in heroes: alone in his room after his apparent screw-up with Governor Ozio's son Jimmy (Robert Cicchini), he's still stinging from Stanton's rebuke in the car and having to search for the cell phone Stanton petulantly threw out the window. Henry finds himself captured by a late-night cable screening of the final sequence from *Shane* (George Stevens, 1953); Henry idly but plaintively echoes young Joey (Brandon deWilde) when he says, "Come back, Shane—and run for President."[10] Henry is looking for an unimpeachable hero, and he seems immune to the heart-rending ambiguities with which Alan Ladd's exit at film's end leaves not only Joey but, of course, the audience. Yet at a particularly vulnerable moment in Stanton's campaign, when Henry has become increasingly tainted by Stanton's grimier personal failings and political expediencies, Henry finds himself riveted by a late breath of fresh air from an opposing camp, the idealistic political rhetoric of former Governor Fred Picker (Larry Hagman, deft in a complex minor role). And when Picker, too, ultimately emerges as all-too-human, Henry has yet another model, perhaps the most complicated of all, emerge in completing his bildungsroman journey: Libby Holden, queen of the True Believers. Henry travels a different route than typical Nichols characters like the Stantons and Libby. Older but not necessarily wiser, they must wrestle with what reification has done to them and decide whether their lives will have a distinctly different second act. Henry is still learning what reification is, so that he can make the most appropriate choices at this, the climactic crisis of his life's first act. *Primary Colors* charts the progress of Henry Burton from a man-child passively expecting a hero to a man disillusioned in the very best sense and ready to proceed without heroes as an illusory source of meaning.

* * *

Henry Burton begins *Primary Colors* in circumstances of privilege and power similar to Nichols' most celebrated protagonist, Benjamin Braddock (Dustin Hoffman) of *The Graduate*. He has been educated in privilege, and his cultural inheritance from his family has largely set the agenda for his identity. The Braddocks are in the conspicuous-consumption business, and thus Benjamin returns home with the weight of a future of material accumulation awaiting him. The Burtons are leaders in political action, and Henry has begun to assume this mantle. Henry's grandfather was a voice of the Civil Rights movement in the 1960s—he inspired Jack and Susan Stanton, Howard Ferguson, Richard Jemmons, Libby Holden, Susan's aide Lucille Kaufman (Caroline Aaron), all of whom, as a kind of pro forma salutation upon meeting Henry, pay homage to Henry's grandfather's enormous influence on their own political lives. Henry lives in the shadow of this legacy of rectitude. It has laden him with that most worthwhile of burdens: to spend a life in doing good. As such, he begins *Primary Colors* out ahead of where many Nichols protagonists, Benjamin Braddock among them, have advanced to by the *end* of their respective narratives.

Yet all is not well for Henry. He has come to Harlem to watch Jack Stanton's political performance art with an adult literacy class because he is disillusioned by the self-congratulatory routine of Congressman Adam Larkin, on whose staff he has been laboring. As he explains it to Susan, the Congressman has settled for being a fly in the ointment rather than a true difference-maker: "[W]e'd win, and we'd be gutted in the Senate. We'd settle for their version, and then the White House would veto, which we knew from the start. Then what? We'd celebrate our great moral victory. We forced the veto." The emptiness of such victories has clearly left a bad taste in Henry's mouth. He dismisses Congressman Larkin with a backhanded compliment: "He taught me a lot, but it was all the same."

The motif of education runs through *Primary Colors*, introduced by Klein in his novel and wisely retained by May. As such, it takes its place in a long-standing commitment by Nichols to this motif in his work, in direct contextualization of narratives within educational settings including *Who's Afraid of Virginia Woolf?*, *The Graduate*, *Carnal Knowledge*, and *Regarding Henry*; others, like *Biloxi Blues* and *Working Girl*, allude heavily to educational preparation for adult life. *Primary Colors* begins, of course, with a visit to a school, but to a specific kind of program, targeting adult literacy, which instantly foregrounds the notion that education may not always have its ideal effect. As the adults tell their stories of being passed up and passed over, we may think their stories have little to do with the formation of agile minds like Jack Stanton's or Henry Burton's. Yet the bildungsroman tradition in which the narrative of *Primary Colors* unfolds is, essentially, a tale of a young protagonist's education, structured on the character's moral development. When Richard bursts into the campaign, he's a nightmare of unrefined characteristics: uncouth and vulgar, a sexual predator in the office within his first five minutes. Yet he also knows instinctively that something has gone wrong in Henry's education, targeting the privileged exclusivity of Henry's prep-school days at Connecticut's prestigious Hotchkiss, a school whose demographics and production goals would be similar to those of the school to which Henry and Sarah Turner have committed their daughter Rachel before retrieving her at the conclusion of *Regarding Henry* (1991). Richard outrageously claims to be "blacker" than Henry, despite Henry's obvious racial and genealogical "qualifications"; at Fat Willie's chicken shack, Henry is far more ill at ease than either Stanton or Richard. Being black isn't what Henry must learn, however; what Hotchkiss and the Ivy League and his apprenticeship with Congressman Larkin have failed to teach him is the difference between abstraction and the real world. Scandalized by the dirty tricks a Democratic candidate has pulled in bankrolling the doctoring of the alleged Cashmere McCloud sex tape, he whines to Libby, "[W]e can't let them get away with this. Come on, this cannot be a world that lets them get away with it." Libby chastens him rhetorically: "Oh my, imagine a black boy saying that." Libby is one of Henry's key instructors in an adult crash course in *reality* literacy.

The education motif so permeates the structure—all the candidates are preoccupied with education reform; they all court teachers' unions; many of the political events, including most prominently the primary debate that marks Jack Stanton's first campaign victory, take place in schools—that, at the climax, all four of the central characters (Jack and Susan, Libby, and Henry) must take a "test," Libby's word for the ethical choice to which the campaign has brought them all. Libby's comic melodramatics ("We are testing our limits. We are in the pits. Remember 'Limbo Rock?' In other words, 'How low can you go?'") also paraphrase the process of dramatic discovery Aristotle termed anagnorisis, which is, fundamentally, a process of education: "This is it—graduation day," Libby says. "They graduate, or I do. Tell the truth, Henry: i'n't that what you're really after, too?" It is in fact precisely what *Primary Colors* is after, and in the notion of graduation, we once again hear the echoes of Nichols' Hollywood legacy from his earliest Hollywood films and their collegiate contextualization, the archetypal story of "commencement" and the ambiguity of being passive as one's life *commences*. As *The Graduate* opens, Benjamin has just come home from his commencement and curled up passively in a reversion to childhood; in the film's second half, he may *look* more active, but without a "definite plan" (which Elaine demands him to strategize when she comes to his Berkeley boarding house) to guide his path, his frenetic motion remains the equivalent of running in place, and at the film's end, he remains the same essentially passive person he was as the film opened, under the sway of larger cultural forces of reified conformity. The best he can manage at the film's end is to run away from his and Elaine's parents, though Nichols' own condemning comment on Benjamin's future is that Benjamin and Elaine *become* their parents[11] (as, long ago, the children at the beginning of Nichols and

May's "Pirandello" grow up to bicker as they'd once mimicked their parents doing). Benjamin has earned the grades, but he has done so in a system that rewards conformity. *The Graduate* has offered several traps of conformity to avoid, not alternative models to replace those traps.

For Henry in *Primary Colors*, his bloodline and education have offered him a calling card to further, even more privileged access than he has already enjoyed. He has not come calling at the highest levels of the Stanton campaign; he has been recruited. Klein's (and subsequently May's) narrative goes to great pains to demonstrate just how passive Henry is in the transition from Larkin Congressional staffer to Stanton Presidential aide. For all intents and purposes, Henry is kidnapped from his previous life—the political science classes he teaches, his girlfriend who writes for the *Black Advocate*, and the Congressman himself have all been abandoned without so much as a change of clothes. Much of this is done essentially against Henry's will—certainly without a "definite plan." He stops home briefly after the literacy event that opens the film, but only to tell his reporter-girlfriend March (Rebecca Walker) that Stanton wants to talk to him about a job; he's swept from that non-meeting with Stanton onto a plane to New Hampshire where Stanton falls asleep on his shoulder and thence, with no decision-point on Henry's part, into the rhythms of life as a staffer, attending meetings, opening campaign offices, training workers. Indeed, the first real choice Henry has to make is one where he chooses to remain passive, when he learns of the McCullisons' paternity claim on Stanton.

In a large cast dominated by white people (whatever Richard's claims), the few scenes where Henry is proximate to other African-Americans take on a greater resonance. In the opening sequence at the literacy program in Harlem, the black and brown faces around the table provide a halting but moving testimony to disenfranchisement. The cutaways from their unfortunate tales of institutionalized illiteracy to Henry's eyes, shining with tears he struggles to blink back, reveal Henry's willingness to recognize, with a mixture of empathy and benign condescension, *There but for the grace of a charismatic grandfather go I.* Yet when he's taken away from the Northeast and dropped into the close, steamy environment of Jack Stanton's South, Henry is indeed less "black" in terms of inherited roots in socio-economic minority powerlessness than Stanton or Richard. The first chicken-shack summit, when Henry meets Fat Willie (Tommy Hollis), quickly devolves into what Susan archly calls a "Mamathon," as Willie, Jack, and Richard each attempt to outdo the others in tales of the sanctity, forbearance, and suffering of his mother. Nichols and Director of Photography Michael Ballhaus shoot the scene from two angles to accentuate Henry's alienation: the first is Henry's point of view, seated at one of Willie's backyard picnic tables, angled up at the three men at the table's other end. As the "Mama" talk becomes more heated and then spills over into a spirited chorus of "You Are My Sunshine," the men stand, arms linked; we see Henry from their high-angle point of view, down on his glum, solitary, non-singing figure. He's the minority, but it has nothing to do with the color of his skin: Henry is a Northerner whose mother farmed him out to be boarded and bred for success while she was bagging a Braddock-worthy lifestyle (à la *The Graduate*) in Beverly Hills.

When Henry has his first opportunity to choose, it's because Fat Willie has sought *him* out—more of his being acted upon rather than his acting. Willie's story of his daughter Loretta's pregnancy disappoints Henry; it's impossible not to be conscious of the echoes of the plantation in a powerful, middle-aged Southern white man potentially having his way with a nubile 15-year-old black girl of small social means. He's already had to negotiate his disillusionment about Stanton's unrestrained appetites, which are readily, boldly on display the day and evening of their first introduction to each other, when Stanton seduces the clumsy schoolteacher with the long legs, Marian Walsh (Allison Janney). By the time the Cashmere McCloud (Gia Carides) scandal hits, Henry is no longer satisfied with having the trumped-up charges discredited, because the hairdresser's story rings true. He, Richard, and Daisy go to see Susan precisely because they are convinced Stanton is not innocent, whether they have managed publicly to dodge the Cashmere McCloud bullet or not. Henry has looked the other way at Stanton's draft record and shady backroom deal with the mayor of Chicago in 1968 to have an arrest expunged; he has managed to stomach the serial philandering and what impact it may be having on Susan; he has ignored Stanton's crowd-pleasing willingness to distort the facts (as in the whoppers he tells about his "Uncle Charlie," who may or may not even be a blood relation but whose gameness to have his past shaped and reshaped to meet Stanton's immediate demographic needs makes him more useful to the campaign than if he were merely kin). If Henry the "True Believer" has been seeking a paragon, he has yet to find him when he works for Stanton. Yet Henry believes nonetheless that Stanton, despite the petty deceit and endless womanizing, is at heart *real*.

There's a scene that comes in the midst of the Cashmere McCloud crisis, when Susan, sick of the hand-wringing of the staff as they contemplate Stanton's incorrigible character, venomously denies the allegation of her former hairdresser and encourages anybody who doesn't believe her to get out. She cooks up the *60 Minutes* appearance on the spot (and subsequently sells her faith in her husband convincingly, though when the red light blinks off she snatches back the hand she'd graciously extended to Jack on-camera; Henry, taking in the couple's performance on television with a cross-section of the American public at a bar, is struck by the on-lookers "rating" the Stantons "like so many Siskel and Eberts"[12] on superficial qualities of appearance). While Susan is haranguing the team's shaky resolve and strategizing about the television mea culpa, Henry turns away to the hotel room window, which overlooks the parking lot and, as it happens, a compact Krispy Kreme donut shop at the lot's far end. The "kindness" that Nichols found embedded in this scene "let me know I could make the movie."[13] The donut shop glows an unhealthy, toxic shade of green in the distance, as if radioactive with bad cholesterol and empty calories, and the camera begins a slow zoom to a full shot of the building as Henry enters it, where we see a solitary customer, Stanton, perched on a counter stool. Stanton, as usual, is at his most comfortable when keeping company with the salt of the earth, in this instance a permanently disabled young counter attendant named Danny Scanlon (Scott Burkholder), whose single-minded devotion to duty ("Apple fritter?") so annoys Henry that he winds up snapping at Danny. In the simple act of accepting, at that moment, an apple fritter he neither wants nor needs from Danny, Stanton is ennobled in Henry's eyes. This is habitual decency, not vote-grabbing per the odd, involuntary pandering that Senator Keeley (Gene Hackman) attempts in *The Birdcage* as he tries to rush his family from the Goldmans' house. Keeley is not a natural politician; Stanton's small gesture of kindness to an utterly inconsequential man like Danny Scanlon reminds us that, for all Stanton's shortcomings, "politician" and "polite" are not mutually exclusive. Inspired by this kindness he has just witnessed, Henry encourages Stanton to remember that the Governor's suffering at the hands of the scandalmongers is "nothing compared to what average folks are going through, losing their jobs, losing their homes. Keep that in your mind. Keep 'the folks' in your mind." Ironically, Henry would know little or nothing about "the folks" if not for his work with Stanton, and he has only been prompted to "remind" Stanton of the true object of his calling as a politician because he has himself been reminded by Stanton's instinctive empathy with one of the plainest and least distinguished of "the folks." Stanton's next speech is one of Travolta's most moving in the entire film. "For me it's always been about them, like this Danny Scanlon, worked every day since he was 14, couldn't get insurance, couldn't get his leg fixed right. Doesn't complain, doesn't do anyone any harm. Achin' to do good. God—if you let a man like that go down, you don't deserve to take up space on this planet, do you?" Henry assures him, "We won't let him go down." If Henry truly feels this, and he may in fact still only understand it as an abstract "good," he does so (or will do so) because he has learned it from Stanton. Nichols closes the scene with Ballhaus' gorgeous final exterior shot of the shop, this time from a new angle that transforms the framing into a variation on Edward Hopper's 1942 *Nighthawks*. The image thus projects the ambiguity of Henry's hopeful claim against the spiritually impoverished alienation of Hopper's world, where people huddle silently together against the storms of life. Henry sits by Stanton in a humbled act of mimicry, in the sort of place he'd never before have been caught dead, because Stanton is transforming Henry's abstract notions of service into a servant's humble instincts.

If Henry has been passively conveyed into working on the staff of Jack Stanton, it may at least be possible to say in Henry's defense that he is willing to submit because he senses in Stanton the spark of a man who understands power as a means, not an end in itself. During his first long conversation with Susan after he has been spirited away from his old life by the Stanton campaign, Henry probably comes as close as he ever does to an actual interview for the position into which he has passively stumbled. Her question, "So why are you here?" implies that he has made active choices that have brought him to this place; his answer reveals his willingness to suspend disbelief in order to believe: "I was always curious to work with someone who actually cared ... I mean, it couldn't always have been the way it is now." (His reference is to their earlier discussion of the commodification of politics, of power and victory as ends in themselves.) "It must have been very different when my grandfather was alive," he continues. Citing John F. Kennedy's rhetoric of "destiny" and "sacrifice," he confesses that the words have been emptied of the values they may once have conveyed, in the time of his father and his father's father. "And okay, maybe it was bullshit with Kennedy, too, but people *believed* it, and I guess that's what I want. I want to believe it." He yields to the Stanton campaign's forceful overtures because he is a True Believer.

The cautionary tale of *Primary Colors* is that even good intentions may be co-opted, distorted, made over into illusion. Henry's solemnizations of his political philosophy are as plain as black and white to Richard—but they are just as evident to the Stanton campaign, which has, whatever Henry's obvious skills and smarts, promoted him as a rookie to the political big leagues because, as Henry's girlfriend March has warned him from the outset, "Stanton wants to use the grandson of a Civil Rights leader, a black man in politics, as a vote-getter." Stanton may eventually come to love Henry, to think of him as family, but what he loves in recruiting Henry is the *idea* of Henry. Stanton is a "pro," as Richard Jemmons would use the term. He will surrender himself to the expediency of the moment, and he expects nothing less from his staff. And so Henry, over time, learns what it means to be a "pro," and comes to hate it. When Fat Willie seeks out *Henry*, not long-time friends Jack, Susan, Howard, Richard, or any of the other white faces in the cloud of operatives around the campaign, Henry's default as a Stanton "pro" is to fix problems, as the other staffers routinely do. Yet Henry knows this one is different the same way Fat Willie does, and Henry confronts Stanton in a public bathroom where Nichols and Ballhaus use mirrors to multiply and diminish Stanton's image while Henry extracts a compromised avowal of innocence. Stanton works on Henry with both hands, his left hand administering what Howard has termed its magic on Henry's shoulder. "You never have to be ashamed to be a part of this campaign," Stanton assures him. Howard, who has been guarding the bathroom door against security leaks, breaks up the tête-à-tête, as if he and Stanton have devised a telepathy that rescues Stanton from uncomfortable clinches. That first afternoon at the adult literacy event, Henry thought they should "rescue" Stanton from the people: "Let's get him out of here." But Daisy assures Henry that Stanton "likes" the communion with the people. The difference is that, in that earlier communion, the terms were all Stanton's, predicated upon a moving but cynical distortion of Uncle Charlie's misfortune; in the confrontation with Henry, Stanton can only count on Henry's dogged willingness to believe.

Henry goes with Howard Ferguson to coerce, however gently, Fat Willie's consent to have his daughter submit to the amniocentesis that will clear Jack Stanton. Willie innocently asks what such a test involves, and as Howard explains the procedure—a long needle that probes Loretta's womb—the shot/reverse shot involves the two black men who aren't speaking. Henry puts on a brave, accommodating face, as if this is the sort of business an energetic young political operative conducts every day of the week along the Presidential campaign trail. All the other adjustments and compromises Stanton's character has required of Henry were easy enough to rationalize. But Fat Willie has reached out to Henry as a fellow black man for justice, and Henry has merely served as Howard's silent sidekick, smiling his encouragement to secure Willie's consent for this latest penetrative violation of his daughter. Henry's complicity literally sickens him. It is Henry's worst moment representing Stanton, despite the variety of other awkward compromises the campaign requires of a "pro." It is also one of Stanton's worst moments, as bad as the moment with Danny Scanlon at the Krispy Kreme was good, made all the worse by Stanton's craven absence from the scene. Never has Henry's color been more an issue, and for less noble cause. Henry has become Stanton's token proxy, with the result that the McCullisons *and* Henry are equally exploited. If this were one of Libby's "tests," everyone would fail.

While the main motif of *Primary Colors* is the classroom and its "tests," the secondary motif is the bedroom. In *Primary Colors*, the realities of campaign life blur the boundaries of what is public and what is personal or private. With perfunctory frankness, the narrative lets drop casually the sexual pairings of, for instance, Henry and Daisy, and Libby and Jennifer (Stacy Edwards). They wander in and out of each other's bedrooms because they live in hotels, where bedrooms are the common areas. It's an effective evocation of the objectification of political life, the opening up to media and popular scrutiny what otherwise would not properly be consumable, and the scrambling to project favorable images that often bear little resemblance to the truth. At one point, just as the Cashmere McCloud story is about to break, the unlucky task falls to Henry to break the news of the impending public scandal to the Stantons. As he interrupts them in their early morning domesticity of preparing their public faces, they are sharing a phone call with their son Jack, Jr., who has made the swim team at school. There is a natural intimacy about the moment that makes Henry doubly hesitant to break in with his news. When he delivers it, as he is coaxed to do by them both, he bears witness to Susan's crisp, compartmentalized rage as she slaps her husband's face. It isn't the first spat he's witnessed (that was within his first hours with them, on the tarmac in the middle of the night in New Hampshire), but it is, nonetheless, the first to take place in the domesticated sovereignty of their bedroom. The deal with Fat Willie has been guarded with great care: only Stanton, Howard, and Henry know about it. When Willie's wife appears on the Stantons' doorstep, she seeks her own source of minority solidarity with Susan, accepting no substitutes (as Willie had earlier reached past all others to Henry). Richard can read in Henry's face that her presence poses some unspoken threat, but can't get Henry to divulge his conspiratorial complicity. The campaign has kept secrets before; they've worked on Stanton's behalf to keep secrets from Susan—but now the conspiracy of misinformation has infected the campaign itself. They're lying to one another. Susan waits to speak to Henry about what she's learned from Willie's wife until he's alone in *his* room, Daisy elsewhere, and then she slaps *him* just as she had her husband, and the symbiosis is complete. Henry as Stanton's proxy has sinned against the McCullisons and Susan, but he receives their respective rebukes not only as Stanton's proxy failure but as a failure in his own right. In Libby's parlance, Henry has failed a test, and Willie and Susan have delivered their judgment on his performance.

It's no coincidence that, as Henry enters this new trough in his confidence, Stanton is worthy of his faith; this is the mixed bag of Jack Stanton. Senator Harris (Kevin Cooney) succumbs to his two heart attacks, and Stanton pulls the campaign's attack ads. But a new man enters the race who seems even nobler in his politically principled commitment to raising the standard of discourse: Harris' wife (Bonnie Bartlett) anoints Fred Picker (Hagman) to stand in for her husband in the campaign, and his introductory set of canny political moves provoke the grudging admiration of Stanton's inner circle because they are strategic without being Machiavellian. Richard, for instance, is in awe of Picker's aplomb on *Charlie Rose* as he addresses his withdrawal from public life twenty years ago. Picker's entrance into the race has an almost alchemical impact upon the Stanton campaign. The Stantons bring in Norman Ash (Robert Klein) to advise them on weathering the Loretta McCullison pregnancy scandal; Richard hurls rare superlatives one after another at Picker, their opponent, and then bows out of the Stanton team, taking Daisy with him. And Henry, briefly but decisively, transfers his True Believerism from Stanton to Picker. The defining moment in Henry's infatuation with Picker comes in listening to Picker at a rally in Connecticut (while the Stantons are being shouted down by an angry feminist mob in New York City). "The world is getting more and more complicated," Picker tells the rally audience, "and politicians have to explain things to you in simpler terms, so that they can get their little, oversimplified explanations on the evening news." As Nichols and editor Arthur Schmidt cut to Henry watching from the crowd, Picker warns that mudslinging comes from a breakdown in the resolve to "explain things," likening what results to professional wrestling: "It's staged, it's fake, and it doesn't mean anything."

For much of the primary season, Jack Stanton has agreed. When his staffers have counseled attack, he has countered with staying on message, resisting the cultural default to "go negative." As we learn at the film's climax, Stanton's history with Libby dates back to the indelible impression he made on her when he challenged Susan, Libby, and himself, as young idealists starting out in politics, not to conform to the usual mudslinging practices of political objectification. As Henry vacillates between Stanton and Picker as icons, we learn that Libby has been there and done that long before him: a long-time friend of the Stantons, she was also one of the original "Picker People." Only later, in retrospect, do we recognize her fierce and unreasonable allegiances to imperfect leaders are what have driven her mad. Despite the take-no-prisoners aggression of her political moves, Libby is at the furthest remove from what Richard would call a "pro." He has defined this genus of political operative by strolling into the room Daisy and Henry have taken to cohabiting and flopping down on the bed beside them to talk about future options. Daisy and Richard, knowing the days of this campaign have grown short no matter how it ends, are doing what pros do, looking ahead to what comes next, committed only to serial commitment. "Stop with the 'when-this-is-over-we-are-pros' crap," Henry tells them. "Maybe *you're* pros, but I've gotten emotionally involved." Richard chides him, "A pro knows how to say goodbye." Richard and Daisy provide a way for Henry to be in the world, at one emotional remove from full commitment, and it's a model Henry rejects. Like Libby, he has decided to lead with his heart, the apparent modus of Jack Stanton himself. Fred Picker suddenly seems the better option to Henry not because he cares more deeply or has more substance than Stanton, but because he has almost no substance at all, and Jack Stanton has become far too real to be Henry's version of *Shane*. For Henry, Picker is a sub-conscious return to the abstractions with which Henry started, his reticence to be a politician as he enters the race for America's highest political office a cleansing agent to Henry, whose hands have been so dirtied by his work on the Stanton campaign.

When Picker appears with Stanton on *Geraldo* and *protects* his opponent from the worst of the salacious gossip Rivera is poised to smear in Stanton's face before the cameras, Henry interprets the act as heroic instead of reading within it some hidden agenda. Richard allows that it's a first, but he has already begun exploring various reasons for the extraordinarily apolitical gesture of a politician in sight of the White House taking his foot *off* of his opponent's throat. Henry, starry-eyed, says, "Maybe this *is* the first time. Maybe Picker's an original, the real thing." Richard resurrects his old insult for Henry, calling him "Hotchkiss," his way of demeaning Henry's ivory-tower perspective on the way most people live their lives. He diagnoses Henry's "galloping T. B." or "True Believerism" as a weakness: "You talk like a pro, you act like a pro, but inside you're just like Libby, who actually goes crazy when her candidate turns out not to be the rock her church was built on." Richard enigmatically predicts there is more to Picker's behavior than meets the eye, and then Richard walks away, just as the campaign enters its final crisis, and having acknowledged his pro's suspicion of Picker's magnanimity *and* Libby's earnestness. Richard and Daisy leave behind them what people like Libby and Henry drive towards: the truth beneath the carefully maintained façade of Picker's rectitude.

Picker and the Stantons, Richard and Daisy and Norman: these are all people who understand reification's "game," as Libby refers to it, and as Henry and Stanton call it in their final dialogue at Picker's plantation when Henry submits his resignation. They know that politics as it is practiced in the real world is typically pure commodification, and the product is being marketed to consumers who want as little substance as possible. This is the discouraging reality Henry observes as he watches the Stantons' *60 Minutes* spinfest with a cross-section of the American public in the diner. The audience is only interested in weight, hairstyle, and who did what with whom. It's the wan version of reality that Picker himself decries in his address at the rally in Connecticut, when he talks about substance reduced to pro wrestling, because "it seems it's the only way we know how to keep you all riled up." When Norman Ash carries forward Richard's parting insight, that politicians always have an ulterior motive for what they do, particularly when they act against the political grain as Picker has done, the Stantons are now close enough to their ultimate goal (for which they've endured all the ritual humiliations of the system's process) to set aside their reified insight about conformist objectification. They are in whatever-it-takes mode. Stanton's new charge to Libby, his in-house pit bull, is to bring down Picker.

The final confrontation of the old friends comes in the kitchen of a rented house, a facsimile of domestic intimacy. Libby has found what Richard knew would be there, and even Picker's dirt is ambiguous: he did not influence-peddle as Governor of Florida, but he devolved into undignified gubernatorial behavior plenty big enough to destroy him (and, as collateral damage, his family). Sitting with an AIDS-afflicted black man in a halfway house in Miami, Libby and Henry learn the sordid truth about Picker in the sex-and-drugs 1970s.

Delgado looks Henry over and asks if Henry is Picker's new flavor. What they've learned from Delgado and from Picker's brother-in-law Eddie Reyes fills a fat dossier that Libby slaps down on the rented kitchen counter in front of the Stantons, a meal for them to consume or to be consumed by. "Now what do we do with this?" Stanton asks in faux-innocence. It's up to Susan to mutter about leaks to the *New York Times* and *Wall Street Journal*. The contents of the dossier, if permitted to leave this kitchen, ensure the nomination.

"We don't do this sort of thing," Libby protests, but Stanton again wedges the door open so Susan can kick it wide. Of Stanton's roseate charge to them two decades ago "to make it clean, because if it's clean, we win, because our ideas are better," Susan now says, "We didn't know how the world worked." "'To me,' Nichols says, 'the killer moment is when Emma says in the kitchen, *We didn't know how the world worked. Now we know.* Because I think it's true for all of us. I think most people feel that way: *I'm sorry to have learned what it's really like.*'"[14] Susan's statement reflects a reified defeatism, and it effectively kills Libby. Libby's final gambit is to blackmail her old friends: she hadn't only been digging Picker's dirt. Presenting her evidence that Stanton had Uncle Charlie submit his own blood in place of Jack's, Libby angles to end Stanton's political career quietly rather than see it detonated by Stanton's raging libido and the couple's lust for power. Susan, incensed, confronts Libby: "You would do that. You would end his political career." Libby unmasks the full corruption of the Stantons' proximity to power: Stanton has become a grotesque of fellow feeling, able to empathize with the common man but not with the extraordinary pain to which he's subjected his wife. As Libby sums it, "That's why you can still talk in that tenderhearted voice about being in it for 'the folks.' Susie here can only talk in that voice from hell about your political career." Libby exits, and as Susan instinctively turns to Henry to pitch strategy for leaking the contents of the Picker file, Henry wordlessly follows Libby, leaving the Stantons in the ashes of their triumph. In Stanton's union speech in New Hampshire, Nichols and Ballhaus have created a faint homage to the monomaniacal rally of Charles Foster Kane on the eve of his certain election to the governor's mansion, an election ultimately skewered by Kane's foibles and pride. The rhetorical question of both *Citizen Kane* and *Primary Colors* is as old as the gospel of Matthew: *What shall it profit a man if he shall gain the whole world but lose his soul?*

No one has lost more than Libby, however, and we begin now, with Henry, to see the wisdom in moderating the excesses of Libby's devotion with the temperance of Richard and Daisy's professionalism. As outré a personality as Richard often has been, he has also offered Henry the sanity of skeptical perspective; Libby has offered only the madness of devout belief. Richard is no more a final word on how to be in the reified world than Libby, but each affords Henry a fragment of a more hopeful and productive synthesis, acknowledging reified anxiety but leveraging it for redemptive possibility. Libby's exit is, of course, of the most dire and final sort, though it is only a typically more dramatic version of Richard's own response. Both Richard and Libby check out, not to be seen or heard from again in the narrative, though in each case, their influence lingers on in the minds of their colleagues long after they have gone. Each is, ultimately, a statement of recusal from ongoing confrontation and struggle with reified conformity. In fact, Libby's suicide may be understood in this light as a failure of resolve; she destroys herself rather than "destroy this village," and by putting the Picker and Stanton dossiers in Henry's hands, passes the responsibility for "saving" the village on to him. When Libby learns the dirt on Picker, she concludes, "He should never have gotten back into the game." Her threats to the Stantons suggest she's drawn similar conclusions about them. And she ends all her own game-playing forever.

Thus the bildungsroman narrative, for all its interest in the reconsidered lives of the established older generation, comes down to Henry's choices about himself and the world. He goes with Stanton to the door of Picker's plantation; he watches his once and future icon hand over a political death sentence to another would-be icon. Stanton's hand reaches out to Picker as he breaks down, and what Henry sees are not icons but simply gifted, foolish, flawed men, prodigal with their opportunities and chastened by their uncontrolled urges ("I could handle anything but cocaine," Picker says, and the mysterious and confounding force of his appetites could be a paraphrase of Stanton's own dilemma). It is impossible to see them as powerful in such a moment, unless we are willing to redefine *power*. After they leave Picker, Henry resigns, but Stanton resists, offering wheedling incentives to bring back Richard and Daisy. Henry only responds that Stanton has "flunked" Libby's test, but Stanton counters, flaunting his awareness of his ambiguity of character, "Yeah, but just now I passed it, so which grade do I get, Henry?"

As we have seen in the ambiguous endings to film after film in Nichols' canon, he is loath to be the one to pass out final "grades" on his characters. His resolutions are so frequently ambiguous because, as his director-surrogate Lowell Kolchek (Gene Hackman) put it in *Postcards from the Edge*, true character development does not adhere to the aesthetic model. We can't simply loop our own mistakes or wait for the third act to resolve our problems. "Growing up is not like in the movies," Lowell says, "where you have a realization and your life changes." In the final moments of *Primary Colors*, Henry wrestles with a suddenly frank and unvarnished Jack Stanton, in full command of his reified faculties once again after allowing his appetites to destroy his wisdom and a true friend. "This is it, Henry," Stanton says. "This is the price you pay to lead." He cites Lincoln's inevitable compromises in order "to stand in front of the nation and appeal to the better angels of our nature." Implicit in the Lincolnian phrase "better angels" is an essential assumption of the duality of the human soul. In using the phrase, Stanton alludes to his own struggles, despite the titanic force of his originality and spirit, with his own appetites and with conformity to the corruptive seduction of power.

"You know as well as I do there are plenty of people playing this game that don't think the way I do," says Stanton. "They're willin' to sell their souls, crawl through sewers, lie to people, divide them, play on their worst fears—for nothin'. Just for the prize." All of what Stanton accuses these unnamed others is also true of himself, save for the rationale. Henry concludes, "I don't care. I'm sorry, but I'm not comparing the players. I don't like the game." The "game," as it turns out, has a life of its own: sold out by their driver (as the Keeleys were in *The Birdcage*), Stanton and Henry find the media have pitched camp at the foot of Picker's driveway, and Henry must a final time confront the blunt force of Stanton's persuasive charm. "I'm gonna win this thing," he says, "and when I do, we're gonna make history. Look me in the eye and tell me it's not gonna happen. Look me in the eye, Henry, and tell me you don't want to be a part of it." Henry's silent, steely gaze offers only negation. For all Stanton's effort, he never coaxes another word from his aide in this scene. Stanton throws off the rhetorical references to "this country" and "history"; his final plea is purely relational: "You're still with me, aren't you? Say you are. Say it. Say it! Come on, Henry! This is ridiculous. You've got to be with me."

Nichols and Schmidt interchange a series of close-up two-shots from reversed angles to heighten Stanton's expectation and Henry's withheld favor, under the last several of which begin to play the rising strains of the "Tennessee Waltz." Between the two men, linking their faces, comes a straight overhead shot of the Presidential seal, appearing via lap dissolve and

**Late in *Primary Colors*, the motif of education running through the entire film reaches the eval-
uation phase: a "test" that pits principle against ambition. Jack Stanton (John Travolta, right)
fails his test when he decides the dirt his staff has dug up about his opponent's past can win him
the campaign. Confronted by Henry Burton (Adrian Lester), Stanton "re-takes" the test by going
to his opponent's house (background) to hand over the information quietly rather than to the
press. The film ends in the dream-like ambiguity of Stanton's victory and soulful touch: have the
objectifying realities of politics rendered principle merely a fantasy?**

gradually revealing the seal's context: it is the locus of an Inaugural dance graced by the new-
minted President and First Lady. The lack of words, the dreaminess of the dissolve and overlapped music, the essential unreality of this long-sought moment imply a layer of wish fulfillment in this, the film's coda. After all the mudslinging and anger and doubt, the happy
ending. We are perhaps right to be suspicious of its dream-like presentation. Stanton makes
the rounds of the Inaugural's attendees, and we recognize peripheral faces who have made
their contributions to the campaign. Daisy is there, too, an indication that her professional
resolve may have melted in proximity to Henry's True Believerism, and beside her, target of
Stanton's final, two-fisted handshake, is Henry Burton, eyes shining.

The film's relentless desire for resolution in these final images—a Stanton White House;
peace with Henry; a reunion for Henry and Daisy—is ladled on with such speed and in such
volume we can't help but feel ourselves to be manipulated. Is this an ending, or is this a daydream, still on the promenade to Picker's plantation, of what a happy ending looks like to a
True Believer? The caution with which Libby parted forever from Henry, the do-as-I-say-
and-not-as-I-do wisdom of her life of True Believerism, is for Henry to "be careful"; unlike
Libby, a moon reflective of those she orbits and "airless for eternity" without them, Henry
"still ha[s] something of an atmosphere." She urges him to find himself "a life" not predicated

solely on idolatry. The ambiguity of the ending of *Primary Colors* is that its final image *could* convey the impression that Henry has, like Libby, been unable to extricate himself from a lunar-like orbit around the Stantons. Yet the lingering, discomfiting silence with which Henry meets all Stanton's blandishments and cajoling as readily suggests that, at bildungsroman's end, Henry's eyes are opened wide, and if they still appear to shine with the empathy and faith we saw in them during Stanton's performance at the adult literacy event in Harlem, we know how much they have subsequently seen and learned. The force of the will of extraordinary men like Jack Stanton will always be brought to bear upon gifted but comparatively ordinary men like Henry Burton, those necessary to make belief without make-believe. In *Primary Colors*, Nichols and May argue that only the full weight of reified wisdom can provide the potential for perspective such a man would need in order to maintain his own "atmosphere" and not merely capitulate as an extension of another's will or ideology, a danger to which even forces of nature like Libby Holden—and Jack Stanton himself—are not immune.

17

"Like a human being"

What Planet Are You From? (2000)

The title of Mike Nichols' sixteenth feature film, *What Planet Are You From?*, refers to the profound, gendered difference in perspective and thus in communication between men and women, a phenomenon articulated to vast popular influence by John Gray in his 1992 bestseller *Men Are from Mars, Women Are from Venus*. Yet the title could as well have reflected a legitimate question on the part of Hollywood financiers, wondering how Nichols could be serious about moving from the earnestness of *Primary Colors* to the unapologetic silliness of an alien sex comedy. Composed by committee, with four writers sharing credit (including the star/producer, Garry Shandling), *What Planet* seems on its surface more like an early Woody Allen comedy or a Mel Brooks or Carl Reiner film than like a Mike Nichols film. The silliness is not atypical of Nichols; it is present in films as different and made as far apart as *Catch-22* (1970), *The Fortune* (1975), and *The Birdcage* (1996). Yet *What Planet* ultimately yields less substance than any of these earlier films, despite the fact that "the movie wants its satire to be taken seriously."[1] Though boasting Nichols' usual command of Hollywood star power (with Annette Bening from *Regarding Henry* in another major role, alongside prominent Hollywood personalities like Shandling, Ben Kingsley, John Goodman, Linda Fiorentino, and Greg Kinnear), the film has less for them to do than a Nichols film usually does. It's the least substantial film of Nichols' career.

What Planet continues many of Nichols' functional preoccupations: the socially proscribed default toward restless accumulation as a means of compensation for the ache of spiritual emptiness; the objectification particularly of gender and the attendant disintegration of connection and communication that proceeds naturally from a failure fully to recognize personhood. The film ultimately has more in common with Woody Allen's existential laughter than with Brooks' or Reiner's two-dimensional parodic silliness, which parodies genre in the single-minded service of the joke. Even in Nichols' giddiest films (as in Woody Allen's), genre serves metaphor as much as punchline. The high-concept premise of *What Planet* is a comic riff on the gender wars while delighting in sound gags about humming sex organs.

At the center of the film are two characters on accidentally intersecting "missions" (a word ironically used not by the alien sent to impregnate an Earth woman and bring the planet to its knees but by the Earth woman herself, bent on finding some clearer sense of purpose for her life). As he is charged with administering his planet's will, H1449–6 (or Harold Anderson, as Shandling's character comes to be called) is selected for the promise of his "adaptability" and "great capacity for learning." He thus takes his place in a long line of Nichols characters to emerge during his second phase of production as a Hollywood filmmaker, beginning with the protean evolution of Karen Silkwood. Nichols' self-reported project as a filmmaker is to create narratives of "transformation,"[2] and Harold Anderson takes the universality of this thematic preoccupation to a whole new galaxy. Harold's partner in transformation is Susan Hart (Bening), a recovering alcoholic and sex addict so committed to conversion that she's hedged her bets by prominently installing in her bedroom an array of religious votives, icons, and fetishes from an ecumenical spectrum of traditions. When Harold and Susan meet, each is hampered by reified misassumptions. The narrative's arc is for each of them to unlearn as much as they have to learn.

In their very first conversation, Susan poses the title question, a rhetorical exasperation with the problem of interpersonal communication, particularly between the sexes, that also gives Shandling the opportunity to mug shamelessly for the camera. Susan makes sweepingly dismissive generalizations about men, based in her experience of the bottom-feeding predators (like Perry Gordon, Kinnear's character) she has met during her years looking at her life from the bottom of a bottle. As for Harold, his conditioning in the gendered transactions of Earthlings constitutes the film's initial comic set piece: a hologram image of 1950s female servitude (a woman with permed hair at an ironing board) receiving compliments in exchange for sexual favors. Men and women are, indeed, worlds apart in *What Planet*. Michael Ballhaus' camera captures Rita (Harmony Smith), the curvaceous "office manager" at the bank where both Perry and Harold work, from a variety of objectifying angles. Perry's wife Helen (Fiorentino) receives similar cinematographic treatment, and Nichols uses Fiorentino's notorious femme fatale image from earlier films like *The Last Seduction* (John Dahl, 1994) and *Jade* (William Friedkin, 1995) as a further means of establishing how she is typed by the men around her.

For all the sci-fi trappings, *What Planet* is actually much more interested in engaging with the rules of romantic comedy than the overt scaffolding of science fiction storytelling, with which Nichols is even less at ease than with the supernatural horror of *Wolf* (1994). In romantic comedy, the introduced stereotypes and resulting miscommunication create the complications that initially drive the plot, and the sort of personal epiphanies that Nichols is always looking for in his characters provide the resolution to the plot's gendered problems. *What Planet* may be far more slight than the films that precede and follow it in his oeuvre, but it is, at its core, a Mike Nichols film.

* * *

With *What Planet*, Nichols argues that the impulses that plague us—the desire to objectify and consume, to dominate and control—are socialized as well as inherited, and should not be assumed to be uniquely earthbound. If there are other races out among the stars, they are likely to have similar impulses to ours. This is the default plot assumption of H. G. Wells' seminal *The War of the Worlds* (1898), which informed much of the alien-invasion science fiction released during the classic B-movie era of the 1950s, during the Cold War beginnings of space exploration and paranoia about decidedly terrestrial forms of invasion. The civilization to which H1449–6, aka Harold Anderson, belongs is "a thousand years" more advanced than Earth in its technologies, yet Harold ultimately concludes that as a race, they have been complicit in a final, utter self-objectification. Rather than support their assertion of their superiority and thus of their right to domination of Earth per Graydon's vision, Harold argues near the film's climax "we can learn from them and they can remind us of who we were before."

The dystopia Graydon (Kingsley) has created on his planet is dystopic not because it fails to function or even because its inhabitants are unhappy per se (they are neither happy nor unhappy, not having access to emotion) but rather because its essential impulse must always be dissatisfaction: a bottomless desire for "more." In its own way, Graydon's cosmic manifest destiny is no different than the conspicuous consumption of the Braddocks and the Robinsons in *The Graduate* or the Turners and their circle in *Regarding Henry*, to take only two examples from two distinct eras of Nichols' oeuvre. The phallocratic impulse to possessive insertion of one's will knows no boundaries of time or space. "Is that what it's about—more, more, more?" demands Harold of Graydon during their confrontation just after Harold has questioned aloud their planet's domineering mission during a training exercise on the seduction of Earth women. Harold has no stomach for mere conquest any longer; Graydon thinks Harold needs to have his memory wiped. The conceit of brainwashing as metaphor of socialized reification is no less powerful for being a familiar narrative strategy of science fiction's critique of culture. Graydon's impulse to consume alien civilizations begins at home; for the alienated, the alien is everywhere, including his own people. This is why the planet engages in groupthink: to subdue threats to hegemony. Nichols and company get comic mileage out of the bland black uniforms of Graydon's vanishing perspective of minions and their unison responses ("uh-huh") to the female avatar during the training exercises. There can be no deviation from the norm; all must reflect the will of power. To be distinct is to be alien. In this sense, Harold's more or less successful (this being romantic comedy at its most generically fantastical) assimilation into Earth's culture of self-actualization constitutes an act of treachery, because it establishes an alternative to the Graydon way.

There are ideological assumptions made by *What Planet* that place free-market democratic society at the vanguard of self-actualization. When Harold is sent to Earth by Graydon, his assigned alias is given a comfortably bourgeois vocation in the financial world in one of the boom economies of the American economic system: Phoenix, Arizona. Susan, too, has assumed her place in the economy, as a fledgling realtor. For the film's initial theatrical audience, the sight of Annette Bening showing houses would have conjured the profound spiritual dysfunction of her breakout, Oscar-nominated performance as Carolyn Burnham the previous year in *American Beauty* (Sam Mendes), a film Nichols was originally approached to direct.[3] Indeed, it's almost impossible to imagine Mendes' Oscar-winning film without acknowledging what it owes to Nichols and *The Graduate* (as part of Nichols' ongoing body of work in dialogue with the quiet—and sometimes noisy—desperation of reified society). For Harold and Susan, however, the life of material affluence on which they embark with their new son is not in question. What Nichols' film questions is the gendered, habitualized proscription of how they think about and behave with one another.

Socioeconomics has never mattered less in a Nichols film. In the title's riff on gendered politics, the narrative asks most of its questions and draws most of its conclusions about reified behavior based in sexual identity and relationships. While Harold gains access to his adaptive emotional range as a dual-planetary citizen by competing with Perry for the boss' favor and the pay raise to assistant vice president, the film focuses its critique on the ways in which Perry and Harold initially bond but eventually diverge in their understanding of relationship to the opposite sex. When they first meet at the bank, it is ten in the morning, but Harold is ready to procreate. The niceties of the mating ritual have eluded Harold; any time is the right time. His insistent craving for sex even impresses an inveterate horndog like Perry, who can't quite tell whether Harold is serious or not (as it turns out, Harold is *always* serious, which is the source of Shandling's desert-dry delivery as a comedian). Perry is a monster to warm Graydon's cold gray heart; he is, in all the important respects but one, an ideal model for Harold to have attached himself to in pursuing the successful achievement of Graydon's assignment. That single exception is the end product of conquest; Perry is not looking for commitment; like Graydon he's looking for fresh, vulnerable territory to conquer. Yet Graydon *does* seek the perpetuation of identity via reproduction, where Perry would, of necessity, run from such permanence. He assumes false identities rather than making his identity perpetual. In his professional attachments, the common currency of Perry's world is power. His daily assignations with Rita take place in the vault, a literal reassertion of her objecthood (she's "money") and a symbolic statement of his dominion over even his boss' property. When Harold initially meets with Perry, then Fisk, Perry asserts that Rita is "taken," while Fisk asserts that she is "mine." For each man, Rita has no distinctive trait other than her memorable curves. She is not prized for her ability (an active trait) but rather for her *desirability* (a passive trait). In the film's treatment of her, she is a montage of inviting smiles and swinging hips. Possessing her is a statement of mastery.

Helen, Perry's wife, receives similar treatment but many more lines to establish an inner complicity with her objectification. She and Perry are well matched; she objectifies him as much as he objectifies women. For Helen, the allure of Perry (which otherwise would probably have escaped us) is in his daily, all-day proximity to money. Her sex addiction is more specialized than Susan's; while Susan falls under the spell of alcohol and surrenders to the disreputable (in the tradition of her mother's succession of bad taste in men), Helen is a fool for financiers. (One assumes she may have become acquainted at some point with Don Fisk's weekend condo as well.) Perry's relationships with men, on the other hand, are all about peer competition and domination. For Fisk and Perry, Rita is an alluring battlefield, and their repeated penetrations of her a way of "sticking it to" each other. Perry's apparent interest in Harold ultimately reveals itself to be manipulative self-interest; everything in reach is his, including Harold's masterful third-quarter report. When Harold calls him on this dishonesty, Perry without reflection is able to fall back on a claim of all he's done for Harold; challenged to name something, Perry is initially at a loss, through we understand how different the two men have become when Perry eventually reminds Harold he took him to the place where he met Susan, his wife. Harold has to grant him this; he's already learned more about love by this point than Perry is ever likely to know. Perry fades away during the film's final third, as the focus shifts permanently to the war of wills between Graydon and Harold. At the renewal of vows at film's end, Perry is a wedding guest, seated between Rita and Helen in a cheerfully and perpetually objectified ensemble. Perry is the comic-narrative parallel to Jack Nicholson's character Jonathan in *Carnal Knowledge* or Clive Owen's character Larry in *Closer*: grasping, vengefully adversarial, the very image of the misanthropic malcontent.

Susan enters the narrative, like all the women introduced in the film, through Perry's and Harold's objectifying eyes. "The set-up allows 'Planet' to leer at women and then ridicule that impulse," writes Elvis Mitchell.[4] Their presence at the AA meeting has already relegated her to objecthood; in Perry's cynicism, the vulnerability of the recovering addict makes for especially easy prey. The two men perch at the room's periphery in judgment of all they see. When Doreen (Jane Lynch) introduces herself, she quickly identifies herself as lesbian, and Perry dismisses her with pejorative slang. Susan is next; from Perry and Harold's perspective, we watch her stand up and move to the podium. "Hello," says Perry, "get the bread—I see something tasty." In Perry's imagination, women are to be consumed and, the metaphor organically concluded, eliminated. Her address to the meeting introduces her victimhood, and Perry comments, "I like what I'm hearing" just as Susan declares, "But all that's changed now." She tells a story of waking up in an unfamiliar city next to an unfamiliar man and concludes, "I stopped putting myself in situations where I couldn't respect myself so others didn't respect me." To Perry's disappointed dismissal, "She wants respect—cuts me out," Harold demands silence. He isn't yet any different than Perry—but he sees what a liability Perry might prove to be.

In her own way, Nadine Jones (Caroline Aaron, another small-part Nichols regular) is just as locked into default assumptions about sexual identity and relationships as Perry. She has bagged Roland (Goodman) as her husband via an affair that breaks up his previous marriage. When he's distracted by his first interesting case as an investigator, she can only understand it as a loss of agency to another object of desire. In the comic extremity of tone in *What Planet*, Nadine comes to find it preferable to think that she's being supplanted by a more desirable woman—a Rita—than by the naked man whose picture she has found hidden under Roland's winter pants. Roland, for his part, has long since taken Nadine for granted, forgetting their anniversary, failing to listen to her concerns. At film's end, however, he demonstrates his ongoing commitment to his marriage by looking for ways to share with her the truth of what has preoccupied him, a professional reengagement that poses no threat to their relationship. At the same time that Harold is telling "the truth" to Susan, Roland wants Harold to come home and tell this same truth to Nadine. That the "truth" comes in the form of a bright white light is a comic acknowledgment of the traditional symbolism of illumination; that it comes from Garry Shandling's nose is indicative of the film's essential silliness of tone.

In his subsequent conversations with Susan, Harold evinces a simple candor so "alien" that Susan is disarmed by it and eventually comes to understand it as knowing, deconstructive irony. Asked what his "mission" is on their first dinner-date, Shandling as Harold vamps his double-take before saying, honestly enough, "I believe I was put here on Earth to have a child." Her response, that she's "never heard a man say that," begins to suggest something out of the ordinary about him, but her instincts recommend similar candor: "I don't trust you [...] because all men are the same. They say whatever they have to to get into your pants." (Variations on this line ensue throughout the film.) "That's terrible," he says in reply to her condemnation of his gender, "but what would it be? [...] The thing I'd have to say to get into your pants." Harold seals the inquiry with Shandling's trademark ingratiating-aggressive toothy grin, and Susan laughs, assuming that Harold is making a joke at the expense of all those tiresome, predictable one-track minds she has previously dated.

She takes him home, but with no default intention to bed him. Like Rachel Samstat (Meryl Streep) in *Heartburn*, she's into "fixing up" her living space as an analog of renovating her life, and as such, the breakfast nook, painted and repainted to express her volatile moods, is the central symbol. Harold makes an innocently ingenuous suggestion that she interprets as a philosophical insight: "Why don't you take that arch-thing out altogether," he says, indicating the trompe l'oeil image of a window on the world she has painted into the wall. "I have a feeling what's out there is more interesting anyway." In the bedroom, inquiring about her array of religious iconography on the chest, he advances on her sexually. "You don't care about any of this," she concedes forlornly. "You're just tricking me." She scares him away to a consultation with Graydon when she confides the vow of celibacy she's taken until marriage. Yet alone in her breakfast nook, contemplating yet another makeover, she instead begins to tear down the wall, discovering, just behind it, a beautiful arched window with a view to the Phoenix Mountains. It sends her back to him to ask him to lunch, but before she can, he says, "Would you think about marrying me?" In the literalism of his alien logic, he understands this to be the commodified terms she has proffered for sexual license. She smiles knowingly and says, "All right, I deserved that. [...] Everything I said the other night was such a turn-off. I went completely overboard." But she's in with the champ of overboard; she's misheard his earnestness as irony again, and as he drops to a knee to make clear how serious he is about his proposal, she has to reorient herself to the unpredictable nature of this new man in her life. Ironically, he begins to break down her gendered objectifying of him (all of which is actually well-deserved) long before she is able to make any headway beyond his Graydon-trained and Perry-reinforced objectification of her.

Beyond these situational ironies, the script delights in the verbal ironies of woman-alien dialogue. After their physically demanding honeymoon and a failed pregnancy test, they have their first quarrel. She's (rightly) feeling herself objectified as pure womb and demands that they talk. The scene takes the form of an advanced training session like the ones he undertook on his home planet, but without Graydon's monomaniacal focus. "This might be a good time to sit next to me and try to comfort me," she suggests; he fails the test when his procreative mission reasserts itself. She shrugs away from his ill-timed groping and encourages him to talk to her "like a human being." This prompts another consultation with Graydon. Later, when Harold learns he's been passed over for the vice-president promotion at the bank, a position that should be meaningless to him given his original mission, he comes home to Susan; in his frustration, he's crying (which he mistakes for blood). She comforts him with the admonition, "You're being too hard on yourself. You're just human, that's all." These characterizations of Harold's latent "humanity" are not played solely or perhaps even primarily for laughs; they are markers of his progress from the reductive state of sperm-gun to something multi-dimensional. The segue to a cosmic starscape for once has nothing to do with Graydon and everything to do with the journey Harold has embarked upon *after* teleportation. "I always feel so much better when I'm with you," he says to Susan, and insists without irony that he has no motive but to state this fact. Their tenderness provokes the first non-mission-based stirring of Harold's libido (irrelevant in Graydon's terms, now that Susan is pregnant), with the result that, after hundreds of "insertions," they make love for the first time.

"'Most young men think about sex, and think that women are sexual objects,'" says Shandling. "'And as we get older, we realize there are elements that are far more important.'"[5] Graydon is, in fact, as one-dimensional as his one-track mission. Kingsley, stiff and terse, his bald head gleaming, is the physical embodiment of phallocracy, a talking analog of the evolutionary drive to reproduce. The columns of rank and file arranged interchangeably in the training amphitheater are the organisms of hypothetical fertility, like spermatozoa awaiting their billions-to-one shot at the egg. Not as literal as Woody Allen's sketch as the reluctant sperm cell in *Everything You Always Wanted to Know About Sex* But Were Afraid to Ask* (1972), the visual and dramatic treatment of Graydon and his command is ultimately a stylized representation of the male sex urge and patriarchal hegemony. Nichols frames the scene in which Harold discovers a new motivation for sex—not phallocentric primacy but an expression of tender and intimate regard—with a return to the cosmic starscape he's always contemplating, Harold's home. His joy at being with Susan is tempered only by his uneasiness about the consequences of his now housing two such profoundly incompatible urges: the prerogative to subdue and exploit at war with the privilege to commune and cherish. His remote agenda remains Graydon's rigid will for him; but Harold has also discovered a new home here, which *What Planet* underscores with a jump cut to the house Susan's still trying to sell, and which Harold surprises her by asserting that they should buy out from under her hesitating, sniping clients.

Harold's transformation is even more extreme than Susan's only because he is extraterrestrial. In coming to a committed relationship, they each must liberate themselves from the default inculcation of their culture. In this sense, a Nichols film once again foregrounds the motif of education—as often a process of *un*learning as of learning. This is the transformative quality Bewes finds alive in reified anxiety.[6] Susan is able to articulate her complicity in her objectification in front of the AA meeting. For Harold, the process is only beginning as he listens to her bold, self-critical words. Susan accurately presumes Harold, like other men, to be motivated by "tricking" her; this is mandated policy from Graydon, who has sworn Harold to secrecy as part of the conspiracy of conquest and counsels Harold to the further duplicity of an affair when Susan is not immediately fertile. But in the best sense of the generic conventions of romantic comedy, Susan feminizes Harold. One of the first markers of this transformation is his turn towards self-revelatory candor as an improvement upon his earlier, merely ingenuous candor, as when he inquires what he would need to say to get into her pants or when he proposes to her as a means of ensuring his access to sex. "I don't know who I am anymore," confides a Harold in transition, deviating from the phallocratic prerogative, in which identity is as simple as sex drive. Later, seeing Graydon hovering in the maternity ward, he resigns himself to the fate of his original mission, but can't bear not to say goodbye.

H14496, aka Harold Anderson (Garry Shandling, who also co-wrote the script) performs instructional role-plays with a holographic avatar of Susan Hart (Annette Bening), the woman he has met, married, and impregnated, for the massed citizens of a planet of cloned men bent on colonizing Earth by reproduction. Harold has swiftly adapted to Earth's individual liberties, and his instruction reflects what he has learned about objectifying women and his own planet's conformist practices. He inadvertently causes the violent overthrow of his planet's hegemonic ruler in *What Planet Are You From?*

"Maybe I should have just left," he says, as he watches Susan's heart break. "This seems much worse." Back on his planet, Shandling also gets comic mileage out of delivering lines traditionally assigned by genre formula to women: "You know, if you don't talk to me, I won't know what's wrong," and "See what you did? I told you you were scaring the baby."[7]

When Harold takes over the instruction of Graydon's rank and file spermtroopers after his return, he brings an enlightened perspective to the curriculum. The men make the same mistakes he did when confronted with the melodramatic verbal irony of a woman's anger. Urged by Susan's hologram to "go" and shop for a new remote control, they of course interpret her literally. "There's a whole layer here you're missing," Harold instructs them. In *Postcards from the Edge*, Suzanne Vale (Meryl Streep) encounters a Malibu version of Perry Gordon in Jack Faulkner (Dennis Quaid). Still wearing her cop uniform from a day's work on a bad buddy-cop movie, she launches a rhetorical assault against him with the claim that she isn't bothered by his sleeping around but by his lying about it; he summons a vindicated indignation when he counters by calling *her* the liar: she *is* bothered by his promiscuity and—the coup de grâce—by her certainty that he will, someday sooner or later, leave. Ever the opportunist, this is Jack's opportunity to show Suzanne the door, proving to her how committed he is to full disclosure of himself: he would never lie about what a liar he is. Later in the same film, Lowell Kolcheck (Gene Hackman) offers Suzanne a different, more stable image of manhood, albeit with no sexual strings attached. Lowell talks to Suzanne about dramatic structure, specifically recognition, Aristotle's concept of anagnorisis; his claim is that, unlike in art, self-realizations and transformation are far less instantaneous in life. They take time: character evolves in process. In his indoctrination sessions back on his home planet, Harold is able to draw similar conclusions about the nature—and necessity—of transformation. "Human relationships are filled with conflict," Harold observes to the spermtroopers. "The whole planet is filled with conflict. Not that that's a bad thing, because it's through conflict that we learn about ourselves." This causes an unsettled stirring in the ranks, the beginning of the end of Graydon's phallocratic reign. The spermtroopers want to become men like Harold. The title of the film quotes a question Susan asks Harold, but in its playful way, the second person pronoun addresses the audience as well. Harold's meta-statement, near the crisis of the film, foregrounds the journey an audience takes with a filmmaker each time it submits to the flow of narrative.

Abundant comic evidence exists in their exchanged wedding renewal vows that both Harold and Susan remain works in progress. Susan acknowledges her need for continuing growth and evolution when she refers to the universe as "one big, screwed-up place where everyone's trying to work out their problems. But I'm honored to work them out with you." Harold is typically even more direct, confessing that he only married her at first "to get into your pants." He follows up by launching into a familiar cliché capped by Harold's brand of full disclosure: "Now I'm [marrying you] because I want to spend the rest of my life getting into your pants." Though more heartfelt than his perfunctory Vegas-strip avowal, his disarming honesty reveals that his ingrained instincts remain. The film's coda ends on a road, and with talk of commuting—more journeys still to come as a couple begin negotiating their married life together. The concluding bickering of the newlywed new parents manifests the human (and humanized) pace of our progress, where democratic conflict trumps the reified illusion of conformist harmony. As Lowell concludes in *Postcards*, transformation isn't instantaneous but a process of becoming. Susan has no firmer an idea of what love is than an alien. But they're learning together.

18

"A little allegory of the soul"

Wit (2001)

Although released within a year of one another, *Wit* and its predecessor in the Mike Nichols canon, *What Planet Are You From?*, seem worlds apart and form a boundary between Nichols' long mid-career phase and a reassertion of the gravity of his early filmmaking. Lee Hill concurs that the move from trivial sci-fi sex farce to his HBO dramas signals "yet another major shift in his work."[1] The earlier comedy was initiated for the cinematic screen as a star vehicle for Garry Shandling. The later drama, which Caryn James in her review in the *New York Times* called "a dynamic addition to [Nichols'] ever-fresh career,"[2] began life on the stage and eventually, when it reached Broadway, won its playwright Margaret Edson the 1999 Pulitzer for Drama, as well as numerous other prizes. The plot of *Wit* is exceedingly faithful to Edson's play; the only significant excisions are some of the more static exegeses of Donne's poetry. While a teacher by vocation, Edson is not, as one might reasonably assume, a professor of literature presenting Vivian Bearing (Emma Thompson in the film) as a kind of avatar. Edson's insight into the world of medicine about which she writes results from when she worked in an AIDS and cancer research hospital; she has taught various levels of grade school as well as kindergarten, undoubtedly a source of her appreciation for the timeless wisdom she gleans from Margaret Wise Brown's classic early-childhood picture book, *The Runaway Bunny* (1942).

When Colin Callendar of HBO approached Edson with his desire to adapt the play for television, she worried that the filmmakers "'would have to jazz it up, add different themes and different places and a car crash.'"[3] But she hadn't taken into account the possibilities inherent within "television's intimacy, [which] creates such a raw, private encounter with Vivian that we seem to be peering into a soul as embattled as its body."[4] When Callendar recruited Thompson, and she in turn recruited Nichols, who had directed her in *Primary Colors*, Edson began to breathe easier. So, it seems, did Nichols: "'There was no opening weekend to worry about, nothing else to worry about except the piece itself.'"[5] David Thomson minces no words in claiming that *Wit* "made so many of [Nichols'] recent movies look fussy and decorative. *Wit* trusted the aching iron of its subject and the steel of its players. I think it is the best work he has ever done."[6] *Wit* initiated an important association for Nichols with HBO, during which he adapted two late-twentieth century stage masterpieces of decidedly different scale, one a chamber drama, the other, Tony Kushner's *Angels in America*, nothing short of a multi-generational epic. While *What Planet* is, above all, silly, *Wit* and *Angels in America* deal quite literally with matters of life and death. This seeming dichotomy of tonal and thematic approach is in fact the Nichols way. While Nichols would make an enormous amount of money mounting the *very* silly 2005 Broadway production of *Spamalot*, which continues to tour around the world, he has also dedicated himself to drama of the greatest gravity. The same year he released *Wit* on HBO, he was reviving Anton Chekhov's *The Seagull*. Other Broadway revivals include Clifford Odets' *The Country Girl* in 2008, Arthur Miller's *Death of a Salesman* in 2012, and Harold Pinter's *Betrayal* in 2013. If Nichols' 2000 sci-fi romantic comedy hybrid and his 2001 death-and-dignity drama have anything at all in common, then, it is because they reflect the stylistically eclectic but thematically consistent work of their director. Both *What Planet* and *Wit* use the motif of educational training as a metaphor for the liberating potential of reified anxiety.

Dr. Vivian Bearing (Thompson) is a teacher of 17th century Metaphysical Poetry, specializing in the work of John Donne. As the film opens, she is surrendering herself into the hands of another teacher, Dr. Harvey Kelekian (Christopher Lloyd), who runs a cancer research unit. John Leonard calls him "amiably remote, a tourist of suffering—patriarchy's smiling face."[7] Both Vivian and Kelekian are eminences in their respective fields, driven almost exclusively by the desire to command "knowledge." In *Wit*, knowledge is so highly prized that it objectifies all in its path, making Vivian and Kelekian stringent but one-dimensional mentors. Each will sacrifice the individual soul in front of him or her for the

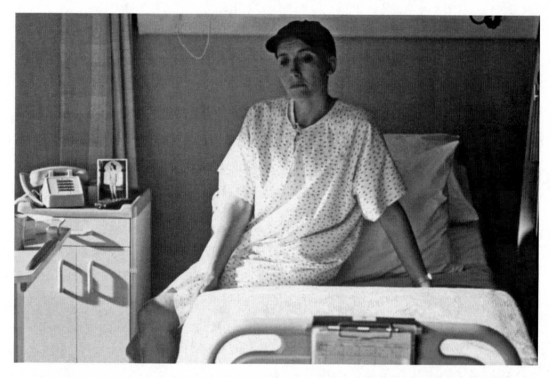

The physical metamorphosis Dr. Vivian Bearing (Emma Thompson) must undergo in her battles with cancer, with experimental treatment *for* cancer, and with the men conducting the experimental research on her body moves her from the rarefied, cap-and-gown world of university life to the ballcap-and-gown humbling of hospitalized weakness. What matters as much to Thompson and Nichols, who co-adapted Margaret Edson's stage play *Wit* for HBO, is a spiritual transformation, in which a woman isolated by her superior intellect finally sees the dangers of living among abstractions, as well as the value of "kindness."

abstracted object; Vivian will humiliate students uncommitted to her scholarly project, while Kelekian will conveniently ignore the agony of his research subject for the "good" of what he can learn about her pain for future treatment protocols. Kelekian, a doctor of medicine, cares more for data than his patients; Vivian, a doctor of philosophy, cares more for words and their poetic application than she does for the individuals entrusted to her instruction. Each is in a profoundly humanizing field of endeavor, yet each has missed the forest for the compelling vision of this or that isolated tree.

Two secondary characters bear witness to these single-minded servants of knowledge. One, Dr. Jason Posner (Jonathan M. Woodward) is in the unique position of having studied with each. The other, Susie Monahan (Audra McDonald), is the only one of the narrative's four central characters not holding the terminal degree in her particular discipline. Edson's play identifies her as having earned the credential of R. N., the baseline health-care qualification of Registered Nurse, as well as the B. S. N., the liberal arts undergraduate degree in the field. Jason is Kelekian's star pupil, already thinking out beyond the bounds of his current appointment to when he will have his own lab, his own research projects. He typifies his mentors' application of knowledge—not only Kelekian's, but also Vivian's—in that he is an exceptional academic performer with tunnel vision. He lacks a sense of what medicine and literature are actually *for*. Each seems to him a purely intellectual challenge, a "puzzle," in which, as he describes it to Susie, "The puzzle takes over. You're not even trying to solve it anymore." Neither literature nor medicine originates in the vacuum of pure abstraction, however. Each is an art meant to bring order to human dilemma. Each is meant to *deepen* our humanity, not marginalize it.

In this sense the hero of *Wit* is its "lowliest" character in terms of credentials and qualifications but whose quotient of humanity far exceeds any of her professional or intellectual superiors. Susie ministers to Vivian when knowledge fails. Jason illustrates to Vivian what she has failed to teach him when he was on her roster in college, because she has first failed to learn it herself. Susie helps Vivian find the dimension she's been missing in Donne's poetry, what Vivian's own brilliant mentor, E. M. Ashford (Eileen Atkins), calls "truth," confounding Vivian by telling her that the term paper she's been laboring over is "not the point." The reified striving and the objectification of all knowledge by Vivian and Kelekian and their talented pupil Jason is put into the balance against Susie's competent compassion and found wanting. "Now is not the time for verbal swordplay," Vivian concludes, commencing her slide towards death. "Now is a time for simplicity. Now is a time for, dare I say it, kindness."

* * *

Wit is, without question, the simplest of Mike Nichols' twenty films. A long, one-act drama on the stage, it has a similar, virtuosic chamber intensity on the screen. Emma Thompson, as Dr. Vivian Bearing, addresses the audience just as Kathleen Chalfant had in creating the role on Broadway. The narrative is thus a kind of "Last Lecture," which Nichols and Edson accentuate by having Vivian, desperately receding into her own head for refuge from the twinned tortures of toxic therapies and even more toxic doctors, lecture a hall of students in hospital gown. The lecture is actually an inquiry: Vivian remains a student until the last, and only in the clarifying simplicity of her intimacy with onrushing death does she finally learn the wisdom that Donne (and her mentor, Professor Ashford) have long offered her.

Her cancer aside, Vivian and her physicians (Dr. Harvey Kelekian and his most able current research fellow, Jason Posner) all suffer from the same disease: commodification. The scientists are a classic case of scientific alienation: in their pursuit of therapeutic solutions, they have inverted the objectives of medicine. Ideally, medicine is an art meant to minister to human need; in Dr. Kelekian's practice, medicine has become an end in itself, and the patients the means to that end. Kelekian's greatest praise ("Excellent") is reserved for those stouthearted patients like Vivian courageous and "tough" enough to undergo the rigors of his indicated regimen at "full throttle." There is an unspoken understanding to their relationship: neither Kelekian nor the patient expects the outcome to be bright, but it may constitute "a significant contribution to our knowledge." The opening images of the film offer the close-up shot/reverse shot intensity of an Ingmar Bergman existential conversation, as Vivian and Kelekian parry language to negotiate the power dynamic of their brief future relationship. His condescension as a scientist never wavers, but when she draws a parallel to her own condescension towards the inadequacies of students, the two eminent intellects briefly but unmistakably meet on something like common ground. In the subsequent humiliation to which she is assigned as an objectified specimen during the clinical "Grand Rounds" of the research fellows, she retains this dual relationship to Kelekian: a piece of cancerous meat to be palpated and quantified, but also the rare person who shares his overwhelming frustration of living among one's intellectual inferiors. Understandably, this is no basis for meaningful bonding. They admire each other, distantly, as disciples of "knowledge" in its distinct forms, but Kelekian also appreciates her, abstractly, as a patient yielding maximum data. As his protégé Jason plaintively observes, "I wish they could all get through it at full throttle. Then we could really have some data."

The contours of Vivian's reification are subtler than that of the scientists. After all, she is a distinguished humanities professor, and may thus be expected to have a more sophisticated grasp of the human condition than a scientist addicted to the minutiae of research. Yet Vivian's cold prickliness (as portrayed by Thompson using her precise, nasal elocution to savage the technicians at the hospital as she'd once skewered her students) soon reveals an intensely isolated person, one who has taken her cues from her father (Harold Pinter), who by his own admission hadn't suffered well fools and their boring after-dinner conversation. In the stage play, one actor plays both Kelekian and Vivian's father, conflating detached, patriarchal authority[8] (Nichols separates their casting to eliminate cinematic confusion, but imperious patriarchy attaches to both roles). Words, and their artful arrangement in literary form, become in the Bearing household a walled defense, or the "verbal swordplay," of "wit." The title of the film bears witness to the ambiguous complexity of this concept: Vivian has used "wit" as an island from which to gaze impassively at the world and at herself, intent only upon the meritocracy of knowledge. Jason's admiration for her, as he attests to Susie, is that "she was a great scholar. Wrote tons of books, articles, was the head of everything." He concludes, "*Enzyme Kinetics* was more poetic than Bearing's class." Of all the indignities Vivian is made to suffer by her illness and its aggressive experimental treatment, this must surely be the most painful of all: Jason was an excellent student who learned nothing, because, as Vivian comes to understand, she herself lacked the humanizing perspective within which to impart Donne's true "wit," what Professor Ashford calls "truth." (Her professor may have felt as frustrated with Vivian as Vivian feels with Jason—maybe more so, since Jason makes no pretense to being an expert on the Metaphysical Poets.) Vivian's humbling insight as she dies is that her career as a scholar and teacher has been, until its final moments, lost in empty striving.

For all her contempt for Jason (reflexive once she knows he was once a student of hers, then grounded in the unfeeling ineptitude of his bedside manner), what Vivian comes to recognize is that they have much in common. Her introduction, via flashback, of her own failed relationships with students comes after an exchange in which she tentatively seeks empathy from one of her doctors. Kelekian, she has long since determined, is a lost cause, far too full of himself and his research to understand the cruelty of his persistent challenge to keep going "full throttle." Having just completed the ideal specifications for treatment, the eight "full doses," she announces, "I have broken the record. [...] Kelekian and Jason are simply delighted. I think they see celebrity status for themselves" when they publish the results her life and death represent. Her reified anxiety as a commodity expresses itself most eloquently in the reduced realization of what her "significant contribution to knowledge" will be: "I flatter myself. The article will not be about *me*; it will be about my ovaries. It will be about my peritoneal cavity, which, despite their best intentions, is now crawling with cancer. What we have come to think of as *me* is, in fact, just the specimen jar, just the dust jacket, just the white piece of paper that bears the little black marks." Her physicians have failed to see *her* in much the same way as she has failed to see her students, or, for that matter, the "truth" in John Donne's "wit" as expressed in something as otherwise pedantic as the preference for a comma over a semi-colon (her professor's strident distinction in Vivian's flashback to studying with Ashford).

Having despaired of invoking Kelekian's humanity, Vivian makes a tentative inquiry into Jason's. He has just condescended to Vivian yet again, when she inquires about the current function of her kidneys. Admitting to "simplifying" the concepts so she can grasp them, he admits he's "supposed" to do so: "There's a whole course on it in med school. It's required. Colossal waste of time for researchers." Implied in this last aside is an entire philosophy of the practice of medicine, one that so entirely objectifies the patient as a commodity to be bartered with death for knowledge that he can't see the irony in his confessing his perspective *to* one of the patients as he turns her into data. Nonetheless, she pursues her line of inquiry, asking him to explain his vocational impulses, and he makes what in any context is an extraordinary declarative utterance: "Cancer's the only thing I ever wanted." His sheer ignorance of the connotative power of words is absolute: there are no circumstances under which such a syntactical arrangement should be constructed. The very best interpretation one may allow is that he invites the challenge of this physiological assault on the species, because only knowledge can lead to a cure. Faced with a confrontation with his words, Jason would surely align himself with this interpretation. But in his level of alienated abstraction from the realities of his life amidst epic human suffering, he blunders on, speaking with undisguised admiration for the insidious, adversarial intelligence of "the malignant neoplasia." Her cancer, and that of the other patients in Kelekian's lab, is about *Jason*, in his battle of wit and wills with malignancy. Searching for a word adequate to his admiration for cancer, he's momentarily at a loss, and Vivian's sardonic suggestion is "awesome." He accepts it gratefully and without noticing her invitation to self-knowledge. He tells her of his dream of running his own lab, "If I can survive this ... *fellowship*." Beyond the ironies of his use of the word "survive" in the presence of Vivian, who is being made with every passing hour to understand that she will *not* survive, *Wit*, through Jason's and Vivian's very distinctly, profoundly alienated characters, shows us the ironies of "fellowship": the word connotes collegiality, a union—what Vivian sarcastically refers to in the next line as "The part with the human beings." Jason, still tone-deaf to everything but what harmonizes with the song of himself, simply accepts what she has pejoratively inserted, saying, "Everybody's got to go through it. All the great researchers."

Vivian has already quoted to us, at the beginning of this scene, from a 1609 poem of Donne: "This is my playes last scene, here heavens appoint/My pilgrimages last mile"; she has begun to reveal to us, beneath the cool, clinical scholarly distance of the relationship she has maintained with the world, the terror of a soul at the brink of its mortality. To haughty, non-ironic Jason, she poses this question: "And what do you say when a patient is ... apprehensive ... frightened?" He can only see himself reflected in the question, and so he does not make the patient-centered response, "Of what?" to locate the source of the patient's emotional distress. Instead, Jason's response to her question is the question, "Of who?" It seems he is finally prepared to understand the insult she's been trying to deliver all along, inferring from her question that patients might be scared of *him* and his ghoulish treatments. "I just ..." she begins, then, knowing that he has already failed her test, relents: "Never mind," she says, a cue indicated in his clinical pathology for patient disorientation. Unable or unwilling to recognize her quite-lucid distress signals, he instead interprets them as onset dementia. He cannot be taught any more than Kelekian, and at this late stage she lacks the stomach it would take to overcome his objectifying density.

When Jason leaves (out of sight of the patient, he begins combing his hair, a monster of youthful narcissism), she's left alone with us, her mute witnesses to their joint failure, teacher and pupil. "So," she begins. "The young doctor, like the senior scholar, prefers research to humanity. At the same time the senior scholar, in her pathetic state as a simpering victim, wishes the young doctor would take more interest in personal contact. Now I suppose we shall see how the senior scholar ruthlessly denied her simpering students the touch of human kindness she now seeks." What duly ensues are flashbacks to her unfeeling cruelty and intolerance as a professor whose first and only duty is to reverence for her subject matter, not those subjected to her instruction. With her own students, Vivian assumes a bullying status: "I'll give you a hint. It has nothing to do with football."

Though Nichols and Thompson substantially elide Edson's classroom flashback, with its long dialogue about Donne's "complicated" use of "wit," the most significant subtraction from Edson's stage play in the completed film is a reference Vivian makes about *Susie*, shortly after the academic flashbacks are over, but very much in the same key of objectifying dismissal. The flashbacks have, notably, left the professional connoisseur of language short of an adequate alibi: "I don't know. I feel so much—what is the word? I look back, I see these scenes, and I ..." she trails off, knowing full well her failure of humanity in her humanities classroom. Then she gets Susie to come to her room. She finds, after all, that what she needs is company, an ear to listen, and soon she is making unprecedented confessions to her compassionate nurse, through tears: "I can't figure things out," and "I don't feel sure of myself anymore." Susie listens; she pets Vivian's arm; she proffers first a tissue, then a popsicle. (While Susie is fetching the popsicle, Vivian provides us with a therapeutic rationale for its useful physiological effects for her system, self-conscious about the child-like display of yielding to the simple pleasures of a frozen novelty.) As the two women subsequently share the popsicle, Susie addresses what the doctors have not: Vivian's small measure of sovereign control over her own death. "I wanted to present both choices," she tells Vivian, "before Kelekian and Jason talk to you." Vivian has already prided herself earlier in the conversation about her ability to "read between the lines" of the doctors' pep talks to the dire truth of her condition. Now she does the same with Susie, acknowledging Susie's unspoken antagonism to the doctors' desire to prolong their patients' lives. Susie is too professional to say it directly, but we, too, can read between the lines to understand Susie's disapproval of her superiors' commodification of illness: "[T]hey like to save lives," she begins diplomatically, but immediately reveals her horror at their mixed motives: "So anything's okay, as long as life continues." "Life" is the linguistic abstraction the lab has adopted to keep the patient's misery at bay.

Susie's interpretation grows darker still: "But they always ... want to know more things." Rallying to this default of her own, Vivian says, as if in the doctors' defense, "I always want to know more things. I'm a scholar." Susie, exquisitely attuned to her patients, respectfully backs away from the line of critique she has initiated; she interprets the first-person vigor of Vivian's response as a desire to cling to what still remains of her diminishing, anguished life. She circles back to her original line of inquiry: Vivian's empowerment in her own end-of-life decision. Vivian adamantly expresses her desire to be DNR, "no-code," free to die when her body is ready, and Susie carefully reviews the choices with her several more times; the repetition would seem patronizing were it not for the utter gravity of what they are discussing. Susie collects their popsicle sticks and turns to go, but Vivian can't help herself: "Susie? You're still going to take care of me, aren't you?" Susie responds warmly, "'Course I am. Don't you worry, sweetheart."

When Susie exits, we encounter the single largest break Nichols and Thompson's adapted screenplay makes with Edson's original stage script. The alteration is largest not because it elides the greatest volume of original material, but because it is the one most central to the interpretation of Vivian Bearing's evolution as a character. When she is alone again, Vivian instantly sets to a meta-reflective recasting of her self-betraying performance of weakness: "Well, *that* certainly was a maudlin display. Popsicles? 'Sweetheart?' I can't believe my life has become so corny." Her last lines exchanged with Susie—indeed, the entire scene, the longest and warmest depiction of human intimacy in the film, has been self-betraying in two very different ways: in Vivian's own mind, she has treacherously betrayed her commitment to the absolute independence of her personhood; but to Susie and us, she has revealed her vulnerability, the humanity so long held in check by an abstract devotion to language and idea. In Edson's stage version, she goes on to explain this breakdown in "tone" as a product of simple minds: "my brain is dulling, and *poor Susie's* was never very sharp to begin with."[9] Coming as late as it does, with only a fifth of the play remaining, the condescension is particularly awkward and unsympathetic. It suggests Vivian remains unreconstructed in her defensive isolation until the final vision, before her death, of her beloved Professor Ashford cradling her. But in fact Nichols' film version, by leaving this demeaning slur out, renders Vivian as a more convincingly gradual learner, moving from the extreme of her painfully arch treatment of her students (including Jason, with whom we are at times so exasperated that we are tempted to believe he deserves it) to allowances for human imperfection, her own and others.' Removing the insult while retaining her self-consciousness of this chink she has displayed in her armor raises the possibility of her character beginning to recognize the crucial role Susie has by this point come to play in Vivian's denouement. Her monologue grudgingly indicates as much; the screenplay eliminates the slur on Susie's intellect but keeps the spirit of the speech as a whole, which moves from self-mockery of her "maudlin" turn to a dismissal of her life's work as a source of comfort and finally, on to her call for "kindness."

Vivian's conclusion to her "last lecture" comes well before the film's conclusion. After the call for "kindness," she condemns the cult of intellect, which includes not only herself but also Kelekian and Jason, all of whom have privileged "knowledge" above the human person. "I thought being extremely smart would take care of it," she confides. "But I see that I have been found out." Now, in her concluding address to us, we find her, in close-up, curled against the pain wracking her insides and finally, fatally, at a loss for words. The best she can do is a final analogy, not to help us understand the pain, but to help us understand her failure to surmount it through knowledge: "I'm like a student and this is the final exam and I don't know what to put down because I don't understand the question and I'm *running out of time.*" Knowing what we know of Vivian Bearing's life, this can't be a familiar experience for her. What it indicates is her default resistance to grasping the "truth" that Professor Ashford had offered to her long ago, in the conference about Vivian's meticulous but somehow still careless term paper, which ought to be "ultimately about overcoming," in Professor Ashford's words, "the seemingly insuperable barriers separating life, death, and eternal life." As it turns out, there were other human barriers Vivian failed to negotiate as well, creating her insuperable pedantry. As she prepares to cross Donne's barrier between her life and what comes after, the other barrier—the one that has kept other people at bay—also crumbles; she is prepared, however "maudlin" she finds it, to surrender herself into the tender hands of Susie, who doesn't know what "soporific" means, and who doesn't need to in order to minister to Vivian.

Furnished her first sustaining dose of morphine, Vivian is able to laugh at Susie's ignorance of the word Vivian's father had taught her at five. Susie, finally getting the joke, responds in good-natured self-deprecation: "Well, that was pretty dumb," but Vivian, significantly, does not pile on with a sardonic aside, as she doubtless once would have done, instead distinguishing "funny" from "dumb." The moment is an extraordinarily apt evocation of Vivian's character, mid-evolution: still pedantic in her distinctions between words, but in pursuit of what small measure of tenderness she can offer in return to her only friend in the world. Susie, ever the cancer-ward politician, as she must be in negotiating the ego air-space around men like Kelekian and Jason, allows that it *is* funny, "in a dumb sort of way. I never would have gotten it. I'm glad you explained it." The last words of Vivian's life spoken in full coherence are simply a reminder, to Susie and to herself, "I'm a teacher." But the claim may never have been more fully, redemptively true than in this final lucid moment before the morphine and death overwhelm her. She has refused the bait of Susie's error; she has insisted, in a teaching moment, that Susie laugh with her—rather than settling for sarcasm, in which wit laughs alone. Vivian has never seemed so happy or so *kind* as in this moment, precisely because she does not—cannot any longer—think of her nurse as "poor Susie."

Nichols' use of camera movement, music, and editing in this last moment of Vivian's conscious life is in poetic contrast to his use of film language earlier in Vivian's ordeal. The film, opens, for instance, with the discordant stridency of scraped strings and, as the titles play, a disorienting, soft-focus view of a cityscape (we soon learn it is the view from the office window behind Kelekian's desk). The camera does not move in this opening scene; rather, Kelekian in close-up, hard focus suddenly invades the soft-focus frame. He literally gets in Vivian's face, threatening and cajoling her to submit to the will of his experimental regimen. Nichols and editor John Bloom render this scene as a remorseless series of close-up shot/reverse shots, crisply corresponding to the "verbal swordplay" of these two intellects, but when she signs the "Informed Consent," it feels like a capitulation. Nonetheless, the solitary close-ups underscore the essential alienation each demands in human encounter. In the closing of Vivian's conscious life, Vivian and Susie are mostly rendered in intimate two-shots that underscore a newfound communion. And as they share a cleansing laugh (again, one suspects this sort of friendly shared laughter is an unfamiliar but suddenly welcome experience for Vivian), the camera tracks slowly, deferentially out of the room. Vivian's breathing slows towards unconsciousness, and on the soundtrack, the earlier, stringed tension of the film has dissolved in a gentler, fuller orchestration, with strings that no longer grate as in the opening of the film but sustain themselves alongside the camera's recessional flow. Susie closes Vivian's curtain.

Jason enters the film (and Vivian's room) twice more after Vivian has "departed" as his sparring partner. The first time, he's with Susie. He seems much more at ease now that Vivian's psychological state matches his emotional interest in that state. The near-actionable abuses of his earlier pelvic exam have been replaced by a cheerful recording of her continued disintegration: "Let's up the hydration," he says to Susie. "She won't be drinking anymore." Susie insists on continuing to address Vivian directly, though Jason actually *mocks* her for it. (If the incident still to come with Professor Ashford should be understood as a morphine dream, then it is accurate to understand Vivian's state as Susie does, rather than as Jason does, as that of a person whose mind remains alive. In any case, as Susie reminds him, "It's just nice to do.") Susie and Jason talk about Vivian and Donne, Jason typically showing off, bragging about an idea from one of the papers he wrote for class. The point of the scene is a referendum on how poorly Vivian has taught Jason Donne's work. Jason praises Donne's "complexity" for its own sake, for "the complications of the puzzle." When Susie asks if Jason believes in what he has termed "the meaning of life garbage," he can't resist another dig: "What do they *teach* you in nursing school?" It's condescension worthy of his one-time literature professor. Susie is too embarrassed by her sentimentality to tell Jason why she lingers when he leaves: she wants to rub lotion into Vivian's skin, unwilling to see Vivian as anything less than a person long after she is nothing but pure, inarticulate specimen for research.

We have encountered a series of "lasts" already in *Wit*'s final scenes: Vivian's last monologue delivered to us as she lectures on Donne and death; Vivian's last conscious exchange (her final teaching moment with Susie). In the scene in which E. M. Ashford makes her visitation, we are offered something like the surreal strangeness of Yossarian's post-knifing hospitalization in *Catch-22* or Suzanne Vale's post-overdose hallucination of Nancy Reagan in the Hall of Overdosed Stars in *Postcards from the Edge*: the idyll with Professor Ashford is Vivian's final coming-to-terms with a reality long resisted. Whether or not her professor's appearance is literal or an unconscious conjuring,[10] Professor Ashford continues to offer to Vivian what she has always offered, the simplicity of truth within the complexity of the "puzzle." A trace of the mentor-pedant persists in Vivian's comical projection of Professor Ashford opening *The Runaway Bunny* not to the first page of the story, but to its bibliographical details recorded on the copyright page. Most poignantly, she also imagines her professor making a kind of running literary commentary on the text as she encounters it: midway through, Professor Ashford has caught the pattern of the narrative hide and seek plot, and she pauses to muse: "Look at that. A little allegory of the soul. No matter where it hides, God will find it. See, Marian?" In Vivian's earlier flashback to that failed term paper, having been counseled by her professor to postpone her revision for some time with friends, Vivian instead returns to the library to plug away at the essay, not understanding that her professor has given her isolated student a second, more vital assignment. Vivian, in her last unconscious glimmering of sentience, remains her professor's diligent student, finally prepared to work past the "insuperable barriers" she has laid down against truth to encounter the "wit" Donne and Professor Ashford have long held out to her. And then, as Professor Ashford parts from Vivian, or more accurately as Vivian parts with this life, she quotes not Donne but Horatio's benediction over Hamlet: "And flights of angels sing thee to thy rest." The Donne scholar, so sniffy about Shakespeare all those years ago in her office, can summon no more soothing words or thought at life's end than Shakespeare's vision of solace in angelic contact and communion. The line's appeal to Nichols and Thompson continues on beyond this film into their next work together, *Angels in America*. The two films dialogue with one another in substantial ways, not only through Thompson's metamorphosis from dying woman to her multiple roles in the epic, including the literal, titular presence as The Angel, but most relevantly in the ministering role she plays in answer to Susie Monahan's powerful presence in *Wit*: as the nurse Emily, Prior Walter's metaphorical angel of mercy that helps summon his vision of The Angel. "Time to go," Vivian's projection of Professor Ashford announces; as she slips almost soundlessly out of her curled position around Vivian, she is a spirit departing, the spirit of Donne and Ashford and, belatedly, Vivian Bearing, at one with their Wit. A solo piano plays, and the camera again glides away, but this time it remains in the room with Vivian to witness her last, peaceful breaths. "A little allegory of the soul": the self-imposed barriers of intellectual imperiousness are no match for the heart's cry.

In *Wit*'s final scene, we see dramatized Vivian's earlier epiphany that "being extremely smart" can function as an ironic barrier to the sort of humanizing insight that Professor Ashford sees in Donne and that Susie sees when she looks at her patients. Intellectual gifts have driven Kelekian, Vivian, and Jason to lives of hierarchical striving. When Vivian indulges a reverie about how her death will affect her professional discipline, she imagines a feeding frenzy of her former students, who "would scramble madly for my position." To assuage their guilt, they would perform the expected part of the aggrieved, in a tribute that "would be short. But sweet. Published *and* perished." Kelekian, at the top of his discipline's food chain, works his junior fellows until, if they are fully with the program (as Jason is), they can dream only of "surviving" to run their own boot camps. Lost in all this reflexive striving for supremacy of a subject is a sense of their professions as humanizing gifts in the world; what is left is getting, or staying, ahead. Jason comes into Vivian's room for his latest data harvest, his rote "How are you feeling today?" met by a not-unwelcome silence, only to discover Vivian's corpse is no longer yielding data. He defaults to the team instinct to conserve the specimen, thus violating Vivian's express desire to Susie to "let it stop." The ensuing battle for Vivian's body waged in the isolation chamber is the closest Nichols' contemplative film comes to a moment of action. Jason tears open Vivian's gown, exposing her to the camera as she has not been exposed throughout the long, depicted ordeal of her treatment. He administers CPR and awaits the code team. Susie takes as her cause the rights of her dead patient and tries but fails to call off the code order. She finally, physically, gains Jason's attention, and he helplessly joins her in trying to stop the further invasion of the code team. Only one thing gets their attention: a doctor's career-determining confession that he's made a mistake. The leader of the code team (David Zayas) pauses at this rare admission of human frailty, and Susie's voice finally becomes hearable. Still, the team leader's response is instantly to revert to hierarchy: "Who the hell are *you*?" he brusquely demands. With all her dignity summoned against hegemonic practice, she identifies herself: "Sue Monahan, primary nurse." Jason is of no help to her, but she has the totemic power of Kelekian's signature on the DNR form, which she brandishes like a weapon. The code team angrily stands down. In Edson's play, Vivian rises at this point, enveloped in a flash of white light before the stage blackout, the soul's release from its mortal prison. In the film, Nichols and Bloom transition by dissolve from Vivian's expired form to a black-and-white photograph of Thompson as Vivian, in the full powers of her professional intelligence, as she recites a final time Donne's "Death Be Not Proud." Pride, it seems, must be devoured if Death is to be laid low: before Death is properly humbled on Donne's terms, Vivian Bearing must encounter her own limits. Ironically, only in relieving herself of the illusion of independent and isolated authority does she encounter something closer to true agency, the triumph of her spirit.

Having explored in *Wit* a work of theater with the intimacy and compressed intensity of a chamber ensemble, Nichols would next embark on a work of genuinely epic, operatic scale, the six-episode cycle of Tony Kushner's *Angels in America*. What the plays share in common is their visionary exploration of "the seemingly insuperable barriers separating life, death, and eternal life." In Nichols' hands, the critique of reified culture becomes a dialogue between the two films. Nurses are at the metaphysical center of therapeutic action in both films, serving as diplomatic agents between power and the powerless. As cast by Nichols, Susie in *Wit* and Belize in *Angels in America* are given signifying minority status via actors of color—Audra McDonald and Jeffrey Wright—further underscoring their traditional function in reified systems as marginal. Yet each asserts the moral conscience of his or her narrative, serving as the embodiment of transformative, redemptive possibility in the morass of human subjugation to hegemony. They are the heirs, in Nichols' oeuvre, of Bradley (played by the African-American actor Bill Nunn) in *Regarding Henry*, whose counsel to Henry Turner (Harrison Ford) long after Henry no longer needs physical rehabilitation is a declaration of war on all systems of objectification: "Don't listen to nobody trying to tell you who you are." Together Bradley, Susie, and Belize offer a vision of hegemony symbolically subverted by the traditionally powerless, and with Emily (Thompson) in *Angels in America*, they project the humanizing power of ministering earthly "angels." In a two-year sequence of releases for HBO that saw a major Hollywood director make a significant career shift using a new medium, *Wit* serves as the profound and moving overture to the grand scale Nichols would achieve in *Angels in America* on the themes of reification and redemption.

19

"Threshold of revelation"

Angels in America (2003)

"When I started to write these plays," comments Tony Kushner of *Millennium Approaches* and *Perestroika*, the two mammoth parts of his epic *Angels in America* (1993), "I wanted to attempt something of ambition and size even if that meant I might be accused of straying too close to ambition's ugly twin, pretentiousness."[1] He wrote the play in the last years of the 1980s, a time of seismic change in world history. "I think the play is about what was happening, about the end of containment as an ideology," he told Susan Cheever just before its debut on Broadway. "Containment is the idea that there is some sort of viral presence in the body or the body politic that has to be proscribed or isolated or crushed. Containment demonizes the other, whether it's Communism or AIDS or Jews. It's a politics that comes completely out of fear as opposed to out of hope."[2] In adapting Kushner's play into a six-part mini-series for HBO, Mike Nichols necessarily reduces some of the grand, spectacular artifice of the staged performance, replacing it with the special effects with which the modern cinematic audience has been spoiled; as Ken Nielsen, Daniel Mendelsohn, and others have pointed out, there is a majesty to the live illusion of an angel's appearance and levitating flight that the computer-aided effects available to the filmmakers can't quite duplicate, even as they seem to create more persuasive illusions.[3] Nichols and Kushner (who adapted his own work for the screen) also reduce the original play's political dimensions to a more human scale. Although the second half of *Angels* still references the political evolution of the Soviet Union in the title *Perestroika*, the first scene of that play, featuring "the World's Oldest Bolshevik," Aleksii Antedilluvianovich Prelapsarianov, is one of the few complete excisions of Kushner's adapted screen version. This is consistent with Nichols' sensibility as a filmmaker. His early counter-cultural touchstones, *The Graduate* and *Catch-22*, collectively make zero direct references to the seismic revolutionary dissent around them. While more overt in their political posturing, films like *Carnal Knowledge*, on the sexual revolution; *Day of the Dolphin*, on environmental exploitation (also a sub-theme of *Angels*); *Silkwood*, on the risks of nuclear power; and *Primary Colors*, on the problems of the democratic process itself, do not suffer from a reduction of their op-ed functionality. Rather, all these films (including *Angels*) dramatize the continued veracity of the 1960s insight that the personal is the political. Kushner says that his initial impulse in writing *Angels* was as a "response to the Reagan counterrevolution, which began in response to the great cultural revolution of the 1960's.'"[4] Despite its enormous scope, *Angels* on stage and on screen is about individuals under pressure, accepting or resisting transformation. Nichols told Kushner, "As far as I'm concerned, this is a story about intimate human relationships, and that's what I'm going after.'"[5] Three decades after the play's first public performances, John Lahr concludes, "The genius of the play lies in the marriage of Kushner's informed mind with his informed heart."[6] Such is the quality of Nichols' own genius, which made for a rare and potent pairing as they collaborated. The film ultimately broke the record, held since the 1970s by *Roots*, for the most Emmys awarded to a program in a single year. It won 11 of the 21 categories in which it had been nominated, including all the major awards. Meryl Streep said, "I think it's the crowning achievement of Mike's career."[7]

Nichols' career has been dominated by the power of the performances he commands. He has always attracted great actors, who have returned to him because of the work he coaxes from them (Streep's appearance in *Angels*, for instance, was her fourth with Nichols). His films are about people, not politics, aiming for the heart first to reach the head. Ironically, considering the size of the project, Nichols identifies his motivation in adapting *Angels* as a desire to do the "smaller things" that Edson's and Kushner's plays represent, narratives "you really can't expect to be blockbuster hits in theaters. Nobody is going to see *Angels in America* if it's six hours long, and it should be six hours long. And nobody's going to pile in to see *Wit* and watch this woman die. It's great to have an intelligent, if you will, elegant place to help you. I love television."[8] Kushner's first draft of the screenplay for Nichols attempted to open out the action to a cinematic mise-en-scène: "I added things in, trying to be responsible—opening it up and moving it around, and cars, and this and that. Mike pretty systematically went though all of that and said, 'I'm not really interested in this. Let's go back to the play and look at how you did it in the play.'"[9] As a six-episode film in Nichols' hands for HBO, *Angels* is an epic chamber study of three characters in advanced stages of illness—Prior Walter (Justin Kirk) and Roy Cohn (Al Pacino), who have AIDS, and Harper Pitt (Mary-Louise Parker), who has debilitating depression—all of whom become visionary seers as a consequence of their suffering; it's also a study of three characters in advances stages of denial (in addition, of course, to Roy and Harper)—Joe Pitt (Patrick Wilson), who is in the closet where his politics and religion have kept him; Louis Ironson (Ben Shenkman), who is out of the closet but unable to commit to the hard work of love; and Hannah Pitt (Meryl Streep), who may be as unwilling to consider the realities of her *own* sexuality as she is her son Joe's. This list of characters excludes one remaining major character, Belize (Jeffrey Wright), and one remaining major screen force, the Angel (Emma Thompson), the two most obvious angels of *Angels*. Belize is the registered nurse who cares for both Prior (out of love) and Roy (out of duty), "the story's earthbound ministering angel."[10] Thompson, like Streep, plays three roles in the Nichols production, but unlike Streep, who embodies Hannah as she labors towards enlightenment, Thompson's roles are static, secondary to the characters emerging around her. She plays the most obvious manifestation of the title, and yet her winged, celestial Angel is, though attention-grabbing,[11] decidedly an observer of the "great Work" which she heralds. The angels, Nichols and Kushner fervently argue, are not only among us, but in some cases *are* us, thanks to the redemption inherent in reified wisdom.

Indeed, each of Nichols' two celebrated films for HBO is, in addition to being an adaptation of a successful stage drama about death, an examination of how mercy is the most potent therapy available in situations of literal and existential life and death ("where love and justice finally meet," as Belize says, in "forgiveness"), and both offer extended scrutiny of health care on its front lines, among the nurses who tend the dying on their passage to the next world (or their return to this one). In *Wit*, Susie (Audra McDonald) is as mild and unprepossessing as her name, submissive to the systemic powers that be, until she finds the tension between caring compassionately for the patient while also following the dictates of her superiors too great. At such times, she counsels Vivian (Thompson) against the wisdom of an eminence like Dr. Kelekian (Christopher Lloyd), or reprimands a pompous Kelekian-in-training like Jason (Jonathan M. Woodward), whose bedside manner is held in store for the funding representatives—the people with whom he has a commodified future. In *Angels*, Belize is prepared to risk his professional reputation for the larger principle—affirming life— he has felt himself called to serve. This means he is prepared to claim and distribute illegally obtained drugs for dying friends; it also means that he dispenses mercy rather than justice to Roy, a man whose life is a violation of all Belize's own personal principles. *Wit* and *Angels* offer a vision of human redemption much broader than the health-care industry yet given metaphoric power within the aptly named confines of "intensive care."

As a stage play, *Angels in America*'s construction is remarkably cinematic, particularly adapting the "split scene" technique of two simultaneous or comparative actions (which happens in nearly every Act of the original play). "Some aspects are written so they're partly movie to begin with," says Nichols. "For instance, the two couples breaking up at the end of the second hour of the first half. These were already intercut [in the stage version]. But on the stage, the couple that didn't have the lights on them had to freeze and wait. Well, cutting back and forth is a little more suited to that kind of going back and forth."[12] Kushner was also influenced in his ensemble storytelling by the group narratives of Robert Altman, the first director with whom Kushner discussed a possible adaptation.[13] The most important formal convention of the play that Nichols and Kushner are careful to carry over into the filmed adaptation is the shape-shifting quality of certain performers. This convention is a much more routinely accepted practice of the stage than of cinema, and Nichols predictably reduces some of the double-duty of the actors to the overlaps that carry the most symbolic heft. (The one such instance of an actor's double-duty in the stage play of Edson's *Wit*, the roles of Dr. Kelekian and Vivian's father played by a single actor, are assigned to two men in Nichols' film version.[14]) Yet for Kushner, Nichols' insistence that the doubling (or tripling) of actor's roles needed to remain a sensational part of the film was the clearest indication that Nichols was the right person to work with: "It never occurred to me that [a film director] would do that. And I immediately thought, 'OK, this is the person that should make this.' It's celebrating the artificiality of the event."[15] The "artificiality" thus foregrounds the empathic "Great Work" of human imagination in understanding human suffering and creating a compassionate response.

In the stage play of *Angels*, for instance, the same actor who portrays Prior's hospital nurse, Emily, plays the Angel, and Nichols is right to hold onto this double-duty for Thompson. There is an inherent narrative logic to this versatility: Emily is, prior to Hannah Pitt's entrance into Prior Walter's life of affliction and abandonment, one of only two steadying, caring presences (the other, Belize, is so dourly opposed to Prior's visionary episodes that Prior unconsciously could not project Belize into such an image). His first visions of the Angel (before this there is only a Voice) come after his first emergency admission to the hospital, where Emily serves as his on-call caregiver (Louis has absconded and Belize must depart for the night); later, she is the one seeing to Prior's out-patient examinations (and speaking in tongues), and she is on call when Hannah brings him back to the hospital with his relapse. As in Nichols' preceding HBO film, *Wit*, there is no more crucial avatar of human mercy than the floor nurse of an ICU. In *Wit*, Susie is the sole of compassionate competence, her only agenda to care for her patient. It is, in the best sense, a vocation. Emily, like Susie, is doing her job—"doing good," with intelligence and grace in equal measure. It is little wonder, then, that when an Angel appears to Prior Walter in unconsciousness, she should appear in a hyper-glamorized variation (like Prior's projection of his own Norma Desmond queendom in his shared vision with Harper) of Emily's sensibly restrained handsomeness. Where Emily is crisply business-like in her conduct and no-nonsense in her self-presentation (no makeup, hair tied back neatly), the Angel is a *Vogue* magazine representation of female erotic power in sheer, clinging white gown and long, curled, windblown tresses. She is a vision at once terrible and desirable, and as she could not be Belize (who dismisses such visions out of hand), she also could not be, for instance, an eroticized version of Louis. Louis is anything but a ministering angel; the one time Louis appears in one of Prior's visions, he descends a Busby Berkeley stairway from the stars to dance with Prior, but the vision literally evaporates, leaving Prior in a post-hallucinatory heap on his apartment floor. Emily's persistence of caring makes her the steady image of the Angel.[16]

Similarly, Harper Pitt remains so besotted by Joe that, even after confronting the specter of his closeted gayness in the narrative's first dream sequence (the shared vision with Prior, who appears as nothing less than her post–Salt Lake stereotype of flaming homosexuality), Harper is unable to imagine herself out of the closet where Joe has hidden himself for so long. Mr. Lies (Jeffrey Wright, doing his own bit of virtuoso double-duty), her narcotic "travel agent," quarrels with her about the illogic of her Antarctic dream: "This is a retreat, a vacuum; its virtue is that it lacks everything: deep-freeze for feelings. You can be numb and safe here; that's what you came for. Respect the delicate ecology of your delusions." She circumvents his literal (no Eskimos in Antarctica) and emotional (no self-defeating, pain-inducing attachments, please) logic by imagining an Eskimo into the Antarctic whiteness— but the Eskimo she conjures is still Joe, played by Patrick Wilson wearing a billowing, Harper-stereotyped parka. Later, when she shelters with Hannah and is induced to tag along under Mother Pitt's watchful eye at the Mormon Visitors Center in Midtown, even (or perhaps especially) the "dummy" in the pioneer diorama has been manufactured by Nichols' production designers to look exactly like Joe. And as Harper is incapable of escaping Joe, Louis is incapable of escaping Prior; after abandoning his ailing partner at the hospital, he adjourns to Central Park's "Ramble" hoping for some eroticized punishment, which he encounters in the form of a leather-clad, bearded Justin Kirk, eager to dole out some role-played abuse.

The premises of *Angels* are largely based in such shape shifting, and thus there is a formal elegance to the functional flourishes of actors' multiple roles. The purest metaphorical association to be made in relation to the characters' shape shifting is to the homosexual closet. Early on, sitting together in a tony straight bar while Roy tries to woo Joe to Washington (and thus, inevitably, also to bed), Joe confesses how difficult it was for him in Salt Lake "[t]o pass." Roy's radar is instantly alerted to this coded language, and he repeats the word with sensual delicacy before asking, "Pass as what?" Joe, defaulting to cover, weighs his words carefully before replying, "As someone cheerful and strong." As he comes closer to approaching and even opening the closet door, Joe remains all but paralyzed by the consequences of such self-revelation. His Mormon upbringing has taught him this is a path to damnation; his father, now deceased, was incapable of loving him, we understand, because of his *tendencies*. Most immediately, such a revelation will explode Joe's illusion of a heterosexual marriage and jeopardize his bright political future in the Reaganized right. Louis Ironson has distanced himself from his Jewish family, as presumably (since we see or hear no reference to them) Prior Walter has distanced himself from the Mayflower Walters. Neither Prior nor Louis hides his sexual identity, but both live the ostracizing consequences of this identity, just as Joe fears he would have to if he stops trying to "pass."

If Kushner's gay characters constitute a continuum of Prior's prophecy of progress, or

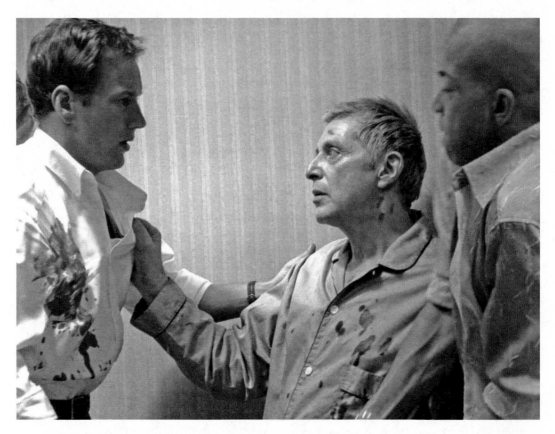

Infections, only some of which are biological, run rampant in *Angels in America*, set during the mid–1980s, the darkest days of the AIDS crisis. Roy Cohn (Al Pacino, center) is dying of AIDS, though his high-profile status as conservative ideologue and one-time consort of Joseph McCarthy makes this impossible for him to admit. In a scene of gothic horror, Roy's protégé, Joe Pitt (Patrick Wilson, left), comes to Roy to report the end of his own long campaign against his nature; Roy reacts so violently to Joe's coming out that he jerks the I.V. from his arm, spraying Joe and his nurse Belize (Jeffrey Wright) with infected blood.

ineluctable human "motion," Roy Cohn is of course the reactionary throwback, willing to lecture his long-time physician about why, despite serial treatment for homosexually-transmitted diseases, "Roy Cohn is not a homosexual." His speech at the end of episode one of Nichols' film (right down to the self-objectifying use of the third-person) is as baldly revealing a statement of the corrosive devastation of unredeemed reification as Nichols has ever recorded in a film. Joe comes next in the continuum: to Roy's death-bed horror, which becomes a literal horror scene of infected blood spurting onto the floor and Joe's shirt, Joe is able to speak his identity aloud, but is sent reeling back towards the closet by the confused ideology he and Roy share, the result of being mentored in intolerant fascism. Xenophopia is as rampant an infection in this scene as AIDS itself. When last glimpsed in Nichols' film, Joe is headed down into the subways of Moloch, in the shaming grip of what he still sees as his affliction. Though liberated, Louis remains trapped between great gusts of political abstraction and a desire to evade words entirely: "Words are the worst things," he says, seducing Joe. "Breathe. Smell. [...] Let's stop talking. Or if you have to talk, talk dirty." This is, decidedly, *not* a paraphrase of the Angel to both Prior and Hannah: "The Body is the Garden of the Soul." Implicit in Louis' urging is a desire to ignore, to *not know*; this is why, despite the floods of information and opinion he can pour forth at will, he can remain so uninformed, so ignorant of even those closest to him. He has no clue about Belize's romantic life, and no inkling that Joe has attached himself to Roy Cohn, Louis' self-described idea of "the worst human being who ever lived." He has no idea that his lover is directly responsible for writing "an important bit of legal fag-bashing" in a military case. Louis remains afraid of much *lived* truth, content to assemble what Belize calls his "Big Ideas" as a safely abstracted version of reality. Unlike Roy, Joe and Louis remain works very much in "progress," though in Kushner's lexicography, such a term is not without "hope," another of Kushner's most cherished words.

The continuum of reified "progress" thus yields Belize and Prior, the former lovers and forever friends, as the prototypes for the future of human tolerance. Belize is, in this context, the Realist and Prior the visionary Idealist. To Louis, Belize unwinds the synopsis of an imaginary "bestselling paperback novel" about American racism, *In Love with the Night Mysterious*, a condemnation of all the patronizing platitudes of the white hegemony. Belize is unconvinced by the prospect of systemic change. He anticipates no revolutions. Caught up in the pragmatism of his profession, he knows Louis can only love "America" from a distance, "too far off the earth to pick out the details," while he hates America: "It's just big ideas, and stories, and people dying, and people like you. [...] I *live* in America, Louis; that's hard enough. I don't have to love it. You do that." No one is more engaged in the hard work of day-to-day living than Belize, working his hospital shifts and then, in his down time, nursing his sick friends like Prior. Despite his apparent political despair, Belize evinces a love and compassion that exceeds the capacities of anyone but, perhaps, Hannah—and no one has sustained this fully realized life longer. Unlike Belize, Prior is given to prophetic optimism, born in defiance but borne forward in what he perceives by the film's epilogue to be both personal and *systemic* progress: "[W]e are not going away," he says of the AIDS generation at the narrative's coda by Central Park's Bethesda Fountain. "We won't die secret deaths anymore. The world only spins forward. We will be citizens. The time has come."

Of the two women Kushner includes among his seven major characters, both bear the patriarchal name of Pitt, an immediate mark of the objectified shape shifting imposed upon them by hegemonic dictates, yet both women by narrative's end have found reinvention easier than Joe, heir to Pitt patriarchy and, at least demographically, the most privileged of the three (via gender and education). Harper has tried to medicate herself into inner peace with her life: young, upwardly mobile, free of the rules of Salt Lake expectation (if not of its inculcation), but married to a gay man. Joe admires her for how "she was always wrong, always doing something wrong, like one step out of step. In Salt Lake City that stands out." One may infer that each was the other's ticket out of the stultification they'd inherited. Harper is content at first to live in the same profound denial as Joe, but she becomes increasingly convinced of the necessity of Truth, eventually stripping herself before Joe and demanding that he confess what she has always, instinctively known: that he sees (and thus feels) "nothing" when he looks at her. Compared to Joe's equally dramatic but ultimately empty episode at Jones Beach when he strips off his Mormon underwear (his protective "second skin" prophylaxis against the corrupting influences of the world) to proclaim his possessive love for Louis, Harper's act of stripping is a re-assumption of her true and best shape, while Joe's is an unmasking of his failure to commit to any identity unmediated by the desires and defaults of others. He can never quite glimpse himself in a mirror for all his anxious, restless searching for what others want to see and what he wants for them to see in him. (And when, fleetingly, he does truly see himself, most often with Harper or his mother, he is shamed into silence and recession.) Nichols and Kushner give us a final monologue with Harper on a journey, up near her beloved, endangered ozone, buoyant with hope and, for the first time, *self*-possession rather than possession by others.

Angels in America's most striking single transformation, however, in a narrative rife with shape-shifting metamorphoses, belongs to Nichols' favorite actress, Meryl Streep. If Thompson, so moving in *Wit*'s lead, is given the flashy pyrotechnics of the Angel, the steady empathy of nurse Emily, and the comic grotesquery of playing a homeless Bronx street person straight out of Beckett, Streep nonetheless does the heavier lifting. In embodying Rabbi Isidor Chemelwitz and Roy Cohn's nightmare of Ethel Rosenberg, she is nothing less than the voice of history, another harbinger, like the Angel, of Walter Benjamin's image of modernity as a "storm" of catastrophic "progress"[17]; but among the six significant characters the two women portray, none is more vital to the function of *Angels in America*'s drama than Hannah Pitt, who moves, by the accidents of grace and serendipitous duty, from dowdy prairie stolidity to stylish Manhattan sophistication and, more important, from cold alienation to warm compassion (and even, with the Angel, hot passion). As Nichols and Kushner are at pains to make clear, she always had these qualities within her. In essence, she becomes Meryl Streep before our eyes, the very best gift Nichols could imagine for a character.

Fisher argues that "*Angels in America* is most often identified as a gay play, and it is indeed a reflection of reinvigorated homosexual activism of the early AIDS era, but Kushner moves beyond the political liberation of gays and the crisis of AIDS toward an exploration of the boundaries of gender (one of the play's conceits is that all of its characters are acted by a corps of eight actors, with men playing women and women playing men in some cases)."[18] What Nichols sees beneath all this shape shifting in Kushner's script, what remained consistent from the gendered dilemmas to the ethnic, political, religious, and materialist anxieties of the stage play, is the consistent problem of objectified, categorical assignment of identity and subsequent behavior. Hegemonic control, labeled "power" by ideologies as polar in opposition as those of Roy Cohn and Louis Ironson, sets "the limits of tolerance" and thus assigns proscribed identities to those who acquiesce and those who rebel. The only effective recourse against such ingrained, systemic practice is the redemptive "hope" (as Prior terms it on several occasions) of the Truth, not Joe's shamed capitulation to a secret life like his mentor Roy, nor Hannah's old, pre-transformation philosophy: "with faith and time and hard work you do get to a point where the disappointment doesn't hurt so much, and it gets actually easier to live with. Quite easy. Which is, in its own way, a disappointment."

There is another way to transformation, *Angels* argues, difficult but not fraught with the mutilating violence of Harper's vision, talking with the Mormon mother of the diorama (in which the "something for real" she sees in how people change is "Just mangled guts, pretending"). There is a transformative power latent within the imagination, which, especially through the visions of Roy, Harper and Prior, takes on increasingly prophetic properties as the narrative unfolds. At first, as in Prior's and Harper's shared hallucinatory dream, imagination is simply a function of grasping what *is*; later, as their visions evolve, the imagination becomes the conduit of what can—perhaps even *will*—be. And so Prior, whose imagination has summoned an Angel to call him to the "Great Work," ends with both a benediction ("*More Life*") and an invocation ("The Great Work Begins"), directed not at any other character in the narrative but, via direct Brechtian address, to the camera and thus the audience, the film's mute, passive witnesses, asked now to forsake our muteness and passivity and to carry forward the "Great Work" of redemptive imagination into the real world in which we must, like Belize, *live*. The film thus stands as a grand, non-ironic answer to the rhetorical ironies of Nichols' most famous film, *The Graduate*, which offered no positive alternative to Benjamin and Elaine, its hapless hero and heroine, just a forlorn passivity and the director's prophetic pronouncement upon their inevitable surrender to commodified identity. *Angels* finds Nichols happily attuned to Kushner's evangelistic fervor, content to leave his trademark concluding narrative ironies embodied in the "works in progress" of Kushner's characters alone, not his point of view on them. What ambiguity remains is left to whether Harper and Prior, the film's two seers who address the camera, are reaching the reified but as-yet unredeemed, or ecstatically preaching to the choir.

* * *

The plot of *Angels in America* is so large and multi-layered that it ought to be unfolded and followed like a map, using character arcs as various routes. For the purposes of this study, the three visionaries (Prior, Harper, and Roy) will receive primary examination; Joe, Louis, Hannah, and Belize all merit substantial consideration as well. As in *Catch-22*, where much of what we see is Yossarian's fever-dream of an already absurd military system, the value of reviewing plot in *Angels* is to establish a baseline for understanding and interpreting what we see and hear.

In Kushner's original creation for the stage, *Angels in America* is a cycle of two sprawling, full-length, multi-narrative plays, the first of which, *Millennium Approaches*, unfolds in three acts whose internal scenic ordering Nichols and Kushner adhere to with few deviations in creating the first three of the six episodes of the filmed version, "organized around a series of abandonments and escapes."[19] The second play of the cycle, *Perestroika*, is comparatively much altered, with major scenes excised or revised, scenes re-sequenced, and some of the play's geopolitical resonances (as the second play's title had heralded) reduced or omitted.[20] *Perestroika*, unlike *Millennium Approaches*, was less neatly constructed into relatively equal Act-length units, and this necessitated many of the adjustments the filmmakers faced in attempting to render as literally faithful an adaptation as transtextuality permits, ultimately whittling the second play's five acts to three episodes, "organized around a series of unexpected scenes of forgiveness [...] meant to make us think about change and redemption."[21] Mendelsohn argues that the flaws of *Angels* are located in the second play, *Perestroika*, "because it has the much trickier job of putting something in the place of what 'Millennium Approaches' has swept away."[22] As we have seen in discussing the breadth of Nichols' career, his first phase was apt simply to demonstrate the failures of culture in negative satires that did not propose alternatives; as he became more desirous of proposing those alternatives (compassionate understanding and commitment to community and personal relationships in place of the consolations of material accumulation and the exercise of power) during his second phase, he became more and more susceptible to accusations of sentimentality (as Mendelsohn accuses Kushner[23]). James Fisher argues that, in fact, "Kushner darkens the tone in *Perestroika*,"[24] yet the ultimate intent is, as Kushner himself has labeled the play, comic: "*Perestroika* is essentially a comedy, in that issues are resolved, mostly peaceably; growth takes place and loss is, to a certain degree, countenanced."[25] Fisher concludes, "[A]t least some of its characters offer hope, imagining redemption through courage to abandon the cold comfort of familiar pain and outmoded beliefs, to cultivate forgiveness, to feel for fellow sufferers, and to develop a personal code of behavior based on compassion and a will to function in a strange new world."[26] Discussing what attracted him to the play, Nichols told *Interview*, "This was one of the rare plays, maybe the only play I've ever seen, in which acts of kindness were such a major event."[27] The idea was no doubt much on his mind because of his recent work with *Wit*, in which Vivian Bearing, stripped of her wit's defenses, says from the depths of her harrowing, "Now is a time for simplicity. Now is a time for, dare I say it, kindness."

Kushner was concerned that *Angels* retain its relevance despite the ten-year lapse between the original stage productions and the screen adaptation, given the changes in social fabric: "AIDS treatment became more efficient, the Cold War faded into memory and though often demonized during election campaigns in America gay men and lesbians slowly gained visibility in the legal system."[28] He needn't have worried. The play works as bracing recent history, "a searing indictment," according to Frank Rich, "of how the Reagan administration's long silence stoked the plague of AIDS in the 1980's,"[29] when 24,000 people died prior to Reagan's first public reference to the epidemic in 1987, six years into his presidency: Kushner's "message" was "that what the AIDS crisis was revealing wasn't a moral flaw on the part of gay men, as the conservatives running the country would have it, but rather a moral failing in America itself."[30] Yet the play also remains regrettably evergreen in dramatizing ongoing objectifying persecutions: "The category of the sodomite is still a social necessity," writes Richard Goldstein, "as the ferocious battle over gay marriage attests."[31] "[T]he millennium has come and the rights of gay citizens are still a work in progress," wrote John Lahr in 2010, during the Broadway revival of *Angels*.[32] Kushner himself has said, "'We have this idea that we cycle through political moments very rapidly [...] We're still living in the late '80s."[33] At bottom, the timelessness of the work is located in the primacy it places upon mercy over power: "It uses the basic tool of drama," says Kushner, "which is empathy and compassion, and says, 'This kind of suffering was the consequence of this kind of oppression.' After all, you can immediately sympathize with what Nora is going through in [Ibsen's] 'A Doll's House.' You don't need to be in a pre-feminist era. You get it because the play makes you get it."[34]

Prior Walter. The first of the narrative's characters to whom we're introduced in Nichols' film are Prior Walter and Louis Ironson, who have been romantic partners for several years when two seismic events trigger the characters' initial reactions and thus, the plot. Louis, a well-informed but professionally undistinguished aide in the district court house, comes from a very traditional Jewish family whose matriarch, Louis' grandmother, has just died. Fisher presents "Sarah Ironson's passing as a representation of the death of the modern American past"; he argues that the main subtext of the rabbi's eulogy is "[c]hastising his listeners for ignoring the lessons of the past,"[35] the first of many demonstrations of the futility of failing to heed reified wisdom. By dint of his sexual orientation, Louis has long been estranged from his family, including his grandmother, and at her funeral sits with Prior apart from the other mourners. (One gets the sense that, while his father shows an uneasy reticence around his son, Louis is largely responsible for his estrangement: the women of the family, presumably his mother and sisters, implore him after the memorial service to proceed with them to the interment.) Prior is the estranged scion of a venerable northeastern family, subsisting on a small family trust.[36] He injudiciously (but with maximum drama) chooses the moments after Louis' grandmother's funeral service to tell Louis he has begun to manifest Karposi's sarcoma, or K.S., lesions associated with the AIDS virus (and which, in the heightened emotional urgency of Prior's references may be misheard, appropriately enough, as the word "chaos"). "I'm going to die," he tells Louis, while all around them, New York at the edge of Central Park teems with life. Alarmed, Louis wants to know why Prior hasn't told him sooner, and Prior explains that he was afraid Louis would leave him, a well-grounded fear. For now, Louis only leaves him to run for the bus that will take him to the cemetery.

Prior has a battery of medicines, both to promote health and decrease pain, and this potent cocktail begins to brew a sequence of increasingly grandiose visions in his head, the first of which is visited upon him alone in his apartment, presumably while Louis is still away with his family. In his dream/hallucination, he is far more stereotypically a "queen" than he presents in his waking life (we learn that he and a former lover, Belize, were drag queens, but while neither is in the least apologetic about lifestyle, neither is quite so flamboyant either). In the dream, Prior is at a cosmetic vanity suite worthy of Norma Desmond in *Sunset Boulevard* (Billy Wilder, 1950), and indeed, the sequence, rendered in luminous black-and-white on an expressionistically gothic set, plays as Prior's self-projection into Wilder's world of gothic silent-movie phantasms. Prior is interrupted at his primping by the arrival of Harper Pitt. It's important to recognize that both participants are at their most glamorous in this scene, and that the shared episode is a "shared vision." Harper has already been introduced to us as the unhappy wife of a closeted gay man climbing the ladder of American influence; she is nearing a crisis point as momentous as Prior's, and like Prior, ingests significant quantities of pharmaceuticals—in her case, psychotropic therapy for her depression.

An important point to establish in reading any Mike Nichols narrative is the point of view that controls our access to information about the characters and their reality. As we have seen in *The Graduate*, for instance, point of view promotes the prejudices and distortions implicit in Benjamin's perspective while also ironizing that perspective, so that we see Benjamin as self-serving, self-pitying, and largely passive. Similarly, in *Postcards from the Edge*, Suzanne's personal collapse leaves her—and us—struggling to distinguish among on-screen performance, off-screen social performativity, and more dramatic bursts of drug-addled psychosis. There are good reasons to understand *Angels* as "belonging," first and foremost, to Prior Walter. His character is on screen in the film's opening and closing scenes, and at the closing, he appears to be orchestrating the concluding action by coaxing other characters to speak, as he does, to the camera, to us. He literally has the film's last word. Yet Harper should not be ignored as a second primary perspective in the film, as she is the other character who initiates substantial direct address to the camera; indeed, the harmonic optimism Harper and Prior both give voice to in their respective final scenes addressed to the audience counterbalances the sense of alienated devastation each feels in the film's opening scenes, and which precipitates their joint hallucination. (Roy, the film's third prophet, also briefly—obscenely—addresses the camera.) Yet the very artificiality of a joint hallucination shared by two central characters who have never met and who will never meet (in the original play, they meet twice more in shared hallucinations, once at the Mormon Visitors Center and once in heaven) asserts an omniscient other whom we can characterize as authorial. This dream meeting between the two central characters who don't have any plot-based contact with each other is a confection of Kushner's, and it suggests that, beyond the surrealism the narrative routinely inserts within its realistic slice-of-life rendering of America in the early years of the AIDS epidemic, Kushner comments on his own work: the surreal joint hallucination is the film's earliest "threshold of revelation," in which what is revealed is the alliance of the two most important characters who never otherwise overlap, an alliance less about their connection to each other than about their connection to the authorial point of view in *Angels*.

Actually, each initially rejects the other's "revelation": Harper's hallucination reveals to her, through "Prior," that her husband Joe (Patrick Wilson) is gay, while Prior's hallucination reveals, through "Harper," that, "deep inside you, there's a part of you, the most inner part, entirely free of disease." This is a message he will need to cling to as he descends, since Louis continues to recoil from his illness. As the second episode opens, Prior has a physical crisis that lands him in the hospital, and Louis finally abandons him to the care of paid professionals like Emily (Thompson's first appearance), so crisply efficient and so thoroughly unimpressed by his genealogical bona fides. To Emily, Prior is just another dying man—nothing more, but more important, nothing less. Belize comes to visit and to assume the role of primary emotional support that Louis has vacated, and Prior confesses that the drugs have him hearing voices that he won't have Belize report, since "It's all that's keeping me alive." After Belize leaves, we hear the voice as well, promising further revelations of "A marvelous work and a wonder we undertake." His condition stabilized, Prior returns home, where he dumps Louis' photo and is visited by the ghosts of two "prior" Walters, ancient ancestors each of whom has died of his own era's plague, though they distinguish Prior's plague as the consequence of "venery." At this point in the narrative, Prior rarely has a scene unpunctuated by surreal vision; on his next routine check-up as Emily's outpatient, she lays her hands on him and he gazes up at her, absorbing her cool manner and handsome features, then she begins to speak in tongues, and the floor of the examination room splits open to reveal a celestial book, flaming on a pedestal. This moment is Prior's first equation of his muse with his vision. Back at home as *Millennium Approaches* ends in the third episode of Nichols' film, Prior climbs into bed, exhausted by the hospital visit but even more by the weight of his visions, which culminate in the scene in which, as he throbs under the effects of the medicine, the Angel (Emma Thompson) first appears, descending through the ceiling that has burst open, proclaiming him a "Prophet" and announcing, "The Great Work begins."

As *Perestroika* opens, Prior awakens from this extended vision, physically, emotionally, even sexually spent (he's had a nocturnal emission, tactile evidence for Prior of the vision's "reality"). The next time he is with Belize (at a drag queen's funeral, presumably from AIDS), he confesses to Belize his conviction that his dream "really happened." He unfolds the tale in the manner of an ancient mariner, and Belize, listening empathically but incredulously, attempts a medical explanation. "This is just you, Prior, afraid of what's coming, afraid of time. You want to go backwards so bad you call down 'an angel.' [...] There's no angel." Prior has described to Belize the visitation of an angel who refers to herself in quadruplicate as "I I I I," an allusion to the multiple, shape-shifting identities *Angels* offers the audience diegetically in, for instance, Prior imaginatively transforming his hyper-competent nurse, Emily, into a celestial herald of the truths about himself and his culture he knows, underneath all, to be self-evident (like Harper's acknowledgment that, in his "most inner part," he is entirely whole). In addition, the Angel's multiplied identity suggests the dynamic nature of drama itself, as Kushner's characters morph in unpredictable ways that surprise them (as in, particularly, the alchemical transformations in both characters after Prior first encounters Hannah Pitt at the Mormon Visitors Center). In Prior's dream, he wrestles philosophically with the Angel, refusing to "submit to the will of heaven," instead causing "revision in the text" through exercise of his will. The Angel and Prior are joined in the air in an ecstatic revelation (the climactic moment in Prior's wet dream) that the Angel sums as, "The Body is the Garden of the Soul." The Angel commands Prior as Prophet to urge the human race to "stop moving," her allusion to "Sleeping Creation's Potential for Change," again foregrounding the prominence of human plasticity. As Prior ends his recounting to Belize, he describes a last tender exchange with the Angel, in which she refers to him as "Jonah," the most unwilling of the Hebrew prophets, and promises to remain constant even if that involves flexibility of her own: "Hiding from me one place you will find me in another." (This is a fair paraphrase of the plot of Margaret Wise Brown's children's book, *The Runaway Bunny*, which Margaret Edson works into the last moments of Vivian Bearing's life in *Wit*, and which Vivian's vision of her professor deems "A little allegory of the soul." Like Vivian, Prior is near death's door and doing soul-work.) The Angel equates Prior's imagination with empathy, a central characteristic of Kushner's vision of full humanity: "You know Me, Prophet: Your battered heart, bleeding life in the universe of wounds." In essence, she has identified herself as the manifestation of his "most inner part," which Harper has already assured him remains pure of disease, and this is why we must sympathize with Prior when he rejects Belize's perfectly accurate but non-visionary interpretation of the "Angel": This *is* indeed "just" Prior, but it is Prior's full flowering from the understandable terror and self-pity of an AIDS death-sentence to a prophetic vision of an enlightened culture where disease is treatable and difference not merely tolerated but accepted.

Prior takes to dressing in a monk's cowl, his "Prophet" garb. Louis asks to meet, and in Washington Square, confesses he's seeing Joe, a "sensitive gay Republican lawyer," for "companionship." Prior tells him not to come back until he has "visible" evidence of suffering—otherwise it's just "the idea of crying [... o]r the idea of love." Prior begins stalking Joe, and confronts him incoherently in Joe's office in the courthouse. His venting fails to cure his obsession, however, and he tails Joe to the Mormon Visitors Center where Joe checks in with his mother, Hannah, who has been volunteering there after her arrival from Utah. Once Joe leaves, Prior accosts him in much the same manner as he'd attacked Joe, but his diminished physical strength coincides with his lost appetite for "haunting" the Pitts. He collapses, feverish, in Hannah's arms, and she gets him into a taxi and back to Emily at the hospital. He finds himself talking to Hannah about his vision of the Angel, and she relates it to her Mormon knowledge of biblical visions and the experience of Joseph Smith, whose "great need of understanding" created the vision of the angel, which, she adds, "was real." Like Belize, she seeks a conclusion about the Angel that accords with lived experience: An angel is just a belief, with wings and arms that can carry you. It's naught to be afraid of. And if it can't hold you up, seek for something new."

Prior asks Hannah to stay, surprising them both, and so she is there in his hospital room when the Angel pierces the ceiling, no longer clad in her customary white. As Prior had once shared an hallucination with Harper Pitt, he now shares one with Hannah, who shrieks in terror at the Angel's entrance; her only advice for Prior is from Genesis 32:26: he should demand, while wrestling with the Angel, "I will not let thee go except thou bless me.'" Wrestled to a draw, the Angel produces a celestial ladder, which Prior climbs to heaven, leaving Hannah alone with the Angel and her own threshold of revelation. Heaven, as Prior and Belize (summarizing it for Roy Cohn) have both imagined it, shares characteristics with San Francisco (the Golden Gate Bridge is prominent), though filming at Hadrian's Villa in Tivoli, Italy, creates an impression of ruined classical grandeur, and the surcease of time—the Angels of the Council of Continental Principalities suggest that Prior rest in "the Tome of immobility, of respite, of cessation." Their siren song, in other words, is the end of a struggle: Death. Prior rejects the temptations of their counsel and instead, knowing the consequences of his choice, demands "more life."

In one of the most ingenious visual moments in the film, Prior wades through the iconic long pool at Hadrian's Villa, near one end of which awaits his hospital bed. When he stretches himself upon it, the non-diegetic soundtrack music is replaced by diegetic labored breathing and the beeps and whirs of medical equipment. He awakes, having survived his infection's worst night, bathed in sweat, his fever broken. Belize dozes in the chair beside the bed; Hannah has taken a bathroom break; Emily is delighted by his recovery; Louis arrives, visibly bruised by a contentious breakup with Joe, and asks to be taken back. While Prior embraces him in forgiveness, he simultaneously refuses Louis' entreaty. When last we see Prior, it is four years later, in 1990, and he is with his friends Belize, Hannah, and Louis on his birthday; they have agreed to meet at his "favorite place in New York City—no, in the whole universe, the parts I've seen": the Bethesda Fountain in Central Park, overseen by the Angel that has featured prominently in the titles sequence to each of the film's six episodes. Prior clings stubbornly, reverently to life, though hobbled to dependence on a cane and eyeglasses. His final prophecy is Kushner's: "We will be citizens," followed by a final benediction upon us, "*More Life*," capped by an exhortation: "The Great Work begins."

Harper Pitt. Harper Pitt also has the opportunity to prophesy as the result of her visions. Her journey is, if anything, more dramatic than Prior's. A wayward Mormon, Harper has presumably married as a means of escape from the stultifying legalism and insularity of devout Mormon life. She and Joe have an apartment in Brooklyn, in which she hides all day in a tranquilized haze, fearing men with knives in the bedroom and waiting for Joe to come home and grant her a "buddy kiss," their non-erotic method of greeting each other within the role-play of husband and wife. Alone, she gets tips on pleasing her man from Dr. Ruth's syndicated sex-talk radio show and talks to Mr. Lies, a smooth-operating "travel agent" who disappears whenever Joe arrives home from one of his "long walks." Joe has been the recipient of a job offer to work in the Justice Department, made in proxy by Roy Cohn, which would necessitate a move to Washington, but Harper balks, claiming they're "happy enough. Pretend-happy." They bicker about who's to blame for their obvious unhappiness, and Joe is unreceptive when she attempts to apply her newfound knowledge from Dr. Ruth; they settle for a "buddy kiss." This latest unhappiness leads to Harper's increased pill popping, and thus to her shared hallucination with Prior in which she first confronts the specter that her husband is a "homo" (less Prior's default diction than Harper's). When next we see her with Joe, he's been "out" again until late, and she has purposely burnt his dinner in reprisal. She badgers him but can't quite confront him until he badgers her: "Are you a homo?" she says, using the same word she'd imagined Prior using in their shared hallucination; Joe half-heartedly continues to observe the formalities of denying the truth and urges that they pray for strength. He accuses her of speaking the truth as the agent of his destruction; she claims to be pregnant, which Joe grasps at hopefully as an emblem of his "normalcy," and she descends a spiral into an increasingly disorienting altered state. She wants Joe to leave, and when he insists he won't, because he believes remaining with her is the key to retaining the appearance of normalcy, Harper calls for Mr. Lies and disappears, via the refrigerator, into the surreal hallucinatory wastes of "Antarctica."

As presented in the film, Antarctica is an obviously unreal location, a barely disguised stage set filled with half-digested stereotypes of what Antarctica might be. Mr. Lies explains her current circumstance as "a retreat, a vacuum; its virtue is that it lacks everything: deep-freeze for feelings." Yet against all the protestations of his logic, she makes an Eskimo appear beyond his indigenous territory to be her mate and make babies. The Eskimo is Joe, and she wanders off after him, much to Mr. Lies' exasperation. Later, she returns to Mr. Lies with a blue spruce tree she has gnawed down "like a beaver" and wants to burn for warmth; Joe the Eskimo returns to tell her he's having a "scary-fun [...] adventure" that he doesn't want her to see. We discover the literal depths of Harper's delusion when she's arrested in Brooklyn with a tree stolen from the Botanical Gardens Arboretum. Her mother-in-law Hannah, who has just arrived in New York to confront her son about his drunken admission that he is gay, collects her at the precinct and brings her home to the apartment in Brooklyn. After she begins volunteering at the Mormon Visitors Center, Hannah brings Harper with her to work, where Harper sits in the empty auditorium eating junk food and contemplating the next objects of her hallucinatory imagination: the diorama of the Mormon pioneers. An exhibit of dressed dummies grouped as a family in a covered wagon serves as the visual aid to the center's dramatization of the arduous journey west towards freedom. She notes an "incredible resemblance" between Joe and the "husband dummy" in the diorama and waits for the "mute wife" to speak; when the wife finally does, she dismisses Harper's polite cliché of a question and demands to know what truly preoccupies Harper, leading to a purposeful discussion of how people change. The wife describes a horrific divine intervention by a "huge filthy hand" that splits people open and yanks out innards, after which "[i]t's up to you to do the stitching." Harper nods and finishes for the wife: "And then get up and walk around. Just mangled guts, pretending."[37]

Harper becomes increasingly self-possessed and lucid from this point forward: no more over-reliance on pharmaceutical escape (thus no more Mr. Lies, Eskimos, or psychotic incidents with coniferous trees). Hannah tries to give her a pep talk about resignation to "disappointment" that undercuts itself, leaving Harper to conclude "[a]nything can happen. Any awful thing." Joe finds her up on the roof of their apartment. The inference is available that she has been contemplating "the end of the world" as represented by an end to her life, via a single step out into the air. She intones a doomsday litany to Joe, who takes her home to bed for make-up sex that, for the last time, goes disastrously wrong and becomes break-up sex. He announces he's going out, "to get some stuff I left behind"—still talking in code about who he is. She confronts him as he dresses, dropping the bed sheet and demanding he look at her and say what he sees. Badgered into a response, he finally admits, carelessly, "Nothing," and, then, seeing its truth, says with greater conviction, "Nothing. I see nothing." This finally cures Harper. She thanks him "finally," for "the truth." Good to his word, he goes "out," and when he returns after the devastating break-up with Louis, she hands him her pill bottle and demands his credit card until she's established herself elsewhere. When last we see her, she's flying to San Francisco and relating a dream in which the ruined ozone layer she's been fretting about throughout the film has been repaired by the bond of "a great net of souls" rising from the earth, who share in common their deaths after outrageous suffering. She pronounces life to be "a kind of painful progress."

Roy Cohn. The third in *Angels in America*'s troika of visionaries is Roy Cohn, described by Kushner in his notes for the original play as "a New York lawyer and unofficial power broker"[38] whose depiction, while based in "the historical record," is nonetheless an act of Kushner's imagination. Kushner's Roy Cohn is a volcanic presence in the film. As the film opens, Roy is intent on luring Joe, a bright, handsome, malleable, closeted attorney, to Washington to be his man in the Justice Department, part of Roy's unofficial right-wing insurgency abetted by the Reagan administration. All his wheedling of Joe has an overt object (a Machiavellian strategy to control Joe so that Joe can influence Roy's jeopardized standing with the New York Bar Association), but it also has a subtextual goal (homosexual procurement). Joe is so deeply in the closet that he attaches an avuncular care to Roy's ardency. Roy is frustrated that Joe hesitates; Joe's wife, Harper, must be consulted before he makes any decision. Joe, as a committed Mormon, is also made uncomfortable by Roy's manner, which is pyrotechnical in its foul-mouthed blasphemy while working the touchpad of his office telephone, greasing the political skids. When next we see him, Roy is in consultation with his long-time personal physician, Henry (James Cromwell). Like Prior, Roy manifests the K.S. lesions, prophets of the AIDS virus. While Henry attempts to address possible therapeutic steps with Roy, Roy lectures Henry about "clout," which Roy possesses—only because he has never permitted his social identification as a gay man. He insists on a label as a man suffering from "liver cancer," not AIDS, and threatens to ruin Henry unless he accepts this as the official diagnosis. "Kushner's conception of Roy as the symbol of bad faith at the top of the American power structure suggests that his corruption and hypocrisy ultimately infect society as a whole, as AIDS infects him."[39]

Roy continues his wooing of Joe, encouraging him to turn his marriage over to Roy, " the best divorce lawyer in the business," and playing his "cancer" card as a means of eliciting a deal-sealing sympathy. After learning of Joe's vulnerability as a result of an unloving military father, Roy unleashes his philosophy of life as "full of horror" and urges Joe to "let nothing stand in your way," citing his own mentors, "powerful, powerful men. Walter Winchell, Edgar Hoover, Joe McCarthy most of all." (Working for McCarthy, Roy was instrumental in the deaths of Julius and Ethel Rosenberg; he admits to Joe that he tampered with the trial judge via ex parte communication every night on the telephone.) Continuing his recruitment, Roy takes Joe to dinner with Martin Heller (Brian Markinson, in his fourth of five small character parts played for Nichols), another eager conservative bureaucrat Roy has anointed while he was on the way up. Roy's commanding relationship to Martin (he receives a back rub from Martin in a crowded Manhattan restaurant) forecasts Joe's own future role. The conversation reveals Martin's willingness to perform dirty legal tricks for Ed Meese in the Justice Department; dismissing Martin, Roy makes explicit his political interest in Joe: he expects Joe to perform dirty legal tricks for Roy, specifically tampering with and fixing the investigation leading towards Roy's disbarment.

After time to think it over, Joe comes to Roy's brownstone to turn down the job offer to work for the Justice Department. Roy, by now a very sick man on the precipice of his final hospital stay, summons all his vitriol to insult Joe, nearly goading Joe into hitting him before Joe runs away. Collapsed in professional and physical ruin, Roy is visited for the first time in the film (though his familiarity suggests it is not the first time in his life) by the ghost of Ethel Rosenberg (also played by Streep), who passes through a solid door to sit in a living-room chair. Her death is on his hands; it has also made his name, given him "clout." He is defiant. To Ethel, to the camera, hence to the world, he assumes a posture of adversarial confrontation, flipping us the bird and insisting he is "not afraid." Ethel delivers to Roy the same message Prior's Angel delivered: "History is about to crack wide open. *Millennium approaches.*"

Roy has been hospitalized by the beginning of Part Two of the film, *Perestroika*, and Belize is doing the thankless work of caring for him. Roy has pulled strings to get in on an experimental drug trial (AZT), and he introduces himself to Belize with an extraordinary string of racial invective calculated to show Belize "who's boss." Yet, perhaps because he understands Roy's fear as a gay man entering the final battle with AIDS, Belize offers Roy two crucial pieces of advice about his treatment: to forego radiation therapy to maintain his T-cell count, and to pull any further strings he has to get the "real drug," not the placebo, in the study's "double blind" methodology. Roy recognizes Belize's disdain, but takes the advice, calls Martin, and gets his own private stash of AZT, which he keeps locked in a refrigerator in his room (wearing the key on a necklace). Ethel makes frequent visits to this room, to update Roy on the "disbarment committee meetings" convening in Yonkers (without Joe Pitt to fix things).

Ethel's presence is directly correlated to Roy's lucidity: like Prior and Harper, Roy is the other character in *Angels* on a heavy pharmaceutical regimen, one that, for Roy, eventually is dominated by morphine. In Roy's last days, Ethel is an avenging dark angel, while Belize is a reluctant angel of solace and mercy, even if Roy refers to him as his "negation." Roy's death scene begins with Ethel announcing Roy has been disbarred; he had hoped to die still a member of "the only club I ever wanted to belong to." Ethel (Roy's hallucination) confesses to vacillating between forgiveness and vengeance, though she appears to "take pleasure" in Roy's "misery." Roy feigns—in his delirium—a disoriented confusion of Ethel with his mother, and coaxes a sympathetic Yiddish lullaby from her before claiming in triumph that he has finally made "Ethel Rosenberg sing." His punning allusion to confession is his final burst of energy before he dies. After his death, Belize steals the key from around Roy's neck and asks Louis to mule the drugs out of the hospital for dissemination to Belize's less-fortunate friends, like Prior, who are not part of the tiny AZT trial. But he also has Louis pray the Kaddish for Roy; the ghost of Ethel Rosenberg, and of the past that lingers in Louis via women like his dead grandmother, is so palpable a presence in the room that it helps Louis, the most secular of Jews, to recall the words.

Joe Pitt. Each of the three non-visionary primary characters—Joe, Louis, and Hannah—is offered the opportunity to grow during the course of the film; the fact that Louis and Hannah appear as part of Prior's inner circle of friends in the film's epilogue indicates that they have responded positively to what life has offered them, while Joe remains lost. Joe begins the narrative as a swirl of contradictions: a married man in the closet; a deeply religious Mormon convinced by the conflict between his beliefs and desires that he is outside God's will; a fervid conservative who persecutes the poor and disenfranchised via the law, even as he himself feels increasingly alienated from the platform of his political party because of his sexual orientation. Offered a job by Roy, a right-wing icon of Joe's, he finds himself unable to accept the position because of his wife's depressive dysfunction and his dawning sense of Roy's spiritual bankruptcy. As his marriage crumbles, Joe has a chance meeting in a court-house men's room with Louis, who is weeping for Prior's illness and his own weakness as a supporting partner. The two are immediately attracted to each other, though Joe can't fully understand the attraction, and Louis toys with him in the guise of political banter. Joe has taken to Central Park's "Ramble," a gay stroll-zone, though as yet only to window-shop. On one such late-night cruise, he drunkenly calls his mother Hannah in Utah to confess he's gay. Kushner plumbed his own past for the emotional extremities of this scene:

> After four years in the closet as an undergraduate and another three years of hiding a secret sex life, Mr. Kushner went to a phone booth at the corner of Seventh Street and Second Avenue in Manhattan to call his mother and tell her he was gay. Mr. Kushner's mother burst into tears. "I told her to stop," he remembers, "and I wrote them the angry letter that you write." Eventually his parents came to terms with his sexual orientation, leaving him to wrestle with what it means to be gay in America.[40]

Hannah coldly refuses to hear what Joe is trying to tell her from his great geographical and psychosexual remove; she instead condemns his drinking. She also vows to come east immediately. When Louis and Joe next chance to meet, on a bench outside the courthouse at lunchtime, each has been further reduced by his personal failure in commitment to a love relationship, and they warily begin to express themselves to one another. Joe is eating piles of vendor food and chugging antacid liquid for what will become his bleeding ulcer. Learning of Roy's hopes that Joe can be his political fixer and that Roy illegally influenced the Rosenberg trial, Joe declines the job offer from Roy. Roy taunts Joe nearly to violence. He runs off, stalks Louis to the Ramble, and allows himself to be picked up.

The two begin a purely carnal relationship without delving for an instant beneath the skin, into each other's inner lives, which is how Louis is unaware of the reactionary conservatism of Joe's politics. Joe comes to believe he is passionately in love with Louis, which Louis dismisses as "the gay-virgin thing," until Joe, on a wintry day at Jones Beach, uses the object lesson of stripping himself naked—even his "Mormon underwear"—to demonstrate he is "flayed" of his past. He espouses a philosophy much like Roy's, urging Louis to get out from under the weight of Prior's illness and pursue his own desires. Just as the philosophy, in its naked self-interest, drove Joe away from Roy, so it does to Louis, who has already decided he must see Prior again. Joe, convinced he's finally found himself, goes to see Roy in the hospital, knowing Roy will understand, since he now understands that Roy, too, is gay. He tells Roy he has left Harper and is living with a man, and Roy in disgust commands him to resume his marriage, extricate himself from his other entanglements, and never "talk to me about it. Ever again." It is Joe's last communication with Roy in the film (the play allows a final haunting of Joe by Roy, in which Roy leaves Joe with the thought, "You'll find, my friend, that what you love will take you places you never dreamed you'd go"[41]). Joe spends the last episode of *Angels* wandering the poles—innate and constructed—of his sexual identity. Harper frankly confronts him, stripping herself before him the same way he laid himself bare for Louis. She recognizes in his recoil from her naked beauty "The Truth" of their illusory marriage, and Joe leaves, "to get some stuff I left behind." (There is no sense by the film's end that he has found what he went out to retrieve.) He attempts to return to Louis, who has finally done his research on Joe, and who provokes Joe into beating him up as Louis banishes him forever. Joe does in fact return again to Harper, his "good heart." While he has "changed," he doesn't yet understand how, and he begs her not to leave him. "Only you love me," he tells her, "out of everyone in the world." But Harper is finally past Joe; she takes his credit card and leaves him her pills. We glimpse one last time, with Hannah, a chance meeting on a Brooklyn street corner where a chorus sings "Shall We Gather at the River?" and it appears Hannah is trying to prove him wrong, to show that someone still loves him; but it also appears Joe in his shame may not be ready yet to acknowledge this.

Louis Ironson. Louis, unlike Joe, is not ambivalent about his orientation, only about commitment. He rejects Prior because the work of supporting a dying loved one is too immersed in the real—the sights and smells of AIDS. When he leaves Prior at the hospital, he goes to the Ramble and picks up a leather-clad man who looks, despite his rough-trade ensemble, like Prior. Louis can't fail to see his lover's face as he betrays him, and he demands to be punished. He moves out of Prior's apartment and into a small hole in the wall, all he can afford on his menial salary, and when Joe follows him onto the Ramble, Louis takes him home and seduces him with patter about smell and taste as the most erotic senses (the very ones he could no longer bear to direct at Prior). Louis meets several times with Belize during his estrangement from Prior to try to work through what's happening to him and to find out how Prior is doing, but these meetings go poorly for Louis: Belize dislikes Louis because he's a pompous windbag, an unintentional racist, and a traitor to Belize's dear friend, and he subjects Louis to withering critiques that Louis accepts as his due. Louis eventually coaxes Prior into meeting him in Washington Square, but Prior only flagellates him, challenging Louis not to return without evidence of his suffering. Louis' policy of not talking with Joe about who they are and what they want from their relationship backfires: after Belize discovers Joe visiting Roy and identifies him as the man who stole Louis from Prior, Belize tells Louis who Joe really is, his final and most devastating critique. In denial because Joe seems so "nice," Louis nonetheless researches Joe and discovers he has legally defended the exploitation or persecution of the vulnerable (children, gays), and that he is, at the very least, the political bedfellow of Roy Cohn. He goads Joe not only into a breakup but into a beating he can take back to Prior as literal evidence of his suffering. Significantly, Prior embraces and forgives him while also, careful of his heart, refusing to forget what Louis has done. (Something similarly complex happens between Louis over Roy's dead body: Louis aids in stealing all the AZT Roy will no longer need, but also performs the Kaddish for the man he has called "the polestar of human evil.") The last image of Louis is in the Park four years later, with three friends—Hannah, Belize, and Prior—all of whom could bear a grudge but don't, instead good-naturedly accepting what appear to be his overbearingly permanent yet forgivable faults.

Hannah Pitt. Neither Hannah nor Belize enters the film until the second episode (though we have of course seen both actors in episode one: Streep is the aged rabbi at the funeral, and Wright is Mr. Lies). They enter the film from vastly different ideological, demographic, and personality types, but what drives them into the narrative is the same: each has responded to the call of a desperate loved one. Joe has drunkenly called his mother from Central Park to confess his feared sexual orientation, while Prior has called Belize from the hospital because Louis has abandoned him there. Hannah arrives in New York from Salt Lake City with unwieldy baggage—two enormous suitcases—and promptly takes the wrong bus, all the way to the Bronx, where she must coax sense from a crazed street person (Thompson) in a vacant lot to tell her where she is and give her directions to the Mormon Visitors Center, since the vagrant has no idea how to reach Brooklyn. She finds her family's life in shambles, her son disappearing for days at a time, her daughter-in-law dazed and confused by depression and medication. Hannah is hopeless at ministering to either of them and also pronounces herself "useless" to the Visitors Center, where she volunteers. However, when Prior stalks Joe to Hannah and then bursts in to rant at her about her son, she finds, of all things, that she is a source of solace and strength to this angry, sick man. Together they endure the terrible, wonderful visitation of the Angel to Prior's hospital room, where she is not simply a passive witness to Prior's vision; the Angel is also there to address her. After Prior ascends the celestial ladder, the Angel remains behind, an ultra-glamorous vision that enchants Hannah and induces an orgasmic embrace. As with Prior, the Angel reminds Hannah "[t]he Body is the Garden of the Soul." When Prior recovers from his fever, Hannah is there with Belize. She excuses herself, confessing to having had "the most *peculiar* dream," but promises to return; she becomes one of Prior's best friends, one of the three people with whom he wants to spend his birthdays. She has blossomed from dowdy Utahn to stylish Manhattanite.

Norman Arriaga, aka Belize. Belize does not embark on as traditional a trajectory of character development as any of the preceding six; "he has already arrived at his full humanity," writes Nancy Franklin.[42] The dilemmas with which Belize is faced, particularly as a health-care professional who must balance his personal feelings with nursing care of Roy (a man to whose life and politics he bitterly objects), make Belize's choices the most crucial of the narrative. Belize has two main objects of animus in the action of *Angels*: Roy, a patient to whom he's assigned, and Louis, the man who broke the heart of Belize's good friend (thus also making Belize's own life harder, since Belize must step into the void left by Louis). Belize makes no pretense that he's anything but antagonistic in his dealings with Roy and Louis, yet he rolls up his sleeves and deals with them both as honestly as he can. Despite his feelings about Roy, further enflamed by Roy's racial stereotyping and imperious demands from his hospital bed, Belize nonetheless offers him insider wisdom about the therapeutic regimen he's about to undergo. Later, he reluctantly holds Roy in the worst of his pain and delirium. With Louis, barely reining in his hostility, he endures Louis' rants and tries to reason with him about Louis' unreasonableness. He enlightens Louis about Joe's full story (even if he clearly enjoys battering Louis with the word "buttboy"). And in Roy's death, Belize connects the two people to whom he's most opposed when he summons Louis to the hospital to steal Roy's drugs and, at the same time, pray the Kaddish over Roy. After his ordeal in attending Roy's entrance into eternity and welcoming Prior "back to the world" (as fair a trade as Belize is ever likely to see in his life), Belize excuses himself to "go home and nurse my grudges." This is what makes Belize so ideologically alive as a character: he tends with equal care to ideas *and* the real world. Thompson recalls mulling the question of the play's meaning with Nichols for "months," and she recalls the conclusion Nichols drew: "'It's about citizenship,' which is a concept that I think we're losing fast. The notion of moral responsibility and living in a society to which and for whom you are responsible. The effects of our daily actions are no longer credited with the power to form our character. What's credited are possessions and status and acquisition."[43] Despite all the pyrotechnical fireworks of the Angel and the visions of Prior, Harper, and Roy, this moment, of Belize's sublimation of his own impulses to the needs even of those he most reviles in his community, is the inmost beating heart of Nichols' and Kushner's *Angels in America*. Prior's "Great Work" is the promotion of "*More Life*"; Belize is the lived reality of that philosophy.

* * *

   Angels in America is unmatched in Mike Nichols' oeuvre in capacity and complexity. Critics routinely declare Kushner's play to be among the most important of the American 20th century; "*Angels in America* is clearly the most important American play since Edward Albee's *Who's Afraid of Virginia Woolf?*"[44] The two plays psychologically form a mighty set of bookends on Nichols' filmography. The bitter comedy of Kushner's drama is the tone with which Nichols made his name as a filmmaker, but there is extraordinarily heartfelt sentiment in *Angels* as well, and this characteristic, which became ascendant only in Nichols' second phase as a filmmaker, gives *Angels* a compassionate dimensionality it would otherwise have lacked had it devolved toward ideological screed or dyspeptic lamentation. It's where the film might have ended up had Robert Altman made it, as he was in talks with Kushner to do.[45] Joe's politics are as egregious to Kushner (and Nichols) as they are to Louis (once he's made to look squarely at them by Belize); yet the difference is that Louis only wants to be cleansed of the stain of his involvement with Joe, while Kushner and Nichols can't dismiss Joe so easily. And Pacino's figure of Roy Cohn in all his charismatic, malevolent energy fascinates precisely because we glimpse the mortal terror beneath his vehemence. He's the narrative's most notorious victimizer and most pathetic victim. As such, *Angels in America*'s most essential scenes do not involve either of its visionary prophets, Prior or Harper, as compelling as their stories certainly are. The narrative's most essential scenes pit Roy against Belize, since these are the two "professionals" whose philosophical convictions are at stake in fiercely performed vocation, one as dead wrong as the other is right.

   Kushner says, "I wanted [Belize] to be the ideological counterweight to Roy, that there were two people in the play who were not lost and inert and swimming around deeply confused. I wanted there to be two people, one of the Left and one of the Right, who had a very clear moral compass and knew exactly where they were in the universe at all times."[46] Despite their vast ideological and moral differences, Roy and Belize share a similar assessment of the modern world, though their crucial divergence comes in how each responds to his dim view of our experience. For both, existence is filled with suffering. But while Roy counsels manipulation, centered first and only on self, Belize devotes his life to service. Belize wants to make the inevitable suffering easier to bear; Roy wants to commodify even suffering's inevitability, to use it to his advantage. And each has a hapless mentee to whom he espouses these principles: Roy has Joe; Belize has Louis.

To Joe, his latest protégé, Roy becomes increasingly direct in his depiction of existence: "I'm not afraid of death. What can death bring that I haven't faced? I've lived. Life is the worst. Listen to me—I'm a philosopher. [...] Love: that's a trap. Responsibility: that's a trap, too. Like a father to a son I tell you this: Life is full of horror. Nobody escapes, nobody. Save yourself. Whatever pulls on you, whatever needs from you, threatens you. [...] Let nothing stand in your way." If such a speech weren't dark enough, its cynical subtext reveals a bottomless swamp of predation. Roy delivers this speech to a young, impressionable man Roy hopes to use and discard not once but twice: as his "buttboy" (in Belize's deliberately indelicate diction) and as his dirty-tricks appointee to the Justice Department to become Roy's kept guardian angel. One need look no further than Martin Heller, a former protégé/buttboy of Roy's, for a foreshadowed glimpse of the objectified system of relationship-barter that Roy practices. After Roy has summarily excused Martin from the table ("Take a walk, Martin. For real"), Joe voices his heartfelt, principled objection to the obstruction of justice Roy has attached to the plum appointment he's offering. Joe asks why Martin isn't able to perform this service for Roy (an ethical slippery slope of a question), but Roy waves away the idea like a bad smell: "Grow up, Joe. The administration can't get involved." Joe, still obtuse about the nature of the political quicksand he's edged near, posits, "But I'd be part of the administration. The same as him." Impatiently, because of his irritation at saying what ought best to remain unsaid, Roy lectures him, "Not the same. Martin's Ed [Meese]'s man. And Ed's Reagan's man. So Martin's Reagan's man. And you're mine."

Thus is made concrete one half of the Faustian bargain that sits on the table between Roy and Joe from their opening scene in the film, when Roy punctuates the offer with a gay-subtext sweetener that, on a sub-committee's transcript or in a tabloid quote, could be reasonably interpreted as "fatherly" warmth: "It's a great time to be in Washington, Joe. [...] And it would mean something to me. You understand?" Joe's hesitation is the caution of a man in the closet, who does indeed understand, at some level he does not allow out into the daylight, who already knows instinctively what Roy is trying to teach him, that relationships are just another of life's "traps." Joe's legal instincts parse every potential response before floating a tentative, generic expression of appreciation while working in an allusion to his wife. At the dinner with Martin, just *after* Roy extracts Martin's humiliation by commissioning a public backrub and just *before* he tells Martin to disappear, Roy describes Joe's role as a well-placed friend," a purveyor of "clout" who could provoke "fear" in the "genteel gentleman Brahmin lawyers" of his disbarment committee. Joe counters with the politically expedient feint, "I don't understand." Ignorance has been Joe's ally in his war against himself (as he prays "for God to crush me, break me up into little pieces and start all over again"); he has hoped to ignore his instincts and pretend his way into conformity with the majority values of hegemony his mentor appears to uphold. To Joe's careful admission of ignorance, Roy counters, simply, "You do." Roy knows Joe has always *understood*; Joe seems genuinely astonished when people like Roy and Louis (and, when she can finally admit it to herself, Harper) can so easily and accurately identify what he has desperately thought he could conceal. (Joe's greatest disappointment is that he hasn't been more successful at negating his identity; his mother Hannah's greatest "disappointment," as she tells Harper, is not "how disappointing life is," but that "it gets actually easier to live with. Quite easy. Which is, in it own way, a disappointment." That she can express this is a redemptive key to her reified awareness; it makes it possible for her to advance to her own "threshold of revelation." Joe can't quite bring himself to acceptance of what he has grudgingly admitted about his identity at the end of the narrative, which is why he remains lost, while Hannah finds herself.)

What Roy Cohn articulates in *Angels* and, for all his closeted hypocrisy, lives out in his professional vocation, is an expression of pure power. In muscling his long-time doctor, Henry, into a public misdiagnosis of his illness, Roy reveals his reified understanding of the hegemonic world within which Roy has ascended to a position of influence. Discoursing on the function of "labels" in social practice in what Alessandra Stanley calls "one of the most richly imagined meditations on power ever shown on television,"[47] Roy provides a concise semiotic analysis: "[Labels] tell you one thing and one thing only: where does an individual so identified fit in the food chain, in the pecking order?" In both the familiar metaphors Roy uses, he has implied a social Darwinist's perspective on human relationships. He answers his rhetorical question with a summation of a worldview: "Not ideology, or sexual taste, but something much simpler: clout." Inserting himself as an object lesson into this philosophical formula, he says, "Homosexuals are men who know nobody and who nobody knows. Who have zero clout. Does this sound like me, Henry?"

Henry must of course concede that, within this pretzel logic, Roy most assuredly cannot be labeled a homosexual, though Henry holds the trump card: Roy's disease, which can be re-labeled but not willed away. The body, both for good or (literally) ill, possesses a reality that Roy and Joe can't deny, despite their insistence (Roy via semantics, Joe via prayer and marriage); and that Harper can't deny either, despite her desire to be *freed* of desire for Joe; and that Hannah can't deny with the Angel, despite her resignation to the "disappointment" of the culturally bound, legalistic teachings of her church; and that Prior can't deny, as his physical disintegration begins to entice him with a longing for death. As the Angel verbally instructs both Prior and Hannah, "The Body is the Garden of the Soul." The Body is a threshold of revelation, and to deny its truths is to invite ruin. The Body is the reason why three characters routinely experience visions: each is under the influence of narcotic therapies that reach the mind via the body. To deny the Body is to deny reality. No one is as *honest* about denying reality as Roy: "I want you to understand," Roy tells Henry, using the threat of his career-destroying influence to buy Henry's cooperation with his ruse. "This is not sophistry. And this is not hypocrisy. This is reality. [...] Because *what* I am is defined entirely by *who* I am." It is a profound assessment of reification, but in its absolute capitulation to the powers that be, it is both a statement about social reality and a complete inversion of the reality that social objectification has sought to manipulate.

In Roy's argument is a life's work—Kushner's, but also Nichols.' It is a clear, coherent, unblinking identification of the systemic operations of objectification. Roy's statement is profoundly accurate. "Who I am" is, indeed, a signifier of identity. The problem comes in looking at his statement in the larger context of an argument that surrenders autonomous self-definition to definition by cultural decree. Brought to his knees by illness and Joe's failure to comply with the rules as Roy has made them up, Roy challenges Joe with the realities of power: "You want to be nice, or you want to be effective? Make the law, or subject to it. Choose." In a narrative immersed in irony, this is a deep-water marker: Roy himself has tried his whole life to have it both ways, to rule and to be ruled. Ethel Rosenberg, the figment his sub-conscious summons to pronounce judgment not just on his disbarment but on history itself, concludes, "Better he had never lived at all." The final irony of Roy's tormenting, tormented life is that, even in delirium, his default remains self-deception. Ethel is his sub-conscious projection of his legacy: the man who killed Ethel Rosenberg. His dying act is to feign vulnerability and contrition (repeating the word "sorry" three times after confessing, in apparent contradiction to his defiant claims of fearlessness throughout the narrative, that he is "scared") before sitting bolt upright, with Belize looking on, as he taunts Ethel for having "fooled" her. Nichols has carefully cut to medium shots in every one of Ethel's appearances, to reveal that Roy is talking to empty chairs, to the air, to himself. Roy Cohn has spent a lifetime fooling no one but Roy Cohn.

While Belize has a similar understanding of the debilitating effects of objectification in the world, what he does with this knowledge makes him Roy's antithesis in the film. No one is as honest about *affirming* reality as Norman Arriaga, which extends to his having renamed himself during his drag days, a moniker he retains now that he is, mostly, post-drag. The assumed name is for Belize an assumption of a dimension of his *reality*, not a distancing layer of artificiality. (Nevertheless, the two names are a reflection of how he relates to the world; paraphrasing the old joke, he is Belize to his friends, so Roy can call him Norman Arriaga.) Insisting, in the face of Louis' gassy essaying about race in America, that the problem is far worse than Louis can know, Belize says, "I *hate* America, Louis. I hate this country. It's just big ideas, and stories, and people dying, and people like you. The white cracker who wrote the national anthem knew what he was doing. He set the word 'free' to a note so high nobody can reach it. That was deliberate. Nothing on earth sounds less like freedom to me." Belize, although clearly well read and intellectually sophisticated, is often contemptuous of the abstracting tendencies of intellectualism, as embodied in Louis Ironson. Kushner gives Louis long, tiresome speeches filled with qualifiers and sidebars that Nichols allows to balloon the air of a close-up take until Belize, in a cutaway from Louis, deflates his disquisitions with a needle-sharp critique. As Belize insists upon airing his own perspective with Louis and then, later, also with Roy, rather than simply deferring to the "*awesome* spectacle" of Louis' opinions or the corrosive deluge of Roy's taunting hatreds, Belize's anger and his distrust of definitive "answers" from *any* point on the ideological spectrum become increasingly apparent. He finds the hypocrisies and cant in both Louis' earnest, bookish liberalism and Roy's misanthropic fascism. Asked by Louis to tell Prior, from whom Louis remains estranged, that he loves him, Belize says, "I've thought about it for a very long time, and I still don't understand what love is. Justice is simple. Democracy is simple. Those things are unambivalent. But love is very hard. And it goes bad for you if you violate the hard law of love."

Ambiguity, then, and human ambivalence in response to it, is the defining characteristic of reality for the most realistic character in *Angels*, created by a writer who defines himself as a "narrative realist."[48] The labeling of reality, as Roy Cohn explains it in hamstringing his own physician, necessitates the taming of reality into neat, confining cages. Labels as Roy understands them *defeat* reality, make it subject to hegemonic control. At some level, below the virile defiance masking his deeper denial, Roy knows this to be true. The last time he sees Joe, for instance, when Joe comes to visit his hospital room, Roy persists in his paternal pretense with Joe, laying his hands on him to bestow a blessing, like blind Isaac hoodwinked by Jacob. Roy even acknowledges the deliberateness of his gesture as biblical allusion, characterizing Joe/Jacob as "ruthless [...], some bald runt, but he laid hold of his birthright with his claws and his teeth." Just after this impromptu ceremony, however, Joe feels compelled to speak the truth of what they have always "understood" about each other. (Indeed, it is ultimately easier for Roy and Joe to speak of the conspiracy to obstruct justice than it is for them to speak of their sexual orientation.) Joe announces, as much with relief as triumph, that he has left Harper to live with a man. Roy's reaction is cataclysmic, scarring. Up out of bed, he pulls free of his IV, spraying his diseased blood all over Joe, the room, eventually Belize. He rails at Joe, "I want you home. With your wife. Whatever else you got going, cut it dead. [...] Do what I say, or you will regret it. And don't talk to me about it. Ever again." As a curse, this response far outweighs whatever "blessing" Roy might have intended upon Joe. Roy has labored to instruct his protégé, and the ambiguity of his hard-won wisdom is both to "let nothing stand in your way," to be fearless, and conversely to fear any false step that could provoke a damaging enculturated label. Roy's reified fear is an even more deadly contagion than his infected blood.

Louis has personality correspondences to both Roy and Joe, the two men in the narrative who most horrify him, and Belize has called him out on the salient characteristics in each case. Roy, Joe, and Louis are all members of the legal profession (Louis in a much lowlier caste, which Joe cruelly acknowledges as their relationship is ending), and all carry from their profession as much as their orientation a wary mistrust of words. For Roy, words are misleading, and power comes in being the one to choose and label words rather than having them assigned to one: "Make the law, or subject to it." One of Roy's cardinal laws is never to be associated with homosexuality, synonymous with enculturated disenfranchisement. But when Joe speaks the love that ought not speak its name, Roy's motives in stifling him are as much to censor the label that will attach to Roy, a known associate of Joe's, as to his protégé. Joe has practiced this linguistic caution until now, but ironically, his effusion over discovering his sexual identity has led him to "flaying" away his masks to stand naked in his identity. Of all people, it's Louis, compulsive opinion-spouter, who counsels Joe on their first night together to "stop talking." The moment is soused in physical desire, but the effect is as disastrous in its revelation of spiritual vacancy as that crucial moment in *The Graduate* when, at the end of the long, futile attempt at a "conversation," Benjamin asks Mrs. Robinson that they "not talk at all." Louis, like Roy and Joe, desires to avoid the realities he fears or finds inconvenient. This, too, distorts reality; to avoid all pretense of labels is in its own way as self-deceptive as Roy's semantic gymnastics. And when Louis tries to talk with Joe, what spills out are the abundant labels that spring readily to mind in relation to Joe ("married probably bisexual Mormon Republican closet case"), a veritable labeling lampoon that can't do anything but discourage Joe from attempting disclosure.

Like Joe, Louis takes comfort in abstraction and blanches when confronted with reality. Joe is able to write legal arguments for Justice Theodore Wilson of the Second Circuit Court of Appeals siding with a corporation that has endangered the health of children and, even closer to home, with the military against a gay soldier, because of an ideological orientation to the law. As if this might serve as a defense, he counters Louis' accusations with, "It's law, not justice; it's power, not the merits of its exercise." This is the gospel of hegemony, whose chief evangelist in *Angels* is Roy Cohn, who is on record as having told us all (directly to the camera) to "go jump in the lake," among less polite imperatives. In fact, Roy is nothing less than an ideology of one, as he tells Joe: "*save yourself*." Joe's horror of Roy deepens the more he listens to his mentor talk, and yet he internalizes every word and can fluently paraphrase when it comes time for him to attempt some manipulation of his own. Roy has said, "[D]on't be afraid to live in the raw wind, naked, alone." Standing on Jones Beach with Louis in winter, stripped naked, contemplating Louis' news that he has to see Prior again, Joe assumes the wheedling role with which Roy once plied him: "Sometimes self-interested is the most generous thing you can be. [...] You ought to think about [...] what you're doing to me. No, I mean ... what you need. Think about what *you* need. Be brave." Nichols treats the ending of this scene from a helicopter, zooming away from Joe, whose adoptive ideology of one has left him a small, solitary figure, alone and shivering at the end of the land.[49]

The two dramatic forces at work on Louis in the film are Roy's law of one (from which Louis recoils in bleeding-heart guilt even as he is powerless not to exercise it in abdicating his responsibilities to Prior) and Belize's ideology of "love and justice." If Roy and Belize represent the "polestars" of human response to the dehumanizing effects of the modern world, Louis is the character who struggles most consciously with where he fits on this continuum. At his grandmother's funeral, he's already anxiously attempting to confess sins of self-interest he has yet to commit; "Worse luck for you, bubbulah," Rabbi Chemelwitz tells him: "Catholics believe in forgiveness. Jew believe in guilt." This remains Louis' pattern in the narrative: helpless captivity to self-interest followed by reckless surrender to self-punishment. When the condom used in the rough-trade assignation on the Ramble after he leaves Prior breaks, Louis insists they continue and expresses a wish to be infected. His most notorious self-inflicted punishment is when he tears down Joe's veneer of responsibility in this violence. Before Louis inflames Joe to violence, Belize inflames Louis. The repetition of the derogatory "buttboy" to describe Joe, for whom Belize has no specifically personal feeling, is instead a label Belize intends to defame Louis, reminding Louis of a hierarchy in which Roy is more important than Joe and Joe is more important than Louis, even though Louis considers himself morally superior to Roy and thus, after Belize's revelation, to Joe. Belize is harder on Louis than on Roy, because he knows Roy is a lost cause, and because he believes Louis can do better. The time Belize spends with Roy is the generosity of vocation; the time he spends with Louis is the generosity of friendship, however adversarial. "You come with me to room 1013 over at the hospital," he says to Louis, even before he hatches the specific plot that calls Louis there. Belize is being rhetorical about Louis' penchant for abstractions like "love" and "America." He says, "I'll show you America," meaning Roy Cohn: "Terminal, crazy, and mean. [...] I *live* in America, Louis; that's hard enough. I don't have to love it." The characterization of Belize's relationship to the world may also stand as a description of his relationship to Louis: *lived*, not merely spoken, commitment. Earlier he's told Louis, "I've thought about it a very long time, and I still don't understand what love is." Actually, Belize *does* understand—he's just uncomfortable with the abstracting label. With Roy even more than with Louis, Belize meets his greatest test as an agent of love in the world, but it's an act of Belize's creative imagination that transforms death into multiplied life, forgiveness, love.

The seeds of this imaginative work on Belize's part are a long time in gestation. His first meeting with Roy goes about as anyone might reasonably predict. Roy asserts a label-based hegemonic assumption of superiority over a mere servant (in a later conversation, declaring he is "not moved by an unequal distribution of goods on this earth," he identifies himself as worthy of a "footnote" in "history," while reminding Belize, "you are a nurse, so minister and skedaddle"). At first blush, when Roy tells Belize during their initial dialogue that he is "not a prejudiced man," it seems pure self-delusion. Yet he goes on to explain, "These racist guys, simpletons, I never had any use for them—too rigid. You want to keep your eye on where the most powerful enemy really is. I save my hate for what counts." Roy is too reactionary to be "rigid"—what has given him "clout" is his ability to remain attuned to hegemony's shifting shape and to conform himself to those values. There is nothing extraordinary about any of this. What is extraordinary is Belize's response to Roy's aesthetic of "hate," which Jeffrey Wright delivers with little of Belize's campy drawl: "I think that's a good idea, a good thing to do, probably." In the pause that follows, Nichols and Kushner allow us more than adequate time to reflect that Roy is Belize's natural, cultural-bound enemy, and that Belize is in a unique position to deliver his hate to "what counts." (Belize reminds Roy—and us—of this fact when inserting the I.V. in Roy's arm, warning that there are two ways he can administer the needle, one merciful, the other bringing torment.) The hiatus in their dialogue appears to be a moment when Belize can calculate a suitable revenge against this powerfully antagonistic force, this traitor who hates traitors. And then Belize delivers his medical tips to Roy on how to stay alive. What we realize is that, beyond the theatrical fanfare of narcotics-based visions of Angels or ghosts or Eskimos, beyond the magnetism of Roy Cohn's evil, we've been watching a very human struggle between the polestars within one man, Belize. The forces of "more life" win. What Belize has *saved his hate for* is "what counts": death, not labels or ideologies. It is the triumph that foreshadows all the small, seemingly insignificant triumphs over which Belize will preside in the future.

Belize is not beyond making deals with the devil in the name of life. When he tells Roy about the methodology of the "double blind" trial, it's possible that his imaginative calculus has reached beyond Roy to other victims that might conceivably benefit down the road from Roy's influence and successful score of a private stash of AZT. Even if this isn't something Belize concretely imagines as he tips Roy, it's something he's begun actively negotiating after the stash arrives. Roy blackmails Martin Heller with what he knows about Iran-Contragate; Belize dares Roy to blow the whistle when Belize demands a cut of the drugs for his ailing friends. They exchange the most colorful litany of derogatory labels to be found anywhere in the six-plus hours of *Angels*, their hate simmering into an understanding that ends in a deal being struck. Such a deal is beneath the ethics of Belize's profession, but in the situational ethics of Belize's life as a gay health-care worker surrounded by dying friends (like Prior), Belize weighs the balance and takes his illicit cut from Roy's illicit windfall. Later, Roy descends into a morphine twilight in which Belize is the "bogeyman, [... t]he Negro night nurse, my negation [...], come to escort me to the underworld." Belize, we understand, is not quite Belize in this scene; he's become partly Roy's vision of encroaching Death. Roy grabs Belize in an embrace that is ambiguously both contact between health-care worker and dying patient and a sexualized solicitation, demanding to know about the afterlife. Belize unfolds a vision of San Francisco in romanticized ruin, characterized by "racial impurity and gender confusion. [...] Race, taste, and history finally overcome. And you ain't there." Belize is Roy's "negation" in this vision because Roy feels the weight of an imminent judgment embodied in Belize's unhidden animus. As this scene ends, with another nurse walking the wandering, addled Roy back to his bed, Ethel has joined Belize in the hallway, two angels of death (from Roy's point of view) keeping watch over their charge by night. After Roy has his sensational reaction to Joe's coming out, Belize is left to mop up the physical and psychological mess. "Mocked and reviled all my life," Roy mutters, and Belize, cleaning Roy's toxic spill, says, "Join the club." Roy predictably turns on him: "I don't belong to any club you could get through the front door of. You watch yourself—you take too many liberties." In the next moment, wracked by a spasm, he is clinging like a child to Belize, who immediately recoils but, again, in reluctant default compassion, allows himself to be held.

Belize, who sees the world more clearly than any other character in *Angels*, has no "visions." He isn't loaded up on drugs like Prior, Harper, or Roy, but in the most practical terms of the drama, he has less need to see the extraordinary to apprehend the real, since he has already been apprehending the real for some time. In his dialogues with both his nemeses, Roy and Louis, his race is a common subject. Elsewhere in the film, Hannah scolds her son, assuring him "[b]eing a woman is harder," but the film suggests Belize's status as a black man may be harder still, and a source of the unblinkered realism with which he views the world (he mocks white perspectives of both genders in his imaginary synopsis of the "bestselling paperback novel, *In Love with the Night Mysterious*"). He is the only one with Roy as this infamous, reviled man draws his last fearful, fearsome breath, though in Roy's dying vision, he's accompanied by Ethel, who "came to forgive" him but, a product of his fevered brain, can only enjoy vengeance. Over Roy's dead body, Belize is a mass of contradictory impulses, gently closing Roy's eyelids and folding Roy's hands to the chest, then ruthlessly snapping the drug key from the dead man's neck. Summoned by Belize to stand before Roy's corpse, Louis wonders why Belize would choose him ("Why me? You hate me"—to which Belize does not protest). But this is how Belize's imagination works. As a good nurse, his work is healing. He doesn't call forth elaborate prophetic or paranoiac visions but instead reconciles. He has brought together the two men who best recognize Belize's animus so that he may join them to one another in an act of mercy and forgiveness.

Louis, predictably, balks: his principles won't let him recite words of a tradition he's long since left behind, especially for an arch-enemy like Roy Cohn. "Louis," says Belize, "I'd even pray for you." And so, finally, Louis understands Belize's hierarchy of "grudges," in which the abstracted, second-hand evils of a Roy Cohn, which may hardly be overlooked, must always come second to the real evil done to a loved one. Belize hates Louis *most*. Yet he hasn't called Louis to this room to condemn him or to coerce him to serve Roy's soul. Belize has brought Louis to a "peace" summit. Of Roy, Belize says, "He was a terrible person. He died a hard death. So maybe [... a] queen can forgive her vanquished foe. It isn't easy; it doesn't count if it's easy. It's the hardest thing: Forgiveness. Which is maybe where love and justice finally meet. Peace, at last. Isn't that what the Kaddish asks for?"

Louis attempts a few last excuses, but Belize wills him into this imaginative act he's devised, this peacemaking: "Do the best you can." A facial tissue draped over his skull, Louis falters his way into the first lines, and Ethel's ghost, in the manner of the ghost of Louis' dead grandmother, miraculously feeds him the rest. To this point in the film, Nichols has been artful in intercutting Ethel's subjective reality for Roy with objective shots of empty rooms. Now, Roy is gone; so, then, Ethel should be gone. There can be only one explanation for this persistence of vision, the same explanation that brought Prior and Harper to their shared hallucination, even though they never meet beyond it: we are in the imaginations of Mike Nichols and Tony Kushner, willing Louis toward the "threshold of revelation" we desire for all protagonists and, vicariously, for ourselves. This is the "Great Work" which has begun. Belize nurses his grudges with the therapeutic intervention of his imagination's capacity to forgive; Kushner and Nichols do the same. Nor does the "Great Work" end: a change Kushner and Nichols make to the original stage play for the film indicates this, after Belize thanks and even mildly praises Louis while loading his backpack with the looted drug hoard. In the play, Louis' parting punch line, good for comic relief after the scene's climactic intensity, is to correct Belize: "Fine? What are you talking about, fine? That was fucking miraculous."[50] Indeed, Ethel's apparition and intervention *is* miraculous, every bit as much a *deus ex machina* as an Angel that can summon the Continental Principalities for Council with the Prophet. They are miracles of the imagination. But in the film, the word "That" becomes "I." Louis walks away impressed with *himself* rather than his momentous participation in unmerited mercy (both as bestower and recipient). Louis remains a work in "progress"—as do we all: the true subject of Kushner's "Great Work."

Nichols and Kushner introduce the vitality of imagination's humanizing power early in *Angels*, and it gradually builds to become the central, transforming force of the project, the source of prophetic vision and truth. The film begins with a funeral homily, and unless we've read the press about the production, we are likely to miss the fact that the gnarled rabbi delivering the words is the first screen persona of Nichols' favorite actress, Meryl Streep.[51] Those who have carped that a cinematic rendering of *Angels* will, inherently, be less "magical" in its performance of, for instance, the Angel's appearances, because we are conditioned to expect cinema's "magical" properties, miss the point that Nichols and Kushner have retained safeguards against our jaded expectation of cinematic illusion. It's less important that the "miracles" be rendered realistically in the film (as indeed they are not: for example, while Thompson's wires are not perceptible, as Kushner instructed the Angel's wires *should* be on stage,[52] neither does her flight have the naturalistic fluidity of blockbuster CGI; and Harper's "Antarctica" is the stagiest artificial set in the entire production, one of the most awkward of Nichols' entire *career*—but purposefully so, since it is a product of Harper's parochial experience). What is of central importance for Nichols' televised cinema, ironically, is retaining the *artificiality* of the play, its *imagined*-ness. The preeminent quality of the cinematic production that retains and thus promotes this artificiality is the multiple-role casting of Streep, Thompson, Wright, and, in smaller scenes that correspond to the fraying logic of Louis and Harper in their emotional extremity, Kirk (as the rough-trade pick-up in the Park) and Wilson (as the first Mormon Eskimo in Antarctica).

From the perspective of confecting a believable cinematic illusion, it is not only unnecessary but counterintuitive to place Streep in the opening scene with a long monologue's time to scrutinize her in her get-up as the octogenarian rabbi presiding over Louis' grandmother's funeral. Better that Nichols and Kushner should cast a seasoned older Hollywood man in the role than *any* actress, let alone one of the most legendary actresses of her era, especially if she's already got a sizable part to play later on. It would be far more believable, if the object is illusory cinematic "magic," to cast an 80-year-old man from Actor's Equity. Likewise, even if it makes "sense" that whatever actress plays the relatively small role of Prior's nurse, Emily, would also play his immense, imaginative projection of her in his drug-induced visions, it makes no sense for that same actress to play an entirely unrelated cameo as a psychotic Bronx street person.[53] Streep should, by the sensibility of Hollywood illusion, play one role; Thompson arguably should play two; in no case should either woman play three— but both do precisely this in Nichols' film. While there is publicity to be mined in such stunts of casting (only if the acting is up to the challenge—and it is), what makes the task worth taking on is the formal emphasis it places on transformative shape shifting and imaginative mutation, a "Great Work" shared by Nichols, Kushner, the actors, and us. "*Angels* was one of the first popular plays to draw a connection between race, gender, and sexuality," observes Richard Goldstein. "It took the new identity politics incubating in the academy and brought it to Broadway. At the same time, it performed a critique of identity politics by portraying the complexities and multiplicities that come with simply existing."[54] We are asked, with plenty of thespian chops and film craft brought to bear, to imagine Streep as an 80-year-old Yiddish man, a middle-aged Mormon matriarch, and a notorious American traitor executed half a century ago. Streep's shape-shifting presence is an invocation to what Kushner calls "empathic imagination,"[55] whose "Great Work" is the object of this play, as its subjects are "love and justice."

Kushner has argued that his idea of narrative "requires an essential gullibility that you can't get through life without having." And yet we must be simultaneously susceptible and discerning. Citing Brecht (and Marx), Kushner contends "we have to learn how to look beneath [...] surface effects [in culture] to locate and understand the sources of their [...]

power."[56] The ultimate goal of theater in the Brechtian (and Shakespearean) tradition, Kushner asserts, is "to enable you to see the familiar as strange and the strange as familiar, so that you greet reality with an appetite to interpret it."[57] Interpretation is thus also an act of imagination. *Angels* is an exercise in this essential looking, in which we both believe all that we see (and are thus made to feel) even as we see through the cinematic illusions. Kushner has Prior make an extended allusion to the 1939 Hollywood classic *The Wizard of Oz* at the end of the film, after his long night's wrestle with death: "I've had a remarkable dream. And you were there, and you, and you! [...] And some of it was terrible, and some of it was wonderful, but all the same I kept saying, 'I want to go home,' and they sent me home." *The Wizard of Oz* creates a tension between reality and illusion that clearly has warmed Kushner's heart. His narrative asks us always to pay attention to the "man behind the curtain," or the mask, or the posed identity. Nichols and Kushner implore us to continue the "Great Work" of understanding illusion and choosing reality; of understanding power and choosing justice, mercy, peace.

Roy's imaginative work is undone by the reified defaults he has set up even in his subconscious mind. Not even delirium on the threshold of death permits Roy access to the threshold of revelation. He can imagine heaven, but he must also imagine a "negation" that not only bars him from it but also does not appeal to his conformist instincts; he mistakes for hell the vision of San Francisco as heaven that Belize unfolds. He can imagine forgiveness, too, but he must also imagine having "fooled" mercy as a means of maintaining the illusion of power. Despite the redemptive possibilities inherent within reification's self-knowledge, Roy never stands a chance; he is forever too occupied by his desire to remain a member of hegemony's "club." He is his own imaginative negation. The comparatively less-flashy and deliberate imaginative work undertaken by Belize in Roy's hospital room, "where love and justice finally meet," is at the deepest heart of the play, yet this does not mean that the more eye-catching, sub-conscious imaginative work of Harper and Prior can be neglected. *Angels* moves from bed to bed in a succession that is never lascivious. The truth Harper literally uncovers with Joe in their bed the final time they try and fail to make love is vital to her future. The truth Roy refuses to see on his deathbed, within his own delirious unconscious, is his commitment to remaining undone to the last. And the truth that Prior discovers as death's "cessation" tempts him during his darkest night abed in the hospital is that "desire" is "what living things do. [...] I've lived through such terrible times, and there are people who have lived through much worse, but ... You see them living anyway. [...] Death usually has to *take* life away. I don't know if that's just the animal. I don't know if it's not braver to die. But I recognize the habit. The addiction to being alive. We live past hope. If I can find hope anywhere, that's it, that's the best I can do. It's so much not enough, so inadequate, but still ... Bless me anyway. I want more life." Prior's imaginative visions transform him from an angry, self-pitying victim into a man of purpose, who moves from wanting to die to resisting the Angel's offer of death's "respite." Harper's imaginative visions transform her from a craven, pill-popping victim into a woman of purpose, who moves from wanting to hide in her room and lie about her "buddy" to resisting the narcotic "deep-freeze for feelings" and choosing instead the "painful progress" of "[l]onging for what we've left behind, and dreaming ahead." Their imaginative work would be valuable if all it had accomplished was their own *personal* transformation, but as with Belize, whose imaginative work reaches beyond himself to spread therapeutic mercy even to those whom he hates, Prior and Harper are directly responsible for the reified redemption of Hannah Pitt.

The two central women in *Angels* are the two characters most dramatically transformed by their experience, which is consistent not only with Kushner's assertion, via Hannah, that modern life is "harder" for women, but reflects a long line of transformed women in Nichols' film career, beginning with Streep in *Silkwood* right through Thompson in *Wit* (and whose progenitor in Nichols' cinematic imagination is Maggie Terrell in *The Day of the Dolphin*). Harper begins the film as a housewife crouching in her Brooklyn apartment, incapable of making jello. She's terrified of "men with knives" and the rending of the ozone layer. When she hears sex tips on the radio, she memorizes them like a recipe, but she has as much trouble pleasing Joe as she does trying to firm up her gelatin. In her shared hallucination with Prior, she reveals her parochial understanding of sexuality: "In my church we don't believe in homosexuals." (She's also said she doesn't believe in addiction, for what that's worth.) Prior's response, "In my church we don't believe in Mormons," has Harper going for a moment before she laughs and says, "Oh—I get it." What comes next is the crux of this theatrically expressionist scene, which Nichols has formally gone to great pains (monochromatic photography, non-realistic dream space, flickering candles, eroticized presentation of Prior and Harper as queens in their distinct keys) to project as artificial, a beautiful series of visual clichés. Harper identifies what we're watching as a "hallucination," and she begins to question the limitations of her imagination:

> I don't understand this. If I didn't ever see you before (and I don't think I did), then I don't think you should be here, in this hallucination, because in my experience the mind, which is where hallucinations come from, shouldn't be able to make up anything that wasn't there to start with, that didn't enter it from experience, from the real world. Imagination can't create anything new, can it? It only recycles bits and pieces from the world and reassembles them into visions. [...] So when we think we've escaped the unbearable ordinariness and, well, untruthfulness of our lives, it's really only the same old ordinariness and falseness rearranged into the appearance of novelty and truth. Nothing unknown is knowable.

This is an enormously rich series of despairing observations, relevant not only to rendering the poverty of a fundamentalist life but also illuminating the experience of most of the other major characters in the film. Harper enters into the monologue with the assumption that, because she does not "believe" in (read: approve of or condone) certain phenomena (addiction, homosexuality), these phenomena have no relevance to her understanding—indeed, do not exist, at least in her world. Yet as she goes on, she acknowledges "untruthfulness" and the desire for "escape" as commonalities of experience, and concludes that such defaults make truth untenable. Ironically, articulating this truth—that we harbor the instinct to distort reality for our own purposes—makes other truths possible. It's not coincidence that Prior and Harper reach the "threshold of revelation" immediately after she's put these "depressing" truths about "falseness" into words. Prior, her projection of stereotypical homosexuality, reveals to her what she knows and has refused, in the "untruthfulness" of her marriage, to "believe": that Joe is in the closet and her marriage, her life, a lie. She in turn imparts to Prior, in his own dream-vision, the assurance that, despite the contamination of his body (and Louis' recoiling from its unpleasant reality), "there's a part of you, the most inner part, entirely free of disease." Each of them will take this essential kernel of revelation and, not without struggle (which is narrative, which is life), grow a new existence from it.

When Harper begins challenging the version of reality she has assembled (with the collusion of her closeted husband and the Mormon church), everything and everyone is suddenly up for her scrutiny. Joe is the most immediate target of her scrutiny, though her recognition that it's her "buddy" of whom she's been terrified (he's "the man with the knives") sends her reeling into the deep-freeze of her narcotic escape. Her sojourn with Mr. Lies, however, ends in frustration for them both. Harper's delusions, like Roy's, reflect both her true desires and her carefully constructed defaults. Unlike Roy, Harper manages to circumvent these defaults and arrive at truths she can bring back with her to the real world, the world that has all along informed her imaginative life. In "Antarctica," she immediately begins to interject imaginative flourishes. It's too cold (all the better, Mr. Lies reminds her, to numb feelings), so she wants to build a fire. She also wants to marry an Eskimo (comically reflective of her ignorance) and start a family, and Mr. Lies scolds her, reminding her to "[r]espect the delicate ecology of your delusions." Harper's potent love for Joe and desire for a nuclear family trump the deep freeze, and an "Antarctic Eskimo"—Joe—arrives, confounding the smooth, unflappable (even *tranquil*) Mr. Lies: she's a better liar than he is, because beneath her lies always throbs the insistent reality of her unexamined life. By the time she emerges from the freezer, however, she's Brooklyn's newest homeless person, trying to start a bonfire with public property, and she's returned to her apartment where she shares living space with yet another reality-denying Pitt fundamentalist. It's important to note that her Antarctic idyll melts before Mother Pitt barges into her life: she answers Joe the Eskimo's announcement that he's having an "adventure" with an assurance that his un-closeted life can't be "worse than what I imagine." Inexorably, via her imagination's recalibration towards truth, Harper pulls herself against the tides of illusion.

With Mother Pitt, who shelters against the realities of New York at the Mormon Visitors Center, Harper finds a negative model, but the "Mormon Mother" in the Visitor Center diorama offers another perspective. All three Pitts have enacted a counter-journey to the one celebrated in the diorama: Joe, Harper, and now Hannah have all trekked east in search of a better life (Joe notes cruelly of his mother, "You sort of bring the desert with you"— though to be fair, all the Pitts do, as their name implies: each is in his or her own distinctive slough of despond). Hannah's square-jawed resolve dovetails in Harper's imagination with the doughty Mormon pioneers, whose hard-headed resolve saw them past the obstacles of persecution, flood, drought, illness, and the mountainous gateway to their western Eden in desert Utah. Although greatly reduced in scope from the stage version (and without a second hallucinatory visit with Prior), Harper's visions in the diorama room in the film produce a similar effect: they are Harper's internal monologue externalized as a dialogue between Harper and the pioneer wife she comes to understand as her doppelganger (even though it's the "dummy husband" who more nearly approximates *Joe*; when the Mormon Mother, played by Robin Weigert, comes to life and begins talking to Harper, she bears only the vaguest resemblance to Mary-Louise Parker: she's plainer and thicker, but of similar age and temperament). Harper asks an innocuous cliché: "Was it a hard thing, crossing the prairies?" but the Mormon Mother won't allow her such an easy out from the hard work of her imagination: "You ain't stupid. So don't ask stupid. Ask something for real." This hallucinatory exchange finally verbalizes the trend of all Harper's hallucinations, against her wishes and perhaps even against her better judgment, towards the "real" and away from the "untruthfulness" of the objectified life she and Joe have shared. It's at the end of this penultimate episode of the mini-series that she confronts Joe with the accusation of her naked body and elicits from him the "Truth" that she is "nothing" for him. Although devastated, even stunned into temporary immobility by this truth (she still stands naked in the doorway after he has left), she thanks him as he goes. The moment has left her, in the best, most literal sense of the word, disillusioned. Whatever spell she and Joe (and her received beliefs) have cast together over themselves, the spell for her has broken and, drug-free, she is able to leave Joe (still begging to stay and cling to the tatters of his own illusions), the prison-keep of their apartment, and New York. She retraces the pioneer journey west at film's end, on a night flight to San Francisco, blazing her own trail against her reified inheritance. Beaming out at us from the portal of her window-seat, she's lit by the setting sun and an inner radiance. She looks better, healthier, than at any other moment in the film, including the projected glamour of her first hallucination, shared with Prior. She is real, and having witnessed her own mending, can now envision (without drugs) a more wholesale mending that encompasses not only suffering souls but the natural world.

If encounter with reality has given Harper a flattering makeover, it's a minor alteration compared to the physical transformation of her mother-in-law. Our first glimpse of Hannah is when any of us would be at our least presentable, awakened from sleep in the middle of the night. Her hair is a lifeless tousle, her features blurred, her robe bunched around thick, midlife dimensions. Her impatience with her son's distress is as unattractive as her appearance, as she scolds him for calling her so late, for his embarrassing talk about his father and himself, for his drinking (which she implies, as a last word, is the root of all the phone call's litany of problems—"Drinking is a sin. A sin! I raised you better than that"—when in fact it's merely the least serious of his many symptoms; Joe is in no danger of addiction to any substance but fast food). Arriving in New York, she's literally weighed down by baggage, and though she gets results, as when she barks at Thompson's homeless woman until Hannah has a route out of the Bronx, she continues to manifest as unappealing (assuming that everyone ought to speak English, the one language she knows, and outraged that an immigrant bus driver allows her to become so lost). When Prior first meets her, at the Visitors Center to which he has been led in stalking Joe, he exchanges insulting assumptions with Hannah, although plain-speaking Hannah is actually *less* direct than Prior. At first she only attempts to ignore him, then to shoo him away. When it is clear that he is here because of Joe, she inquires, with palpable distaste, "Are you a … a homosexual?" When he confirms her diagnosis, she asks if he is "typical," and sizing her up, he begins his counter-assault: "Oh, I'm *stereo*typical," and cites the profession of hairdressing as an example. She immediately takes the bait (as Harper had earlier, in her stereotyped hallucination), asking if this is what Prior does for a living (and unlike her daughter-in-law, failing even in delayed reaction to see the joke). His eyes darting appraisingly over dowdy hair, features, and ensemble, he says, "Well it would be your lucky day if I was, because frankly …"

At this moment, something in Prior seizes up, and his change begins. From the beginning of the film, he has been a mixture of terror and rage, most often aimed at Louis in symbiotic tandem with the reality of his AIDS diagnosis sinking in. Louis' hints about abandonment serve as Prior's presentiment, something he doesn't have the courage to treat as prophecy, and thus he makes no emotional or practical preparation for its fulfillment. After Louis has left him alone with his illness, then has the temerity to resurface and tell him about Joe, Prior's outraged self-pity reaches its apotheosis: "There are thousands of gay men in New York City with AIDS, and nearly every one of them is being taken care of by … a friend or by … a lover who has stuck by them. […] Everyone got that except me. I got you." This has the predictable (and desired) effect on Louis, whose impotent tears become Prior's next target. This is when he banishes Louis, telling him not to return without visible evidence of his suffering. There is no doubt that Prior has been treated unfairly, both by life and Louis. Yet he has not been abandoned. Aside from the compassionate care he is receiving at the hospital, he has a constant and steadfast friend in Belize, and he has no reason to think Belize will not stick with him no matter the cost. For much of the narrative, Prior behaves badly, and his behavior (already eccentric with his insistence upon the monk's cowl as his public persona) sinks still lower when he destroys his delicately stabilized health by stalking Joe, humiliating himself and Belize at Joe's office at the courthouse, and essentially indulging in a multi-borough tantrum. Launching into a bitchy insult of an unsuspecting stranger, as he's about to do when confronting Hannah, is when he finally hits bottom, and Nichols and Kushner literalize this by having a feverish spell knock him to the floor, and thus into Hannah's capable hands.

The dialogues they have are quite unlike those of any other ideologically opposed individuals in the film. Louis and Belize (who aren't even that opposed ideologically) snipe at one another because of Louis' pomposity and Belize's righteous anger on behalf of Prior (he's also disgusted that Louis has shown so little interest in Belize himself as a person that he has no inkling of Belize's personal life and wrongly assumes his antagonism towards Louis is because he still holds a torch for Prior). Roy and Belize, of course, hurl colorful abuse at one another, and although Belize bestows typically empathic physical care, neither allows this to soften his personal antipathy towards the other. Louis and Joe avoid substantive discussion of their differences altogether until it's too late, and all that's left to them is violence. But Hannah and Prior transform each other by speaking and listening to the truth of each other in newfound mutual respect. It may be possible to see some of the groundwork for Hannah's transformation in the time she spends alone with Harper, especially when Harper assures her mother-in-law that only Hannah is more out of place in her life than Harper is, and when Hannah confides aloud her "disappointment" at having accustomed herself to "how disappointing life is." Harper is hardly a prophetess at this point; she's just barely verbal. Yet there is a submerged tremor of suffering and outrage in Harper that leaves Hannah pensive. Hannah is as frigid emotionally as Harper has imagined she'd like to be; seeing her mother-in-law is her final cure for desiring the deep-freeze. Yet *neither* woman ultimately desires the cold. Talking with Harper, Hannah is franker about her life than ever before; Prior occasions Hannah's further thaw in ways her own son and daughter-in-law cannot, so ingrained is their history with each other. Warming to Prior promotes the heat of her wrestle with the Angel, as well as the possibility that Hannah may one day be able to share her warmth with Joe, the man lost out in the cold at narrative's end.

Sitting in Emily's examination room with Prior at the hospital, Hannah muses, "When I got up this morning, this is not how I envisioned the day would end." Delivered by Streep in that clipped, heartland plain-speak, the line is comic relief, but contextually at this point in *Angels*, with its obsessive motif of the relative limits and limitlessness of the imagination, the comment is also her referendum on her own emptiness. Hannah couldn't navigate her own way out of the Bronx, let alone existential alienation. However, she is prepared to voice not only her reified circumstance but her "disappointment" with this predicament, leaving her open to seek alternatives beginning with the expansion of her consciousness. She is far from the Mormon safe house she has defaulted to on the West Side: she's in the hospital, holding the hand of a terrified AIDS sufferer. The walls of the tiny room she's lived in for five-plus decades haven't so much expanded as exploded. Introducing Hannah to Emily, Prior says, "This is my ex-lover's lover's Mormon mother." After a comic pause, Emily says, "Even in New York in the eighties, *that* is strange." Prior, who has earlier attempted to tell Belize his vision of the Angel (to practical-minded Belize's resistance), now unburdens himself to Hannah, whose grounding in the eschatological mythology of the Latter-Day Saints makes it comparatively easy for her to talk about angel appearances. Despite avowing his own experience, he finds her description of Joseph Smith's vision "preposterous." Mother Pitt admonishes him: "It's not polite to call other people's beliefs preposterous." She adds that Smith's vision was the product of "great need for understanding," certainly a quality that would describe most characters in the film. "His desire made prayer. His prayer made an angel. The angel was real. I believe that." Astonishingly, Prior says, "I don't," even though he has made this verbatim assertion to Belize and then Hannah about his *own* angel. When he explains himself by labeling "repellent" her presumed system of belief, she demands to know: "What do I believe?" He responds with the cliché cop-out, "I can just imagine ..." Hannah firmly corrects him, using his own diction: "No, you *can't* imagine the things in my head. You don't make assumptions about me, mister; I won't make them about you." For the first time, Prior actually sees *Hannah* rather than his objectifying projection of her. A moment later, she confesses to a failure of imagination about her son Joe's sexuality, not because of a culturally received aversion but rather because, "for me, men in *any* configuration ... well, they're so lumpish and stupid." (Having expressed these thoughts aloud serves as a segue to what she discovers about herself with the glamorous, amorous Angel in her shared dream with Prior.) Prior regards her with even greater seriousness now, and he says, in reified self-consciousness, "I wish you would be more true to your demographic profile. Life is confusing enough."

Together on their shared "threshold of revelation," waiting for the hospital to find him a room, they begin to talk more easily, even to share a laugh over what God does to recalcitrant prophets ("feeds them to whales"), but Prior's laughter ends abruptly in a coughing fit that sends him spiraling back towards the mire of self-pity. Hannah has already admitted earlier that she doesn't "have pity. It's just not something I have," and as he foretells his certain death, she interjects, "You shouldn't talk that way. You ought to make a better show of yourself." If she'd only spoken the first sentence, it might have been construed as pity and thereby invited even more wallowing in woe, but by adding the second sentence, she makes the first sentence a critique of his attitude, not a pep talk about his illness. Prior tries to cow her by flashing his K.S. lesion, now nearly the breadth of his chest, and, without dismissing it, she refuses to make it totemic: "It's a cancer. Nothing more." And then, making a full thought of the phrase, so it can't be construed as a misunderstanding of the gravity of his situation: "Nothing more human than that." Once again, she makes a motion to leave, and Prior asks her to stay. "You comfort me. You do—you strengthen my spine." After he has weathered his dark night with the Angel, as Belize welcomes him "back to the world" and Emily proclaims "the dawn of man," Prior wants to know where Hannah is. Belize explains that she's just stepped out to the rest room, but follows incredulously with the question, "Where did you find *her*?" With a warmth that admits none of the chilly irony with which Belize and Prior can sometimes regard the world together, Prior says, "We found each other." The phrasing permits two interpretations: each has identified, against all the odds of objectified expectation, a friend; each has located the other who was, at the time, stumbling and lost. What happens to them during their shared dream with the Angel is nothing less than awakening— for Hannah, a sexual awakening only suggested rather than fully explored by the narrative (reflecting Hannah's natural reticence); and for Prior, an existential awakening to the preciousness of life, which compensates for its absurdity and suffering.

At the end of the film, after the apocalyptic storm of the Millennium's advent gives way to the restructuring perspective of Perestroika, Nichols and Kushner afford both visionary Prophets a last word, even though Belize has already intoned the words at the core of *Angels*— "love and justice," "forgiveness," "peace"—that weather even apocalyptic storms. Harper speaks to us from the calm of the tropopause, a liminal space of "safe air" from which she can contemplate an imagined mending of all that is broken, torn, and wracked. She knows she must descend again into the "painful progress" of the world, but for the first time, this prospect invigorates her. If Harper prophesies, Prior is *the* Prophet, the one who dresses the part, who understands suffering because "I am a gay man, and I am used to pressure, to trouble." Offered celestial nepenthe in his dream of heaven, Prior literally rages against the dying of the light, demanding that the Council of the Continental Principalities take the absentee deity that allowed "all this destruction [...] all the terrible days of this terrible century" to "court," should this absent creator return "to see [...] how much suffering his abandonment had created, if all he has to offer is death" as compensation for pain and suffering. It is Prior's way of making "a better show of" himself, as Hannah has advised. The second episode of *Angels* ends with Prior saying, "I wish I was dead." Here in the final episode, confronting what he has precipitously wished for, Prior observes that most people who have lived "through much worse" refuse to surrender to death, and he opts for "hope" and "more life." No more dramatic "transformation," Nichols' stated object of his filmmaking, could be imagined.

Two gay young men wrestle with an angel in *Angels*. Joe Pitt wrestles to deny his life, to fight "with everything I have, to kill it." Prior wrestles to wring from immortality's "cessation" the privilege and burden "to be alive." As the Angel bestows the sign of blessing, with Millennium's storm still crackling, she's left alone in the ruin of heaven, as Prior turns and strides in resolution away from her towards his life-bed, once assumed to be his deathbed, in one of the most beautiful and logically elegant sequences of the entire film. *Angels* is constructed as an intricate series of mirrors: Harper and Joe both stand naked before their illusory loves and are left humiliatingly abandoned, invited to disillusionment; Joe and Prior both wrestle with angels; Prior and Hannah both discover the body's connection to the soul through ecstatic union with the Angel; and so on. At the film's climax, the thunder of Millennium roaring over Manhattan, two gay men confront Death in hospital rooms, attended by Belize. Roy yields to the angel of Death, while Prior's wrestling produces a truce and a blessing. The Angel's blessing is her last act in the drama—she won't be seen again; after this, Thompson is "plain" Emily. While Harper and Prior continue to prophesy, they do so without the cinematic pyrotechnics to which the narrative has been accustomed. What remains is the film's self-conscious artificiality, which underscores the narrative's "double vision," as Kushner calls it, with "empathic imagination" and "skepticism" equally invoked. "I believe in the power of theater," and by extension, the cinema, he says, "to teach and to heal through compassion, through shared agony. And it also offers a way of developing critical consciousness."[58] In this sense, Kushner's "double vision" promotes the imaginative work entailed within reification's redemptive dimension, which invites us to understand our objecthood and to imagine alternatives. Within moments of regaining consciousness after his near-death experience, Prior has become Dorothy, regaling a coterie of loving, familiar faces with his tale of having seen them in his "remarkable dream." The aggressive and comic allusion to *The Wizard of Oz* is an internal deconstruction of the "realities" of heaven we have just witnessed in Prior's company. The allusions continue: saying goodbye to Hannah (who has also had a "remarkable dream") but only allowing her to leave if she reassures him she will return, Prior trots out the familiar parting meditation of that notorious dreamer and drama queen, Blanche DuBois: "I have always depended on the kindness of strangers." Hannah, who really must brush up her Broadway literacy with her newfound gay friends, bristles, "Well, that's a stupid thing to do." But it has become both Prior's *and* Hannah's new strategy for coping with life's confusion and alienation.

The brief epilogue in Central Park returns us to a site (and sight) that has become familiar to us as we journey through *Angels*, since the Angel gracing the Bethesda Fountain

The Bethesda Fountain is the symbolic center of Central Park, which is the symbolic center of public community in New York, which is the symbolic center of American culture. The fountain and its angel also serve as the setting for the coda of Tony Kushner's *Angels in America*, adapted for Nichols and HBO. In having his four friends meet at the fountain, with its biblical allusion to ancient Jerusalem's civic center of healing, Kushner invokes a prophecy of expanded citizenship, a "kindness" (as Nichols calls it) that locates all benevolent action between people in our species' essential equality—our shared *kind* (photograph by the author).

is the climactic image of the title sequence that opens each of the film's six episodes. Mendelsohn calls the title sequence "one of the most moving moments" of the entire production, "suggest[ing] something essential about the mighty scope both of Kushner's concerns [...] and of the drama he's written."[59] In a seamless, bravura use of CGI and form cutting, the sequence begins over the Golden Gate Bridge in San Francisco, moves over the Angel Moroni atop the Mormon Temple in Salt Lake City, past the Gateway Arch of St. Louis and the skyscrapers of Chicago to dip out of the clouds once and for all above the Financial District in Manhattan (a shot similar to the one at the end of *Working Girl*, with the difference that the shot moves uptown and into the park rather than out into the harbor), ending in a zoom to a computer-generated close-up of the Bethesda Angel, which, just before the titles end, shifts ominously into motion. Nancy Franklin writes that when the angel "lift[s] its blank, grave eyes to stare into your own," the effect is to include, or perhaps indict, the audience: "'Yes, you,' the eyes seem to say. 'This is about you, too.'"[60] The closing scene of the film of course permits no such CGI "magic," but it is no less self-conscious of its artifice. In fact, the epilogue is among the most artificial sequences of the film. The site is one of the loveliest in the Park, a complex dialogue between the fountain and its central sculptural element, the angel sculpture of Emma Stebbins (first woman to create a public sculpture in New York[61]), the Lake and boathouse, the Bethesda Terrace, and, presiding over the skyline, the monumental apartment towers of the West Side. It is a central locus of the Park not only in terms of geography but also in psychological and symbolic terms. The project's chief planners, Frederick Law Olmstead and Calvert Vaux, called the Terrace and Fountain "the heart of the park"[62]; the allusion to Bethesda accesses the fifth chapter of the Gospel of John, with the story of the public pool in Jerusalem which was reported to have healing powers and so had become the locus of many of the disadvantaged of the city. "It is not surprising to speak metaphorically of [...] religious symbolism at the heart of Central Park. The Park was created to be a moral landscape."[63] Nichols and Kushner are equally interested in establishing a moral geography for a transformed culture. As Central Park is at the symbolic and geographical heart of democratic Manhattan, free and open to all, so the Bethesda Complex—not Wall Street or any of the city's many cultural institutions—is Nichols and Kushner's civic center. Kushner chooses this place for his closing scene of regenerative prophecy because it is so centrally symbolic to the identity of the metropolis, which is as much in evolution as any of the characters.[64] The location of the final scene of *Angels in America* weaves a poetic web of historical allusions—ancient Jerusalem, Old New York, the 1960s counterculture, post–Reagan advancements in AIDS research—to community healing.

In early versions of *Angels*, Kushner had Prior make the claim that the complex was a memorial to the Civil War dead, contextually freighting the site with Prior's vision of a second civil war, passively waged against the homosexual community as society ignored the AIDS scourge; when Kushner was corrected about the "purpose" of the Bethesda Complex, which makes no mention of the Civil War, he removed this allusion from the play. What replaces the allusion is Prior's more poetic observation that angels "commemorate death but they suggest a world without dying." Given the context of the scene within the narrative, a four-years-on coda in which death has not claimed Prior, he remains a prophet but in a less strident key. He has matured into his role, and he presides over the scene, in character but post-drama, directly addressing the camera and orchestrating the direct addresses of his friends. It is his birthday, four years after his near-death deal with the Angel, and his desire remains consistent: for healing and wholeness, for "*More Life*." Of the four friends assembled, Hannah is the most changed, "noticeably different," in Kushner's original stage play description: "she looks like a New Yorker, and she is reading the *New York Times*."[65] Fisher writes, "A wiser, more sophisticated Hannah asserts Kushner's view of the interconnectedness of all humanity, regardless of race, sexual preference, religion, or politics and of the primacy of loyalty and commitment to others and to society."[66] In our last glimpse of her four years earlier, Hannah has encountered Joe by chance in Brooklyn, both of them on the outside of a street-corner Mennonite chorus,[67] and Hannah has made tentative overtures to be there for him as she has been for Prior. That he neither appears nor is mentioned in the film's epilogue suggests he may still be wandering, as we saw him last, disappearing down into the underground precincts of the subway and his shame.[68] Perhaps surprisingly (given Prior's rejection of Louis' renewed overtures of love), Louis is present in the coda—Prior has rejected Louis *only* as a lover, confounding expectation and testifying to Belize's ideology of "forgiveness." Louis and Belize, who is the one constant angel of Prior's past, present, and future life, continue to irritate one another (and to abide each other, for Prior). The last action mirrored in the film is the blessing: Nichols visually alludes to the Angel's blessing on Prior "in heaven" by framing Prior as he delivers a blessing to us in close-up with the Bethesda angel over his left shoulder. His defiant prophecies about the reified redemption of the marginalized form the bulk of his parting homily, in which he asserts "we are not going away," and "we will be citizens." Nichols says "being a citizen" is the "main subject" of *Angels*, and he was struck by the centrality of "kindness" in the dramatic architecture of Kushner's narrative.[69] The connotative inference in the word "kind" of a relationship between benevolence (to be kind) and kinship (to be of a kind) offers perspective on the vision of *Angels in America*. Citizenship is a shared understanding of "kindness" in all its forms, and the wisdom of reified awareness transcends constructed prejudice in hope of an encompassing fellow feeling.

Prior leaves us with more than mere prophecy, however; he transfers his blessing on to us, as a great work of art must. With his final words, "The Great Work Begins," Prior Walter closes Nichols and Kushner's great work. These are the words imagined by Prior in his dreams of the Angel, a self-exhortation to prophetic life, to dream past his visions into the real light of day. In this final, daylight, direct address to the audience, Nichols and Kushner offer to us in *Angels in America* the invitation to cross the "threshold of revelation," commissioning a continuation of the "great work" begun vicariously, magically in their art, to awaken us to the redemption latent in our reified world. "'It's the thing I'm the proudest of,'" Nichols has said of his epic.[70] In the Great Work of the imagination begin responsibilities.

20

"RU4 real?"

Closer (2004)

Maintaining his torrid production pace from the release of *Wolf* (1994), a decade in which he directed five theatrical features, a cable feature, and a six-episode cable mini-series, Mike Nichols worked with British playwright Patrick Marber to adapt his intense chamber drama, *Closer*, which debuted at London's National Theatre in 1997 and ran for well over a year in a series of venues culminating in transfer to the West End and then Broadway, where Nichols invited Marber to breakfast in 1999 and asserted his claim on the play.[1] Both play and film span the four years that Dan (Jude Law) and Alice (Natalie Portman), who meet quite literally by accident, when she is struck by a London cab while making eye contact with him, know each other before parting company forever. Although he cut "about 35 per cent"[2] of the play, excising entirely one of the stage play's original twelve scenes (Scene Nine) and substantially revising the final scene, Marber maintained the essential integrity of the original. "For a ninety-minute Hollywood film made in 2004 to contain only a dozen scenes/sequences, all lasting between five and eleven minutes, is extremely rare—and shows how determined Marber and Nichols were to avoid the traditional approach to filming plays [... by] break[ing] them up into sequences of shorter scenes set in several locations."[3] Upon the film's release, many critics instantly connected *Closer* back to two early, chamber-ensemble casts from Nichols' first phase as a filmmaker: *Who's Afraid of Virginia Woolf?* and *Carnal Knowledge*. In significant formal and thematic ways, *Closer* is a revisiting of these earlier Nichols films; however, while Marber knew the Albee play and Nichols' famous adaptation, he was introduced to *Carnal Knowledge* during discussions with Nichols before they collaborated on the adaptation; "'I subsequently saw the film and could understand why Mike thought I had. It's a very tough four-hander about misogyny.'"[4] Both *Carnal Knowledge* and *Closer* are chamber ensembles limited to four main characters; indeed, the earlier film introduces three minor but important characters (Cindy, Jennifer, and Louise) relatively late in the film, while *Closer* is even more insular: only the four main characters matter. "[T]here are virtually no other speaking parts [beyond the four principals in *Closer*], which is fitting given the quartet's seamless absorption in themselves and one another."[5] Both narratives unfold over years (in *Carnal Knowledge*, decades). Unlike most of Nichols' films beginning with 1990's *Postcards from the Edge*, which typically offer at least one character (and sometimes more) moving in reified wisdom from social proscription towards self-actualization, neither *Carnal Knowledge* nor *Closer* offers optimism about progress in the gender wars or in its characters' evolutionary capabilities.

Almost all interactions between the four principals in both these Nichols films may more appropriately be termed transactions—commodifed gambits in which the objectives are possession and evasion, manipulative deception and aggressive domination, all fueled by terminal self-interest. The four principals in *Carnal Knowledge* are all in their own ways among the socially entitled: Sandy (Art Garfunkel), Jonathan (Jack Nicholson), and Susan (Candice Bergen) as students at exclusive, tradition-bound Northeastern colleges, and Bobbie (Ann-Margret) as a cover-girl model. Marber introduces a complicating dimension of class struggle to the gender wars: while Dan and Anna (Julia Roberts) have the luxury to indulge their artistic temperaments (Dan as an obituary writer moonlighting as a novelist, Anna as a successful photographer), Larry (Clive Owen) and Alice are self-conscious about their status; Larry refers to his "working-class guilt" about the *au courant* furnishing of his and Anna's bathroom, and Alice theorizes that she has lost Dan to Anna "because she's successful." While Larry has enough disposable cash as a dermatologist with his own surgery to carry (and unload) hundreds of pounds of currency on one private dance by Alice, Alice has made enough money as a stripper (from obsessed men like Larry) to splurge on an anniversary vacation trip with Dan to New York. Ultimately, class conflict does not fuel the machinations of the four characters in *Closer*; as in *Les Liaisons Dangereuses*, the 1792 epistolary novel by Pierre Choderlos de Laclos, money may provide the assumption of entitlement, but the motivations run deeper, to gendered resentments, fears, and aggression. *Carnal Knowledge* and *Closer*, films at opposite ends of Mike Nichols' long and productive Hollywood career, each argue that our innate instincts in mating are commodifying territorial predation. Sam Davies writes, "The title is a piece of mordant authorial irony. The characters seek intimacy, but the denouement, and the Jacobean sexual treachery that leads to it, argue such intimacy is, if not impossible, probably illusory."[6] Anthony Lane observes that the title of *Closer* "could stand for [Nichols'] whole career" as "an intimist director who is far happier finding dirty laughs in a closed room" than on a broad, exteriorized canvas.[7]

In practical terms for Nichols, *Carnal Knowledge* and *Closer* serve as logical next projects after quixotic directorial ambitions. Nichols' long, self-imposed exile in the Mexican desert making the sprawling, complex, surreal *Catch-22* required commitments of time and energy he needed to conserve in his next project if he was to regain the industrial capital in Hollywood that he'd earned in the extraordinary popular success of his first two films, particularly *The Graduate*. And in taking on a cultural behemoth like *Angels in America*, Nichols once again risked his reputation (as he had with *Catch-22*) in adapting a bellwether ideological work of immense formal proportions about which everyone had strong feelings. *Closer*, like *Carnal Knowledge*, was a move from an enormous cast to a chamber ensemble, from a picaresque series of dreamscapes to a realistic slice of the way we love now, with a bleak outlook on the possibilities of "transformation"[8] via reified wisdom.

In *Carnal Knowledge*, the characters are aware from the earliest moments of the film of their performative roles in society (as evidenced by Sandy and Susan's flirtatious deconstruction of the mixer at which they meet and begin to perform their roles, or Jonathan and Bobbie's flirtatious deconstruction of romance on their first date, playfully moving from first passion through marriage to acrimonious divorce). Yet this knowledge fails to prepare them adequately to act outside of these roles, and Sandy's apparent liberation late in the film from his patriarchal defaults is likely another phase of an essentially weak and easily manipulated person, now under the sway of a hippie teenager, his "love teacher." Jonathan is in thrall from beginning to end to the most literal interpretation of gender-based hegemony (he literally scripts phallocratic performance at film's end); he lives in terror of female sexual autonomy and thus commits himself to dissection of women via erotic synechdoche (his big-breast fetish), since he believes women are sexual terrorists bent on doing the same to him (his "ball-buster" paranoia). Despite their intelligence and privilege, the people in *Carnal Knowledge* remain ignorant of the "knowledge" they can articulate, retreating into rote performance of the very roles they'd once playfully critiqued.

Likewise, in *Closer*, "Alice" and Dan predicate their relationship in a fantasy construction of one another so total that "Alice" isn't even Alice's name; Alice's fiction is that Jane Jones can truly love a man "forever" under a name she has assumed while looking at a memorial plaque on a London garden wall. Could they ever have been married, or even passed through customs inspection together? (Is this in fact why Alice invents a controversy they cannot overcome on the night before flying overseas?) Dan's fiction is that Alice is his possession ("mine," he tells the cabbie) from the first moment he sees her and takes his confessed liberties by kissing her while she is unconscious beside him (if indeed she is) on the ride to the hospital. In their mythological nostalgia for meet-cute inevitability, they inadvertently betray commentary on the poorly concealed truth of their feelings, beyond the romanticized constructions they overlay on their reality: they have a rehearsed litany of trivia ("What was in my sandwiches?" "What color was my apple?"), and when Alice correctly answers the question, "What were your first words to me?" with "Hello, Stranger," Dan playfully comments, "What a slut." This is, in fact, precisely what each has feared about the other from their first meeting: she has known she would lose him because she can't share in his inner life as a cultured woman like Anna can; he has known he can not trust her because of her unsettling combination of immediately assumed intimacy and unapologetic revelation of her stripper past. And when Dan, in their nostalgic trivia trips, tells his story of kissing her in the cab to the hospital, which he presumably is recounting as another part of this mythologizing litany, she playfully interjects, "You brute," precisely the conclusion she draws—in dead seriousness—as their relationship ends several minutes later, when he acquiesces to her taunting demand to hit her, since "that's what you want."

Anna also sees clearly but in her complicity refuses to see that she has been objectified as a desirable pawn in the territorial battles of Dan and Larry. Larry does the same to Alice, and Alice is even more active in her complicity than Anna to abet Larry's objectification of her. Nichols has said "the film is about how powerful people deal with 'being in the power of someone else.'"[9] In such to-the-death competitions, there must be a victor, and in Larry, *Closer*'s "most obnoxious and least deluded character,"[10] Marber has created a misanthropic equal to *Carnal Knowledge*'s Jonathan, a terrorist of the emotions with a "caveman" point of view on sexual politics. "Even *Closer*'s self-styled caveman might blanch" at some of Jonathan's concluding self-pronouncements on phallocracy, "yet Jonathan's plight can be viewed as a salutary warning of where Larry's relentless objectification of women [...] might lead him ten years down the line."[11] Like Jonathan, Larry remains resolutely unreconstructed. Larry delivers an important, terse summation of reified despair in the last scene of Marber's stage play, lost to the adaptive revision but still present in the spirit of the screenplay: "Everyone learns, nobody changes."[12] There can be no bleaker understanding of human existence in the cinematic world Nichols has created over the past half-century: that a man (or woman) can understand the need for change and the means of his transformation, yet retreat into the systemic defaults of objectified control, settling for "victory" in exchange for his soul.

* * *

A familiar Nichols touch—the circular soundtrack—brings us into *Closer* even before the titles begin. The mournful tempo of Damien Rice's spare, plaintive "The Blower's Daughter" accents well the slow-motion photography introduced in the opening montage, a variation of the old cinematic cliché of lovers moving towards each other from opposed angles. Centered in cross-cut shots of crowds on London's pavement are Alice, instantly striking with her dyed hair, tacky faux-fur coat, and mini-skirt, and Dan, far less noticeable save that his place on screen and in his respective sidewalk crowd is a form-cut replacement of the spot where we've just been watching Alice. The variation on the standard Hollywood visual trope of reunion is that these two have never met: they look at the camera, and what they see, as each approaches the curb to the traffic street that separates them, is each other. Indeed, as Rice's chorus, the five-times repeated "I can't take my eyes off of you," ends in a sixth repetition cut short to begin the second verse, Natalie Portman as Alice and Jude Law as Dan have moved into close-up range of the camera and, with proximity, into the forthright and smiling gaze of what appears to be recognition. Rice's second verse begins in a statement of self-fulfilled prophecy that never finishes—Alice, the young American new to London, has stepped out into the street after looking the wrong way, and our first shot at normal speed interjects the unconventional: a crane shot from several stories directly above where Alice lies prone on the street. The new angle asserts a disassociating, clinical distance on what we thought we were watching unfold, a radical rupture of narrative rhetoric that alerts us, for the first of many times, to deceptive practice: our assumptions about what we see ought not to be trusted.

The sequence, which does not appear in Marber's stage play except as immediate backstory to how these two strangers end up waiting together in the hospital for her treatment of a minor leg abrasion, is a valuable addition to the narrative's examination of the corrosive dangers of wishful thinking aided by willful ignorance of the real. The formalist accenting of the opening shots—slow-motion cross-cuts followed by the God's eye view—invites an ironic distance on what we're watching. There is a romanticized nostalgia in the audience as two recognizable Hollywood faces approach one another; further complicating the effect is our learning eventually that both these characters, Dan and Alice, like to indulge themselves (and each other) in romanticized nostalgia—though of the two, Dan is the more susceptible, as his return to haunt Postman's Park in the film's epilogue suggests. As in *The Graduate*, which opens and closes with Benjamin Braddock (Dustin Hoffman) enveloped in Simon and Garfunkel's "The Sounds of Silence," passively conveyed into a future he hasn't chosen, *Closer* begins and ends with "The Blower's Daughter," its refrain repeated enough times to connote helpless psychological obsession. *The Graduate* presents the illusion of movement in the freneticism of Benjamin the Track Star's mad dash throughout the southern half of California, yet, upon reflection, one is left to conclude that Benjamin is merely running away, without any positive objective in mind. In *Closer*, the narrative's full-circle return leads us to Alice on Broadway, again the beautiful face in the crowd as the lyric's obsessiveness repeats. Once she is off screen, the narrative ends, and the credits begin scrolling on a black screen; the song reaches its final chorus, where "eyes" is replaced by "mind": a fair assessment of Dan's state at film's end, since he will never see Alice again except in the haunting of his mind's eye. If Alice's sidewalk stroll in slow-motion is the clearest visual repetition of the film's opening, Dan's psychological repetition as he haunts and is haunted by Postman's Park is the film's adamant statement of Larry's idea, in the play, that "everyone learns, nobody changes." It is a pessimistic artistic rendering of reified stasis, the flip side of the free flow of reified wisdom in many of the films in the second half of Nichols' career. *Closer* serves as additional, cautionary tempering of the optimism of films like *Regarding Henry* and *The Birdcage*. In his previous film, the epic *Angels in America*, Nichols conveyed the full, career-long complexity of his vision, the tempered optimism that reification can, beyond its social imprisonments, also bring the insights necessary to liberation. While Prior Walter (Justin Kirk) and Hannah and Harper Pitt (Meryl Streep and Mary-Louise Parker) experience an enlightening revision of identity in relation to the objectifying world around them, Roy Cohn (Al Pacino) and Joe Pitt (Patrick Wilson) are held fast by their reified bonds. In *Closer*, *no one* escapes the iron grip of reified entrapment.

Despite his shape-shifting predilections as a novelist (and in online chatter assuming promiscuously libertine female identities), Dan may have more opportunity to learn and change than anyone in the film; at the very least, his moments of recognition are most formally underscored by Nichols, using mirrors as Lacanian signifiers of arrested self-formation, invitations to see himself and failing to see. "Nichols, Goldblatt, and the production designer Tim Hatley find visual equivalents for *Closer*'s examination of the slippery nature of identity: the reflections of faces in mirrors in Dan's flat, the strip club, the airport hotel, in Anna's camera lenses, computer screens or in the glass walls of the Aquarium tanks; the translucent walls of the private room in the strip club."[13] When Dan waits for Anna to arrive at the opera, he is aware of the errand she's been on that day, trying to extract Larry's signature for the divorce that will leave Anna free to be with Dan. He has little sense as yet of Larry's capabilities as an artist of revenge; when Anna comes running up the stairs with her one-word explanation of her lateness ("Traffic"), and when she is vaguely evasive in accepting his toast on her success in securing the signature, his imagination turns to what *she* is capable of, rather than what Larry is capable of: she has repeatedly deceived Larry with Dan. In the men's room, he regards himself in the mirror. He is looking at a treacherous person, who is in love with a treacherous person who has been married to a treacherous person. And he bursts with accurate accusations when he returns to the table and, in so doing, drives her away. In "a superb addition to the play, giving us a preparatory, and slightly ominous, glimpse of the couple's domestic life,"[14] mirrors are prominently framed features of mise-en-scène in Alice and Dan's preparations to attend Anna's show, "Strangers": in a complicated visual composition, both Dan and Alice appear in his bathroom mirror, Alice self-conscious about his potential for treachery with Anna because she herself has been deceiving him all along, pretending to be a foundling. A mirror, yet to be mounted in Larry's surgery, dominates mise-en-scène in the shot after Anna has slept with Larry and finally gains his signature on the divorce papers, per the Machiavellian deal he has struck with her. Intercut as a flashback to her confrontation with Dan after his own moment of conviction in the opera bathroom mirror, the immersive presence of Mozart's *Così fan tutte*, a sonic mirror of their infidelity, merges their similarly corrosive insights about themselves and, inevitably, each other. Late in the film, on the eve of his trip with Alice to New York in celebration of their four years (mostly) together, Dan again confronts himself in a mirror—this time in a hotel elevator, having just pushed Alice further with possessive accusations than he had any right to do. He's been wearing contacts, but he has just taken his "eyes out," the euphemism for switching to glasses but the accented metaphor for default blindness to the consequences of the objectifying impulse. His relation to the elevator mirror is identical to the camera's capture of his moment before the lavatory mirror at the opera while he was still with Anna. Regarding himself again, he now has learned what his hypocritical possessiveness has done to one relationship, though as he was hectoring Alice with his "eyes out," he couldn't see it, blind to all but his presumption of ownership. Chastened by giving himself a good look, he returns with his ill-gotten prop of a rose as peace-offering, only to find that he has done it again, driving Alice away as he'd driven Anna away.

As Dan had said to Anna during their confrontation, Larry is the only one who "understands" him; Dan acknowledges how "clever" Larry is: "I almost admire him." To get "truth," he will have to go to Larry, who describes himself as "a clinical observer of the human carnival." The "truth" that Larry understands and Dan learns (without either of them changing) is that of the "caveman," as Larry calls himself. The caveman is, above all, territorial. Survival, let alone profit, may be measured in whether one has gained or lost turf, property, goods. Larry is ambitious, having raised his status from working-class origins (still abundantly evident in his broad accent) to life as a physician—a dermatologist, an expert on skin, on surfaces. Yet when we see him at work the first time, what occupies his consciousness is not his patients (a distraction he attempts to deflect as quickly as possible) but fantasies of sexual mastery and conquest. For Larry, women are objects. Certainly this is displayed in his behavior in the online chat room with Dan, and in the private room with Alice at the club, where women are reduced to fetishized anatomy to be revealed in slow, ritualized tease. Ultimately, it is his use of the two women in the film that most clearly displays his objectifying, commodifying instincts. The night he returns from his conference in New York, he has a confession to make: he has had sex with a working girl at the Paramount Hotel. Although he understands Anna may attach consequences to this behavior, it has not prevented him from acting on his desire; he claims to be telling her the truth now because he loves her. The obvious objection would be to wonder why his love could not stop him from pursuing this unfaithful course, but this becomes a minor consideration when weighed against his appalling hypocrisy when Anna makes her own confession. He knows that she struggles with self-image and depression (she's even been subject in past relationships to physical abuse); he briefly attempts a pep talk: "Anna, you're making the mistake of your life. You're leaving me because you think you don't deserve happiness, but you do." Then he stops himself, and as Dan is compelled to accuse both Anna and Alice, so Larry now accuses Anna, having finally understood the mystery of her redressing after her bath. He is as relentless as a detective with his detailed (and eventually comparative) questioning, and Anna finally asks, "*Why is the sex so important?*" Larry's subsequent "caveman" explanation stands as much for Dan as himself (because he "understands" them both): Anna is contested territory between the men. And so Larry goads Anna into ever more humiliating revelations, until she has been reduced to attack, which in turn reduces Larry to adversarial, marauding caveman. For Larry, attack is truth, because life is predation. He spits at both Alice and Anna at the height of hostility with each, "Thank you. Thank you for your honesty." The context both times is his having goaded them to reductive insults, justifying his own atavistic reversion. After Larry confesses to Dan that he's slept with Alice, Dan asks what he and Larry always ask when confronted with evidence of having been cuckolded: did she enjoy it? Larry assures him that his objective was not "to give her a 'nice time'" but to injure Dan: "A good fight is never clean." Larry thinks of Anna and Alice as property to be vandalized.

Dan, who knows that Larry "understands" him, has a similar response to women (beneath the appearance of a sensibility of greater tenderness). When he first meets Alice, he takes the "waif" under his wing, assuming a proprietary paternalism that allows him instantly to claim her as "mine" to the cab driver, whose question about Alice reflects his own possessive understanding of love. "Is she yours?" may be an innocently Anglicized shorthand to ascertain relationship status, but it nonetheless yields troubling linguistic assumptions about power. In exploiting Alice's life for his art, Dan aestheticizes Alice's troubling past—it is likely easier for him to think of her hyper-sexualized experience as his fiction rather than her fact. What's more, during his conversation in Anna's loft while having his jacket photo taken, he translates this literary co-opting of Alice's experience into erotic capital he can then use in betraying her by seducing Anna. (As it turns out, he's not even a very good novelist; he's only managed to find good "material.") Dan grows tired of his possession of Alice, not on any enlightened political ground but in the way that materialism always breeds exhaustion and restless desire for something new, as a person might tire of furniture, or seek to trade in an old car on a newer model. He enters into an affair with Anna and, later, into fantasies online; he parts ways with Alice, drives Anna away, and eventually drives Alice away again. A life predicated upon acquisition, ownership, and accumulation is a life of craving for the next unpossessed object; the clearest evidence of this is that Dan understands best what a woman has meant to him only after he has "lost" her (sometimes more than once).

In that first, immediately flirtatious conversation with Anna at her studio, each is quick to accuse the other of "stealing" as a means of artistic creation. Having learned that the heroine of Dan's book, *The Aquarium*, is based on a woman named "Alice," Anna asks, "How does she feel about you stealing her life?" Dan corrects her: "*Borrowing* her life"—then he looks for his opportunity to deflect the accusation with an equivalence of Anna's stealing people's likenesses in her photographs; she parrots his own correction ("*Borrowing*") to their mutual amusement. Yet in what sense (other than perhaps a royalty) is it possible to talk about a reciprocal exchange on "borrowing" a past or a likeness? In fact, Dan and Anna recognize in each other (as Dan and Larry recognize their shared "caveman" identities) the shared instinct for commodification of individuals in their art. The creative distance necessary to abstract the real into a formalized artifice makes, when done well, its own truth. Yet Dan and Anna exemplify the danger of exploration inherent in commodifying reality: while bonding over their artistic instinct, they fail truly to feel the gravity of the real woman they betray. After Alice arrives and shoos Dan away so she can confront Anna about the seduction she senses has taken place between Dan and Anna, Alice renders herself for Anna as object to be aestheticized. She is complicit in her own objecthood when, shedding tears by the window, she insists Anna photograph her. The moment seems genuinely to move and inspire Anna—but doesn't keep her from sleeping with Dan. Later, at the opening to Anna's exhibition, "Strangers," long before she learns he is the artist's boyfriend, Alice deconstructs Anna's show for Larry. Those "who appreciate 'art,'" she says, "say it's beautiful because that's what they *want* to see. [...T]he people in the photos are sad and alone, but the pictures make the world *seem* beautiful. So the exhibition is 'reassuring,' which makes it a lie, and everyone loves a big, fat lie."

Alice would know, of course. Her identity from first to last in *Closer* is a construction, a "big, fat lie" for people to love. In nearly every episode of the film, she has "made herself over"—especially her hair, but also clothes, make-up, even body language. Wearing a ridiculous platinum wig in the scene with Larry at the strip club does not prevent her from wearing a longer, blonder wig at the club when Dan subsequently tracks her down. These "makeovers" are a part of her re-creative "armor," as Larry calls it when referring to the aliases the girls at the strip club adopt. All these surface efforts of re-creation are intended to guard against genuine commitment and avoid "shame" about self-commodification. The characters in *Closer* lie with such frequency and alacrity that, as observers, we begin to suspect that anything they say is as likely to be a lie for unknown, ulterior motives as it is to be the truth. Which of the sparse "facts" Alice tells Dan at their first meeting is true? Is it really Anna's "birthday" the afternoon she and Larry accidentally meet at the Aquarium? Does anyone ever really love anyone, just because they claim to do so? This is Alice's condemnation of

At the opening of a portrait exhibition entitled "Strangers" (which could have been the title of Nichols' film, instead of the ironic *Closer*), two masters of manipulative autonomy meet. Larry (Clive Owen) and Alice (Natalie Portman) see the objectifying nature of the world better than their romantic partners, affording them control of their relationships. This remains their consolation in the inevitable collapse of the illusion of love, which cannot coexist with manipulation. The ambiguously exploitative image of Alice on the wall recalls a similarly displayed image of Bobbie (Ann-Margret) in *Carnal Knowledge*, the film from early in Nichols' career to which *Closer* so closely corresponds.

Dan, just before erasing him from her life: "Where is this '*love*?' I can't see it, I can't touch it, I can't *feel* it. I can *hear* it; I can hear some *words*, but I can't do anything with your easy words." Who is "Alice," however, to be making such a self-righteous claim? There is no bigger, fatter liar in *Closer* than "Alice Ayres," with her continual, four-year deception.

In *The Graduate*, Buck Henry and Nichols set up as the centerpiece of their film an extraordinary ten-minute scene at the Taft Hotel in which, after half a summer of joyless erotic congress, Benjamin insists to Mrs. Robinson that they legitimize their relationship via "conversation." Implicit is the assumption that the shared self-revelation of dialogue begets meaning, and this is borne out (although hardly as Benjamin in his naivety had intended) in their ensuing exchange. The conversation at the heart of *The Graduate* is the most traditionally dramatic episode of the film: two characters alone together, revealing themselves to each other (and us) via their words, until they can no longer stand it. "Let's not talk at all" is Benjamin's profoundly disillusioned summary of what the conversation has taught him; he longs to retreat back into illusion, and thus the second half of the film is the result, with its pretty, fantasy images of boy-girl romance and rescue. *Closer*, originally a stage play, is necessarily stocked with such dysfunctional conversations, yet one in particular, which Lane calls "the core of the picture,"[15] creates an interesting study in contrasts between two masters of manipulative objectification: the strip-club conversation between Larry and Alice, during which, outraged by Alice's ironical, performed lines, Larry fumes, "I'm trying to have a conversation here!" The ironies of this scene are as thick with murk as the lighting and sound systems of the club. Two people speak the truth past each other, revealing nothing. In *Closer*'s "examination of the way modern people talk their way through and around treachery—simultaneously seeking and sabotaging intimacy,"[16] the club scene verbalizes all the desires and defenses of these brutal, brutalized people. Not even Anna and Larry's sordid, blue confessions of infidelity to one another upon his return from his conference in New York have the same multi-dimensional effect: their break-up scene is designed for maximum injury; the club scene's injuries somehow manage to reveal (to us, though not to each other) the yearning beneath the savagery. "The characters in "Closer" don't wound each other with deceit, like most couples do," writes Sean Smith. "They brutalize their lovers with truth."[17] Yet, as Dennis Lim points out, "Brute honesty is simply the purest form of emotional deceit."[18] It's only much, much later, as she returns to her native country, that we know "Alice" has stripped herself bare before Larry at the club—offering him that most totemic of her possessions, her true identity, confident that he can't possibly believe her.

There are layers within layers of deception in their situation in the "Paradise Suite," one of eight such identical private performance rooms in the club. Underlying all, of course, is Alice's identity as "Alice," eventually revealed by the film's denouement to be a construction. There is also, on her side, the performed fiction of her identity as a "private dancer," an even more blatant complicity in self-commodification than her yielding herself as "slut" to Dan's pen or as "sad" to Anna's camera. She strikes a series of poses for Larry in the "Paradise Suite," some at his direction, others her exceedingly rote, professional contortions. A further layering of deception has its source within Larry: it is never clear whether, in pursuing her within and beyond the "Paradise Suite," he feels any genuine attraction to her at all, or whether he has only pursued her, as he claims to Dan, as a means to further vengeance ("It's not a war," Alice claims at one point during their conversation, and Larry laughs). All Larry's protestations of love and of desire to see her may only be attempts to establish feigned intimacy; ironically, the usual reason a man performs emotional connection as a deceptive act is as a means to the end of sexual gratification, an abstracting of the woman as sex-object. Larry's deception, however, may be even *more* abstract: the sex act *itself* may not be the point, either, but rather merely an act of aggression against another person (Dan) not even present. This is why Alice seems so hurt when Dan reveals at the end that Larry has used her not as a *sex* object (which, after all, she herself has fostered as a stripper and which thus affords her the illusion of power) but instead as a *revenge* object, denying her even the illusion of control. "Why did he tell you?" she asks. "How could he?" Given that she is in the midst of leaving Dan, there should be more than enough emotional upheaval for her to process. That she lingers over this bombshell suggests how deeply Larry has deceived her and she has deceived herself about the "power" she possesses. Her only trump card is to rely upon the power she holds over them all concerning her identity: she is inviolable because she is unknowable.

Larry begins the Paradise Suite conversation with a ridiculously glib utterance: "I love you," to which Alice responds precisely as she would to an erotic compliment, or to cash: with a crisp, professional "Thank you." She collects his money, words, and *gaze* as tokens of her assumed control over her objecthood; she understands herself to be in charge, and she maintains the further "security" of the cameras that watch and restrain client behavior. Larry becomes more heated—or at least performs the role of the overheated male—when attempting to approach the "reality" of Alice rather than the "performance" of the private dancer.

At one point, she asks him his profession (though she in fact reveals later that she already knows he's a dermatologist), and he seizes on this as evidence of a non-professional curiosity about him: "It's a chink in your armor," he says, referring to the dancers' inevitable desire to remain anonymous to fend off unwanted suitors beyond work. "I'm not wearing armor," she protests, twisting it towards a provocation she can control, considering how little she actually *is* wearing. "*Yes you are*," he insists, and he focuses upon her stage name, "Jane," as evidence to support his supposition. When she avows that Jane is her real name, the brokenness of the commodified environment in which they encounter each other is so profound that he can parry, with confidence, "We both know it *isn't*." Neither knows a thing, in actuality, about the other, because the "relationship" has been forged in the corrosive mutual mistrust of power.

The enormous outlay of cash that changes hands cannot buy him any other name, though we understand by film's end that he has paid repeatedly for a truth he cannot or will not believe (or perhaps has only pretended to care about to begin with). Later, he amends his initial protestation of love to something that, even in hindsight and at face value, we can believe: "I love everything about you that hurts." What he intends here is an equation of their powerlessness, the two jilted lovers of Anna and Dan. Larry can appreciate when people hurt. However, since Alice refuses to be jilted ("*I'm* the one who leaves," she tells Dan, and does so the instant his back is turned), she is constitutionally incapable of thanking Larry for this particular compliment. But just as she hides in plain sight behind her real name, this may be the closest Larry comes to revealing *himself*: he responds to the suffering of others; it is how he gets what he wants. The important differences between Benjamin's conversation with Mrs. Robinson in *The Graduate* and the conversation Larry claims he is "trying" to have with Alice is that Benjamin actually wants—however misguided—to establish a justifying intimacy with Mrs. Robinson, and the conversation in the Taft Hotel room literally reveals all about what they have been doing together all summer. Neither Larry nor Alice genuinely seeks contact in *Closer*, and so it is no surprise that all remains concealed between them. The most important parallel between these two great set-piece conversations at opposite ends of Nichols' long Hollywood career is that both establish clearly that when the conditions for intimacy are absent, replaced by commodifying barter and manipulative grasping for control, all that can result from such a conversation is frustration and silence. "Let's not talk at all," a wounded Benjamin mutters as postscript, and in *Closer*, Larry commands Alice to perform a silent striptease, his money having bought him the illusion of control.

Marber's title has obvious ironies, given the chilly atmosphere of the narrative's failed relationships and emotional frigidity ("You're cold," Larry pronounces upon Alice in the Paradise Suite; "You're all cold at heart"—but it is a diagnosis that as easily fits the caveman's mentality of love as war). The comparative form of the word "closer," however, is left ambiguously vague: closer than what, or *to* what? Marber attributes the title to an intended allusion: the British band Joy Division's 1980 album, awash in morbid assumptions of doomed love.[19] Within the context of the film, the title projects the paradox of wearing metaphorical "armor" while at the same time seeking contact. Alice is thus the perfect embodiment of the title's ironies. At once, she projects an image of total fidelity ("I would have loved you forever") and utter alienation (she has never revealed her name, most basic tenet of identity). Even her "forever" declaration comes freighted by the conditional tense—hardly an uncompromised commitment. Her commitment is always and only to the inviolability of herself, maintained through concealment of herself, even at her most naked (in the strip club, stating her real name). Perhaps this commitment to self-concealment and re-packaging of identity is why she moves from stripper to food service and back again: each is a job she is more likely to be able to negotiate off the books, avoiding issues of identity, than if she'd dedicated herself to a job with the promise of future advancement. Alice does not *believe* in future advancement, only knee-jerk rebooting of identity.

It is possible to understand all the relationships in *Closer* as invitations to self-reflection. Dan has acknowledged this when he says that Larry "understands" him, but he has also demonstrated it when, in looking himself in the eye while in the lavatory at the opera house, what he sees reflected there are Anna's infidelities. It's why Nichols has saturated the film with Mozart's *Così fan tutte*: inconstancy is in the air these people breathe, and in the hermeticism of their shared chamber drama, the air is simply recirculated among them until it has poisoned them all. Dan and Alice in particular are attracted to Mozart's opera buffo: it's as likely to enter a scene diegetically, because the characters have actively sought to listen to it, as non-diegetically, because Nichols has selected it for its choric commentary on the characters from beyond the world of the film. Like "The Blower's Daughter," used non-diegetically to bookend the film, *Così fan tutte* is employed to pervasive, compulsive effect, like the lovers' treachery and fear of treachery. Alice takes one look at Dan after his shoot with Anna and knows she had better listen carefully to what they say to each other; her own foundational lie, perpetuated for four years, fine-tunes her ear to detect false notes in others' voices. Anna and Dan instantly see the exploitative impulse of the artist in one another; Anna and Larry intuitively detect the strangeness in each other's choice to bathe late at night and then dress again. With all the powerful insight each of them brings to the subjects of deception and infidelity, it's a wonder that they are so often vulnerable. Ultimately, the two more traditionally privileged individuals, Dan and Anna, are least resilient. Their deceptions are of the heart, deceiving others to be together, and their greatest deception is of themselves: that they can be at peace together, each knowing what they were capable of once. Larry and Alice are more accomplished at this game of emotional survival than either Dan or Anna; in the Paradise Suite, with an admiration for Alice he doesn't even attempt to conceal, Larry says, "You're strong." What more admirable quality for a caveman to contemplate? Strength is Larry's chief characteristic as well, though others might more likely perceive it as ruthlessness or savagery. "Without forgiveness, we're *savages*," Larry tells Dan when they talk about their women at Larry's surgery, but after he "prescribes" Alice for Dan, he poisons Dan with the revelation of having slept with Alice, too. Undercutting his earlier claim about forgiveness and his own civility, Larry says, "I'm just not big enough to forgive you." Strength is his weakness: he has to win. Larry lays claim compulsively to his inner caveman. He sleeps peacefully at film's end because he has come to terms with the limitations of love, settling instead for manipulative possession. He owns them all: Anna, despite his abuse, continues to share his marriage bed; he stuns Alice with his ability to manipulate her into the revenge sex she's already announced to him, in the Paradise Suite, will never happen; and Dan is ruined for love, having lost both women he thought he could have and hold. With each of the three, Larry assumes a very personal, possessive control, and the compulsion to do so is, ironically, most acute in relation to Dan. Responding to what he's read in the body language between Anna and Dan the night of her exhibit opening, he allows the learned refinement of his educated accent to slip back to its most antagonistic blue-collar roots: "I could 'ave 'im. [...] If it came to it, in a scrap, I could 'ave 'im." As in the cabbie's inquiring of Dan, "Is she yours?" when driving Alice to the hospital, Marber finds embedded within the idiomatic absurdity of Larry's non sequitur claim the etymological truth: a bald statement of possessive dominion, predicated in atavistic strength, power, caveman savagery.

It isn't surprising that Nichols and Marber, having found the victor in the "war" these four participants have waged, do not linger long on Larry's peaceful slumber at the end: there is no need to because Larry is everywhere: he "has" them all. He coerces Anna to become his "whore," and though she has the signed divorce papers to show for it, she can see Dan's love "draining out" of him as if from a wound. Disgusted by her, he says, "All I can see is *him* all over you." After he has lost Alice, Dan again can see only Larry: "he wanted *this* to happen." Nichols and Marber do not need Larry to be active in the epilogue, because his caveman strength has set in motion the self-inflicted ruin of all the other participants. This is an instinct Marber carries over from the stage play: Larry is on stage just long enough in the final scene so that he can make a very obvious exit. Larry is not so unambiguously the "victor" in the play as he is in the film, however: he and Anna are not together, his surgery and subsequent romantic relationship have failed, and he expects not to have long-term love in his future. While he and Anna share a marriage bed in the concluding montage of Nichols' version, the doom is palpable. Acknowledging *Closer*'s irony, A. O. Scott observes, "in the end, its plot conforms to the basic rules of comedy without offering much in the way of consolation."[20] The biggest change in the ending involves Alice, who in the play has died in another street-crossing accident, this time back in the U.S.; Dan has been notified (and thus learns her real name) because his address remains among her effects. This creates a more sentimentalized vision of Alice/Jane in the play version, providing evidence of her retained flame for Dan; it also recasts the opening "accident" in the new light of a second, identical accident, suggesting that what appeared to be a careless act may have been premeditation— if not the first time, then perhaps the second. Returning via Nichols' film to a renewed exploration of the characters, Marber uncovers a second interpretation of their fates. Of these, clearly the most radically transformed from the play's conclusion is Alice, who is buoyantly, defiantly alive in the film's last shot, and with no implied residue of sentimental attachment to Dan. Although hurt by men before London, and hurt by at least two men in London, she remains sovereign in the hoarded truth of herself, a vision in slow motion of youthful strength and beauty. What lingers, however, is the wistfulness (and, perhaps, sincerity) of her question, when Dan announces he's breaking up with her to be with Anna, "Why isn't love enough?"

Her question reveals Alice in all her ambiguous and ambivalent complexity: a passionate, strong woman willing to commit years of her life to a relationship without ever, in her vulnerable terror of weakness, taking off the "armor" of an instinctively improvised name. In a narrative in which everyone sees the duplicity in others by having lived so long and contemplated so intimately one's own duplicity, her question haunts her. Dan's infidelity condemns her own deceptions. She may not know the answer to the question, but she knows the truth of what has provoked it. Her tragedy, whether she lives (as in the film) or dies (as in the play) is most profoundly located in the self-knowledge that either way, she is emotionally dead: her absolute need to control all contact makes contact impossible. She is "Alice" because she has known all along "love" was not enough, and therefore she can never be Jane with someone else.

Dan claims a different premise for what civilizes us than Larry's claim of "forgiveness." In his final, fatal missteps of a self-fulfilling doomed relationship with Alice, Dan claims that without the *truth*, "we're animals." Truth is the redeeming possibility within reification—one's awareness of complicit surrender to systems of destructive objecthood. In his magnum opus, *Angels in America*, Nichols offered us characters stuck in reified stasis like Roy and Joe and others (Prior, Harper, Hannah, Belize) capable of transformation because they encounter not one or the other but *both* of these civilizing influences Larry and Dan articulate. Belize is the film's most profound example of this civility—able to express forgiveness even as he continues to nurse grudges—and Prior manifests this same civility in his willingness to reclaim Louis as a friend despite the enormity of the wrong Louis has done him. What *Angels* prophesies is emergent kindness, an expanded definition of "citizens." As in *Carnal Knowledge*, Nichols' earlier chamber drama on the alienating destruction wrought by objectification, reified truths are everywhere in evidence in *Closer*, but the principals are too fragile or threatened to act in anything but savage, isolating self-defense. The truth, co-opted for possessive manipulation, is at best half-truth, and nowhere near love. Larry's manipulative power comes in using the truth to destroy. Anna, Alice, and Dan all prove capable of breathtaking cruelty and manipulative abuse, even if it is not quite as close to the surface in any of them as it is in caveman Larry. Dan and Alice may appear, in their rekindled romance, to have combined the civilizing agents of truth and forgiveness, but in their final hour together, what they have used to mend their brokenness is illusion: their long-nurtured desire to mythologize (and thus distort out of recognizable correspondence to the realities they fear) their romance of the "Waif" and the "Knight" (words Alice uses in the opening scene of the play[21] and film). The story they tell each other in their oft-rehearsed, meet-cute catechism seeks to cover the badly concealed brittleness of their connection, in which he has shut her out of his past (the burial of his father) almost as completely as he's been shut out of hers. They have found each other to shelter together a while from the storm, full of the knowledge that love is not enough. They only have fantasy to impose as an alternative to facing their fears—the fantasy of the fated collision of strangers. (And when the fantasy of "Alice" ends, it's "Welcome back, Miss Jones.") Like Larry, Alice understands another, equally bankrupt alternative: autonomous control. If Larry can "'ave" Dan, so can she; the reprise of "The Blower's Daughter" at film's end assures us that she does. Her image as she strides through Times Square bespeaks self-possession. She has made herself over yet again. It will have to do.

21

"We'll see"

Charlie Wilson's War (2007)

Mike Nichols' 20th feature film finds him back inside the Beltway where, a decade earlier, he'd examined the compromises of the Presidential campaign trail in *Primary Colors*. Like that earlier film, *Charlie Wilson's War* is about outsiders impinging upon hegemony— and the ways in which hegemony inevitably impinges right back. "The following is based on a true story," we're told near the beginning of the film; a disclaimer as the closing credits end adds: "While this picture is based upon a true story, some of the characters have been composited or invented, and a number of incidents fictionalized." Nichols knows that what is central to making his fictional films work, even when based on factual events, is "'at what point you liberate the story by finding central conflicts and central metaphors.'"[1] Like *Silkwood*, the film is not primarily intended to provide a documentary, historicizing function. Its appearance in Hollywood, however, at the tail end of a long, grim season in Fall 2007 of U.S. foreign-ops films—including *In the Valley of Elah* (Paul Haggis) and *The Kingdom* (Peter Berg), both released September 28; *Redacted* (Brian De Palma, released October 10); *Rendition* (Gavin Hood, released October 19); and *Lions for Lambs* (Robert Redford, released November 9)—all but ensured Nichols' film (released December 21), the best and most complicated of the pack, would meet with critical and box-office exhaustion. It's a film that deserves to be reconsidered, especially as the U.S. quagmire in Afghanistan spreads wider into its second decade.

The plot of *Charlie Wilson's War* is predictably complicated, considering the international conspiracy against Communism that it depicts, though Aaron Sorkin's rapid-fire screenplay manages to capture both the flavor of the personalities and some inkling of the complexity of their entanglements in a crisp 105 minutes and is "more of a hoot than any picture dealing with the bloody, protracted fight between the Soviet Army and the Afghan mujahideen has any right to be."[2] As in the analysis of earlier political or biographical films by Nichols, this examination of *Charlie Wilson's War* will focus not on the veracity of the biographical or historical elements of the story but on how the film explores Nichols' characteristic preoccupations with the human condition bound within constrictive social structures. In the three main characters of the film—Charlie Wilson (Tom Hanks), a playboy Texas Congressman who calls in all his political I.O.U.'s to fund a covert alliance with the Afghan mujahideen against the Soviet Union; Joanne Herring (Julia Roberts, in her second consecutive starring role for Nichols), the Houston billionaire socialite whose reactionary right-wing politics fuel her anti–Communist passion; and Gust Avrakatos (Philip Seymour Hoffman), a rogue CIA operative with anti–Communist passion and no interest in agency politics—Nichols and Sorkin, working from Crile's propulsive 2003 exposé, offer three distinct versions of the reified individual, each locked within objectified, objectifying positions of influence.

As presented by George Crile in the book Sorkin adapted, the public record reflects the unlikely conspiracy of three people whose cultural stratifications should have provided no entrée to one another: the natural objectifying order of class structure typically would have operated to insulate Herring in her enormous wealth, Wilson in his modest middle-class Texas origins as son of a timber-company accountant, and Avrakatos as the second-generation son of a "Greek soda-pop maker." What unites them is ideology: opposing foreign incursions of Communism during the Cold War that threaten American interests. As the narrative of *Charlie Wilson's War* begins, the Soviets have long since marched into Afghanistan, and Congress has earmarked $5 million in token military aid to fund Afghani resistance. The anti–Communist rhetoric that flows freely from all the important players in the covert initiative that directly leads to the first defeat of the vaunted Red Army serves as bond between strange bedfellows; the phrase "kill some Russians" is the verbal equivalent of a secret handshake.

Beyond a willingness to depersonalize and thus objectify the enemy to bend it to one's will, what these three principals share is strategic placement within the structures of American authority—Herring via the ultimate clout of capital, Wilson and Avrakatos via tenuously assigned stations within governmental hierarchy. Yet *Charlie Wilson's War* quickly establishes all three as unconventional avatars of hegemony, who must slyly use the system against itself in order to accomplish their goals. Of the three, Avrakatos emerges as most aware of reified reality, acutely sensitive to the dangerous ramifications of what they are enacting in Afghanistan's war with the Soviets if they are not prepared to enact equally far-reaching, transformative post-war development once the country is freed from Soviet tyranny.

Joanne Herring as portrayed by Julia Roberts is a high-rent variation on Roberts' Oscar-winning portrayal of the title character in *Erin Brockovich* (Steven Soderbergh, 2000), with her broad mouth, brass, and mountainous décolletage. Her money and socialite connections give her access to power that is just as swiftly undercut by gendered traditionalism. Rather than disguise herself as a man in conservative clothing and behavior, however (which, in any case, in her reactionary Texas circles, would not fly), she accentuates her physical and monetary assets, unapologetically sexualized and commodified. If Charlie charms and Gust bulldozes to get their respective ways, Joanne Herring seduces. She has recognized that what she wants will necessitate strange bedfellows, and that, in the realities of patriarchal sexual politics, the bed may sometimes be a literal one.

Gust Avrakatos is "coarse," as Cravely (John Slattery), a patrician CIA supervisor, calls him. The word is freighted with intended cultural baggage referencing Avrakatos' ethnicity; his blue-collar, "street" sensibility; and, of course, his impolitic preference for unvarnished truth over unctuous conformity. He is easy to dismiss, despite his bristling intelligence, because intelligence that bristles is no more welcome in the polarizing simplification of political ideology than it is anywhere else. Gust is a constant, reified threat to entrenched, complacent hegemony—a direct invitation to be summarily, categorically dismissed. There is, of course, no social position more desirable to a covert operative than to be dismissed, and Gust uses his persona non grata status in the Company to make things happen in Central Asia. Whether entirely organic, entirely manufactured, or (what is most likely) a combination of the two, Gust's iconoclastic antipathy to the inbred, silver-spoon fecklessness of what he encounters in the U.S. Intelligence community makes him well qualified to elude foreign radar but also his own meddling bureaucracy. Tragically, as he notes at the end of the film, that bureaucracy to which he and Charlie Wilson turn over their operation will scuttle what they have managed to effect, precisely because it is unable or does not *wish* to see the irony of what Gust cannot help but see: our country's dangerously short attention span and our aversion to a Soviet ideology that intervenes on foreign soil purely from self-interest will lead to our pursuing a course identical to the one we have opposed in the Soviets.

Charlie Wilson, the man whose "special recognition by the "Clandestine Service" operates as the ironized frame for the narrative (the recognition seems simultaneously more deserved and more ambiguous when we return to it at film's end), is as savvy an opportunist as Joanne Herring or Gust Avrakatos. He appears to the Beltway as "Good-Time Charlie," an unreconstructed man's man, boozing, womanizing, for sale not just to the highest bidder but to *all* bidders, and content simply to collect political I.O.U.'s from congressional colleagues who have long suspected he has no agenda to promote and therefore no reason ever to cash in those accumulating vouchers. He has a scandalous penchant for objectifying women ("You can teach 'em to type, but you can't teach 'em to grow tits"), matched only by his scandalous indifference to scandal (his affectionate name for one of the youngest members of his glamorously curvy staff of "Charlie's Angels" is the deliberately provocative "Jailbait"). He allows himself to be exploited by Joanne; indeed, his entire operation is soaked in exploitation, in which the historical antagonisms of Christian, Muslim, and Jew are co-opted by yet another, purely ideological antagonism, towards Communism. As an Egyptian and an Israeli hurl teeth-bared accusations at one another across a cocktail table pressed into covert duty as negotiating table, Charlie utters the mind-bogglingly pragmatic remark, "None of this is important." The best that can be said for such an opinion is that it is fueled by the haste of a salesman knowing a deal is imminent and can easily crumble. The film demonstrates what Nichols has brought to life in a wide variety of dramatic contexts: objectifying points of view, whether appropriated for domination, dismissal, or demonization, always promote myopia, even blindness, to the realities of one's own situation. By the time Gust warns Charlie, standing on Charlie's Washington balcony apart from the victory celebration over the Soviet retreat, that the vacuum of leadership after the Soviets are gone is as terrifying as the Soviets' presence, it is too late for Charlie to parlay any more political favors. He has used his I.O.U.'s on the easier sell: hating the Soviets. There's nothing left to induce colleagues to care about a "-stan" that has receded into the indifference of American geographical insularity. Charlie has become the "Congressman from Kabul," crying in the wilderness a jeremiad of "what we always do" and (by ignoring the redemptive possibilities inherent in such reified awareness) will inevitably do again.

* * *

In terms of the ironic ambiguity of their narratives, *Charlie Wilson's War* displays a complexity that rivals any of Nichols' most accomplished films. *Primary Colors*, the most direct precedent in the Nichols' canon to *Charlie Wilson's War*, presents John Travolta as a charismatically likable but eminently corruptible Clintonian figure and leaves us in its concluding images uncertain whether we're watching an apotheosis or a fantasy. Travolta and Hanks deliver performances that command our sympathy even as the cinematic context makes a case against the central character. *Charlie Wilson's War* takes it narrative to even deeper exploration of ambiguity, because the former Congressman cooperated with the film production and was a presence on set. Should *Charlie Wilson's War* turn out to be Nichols' valedictory in Hollywood, it will be an apt last word. Nichols' entire career in filmmaking has been an exploration of the redemptive possibility of awareness within the processes of reification, with some protagonists refusing the overture to awakening and others embracing their transformation. *Charlie Wilson's War*, as a true story of ideological patriotism and good will pursued with blinkered monomania, offers a complexity of response to American intervention in the Arabic world much richer than the typically somber left-wing platitudes of the films that preceded it during the spate of politicized cinema released during the Fall of 2007. Hanks' undervalued performance, like Travolta's, commands our sometimes-unwilling affection. These are deeply flawed men who know they are flawed, working within systems as deeply flawed as they are. In having the former Congressman on set and ending the film with Wilson's own critical pronouncement upon himself and his legacy, Nichols unifies life and art in promoting his auteurist themes: it's one thing when a fictional character sees the ways in which he has failed and speaks truth to power. There's an added dimension when that character's analog in the real world does the same thing. Charlie Wilson is a real-life Mike Nichols protagonist.

The film presents a morass of entrenched social objectification. Beyond the framing event (Wilson's commemoration by the Clandestine Services), the film's decade-long flashback opens with Wilson up to his armpits in the stuff of awkward political imagery: naked in a Vegas hot tub with a sleazy independent television producer, a *Playboy* cover girl, and two strippers. Women are bartered—happily barter themselves—with ease throughout the film, beginning with this first scene, which is about deal making, with Crystal Lee's nudity the initial item on display. Wilson's congressional career has afforded him a license to chase women, many of whom he has caught by *employing* them on Capitol Hill. Charlie's "Angels," the tight-skirt-and-décolletage crowd that staffs Wilson's offices, are capable aides complicit in the objectifying terms of their employment. When Jane Liddle (Emily Blunt) accompanies her father to Charlie's office, she dresses conservatively, a desexualized performance that Charlie and the Angels leer at; inevitably, Jane winds up in skimpy lingerie in Charlie's apartment.

As Charlie's administrative assistant, Bonnie Bach (Amy Adams) brings a fresh-faced fervor that is clearly professional and may or may not also be personal. Bonnie's wardrobe is also snug-fitting, but at least conservative in palette, since she is seen more consistently in congressional corridors beyond the office suite. She travels with Charlie to Joanne's house in Houston, and to President Zia's palace in Pakistan. She sees what he sees in the Afghani refugee camps in Peshawar, and she is just as visibly moved. While she and Charlie banter, only once is their flirtatious give-and-take clouded by genuine criticism of her boss: when the scandal involving Paul Brown (Brian Markinson), the TV producer from the Vegas hot tub, first breaks. Pausing in profile at the door to his office before retiring to help put out another fire lit by his perpetually hot pants, Bonnie poses in alluring disapproval: "You never should have been in the same room, Congressman," she says. She's right—yet this is a woman who exits Wilson's inner office to resume her work in a harem that includes a staffer affectionately nicknamed Jailbait. They are all very much aware of their packaging, and, given Bonnie's reasonable conclusions about what is happening upstairs in Joanne's mansion while she waits patiently downstairs among the faithful thoroughbreds, her criticism could actually be rephrased as a critique of Charlie's need to maintain higher standards in his womanizing. Hot-tub strippers are in bad taste; women like Joanne or the Angels reveal a discriminating palette. Midway through the triumphal montage, which leads from Charlie lobbying his congressional colleagues for increased aid to the success of the covert operation, we are treated to a long, close-up, tracking shot of Bonnie's tight gray skirt as it swishes through the corridors of Congress. She bears a note from Gust, and she's well aware of its contents: its assurance of a first destroyed Russian craft has put some extra sashay in her stride. She wends her way past several dozen offices and individuals, a pert blonde missile seeking the heat of her man. When he takes the note from her, she gazes up at him in expectation, and her waiting is rewarded: he lunges at her as if in an assault and dips her into a soul-kiss.

When Bonnie accompanies Charlie to Houston, she's palpably uncomfortable in the home of a right-wing reactionary like Joanne. Yet at least some of her discomfort is about her being supplanted as the target of Charlie's charm and ardent glances. Before Joanne makes her predictably grand entrance, trailing whippets, Bonnie must negotiate the iconography of Joanne, in the form of a variation on John Singer Sargent's *Madame X* (1883–1884) with Joanne's likeness attached to the notorious bare-shouldered society-woman portrait. Accentuating the performativity of her role as a powerful woman in patriarchy, Joanne is a compendium of Roberts' star tropes: "Not many movie stars have the wit or the moxie to embrace the camp elements of their own personas, and the character is clearly something of a performer in her own right."[3] Charlie regards the painting admiringly; Bonnie eyes it nervously. Outside, an auction is underway in the garden, and a beautiful dancing girl (Carly Reeves, niece of Hanks) in Oriental harem costume is the next "lot"; inside, Charlie attempts to ease Bonnie's misgivings as they wait for their hostess. Referencing the cultural misogyny of Central Asia, Charlie lamely attempts a pitch for an enlightened Joanne: "One of the things she's trying to do over there is liberate the women." Bonnie smirks, "And what better way than through a slave-girl auction." The idea lingers in her mind after she's in Joanne's presence. Joanne sweeps across the room to within inches of Charlie; Nichols and Stephen Goldblatt (Nichols' director of photography on each of his last three films, beginning with *Angels in America*) pointedly frame the encounter so Bonnie is caught in the center of the composition, squeezed out by the two overwhelming presences facing one another in profile.[4] When Charlie introduces the two women, Joanne never shifts her none-to-nose gaze from Charlie while saying a rote, "Nice to meet you." When finally she deigns to regard "Bobbie," it's to order a specially blended martini; Bonnie sounds petulant in asserting that she isn't the Congressman's "slave" but rather his "administrative assistant." The barb fails to bite: Joanne knows exactly how to handle a bright, pretty young rival for the room's attention. She reasserts her rank, and Charlie gives a barely perceptible nod that indentures Bonnie to Joanne's will—because that's precisely where Charlie will always find himself. When Joanne leads Charlie upstairs for more intimate negotiations, Bonnie is left holding the martini. She ultimately settles among the hounds in a pile-up of fidelity at the bottom of the stairs, all of them awaiting their masters.

For all the glimpses inside the conference rooms and inner offices on Capitol Hill and at CIA Headquarters, there is no person depicted as wielding power more forcefully and with less surrendered to compromise of what she wants than Joanne Herring, because she commands the social and political standing that comes with access to more money than all but five women in the state of Texas. The attraction of Joanne Herring and Charlie Wilson is strictly commodified by the influence each commands; they otherwise would have as little to say to each other as Mrs. Robinson and Benjamin in *The Graduate*. They are not the strangest of "bedfellows" in this political intrigue they've initiated (which ultimately requires the pairing of ancient national enemies), but they are unquestionably the strangest to *literalize* the expression. When first we see them together, in this scene with Bonnie, there is audacious impulse implied in Joanne's inviting powerful, moneyed people to her house and then slipping away long enough for bed, bath, and barter with Charlie. As in the carefully constructed

In a comic composition from *Charlie Wilson's War* that appears to be equal parts love match and prizefight, Charlie Wilson (Tom Hanks) and Joanne Herring (Julia Roberts) go toe-to-toe to get what they want from each other. Caught in their crossfire is Bonnie Bach (Amy Adams), Charlie's pretty, pert administrative assistant, who seems to understand better than her boss that, for all his power as a six-term congressman, he's probably out of his league with a billionaire king-maker like Joanne. By the time Charlie himself realizes it, he's brought down the Soviet Empire in central Asia but is powerless to counter the sweep of the Taliban into the ideological void.

mirror shots in *Closer*, Nichols and Goldblatt offer visual cues to the deceptive method beneath Joanne's mask of carnality. As we learn by the end of the film, she has fantasized about the Fall of Communism during her trysts with Charlie. Two times in the film we see Charlie in his apartment, on the telephone with Joanne. The first is when he has just finished showing lithe Jane Liddle the potency of the Washington skyline, all gleaming White House and, rising high above it, the Monument (contextually, a comic wink and nudge at phalloc-racy). Joanne's timing in telephoning is emblematic of Charlie's capitulation to Joanne's siren call: he'd put off any other alluring woman for the bird literally in hand, but Joanne's allure transcends mere sexuality. The party he agrees to attend by the end of her phone call is the inception of the narrative's intrigue, and their sexual tryst is more than just the first meeting that will produce the operation: it is the film's first deal. It's the only time Charlie gets more than he gives with Joanne; all that she has previously given has been invested in anticipation of what Charlie can eventually give her. As Charlie gives and gives in Congress, collecting chits for which he has no particular strategic purpose earmarked, Joanne has lavished the support of her rich contacts in sustaining Charlie's long, undistinguished congressional run. Charlie likes to believe he's still in office because his constituents have simple needs and his deep-pockets supporters, most of whom are Jewish, like his pro–Israel activity (which, as his deals with Egypt and other Israeli antagonists indicates, is yet another superficial performance). In fact, as Joanne reminds him, he's where he is, relaxing in her bathtub, in his sixth term on Capitol Hill, because she has supported rather than opposed him.

Their "relationship" is thus purely transactional, though this does not stop Charlie from being fooled by its illusion of intimacy. The second time that Nichols and Sorkin show Charlie and Joanne talking on the phone, the covert operation is all but over in the spring of 1988, and Charlie is the odd man out of Joanne's sleeping arrangements. This time, significantly, it's Charlie who has dialed; there are no pretty young things distracting him; he's moist-eyed, and he's been drinking. We assume that something terrible may have happened with their operation, though it's hard to imagine anything stopping the juggernaut they have unleashed, and besides, in this "true story," we already know the outcome. "Where's it at, Charlie?" she says, and in a small voice, implying the reciprocity he has come to enjoy but fears has ended, he asks, "Am I ever gonna see you nekkid again?" Only *her* question gets an answer: he reports that Congress has just increased appropriations to $500 million; matched by their Middle-Eastern conspirators, this makes a billion dollars invested in countering Communism in Central Asia. This is Joanne's idea of pillow talk, where size definitely matters: "There's never been anything like it," he adds. While they exchange warm assurances of missing each other, Nichols and his editors, John Bloom and Antonia Van Drimmelen (the team who worked with him on each of his last four films beginning with *Wit*) end Joanne's side of the scene with a new medium-shot that reveals her husband for the first time, slumbering beside her, wedding ring dully glinting on his finger in foreground soft-focus as Joanne dismisses Charlie: "I gotta go." Charlie has only been a bedfellow while he had something she needed. There is a clear distinction between what each misses in the other. She misses the eroticism of covert power, wielded absolutely in the white-hot foreplay of making the deal together in secret and on the grandest of scales. Having achieved a political goal he scarcely could have dreamed a decade before, he misses something much more human-scale, and his near-weepy loneliness is a personal disillusionment that parallels the political disillusionment he'll soon experience on the Hill. Everyone has taken him for what they could get, and while he can be accused of the very same thing, he's coming to terms with the emptiness of contact that aspires to nothing beyond transaction. Charlie is left holding the phone. We see another boozy, moist-eyed shot of Charlie just before the film returns to the commemoration ceremony, another late night in Washington: Charlie is slushy with all the deal-making and how little it feels like he's accomplished in light of his failure to reconstruct something positive in Afghanistan, now that he finally understands and desires a moral and ethical imperative. Without ever picking up or even so much as looking at the phone, Hanks calls to mind the same air of disillusioned resignation Charlie felt after that second phone call with Joanne: now he's been dumped by Joanne *and* Congress.

Joanne, the Texas beauty queen, knows how to package herself because she's never known anything else. She out-provokes even the Angels in her cleavage display, her sexualization of her persona more aggressive than the Angels because they are wearing the uniform that Charlie has cheerfully abetted, while Joanne answers only to herself. The difference between Joanne and the Angels, as she makes clear at the pub in parting from them the night before she flies with Charlie, Gust, and Doc Long (Ned Beatty) to Pakistan, is that they are "sluts." Her power permits the distinction, though there is of course more physical evidence of slatternly behavior by Joanne in the film than by all of the Angels combined. They are obediently eroticized; Joanne is formidably erotic. When called on her obviously exploitative presentation of herself, as she is by that noted non-prude Gust Avrakatos (who warns her before they fly to Central Asia to dress more modestly), she scolds him indignantly about her experience and good sense (and indeed, when she tours the Peshawar refugee camps, she has swathed herself head and shoulders in a stylish navy headscarf; as usual, Joanne is alluring even when purposely dressed for neutrality). To have Roberts play Joanne is to access her back-catalog of physiologically assertive women, from Vivian Ward in *Pretty Woman* (Garry Marshall, 1990) to *Erin Brockovich* to Tess Ocean in Soderbergh's *Ocean's Eleven* (2001) and *Ocean's Twelve* (2004). Joanne enters her scenes and commands men's gaze as a celebrated Texas billionaire beauty queen—or as the megastar Roberts—has earned the right to do. (Hanks' casting is also pointed, accessing Hanks' Jimmy-Stewart warmth to give Charlie an unpretentiously well-meaning decency, even at his most lost and misbegotten, at coke parties with strippers and arms deals with dangerously mercenary men.) At the refugee camp with Charlie, Gust, and Doc and his wife (Nancy Linehan Charles), Joanne gets in character with the shawl pulled tight to her skull, pretending for the moment to be the sweetly submissive woman Central Asian culture demands, rather than the brassy ideologue she in reality is, secretly driving America's largest covert action. Doc has predictably been moved by what he has seen in the camps, and he needs Joanne's urging to get up and speak to the assembled crowd of turbaned onlookers. They've been "sittin' here," she says, "and bleedin', and waitin', and prayin' for you—it's only gonna be a man like you that can save them." Charlie watches in awe; he knows if she can get Doc to speak to the crowd, he's on the hook. As a politician who has made public promises, he won't be able to have second thoughts and back out on the long plane ride home. Gust looks on from behind mirror shades that conceal bemused disgust. He usually can't help saying what he thinks, but he knows if he undercuts her cynical ploy, he could jeopardize funding for the operation. Joanne cinches the hold she has on Doc with an appeal to his meekly grandmaternal wife: "We know, don't we, about our men— what they can do when they summon themselves." In fact, Doc has done nothing but allow himself to be pushed and prodded to this point. Joanne uses the packaging of patriarchy to convince men they're doing their *own* will, not hers.

Doc readily submits to the traditional role-playing Joanne has initiated, because he is an old-fashioned, "church-goin'" sort. He betrays intense ideological alienation from the strange bedfellows Charlie is assembling in Jerusalem and Islamabad and Cairo: "You want to put $80 million in the hands of those people?" Charlie recoils at the familiar, derisive referent: "Doc, now, if you took a trip to the border with me, you'd stop calling them 'those people.'" (Of course, Charlie alone *cannot* convince Doc to see for himself; only Joanne can make this happen, by packaging her financial clout in coquetry. There would be feminist authority to such potency if she weren't trading in sexual favors and demeaning stereotypes to accomplish her goals.) One of the great ironic set pieces of the film comes when Doc accedes to Joanne's coaxing and stands up with the microphone. He compares himself and his personal privations to those of the refugees, an appalling analogy until he explains, via translator, that his son was wounded in Vietnam fighting "against Soviet oppressors." Charlie exclaims in surprise to Joanne, who, typically, is several steps ahead of the men: it's another part of her due diligence that she has waited for the right time to use this personal pain of the Long family in manipulating Doc, the same way she knows how to push Charlie's buttons. (Her coldness and antipathy to Gust are the flip side of this: Gust sees through everything she does but is already in line with their objective and needs no sex-based wrangling by Joanne; she curtly brushes off his solicitation the night before their trip.) Doc stands before the mujahideen and promises guns and training; when the hush of the relayed translation explodes in a fist-pumping roar of approval, Doc feels the rush of a revivalist call-and-response and thrusts his fist into the air in solidarity. Commenting to Joanne on Doc's vow to always be on the side of good, on *God's* side, Charlie says, "I think what's got Doc worried is that, sooner or later, God's gonna be on *both* sides." This acknowledges Joanne's and Doc's rabid, Christian-Fundamentalist hatred of atheist Communism locking arms with rabid, Islamic-Fundamentalist hatred of Communist invasion. Doc concludes his impromptu pep rally with lines he could comfortably deliver from the bully-pulpit of his home church: "This is good against evil. And I want you to know that America is always going to be on the side of the good, and God will always punish the wicked." As the crowd goes wild at the translation of these incendiary words, Gust and Charlie exchange an ambivalent look, as much as to say, *What sleeping giant have we not only awakened but armed?* Soon, having defeated "those people" of godless Communism in the Soviet Empire, "those people" of Afghanistan will turn on us, just another affluent, heedless nation of "those people" of the West, infidels whose materialist decadence and overstepping interventionism they abhor.

Nichols deftly treats the counter-attack by the mujahideen against the Soviets as a David vs. Goliath underdog tale an audience can't help but be compelled by: two neophyte Afghanis, a newly delivered missile launcher wielded awkwardly in their arms as a Soviet air squadron murders innocents in an Afghani hill town, perform an endearing Central Asian vaudeville routine before managing to blow up one of the marauding helicopters. Two more freedom fighters join the original two on their hilltop, each more confidently brandishing a missile launcher. Two more Russian helicopters perish, and the four men on the hilltop indulge themselves in a small rally of self-congratulation. "The scenes of Afghans blowing Soviet helicopters out of the sky feel cheap, cartoony, but they have an afterbite. After you've finished cheering, you remember the same fearless holy warriors are shooting at our guys now."[5] All the while, the propulsive soundtrack score, by James Newton Howard, features an unlikely melding of Eastern tablas to one of Western Christianity's great, triumphalist choruses, "And He Shall Purify ..." from Handel's *Messiah*. The formal irony underscores the dramatic irony that these two forces may only be united when taking objection to still another force. They all desire to "kill some Russians," but when their tenuous shared objective is achieved, they risk no further distraction from objectifying and thereby demonizing one another.

Charlie has been naïve enough to believe historical antagonisms can be pronounced irrelevant: If there is a "transformation" in Charlie (as Nichols' films typically at least invite protagonists to contemplate[6]), it is Charlie's disillusionment. As the film begins, the commemoration ceremony can only have a face-value meaning: the victory of an ideology, and the celebration of the enormous role one unassuming man had in that triumph. As the film ends, the flashback has revealed to us the ambiguity of what Charlie sees as he looks out over the assembled crowd and looks back over the crowning achievement of his life's work. From Joanne but also from Gust (both of whom smile up at him from the assembly, for their own reasons), Charlie has nurtured his sense that, as Nichols himself admiringly says of the real Wilson, "The possibility of making a difference still exists."[7] That difference, however, can never be more than incidental; it is not systemic. The world turns to its reified defaults—grasping for power, relishing privilege, fearing the other, loathing what challenges orthodoxy. From Larry Liddle (Peter Gerety) whining in Charlie's office about the free-speech police of the ACLU to Zvi (Ken Stott), Charlie's Israeli arms connection, trading ancient antagonisms with a member of the Egyptian defense ministry, Charlie can't understand why we can't all just get along. He's the kind of person who rarely meets a man he doesn't like; he and Gust have a disastrous first impression of one another but are able to bond because Gust seemingly dislikes everybody, and this fortunately for Charlie includes Islamabad Station Chief Harold Holt (Denis O'Hare), the one person in the narrative whom Charlie clearly can't stand, either. To Larry, Charlie offers no accommodation, only the assurance that, when Larry moves his nativity scene off of public property onto the grounds of one of the 38 churches that can serve as the more appropriate host of the crèche, "Everybody lives." His assessment is accurate. But these are also the low stakes he's typically played as a ne'er-do-well politician along for the ride. He's not foolish enough to make the same sweeping claim about the Israelis and the Egyptians, but, to shift their historically intractable animosity back to the matter at hand (covert arms-laundering arrangements in the service of killing Russians), he makes an equally extraordinary claim about their mutual fear and loathing: "None of this is important." What he means, of course, is that none of this is *relevant* to his deal getting done, or, perhaps, that none of their antagonisms is important to *him*. But it's the sort of mistake made in haste that he gets to regret over time.

When Gust pulls him aside on the balcony and finally tells him the rest of the "Zen master" story he's had in his hip pocket since the first time they met, Charlie pleads that he's "stupid" and therefore can't negotiate the story's parabolic complexities. It's an important moment in the film, because a more conventional telling of Charlie Wilson's story might have cut directly from the victory celebration in Charlie's living room (Charlie getting his last kiss from Joanne, Gust delighting the celebrants by hurling performative obscenities at the Russian evacuation televised on the CBS Evening News) back to the awards ceremony, the frame of the film's narrative, thus implying in the triumphalism of Western capitalist democracy only what the master of ceremonies has claimed at the film's outset: that they are here to honor Charlie's integral part in "the defeat and break-up of the Soviet Empire, culminating in the crumbling of the Berlin Wall, [...] one of the great events of world history," and "Without Charlie, history would be hugely—and sadly—different." Instead, the film spends an additional five minutes with Charlie in his flashback before sending us all back with him into the film's present moment, for his "special recognition." The aftermath of the Soviet defeat is the defeat of Charlie Wilson's illusions, and the beginning of wisdom. In the last five minutes of his flashback, rather than in a ceremony of the "Clandestine Services," Charlie has his "special recognition."

The film has faded to black with Charlie alone on his balcony, startled to attention by Gust's having tossed away Charlie's whiskey and made him look at the reality of what they have accomplished: so much, and not nearly enough. We might reasonably expect that this is the film's ending: Gust's Zen master has posed his final "We'll see" proposition, an invitation to us all to overlay our historical hindsight on what we've seen and heard and not to mistake any *latest* development for *last*. But part of the opening rhetoric of the film is to frame its events within the self-conscious, reifying glare of "world history," among the people of the Clandestine Services who flatter themselves that they make that history. Sorkin's script isn't finished with either Charlie or history, however. Charlie did his part to topple the Soviet Empire; history must acknowledge this. In his obituary in the *Economist*: "It was he who organized and largely procured the money for the CIA's most successful covert operation, the backing in the 1980s of the mujahideen of Afghanistan in their war against the Soviet invaders. [... H]e had put up two fingers to the devil and at least some of his works."[8] But where is the wisdom to be extracted from this? Whence Nichols' characteristic examination of the possibilities of "transformation?"[9] Charlie's chance at reified insight comes when he returns to his congressional colleagues. In the very same committee room in which he'd once "doubled to $250 million," he can't raise a paltry $1 million for school reconstruction. The room is mostly empty. Nichols and Goldblatt assign Hanks a close-up so he can go to work on a brief but summative assessment of the process of reification: "This is what we always do: we always go in with our ideals, and we change the world. And then we leave. We always leave." The representatives across the room from him, ten years later and after countless media reports and political briefs, still have no more grasp of the Islamic world than sleazy TV producer Paul Brown in the long-ago Vegas hot tub, who confused "mujahideen" for "priest." Charlie knows the difference between "Pakistan" and "Afghanistan," correcting his congressional colleague. He has *made* a difference in the world. And yet that difference must beget additional adaptive changes in a recognition that, in the game of conflicting ideologies, "the ball keeps on bouncin.'" Charlie Wilson was able to "make a difference" in the Cold War precisely because there *was* a Cold War, and he was able to tap into and manipulate the appetite shared by many, himself included, to "kill some Russians." He was able to use the instinctual stereotyping of "those people" to destroy "those people."

    One could argue that Nichols' film has an incoherent perspective on Charlie Wilson's place in history—that he helped end the Cold War, or that he was a warmonger; that he was a lucky opportunist, or that he was a cunning strategist; that he willfully worked near-miracles in summoning cooperation between ancient enemies, or that he inadvertently ushered in a new "hot" era of conflict between East and West. Nichols himself sounds, in his typically dignified, well-spoken way, like a political fanboy of Wilson's when summing the Congressman's remarkable accomplishment, yet ultimately what matters is the formal statement of the film. Nichols is a filmmaker, not a historian. Sorkin's narrative as presented by Nichols offers, especially in its ending, an ironic ambiguity familiar to many Nichols films. In that final, brief, late-night interior shot back in Charlie's living room, after being stonewalled by Congress in making his Gust-Avrakatos pitch to "give 'em hope" in Afghanistan before the "crazies" roll into the void, a disillusioned Charlie mulls all he's seen and done. He has been relieved of the illusion that, in the world's complexity, such a sweeping "difference" as the one he's made will ultimately transform hearts and minds. And so, when we return to the commemorative celebration and the film ends, we understand the mask of humility he presents to the crowd as what true humility looks like, the kind that can only come from a reifying glimpse of the "endgame." We don't hear what he says when the ovation ends; it doesn't matter what Charlie might say to such a crowd under such circumstances, because they wouldn't hear the truth his "special recognition" has afforded him. What matters is what Nichols and Sorkin end with, the real Charlie Wilson's pronouncement upon the wonders and the failures of his legacy, which lingers in the mind less as a "We'll see" than the reified wisdom of "We've seen."

22

Tempered Optimism

The Cinematic Legacy of Mike Nichols

The path Mike Nichols took to his career in filmmaking is, if atypical, hardly unique. While most directors come to their craft now through writing for the screen, and some continue to arrive through editing or camerawork, the path through theater to cinema is the one Ingmar Bergman took. It was Elia Kazan's route. In a brief, meteoric way, it was Orson Welles' route, too. While there was and will remain only one Welles, there is actually an illuminating analog to be found in comparing the careers of Welles and Nichols, the wunderkinds of theater and performance wooed by Hollywood into a new life. Andrew Sarris writes of Nichols' early films, "No American director since Orson Welles had started off with such a bang."[1] Sarris ultimately forgives the idiosyncratic failures of Welles' later life because "Welles had followed his own road, and that made all the difference. Nichols seems too shrewd ever to get off the main highway [, ...] incapable of the divine folly of a personal statement."[2] Welles' prodigious gifts were, like Nichols,' established in a variety of entertainment settings (radio, stage, and cinema for Welles; stand-up comedy, stage, and cinema for Nichols). Each was a powerful force in New York theater: Welles with Roosevelt's Federal Theatre Project (part of the WPA), Nichols mounting a series of hit Broadway comedies in unofficial partnership with Neil Simon. Both Welles and Nichols learned the value of ensemble: working with a select group of talented cast and crew, building relationships that deepen from one project to the next. They also understood the value of creative control, and when Hollywood came calling, each made final-cut authority one of the deal-making requirements. Hollywood both made Welles a legend and soon afterwards destroyed him (with his own reckless assistance); this is where the comparison of the two careers becomes most instructive. Welles made a politically impractical masterpiece, *Citizen Kane*, which antagonized William Randolph Hearst, one of the most powerful men in the media and entertainment industries; the film's avant-garde formalism and dour ecclesiastical pronouncements upon materialism and alienation kept the ticket-buying public at bay. Nominated for nine Academy Awards, it won only the Best Writing (Original Screenplay) category for Welles and Herman Mankiewicz (the authorship question serving as the most hotly contested point in *Raising Kane*, Pauline Kael's sloppy but charismatic polemic attacking the auteur theory). Welles' follow-up, *The Magnificent Ambersons*, was one of the most notorious of all Hollywood battles for creative control, a battle (and war) Welles emphatically lost. His life devolved over the decades into sniping resentment and fringe filmmaking in indie Europe and genre Hollywood. His appearance as General Dreedle in *Catch-22*, scowling furiously through his scenes, was a tortuously ironic experience for Welles, since he was only doing it for the money (always trying to raise capital off of his outsized personality to fund a quixotic project), didn't believe Nichols was up to the task of adapting such a complex and important book, and had dreamed for a decade of adapting the book himself, to no avail.

Nichols also made an enormous and immediate splash in Hollywood upon his debut, but while Welles was making enemies, Nichols took an already familiar and revered property, Edward Albee's *Who's Afraid of Virginia Woolf?* (1962), and cast Hollywood royalty—Elizabeth Taylor and Richard Burton—at his film's molten core. It was a can't-miss proposition (dangerous in its own way, of course, because of the danger that one might miss anyway), and Nichols' golden Broadway instincts did not fail him: his debut earned 13 Oscar nominations (including Best Director), winning in five categories, and satisfying box-office expectations. *The Graduate*, Nichols' second film, was a box-office phenomenon. The trajectories of the two careers could not have looked less similar after two films: Welles in a self-imposed exile in South America, licking his wounds after the eviscerating studio re-cut of *The Magnificent Ambersons*, Nichols at the vanguard of a counter-cultural wave hitting Hollywood's shores as he prepared to take on the adaptation of a revered novel, *Catch-22*, that the counter-culture had embraced and that the prevailing insider wisdom whispered couldn't be filmed.

Welles condescended to everyone, including his director, while on the *Catch-22* location shoot in Mexico. People typically cherish their time spent working with Nichols, as evidenced by the repeat collaborations with some of the most important actors and most accomplished technicians of two Hollywood generations. "'No matter what happens to Mike Nichols,'" attests his long-time costume designer Ann Roth, "'he will always be a director that anybody wants to work with.'"[3] Most of *Catch-22*'s cast and crew tolerated Welles' blowhard interventionism because of Nichols' own deference to Welles' legend. Some made fun of Welles behind his back; Alan Arkin had nothing to do with Welles at all. The contempt for General Dreedle radiating from the men was apparently an easy emotion for the company to access, and Nichols wisely used it to fuel Welles' scenes. As discussed in Chapter 4, Welles' imposed innovation in having Cathcart and Korn "run" in place on a platform behind Dreedle's jeep produced a ridiculously artificial effect; Nichols diplomatically allowed the master's whim and subsequently used the hapless shot to his advantage, as another layer of the narrative's unreliably surreal imagery. This is a microcosmic example of the difference between Welles and Nichols: the autocratic authoritarian who presumes to know better than anyone, and the accommodating charmer who manages to get what he needs from even the most difficult personalities. It's why Nichols made it back from the desert to find himself eventually returned to Hollywood's good graces, the best actors clamoring to work for him and producers green-lighting his budgets, while Welles continued to be a disapproving voice in the wilderness who couldn't get Hollywood to write a check. Nichols recalls, "Orson Welles once said to me that some lives start at their apex and then gradually descend, and he wouldn't have it any other way [...]. Well, that's not my opinion of my life or my work.'"[4]

In the generation after Nichols, the British director Sam Mendes most nearly approximates the professional route taken by Welles and Nichols. Another young genius, he was directing Judi Dench in *The Cherry Orchard* in the West End at 24, and he was soon a star of the Royal Shakespeare Company and then artistic director of London's prestigious Donmar Warehouse theatre. He crossed the Atlantic with a revelatory revival of *Cabaret* on Broadway, and when Hollywood inevitably came calling, chose as his debut feature Alan Ball's *American Beauty* (1999), originally offered to Nichols by Steven Spielberg and Dreamworks.[5] Søren Birkvad projects *American Beauty*'s debt to *The Graduate* as "the execution of Ben and Elaine's misery thirty years later."[6] *American Beauty* was eventually nominated for eight Academy Awards, winning five. Welles, Nichols, and Mendes were each nominated as Best Director for their first Hollywood production, but only Mendes won; Nichols had to wait for *The Graduate*, and Welles was never nominated again by the Academy in any category. Best of all for Mendes (as a predictor of Hollywood authority and longevity), his film was a certifiable blockbuster of the proportions of *The Graduate*, a film to which it owes a thematic and stylistic debt.[7]

In the decade and a half since that auspicious debut, Mendes has released five more films. His second feature, *The Road to Perdition* (2002), was an adaptation of Max Alan Collins' noir graphic novel; awarded a production budget totaling nearly nine figures, Mendes' film underperformed. Another pricey genre film, the Desert-Storm war drama *Jarhead* (2005) did less well, both critically and at the box office. Mendes scaled back on budget ($35 million, roughly half what he worked with on *Jarhead*) for his much-anticipated 2008 adaptation of Richard Yates' 1961 novel *Revolutionary Road*. It was, again, a disappointment for investors. His fifth film, *Away We Go* (2009), from an original screenplay by Dave Eggers and Vendela Vida, halved the previous budget again (to $17 million) and still failed to recoup its investment; the film's aesthetic was "indie," an odd development from a filmmaker whose first four features were all high-gloss studio work. (If anything, *Away We Go* is even more directly the offspring of *The Graduate* than is *American Beauty*.) In his first decade of filmmaking, Mendes had made five films, all accomplished, intelligent work, and had reaped such progressively diminishing returns (he couldn't keep halving budgets indefinitely) that his career was in crisis. What came next was not anticipatable: Mendes became the new director of the James Bond franchise, far and away the most talented director in the series' long, inconsistent history. The surprise of this selection would be literally akin to Mike Nichols agreeing, in the fug following the poor reception of *The Day of the Dolphin* and *The Fortune*, to direct Roger Moore in *The Spy Who Loved Me* (1977) or *Moonraker* (1979), instead of entering into his eight-year Hollywood aphasia. Mendes received a $200 million budget for *Skyfall* (2012) and returned a spectacular profit and even some Oscar bling. Nichols never stopped being the director of *The Graduate*, for better or worse. Mendes, the director of *American Beauty*, will now be the director of *Skyfall* in the minds of all but a few Hollywood historians.

The comparisons of Nichols to Welles and Mendes suggest as much about the Hollywood industry as they do about Nichols. Hollywood filmmaking is an essentially conservative business, in which mavericks will always be the exception to the golden rule of the remake, the sequel, the formula. Welles, too smart for his own good, set fire to bridges while still traversing them, and only once, in his very first feature, *Citizen Kane*, did he manage to deliver a film to the audience unscathed. Mendes, smart enough to understand the shifting industry paradigm (during his career he has witnessed the expansion of blockbuster franchising and the transfer of intelligent filmed drama from theatrical to television production), threw in his lot with the Hollywood superhero factories. He selected a franchise that offers promise for human-scale drama and geopolitical commentary. Nichols, smart enough to know how to cooperate with the bean counters who aren't as smart (or are smart in profoundly different ways), by and large made the films he wanted to make, consistent with a worldview. Not all were of uniform ambition or accomplishment, but it's the rare filmmaker who never misses when he or she releases films regularly, as Nichols has with the exception of the long gaps from 1975 to 1983 and after 2007.

Since releasing *Charlie Wilson's War*, Nichols has reportedly been attached as director to several intriguing projects consistent with his thematic preoccupations, including an adaptation of Patricia Highsmith's 1957 novel, *Deep Water* (the next book she published after 1955's *The Talented Mr. Ripley*) and an English-language remake of Akira Kurosawa's classic crime drama, *High and Low* (1963). In Spring 2013, he was announced to direct an adaptation of Jonathan Tropper's 2012 novel, *One Last Thing Before I Go*; set to produce was J. J. Abrams, with whom Nichols worked two decades earlier on *Regarding Henry*, at the beginning of Abrams' Hollywood career. At seven years and counting, the hiatus between *Charlie Wilson's War* and a next feature film is already the second longest of Nichols' career; only the gap between *The Fortune* (1975) and *Silkwood* (1983) stretched longer. As in that earlier film-making silence, however, Nichols has remained active in theater at the highest levels, though in slightly slower motion as a man transitioning from his seventies into his eighties than during that first hiatus when, in his mid-forties, he launched an average of a play a year either as director (including David Rabe's *Streamers* in 1976) or as producer (including *Annie* in 1977), while also producing the television series *Family* for ABC. In Spring 2012, he brought Philip Seymour Hoffman to Broadway as Willie Loman in Arthur Miller's *Death of a Salesman*, and both Hoffman and Nichols won Tonys. Nichols, who as a teenager saw the play in its original production with Lee J. Cobb, describes it in terms that dovetail with the thematic preoccupations of his own oeuvre: "'*Salesman* is more relevant now than it was even then. Everybody wants to be known. Everybody's a Kardashian. We are a nation of salesmen. Arthur Miller knew what was coming.'"[8] For Nichols, the revival was his ninth Tony win (seventh as director); Fall 2013 brought a brisk, cinematic Broadway revival of Harold Pinter's *Betrayal* featuring Mendes' *Skyfall* star, Daniel Craig.

Nichols' productions in Hollywood have garnered more than three-dozen Oscar nominations, including four nominations for Best Director (*Virginia Woolf, The Graduate, Silkwood*, and *Working Girl*), and nearly five-dozen Golden Globe nominations (which include his two cable-television productions, *Wit* and *Angels in America*), adding Best Director nominations for *Angels* and *Closer* to the four nominated by the Academy. He's been honored with a Gala Tribute by the Film Society of Lincoln Center in 1999, received the Kennedy Center Honors in 2003, and in 2010 was recognized by the American Film Institute with their Lifetime Achievement Award. His actors and collaborative crew regard him with reverence as a man of taste and intelligence and encyclopedic knowledge.

A. O. Scott, in one of the best critical overviews of Nichols' oeuvre, labels Nichols' legacy "a puzzle. And not because his movies are difficult or abstruse. On the contrary, they are distinguished by a clarity and accessibility that sometimes make it easy to take them for granted."[9] It is a curiosity that such a brilliant and inventive improvisational comedian turned away from creating original stories on his own. When he transitioned from stage performance with Elaine May to stage direction, the move may have appeared more natural than his subsequent move from Broadway to Hollywood. Yet the shift from creating to interpreting was his greatest leap as an artist. Scott claims "the identifying trait that runs through [Nichols'] movies—the thing that makes them, in spite of their deference to mightier authorial imaginations, recognizably *his*—may be a modest, unobtrusive but nonetheless palpable intelligence."[10] A film director unquestionably does possess an authority to stamp (or fail to stamp) a work with his or her own brand. My book has argued that Nichols has in fact done this, but almost purely at the thematic level, via an impassioned critique of socially constructed identity in late-capitalist America. Other than the long take and the circular narrative frame, he has not developed a signature style (like Alfred Hitchcock or Robert Altman or Martin Scorsese or Woody Allen); he has not adopted a signature genre (like John Ford or Steven Spielberg or Hitchcock, all of whom transcend their genre's limitations and in any case have freely worked in other genres). Thematic identity is part of the constitution of an auteur, but it is the least likely way to establish an auteurist identity in the popular imagination. "Perhaps he was never the kind of director we thought he was," concludes Peter Biskind. "In the days of *The Graduate*, he was hailed, with typical media hyperbole, as America's auteur, our answer to Truffaut and Fellini. But he never really made 'personal' movies."[11] Scott observes, "Although his films of the 1960's and 70's seemed to define (if also to mock) the attitudes of a rebellious generation, he did not really fit in with the wild children of the New Hollywood. Directors like Martin Scorsese, Francis Ford Coppola and Altman were self-styled and critically designated mythmakers, visionaries and iconoclasts, whereas at his best Nichols has always been an observer, an adapter and an ironist."[12] Biskind speculates that, "with our obeisance to 'sincerity' and 'authenticity,' we are more forgiving of our less commercial filmmakers."[13] As a result, it may be that Nichols will be classified more readily in the critical and popular mind with competent filmmakers of middlebrow box-office appeal like Sydney Pollack and Alan J. Pakula in Nichols' own generation and Robert Redford, Ron Howard, Rob Reiner, and Nora Ephron of the generation inspired by his work. All these directors have made good films, but none has made a film as iconic as *The Graduate*[14] or as ambitious as half a dozen of Nichols' other films.

As a Hollywood player, Nichols has never been either a true blockbuster A-list director or a true art-house darling; he's had films exceed even the most optimistic box-office expectations (*The Graduate* first and foremost, but also *Working Girl* and *The Birdcage*); he's also delivered demoralizing box-office failures (*Catch-22* first and foremost, but also *The Day of the Dolphin*, *Wolf*, *Primary Colors*, and *What Planet Are You From?*). His career as a filmmaker is actually somewhat difficult to analogize to someone in his own era. Among his near-contemporaries, there is no one quite like him: Woody Allen, three years younger, may seem the closest analog (smart, funny, New York, Jewish) both in chronological years and in career sequence (stand-up comic transitioning to theater and then to feature-film direction), but Allen is an auteur in the most literal sense, writing his own films, and has worked at roughly a 2:1 pace to Nichols, twice as prolific in the number of films he has poured forth. For all his talent, Nichols has accomplished less as a filmmaker than Allen. Mel Brooks, six years older than Nichols (smart, funny, New York, Jewish), has a connotative identity as a comedian that, like Nichols and Allen, began in comic performance. Brooks has staked out a narrower vein of humor than either Nichols or Allen, contenting himself with slapstick satire and parody. For all his talent, Brooks has accomplished less as a filmmaker than Nichols. Of all the films of Nichols' career, the one that could most easily be mistaken for a Brooks production, *What Planet*, is Nichols' least successful feature film.

Biskind identifies Nichols' "greatest gift" as "getting the best performance an actor had ever given or, in many cases, would ever give."[15] An actors' director, Nichols has always structured his productions to include time for the cast to ease into their roles and relationships. This often has led him to days or even weeks of rehearsal with the principal players on a film, a holdover value from his success as a theater director. The rehearsals are structured play, with room for inspiration that becomes part of performance. Yet Nichols remains the director, selecting what becomes part of the production when it moves in front of the cameras. It's a recipe for great acting: with collaborative trust established and roles refined, Nichols knows exactly what to tell his crew to look for during shooting. Structured improvisation may sound like an oxymoron, but Nichols has made it work for 60 years, since his days on stage with May after college. Biskind draws a natural contrast between Nichols' methodology and the antic improvisation in the style of his notoriously maverick directorial contemporary, Altman (born six years before Nichols).[16] Jules Feiffer, who wrote *Carnal Knowledge* for Nichols, recalls shooting parts of their film in Vancouver, British Columbia at the same time Altman was filming *McCabe and Mrs. Miller*, eventually released exactly one week before *Carnal Knowledge* in June 1971. "As different styles as possible," Feiffer comments of watching both directors at work. "Mike Nichols organizes everything and knows everything that's going to happen and plans it all; that's the way he thinks and that's the way he works. Altman works in a pigpen"[17] (in which the actors are often improvising not from a scripted but a barely sketched scene). When Nichols' and Altman's anti-war satires faced off in 1970, *M*A*S*H** had already been entrenched in the public imagination for months, and its ragged, fragmented sketchiness, knitted together by witty editing and charismatic buddies (Donald Sutherland as Hawkeye Pierce and Elliott Gould as Trapper John McIntyre) were ultimately easier to warm to than *Catch-22*'s surreal dream logic and the prickly raging of Alan Arkin as Yossarian.

Ultimately, both directors would have difficulty satisfying the mainstream Hollywood audience decade after decade. Nichols took a steadier course than Altman, with fewer films and far fewer experiments. While both men turned to the American theater when Hollywood disoriented them, Nichols had firmer footing there than Altman. Altman made filmed stage plays like *Fool for Love* (1985) that remained stagy; Nichols made *Angels in America*, and the play breathed, rasped, roared. Altman eventually found his way again and made late masterpieces like *The Player* (1992, with its sly allusions to Nichols and *The Graduate*), *Short Cuts* (1993), and *Gosford Park* (2001). They were all Altman films, unmistakably. Most of the bad ones were unmistakably his, too. Nichols never wandered so far from that path of who he was as a filmmaker, but he never had as formally distinctive a voice, either. Comparing him to a wild man like Altman is ultimately fruitless except to demonstrate the more moderate approach Nichols typically took to his filmmaking. The best (and, at times, the worst) that can be said of Nichols the filmmaker is that he was always as good as his material; sometimes he chose Albee, or Kushner; sometimes he ... didn't. Whatever he chose told a familiar thematic story: of men and women snared in reified systems of exploitative complicity and offered transformative insight they can either choose to ignore or to act upon. And unlike Altman, who famously antagonized Raymond Carver by piling up emotional devastation in the stories he selected and adapted for *Short Cuts*, Nichols has generally been faithful to authorial intention in the works he's adapted. Nichols is a tempered optimist: roughly half of his protagonists choose to heed their awakenings and explore redemptive possibility. This still has left him plenty of room to examine lost souls like Jonathan in *Carnal Knowledge* and the damned conspirators in *The Fortune*; Roy Cohn and Joe Pitt in *Angels in America* and the damned conspirators in *Closer*. A familiar technique of Nichols, debuting all the way back in his second film, *The Graduate*, and still in use exactly forty years later, in *Charlie Wilson's War*, is the circular frame, via a repeated soundtrack melody, a repeated action, a return to the opening scene or image. Even when this repetition clearly underscores a protagonist's lostness, his or her failure to break from a cycle that reification invites one to see, Nichols' films still offer the redemptive insight to the audience. Benjamin and Elaine may not be able to imagine their way out of the programming of their socialization, but perhaps the audience can. It's the faith of art. Nichols' darkest endings—Jonathan paying Louise to lie to him in *Carnal Knowledge*; Freddy opting for her life of mutual torment with Oscar and Nicky in *The Fortune*; Roy Cohn sent to hell by his own imagination and Joe Pitt descending to his own personal underworld at the end of *Angels*; the cynical "victories" of Larry and "Alice" in *Closer*; and yes, that final bus ride in *The Graduate*—command us to marvel at lostness, to feel and thus to fear it.

Occasionally Nichols indulges in fairy tales of redemption—Tess McGill in *Working Girl*, Suzanne Vale in *Postcards From the Edge*, Henry Turner in *Regarding Henry*, Harold and Susan in *What Planet*—all of which are mid-career confections meant to reassure the audience that, as Lowell Kolcheck (Gene Hackman), Suzanne's director-friend in *Postcards*, observes, real-life transformation "is not like in the movies where you have a realization and your life changes. You know, in life, you have a realization, and your life changes a month or so later." It is very tempting to conclude, with Suzanne (Meryl Streep), "So I just have to wait a month." This is when Lowell reminds her that transformation is more ambiguous than a generic resolution in cinema and requires "coping." If Nichols occasionally gives us an unambiguously dark resolution of lostness or an unequivocal happy ending, his films more often resign their narratives to the gray area between these artificial assertions of closure, thus calling into question the permanence of even the happiest (or saddest) ending in any of his films. Writing in 1978 about what at that point amounted only to the first phase of Nichols' Hollywood career, H. Wayne Schuth claims, "Nichols' artistic vision seems to be based on an honest look at the grimness and tragedy of the human condition, with a tentative, resolving note of hope and nobility."[18] Nichols' tempered optimism is the only kind available to people who must take as consolation the redemptive possibility inherent in reified awareness. The good news of a Mike Nichols film is the "threshold of revelation" that no longer sugarcoats the "bad news." This phrase, "Bad News," is the title of the first episode of the *Angels in America* cycle; Kushner changes some of the original Act titles in the episodes of Nichols' adaptation, but tellingly, this one remains. For Nichols, the bad news is that we are all subject to the objectifying structures and systems of human society, with its naked manipulation to command dominance politically, economically, sexually. The good news is that, on the "threshold of revelation" inherent within reification, we have access to the full weight of this bad news and can attempt a new course.

"What the director is saying to his audience," Nichols argues, "is, 'This happened to me; did it happen to you too?' Metaphorically, almost always, not literally. The impulse is strong to say to whoever is watching, 'You too?'"[19] Nichols' most iconic film, the one that has resonated most deeply with audiences who have responded, "Me too," remains *The Graduate*. Its drama is to watch a young man labor philosophically through a summer season of "drifting" on this threshold of revelation, aware of the problems of his socialized inheritance but inept at imagining, let alone enacting, some sensible alternative. Yossarian, too, knows the absurdity of reified existence and rails against it from one end of the narrative to the other, to little avail. His escape at film's end is on the same epic absurdity of scale—a tiny man with a tiny oar in a tiny dinghy on an immense, implacable sea—as any absurdity he has encountered in the military. We get to watch Benjamin and Yossarian flounder much longer with the bad news of their reified predicament than in most of Nichols' films. George and Martha in *Virginia Woolf* exorcise their decades of "games" and, in the pale light of dawn, see the scarifying truth of their lost years. Jake in *The Day of the Dolphin* sits in disillusionment east of the Eden of his Terrell Center. Karen in *Silkwood* comes to terms with her complicity in reified systems midway through the film, but in the generic logic of the paranoid-conspiracy thriller, that doesn't mean they're not still out to get her, a fact with which she's still coming to terms as she dies at film's end. Henry Burton in *Primary Colors* must find his way past his raging case of "true believerism" to the same tempered optimism—eyes open—that informs Nichols' point of view in his films. Charlie Wilson looks out at an adoring Intelligence Community and reflects on the cycle of reified mistakes we seem doomed to ignore and repeat, both as individuals and as a nation.

Like Benjamin and Yossarian, the various Prophets of *Angels in America* stand on their own thresholds of revelation early in the narrative. Yet Harper Pitt continues to be afraid of what she has seen in her shared vision with Prior Walter, medicating in hopes of avoiding too-painful confrontation with truths she's known but boxed away, and Prior enters into a Yossarianesque jeremiad against his personal sense of ill treatment until he comes to a recognition of injustice's indiscriminate path of destruction; he gets more perspective from a repressed, middle-aged Mormon woman than he does even from Belize, the reluctant prophet of *Angels*. Prior learns on his threshold of revelation what Harper also learns, that existence offers to those who step over the threshold "a kind of painful progress." With its persistent allusive evocations of Walter Benjamin's "angel of history," *Angels* petitions for "reexamination of cultural certitudes, particularly those in the arenas of politics, economic justice, religion, morality, and sex and gender. A reformed society, as Kushner sees it, must be built upon a progressive, humanist doctrine grounded in the hard lessons of history."[20] Harper steps over the threshold into the responsibilities of revelation when she leaves the deep freeze of "Antarctica"; Prior rejects the Angel's siren song of Death's "respite, of cessation" to receive from Belize, reluctant prophet of the real, his "Welcome back to the world." Roy Cohn is the prophet of illusion: having understood all the realities of reified existence, which he carefully lays out before Henry, his personal physician of decades, he remains literally hell-bent on deception as a philosophical solution; in contrast, Belize is the prophet of disillusionment in the best literal sense of that word. He's hard on Louis Ironson, who needs Belize's hard line, which is too honest to ever call itself tough love. Of all his many criticisms of Louis, however, the most profound is Belize's insistence that Louis is "Up in the air, just like that angel, too far off the earth to pick out the details. Louis and his Big Ideas. Big Ideas are all you love." Belize understands that abstractions are as much a capitulation as any other escape—denial, drugs, Death itself—from the *dis-illusionment* of genuine encounter with the world in all its imperfection. "I *live* in America, Louis—that's hard enough," says Belize. Refusing his Angel of Mercy/Death, Prior announces his own version of Belize's reified and redeemed philosophy: "We live past hope. If I can find hope anywhere, that's it, that's the best I can do. It's so much not enough, so inadequate, but still: Bless me anyway. I want more life." Prior stakes his claim to life "with his eyes firmly fixed on what lies behind him, on the stagnation of stasis. He accepts, and even embraces, the agonies of his life and, as such, achieves redemption born of a renewed hope, even if that hope is burnished with a knowledge that the joy of living is inextricably linked to loss and suffering [... and i]nsisting that no matter what humans are given to endure, belief in progressive change is a path to hope and salvation."[21]

Though it is not chronologically his final work, *Angels in America* has a grandness of size and purpose that, seen in the context of a career, makes a kind of culminating summation of who Nichols has been as a cinematic artist, and he has stated it is his best work.[22] He'd just entered his seventies when he took on the project—a time for self-appraisal and retrospection. Approaching a half-century of having made the world laugh and think, Nichols couldn't have helped seeing an adaptation of Kushner's epic as a work that would cast inevitable light on his larger body of work. He'd attempted something of the sort in mid-career, in *Postcards*, with its cine à clef allusions to filmmaking and, specifically, to *The Graduate*, and featuring a directorial avatar with an Anglicized Russian name: Lowell Kolchek, who articulates the limitations of cinema in exploring life.

In the extraordinary launch of his career, six films in nine years that ranged the spectrum from epic and surrealist to chamber drama and slapstick, Nichols announced a consistent

On the set of his late-career magnum opus, the six-part mini-series *Angels in America* for HBO, Mike Nichols (foreground, right) confers with Emma Thompson about one of her scenes as The Angel. Thompson told Richard Stayton in *Written By* (December 2003), "Mike and I spent months asking, 'What's it really about?' Mike [...] said, 'It's about citizenship,' which is a concept that I think we're losing fast. [...] The effects of our daily actions are no longer credited with the power to form our character. What's credited are possessions and status and acquisition. [... Y]ou do have to, therefore, embrace with open arms and hearts something that examines the processes of being human in an honest way like *Angels in America*." More than any formalist quirk of style, this examination of "the processes of being human," both in ways that damage and ennoble us, is the auteur vision of Nichols' film career.

vision of men and women in reified limbo, some of whom are held fast by systems threatened by any resistance to status quo, the rest of whom remain stubbornly resistant to truths that might otherwise set them free. In a demonstration of the "kind of painful progress" that characterizes our daily encounter with "more life" in all its messy ambiguity, Nichols wrestled his way through the 1980s and 1990s, attempting to articulate the hope he harbored for "transformation,"[23] sometimes too easily, generically won in his mid-career films. As many of his films have structurally traced a circle back to where they began, either implying (as in films like *The Graduate* and *Working Girl* and *Closer*) a failure of progress or (as in films like *Heartburn* or *Primary Colors* or *Charlie Wilson's War*) a resignation to the limits of progress, Nichols' career has returned in his final films to the grand ambition and even some of the dramatic circumstances of his first phase. Like George and Martha in *Virginia Woolf*, Vivian Bearing is a member of academia, a keeper of knowledge, who must come to terms with impermanence and her own objecthood. *Closer* revisits the gendered post-feminist alienation that *Carnal Knowledge* prefigures in the early decades of feminism. And if Charlie Wilson never quite questions the military-industrial complex as Yossarian does, he nonetheless recognizes a systemic absurdity that results in our failure to learn from what "we always do" when we take up arms on foreign soil. Both films focus on earlier foreign interventions by the United States (*Catch-22* in Europe during World War II, *Charlie Wilson's War* during the Soviet War in Afghanistan in the 1970s) as a means of commenting on American entanglements contemporary with the films' release dates (respectively, Vietnam and the War begun in 2001 in Afghanistan). His early films bristled with ambition, and even though rich in comic moments and detail, represent a profound seriousness of intent that rewards renewed study. His late films can be described in similar terms; not all of the films of his long middle period, his most intensely mainstream–Hollywood phase, are either as ambitious or as accomplished.

Nichols will be remembered, with May, as a significant figure in the new stand-up comedy that exploded in American entertainment in the late 1950s and in the 1960s. While these performances have been preserved in recordings, they nonetheless capture moments best experienced as live performance in a particular time and place. He will be remembered for his extraordinary success in Broadway theaters; he's the leading Broadway director of his generation, with almost unerring instincts for what plays on a stage. But of all his accomplishments, the theater work will be the first to fade from cultural memory, because of the essential ephemerality of theatrical performance, art writ in the river of time. Nichols' most durable legacy, then, is the work he has created as a Hollywood filmmaker. Philip Seymour Hoffman, who has worked for Nichols on stage and on screen, calls Nichols "'one of the great artists of the 20th century.'"[24] Beyond *The Graduate*, whose iconic status both assures its permanence in the cultural memory at the same time that it has kept audiences from clearly seeing the film's acidic point of view,[25] Nichols has made several cinematic adaptations of stage plays that will serve as enduring interpretations of important theatrical texts, including two accomplished minor classics, Margaret Edson's *Wit* and Patrick Marber's *Closer*, and two canonical masterworks, *Virginia Woolf* and *Angels*. Despite its box-office failure, *Catch-22* is a major work of the early New Hollywood, as is *Carnal Knowledge*. Nichols made two paranoid-conspiracy thrillers, *The Day of the Dolphin*[26] and *Silkwood*, when that genre was at the height of its popularity; each captures beautifully the ethos of the era of Questioned Authority. *Primary Colors* and *Charlie Wilson's War* were major films that, like *Catch-22*, suffered because of complications with genre packaging (are they comedies or dramas? Are they satiric or heart-felt?). More acutely, both suffered as *Catch-22* had from poor marketplace timing, and all three deserve serious re-evaluation. Of all Nichols' films, *Catch-22* has been the most undervalued, and, with *The Graduate*, the least understood—an ironic phenomenon, considering the global ubiquity of *The Graduate* and the near-total dismissal of *Catch-22*.

It is likely that Nichols' filmmaking reputation, as an intelligent interpreter of others' texts rather than as a generator of his own, has done little to advance his critical reputation. He is perceived as a professional—tasteful, but without a "brand." In 1993, before he made his final eight films (including the two HBO masterpieces), Nichols was pinned down by *New York Times* reporter Bernard Weinraub regarding his legacy; for once Nichols' savoir faire was ruffled as he demanded, "Why should I have to defend myself? Who's still doing it so well after so long? [...] Why do I get punished for making two or three or however many great movies that I'm granted?"[27] Certainly there are other directors of his New Hollywood era who, unlike Allen and Coppola, do not as a matter of course write their own films. Yet most of these filmmakers have staked out a distinctive formal rhetoric or familiar genre conventions (or both) that have "branded" them. One always recognizes a Scorsese or Spielberg film, whether they had any part in the writing or not, as one once recognized the films of Hitchcock or Ford. Is there a Nichols brand? "Mike Nichols is an unquestioned figure in our culture," writes David Thomson, " [...] Yet I find it hard to grasp a him in there, a movie director: [...] Is there soul, intelligence, theme, or character holding these films together in series?"[28] Altman, Allen, even, in a lesser light, Brooks all project, in a name, a cinematic world and worldview. "Nichols" has been a less precise brand of artistic vision, and the reason for this book. "'If you want to be immortal,' Nichols says, 'stick to one kind of movie. Be the master of suspense. Be our greatest comedian to cause warm laughter. And then all the guys in France with cigarette ashes all over them can make their lists, and the bloggers can write each other about arcana. I say, do something you want to do, as well as you can—who cares if you're immortal?'"[29] It may ultimately be most accurate to say that Mike Nichols is an accomplished New Hollywood professional who has made some major films. "He can go on and on until he chooses not to go on anymore,'" Spielberg has said admiringly.[30] Yet posterity likely will not call Mike Nichols an auteur because of its own hidebound prejudices about what "art" is. This irony will not be lost on a smart man like Nichols: the branding as "auteur," whether bestowed or withheld, may be understood as yet another form of the diminishing objectification to which Nichols' films consistently object.

Filmography

Who's Afraid of Virginia Woolf?
(Warner Brothers, 1966)

Producer: Ernest Lehman; *Screenplay*: Ernest Lehman, adapted from the play of the same name by Edward Albee (1962); *Production Design*: Richard Sylbert; *Director of Photography*: Haskell Wexler; *Editor*: Sam O'Steen; Music: Alex North; *Principal Cast*: Elizabeth Taylor (Martha), Richard Burton (George), George Segal (Nick), Sandy Dennis (Honey); *Running Time*: 131 minutes; *Premiere Date*: June 21, 1966; *DVD*: Warner Brothers Two-Disc Special Edition, 2006

* * *

The Graduate (AVCO-Embassy, 1967)

Producer: Lawrence Turman; *Screenplay*: Buck Henry, adapted from the novel of the same name by Charles Webb (1963); *Production Design*: Richard Sylbert; *Director of Photography*: Robert Surtees; *Editor*: Sam O'Steen; *Music*: Simon and Garfunkel, Dave Grusin; *Principal Cast*: Anne Bancroft (Mrs. Robinson), Dustin Hoffman (Benjamin), Katharine Ross (Elaine), William Daniels (Mr. Braddock), Murray Hamilton (Mr. Robinson), Elizabeth Wilson (Mrs. Braddock), Buck Henry (Room Clerk), Brian Avery (Carl Smith), Norman Fell (Mr. McCleery); *Running Time*: 106 minutes; *Premiere Date*: December 21, 1967; *DVD*: Metro Goldwyn Mayer Two-Disc 40th Anniversary Edition, 2007

* * *

Catch-22 (Paramount, 1970)

Producers: John Calley and Martin Ransohoff; *Screenplay*: Buck Henry, adapted from the novel of the same name by Joseph Heller (1961); *Production Design*: Richard Sylbert; *Director of Photography*: David Watkin; *Editor*: Sam O'Steen; *Principal Cast*: Alan Arkin (Yossarian), Martin Balsam (Cathcart), Richard Benjamin (Danby), Art Garfunkel (Nately), Jack Gilford (Doc Daneeka), Buck Henry (Korn), Bob Newhart (Major Major), Anthony Perkins (Chaplain Tappman), Paula Prentiss (Nurse Duckett), Martin Sheen (Dobbs), Jon Voight (Milo), Orson Welles (Dreedle), Seth Allen (Hungry Joe), Bob Balaban (Orr), Suzanne Benton (Dreedle's WAC), Norman Fell (Towser), Charles Grodin (Aardvark), Austin Pendleton (Moodus), Peter Bonerz (McWatt), Jon Korkes (Snowden); *Running Time*: 121 minutes; *Premiere Date*: June 24, 1970; *DVD*: Paramount, 2006

* * *

Carnal Knowledge (AVCO-Embassy, 1971)

Producer: Mike Nichols; *Screenplay*: Jules Feiffer; *Production Design*: Richard Sylbert; *Director of Photography*: Giuseppe Rotunno; *Editor*: Sam O'Steen; *Principal Cast*: Jack Nicholson (Jonathan), Ann-Margret (Bobbie), Art Garfunkel (Sandy), Candice Bergen (Susan), Cynthia O'Neal (Cindy), Carol Kane (Jennifer), Rita Moreno (Louise); *Running Time*: 98 minutes; *Premiere Date*: June 30, 1971; *DVD*: Metro Goldwyn Mayer, 1999

* * *

The Day of the Dolphin (AVCO-Embassy, 1973)

Producer: Robert E. Relyea; *Screenplay*: Buck Henry, adapted from the novel of the same name by Robert Merle (1967); *Production Design*: Richard Sylbert; *Director of Photography*: William A Fraker; *Editor*: Sam O'Steen; *Music*: Georges Delerue; *Principal Cast*: George C. Scott (Dr. Jake Terrell), Trish Van Devere (Maggie), Paul Sorvino (Mahoney), Fritz Weaver (Harold DeMilo), Jon Korkes (David), Edward Herrmann (Mike), Leslie Charleson (Maryanne), John David Carson (Larry), Victoria Racimo (Lana), John Dehner (Wallingford); *Running Time*: 104 minutes; *Premiere Date*: December 19, 1973; *DVD*: Studio Canal Image, 2005

* * *

The Fortune (Columbia Pictures, 1975)

Producers: Mike Nichols and Don Devlin; *Screenplay*: Carole Eastman (writing as Adrien Joyce); *Production Design*: Richard Sylbert; *Director of Photography*: John A. Alonzo; *Editor*: Stu Linder; *Music*: David Shire; *Principal Cast*: Jack Nicholson (Oscar), Warren Beatty (Nicky), Stockard Channing (Freddie), Florence Stanley (Mrs. Gould), Tom Newman (John the Barber), Richard B. Shull (Chief Det. Sgt. Jack Power), John Fiedler (Photographer); *Running Time*: 88 minutes; *Premiere Date*: May 20, 1975; *VHS*: Columbia Tristar, 1998

* * *

Silkwood (ABC Motion Pictures, 1983)

Producers: Mike Nichols and Michael Hausman; *Screenplay*: Nora Ephron and Alice Arlen; *Production Design*: Patrizia von Brandenstein; *Director of Photography*: Miroslav Ondricek; *Editor*: Sam O'Steen; *Music*: Georges Delerue; *Principal Cast*: Meryl Streep (Karen), Kurt Russell (Drew), Cher (Dolly), Craig T. Nelson (Winston), Fred Ward (Morgan), Diana Scarwid (Angela), Ron Silver (Paul Stone), Josef Sommer (Richter), Sudie Bond (Thelma), Henderson Forsythe (Quincy), E. Katherine Kerr (Gilda), Bruce McGill (Hurley), David Straithairn (Wesley), J. C. Quinn (Curtis); *Running Time*: 131 minutes; *Premiere Date*: December 14, 1983; *DVD*: Metro Goldwyn Mayer, 2003

* * *

Heartburn (Paramount, 1986)

Producers: Mike Nichols and Robert Greenhut; *Screenplay*: Nora Ephron, adapted from her own novel of the same name (1983); *Production Design*: Tony Walton; *Director of Photography*: Néstor Almendros; *Editor*: Sam O'Steen; *Music*: Carly Simon; *Principal Cast*: Meryl Streep (Rachel), Jack Nicholson (Mark), Jeff Daniels (Richard), Maureen Stapleton (Vera), Stockard Channing (Julie), Richard Masur (Arthur), Catherine O'Hara (Betty), Steven Hill (Harry), Milos Forman (Dmitri), Karen Akers (Thelma), Aida Linares (Juanita), Anna Maria Horsford (Della), Kevin Spacey (Subway Thief), John Wood (British TV Moderator), Yakov Smirnoff (Laszlo), Caroline Aaron (Judith); *Running Time*: 109 minutes; *Premiere Date*: July 25, 1986; *DVD*: Paramount, 2004

* * *

Biloxi Blues (Rastar Pictures, 1988)

Producer: Ray Stark; *Screenplay*: Neil Simon, from his own play of the same name (1984); *Production Design*: Paul Sylbert; *Director of Photography*: Bill Butler; *Editor*: Sam O'Steen; *Music*: Georges Delerue; *Principal Cast*: Matthew Broderick (Eugene Morris Jerome), Christopher Walken (Sgt. Toomey), Matt Mulhern (Wykowski), Corey Parker (Epstein), Markus Flanagan (Selridge), Casey Siemaszko (Carney), Michael Dolan (Hennessey), Penelope Ann Miller (Daisy), Park Overall (Rowena); *Running Time*: 107 minutes; *Premiere Date*: March 25, 1988; *DVD*: Universal, 2003

* * *

Working Girl (Twentieth Century–Fox, 1988)

Producer: Douglas Wick; *Screenplay*: Kevin Wade; *Production Design*: Patrizia von Brandenstein; *Director of Photography*: Michael Ballhaus; *Editor*: Sam O'Steen; *Music*: Carly Simon and Rob Mounsey; *Principal Cast*: Harrison Ford (Jack), Sigourney Weaver (Katharine), Melanie Griffith (Tess), Alec Baldwin (Mick), Joan Cusack (Cyn), Philip Bosco (Oren Trask), Nora Dunn (Ginny), Oliver Platt (Lutz), James Lally (Turkel), Kevin Spacey (Bob), Olympia Dukakis (Personnel Director), Amy Aquino (Tess' Secretary), Jeffrey Nordling (Tim), Elizabeth Whitcraft (Doreen), Timothy Carhart (Trask Gatekeeper); *Running Time*: 116 minutes; *Premiere Date*: December 21, 1988; *DVD*: 20th Century–Fox, 2006

* * *

Postcards from the Edge (Columbia Pictures, 1990)

Producers: Mike Nichols and John Calley; *Screenplay*: Carrie Fisher, adapted from her novel of the same name (1987); *Production Design*: Patrizia von Brandenstein; *Director of Photography*: Michael Ballhaus; *Editor*: Sam O'Steen; *Music*: Carly Simon; *Principal Cast*: Meryl Streep (Suzanne), Shirley MacLaine (Doris), Dennis Quaid (Jack), Gene Hackman (Lowell), Richard Dreyfuss (Dr. Frankenthal), Mary Wickes (Grandma), Conrad Bain (Grandpa), Annette Bening (Evelyn), Robin Bartlett (Aretha); *Running Time*: 102 minutes; *Premiere Date*: September 12, 1990; *DVD*: Columbia/Sony, 2006

* * *

Regarding Henry (Paramount, 1991)

Producers: Mike Nichols and Scott Rudin; *Screenplay*: J. J. Abrams (as Jeffrey Abrams); *Production Design*: Tony Walton; *Director of Photography*: Giuseppe Rotunno; *Editor*: Sam O'Steen; *Music*: Hans Zimmer; *Principal Cast*: Harrison

Ford (Henry), Annette Bening (Sarah), Rebecca Miller (Linda), Bruce Altman (Bruce), Elizabeth Wilson (Jessica), Donald Moffat (Charlie), Mikki Allen (Rachel), Robin Bartlett (Phyllis), Bill Nunn (Bradley); *Running Time*: 107 minutes; *Premiere Date*: July 10, 1991; *DVD*: Paramount, 2003

* * *

Wolf (Columbia Pictures, 1994)

Producer: Douglas Wick; *Screenplay*: Jim Harrison and Wesley Strick; *Production Design*: Bo Welch and Jim Dultz; *Director of Photography*: Giuseppe Rotunno; *Editor*: Sam O'Steen; *Music*: Ennio Morricone; *Principal Cast*: Jack Nicholson (Will), Michelle Pfeiffer (Laura), James Spader (Stewart), Kate Nelligan (Charlotte), Richard Jenkins (Det. Bridger), Christopher Plummer (Alden), Eileen Atkins (Mary), David Hyde Pierce (Roy), Om Puri (Dr. Alezais); *Running Time*: 125 minutes; *Premiere Date*: June 17, 1994; *DVD*: Columbia/Sony, 2005

* * *

The Birdcage (United Artists, 1996)

Producer: Mike Nichols; *Screenplay*: Elaine May, adapted from the film *La Cage aux Folles* (Edouard Molinaro, 1978), which was adapted from the play of the same name by Jean Poiret; *Production Design*: Bo Welch; *Director of Photography*: Emmanuel Lubezki; *Editor*: Arthur Schmidt; *Principal Cast*: Robin Williams (Armand), Gene Hackman (Sen. Keeley), Nathan Lane (Albert), Dianne Wiest (Louise), Dan Futterman (Val), Calista Flockhart (Barbara), Hank Azaria (Agador), Christine Baranski (Katherine); *Running Time*: 119 minutes; *Premiere Date*: March 8, 1996; *DVD*: Metro Goldwyn Mayer, 2005

* * *

Primary Colors (BBC and Universal Pictures, among several other production companies, 1998)

Producer: Mike Nichols; *Screenplay*: Elaine May, adapted from the novel of the same note by Joe Klein, writing as Anonymous (1996); *Production Design*: Bo Welch; *Director of Photography*: Michael Ballhaus; *Editor*: Arthur Schmidt; *Music*: Ry Cooder; *Principal Cast*: John Travolta (Gov. Jack Stanton), Emma Thompson (Susan), Billy Bob Thornton (Richard), Kathy Bates (Libby), Adrian Lester (Henry), Maura Tierney (Daisy), Larry Hagman (Gov. Fred Picker), Diane Ladd (Mamma Stanton), Paul Guilfoyle (Howard),

Rebecca Walker (March), Tommy Hollis (Fat Willie), Caroline Aaron (Lucille), J. C. Quinn (Uncle Charlie), Allison Janney (Miss Walsh), Robert Klein (Norman), Stacy Edwards (Jennifer); *Running Time*: 144 minutes; *Premiere Date*: March 20, 1998; *DVD*: Universal, 1998

* * *

What Planet Are You From? (Columbia Pictures, 2000)

Producers: Mike Nichols, Garry Shandling, and Neil Machlis; *Screenplay*: Garry Shandling, Michael Leeson, Ed Solomon, and Peter Tolan; *Production Design*: Bo Welch; *Director of Photography*: Michael Ballhaus; *Editor*: Richard Marks; *Music*: Carter Burwell; *Principal Cast*: Garry Shandling (Harold), Annette Bening (Susan), John Goodman (Roland), Greg Kinnear (Perry), Ben Kingsley (Graydon), Judy Greer (Rebecca), Harmony Smith (Rita), Richard Jenkins (Don Fisk), Linda Fiorentino (Helen), Caroline Aaron (Nadine), Nora Dunn (Madeline), Camryn Manheim (Alison), Ann Cusack (Liz); *Running Time*: 107 minutes; *Premiere Date*: March 3, 2000; *DVD*: Columbia Tristar, 2000

* * *

Wit (HBO Films, 2001)

Producer: Simon Bosanquet; *Screenplay*: Mike Nichols and Emma Thompson, adapted from the play of the same name by Margaret Edson (1993); *Production Design*: Stuart Wurtzel; *Director of Photography*: Seamus McGarvey; *Editor*: John Bloom; *Music*: Henryk Mikolaj Górecki; *Principal Cast*: Emma Thompson (Vivian), Christopher Lloyd (Dr. Kelekian), Eileen Atkins (Prof. Ashford), Audra McDonald (Susie), Jonathan M. Woodward (Jason), Harold Pinter (Vivian's Father); *Running Time*: 99 minutes; *Premiere Date*: March 24, 2001; *DVD*: Home Box Office, 2010

* * *

Angels in America (HBO Films, 2003)
Part 1: Millennium Approaches
Part 2: Perestroika
Producers: Mike Nichols, Cary Brokaw, Delia D. Costas, Michael Haley, Paul A. Levin, Marco Valerio Pugini; *Screenplay*: Tony Kushner, adapted from his play of the same name (1992); *Production Design*: Stuart Wurtzel; *Director of Photography*: Stephen Goldblatt; *Editors*: John Bloom and Antonia Van Drimmelen; *Music*: Thomas Newman; *Principal Cast*: Al Pacino (Roy), Meryl Streep (Ethel Rosenberg/Hannah/

The Rabbi), Emma Thompson (Emily/The Angel/Homeless Woman), Mary-Louise Parker (Harper), Jeffrey Wright (Belize/Mr. Lies), Justin Kirk (Prior Walter/Leatherman in Park), Ben Shenkman (Louis), Patrick Wilson (Joe), James Cromwell (Henry); *Running Time*: 352 minutes (six episode mini-series); *Premiere Date*: December 7, 2003; *DVD*: Home Box Office, 2004

* * *

Closer (Columbia Pictures, 2004)

Producers: Mike Nichols, Cary Brokaw, and John Calley; *Screenplay*: Patrick Marber, adapted from his play of the same name (1997); *Production Design*: Tim Hatley; *Director of Photography*: Stephen Goldblatt; *Editors*: John Bloom and Antonia Van Drimmelen; *Principal Cast*: Julia Roberts (Anna), Jude Law (Dan), Natalie Portman (Alice), Clive Owen (Larry); *Running Time*: 104 minutes; *Premiere Date*: December 3, 2004; *DVD*: Columbia/Sony, 2005

* * *

Charlie Wilson's War (Universal Pictures, 2007)

Producers: Gary Goetzman and Tom Hanks; *Screenplay*: Aaron Sorkin, adapted from the book of the same name by George Crile (2003); *Production Design*: Victor Kempster; *Director of Photography*: Stephen Goldblatt; *Editors*: John Bloom and Antonia Van Drimmelen; *Music*: James Newton Howard; *Principal Cast*: Tom Hanks (Charlie), Amy Adams (Bonnie), Julia Roberts (Joanne), Philip Seymour Hoffman (Gust), Brian Markinson (Paul Brown), Jud Tylor (Crystal Lee), Emily Blunt (Jane), Peter Gerety (Larry), Wynn Everett, Mary-Bonner Baker, Rachel Nichols, Shiri Appleby (Charlie's Angels), John Slattery (Cravely), Om Puri (President Zia), Denis O'Hare (Harold Holt), Christopher Denham (Mike Vickers), Ken Stott (Zvi), Ned Beatty (Doc Long), Nancy Linehan Charles (Mrs. Long); *Running Time*: 102 minutes; *Premiere Date*: December 21, 2007; *DVD*: Universal, 2008

Chapter Notes

Preface

1. Gavin Smith, "Of Metaphors and Purpose," *Film Comment*, May/June 1999, 21.
2. Douglas Kennedy, "From New York to LA," *The Listener*, 16 March 1989, 36.
3. Nichols did, however, direct one film during this hiatus, a concert film of Gilda Radner's comic stage show, called *Gilda Live* (1980).
4. Sean Mitchell, "The One They Ask for By Name!" *Empire*, February 1991, 67.
5. Gavin Smith, "Without Cutaways," *Film Comment*, May 1991, 32.
6. John Lahr, *Show and Tell*, 283.
7. Joan Juliet Buck, "Live Mike," *Vanity Fair*, June 1994, 81.
8. David Thomson, *The New Biographical Dictionary of Film*, 5th ed., 705.
9. Lee Hill, "Mike Nichols and the Business of Living," *Senses of Cinema*, July 2003.
10. Smith, "Without Cutaways," 27.
11. Thomson, 127.
12. A. O. Scott, "Who's Returning to Virginia Woolf?" *New York Times*, 28 November 2004.
13. Smith, "Of Metaphors and Purpose," 21.
14. Joseph Gelmis, *The Film Director as Superstar*, 359.
15. Caryn James, "Death, Mighty Thou Art; So Too, a Compassionate Heart," *New York Times*, 23 March 2001.
16. Buck, 70.
17. Mel Gussow, "Mike Nichols: Director as Star," *Newsweek*, 14 November 1966, 98.
18. Smith, "Of Metaphors and Purpose," 26.
19. Timothy Bewes, *Reification: Or, The Anxiety of Late Capitalism*, 252.
20. Bewes, 253.
21. Bewes, 270.
22. Bewes, 255.
23. Bewes, 255.
24. Smith, "Of Metaphors and Purpose," 26.
25. John Lindsay Brown, "Pictures of Innocence," *Sight and Sound*, Spring 1972, 102.
26. Peter Applebome, "Always Asking, What Is This Really About?" *New York Times*, 25 April 1999.
27. Smith, "Without Cutaways," 36.
28. Benjamin's "future" is here extrapolated from the larger context of the 1963 source novel, by Charles Webb.
29. "Some Are More Yossarian Than Others," *Time*, 15 June 1970, 68.
30. Leslie Aldridge, "Who's Afraid of the Undergraduate?" *New York Times*, 18 February 1968.
31. Bewes, 270.
32. Scott.
33. Lahr, 253.
34. Scott.
35. Interviewed on *Charlie Rose*, April 28, 1998, at the Metropolitan Museum of Art.
36. Caryn James, "Death, Mighty Thou Art; So Too, a Compassionate Heart," *New York Times*, 23 March 2001.
37. Brad Goldfarb and Patrick Giles, "The Angels Have Landed," *Interview*, December 2003/January 2004, 171.
38. Tony Kushner, "The Art of Theater No. 16," *The Paris Review*, Summer 2012, 117–118.
39. James Fisher, *Understanding Tony Kushner*, 55.
40. Goldfarb and Giles, 172.
41. Goldfarb and Giles, 171.
42. Lahr, 279.
43. Mel Gussow, *Edward Albee: A Singular Journey*, 239.
44. Andrew Sarris, *The American Cinema: Directors and Directions, 1929–1968*, 218.
45. A. H. Weiler, "Nichols Meets Jules Feiffer," *New York Times*, 26 October 1969.
46. Howard Taubman, "In Pursuit of Laughter," *New York Times*, 8 April 1968.
47. Barbara Goldsmith, "Grass, Women and Sex: An Interview with Mike Nichols," *Harper's Bazaar*, November 1970, 143.
48. See especially Chapter 2, "Post-*Graduate*," for a review of the critical literature reflecting the film's problematic reception.
49. Nora Ephron, *Wallflower at the Orgy*, 219.
50. Smith, "Without Cutaways," 31.
51. Hill.
52. Richard T. Jameson, "Mike Nichols," *Film Comment*, May/June 1999, 10.
53. Jameson, 10.

54. Thomson, 705.
55. Gerald Nachman, *Seriously Funny: The Rebel Comedians of the 1950s and 1960s*, 353.
56. Hill.

Chapter 1

1. Sam Kashner, "Who's Afraid of Nichols & May?" *Vanity Fair*, January 2013, 102.
2. Robert would also distinguish himself in later life, following a path closer to their father's, as a doctor at the Mayo Clinic.
3. Henry Louis Gates, *Faces of America*, PBS DVD, 2010.
4. John Lahr, *Show and Tell*, 260.
5. Peter Applebome, "Always Asking, What Is This Really About?" *New York Times*, 25 April 1999.
6. A. O. Scott, "Who's Returning to Virginia Woolf?" *New York Times*, 28 November 2004.
7. Gates.
8. Mike Nichols, "*Playboy* Interview," June 1966, 73.
9. Nichols, 73.
10. Lahr, 283.
11. Nichols, 73.
12. Lahr, 283.
13. Lahr, 261.
14. Kashner, 99.
15. Robert Rice, "A Tilted Insight," *The New Yorker*, 15 April 1961, 60.
16. Gerald Nachman, *Seriously Funny: The Rebel Comedians of the 1950s and 1960s*, 327.
17. Nachman, 327.
18. Jeffrey Sweet, *Something Wonderful Right Away: An Oral History of The Second City & The Compass Players*, 85.
19. Nachman, 338.
20. Sweet, 77.
21. Sweet, 75.
22. Sweet, 78.
23. Lahr, 268.
24. Nachman, 341.
25. Sweet, 78.
26. Lahr, 271.
27. Lahr, 273.
28. Nachman, 342.
29. Nachman, 342.
30. Adam Gopnik, "Standup Guys," *The New Yorker*, 12 May 2003, 108.
31. Nachman, 333.
32. Kashner, 102.
33. Leslie Aldridge, "Who's Afraid of the Undergraduate?" *New York Times*, 18 February 1968.
34. Rice, 68, 70.
35. Gavin Smith, "Without Cutaways," *Film Comment*, May 1991, 29.
36. Gavin Smith, "Of Metaphors and Purpose," *Film Comment*, May/June 1999, 21.
37. Sweet, 80.
38. Nachman, 350.

39. Nichols' acting talent has been his most neglected gift during his professional life. Peter Rainer writes that Nichols' rare appearance, as Jack, in *The Designated Mourner* (David Hare, 1997), is "one of the most extraordinary monologues I've ever seen anywhere. [...] On the basis of that performance alone, Nichols stands as one of our finest actors" ("Sitcoms," *New York*, 13 March 2000, 87).
40. However, Nichols and May remained friends and unofficial colleagues throughout Nichols' working life: "I never made a movie without spending a couple of days listening to her, or having her talk to me and the writer," Nichols says in his foreword to May's published screenplay of *The Birdcage*. "The best scene in *Heartburn* came from Elaine asking Nora Ephron questions about her father. In the scene with her father in which he says to her, 'you want fidelity, marry a swan,' that all came from Elaine's questioning of Nora about her real father. On *Wolf*, Elaine [...] did a fantastic rewrite job. But she very rarely takes credit on movies, and I'm sort of proud she took a credit on *The Birdcage*" (xv).
41. Nachman, 351.
42. Lahr, 274.
43. Smith, "Of Metaphors and Purpose," 16.
44. Lahr, 251.
45. Lahr, 277.
46. Lahr, 277.
47. Lahr, 282.
48. Lahr, 285.
49. Lahr, 282.

Chapter 2

1. Mel Gussow, *Edward Albee: A Singular Journey*, 239.
2. Commentary by Nichols and Steven Soderbergh on the Warner Bros. Two-Disc Special Edition DVD, 2006.
3. Gussow, 241.
4. Gussow, 241.
5. Commentary by Nichols and Soderbergh, DVD.
6. Commentary by Nichols and Soderbergh, DVD.
7. Gussow, 236.
8. Commentary by Nichols and Soderbergh, DVD.
9. Commentary by Nichols and Soderbergh, DVD.
10. Harry M. Benshoff, "Movies and Camp," in *American Cinema of the 1960s: Themes and Variations*, ed. Barry Keith Grant, 161.
11. Gussow, 237.
12. Benshoff, 162.
13. Sam Kashner and Nancy Schoenberger, *Furious Love: Elizabeth Taylor, Richard Burton, and the Marriage of the Century*, 144.
14. In her review for *The New Yorker*, Edith Oliver observes that "the most important change of all in the move from stage to screen is that Martha's play has become George's movie." This resonates with the decisions George makes for the two of them at the climax of the evening's games.
15. Commentary by Nichols and Soderbergh, DVD.

16. Bosley Crowther, "Who's Afraid of Audacity?" *New York Times*, 10 July 1966.

17. Kashner and Schoenberger, 148.

18. Commentary by Nichols and Soderbergh, DVD.

19. Commentary by Nichols and Soderbergh, DVD.

20. Timothy Bewes, *Reification: Or, The Anxiety of Late Capitalism*, 255.

Chapter 3

1. Mark Harris, *Pictures at a Revolution: Five Movies and the Birth of the New Hollywood*, 418.

2. Qtd. in Peter Biskind, "Who's Afraid of the Big Bad Wolf?" *Premiere*, March 1994, 60.

3. Bosley Crowther, retiring from his post as film critic at the *New York Times* at the end of 1967, was a prominent early supporter, comparing Nichols to Preston Sturges; his final article for the *Times* was a second, longer rave for the film.

4. Harris, 394–395.

5. Gavin Smith, "Of Metaphors and Purpose," *Film Comment*, May/June 1999, 18.

6. Richard T. Jameson, "Mike Nichols," *Film Comment*, May/June 1999, 10.

7. Richard Corliss, *Talking Pictures: Screenwriters in the American Cinema*, 362.

8. Lyndon Johnson, "The Great Society," in *The Times Were a Changin': The Sixties Reader*, ed. Irwin Unger and Debi Unger, 40.

9. Andrew Sarris, *The American Cinema: Directors and Directions, 1929–1968*, 218.

10. John Lahr, *Show and Tell*, 280.

11. Stephen Farber and Estelle Changas, "Review: The Graduate," *Film Quarterly*, Spring 1968, 39.

12. Rob Feld, "Trouble in Mind," *DGA Quarterly*, Summer 2010, 22.

13. Joseph Gelmis, *The Film Director as Superstar*, 370.

14. Peter Bart, "Mike Nichols, Moviemaniac," *New York Times*, 1 January 1967.

15. Lee Hill, "Mike Nichols and the Business of Living," *Senses of Cinema*, July 2003.

16. Søren Birkvad, "Hollywood Sin, Scandinavian Virtue: The 1967 Revolt of *I Am Curious* and *The Graduate*," *Film International* 9.2 (Issue 50), 2011, 50.

17. Leslie Aldridge, "Who's Afraid of the Undergraduate?" *New York Times*, 18 February 1968.

18. Feld, 22.

19. Murray Pomerance, "1967: Movies and the Specter of Rebellion," in *American Cinema of the 1960s: Themes and Variations*, ed. Barry Keith Grant, 191.

20. Smith, 26.

21. The film I've just described here is exceptionally rare as a narrative ambition, in or beyond Hollywood.

22. Roger Ebert, "The Graduate," *Chicago Sun-Times*, 26 December 1967.

23. Feld, 23.

24. Birkvad, 52.

25. Gelmis, 375.

26. Farber and Changas, 39.

27. Smith, 24.

28. Birkvad, 51.

29. Pomerance, 192.

30. Paul Monaco, *History of the American Cinema: The Sixties, 1960–1969*, 183.

31. Jacob Brackman, "The Graduate," *The New Yorker*, 27 July 1968, 60.

32. Dan Georgakas, "From Words to Images: An Interview with Buck Henry," *Cineaste*, Winter 2001, 5.

33. Aldridge.

34. John Lindsay Brown, "Pictures of Innocence," *Sight and Sound*, Spring 1972, 102.

35. Pomerance, 192.

36. Georgakas, 5.

37. Paul Monaco quotes a letter written to the *Saturday Review*, 27 July 1968, by Sandra A. Lonsfoote of Niskawaka, Indiana: "[*The Graduate*] speaks to us, a generation of young people who refuse to accept the plastics, extramarital sex, and booze given to us by our 'elders.' We, as Benjamin, want more than what many of our critics suspect: we want truth, with all its crudeness, shock, and beauty" (184).

Chapter 4

1. Mel Gussow, *Edward Albee: A Singular Journey*, 237.

2. Dan Georgakas, "From Words to Images: An Interview with Buck Henry," *Cineaste*, Winter 2001, 5.

3. Chuck Thegze, "I See Everything Twice: An Examination of Catch-22," *Film Quarterly*, Autumn 1970, 8.

4. Stephen Farber, "Catch-22," *Sight and Sound*, Autumn 1970, 219.

5. Gavin Smith, "Of Metaphors and Purpose," *Film Comment*, May/June 1999, 26.

6. "Some Are More Yossarian Than Others," *Time*, 15 June 1970, 67.

7. Joseph Heller, *Catch As Catch Can*, 308.

8. Commentary by Nichols and Steven Soderbergh on the Paramount DVD, 2006.

9. Lee Hill, "Mike Nichols and the Business of Living," *Senses of Cinema*, July 2003.

10. Commentary by Nichols and Soderbergh, DVD.

11. Commentary by Nichols and Soderbergh, DVD.

12. Georgakas, 6.

13. Hill.

14. "Some Are More Yossarian Than Others," 74.

15. Thegze, 12.

16. Tracy Daugherty reports in *Just One Catch: A Biography of Joseph Heller* that a total of 18 vintage B-25s, half of Nichols' original demand of his properties department, received loving (and expensive) refurbishment (309), and that one of the planes has taken up permanent residency at the Smithsonian's National Air and Space Museum (314).

17. In *The Graduate*'s "drifting" sequence, Benjamin Braddock's associative mind conflates various kinds of activity: floating in the pool on his raft, floating through his affair atop Mrs. Robinson, and floating through his life mutely watching television and staring at the tele-

vision; cf. John Lindsay Brown, "Pictures of Innocence," *Sight and Sound*, Spring 1972, 102.

18. Nora Ephron, *Wallflower at the Orgy*, 209.

19. Ian Freer, "Nicholsodeon," *Empire*, November 1998, 88.

20. Gavin Smith, "Without Cutaways," *Film Comment*, May 1991, 29.

21. Farber, 218.

22. Thegze, 13.

23. Thegze, 15.

24. Commentary by Nichols and Soderbergh, DVD.

25. Commentary by Nichols and Soderbergh, DVD.

26. Commentary by Nichols and Soderbergh, DVD.

27. Farber, 219.

28. Like, for instance, David Lynch presenting, in a "realistic" context during the coda of *Blue Velvet* (1986), shots of a robin on a branch just beyond the kitchen window, in which the robin is clearly animatronic, its movements unconvincingly automated and wooden. The falseness of the robin ironizes the "happy ending" the film has attached to a vision of horror beneath the surface of an idyllic small town with its white picket fences, rose gardens, and "robins." In addition to its grounding in the Expressionist extremes of noir and European surrealism, Lynch's film is yet another narrative inspired by the vivid suburban palette of *The Graduate*.

29. Heller, *Catch-22*, 440.

30. Heller, *Catch As Catch Can*, 309.

31. Commentary by Nichols and Soderbergh, DVD.

32. Heller, *Catch As Catch Can*, 315.

33. Heller, *Catch-22*, 435.

34. The chaplain's reply has an added subtextual poignancy because the part is hauntingly inhabited by Anthony Perkins, who wrestled with his own socially proscribed demons as a closeted homosexual in Hollywood's image factory.

35. Thegze, 11.

36. Heller, 453.

37. Thegze, 12.

38. Ephron, 188.

39. Smith, "Of Metaphors and Purpose," 21.

Chapter 5

1. Commentary by Nichols and Steven Soderbergh on the Paramount DVD release of *Catch-22*, 2006.

2. Harry M. Benshoff, "Movies and Camp," in *American Cinema of the 1960s: Themes and Variations*, ed. Barry Keith Grant, 164; and David A. Cook, *Lost Illusions: American Cinema in the Shadow of Watergate and Vietnam, 1970–1979*, 99.

3. Peter Biskind, "Who's Afraid of the Big Bad Wolf?" *Premiere*, March 1994, 61.

4. Patrick Marber, *Closer*, 110.

5. Ernest Callenbach, "Carnal Knowledge," *Film Quarterly*, Winter 1971–1972, 56.

6. Commentary by Nichols and Soderbergh, *Catch-22* DVD.

7. Gavin Smith, "Of Metaphors and Purpose," *Film Comment*, May/June 1999, 26.

8. Biskind, 61.

9. Smith, "Of Metaphors and Purpose," 26.

10. A. H. Weiler, "Nichols Meets Jules Feiffer," *New York Times*, 26 October 1969.

11. Paul D. Zimmerman, "Love in a Blind Alley," *Newsweek*, 5 July 1971, 71.

12. Vincent Canby, "'I Was Sorry to See It End': 'Carnal Knowledge,'" *New York Times*, 4 July 1971.

13. Gavin Smith, "Without Cutaways," *Film Comment*, May 1991, 32.

14. Gavin Smith, "Without Cutaways," *Film Comment*, 34.

15. John Lindsay Brown, "Pictures of Innocence," *Sight and Sound*, Spring 1972, 103.

16. Jacob Brackman, "Carnal Knowledge," *Esquire*, October 1971, 46.

17. Brackman, 45.

18. Commentary by Nichols and Soderbergh, *Catch-22* DVD.

19. Feiffer identifies the new time period as "the early sixties" in his published screenplay (1971), 60.

20. Julian Jebb, "Carnal Knowledge," *Sight and Sound*, Autumn 1971, 222.

21. Zimmerman, 71.

22. Jebb, 222.

23. Zimmerman, 71.

24. Feiffer screenplay, 108.

25. David A. Cook, in the volume on 1970s Hollywood in the University of California Press *History of the American Cinema*, calls *Carnal Knowledge* "epoch-making" (324).

26. Canby.

Chapter 6

1. Christopher Sandford, *Polanski*, 137–154.

2. Vincent Canby, "Underwater Talkie: Scott Stars in Nichols's 'Day of the Dolphin,'" *New York Times*, 20 December 1973.

3. Pauline Kael, "The Day of the Dolphin," *The New Yorker*, 31 December 1973, 50.

4. In his 1978 Twayne monograph on Nichols, H. Wayne Schuth quotes Levine as calling Nichols a "'genius'" (126), while Mark Harris in *Pictures at a Revolution* quotes Nichols as describing the association begun with Levine on *The Graduate* as "'scraping the bottom of the barrel'" (71).

5. Henry wryly laments in a featurette on the Image Entertainment DVD of *The Day of the Dolphin* that his "career" voicing animated animals was ruined by this early type-casting.

6. Henry in the Image Entertainment DVD featurette.

7. John Lahr, *Show and Tell*, 283.

Chapter 7

1. Gavin Smith, "Of Metaphors and Purpose," *Film Comment*, May/June 1999, 29.

2. Smith, 29.

3. Peter Biskind, *Star: How Warren Beatty Seduced America*, 200.

4. Mel Gussow, "Nichols, Fortune Made, Looks to the Future," *New York Times*, 3 June 1975.

5. Jacob Brackman, "Carnal Knowledge," *Esquire*, October 1971, 46.

6. Brackman, 46.

7. H. Wayne Schuth, *Mike Nichols*, 60.

8. Paul D. Zimmerman, "Madcap Murder," *Newsweek*, 26 May 1975, 84.

9. Lee Hill, "Mike Nichols and the Business of Living," *Senses of Cinema*, July 2003.

10. Caryn James, "Mike Nichols Surveys the American Dream," *New York Times*, 25 February 1990.

Chapter 8

1. Cathleen McGuigan, "War, Peace & Nichols," *Newsweek*, 17 December 2007, 63.

2. Leonard Quart and Albert Auster, *American Film and Society Since 1945*, 142.

3. Lee Hill, "Mike Nichols and the Business of Living," *Senses of Cinema*, July 2003.

4. Peter Biskind, "Who's Afraid of the Big Bad Wolf?" *Premiere*, March 1994, 61.

5. Mainstream critics like Vincent Canby, writing in the *New York Times*, and Richard Schickel writing in *Time* excoriated the film's imprecisions with the facts; Nichols himself wrote to the *New York Times* in a letter dated December 28, 1983, responding to Canby's attack by reminding Canby that his own review initially praised the film as drama before attacking its reportage.

6. Tom Doherty, "Silkwood," *Film Quarterly*, Summer 1984, 25.

7. Quart and Auster, 142.

8. Quart and Auster, 142.

9. David Denby, "A Life on the Line," *New York*, 26 December 1983–2 January 1984, 97.

10. Lee Hill, "Mike Nichols and the Business of Living," *Senses of Cinema*, July 2003.

Chapter 9

1. Nora Ephron, *The Most of Nora Ephron*, 239.

2. Ephron, 240.

3. Ephron, 240.

4. Ephron, 240.

5. Ephron, 240.

6. Mark Harris, *Pictures at a Revolution*, 360.

7. Harris, 359. Simon submitted original songs for the soundtrack of *The Graduate*, but Nichols ultimately reverted to previously recorded Simon and Garfunkel tracks with the exception of some passages from "Mrs. Robinson." The rejected songs appeared on the 1968 Simon and Garfunkel album *Bookends*.

8. Gavin Smith, "Of Metaphors and Purpose," *Film Comment*, May/June 1999, 21.

9. Walter Goodman, "Romance Narrows the Gap Between Generations," *New York Times*, 10 August 1986.

Chapter 10

1. This does not include the aborted collaboration with Neil Simon on *Bogart Slept Here*, which was to be Nichols' next film after *The Fortune* but which barely made it out of pre-production before stalling.

2. Vincent Canby, "Simon's 'Biloxi Blues,' Coming of Age in the Army," *New York Times*, 25 March 1988.

3. David Denby, "Skirting Trouble," *New York*, 28 March 1988, 98; Jack Kroll, "Basic Training of Neil Simon," *Newsweek*, 4 April 1988, 72.

4. Richard Schickel, "Making a Memoir Memorable," *Time*, 4 April 1988, 77.

5. Lee Hill, "Mike Nichols and the Business of Living," *Senses of Cinema*, July 2003.

6. In an aside at the end, Eugene acknowledges that a "sane, logical, and decent man" replaces Toomey for the remainder of the camp, but they come to miss Toomey: "one should never underestimate the stimulation of eccentricity." Although delivered for a laugh, the line prizes Toomey's distinct personhood, ironically that very thing he'd hoped to drain out of the "boys" in his charge, and which got him unceremoniously dismissed. Nichols reflected this by casting the most indelibly "eccentric" actor in this antagonistic role.

Chapter 11

1. Deron Overpeck, "Movies and Images of Reality," in *American Cinema of the 1980s: Themes and Variations*, ed. Stephen Prince, 197.

2. Leonard Quart and Albert Auster, *American Film and Society Since 1945*, 159.

3. Overpeck, 196.

4. Overpeck, 197.

5. Douglas Kennedy, "From New York to LA," *The Listener*, 16 March 1989, 37.

6. Richard Combs, "Slaves of Manhattan," *Sight and Sound*, Spring 1989, 78.

7. David Denby, "Trading Places," *New York*, 2 January 1989, 45.

8. Combs, 78.

9. Denby, 45.

10. Overpeck, 198.

11. Combs, 78.

12. Overpeck, 198.

13. Overpeck, 198.

14. Oddly, neither David Denby, who adored the film, nor Pauline Kael, who predictably despised it, saw the ending for what it was, a slyly ironic demonstration of the perils of fantasy wish-fulfillment within a corrupted value structure.

Chapter 12

1. Richard Corliss, "Spin and Sizzle," *Time*, 17 September 1990, 70.

2. Carrie Fisher provides running commentary on the film, courtesy of the 2006 Columbia Pictures DVD.

3. 2006 Columbia Pictures edition.

4. Fisher on the 2006 Columbia Pictures DVD commentary track.

5. John Lahr, *Show and Tell*, 273.

6. "Trivia" section of Internet Movie Database entry on *Postcards from the Edge*.

7. Sean Mitchell, "The One They Ask for By Name!" *Empire*, February 1991, 67.

Chapter 13

1. Gavin Smith, "Of Metaphors and Purpose," *Film Comment*, May/June 1999, 21. Georgia Brown also acknowledges this thematic trend in Nichols' work, though she savages *Regarding Henry* in her *Village Voice* review of 23 July 1991.

2. Janet Maslin (*New York Times*, 14 July 1991) writes that *Regarding Henry* functions as "a companion piece" to *Working Girl*, in that "what [Tess] wins through this relentless effort—an executive position, a nice office, her own secretary—is precisely what Henry Turner needs to be freed from."

3. *Regarding Henry* received the worst reviews of Nichols' film career, by far. Even without Pauline Kael weighing in with her typical prejudices against Nichols, the vitriol that this film provoked in critics was mystifying and wrong-headed. Critics largely gave Abrams a pass based on callow youth, reserving the brunt of their attacks for Nichols, whom they thought should have known better than to depict a changed mind and heart via brain damage. Several critics (including David Ansen, Georgia Brown, and David Denby) actually stooped to extremely poor-taste jokes about whether the filmmakers, the audience, or the critics themselves would benefit more from being shot in the head than being made to watch the film; they wailed that the pre-trauma Henry was preferable to the post-trauma Henry, a provocative critical miscalculation if ever there were one, calling into question the moral aesthetics of their critical eye.

4. Gavin Smith, "Without Cutaways," *Film Comment*, May 1991, 36.

5. Smith, 42.

Chapter 14

1. Gavin Smith, "Of Metaphors and Purpose," *Film Comment*, May/June 1999, 21.

2. Anthony Lane, "Howl," *The New Yorker*, 11 July 1994, 84.

3. David Ansen, "Jack Cries Wolf," *Newsweek*, 20 June 1994, 59.

4. Peter Biskind, "Who's Afraid of the Big Bad Wolf?" *Premiere*, March 1994, 58.

5. Georgia Brown, "Where the Wild Things Are," *The Village Voice*, 21 June 1994, 50.

6. David Foster Wallace, *A Supposedly Fun Thing I'll Never Do Again*, 302.

7. Janet Maslin, "Wolf Bites Man; Man Sheds His Civilized Coat," *New York Times*, 17 June 1994.

8. The lapses in the internal logic of the film's genre narrative suggest how at sea comedians of social manners like Nichols and May found themselves in polishing Harrison's story. While Will's ears are so good he can hear conversations or ringing phones behind closed doors, he cannot hear Stewart as he steals up on the guards or on Laura herself. More important, he cannot scent Stewart's approach. Thus he can't warn Laura, who has her dramatic dialogue with Stewart on the barn steps before Stewart attempts to rape her inside the building, before Will's eyes. Most incredibly, the man who knows someone has been drinking because he "can smell it a mile away" does not have any inkling of the severed hand he's been carrying in his jacket pocket since his romp in the park the previous night.

9. Brown, 50.

10. David Denby, "Beastly Boys," *New York*, 20 June 1994, 77.

11. Smith, 21; cf. Joan Juliet Buck, "Live Mike," *Vanity Fair*, June 1994, 81.

12. Lane, 95.

Chapter 15

1. David Denby, "The Beach Boys," *New York*, 11 March 1996, 50.

2. Richard Corliss, "The Final Frontier," *Time*, 11 March 1996, 66.

3. Terrence Rafferty, "Seeing Straight," *The New Yorker*, 18 March 1996, 111.

4. Denby, 51.

5. Gary Susman, "The Birdcage," *The Village Voice*, 19 March 1996, 70.

6. Rafferty, 111.

7. Corliss, 68.

8. Nichols, xvi.

Chapter 16

1. Lee Hill, "Mike Nichols and the Business of Living," *Senses of Cinema*, July 2003.

2. J. Hoberman, "Running for Cover," *The Village Voice*, 24 March 1998, 65.

3. Gavin Smith, "Of Metaphors and Purpose," *Film Comment*, May/June 1999, 30.

4. Hendrik Hertzberg, "Upset Victory," *The New Yorker*, 23 March 1998, 86.

5. Hill.

6. David Thomson, *The New Biographical Dictionary of Film*, 5th ed., 705.

7. David Ansen, "Good Guy/Bad Guy," *Newsweek*, 23 March 1998, 63.

8. Denby, "Young Rascals," *New York*, 23 March 1998, 147.

9. James Kaplan, "True Colors?" *New York*, 2 March 1998, 26.

10. In an interview with Jeffrey Ressner for the Fall 2006 issue of *DGA Quarterly*, Nichols expressed his admiration for Stevens' mythic Western and calls

Stevens' *A Place in the Sun* (1951) the single most influential movie on his experience as a director.

11. Leslie Aldridge, "Who's Afraid of the Undergraduate?" *New York Times*, 18 February 1968.

12. Hoberman, 65.

13. Interviewed on *Charlie Rose*, 28 April 1998, at the Metropolitan Museum of Art. Nichols also cast Rose, playing himself, in *Primary Colors*, interviewing Fred Picker (Larry Hagman).

14. Kaplan, 29.

Chapter 17

1. David Ansen, "Love from Another Planet," *Newsweek*, 6 March 2000, 68.

2. Gavin Smith, "Of Metaphors and Purpose," *Film Comment*, May/June 1999, 21.

3. "Elaine May in Conversation with Mike Nichols," *Film Comment*, July/August 2006, Web only: www.filmcomment.com/article/elaine-may-in-conversation-with-mike-nichols.

4. Elvis Mitchell, "Sent to Earth with Powers and Abilities Far Below Those of Mortal Men: What Planet Are You From?" *New York Times*, 3 March 2000.

5. Bruce Newman, "Relatively Comfortable on the Planet Shandling," *New York Times*, 5 March 2000.

6. Timothy Bewes, *Reification: Or, The Anxiety of Late Capitalism*, 255.

7. Though not intended as a direct quote from an earlier classic, the suspension of Harold and Susan's child in the secure blue light-zone at Graydon's headquarters recalls the star-child in the final shots of Stanley Kubrick's *2001: A Space Odyssey* (1968). That newborn, the next evolutionary phase "beyond Jupiter" for astronaut Dave Bowman (Keir Dullea), is both an end to a journey and the most literalized of new beginnings of Kubrick's famous film. This reflects Nichols' own essential understanding of his narratives as centered in "transformation."

Chapter 18

1. Lee Hill, "Mike Nichols and the Business of Living," *Senses of Cinema*, July 2003.

2. Caryn James, "Death, Mighty Thou Art; So Too, a Compassionate Heart," *New York Times*, 23 March 2001.

3. Marc Peyser, "From Broadway to Boob Tube," *Newsweek*, 19 March 2001, 56.

4. James.

5. Bernard Weinraub, "Little Screen, Big Ambition; Serious Films by Cable Networks Fill a Void Left by Hollywood," *New York Times*, 3 January 2001.

6. David Thomson, *The New Biographical Dictionary of Film*, 5th ed., 705.

7. John Leonard, "The I. V. League," *New York*, 26 March 2001, 125.

8. Leonard, 125.

9. Margaret Edson, *Wit*, 69.

10. Nichols and Thompson could easily have clarified that it is a "real" visit by having Susie show her into the room, but since Vivian has long been in medical isolation, there is no reason to think of this scene as anything but Vivian's last—and successful—attempt at metaphysical *Wit*.

Chapter 19

1. Tony Kushner, *Angels in America*, 284. All my quotations from the film, when Kushner has adapted them verbatim from his play, use Kushner's presentation of syntax and punctuation in the published one-volume edition of the play.

2. Susan Cheever, "An Angel Sat Down at His Table," *New York Times*, 13 September 1992.

3. Ken Nielsen, *Tony Kushner's* Angels in America, 89–90; Daniel Mendelsohn, "Winged Messages," *The New York Review of Books*, 12 February 2004, 42–43.

4. Alex Abramovich, "Hurricane Kushner Hits the Heartland," *New York Times*, 30 November 2003.

5. Richard Stayton, "Flights of Angels," *Written By*, December 2003, 50.

6. John Lahr, "Angels on the Verge," *The New Yorker*, 15 November 2010, 96.

7. Brad Goldfarb and Patrick Giles, "The Angels Have Landed," *Interview*, December 2003/January 2004, 172.

8. Jeffrey Ressner, "Working Man," *DGA Quarterly*, Fall 2006.

9. Stayton, 52.

10. Alessandra Stanley, "Finally, TV Drama to Argue About," *New York Times*, 30 November 2003.

11. Thompson as the Angel is cover-girl to the Theatre Communications Group edition of the published play tied in to the Nichols production, as well as the figure who graces the front of the HBO DVD slipcase.

12. Stayton, 52.

13. Nielsen, 88.

14. John Leonard, "The I. V. League," *New York*, 26 March 2001, 125.

15. David Ansen, "City of Angels," *Newsweek*, 17 November 2003.

16. Other stage doublings would have made less sense cinematically; Martin Heller (Brian Markinson in the Nichols version), who plays an Ed Meese stooge and one-time Roy Cohn protégé, is often performed on stage by the actress who plays Harper; while there may be interesting insights to be made about the feminizing of Martin, there is no need for Nichols to slavishly reproduce all stage effects, some of which (like Parker in male drag) would be *unnecessarily* (rather than fruitfully) distracting to the cinematic audience.

17. James Fisher, *Understanding Tony Kushner*, 50.

18. Fisher, 43.

19. Mendelsohn, 43.

20. The political evolution of the Soviet Union, for instance, has reality in the play only through the allusions of Rabbi Isidor Chemelwitz to Lithuanian Jews languishing in the "shtetl" and in the endlessly opinion-

ated Louis' references to late 1980s current events, particularly the fall of the Berlin Wall.

21. Mendelsohn, 43.

22. Mendelsohn, 44.

23. Mendelsohn, 44.

24. Fisher, 52.

25. Kushner, *Angels in America*, 142.

26. Fisher, 52.

27. Goldfarb and Giles, 171.

28. Nielsen, 90.

29. Frank Rich, "Angels, Reagan, and AIDS in America," *New York Times*, 16 November 2003.

30. Mendelsohn, 42.

31. Richard Goldstein, "Angels in a Changed America," *The Village Voice*, 26 November–2 December 2003, 33.

32. Lahr, 96.

33. James Poniewozik, "Heaven on Earth," *Time*, 8 December 2003, 81.

34. Ansen.

35. Fisher, 44.

36. Kushner, *Angels in America*, 9.

37. It is possible to infer—from Harper's obsession with babies, her description of the invasive hand of God, and her chronic depression—that Harper feels guilt for an abortion or rage at a God who has allowed her to miscarry or forbid her to conceive.

38. Kushner, *Angels in America*, 9.

39. Fisher, 47.

40. Cheever.

41. Kushner, *Angels in America*, 259.

42. Nancy Franklin, "America, Lost and Found," *The New Yorker*, 8 December 2003, 127.

43. Stayton, 54.

44. Andrew O'Hehir, "Wings of Desire," *Sight and Sound*, March 2004, 6.

45. Nielsen, 88.

46. Qtd. in Nielsen, 46.

47. Stanley.

48. Tony Kushner, "The Art of Theater No. 16," *The Paris Review*, Summer 2012, 139.

49. Charlie Kaufman would later use wintry beach imagery to convey similar spiritual extremity and alienation in *Eternal Sunshine of the Spotless Mind* (Michel Gondry, 2004).

50. Kushner, *Angels in America*, 257.

51. In his *Paris Review* interview, Kushner reveals that he, too, is in Streep's thrall; upon meeting her on Nichols' set, he asked if she would play Brecht's great Mother Courage if Kushner translated the play for her, and she did, in 2006 (133).

52. Kushner, *Angels in America*, 11.

53. Indeed, it would actually make more sense for the actress playing Harper to play this cameo, since Harper's derangement moves her perilously close to vagrancy during her adventure at the Brooklyn Arboretum, and Thompson the street person's final words to Hannah are a prophecy of a future of rampant insanity. Nichols and Kushner likely felt the audience might be confused by Hannah not recognizing her own daughter-in-law.

54. Goldstein, 33.

55. Kushner, "The Art of Theater," 118.

56. Kushner, "The Art of Theater," 118.

57. Kushner, "The Art of Theater," 119.

58. Kushner, "The Art of Theater," 117.

59. Mendelsohn, 42.

60. Franklin, 126.

61. Sara Cedar Miller, *Central Park, An American Masterpiece*, 63.

62. Miller, 39.

63. Miller, 33.

64. In their detailed *The Park and the People: A History of Central Park*, Roy Rosenzweig and Elizabeth Blackmar note that the late–1960s counter-culture (including the gay liberation movement) came to adopt the Park—and in particular the Bethesda Fountain—as its public locus in the city: "A park originally designed to exemplify the city's official culture now opened its gates to powerful alternative and oppositional 'counter-cultures'" (493–494).

65. Kushner, *Angels in America*, 277.

66. Fisher, 55.

67. Stayton, 54. While not remotely like the Mormons in dogma, the Mennonites nonetheless project a clannish separation of themselves from secular majority culture that Nichols and Kushner mean to reflect in Hannah, who is on the cusp of an evolution away from such isolation, and in Joe, still paralyzed in place between the closet and the truth of himself.

68. Mendelsohn, a thoughtful gay cultural critic, objects to this treatment of Joe, arguing for Joe as the play's "only truly tragic" character and accusing Kushner of betraying Joe for the sake of the play's structure, in which both Louis and Joe must be condemned for abandoning their lovers (46–47); while Mendelsohn is right to contrast Joe's sexual awakening with Louis' inconstancy, he puzzlingly forgives Joe's devastating legal opinions as the natural consequence of the closet and, most important, conveniently forgets Joe's "desert" temptation of Louis on the wintry beach to forsake Prior, as Roy once tempted Joe to forsake Harper. Joe has the right to assert his sexuality; he does not have the right to suborn Louis' continued infidelity just as Louis is finding his conscience.

69. Goldfarb and Giles, 171.

70. Chris Nashawaty, "Life of Mike," *Entertainment Weekly*, 16 March 2012, 48.

Chapter 20

1. Colin Kennedy, "Love Hurts," *Empire*, February 2005, 74.

2. Kennedy, 75.

3. Daniel Rosenthal, "Commentary and Notes," *Closer*, Student Edition, lxxvi.

4. Rosenthal, lxxxiv.

5. Dennis Lim, "Closer," *The Village Voice*, 1 December–7 December 2004, 47.

6. Sam Davies, "Closer," *Sight and Sound*, February 2005, 46–47.

7. Anthony Lane, "Settling Scores," *The New Yorker*, 24 December 2007, 151.

8. Gavin Smith, "Of Metaphors and Purpose," *Film Comment*, May/June 1999, 21.

9. Logan Hill, "Mr. Nichols and the Vicious Circle," *New York*, 13 September 2004, 51.

10. Lim, 47.

11. Rosenthal, lxxxvi.

12. Patrick Marber, *Closer*, 110.

13. Rosenthal, lxxvii-lxxviii.

14. Rosenthal, lxxvii.

15. Anthony Lane, "Partners," *The New Yorker*, 13 December 2004, 108.

16. Chris Norris, "Closer," *Film Comment*, January/February 2005, 72.

17. Sean Smith, "Coming Attractions," *Newsweek*, 30 August 2004, 46.

18. Lim, 47.

19. Rosenthal, xxiii.

20. A. O. Scott, "Who's Returning to Virginia Woolf?" *New York Times*, 28 November 2004.

21. Marber, 7, 13.

Chapter 21

1. Helen O'Hara, "Patriot Games," *Empire*, January 2008, 84.

2. A. O. Scott, "Good Time Charlie, and His Foreign Affairs," *New York Times*, 21 December 2007.

3. Scott.

4. The movie tie-in edition of Crile's book reproduces this image, but doctored: Bonnie is out, Gust in.

5. David Edelstein, "It's a Gusher!" *New York*, 24 December, 2007, 100.

6. Gavin Smith, "Of Metaphors and Purpose," *Film Comment*, May/June 1999, 21.

7. From "The Making of *Charlie Wilson's War*," a featurette on the 2008 Universal Pictures DVD.

8. "Charlie Wilson," *The Economist*, 20 February 2010, 84.

9. Smith, 21.

Chapter 22

1. Andrew Sarris, *The American Cinema: Directors and Directions, 1929–1968*, 218.

2. Sarris, 218.

3. Peter Biskind, "Who's Afraid of the Big Bad Wolf?" *Premiere*, March 1994, 63.

4. Bernard Weinraub, "Mike Nichols Plans a Career Finale," *New York Times* 15 March 1993.

5. "Elaine May in Conversation with Mike Nichols," *Film Comment*, July/August 2006, Web only: www.filmcomment.com/article/elaine-may-in-conversation-with-mike-nichols.

6. Søren Birkvad, "Hollywood Sin, Scandinavian Virtue: The 1967 Revolt of *I Am Curious* and *The Graduate*," *Film International*, 9.2 (Issue 50) 2011, 53.

7. I discuss this debt at length in Chapter 16, "The Legacy of *The Graduate*," in my 2011 monograph, *Appraising* The Graduate: *The Mike Nichols Classic and Its Impact in Hollywood* (McFarland).

8. Chris Nashawaty, "Life of Mike," *Entertainment Weekly*, 16 March 2012, 49.

9. A. O. Scott, "Who's Returning to Virginia Woolf?" *New York Times*, 28 November 2004.

10. Scott.

11. Biskind, 63.

12. Scott.

13. Biskind, 63.

14. The only possible exception is Pakula's *All the President's Men*. Pakula gave compelling imagery to a story nearly everyone already knew and was compelled by; Nichols took a story almost no one knew and made it iconic.

15. Biskind, 60.

16. Biskind, 63.

17. Mitchell Zuckoff, *Robert Altman: The Oral Biography*, 217.

18. H. Wayne Schuth, *Mike Nichols*, 160.

19. Joseph Gelmis, *The Film Director as Superstar*, 359.

20. Fisher, 39.

21. Fisher, 40.

22. Chris Nashawaty, "Life of Mike," *Entertainment Weekly*, 16 March 2012, 48.

23. Gavin Smith, "Of Metaphors and Purpose," *Film Comment*, May/June 1999, 21.

24. Sam Kashner, "Who's Afraid of Nichols & May?" *Vanity Fair*, January 2013, 170.

25. This is a phenomenon I examine briefly in Chapter 3 but at book-length in *Appraising* The Graduate: *The Mike Nichols Classic and Its Impact in Hollywood* (McFarland, 2011).

26. It is odd that an audience will forgive distant-future science fiction any sort of preposterous premises about technological evolution, but as *The Day of the Dolphin* proposed the unlikely idea of 1973 inter-species communication with dolphins as a narrative metaphor, it was ridiculed in the critical and popular imagination. If one allows the premise and story to proceed, *Dolphin* becomes a fascinating dystopian story of objectification's insidious, invasive toxins.

27. Weinraub.

28. David Thomson, *The New Biographical Dictionary of Film*, 5th ed., 705.

29. Cathleen McGuigan, "War, Peace & Nichols," *Newsweek*, 17 December 2007, 63.

30. John Lahr, *Show and Tell*, 285.

Bibliography

Abramovich, Alex. "Hurricane Kushner Hits the Heartland." *New York Times*, 30 Nov. 2003.

Aldridge, Leslie. "Who's Afraid of the Undergraduate?" *New York Times*, 18 Feb. 1968.

Ansen, David. "City of Angels" [Roundtable discussion with playwright, director and cast of *Angels in America*]. *Newsweek*, 17 Nov. 2003: 54.

———. "Good Guy/Bad Guy." *Newsweek*, 23 Mar. 1998: 63.

———. "Jack Cries Wolf." *Newsweek*, 20 Jun. 1994: 58–59.

———. "Love from Another Planet." *Newsweek*, 6 Mar. 2000: 68.

———. "You Need This Movie Like." *Newsweek*, 15 Jul. 1991: 56.

Applebome, Peter. "Always Asking, What Is This Really About?" *New York Times*, 25 Apr. 1999.

Bart, Peter. "Mike Nichols, Moviemaniac." *New York Times*, 1 Jan. 1967.

Benshoff, Harry M. "Movies and Camp," in *American Cinema of the 1960s: Themes and Variations*, 150–171. New Brunswick, NJ: Rutgers University Press, 2008.

Bewes, Timothy. *Reification, or The Anxiety of Late Capitalism*. London: Verso, 2002.

Birkvad, Søren. "Hollywood Sin, Scandinavian Virtue: The 1967 Revolt of *I Am Curious* and *The Graduate*." *Film International* 9.2 (Issue 50) 2011: 42–54.

Biskind, Peter. *Star: How Warren Beatty Seduced America*. New York: Simon and Schuster, 2010.

———. "Who's Afraid of the Big Bad Wolf?" *Premiere* Mar. 1994: 57–63.

Brackman, Jacob. "Carnal Knowledge." *Esquire* Oct. 1971: 45–46.

———. "The Graduate." *The New Yorker*, 27 Jul. 1968: 34–42.

Brown, Georgia. "Holz N the Head." *The Village Voice*, 23 Jul. 1991: 58.

———. "Where the Wild Things Are." *The Village Voice*, 21 Jun. 1994: 50.

Brown, John Lindsay. "Pictures of Innocence." *Sight and Sound* 41.2 (Spring 1972): 101–103.

Buck, Joan Juliet. "Live Mike." *Vanity Fair* Jun. 1994: 70–82.

Callenbach, Ernest. "Review: Carnal Knowledge." *Film Quarterly* 25.2 (Winter 1971–1972): 56.

Canby, Vincent. "A Triumphant 'Catch.'" *New York Times*, 28 Jun. 1970.

———. "The Attitude Adjustment of a Bullet in the Brain." *New York Times*, 10 Jul. 1991.

———. "'Carnal Knowledge': Nichols Directs Cast in Feiffer's Work." *New York Times*, 1 Jul. 1971: 63.

———. "'I Was Sorry To See It End': 'Carnal Knowledge.'" *New York Times*, 4 Jul. 1971.

———. "Karen Silkwood's Story." *New York Times*, 14 Dec. 1983.

———. "Nichols's 'Fortune' Is Old-Time Farce." *New York Times*, 21 May 1975.

———. "Simon's 'Biloxi Blues,' Coming of Age in the Army." *New York Times*, 25 Mar. 1988.

———. "Underwater Talkie: Scott Stars in Nichols's 'Day of the Dolphin.'" *New York Times*, 20 Dec. 1973.

"Charlie Wilson." *The Economist*, 20 Feb. 2010: 84.

Cheever, Susan. "An Angel Sat Down at His Table." *New York Times*, 13 September 1992.

Combs, Richard. "Slaves of Manhattan." *Sight and Sound* 58.2 (Spring 1989): 78.

Cook, David A. *Lost Illusions: American Cinema in the Shadow of Watergate and Vietnam, 1970–1979*. Berkeley: University of California Press, 2000.

Corliss, Richard. "The Final Frontier." *Time*, 11 Mar. 1996: 66–68.

———. "Spin and Sizzle." *Time*, 17 Sept. 1990: 70.

———. *Talking Pictures: Screenwriters in the American Cinema*. Woodstock, NY: Overlook, 1974.

Crile, George. *Charlie Wilson's War*. New York: Grove, 2003.

Crowther, Bosley. "Graduating with Honors." *New York Times*, 31 Dec. 1967.

———. "Who's Afraid of Audacity?" *New York Times*, 10 Jul. 1966.

Daugherty, Tracy. *Just One Catch: A Biography of Joseph Heller*. New York: St. Martin's, 2011.

Davies, Sam. "Reviews: Closer." *Sight and Sound* 15.2 (Feb. 2005): 45–47.

Denby, David. "The Beach Boys." *New York*, 11 Mar. 1996: 50–51.

_____. "Beastly Boys." *New York*, 20 Jun. 1994: 77–78.

_____. "A Life on the Line." *New York*, 26 Dec. 1983–2 Jan. 1984: 96–97.

_____. "Skirting Trouble." *New York*, 21 (28 Mar. 1988): 97–98.

_____. "Trading Places." *New York*, 2 Jan. 1989: 45–46.

_____. "The Trouble With Henry." *New York*, 22 Jul. 1991: 40.

_____. "Young Rascals." *New York*, 23 Mar. 1998: 82–83, 147.

Doherty, Tom. "Silkwood." *Film Quarterly* 37.4 (Summer 1984): 24–26.

Ebert, Roger. "The Graduate." *Chicago Sun-Times*, 26 Dec. 1967.

Edelstein, David. "It's a Gusher!" *New York*, 24 Dec. 2007: 95–100.

Edson, Margaret. *Wit*. New York: Faber and Faber, 1999.

Ephron, Nora. *The Most of Nora Ephron*. New York: Knopf, 2013.

_____. *Wallflower at the Orgy*. New York: Ace Books, 1973.

_____. "Yossarian Is Alive and Well in the Mexican Desert." *New York Times*, 16 Mar. 1969.

Farber, Stephen. "Film Reviews: Catch-22." *Sight and Sound* 39.4 (Autumn 1970): 218–219.

Farber, Stephen, and Estelle Changas. "Review: The Graduate." *Film Quarterly* 21.3 (Spring 1968): 37–41.

Feiffer, Jules. *Carnal Knowledge*. New York: Avon, 1971.

Feld, Rob. "Trouble in Mind." *DGA Quarterly* (Summer 2010): 22–25.

Fisher, Carrie. *Postcards from the Edge*. New York: Pocket, 1988.

Fisher, James. *Understanding Tony Kushner*. Columbia: University of South Carolina Press, 2008.

Franklin, Nancy. "America, Lost and Found." *The New Yorker*, 8 Dec. 2003: 125–127.

Freer, Ian. "Nicholsodeon." *Empire* Nov. 1998: 88.

Gates, Henry Louis. *Faces of America with Henry Louis Gates, Jr.* Public Broadcasting System, 2010.

Gelmis, Joseph. *The Film Director as Superstar*. London: Pelican, 1974.

Georgakas, Dan. "From Words to Images: An Interview with Buck Henry. *Cineaste* (Winter 2001): 4–10.

Goldfarb, Brad, and Patrick Giles. "The Angels Have Landed" [Roundtable discussion with cast and crew of *Angels in America*]. *Interview* Dec. 2003/Jan. 2004: 170–174.

Goldsmith, Barbara. "Grass, Women and Sex: An Interview with Mike Nichols." *Harper's Bazaar* Nov. 1970.

Goldstein, Richard. "Angels in a Changed America." *The Village Voice*, 26 Nov.- 2 Dec. 2003: 32–34.

Goodman, Walter. "Romance Narrows the Gap Between Generations." *New York Times*, 10 Aug. 1986.

Gopnik, Adam. "Standup Guys." *The New Yorker*, 12 May 2003: 106–109.

Gussow, Mel. *Edward Albee: A Singular Journey*. New York: Applause, 2001.

_____. "Mike Nichols: Director as Star." *Newsweek*, 14 Nov. 1966: 95–99.

_____. "Nichols, Fortune Made, Looks to the Future." *New York Times* 3 Jun. 1975.

Harris, Mark. *Pictures at a Revolution: Five Movies and the Birth of the New Hollywood*. New York: Penguin, 2008.

Heller, Joseph. *Catch As Catch Can*. Ed. Matthew J. Bruccoli and Park Bucker. New York: Simon & Schuster, 2004.

_____. *Catch-22*. 50th Anniversary Edition. New York: Simon & Schuster, 2011.

Hertzberg, Hendrik. "Upset Victory." *The New Yorker*, 23 Mar. 1998: 86–90.

Hill, Lee. "Mike Nichols and the Business of Living." *Senses of Cinema*, July 2003. Web. Available at sensesofcinema.com/2003/great-directors/nichols/.

Hill, Logan. "Mr. Nichols and the Vicious Circle." *New York*, 13 Sept. 2004: 50–51.

Hoberman, J. "Running for Cover." *The Village Voice*, 24 Mar. 1998: 65.

James, Caryn. "Death, Mighty Thou Art; So Too, a Compassionate Heart." *New York Times*, 23 Mar. 2001.

_____. "Mike Nichols Surveys the American Dream." *New York Times*, 25 Feb. 1990.

Jameson, Richard T. "Mike Nichols." *Film Comment* 35.3 (May/June 1999): 10.

Jebb, Julian. "Carnal Knowledge." *Sight and Sound* 40.4 (Autumn 1971): 222.

Johnson, Lyndon B. "The Great Society," in *The Times Were a Changin': The Sixties Reader*, ed. Irwin Unger and Debi Unger, 39–42. New York: Three Rivers Press, 1998.

Kael, Pauline. "Carnal Knowledge." *The New Yorker*, 3 Jul. 1971: 43–44.

_____. "The Day of the Dolphin." *The New Yorker*, 31 Dec. 1973: 50.

_____. "Working Girl." *The New Yorker*, 9 Jan. 1989: 80–81.

Kaplan, James. "True Colors?" *New York*, 2 Mar. 1998: 22–29.

Kashner, Sam. "Who's Afraid of Nichols & May?" *Vanity Fair* Jan. 2013: 94–106.

Kashner, Sam, and Nancy Schoenberger. *Furious Love: Elizabeth Taylor, Richard Burton, and the Marriage of the Century*. New York: It Books, 2011.

Kennedy, Colin. "Love Hurts." *Empire* Feb. 2005: 74–76.

Kennedy, Douglas. "From New York to LA." *The Listener*. 16 Mar. 1989: 36–37.

Kroll, Jack. "Basic Training of Neil Simon." *Newsweek*, 4 Apr. 1988: 72.

Kushner, Tony. *Angels in America: A Gay Fantasia on National Themes*. [Combined Paperback HBO Tie-In.] New York: Theatre Communications Group, 2003.

_____. "The Art of Theater No. 16." *The Paris Review* (Summer 2012): 108–140.

Lahr, John. "Angels on the Verge." *The New Yorker*, 15 Nov. 2010: 96–97.

_____. *Show and Tell*. New York: The Overlook Press, 2000.

Lane, Anthony. "Howl." *The New Yorker*, 11 Jul. 1994: 83–85.

_____. "Partners." *The New Yorker*, 13 Dec. 2004: 107–109.

_____. "Settling Scores." *The New Yorker*, 24 Dec. 2007: 150–152.

Leonard, John. "The I.V. League." *New York*, 26 Mar. 2001: 125–126.

_____. "Winged Victory." *New York*, 8 Dec. 2003: 72–73.

Lim, Dennis. "Closer." *The Village Voice*, 1 Dec. 2004: 47.

Marber, Patrick. *Closer*. London: Methuen Drama, 2007.

Maslin, Janet. "In the 90s, the 80s Turn to Junk." *New York Times*, 14 Jul. 1991.

_____. "Wolf Bites Man; Man Sheds His Civilized Coat." *New York Times*, 17 Jun. 1994.

May, Elaine. *The Birdcage*. New York: Newmarket, 1997.

McGuigan, Cathleen. "War, Peace & Nichols." *Newsweek*, 17 Dec. 2007: 62–64.

Mendelsohn, Daniel. "Winged Messages." *The New York Review of Books*, 12 Feb. 2004: 42–47.

Miller, Sara Cedar. *Central Park, an American Masterpiece*. New York: Abrams, 2003.

Mitchell, Elvis. "Sent to Earth with Powers and Abilities Far Below Those of Mortal Men: What Planet Are You From?" *New York Times*, 3 Mar. 2000.

Mitchell, Sean. "The One They Ask for by Name!" *Empire* Feb. 1991: 66–67.

Monaco, Paul. *History of the American Cinema: The Sixties, 1960–1969*. Berkeley: University of California Press, 2001.

Nachman, Gerald. *Seriously Funny: The Rebel Comedians of the 1950s and 1960s*. New York: Pantheon, 2003.

Nashawaty, Chris. "Life of Mike." *Entertainment Weekly*, 16 Mar. 2012: 44–49.

Newman, Bruce. "Relatively Comfortable on the Planet Shandling." *New York Times*, 5 Mar. 2000.

Nichols, Mike. *Charlie Rose* Interview. 28 Apr. 1998.

_____. "Elaine May in Conversation with Mike Nichols." *Film Comment* (July/August 2006). Available at: www.filmcomment.com/article/elaine-may-in-conversation-with-mike-nichols. Web only.

_____. "On Telling the Real Karen Silkwood's Story." *New York Times*, 8 Jan. 1984.

_____. "*Playboy* Interview." *Playboy* Jun. 1966: 63–74.

Nielsen, Ken. *Tony Kushner's* Angels in America. New York: Continuum, 2008.

Norris, Chris. "Closer." *Film Comment* 41.1 (Jan./Feb. 2005): 72.

O'Hara, Helen. "Patriot Games." *Empire* (Jan. 2008): 81–84.

O'Hehir, Andrew. "Wings of Desire." *Sight & Sound* 14.3 (Mar. 2004): 4–6.

Oliver, Edith. "The Current Cinema: Who's Afraid of Virginia Woolf?" *The New Yorker*, 1966: 64–65.

Overpeck, Deron. "Movies and Images of Reality," in *American Cinema of the 1980s: Themes and Variations*. Ed. Stephen Prince. New Brunswick, NJ: Rutgers University Press, 2007.

Peyser, Marc. "From Broadway to Boob Tube." *Newsweek*, 19 Mar. 2001: 56–58.

Pomerance, Murray. "Movies and the Specter of Rebellion," in *American Cinema of the 1960s: Themes and Variations*, 172–192. New Brunswick, NJ: Rutgers University Press, 2008.

Poniewozik, James. "Heaven on Earth." *Time*, 8 Dec. 2003: 81–82.

Quart, Leonard, and Albert Auster. *American Film and Society Since 1945*. 3d. ed. Westport, CT: Praeger, 2002.

Rafferty, Terrence. "The Current Cinema: Seeing Straight." *The New Yorker*, 18 Mar. 1996: 109–112.

Rainer, Peter. "Sitcoms." *New York* 33.10 (13 March 2000): 86–7.

Ressner, Jeffrey. "Working Man." *DGA Quarterly* (Fall 2006).

Rice, Robert. "A Tilted Insight." *The New Yorker*, 15 Apr. 1961: 47–75.

Rich, Frank. "Angels, Reagan and AIDS in America." *New York Times*, 16 Nov. 2003.

Rosenthal, Daniel. *Closer*. Student Edition. London: Methuen Drama, 2007.

Rosenzweig, Roy, and Elizabeth Blackmar. *The Park and the People: A History of Central Park*. Ithaca, NY: Cornell University Press, 1992.

Sandford, Christopher. *Polanski*. New York: Palgrave Macmillan, 2007.

Sarris, Andrew. *The American Cinema: Directors and Directions, 1929–1968*. New York: Da Capo, 1996.

Schickel, Richard. "Making a Memoir Memorable." *Time*, 4 Apr. 1988: 77.

Schuth, H. Wayne. *Mike Nichols*. Boston: Twayne, 1978,

Scott, A. O. "Good-Time Charlie, and His Foreign Affairs." *New York Times*, 21 Dec. 2007.

_____. "Who's Returning to Virginia Woolf?" *New York Times*, 28 Nov. 2004.

Simon, John. "Our Movie Comedies Are No Laughing Matter." *New York Times*, 29 Jun. 1975.

Smith, Gavin. "Of Metaphors and Purpose." *Film Comment* 35.3 (May/June 1999): 12–30.

_____. "Without Cutaways." *Film Comment* 27.3 (May 1991): 27–42.

Smith, Sean. "Coming Attractions." *Newsweek*, 30 Aug. 2004: 44–47.

"Some Are More Yossarian Than Others." *Time*, 15 Jun. 1970: 66–68.

Stanley, Alessandra. "Finally, TV Drama to Argue About." *New York Times*, 30 Nov. 2003.

Stayton, Richard. "Flights of Angels." *Written By* (Dec. 2003): 47–54.

Susman, Gary. "The Birdcage." *The Village Voice*, 19 Mar. 1996: 70.

Sweet, Jeffrey. *Something Wonderful Right Away: An Oral History of* The Second City & The Compass Players. New York: Limelight, 1986.

Taubin, Amy. "Occupational Hazards." *The Village Voice*, 27 Dec. 1988: 76.

Thegze, Chuck. "'I See Everything Twice': An Examination of Catch-22." *Film Quarterly* 24.1 (Autumn 1970): 7–17.

Thomson, David. *The New Biographical Dictionary of Film*. 5th ed. New York: Knopf, 2010.

Wallace, David Foster. *A Supposedly Fun Thing I'll Never Do Again*. New York: Little, Brown, 1997.

Webb, Charles. *The Graduate*. New York: New American Library, 1963.

Weiler, A. H. "Nichols Meets Jules Feiffer." *New York Times*, 26 Oct. 1969.

Weinraub, Bernard. "Little Screen, Big Ambition; Serious Films by Cable Networks Fill a Void Left by Hollywood." *New York Times*, 3 Jan. 2001.

_____. "Mike Nichols Plans a Career Finale." *New York Times*, 15 Mar. 1993.

Whitehead, J. W. *Appraising* The Graduate*: The Mike Nichols Classic and Its Impact in Hollywood*. Jefferson, NC: McFarland, 2011.

Zimmerman, Paul D. "Love in a Blind Alley." *Newsweek*, 5 Jul. 1971: 71.

_____. "Madcap Murder." *Newsweek*, 26 May 1975: 84.

Zuckoff, Mitchell. *Robert Altman: The Oral Biography*. New York: Knopf, 2009.

Index

Aaron, Caroline 204, 220
Abbott, George 22
Abbott and Costello 139
ABC (television network) 1, 115, 137, 300
Abrams, Jeffrey (J.J.) 170, 172, 173, 175, 300, 318*ch*13*n*3
Academy Awards (Oscars) 34, 36, 38, 75, 89, 90, 103, 117, 128, 137, 150, 168, 169, 204, 218, 287, 297, 299; *see also* Nichols, Mike
Adams, Amy 289, 291
Adams, Caitlin 106
An Affair to Remember 131
Albee, Edward 1, 25, 26, 27, 30, 31, 32, 33, 37, 117, 254, 298, 302
Alger, Horatio 144, 146
All the President's Men 89, 321*ch*22*n*14
Allen, Mikki 170–171
Allen, Seth 53
Allen, Steve 17
Allen, Woody 2, 12, 216, 221, 300, 301, 307
Alonzo, John A. 112
Altman, Bruce 171
Altman, Robert 2, 12, 54, 115, 155, 201, 238, 254, 300, 301, 302, 307
"Amazing Grace" 119, 128
American Beauty 150, 218, 298–299
American Film Institute 3, 9, 300
American Graffiti 114
"And He Shall Purify..." (Handel) 294
Angels in America (Kushner) 236, 237, 238–239, 242, 243, 245, 252, 254, 261, 271–272, 329*ch*19*n*1
Angels in America (Nichols) 1, 5, 6–7, 8, 11, 23, 26, 43, 66, 93, 94, 102, 166, 225, 233–234, 235, 236–272, 274, 276–277, 284–285, 290, 300, 302, 303, 304–305, 306, 319*ch*19*n*1, 319*ch*19*n*16, 319–320*ch*19*n*20, 320*ch*19*n*37, 320*ch*19*n*53, 320*ch*19*n*67, 320*ch*19*n*68
Ann-Margret 6, 75, 81, 82, 84, 274, 280
Annie 1, 115, 300
Ansen, David 318*ch*13*n*3

Antonioni, Michelangelo 9, 117
Apocalypse Now 53
Applebome, Peter 5
Appraising The Graduate 2, 6, 9, 10, 313*ch*1*n*48, 321*ch*22*n*7, 321*ch*22*n*25
"April Come She Will" 43
Aquino, Amy 153
Aristotle 112, 223
Arkin, Alan 5, 54, 55, 57, 62, 69, 82, 298, 302
Arlen, Alice 116, 122, 124, 126, 127, 128
Ashby, Hal 104
Ashley, Elizabeth 22
Asner, Ed 16
Atkins, Eileen 183, 227
Auster, Albert 116, 145
AVCO-Embassy Pictures 52, 75, 102, 103
Avrakatos, Gust 287
Away We Go 299
Azaria, Hank 196

Bach, J.S. 20
Bain, Conrad 161
Balaban, Bob 57, 68
Baldwin, Alec 144, 145
Ball, Alan 298
Ballhaus, Michael 144, 167, 206, 208, 212, 217
Balsam, Martin 55, 57, 67
Bancroft, Anne 38, 121
Baranski, Christine 193
Barefoot in the Park 22
Bart, Peter 39
Bartlett, Bonnie 210
Bartlett, Robin 159, 173, 174
Bates, Kathy 202
Beat Poets 20
The Beatles 21
Beatty, Ned 292
Beatty, Warren 11, 103, 104, 105, 106, 111, 169
Beckett, Samuel 33, 242
Being There 175
Bening, Annette 11, 19, 150, 163, 170, 171, 216, 217, 218, 222
Benjamin, Richard 59
Benjamin, Walter 242, 304

Benshoff, Harry M. 27, 30
Benton, Suzanne 58
Berg, Peter 286
Bergen, Candice 74, 75, 81, 82, 274
Bergman, Ingmar 9, 117, 228, 297
Berkeley, Busby 239
Berman, Shelly 16, 17
Bernstein, Carl 129, 131, 155
Bethesda Fountain (Central Park, NY) 241, 248, 269–272, 320*ch*19*n*64
Betrayal (Pinter) 23, 226, 300
Bewes, Timothy 4, 6, 33, 222
Beyond the Forest 30
Big 175
Biloxi Blues (Nichols film) 4, 7, 22, 116, 137–143, 155, 168, 183, 184, 201, 205, 317*ch*10*n*6
Biloxi Blues (Simon play) 137
The Birdcage 18, 19, 22, 94, 116, 183, 185, 192–200, 201, 207, 213, 216, 276, 301, 314*ch*1*n*40
Birkvad, Søren 43, 50, 298
Biskind, Peter 74, 103, 301
Blackmar, Elizabeth 320*ch*19*n*64
Bloom, John 232, 234, 292
"The Blower's Daughter" 275–276, 283, 285
Blunt, Emily 289
Bogart Slept Here 115, 317*ch*10*n*1
Bogdanovich, Peter 103
Bonerz, Peter 57
Bonnie and Clyde 104
Bosch, Hieronymus 60
Bowen, Roger 10
Brackman, Jacob 50, 51, 76, 79, 107, 108
Bradbury Building (L.A.) 183, 185
Brando, Marlon 15
Brecht, Bertholt 242, 262–263, 320*ch*19*n*51
Brief Encounter 21
Brighton Beach Memoirs 137
Broadway Bound 137
Broderick, Matthew 138, 139
Brooks, James L. 168
Brooks, Mel 3, 104, 216, 301, 307
Brooks, Richard 118
Brown, Georgia 184, 318*ch*13*n*1, 318*ch*13*n*3

Brown, John Lindsay 4, 50, 76, 316*ch*4*n*17
Brown, Margaret Wise 225
Buck, Joan Juliet 2, 4
Buck Privates 139
Burkholder, Scott 207
Burton, Richard 9, 11, 23, 25, 26, 34, 35, 37, 38, 93, 298
Bush, Barbara 198
Bush, Jeb 200

Cabaret 298
La Cage aux Folles 183, 192, 195, 199
Callenbach, Ernest 73
Callendar, Colin 225
Calley, John 52, 73
Camelot 23, 26
Cameron, James 115
Canby, Vincent 54, 75, 88, 89, 90, 105, 139, 317*ch*8*n*5
Carides, Gia 207
Carlisi, Olimpia 59
Carnal Knowledge 4, 6, 7, 9, 15, 26, 56, 63, 72, 73–88, 94, 96, 103, 107, 108, 111, 115, 116, 117, 129, 137, 138, 139, 155, 157, 160, 166, 171, 181, 205, 219, 236, 273, 280, 285, 302, 306, 316*ch*5*n*19, 316*ch*5*n*25
Carson, John David 96
Carter, Jimmy 21
Carver, Raymond 302
Carville, James 203
Catch–22 (Heller) 52, 53, 54, 55, 56, 57, 58, 59, 62, 65, 67, 69, 70, 71, 74, 298
Catch–22 (Nichols) 1, 2, 4, 5–6, 10, 11, 15, 21, 37, 52–72, 73, 74, 75, 76, 77, 79, 83, 86, 87, 88, 89, 102, 107, 108, 115, 116, 117, 126, 138, 144, 153, 160, 165, 171, 190, 193, 201, 202, 216, 233, 236, 243, 274, 297, 298, 301, 302, 303, 304, 306, 315*ch*4*n*16, 316*ch*4*n*34
Central Park (NY) 183, 241, 269–272, 320*ch*19*n*64
Changas, Estelle 45, 51
Channing, Stockard 103, 104, 105, 106, 113, 129
Chaplin, Charlie 19
Charles, Nancy Linehan 293
Chekhov, Anton 115, 226
Cher 117, 124, 128
The Cherry Orchard 298
Chinatown 89, 113
Chopin, Frédéric 20
Cicchini, Robert 203
Cimino, Michael 52
"Cinderella" 10, 137, 144–145, 146, 148, 149, 153, 156, 157, 171

Citizen Kane 212, 297, 299
Cleopatra 26
Clinton, Bill 192, 198, 201, 202, 288
Closer (Marber) 73, 273, 276, 280, 282, 284, 306
Closer (Nichols) 23, 73, 94, 166, 219, 273–285, 291, 300, 302, 305, 306
Cobb, Lee J. 300
Coe, Fred 22
Coen Brothers 113
Coleridge, Samuel Taylor 90
Collins, Max Allan 299
Columbia Pictures 52
Columbus, Chris 198
Colvin, Norm 121
"Comin' Around Again" 63, 129, 131, 132, 136, 150
Compass Players (Chicago) 10, 16–17, 18, 19, 22
The Concept of Anxiety (Kierkegaard) 4
Conrad, Joseph 14
The Conversation 89
Cook, David 316*ch*5*n*25
Cooke, Alistair 17
Cooney, Kevin 210
Coppola, Francis Ford 53, 89, 301, 307
Corliss, Richard 37, 155, 192–193, 200
Così fan tutte 277, 283
The Country Girl 226
Craig, Daniel 23, 300
Crane, Stephen 72
Crile, George 287
Cromwell, James 249
Crowther, Bosley 31, 315*ch*3*n*3
Cusack, Joan 144, 145

Dahl, John 217
Dalio, Marcel 60
Daniels, Jeff 136
Daniels, William 38, 41, 91
Danon, Marcello 192
Davies, Sam 274
Davis, Bette 30, 32
The Day of the Dolphin (Merle) 89
The Day of the Dolphin (Nichols) 2, 7, 72, 87, 89–102, 103, 107, 108, 116, 117, 161, 191, 201, 236, 264, 299, 301, 303, 306, 316*ch*6*n*5, 321*ch*22*n*26
Days of Heaven 118
Death of a Salesman 23, 226, 300
Deep Water 11, 300
Dehner, John 98
Delerue, Georges 90, 91, 94, 95, 1116, 117, 119, 122, 126, 128, 191
Denby, David 128, 139, 145, 148, 191, 192, 198, 202, 317*ch*11*n*14, 318*ch*13*n*3
Dench, Judi 202, 298
De Niro, Robert 115
Dennis, Sandy 26, 34
De Palma, Brian 286
The Designated Mourner 314*ch*1*n*39

De Wilde, Brandon 204
Dick Tracy 169
Dickens, Charles 202
Dickey, James 183
Dietrich, Marlene 25
Doctor Doolittle 90
Doherty, Tom 117
Dolan, Michael 138
Dole, Bob 198
D'Olive, Wendy 61
A Doll's House 135
Donizetti, Gaetano 61
Donne, John 225, 226, 227, 228, 229, 230, 232, 233, 234
Dostoevsky, Fyodor 202
Dreiser, Theodore 72
Dreyfuss, Richard 159
Dubin, Al 107
Dukakis, Olympia 146
Dunaway, Faye 104
Dunn, Liam 60
Dunn, Nora 147
Duvall, Robert 16
Dylan, Bob 69

Eastman, Carole 103
Easy Rider 52
Ebert, Roger 42
Economist 295
Edson, Margaret 1, 225, 226, 227, 230, 231, 237, 247, 306
Eggers, Dave 299
EGOT (Emmy, Grammy, Oscar, Tony) 3
8½ 26
Eliot, T.S. 20
Ephron, Nora 10, 17, 57, 116, 122, 124, 126, 127, 128, 129, 130, 131, 132, 133, 134, 155, 301, 314*ch*1*n*40
Erin Brockovich 287, 293
Eternal Sunshine of the Spotless Mind 320*ch*19*n*49

Faces of America 14
Family 1, 115, 300
Farber, Stephen 45, 51, 54, 64
Feiffer, Jules 17, 74, 75, 79, 80, 82, 84, 85, 86, 129, 155, 162, 302, 316*ch*5*n*19
Fell, Norman 59
Fellini, Federico 9, 14, 15, 26, 75, 117, 171, 301
Ferris Bueller's Day Off 139
The Film Director as Superstar 9
Film Society of Lincoln Center 3, 300
Filmways Productions 52
Fiorentino, Linda 216, 217
Fisher, Carrie 155, 157, 159, 163, 164, 165, 168
Fisher, James 8, 242, 243, 244, 272
Five Easy Pieces 103
Flagler Memorial Chapel (Millbrook School) 172
Flaherty, Pat 107
Flanagan, Markus 138
Flockhart, Calista 193

Flynn, Errol 50
Follies 162
Fool for Love 302
Ford, Harrison 7, 11, 19, 102, 144, 149, 152, 156, 170, 175, 179, 184, 235
Ford, John 300, 307
Forman, Milos 103
Forsythe, Henderson 121
The Fortune 4, 9, 11, 72, 102, 103–114, 115, 117, 129, 136, 137, 139, 157, 168, 171, 216, 299, 300, 302
Fraker, William A. 94, 100, 101
Franklin, Nancy 253, 271
The French Connection 53
Friedkin, William 53, 217
Futterman, Dan 94, 193, 196

Garfunkel, Art 57, 63, 74, 82, 274
Gates, Henry Louis 14
Gelmis, Joseph 9
General Motors 65
Gerety, Peter 294
Giant 118
Gilda Live 23, 313*n*3
Gilford, Jack 57
The Godfather 103, 104
The Godfather II 89, 103, 114
Goldblatt, Stephen 277, 290, 291, 296
Goldstein, Richard 244, 262
Gondry, Michel 320*ch*19*n*49
Gone with the Wind 36
The Goodbye Girl 115
Goodman, John 216, 220
Goodman, Walter 135
Gopnik, Adam 19
Gosford Park 302
Gottlieb, Adolph 175
Gould, Elliott 54, 302
Goya 57
The Graduate (Nichols) 1, 2, 5–6, 7, 9–10, 14, 15, 19, 20, 23, 25, 26, 29, 30, 36–51, 52, 54, 56, 57, 60, 62, 63, 64, 65, 69, 70–71, 72, 73, 74, 75, 76, 77, 79, 81, 83, 89, 91, 96, 98, 100, 102, 103, 104, 105, 107, 108, 113, 115, 116, 117, 121, 129, 131, 132, 134, 136, 137, 138–139, 144, 145, 150, 153, 154, 155, 156–157, 159, 160–161, 165, 168, 171, 181, 182, 184, 190, 191, 194, 195, 197, 200, 203, 204, 205–206, 218, 236, 243, 245, 258, 274, 276, 280, 282, 290, 298, 299, 300, 301, 302, 303, 304, 305, 306, 315*ch*3*n*37, 315*ch*4*n*17, 317*ch*9*n*7
The Graduate (Webb) 25, 36, 37, 38, 313*n*28
Gray, John 216
"Great Society" Speech 38, 116
Griffith, Melanie 10, 144, 146, 148, 148, 149, 151, 156
Grodin, Charles 57
Guaymas (Mexico) 53
Guest, Christopher 106

Gussow, Mel 9, 104
Gypsy 155

Hackman, Gene 16, 155, 158, 166, 188, 193, 199, 200, 207, 213, 223, 303
Haggis, Paul 286
Hagman, Larry 204, 210, 319*ch*16*n*13
Hamlet 31, 233
Handel, George Frideric 294
Hanks, Tom 11, 175, 286, 288, 289, 290, 291, 292, 293, 296
Harper, Tess 119
Harris, Barbara 16
Harris, Mark 316*ch*6*n*4
Harrison, Jim 183, 184, 318*ch*14*n*8
Hatley, Tim 277
HBO 1, 2, 3, 6, 8, 23, 26, 105, 128, 170, 183, 225, 226, 235, 236, 237, 238, 270, 305, 306
Hearst, William Randolph 297
Heartburn (Ephron) 129, 130, 131, 133, 155
Heartburn (Nichols) 17, 63, 116, 129–136, 150, 155, 157, 165, 166, 168, 171, 183, 220, 305, 314*ch*1*n*40
Heaven's Gate 52
Heller, Joseph 1, 5, 52, 53, 54, 55, 56, 57, 58, 59, 62, 65, 67, 69, 70, 71, 74
Hemingway, Ernest 183
Henry, Buck 2, 14, 37, 50, 53, 54, 55, 56, 57, 65, 67, 69, 70, 71, 87, 89, 90, 95, 96, 100, 102, 103, 155, 316*ch*6*n*5
Herring, Joanne 287
Herrmann, Bernard 122
Herrmann, Edward 92
Hertzberg, Hendrik 202
High and Low 11, 300
Highsmith, Patricia 11, 300
Hill, George Roy 103
Hill, Lee 2, 10, 11, 39, 55, 56, 116, 128, 139, 201, 202, 225
Hill, Steven 133
Hitchcock, Alfred 2, 25, 122–123, 300, 307
Hoffman, Dustin 10, 11, 16, 37, 38, 40, 41, 49, 50, 56, 82, 203, 204, 276
Hoffman, Philip Seymour 11, 286, 300, 306
Hollis, Tommy 206
Hollywood 52–53, 89, 102, 115, 117, 121, 131, 299
Hood, Gavin 286
Hopper, Dennis 52
Hopper, Edward 111, 118, 208
"How High the Moon" 139, 140
Howard, James Newton 294
Howard, Ron 301
Hughes, John 139

"I Must Be Dreaming" 107, 109, 111, 112
Ibsen, Henrik 135

"I'm Checkin' Out (of This Heartbreak Hotel)" 169, 184
"I'm Still Here" 162
The Importance of Being Earnest 22
In Cold Blood 118
In the Valley of Elah 286
Industrial Light and Magic 52
Interview 243

Jade 217
James, Caryn 4, 114, 225
Jameson, Richard T. 10, 37
Janney, Allison 189, 207
Jarhead 299
Jarvis, Graham 125
Jaws 103, 115
Jebb, Julian 82
Jenkins, Richard 189, 190
Joffe, Charles H. 19
Johnson, Lyndon B. 38, 116
Joy Division 282
Joyce, Adrien 103, 104

Kael, Pauline 51, 90, 297, 317*ch*11*n*14
Kane, Carol 73
Kaplan, James 203
Kashner, Sam 13, 31
Kauffmann, Stanley 36
Kaufman, Charlie 320*ch*19*n*49
Kazan, Elia 1, 15, 297
Keaton, Buster 104
Kennedy, Douglas 1
Kennedy, John F. 208
Kierkegaard, Søren 4
The Kingdom 286
Kingsley, Ben 216, 217, 221
Kinnear, Greg 216, 217
Kirk, Justin 5, 237, 239, 262, 277
Klein, Joe 19, 183, 201, 204, 206
Klein, Robert 210
Klute 89
Korkes, Jon 57, 62, 93
Kosinski, Jerzy 175
Kroll, Jack 139
Kubrick, Stanley 52, 59, 175, 319*ch*17*n*7
Kurosawa, Akira 11, 300
Kushner, Tony 1, 5, 8, 26, 225, 235, 236, 237, 238, 242, 243, 244, 245, 249, 250, 251, 254, 256, 259, 261–263, 267, 268–272, 302, 304, 319*ch*19*n*1, 320*ch*19*n*51, 320*ch*19*n*53, 320*ch*19*n*67, 320*ch*19*n*68

La Verne (CA), United Methodist Church 47–48
Laclos, Pierre Choderlos de 274
Ladd, Alan 204
Lahr, John 7, 17, 22, 237, 244
Lally, James 146
Landesman, Jay 16
Lane, Anthony 184, 191
Lane, Nathan 193, 196, 198, 199, 274, 280
The Last Movie 52
The Last Seduction 217

Law, Jude 273, 276
Lean, David 21
Lehman, Ernest 25, 27, 30, 31
Leigh, Janet 122
Leonard, John 226
The Leopard 75
Lester, Adrian 203, 214
Lester, Richard 9
"Let the River Run" 144, 145, 148,
    150, 154
Levine, Joseph E. 9, 36, 52, 75, 102,
    103, 316*ch*6*n*4
Liaisons Dangereuses, Les 274
Libertini, Richard 60
Lilly, Dr. John C. 89
Lim, Dennis 281
Lincoln, Abraham 213
Lions for Lambs 286
Lloyd, Christopher 226, 238
Lubezki, Emmanuel 194
Lubitsch, Ernst 14
Lucas, George 52, 115
Lukács, György 4
Luv 55
Lynch, David 316*ch*4*n*28
Lynch, Jane 219

Mackendrick, Alexander 25
MacLaine, Shirley 156, 159, 162,
    164, 168
Madame X 290
Madonna 150
The Magnificent Ambersons 297,
    298
Malick, Terrence 118
Maltagliati, Evi 61
Mankiewicz, Herman 297
Mann Act 103, 105, 106, 107, 109
Manson, Charles 89
Marber, Patrick 1, 73, 273, 274,
    275, 282, 283, 284, 306
Markinson, Brian 189, 250, 289,
    319*ch*19*n*16
Marshall, Garry 293
Marshall, Penny 175
Marx, Karl 262
Marx Brothers 19
M*A*S*H* 54, 65, 201, 302
Maslin, Janet 185, 318*ch*13*n*2
Mason, James 30
A Matter of Position 21–22
May, Elaine 1, 3, 13, 15–22, 37, 183,
    192, 195, 197, 198, 199, 200, 201,
    203, 204, 206, 215, 300, 301, 306,
    314*ch*1*n*40; *see also* Nichols and
    May
Mayer, Louis B. 158
McCabe and Mrs. Miller 302
McDonald, Audra 8, 227, 235, 237
McGovern, George 21
*Men Are from Mars, Women Are
    from Venus* 216
Mendelsohn, Daniel 236, 243, 271,
    320*ch*19*n*68
Mendes, Sam 12, 150, 218, 298–
    299, 300
Merle, Robert 89
Messiah 294

Mexico 10, 53, 74, 89, 115
Midnight Cowboy 58
Millbrook School (CT) 172
Millennium Approaches (Kushner)
    236, 243, 246
Miller, Arthur 23, 226, 300
Miller, Glenn 76
Miller, Rebecca 173
The Miracle Worker 38
Miss Julie 15
Mitchell, Elvis 219
Moffatt, Donald 173
Molinaro, Edouard 192
Moonraker 299
Moore, Roger 299
Moreno, Rita 6, 73
Mounsey, Rob 148
Mozart 277, 283
Mrs. Doubtfire 198
"Mrs. Robinson" 37, 317*ch*9*n*7
Mulhern, Matt 138

Nabokov, Vladimir 14
Nelligan, Kate 185, 187
Nelson, Craig T. 121
New York State Supreme Court
    Building 171
New York Times 19, 31, 54, 88, 105,
    114, 135, 225, 306
New Yorker 15, 19, 50, 202
Newhart, Bob 53, 58, 67
Newman, Tom 107
Newsweek 9, 25
Newton, John 119
Nichols, Brigitte Landauer
    (mother) 13–15
Nichols, Mike: Academy Awards
    (Oscars) 1, 2, 3, 10, 11, 23, 36, 37,
    52, 128, 144, 298, 300; Broadway
    career 1, 2, 9, 22–23, 37, 52, 55,
    103, 115, 226, 297, 300, 301, 306;
    childhood 13–15; chivalric motifs
    47–48, 50, 138; classical motifs
    28, 60, 65, 247; comic career 1, 3,
    9, 10, 13, 15–22, 37, 52, 103, 300,
    301, 306; conspiracy thriller
    genre 89, 116, 306; dancing mo-
    tifs 80; 94–95, 111, 139–140; ed-
    ucation motifs 5, 28, 51, 95, 181–
    182, 204–206, 222–223, 227–
    235; EGOT 3; Emmy Awards 1,
    3, 11, 237; farce genre 108, 113,
    193, 198; Golden Globe Awards
    11, 300; Grammy Award 1, 3, 37,
    52; horror genre 123, 185, 191;
    melodrama 167, 171, 172; per-
    formance motifs 5–7, 31–32, 41–
    42, 45–47, 63, 77–80, 83, 87–88,
    90–95, 98–99, 101, 111–112,
    124–125, 133–135, 142–143, 144,
    145, 148–154, 155–157, 158–169,
    170, 174, 177–182, 186–190,
    193–200, 202, 274–275, 279–
    285, 289–294; reification motifs
    4, 33, 49, 66, 71, 73, 77–80, 83,
    94, 96–97, 99–102, 107–110,
    116–117, 121–122, 124, 132–133,
    139–143, 150, 152–154, 157, 163,

164–169, 171–172, 177–182,
    184–186, 188–191, 193, 197–200,
    205–206, 211–215, 218–223,
    225–235, 239–243, 254–272,
    275–285, 287–296, 302–307; ro-
    mance genre 44, 48, 49, 50, 63,
    65, 72, 74, 76, 83, 113, 131, 144,
    153–154, 163, 185, 217, 276, 285;
    science-fiction genre 217–218,
    321*ch*22*n*26; Shakespearean com-
    edy 192, 199; Tony Awards 1, 3,
    22, 52, 300; war genre 63–64, 66;
    western genre 47; *see also* Nichols
    and May
Nichols, Paul (father) 13–15
Nichols, Robert (brother) 13,
    314*ch*1*n*2
Nichols and May 15–22; "Adul-
    tery" 21; "The Dentist" 21; "Disc
    Jockey" 21; *An Evening with
    Nichols and May* (Broadway
    show) 20–21, 26; *An Evening
    with Nichols and May* (recording)
    21; "Everybody's Doing It" 20–
    21; *Improvisations to Music* 20–
    21; *Mike Nichols and Elaine May
    Examine Doctors* 21; "Mother and
    Son" 21; "Nichols and May at
    Work" 21; "Pirandello" 19–20,
    21, 30, 206; "Teenagers" 17, 19;
    "Telephone" 21
Nicholson, Jack 6, 11, 19, 74, 82,
    84, 94, 103, 104, 105, 106, 129,
    130, 132, 133, 136, 183, 184, 187,
    190, 219, 274
Nielsen, Ken 236
Nobody Loves You 22
Nordling, Jeffrey 145
Norris, Frank 72
North, Alex 31
North by Northwest 25
Nunn, Bill 174, 179, 235

Ocean's Eleven 293
Ocean's Twelve 293
Odets, Clifford 226
O'Hare, Catherine 131, 133
O'Hare, Denis 295
Oliver, Edith 314*ch*2*n*14
Olmstead, Frederick Law 271
Omnibus 17
Ondricek, Miroslav 124
One Flew Over the Cuckoo's Nest
    103
One Last Thing Before I Go 11, 300
O'Neal, Cynthia 74, 75
Orlandi, Felice 60
O'Steen, Sam 28, 41, 47, 52, 53, 57,
    70, 71, 75, 80, 81, 82, 95, 97, 100,
    120, 124, 128, 129, 147, 161, 163,
    181
Overpeck, Deron 145, 153
Owen, Clive 73, 219, 274, 280

Paar, Jack 17
Pacino, Al 6, 93, 237, 240, 254, 277
Pakula, Alan J. 89, 301, 321*ch*22*n*14
Paper Moon 103

The Parallax View 89
Paramount Studios 36, 52
Parker, Corey 138
Parker, Mary-Louise 5, 102, 237, 265, 277, 319*ch*19*n*16, 320*ch*19*n*53
PBS 14
Pendleton, Austin 58
Penn, Arthur 1, 20, 26, 37, 104
Pentagon Papers 89
Perestroika (Kushner) 8, 236, 243
Perkins, Tony 58, 316*ch*4*n*34
Peschkowsky *see* Nichols, Mike, childhood
Pfeiffer, Michelle 19, 184
Piazza Navona (Italy) 53, 59
Picasso 57
Pierce, David Hyde 183
Pinter, Harold 23, 56, 226, 228, 300
Pirandello, Luigi 19
A Place in the Sun 318*ch*16*n*10
Platt, Oliver 146
The Player 155, 302
Plaza Suite 52
Plummer, Christopher 183, 184
Poiret, Jean 192
Polanski, Roman 89, 90
Pollack, Sydney 301
Pomerance, Murray 41, 50
Portman, Natalie 94, 273, 276, 280
Postcards from the Edge (Fisher) 155, 157
Postcards from the Edge (Nichols) 10, 102, 144, 155–169, 170, 174, 184, 186, 188, 190, 193, 213, 223, 233, 245, 273–275, 303, 304
Pound, Ezra 20
Prentiss, Paula 58
Pretty Woman 293
Primary Colors (Klein) 201, 204, 206
Primary Colors (Nichols) 7–8, 10, 18, 19, 22, 94, 116, 183, 185, 193, 197, 201–215, 216, 225, 236, 286, 288, 301, 303, 305, 306, 318*ch*16*n*10
The Producers 3
Psycho 122–123
Pulitzer Prize 25, 225
Puri, Om 183
Pygmalion 147

Quaid, Dennis 186, 223
Quart, Leonard 116, 145
Quinn, J.C. 121

Rabe, David 1, 115, 300
Racimo, Victoria 95
Radner, Gilda 9, 23, 115, 313*n*3
Rafelson, Bob 103
Rafferty, Terrence 198, 199
Raising Kane 297
Ransahoff, Martin 52
Reagan, Nancy 160, 233
Reagan, Ronald 10, 145, 146, 236, 244, 271
Rebhorn, James 127

Redacted 286
Redford, Robert 22, 286, 301
Reeves, Carly 290
Regarding Henry 7, 8, 19, 102, 116, 156, 170–182, 183, 184, 185, 190, 193, 200, 205, 216, 218, 235, 276, 300, 303, 318*ch*13*n*1, 318*ch*13*n*2, 318*ch*13*n*3
Reiner, Carl 216
Reiner, Rob 160, 301
Rendition 286
Renoir, Jean 2
Revolutionary Road 299
Reynolds, Debbie 155, 162
Rice, Damien 275
Rich, Frank 244
Rin Tin Tin 90
Rivera, Geraldo 211
The Road to Perdition 299
Roberts, Julia 11, 19, 274, 286, 287, 290, 291, 293
Rock, Chris 11
Rollins, Jack 17, 19
Roots 237
Rose, Charlie 210, 319*ch*16*n*13
Rosenzweig, Roy 320*ch*19*n*64
Ross, Katharine 39, 49, 50
Roth, Ann 298
Rothko, Mark 175
Rotunno, Guiseppe 75, 84, 171, 172
Rovere, Gina 59
Rubens, Peter Paul 11, 57
Rubinstein, Marty 20
The Runaway Bunny 225, 233, 247
Russell, Kurt 128, 181

Saarinen, Eero 47
Sahl, Mort 17
Saint-Subber, Arnold 22
Saks, Gene 137
Sargent, John Singer 290
Sarris, Andrew 9, 38, 297
Saturday Evening Post 25, 58
Schickel, Richard 317*ch*8*n*5
Schmidt, Arthur 199, 210, 213
Schuth, H. Wayne 2, 303, 316*ch*6*n*4
Scorsese, Martin 300, 301, 307
Scot, Patricia 17
Scott, A.O. 7, 14, 284, 300, 301
Scott, George C. 11, 89, 90, 92, 97, 115, 191
The Seagull 226
Segal, George 26, 34
Sellers, Peter 175
Shakespeare, William 263
Shakespeare in Love 202
"Shall We Gather at the River?" 252
Shampoo 104
Shandling, Gary 19, 216, 217, 218, 221, 222, 225
Shane 204, 211, 318*ch*16*n*10
Sheen, Martin 57
Shenkman, Ben 7, 237
Sherman, Al 107
Shire, David 104
Short Cuts 302
Shull, Richard 107

Siemaszko, Casey 138
Sight and Sound 54
Silent Movie 104
Silkwood 2, 7, 10, 11, 43, 90, 94, 102, 103, 114, 115–128, 129, 131, 136, 138, 155, 157, 165, 166, 170, 181, 183, 184, 193, 201, 217, 236, 264, 286, 300, 303, 306, 317*ch*8*n*5
Silver, Ron 121
Silverstein, Shel 169
Simon, Carly 63, 129, 131, 132, 136, 144, 145, 148, 150, 154
Simon, John 105
Simon, Neil 1, 22, 52, 115, 137, 139, 142, 143, 155, 317*ch*10*n*1
Simon, Paul 47, 132, 317*ch*9*n*7
Simon and Garfunkel 37, 40, 50, 72, 81, 113, 132, 136, 276, 317*ch*9*n*7
Sister Sledge 194, 200
Skyfall 299
Slattery, John 287
Sleepless in Seattle 131
Smirnoff, Yakov 130
Smith, Gavin 2, 76
Smith, Harmony 217
Smith, Sean 281
Smith College (MA) 25, 26, 53, 74, 79
Smothers Brothers 17
Soderbergh, Steven 55, 287, 293
"Solitude" 139, 140
Sondheim, Stephen 17, 162, 169
Sonora (Mexico) 53, 65
Sontag, Susan 15
Sorkin, Aaron 202, 286, 292, 295, 296
Sorvino, Paul 92
The Sound of Music 36
"Sounds of Silence" 40, 43, 50, 72, 81, 113, 129, 131, 136, 168, 276
Sousa, John Philip 71, 72
Spacey, Kevin 146
Spader, James 94, 183, 185, 187
Spamalot 3, 23, 226
Spielberg, Steven 23, 38, 115, 298, 300, 307
The Spy Who Loved Me 299
Stalin-Hitler Pact 13
Stanley, Alessandra 256
Stanley, Florence 105
Stapleton, Maureen 130
Star Wars 115
"Stars and Stripes Forever" 71
Stayton, Richard 305
Stebbins, Emma 271
Stevens, George 9, 118, 204, 318*ch*16*n*10
The Sting 103, 114
Stoppard, Tom 14
Stott, Ken 294
Straithairn, David 118
Strasberg, Lee 16, 22
Strauss, Richard 59, 175
Streamers 1, 115, 300
Streep, Meryl 7, 8, 11, 17, 19, 42, 94, 102, 103, 116, 119, 123, 128, 129,

130, 133, 155, 157, 158, 165–166, 169, 170, 181, 184, 188, 220, 223, 237, 242, 250, 253, 262, 264, 267, 277, 303, 320*ch*19*n*51
A Streetcar Named Desire 8, 15, 269
Strick, Wesley 183
Strindberg, August 15
Sturges, Preston 117, 315*ch*3*n*3
"Subterranean Homesick Blues" 69
Sunset Boulevard 245
"A Supposedly Fun Thing I'll Never Do Again" 185
Surtees, Robert 41, 113
Sutherland, Donald 54, 302
Suzuki, Pat 139
Sweet Smell of Success 25
Sylbert, Richard 26, 53, 75

The Talented Mr. Ripley 300
Tate, Sharon 89
Taylor, Elizabeth 11, 22–23, 25, 26, 30–31, 32, 34–35, 37, 38, 82, 94, 298
Taylor, James 132
"Tennessee Waltz" 213
Terms of Endearment 155, 168
Thegze, Chuck 54, 56, 57, 65
Thompson, Emma 8, 11, 19, 202, 225, 226, 227, 230, 231, 233–234, 235, 237, 238, 242, 245, 253, 254, 262, 264, 266, 269, 305, 319*ch*18*n*10, 319*ch*19*n*11
Thomson, David 2–5, 10, 202, 225, 307
Thoreau, Henry David 193
Thornton, Billy Bob 203
"Thus Spake Zarathustra" 59, 175
Tierney, Maura 203
Time 54
Titian 93
Tonight Show 17
Touch of Evil 158
Travolta, John 19, 201, 202, 207, 214, 288, 289
Tropper, Jonathan 11, 300
Truffaut, François 14, 301
Turman, Lawrence 25, 26, 36
2001: A Space Odyssey 52, 59, 175, 319*ch*17*n*7

"*Una furtive lagrima*" 61
Uncle Vanya 115

United Methodist Church of La Verne (CA) 47–48
University of California at Berkeley 26
University of Chicago 15, 16, 18
University of Southern California 26

Van Devere, Trish 92, 97
Van Drimmelen, Antonia 292
Vaux, Calvert 271
Veber, Francis 192
Vida, Vendela 299
Vidor, King 30
Visconti, Luchino 75
Vitobello, Fernanda 59
Voight, Jon 58

Walken, Christopher 138, 142
Walker, Rebecca 206
Wallace, David Foster 185
The War of the Worlds 217
Ward, Fred 118
Warner Brothers Studios 26, 30, 52, 53, 115
Washington Post 129
Watergate 89, 93, 97, 129
Watkin, David 55
Wayne, John 196
"We Are Family" 194, 200
Weaver, Sigourney 144, 145, 146, 153, 170, 184
Webb, Charles 25, 36, 37, 38, 313*ch*1*n*28
Weigert, Robin 265
Weinraub, Bernard 306
Weisz, Rachel 23
Welles, Orson 2, 9, 12, 53, 58, 67, 158, 297–298, 299
Wells, H.G. 217
The West Wing 202
Wexler, Haskell 26, 31
When Harry Met Sally 131
What Planet Are You From? 4, 11, 19, 104, 183, 216–223, 225, 226, 301, 303, 319*ch*17*n*7
*What You Always Wanted to Know About Sex*But Were Afraid to Ask* 221
Whitcraft, Elizabeth 144, 145
Who's Afraid of Virginia Woolf? (Albee) 22, 25, 26, 27, 30, 31, 32, 33, 37, 38, 117, 254, 298, 306

Who's Afraid of Virginia Woolf? (Nichols) 1, 5–6, 7, 14, 25–35, 37, 38–39, 42, 53, 63, 65, 71–72, 73, 74, 76, 87, 93–94, 96, 107, 108, 115, 116, 117, 139, 144, 157, 160, 165, 192, 193, 195, 205, 273, 298, 300, 303, 305, 306, 314*ch*2*n*14
Wickes, Mary 161
Wiest, Dianne 193, 199
Wilde, Oscar 22
Wilder, Billy 9, 14, 117, 144, 245
Williams, Robin 193, 196, 198
Williams, Tennessee 8, 15
Wilson, Charlie 287, 288, 289, 294, 295, 296
Wilson, Elizabeth 38, 41, 60, 101, 170, 176
Wilson, Patrick 7, 93, 237, 239, 240, 253, 259, 262
Winger, Debra 168
Wit (Edson) 225, 226, 227, 230, 231–232, 234, 235, 237, 238, 244, 247, 306
Wit (Nichols) 1, 8, 11, 23, 105, 225–235, 237–238, 264, 292, 300, 305–306, 319*ch*18*n*10
The Wizard of Oz 263, 269
Wolf 10, 19, 89, 94, 170, 171, 183–191, 193, 217, 273, 301, 314*ch*1*n*40, 318*ch*14*n*8
Woodward, Jonathan M. 227, 238
Working Girl 10, 116, 137, 144–154, 156, 157, 165, 170, 183, 184, 205, 271, 300, 301, 303, 305, 317*ch*11*n*14, 318*ch*13*n*2
Wright, Jeffrey 7, 235, 237, 239, 240, 253, 259, 262
Wyeth, Andrew 118

Yates, Richard 299
"You Are My Sunshine" 206
"You Belong to Me" 150
"You Don't Know Me" 161, 162, 169
"You're So Vain" 150

Zanuck, Darryl 158, 162
Zayas, David 234
Zemeckis, Robet 115
Zimmerman, Paul D. 82, 84, 113